# Chambers
# science
# factfinder

Chambers

CHAMBERS

An imprint of Chambers Harrap Publishers Ltd
7 Hopetoun Crescent
Edinburgh, EH7 4AY

www.chambers.co.uk

First published by Chambers Harrap Publishers Ltd 2006
Reprinted 2006

© Chambers Harrap Publishers Ltd 2006

A CIP catalogue record for this book is available from the British Library.

ISBN–13: 978 0 550 10148 8
ISBN–10: 0 550 10148 9

Image credits

Illustrations of Fibonacci sequence (p492), hydrological cycle (p424) and RNA (p319):
Copyright © 2005 by Houghton Mifflin Company. Reproduced by permission from
*The American Heritage Science Dictionary*.

Illustrations of carbon cycle (p423) and electromagnetic spectrum (p460):
Copyright © 2002 by Houghton Mifflin Company. Reproduced by permission from
*The American Heritage Student Science Dictionary*.

Illustrations of levers (p259), star images (p448), cloud images (p426–7), and
illustrations of geological timescale (p400–1), mitosis (p334), interference (p458),
refraction (p458), diffraction (p459), ionizing radiation (p465), nuclear fission (p467)
and nuclear fusion (p468):
Copyright © 2002 by Houghton Mifflin Company. Adapted and reproduced by
permission from *The American Heritage Student Science Dictionary*.

Illustration of nervous system (p274):
Copyright © 2004 by Houghton Mifflin Company. Reproduced by permission from
*The American Heritage Stedman's Medical Dictionary*.

Illustration of Pythagoras's theorem (p268):
Copyright © 2000 by Houghton Mifflin Company. Adapted and reproduced by
permission from *The American Heritage Dictionary of the English Language*, Fourth
Edition.

Muscles anatomy diagram (p273)
Copyright © www.arttoday.com

Designed and typeset by Chambers Harrap Publishers Ltd, Edinburgh

Printed and bound in Germany by Bercker

# CONTRIBUTORS

## Editor

Katie Brooks

## Managing Editor

Camilla Rockwood

## Contributors

Vicky Aldus
Philip Ball
Ian Brookes
Katie Brooks
Gary Dexter
Alice Goldie
Sharon McTeir
Camilla Rockwood
Howard Sargeant

## Publishing Manager

Patrick White

## Prepress

Heather Macpherson
David Reid

## Prepress Manager

Clair Simpson

The editor would like to thank Jamie Davies, who offered valuable comments on the contents.

# INTRODUCTION

Chambers Science Factfinder, an exciting new addition to the Chambers Factfinder range, provides a wide range of information in one handy volume. Designed to be not only useful but entertaining, the text is peppered with fascinating facts, quirky quotations and ingenious applications that are sure to amaze and amuse.

The opening sections of the *Science Factfinder* familiarize readers with the ideas and language of science. The renowned science writer Philip Ball, winner of the 2005 Aventis prize for science writing, tackles the question 'What is science?', and gives an insight into how scientists think and work, in two introductory articles. An A–Z guide to scientific terms and fields then follows, helping to demystify the jargon that so often makes science difficult to understand.

The middle parts of the book focus on scientific research and those who undertake it. A chronology explores the fascinating development of science from ancient times to the present day, while the human face of scientific discovery is revealed through biographies of notable scientists and details of the prizes they have won.

The later sections of the *Science Factfinder* concentrate on the knowledge and understanding that scientists have gained to date through their research. Key scientific concepts are explained in short summaries, while 14 subject-specific sections provide clear information and handy reference material relating to different areas of science. Topics are arranged to take readers on a journey from the biology of their own bodies, through the chemistry, geology and environmental science that describe our planet, to the physics and mathematics that govern the universe.

Detailed contents pages at the front of the book, as well as an index, guide the reader to specific information throughout the various sections, while cross-references highlight the connections between different aspects of science and encourage browsing. A system of icons relates the information to particular areas of science.

Whether hunting for a specific fact, seeking to understand a particular scientific topic or simply browsing for something new, Chambers Science Factfinder is sure to satisfy.

A system of icons relates the key concepts, reference topics and chronology entries to eight broad areas of science.

Astronomy

Geology

Biology

Mathematics

Chemistry

Medicine

Climate and environment

Physics

Cross-references within each section of the book are in **bold** and relate to the main headings within that section, eg (see **atom**).

Cross-references between sections are in the form **Section: Main heading**, eg (see **Genetics: DNA**).

# ABBREVIATIONS

Abbreviations with an initial Greek letter are listed alphabetically under the equivalent English letter.

For symbols of chemical elements, see **Atoms, elements and molecules**, p364. Abbreviations of units used in the main text are given; for additional abbreviations, see **Measurement**, pp499–504.

Months are abbreviated to the first three letters, eg 26 Nov 1976.

| | | | |
|---|---|---|---|
| a | acre(s) | DC | direct current |
| A | ampere(s); adenine | dm | decimetre(s) |
| AC | alternating current | DNA | deoxyribonucleic acid |
| AD | Anno Domini | DVD | digital video disc |
| AIDS | acquired immune deficiency syndrome | eg | for example |
| aJ | attojoules | °F | degrees Fahrenheit |
| AM | amplitude modulation | fl. | flourished |
| ATP | adenosine triphosphate | fl oz | fluid ounce(s) |
| b. | born | fm | femtometre(s) |
| BBC | British Broadcasting Corporation | FM | frequency modulation |
| BC | before Christ | FRS | Fellow of the Royal Society |
| BCG | Bacille Calmette–Guérin | ft | foot (feet) |
| BSE | bovine spongiform encephalopathy | g | gram(s) |
| c | century | G | guanine |
| c. | circa | gal | gallon(s) |
| C | coulombs; cytidine | GHz | gigahertz |
| °C | degrees Celsius (Centigrade) | GJ | gigajoule(s) |
| CBE | Commander of the (Order of the) British Empire | GUT | Grand Unified Theory |
| cd | candela(s) | Gy | gray(s) |
| CFCs | chlorofluorocarbons | h | hour(s) |
| CJD | Creutzfeldt-Jakob disease | ha | hectare(s) |
| cl | centilitre(s) | HBV | hepatitis B virus |
| cm | centimetre(s) | HF | high frequency |
| cu | cubic | HIV | human immunodeficiency virus |
| d. | died | hl | hectolitre(s) |
| dB | decibel(s) | hm | hectometre(s) (hectares) |
| DBE | Dame (Commander of the Order) of the British Empire | Hz | hertz |
| | | ICM | International Congress of Mathematicians |
| | | ie | that is |

| | | | |
|---|---|---|---|
| IMU | International Mathematical Union | $\mu$T | microtesla(s) |
| in | inch(es) | MW | medium wave |
| J | joule(s) | Mya | million years ago |
| K | Kelvin | N | newton(s) |
| KBE | Knight Commander of the (Order of the) British Empire | nm | nanometre(s) |
| | | NMR | nuclear magnetic resonance |
| kcd | kilocandela(s) | no | number |
| kg | kilogram(s) | nWb | nanoweber(s) |
| kHz | kilohertz | $\Omega$ | ohm(s) |
| kJ | kilojoule(s) | $\pi$ | pi |
| klx | kilolux | Pa | pascal(s) |
| km | kilometre(s) | PCR | polymerase chain reaction |
| kN | kilonewton(s) | PhD | doctor of philosophy |
| kPa | kilopascal(s) | pm | picometre(s) |
| kph | kilometres per hour | POW | prisoner of war |
| kW | kilowatt(s) | pt | pint(s) |
| l | litre(s) | rad | radian(s) |
| lb | pound(s) | Rh | rhesus |
| LF | low frequency | RNA | ribonucleic acid |
| lm | lumen(s) | s | second(s) |
| LW | long wave | sq | square |
| lx | lux | sr | steradian(s) |
| ly | light year(s) | Sv | sievert(s) |
| m | metre(s) | SW | short wave |
| mC | millicurie(s) | T | thymine |
| MF | medium frequency | Tm | terametre(s) |
| MG | megagram(s) | TOE | theory of everything |
| MHz | megahertz | TSE | transmissible spongiform encephalopathy |
| mi | mile(s) | | |
| min | minute(s) | U | uracil |
| $\mu$J | microjoule(s) | UHF | ultra high frequency |
| ml | millilitre(s) | UK | United Kingdom |
| mm | millimetre(s) | US | United States |
| $\mu$m | micrometre(s) (microns) | USA | United States of America |
| $\mu$N | micronewton(s) | USSR | Union of Soviet Socialist Republics |
| mol | mole | | |
| Mpa | megapascal(s) | V | volt(s) |
| mph | miles per hour | W | watt(s) |
| mrad | milliradian(s) | Wb | weber(s) |
| | | yd | yard(s) |

# CONTENTS

# SCIENCE FACTFINDER
## Contents

# SCIENCE FACTFINDER

# WHAT IS SCIENCE?

## The problems of defining science

There can be more than one motive for attempting to define a word. If the word is one that few people have heard of, a definition simply aims to throw light into darkness; if, on the other hand, the word refers to something familiar, a definition may help to untangle common misperceptions – to dispel not darkness, but confusion. Defining 'science' is a task of the second sort. We have all heard about science; we have almost certainly been taught something about it at school; we know that it affects our lives, that it has something to do with technology and something to do with the way the world works. But what is it, exactly?

Most of us could make our way through life without ever needing a more precise definition than the cluster of ideas above. However, it is surely a precarious society that has only the foggiest notion about the most powerful system of thought it has devised. We might be aware that, until we know certain key 'facts' of science, we are ill-equipped to deal with some important aspects of modern life (in areas such as health and the environment, for example). But knowing facts alone may not help us much – we need to know what to do with them, and this can be difficult unless we have some idea of what science itself actually is.

## Science is a human activity

> Science is facts. Just as houses are made of stones,
> so science is made of facts. But a pile of stones
> is not a house and a collection of facts is not
> necessarily a science.
>
> —French mathematician Henri Poincaré (1854–1912),
> La Science et l'Hypothèse (1902).

It is tempting to begin by listing the things that science is not. It is not, for example, a collection of facts, some of which are forced into us at school and then quickly forgotten afterwards. If it is true that this is sometimes the way science is taught, then it is taught badly. The trouble with a collection of facts is that there is often no obvious relation between them. If you can remember the date of the Battle of Agincourt, can you work out the date of the Battle of Waterloo? Of course you can't. History is not a series of dates, and likewise science is not a list of unrelated facts – it is not even the mechanism that produces the list. Science is a particular kind of human activity, one that helps us to see connections between natural phenomena and to alter the world around us in more or less predictable ways.

> Natural science does not simply describe and
> explain nature; it is part of the interplay between
> nature and ourselves; it describes nature as exposed
> to our method of questioning.
>
> —German physicist Werner Heisenberg (1901–76),
> Physics and Philosophy (1959)

# WHAT IS SCIENCE?

Science is not about finding out true things – at least, not if by 'true' we mean that those things never change. Science helps us to find descriptions of the world that seem to work, in the sense that we can use those descriptions to make predictions that are usually pretty reliable, and sometimes astonishingly so. If a scientific prediction fails, it does so because the theory that led to it is imperfect, or even totally wrong, or has been applied to a situation in which it is an inappropriate description of the world. Science itself can't be 'wrong', because it is an activity, not a theory. It would be like saying that tennis is wrong – a meaningless statement. Tennis is sometimes irrelevant to the matter at hand, and tennis can certainly be played badly; but tennis is never 'wrong'.

Calling science a human activity is not a trivial point – it is part of the definition of science. This doesn't simply mean that cockroaches don't do science (in fact, some people might argue that they do), or that science is just a social construct (although the social setting of science inevitably plays a part in shaping it). It means that science is perhaps best defined as the activity that scientists do, just as art is what artists do and religion is what religious people practice. Many people are uncomfortable with this idea. They think that it should be possible to define science in abstract terms, without reference to the routine activities of real scientists. The problem with this approach is that, if you try it, you end up with a definition that bears little relation to what appears in scientific journals. If science is, as some would have it, simply about discovering how the world works, then all the research done on making new drugs and materials, or building ingenious devices from silicon and DNA – all the work that fills pages and pages of journals in physics and chemistry, biology and geology and engineering – isn't really science. Clearly, then, a definition of that sort makes no sense.

## Science and technology

The British biologist Peter Medawar takes the stance that our culture's notions of 'what science is' have become infected with the idea of 'purity', so that the only 'real science' we will allow is that which aims to understand the workings of the universe, and has nothing to do with the grubby business of making things. This distinction, Medawar says, is one motivated by a kind of aesthetic snobbery: it is 'between polite and rude learning, between the laudably useless and the vulgarly applied, the free and the intellectually compromised, the poetic and the mundane.' By avoiding such distinctions, it is possible to consider 'science' and 'technology' as one and the same, or at least as merging seamlessly . Other people, including the British biologist Lewis Wolpert, still argue for separate activities of 'science' and 'technology', the former being straightforward discoveries about the nature of things and the latter being the applications in which we use these discoveries.

> 66
>
> *The first man of science was he who looked into a thing, not to learn whether it furnished him with food, or shelter, or weapons, or tools, or armaments, or playwiths but who sought to know it for the gratification of knowing.*
>
> —English poet Samuel Taylor Coleridge (1772–1834).
>
> 99

> " 
> We shall have to learn to refrain from doing things
> merely because we know how to do them.
> —Sir Theodore Fox, Editor, *The Lancet* (1965).
> "

## Science and morality

The question of whether science and technology are separable has important
implications for the moral responsibilities of scientists. Lewis Wolpert maintains that
'science is value-free, as it explains the world as it is. Ethical issues arise only when
science is applied to technology – from medicine to industry'. However, drawing
such a distinction may be seen as an argument that scientists are above morality,
which is a dangerous thing to suppose. Of course, we can't change the basic
principles of how the world works, only how we choose to harness them. However,
if we try to maintain a rigid separation of these two categories, much (although not
all) of today's 'science' would fall into the category of 'technology': even some of
the most abstruse research in modern physics, for example, often has applications
explicitly in mind. Scientists can rarely tell exactly where their research might
lead, but they often have a fair idea of the possibilities – and so one can argue that
there are moral responsibilities attached to such research well before it reaches an
'engineering' stage.

> " 
> Knowledge is a sacred cow, and my problem will
> be how we can milk her while keeping clear of her
> horns.
> —US biochemist Albert Szent-Gyorgyi (1893–1986),
> in *Science* (1964).
> "

## What do scientists do?

Clearly the question 'what is science?' does not have a simple answer. The
separate, but related, question 'how is science done?' is commonly answered
with references to what is called the 'scientific method' (see **Scientific thought**),
although of course it is one thing to ask how science ought to be done in principle,
and another to ask how it is done in practice. One way to attempt an answer to all
of these questions is to take a look at what scientists actually do and try to work out
what, if anything, their activities have in common.

The first thing to say is that these activities are different today from what they were
a hundred years ago, which in turn differed from those a few centuries further
back. The English philosopher Francis Bacon tried to set an agenda for science at
the beginning of the 17th century by calling for natural philosophers (as scientists
were then called) to make systematic observations and experiments, so that they
could accumulate reliable knowledge about the way things are. People did make
careful observations and experiments before Bacon, but they didn't generally use
them to seek deep understanding. The Babylonians, for example, kept detailed
records of the motions of the stars and planets, and even used them to predict

what their future positions would be. They also developed theories about why the heavenly bodies moved in this way. However, their theories were theological, and could never explain why the planets took the very specific trajectories that they did. Bacon's contemporary, the German astronomer Johann Kepler, on the other hand, used numerical tables of astronomical data to figure out the mathematical laws that could explain the numbers. At that time, Kepler couldn't explain why these mathematical relationships should exist, and this remained a mystery until Isaac Newton, later in the 17th century, proposed a mechanism – the law of gravity – that could account for them.

Theories with the explanatory and predictive power of Newton's were, however, rare in his age. Many of his contemporaries spent their time thinking up interesting 'what if' questions and then conducting experiments to find the answers. This was very much in line with Bacon's model for the practice of science; but, in general, scientific theories don't just 'fall out' of the data.

All the same, there is still plenty of science around today that follows Bacon's model, especially in molecular biology and genetics. Because they do not yet know some of the fundamental principles that govern the systems they are studying, scientists in these fields must rely on the habit of amassing data and looking for patterns that will give them clues about the underlying mechanisms. By contrast, in some other fields, such as evolutionary biology and the earth sciences – geology, oceanography, atmospheric science – the basic principles are fairly well established, but the real world imposes so many complex factors that researchers have to labour to understand each little piece of the puzzle. For instance, it is understood that both Africa and Asia are shaped by the same geological forces but, until they go there, geologists can't be sure exactly what they will find.

Modern chemistry, meanwhile, is mostly about making things – finding new ways to put atoms together to create useful molecules and substances. This sort of 'fabrication science' is also common in areas such as biotechnology and computer science, and is surprisingly prevalent in physics. But in all of these scientific disciplines, the common modern idea of what science consists of – framing hypotheses about the way a system should behave, and then devising an experiment to see if it does – is often indeed the way science is done. (In disciplines such as geology and astronomy, where it is hard to run real experiments, such hypotheses may be put to the test using computer models or scaled-down laboratory models.) It's important to understand that these hypotheses are themselves typically generated as a result of observation or experiment – by scientists exploring a natural or an artificial system, and coming up against something they didn't expect or can't explain. (See **Scientific thought: A matter of fact, or just a theory?**)

This is why puzzles, mysteries and unexplained phenomena are the lifeblood of science. People who are sceptical of what they perceive as science's attempt to corner the market on 'truth' often fail to realize that, when scientists encounter something that conflicts with their theories, collectively they couldn't be more delighted – such conflicts provide fresh material for science to investigate, and the possibility of discovering something new. Of course, individual scientists don't always welcome evidence that their theories are 'wrong' – they are only human, after all.

# SCIENTIFIC THOUGHT

## Seeing beyond the obvious

Because you have to think logically to do science, it has often been said that science is simply well organized common sense. This was the view of the biologist Thomas Henry Huxley, Charles Darwin's supporter in the 19th century, and it was the position taken by the influential philosopher of science Alfred North Whitehead in the early 20th century. But it can be argued that, on the contrary, science requires the precise opposite of common sense – that's not common nonsense, but uncommon sense. The scientist needs to see beyond what is 'obvious'.

It seems 'obvious', for example, that the sun moves across the sky – or, to a rather more careful thinker, that the sun circles around the globe of the earth. This conclusion follows so 'obviously' from what we observe that astronomers didn't realize that in fact the earth moves around the sun until thousands of years after they began to study the heavens. It is 'obvious' that you have to keep pushing an object – you must keep applying a force – if you want to keep it moving. Galileo's genius was to recognize that, on the contrary, a moving object will keep moving forever so long as no forces act on it. A ball rolling over flat ground eventually comes to rest because it is slowed by the force of friction. Without frictional resistance from the ground and air, a ball moving in empty space will never stop.

> **“**
> *That is the essence of science: ask an impertinent question and you are on the way to a pertinent answer.*
>
> —Polish mathematician Jacob Bronowski (1908–74), *The Ascent of Man* (1973).
> **”**

## A process of deduction – or induction?

This was why the 'scientific' theories of the philosophers of antiquity, such as Aristotle, were so often wrong. Their approach seemed sound at face value: they started with axioms or premises that are unquestionably true, and deduced through logical steps what these premises imply. This is called deductive reasoning. It usually worked well enough in geometry, but in physics it was easy to go astray because the axioms were really just guesses, and because what passes for 'common sense' with one person is nothing of the kind to another. Aristotle's explanations in particular were often circular arguments: he said, for example, that stones fall to earth because they tend naturally to have downward motion. They fall, in other words, because it is in their nature to fall. That doesn't get you very far.

> **“**
> *Aristotle maintained that women have fewer teeth than men; although he was twice married, it never occurred to him to verify this statement by examining his wives' mouths.*
>
> —English mathematician and philosopher Bertrand, Lord Russell (1872–1970), *The Impact of Science on Society* (1952).
> **”**

Another problem with deductive reasoning from 'common-sense' premises is that common sense tends to depend on what is widely believed at the time. It seemed very reasonable for the English theologian William Paley at the start of the 19th century to argue that the wonderful 'design' of living organisms pointed to the existence of a Designer, just as a person finding an intricately mechanical watch in the middle of a heath would have to infer the existence of a watchmaker: such a structure is too complex to have arisen by chance, for if you take any part of it away then the whole thing fails. This argument was no longer 'common sense', however, once Charles Darwin had provided a mechanism – natural selection – by which such apparent 'design' could arise spontaneously in nature. (It's worth remembering, however, that even before Darwin, Paley's argument didn't look like common sense to some people, such as the Scottish philosopher David Hume.)

But if common sense is so treacherous a guide, how can people hope to gain reliable knowledge about the world? From the late Renaissance to the Victorian era, most scientists tended to rely on the inductive reasoning advocated by the 17th-century English philosopher Francis Bacon. This assumes that, if something holds true for all the cases that you've come across, then it is universally true. Scientific 'laws' then emerge as generalizations of observations of the world, once you have looked at enough examples. If every river and stream you come across runs downhill, it is a law of nature that 'water runs downhill'. The problem here is that there is no logical reason why this should be so. Even if you spend years finding white swans, that doesn't rule out the possibility that there isn't a black swan somewhere that you haven't yet found. You can't conclude that 'all swans are white'. What's more, it can be hard to spot reasons why your sample is biased (perhaps all black swans live in very remote places, or only come out at night).

Scientists also faced the problem that explanations for observed events are never unique. Both the rotation of the earth around the sun, and the sun around the earth, will explain the sun's motion across the sky – and so, for that matter, will the hypothesis that the sun is a flaming disc borne on Apollo's chariot. To cut through these thickets of possible explanations, scientists in both historical and contemporary times have used a principle called Occam's razor. The English monk William of Ockham (or Occam) proposed in the 14th century that, in philosophy, 'entities should not be multiplied unnecessarily.' In other words, keep things simple – or, as Isaac Newton put it, 'We are to admit no more causes of natural things than such as are both true and sufficient to explain their appearances.' Albert Einstein had a nicer phrase: 'Everything should be made as simple as possible, but not simpler.'

Thus, if there are two scientific theories competing to explain a particular phenomenon, we should choose the simplest. And we should avoid introducing new principles when existing ones will suffice. No one can prove (without further information) that glowing lights seen in the sky are not those of an extraterrestrial spacecraft – but Occam's razor tells us that we should assume, unless we have reason to think otherwise, that they are the lights of, say, a human aircraft, which does not then oblige us to assume the possibility of (among other things) interstellar travel by intelligent beings.

Occam's razor is just a practical tool, not an iron rule. We know of no law that says the universe has to be as simple as possible (although many scientists believe that it is). Sometimes the more complex theory might be the right one. But if scientists do not at least let the principle guide them, science itself will be submerged beneath arbitrary 'explanations'. It is possible that God made humankind, but all the questions this hypothesis raises are avoided if we assume that Darwinian evolution did the job instead – something that it is clearly capable of doing.

## Reasons to be wrong

Because you can never prove that something is 'true' simply by accumulating examples of it being so, the Austrian-British philosopher Karl Popper argued in the 1930s that science doesn't really work by inductive reasoning. Instead, he proposed the so-called hypothetico-deductive method, which says that scientific ideas are always provisional: they can never be proved, but they can be falsified. So scientific theories are tested not by devising experiments which show that they are true, but by conducting tests that could potentially disprove them. In other words, the scientist's task is to conduct a systematic search for those black swans. So long as it survives such searches, a theory can be deemed reliable.

> 66
>
> *Überhaupt ist es für den Forscher ein guter Morgensport, täglich vor dem Frühstück eine Lieblingshypothese einzustampfen—das erhält jung.*
>
> *(It is a good morning exercise for a research scientist to discard a pet hypothesis every day before breakfast. It keeps him young.)*
>
> —Austrian zoologist Konrad Lorenz (1903–89), *Das sogenannte Böse* ('The So-Called Evil', 1963), translated by Marjorie Latzke as *On Aggression* (1966). 99

Popper put his finger on precisely what it is that makes science so powerful: not its veracity, but its scepticism. It never stakes a claim to the truth, but instead recognizes that it represents merely the current best guess, which could be overturned tomorrow. We can scarcely be surprised that science is not always practised this way; scientists inevitably become attached to their ideas and theories, and sometimes choose to ignore evidence of their deficiencies. But that doesn't tend to hinder scientific progress, or not for long, because there is never any shortage of more objective observers who won't tolerate a theory that conflicts with what the real world tells us.

> 66
>
> *An important scientific innovation rarely makes its way by gradually winning over and converting its opponents: it rarely happens that Saul becomes Paul. What does happen is that its opponents gradually die out, and that the growing generation is familiarized with the ideas from the beginning.*
>
> —German theoretical physicist Max Planck (1858–1947), in *Thematic Origins of Scientific Thought* by G Holton (1973). 99

# Scientific Thought

## Perpetual revolution

That, at least, is what scientists hope. But the American philosopher of science Thomas Kuhn proposed in 1962 that scientific advance is not always so relentless and smooth. He suggested instead that the progression occurs sporadically, as fundamental, cherished theories collapse and are replaced in intellectual revolutions that have become known as 'paradigm shifts' – 'paradigm' here means the standard way of looking at things. During non-revolutionary periods of 'normal science', scientists get so stuck in established modes of thinking that they are not even able to formulate the questions that would get them out of the rut. The existing paradigm dominates scientific thought, and almost all scientists follow its precepts unquestioningly. They are engaged in posing questions and solving puzzles within that paradigm.

> "
> *How can we have any new ideas or fresh outlooks when 90 per cent of all the scientists who have ever lived have still not died?*
>
> —British crystallographer Alan Lindsay Mackay (b.1926), in *Scientific World* (1969).
> "

Eventually, however (according to Kuhn), some anomaly emerges that can't be fitted into the prevailing paradigm. This provokes a crisis in science, usually characterized by strong dissent. A new theory is proposed, often by younger scientists, that provides a way out of the crisis – and into a new paradigm. For a time everything is in turmoil, but eventually science settles down to a new normality – one where the 'old' way of doing things is virtually forgotten. Just as it will soon seem odd to people that there was a time when, if you wanted to telephone someone when you were out and about, you had to find a public phone box rather than using your mobile phone, so it seems strange or quaint to scientists after a paradigm shift that certain ideas and theories hadn't always existed.

A classic example of a paradigm shift in science is the development of quantum theory in the early 20th century, which arose from problems in understanding how light ejects electrons from metals (the 'photoelectric effect') and how warm objects emit radiation ('black-body radiation'). Max Planck and Albert Einstein realised that the theoretical problems posed by these phenomena could be solved by assuming that light energy is parcelled into packets known as 'quanta'; that is, light has the properties of particles as well as waves.

Some philosophers have extended Kuhn's ideas to argue that all scientific theories are merely products of their times and cultures, and that there is no reason to regard any particular paradigm as being 'better' than any other. According to this view, science changes but doesn't really advance. This is hard to square with the fact that we now know much more about the structure of the world, from microscopic to cosmic scales, than ever before, and as a consequence science can make much better predictions about its behaviour. Whether we have more wisdom about how to use that knowledge is, of course, another matter.

## A matter of fact, or just a theory?

Scientists make distinctions between ideas, hypotheses, theories and facts which, even if they are not entirely clear-cut, are still useful. These terms could be regarded as successive points on a scale stretching between ignorance and certainty. A scientific idea is like any other idea: it is an interesting thought that is worth exploring further. Could life on Earth have been 'seeded' by organisms from Mars, brought here in lumps of Martian rock that fell as meteorites? That's an interesting idea. A hypothesis states such an idea in more formal scientific terms, allowing you to see how it might be tested. The 'panspermia' hypothesis – a hypothesis that microscopic life from other Earth-like worlds can be deep-frozen in rocks or dust thrown into space by events such as a big meteorite impact, and that some of this debris drifts through the cosmos to Earth where the frozen cells get thawed and brought back to life – was proposed at the start of the 20th century. One way of testing it would be to look for signs of life in meteorites. If you found it, you would then need to be able to rule out the possibility that the meteorite was contaminated with earthly bacteria after it fell. You would also have to think about (and study experimentally) a number of other ideas, such as whether living organisms can survive such a trip through space.

If a hypothesis appears to stand up in the face of many tests like this, it can be granted the dignified status of a theory. This means that it seems to provide a self-consistent and accurate explanation of how things happen, or how they once happened. There is no evidence yet that makes the panspermia hypothesis a theory, but there is plenty of evidence that allows us to talk about Darwinian evolution and general relativity as theories. Scientists now feel justified in using these theories to explain other phenomena. When we say colloquially that something is 'just a theory', we tend to mean that it is just one possibility among others. But scientific theories are more than that. They started out as hypotheses and are now supported by strong evidence, so we can afford to trust them.

Strictly speaking, a scientific theory can never really become a 'fact', because it might always be disproved by further observations. However, some theories are so solidly supported by all kinds of different evidence that scientists feel justified in talking about them as facts – they might regard evolution as a fact, for example. It might not be a fact from a philosophical point of view, but no reasonable person can deny it. Other scientific 'facts' are not explanations, but simply descriptions of nature: it is a fact that the value of $\pi$, the ratio of the circumference to the diameter of a circle, has the value 3.142 (to three decimal places), and we can be sure there won't be a circle found in normal space that has a value of $\pi$ equal to 10. The same is true of other fundamental constants of nature, such as the ratio of the masses of the proton and the electron (subatomic particles that make up atoms). Scientific theories often try to find explanations for the values of such quantitative facts. Much of scientific reasoning, therefore, isn't about looking for facts, but about understanding why the facts are true.

# A

**aberration**    Faults in the image produced by an optical instrument such as a mirror or lens, caused by light focusing on several points or being reflected or refracted by varying amounts.

**abscissa**    In **coordinate geometry**, the *x*-coordinate of a point, corresponding to its distance along the horizontal axis; compare **ordinate**.

**absolute zero**    The lowest possible temperature for all substances, when the **molecules** of a substance possess no thermal energy. A figure of –273.15°C (–459.67°F) is generally accepted as the value of absolute zero.

**absorption**    In chemistry, the process by which one substance is incorporated into the structure of another substance, as when water is soaked up by a sponge; compare **adsorption**.

**AC**    see **alternating current**

**acid**    In chemistry, a compound that forms hydrogen **ions** when it is dissolved in water and reacts with a **base** to form a **salt**. Acids have a **pH** value of less than 7. See **Atoms, elements and molecules: Acids, alkalis and bases**.

**acid rain**    Rain that is unnaturally acidic as a result of pollution of the atmosphere with oxides of nitrogen and sulphur, eg from the burning of coal in power stations and petroleum products in vehicle engines. See **Climate and enviroment: Chemical imbalances**.

**acquired character**    In zoology, a change in a part of an animal's body that occurs during its lifetime, eg an enlarging of a muscle that is frequently used, as distinct from a characteristic inherited from a previous generation; see **natural selection**.

**actinobiology**    The study of the effects of radiation on living organisms.

**adaptation**    In zoology, a physical or behavioural change in an organism that makes it better suited to its natural environment and increases its chances of survival; see **natural selection**.

**adenosine triphosphate**    see **ATP**

**adiabatic process**    In physics, a process in which there is no gain or loss of

**adsorption**　In chemistry, the process by which one substance collects on the surface of another but is not incorporated into the structure of it; compare **absorption**.

**aerobic**　Needing oxygen in order to take place or survive. Aerobic **respiration** is the process by which cells use oxygen to convert glucose into energy, releasing water and carbon dioxide as waste products. Compare **anaerobic**.

**aerodynamics**　The branch of fluid mechanics that deals with the dynamics of gases, particularly the study of forces acting on objects in motion in air.

**aerosol**　A substance, eg mist or fog, that consists of small particles of a liquid or solid suspended in a gas.

**aerospace**　The Earth's atmosphere together with the space beyond it.

**aetiology** or **etiology**　In medicine, the study of the causes of disease.

**affinity**　(1) In chemistry, a force that binds the atoms of a molecule together. (2) In immunology, a measure of the strength of the interaction between an **antigen** and an **antibody** or between a **receptor** and the molecule that binds to it.

**AIDS**　Short for Acquired Immune Deficiency Syndrome; a disease that attacks the **immune system** and makes the body very susceptible to infection. It is caused by the human immunodeficiency virus (**HIV**) and is transmitted through bodily fluids such as blood and semen.

**algae**　A group of simple organisms that contain **chlorophyll**, have no roots, stems or leaves, and live in water or in damp conditions.

**algebra**　The branch of mathematics that deals with the relationships between quantities. It uses combinations of letters, numbers and other symbols to represent quantities.

**algology**　The study of **algae**.

**aliphatic compound**　An **organic** compound in which there are no **delocalized** electrons; compare **aromatic compound**.

**alkali**　In chemistry, a compound that forms hydroxide **ions** when it is dissolved in water. Alkalis are a type of **base** and have a **pH** value of more than 7. See **Atoms, elements and molecules: Acids, alkalis and bases**.

| | |
|---|---|
| **allele** | One of the possible forms in which a **gene** can be expressed in an individual. See **Genetics: Genetic inheritance**. |
| **allotrope** | One of the possible forms that a chemical **element** can have in the same solid, liquid or gas state. For example, graphite and diamond are allotropes of carbon. |
| **alloy** | A mixture of metals, or a mixture of a metal with a non-metal in which the metal is the major component. See **Materials: Alloys**. |
| **alpha particle** | A positively charged particle that is emitted by the **nucleus** of a radioactive atom; see **radioactivity**. |
| **alternating current (AC)** | An electric **current** in which the direction of flow changes at regular intervals; compare **direct current**. |
| **AM** | see **amplitude modulation** |
| **amino acid** | An **organic** molecule containing an amino group ($NH_2$) and a carboxyl group (COOH). Amino acids play an important part in the body's biological processes, often combining in different forms to produce **proteins**. See **Atoms, elements and molecules: Amino acids**. |
| **amorphous** | Existing in a non-**crystalline** or disordered form. Glass is an amorphous solid. |
| **amplitude** | In physics, the height of a **wave** from its average value to its maximum value. |
| **amplitude modulation (AM)** | A method of radio broadcasting in which the size or **amplitude** of the **wave** changes to reflect changes in broadcast sounds, while the **frequency** remains the same. Compare **frequency modulation**. |
| **amu** | see **atomic mass unit** |
| **anabolic** | Causing a build-up of body tissue. Anabolic steroids are **hormones** that promote tissue growth. Compare **catabolic**. |
| **anaerobic** | Taking place or surviving in the absence of oxygen. In anaerobic **respiration**, glucose is not broken down completely, and much less energy is produced than in **aerobic** respiration. |
| **analogous** | Analogous features are physical features that have a similar function but a different evolutionary origin, as have, eg, the wings of a bird and the wings of a butterfly; compare **homologous**. |
| **analogue** or **analog** | Using a physical quantity that changes continuously, as does the position of the hands on the face of a |

traditional clock, unlike the display of a **digital** clock, which changes at intervals.

**angiology**
The study of the structure of blood and lymph vascular systems.

**anion**
An **ion** with a negative electrical **charge**.

**anisotropic**
Having physical properties, eg strength or the ability to conduct electrical current, that are different in different directions. See **Materials: Properties of materials**.

**annihilation**
In nuclear physics, the process in which a **subatomic particle** and its **antiparticle** are destroyed as they collide, releasing a burst of **radiation**.

**annual**
A plant that flowers and dies within a period of one year from germination.

**anode**
The positive **electrode** in an **electrolytic cell** or **voltaic cell**; compare **cathode**.

**antibody**
A defensive **protein** produced in an organism in response to the action of a foreign body, eg the **toxin** of a bacterium. See **Human body: Defence mechanisms**.

**antigen**
A substance that stimulates the production of an **antibody**.

**antiparticle**
The antiparticle of a given particle has the same mass but opposite values for all its other properties, eg **charge**. A particle and its antiparticle destroy each other on contact in the process of **annihilation**.

**apogee**
The point in the orbit of a planet or other body at which it is furthest from the body it is orbiting; compare **perigee**.

**archaea**
A group of single-celled microorganisms that are similar in for to **bacteria** but are not related to them. They are very old in evolutionary terms and gave unusual **metabolisms** and **habitats**. See **Organisms: Archaea Kingdom**.

**Archimedes' principle**
The principle that when a body is wholly or partly immersed in a fluid it experiences an upward force equal to the weight of fluid it displaces. See **Key concepts: Archimedes' principle**.

**arithmetic**
The branch of mathematics that deals with the addition, subtraction, multiplication and division of numbers.

**aromatic compound**
An **organic** compound in which the carbon atoms are arranged in a ring structure with clouds of **delocalized** electrons above and below, as they are in benzene and pyridine; compare **aliphatic compound**.

| | |
|---|---|
| **asteroid** | One of the thousands of rocky objects found in the solar system, normally between the orbits of Mars and Jupiter, ranging in size from 1 to 1000km. Also called a minor planet. See **Space: Asteroids**. |
| **astigmatism** | Unequal curvature of the focusing surfaces of the eye, which prevents light rays from reaching a common focal point on the retina, resulting in blurred eyesight. |
| **astronomical unit** | The mean distance of the Earth from the Sun, about 149 600 000km (93 000 000 mi), used as a measure of the distance between celestial objects. |
| **astronomy** | The study of all classes of celestial object and the universe as a whole. |
| **astrophysics** | The branch of astronomy that applies the laws of physics to the study of stars, **galaxies** and interstellar space. |
| **asymptote** | In geometry, a line that a curve approaches but never touches. |
| **atom** | The smallest particle of an element that can take part in a chemical reaction. It comprises a central **nucleus** containing **protons** and **neutrons**, surrounded by shells of **electrons**. During chemical reactions, atoms lose, share or transfer some of their electrons to become compounds. See **Atoms, elements and molecules: Atoms**. |
| **atomic mass** | see **relative atomic mass** |
| **atomic mass unit (amu)** | A unit of mass equal to one twelfth the mass of a neutral atom of carbon-12, the most abundant **isotope** of carbon. |
| **atomic number** | The number of **protons** in the **nucleus** of an **atom** of an element, equal also to the number of **electrons** orbiting the element's nucleus. |
| **ATP** | Adenosine triphosphate, an **organic** compound that carries chemical energy in all living organisms and drives their biological processes. See **Cells: Cellular energy**. |
| **autecology** | The study of the ecology of any individual species; compare **synecology**. |
| **axiom** | In mathematics, a statement or fact that is accepted as true without being proved. |

# B

**background radiation**  Radiation that occurs naturally in the atmosphere and on the Earth's surface.

**bacteria**  A large group of single-celled **microorganisms** that are found in all living things and natural environments. Some bacteria live as **parasites** and produce **toxins** that cause disease. See **Organisms: Eubacteria kingdom**.

**bacteriology**  The scientific study of **bacteria**.

**bacteriophage**  A virus that infects **bacteria**.

**ballistics**  The branch of physics that deals with the motion of projectiles, eg bullets and missiles.

**base**  (1) In chemistry, any of a class of compounds that react with **acids** and some metals to form **salts**. A base that dissolves in water is an **alkali**. See **Atoms, elements and molecules: Acids, alkalis and bases**. (2) In mathematics, a number that is multiplied by an **exponent**. In the expression $3^2$, 3 is the base and 2 the exponent. (3) In mathematics, a number on which a number system is based. See **decimal, binary**.

**benthos**  A collective name for the immobile animal and plant life that lives on the sea bottom.

**benzene**  A colourless liquid derived from petroleum, used to make various chemical products. The six carbon atoms in benzene are arranged in a ring known as a benzene ring, each atom having a hydrogen atom attached to it. Benzene is an **aromatic compound**.

**beta particle**  An **electron** or **positron** that is emitted during the disintegration of the **nucleus** of a radioactive atom; see **radioactivity**.

**biennial**  A plant that flowers and dies between its first and second years and does not flower in its first year.

**Big Bang**  In astronomy, the hypothetical violent explosion that created the universe, between 12 billion and 14 billion years ago. The Big Bang Theory states that all the matter and energy of the universe was once an unimaginably dense mass and that the universe has been expanding from the explosion of this mass ever since.

**binary**  A system of numbers whose **base** is 2.

**bio-**  In science, the prefix bio- means 'relating to life'. For example, *biochemistry* is the chemistry of living organisms.

**bioassay**
An experiment designed to determine how much of a substance is present by measuring its biological effect, eg on the growth of an organism.

**biogenesis**
The formation of living organisms from their ancestors and of **organelles** from their predecessors.

**biology**
The study of living organisms and systems, with branches including botany, anatomy, physiology and zoology.

**bioluminescence**
The production of light by living organisms, eg glow-worms, some deep-sea fish, some bacteria and some fungi.

**biophysics**
The study of biological phenomena using the laws of physics. The ability of bats to navigate using **echolocation**, for example, would come into this realm.

**biosphere**
The parts of the Earth and the atmosphere surrounding it that are able to support life, generally accepted as extending upwards at least to a height of 10 000m (33 000ft) and downwards to the depths of the ocean, and a few hundred metres below the land surface. The term may also be applied theoretically to other planets. See **Climate and environment: Biosphere**.

**biotechnology**
The use of organisms or their components in industrial or commercial processes, eg the use of genetic manipulation to develop new plant varieties for agriculture.

**bit**
In computer science, the smallest unit of computer information, which is the digit 0 or 1 in **binary** notation.

**black hole**
In astronomy, a region in space from which matter and energy cannot escape. A black hole could be a star or the central part of a galaxy which has collapsed in on itself to the point where the speed required for matter to escape exceeds the speed of light. See **Space: Black holes**.

**bond**
The force of attraction that holds **atoms** or **ions** together to form **molecules** or **crystals**, usually created by the transfer or sharing of one or more **electrons**. See **Atoms, elements and molecules: Chemical bonds**.

**botany**
The scientific study of plants.

**Brownian motion**
The random movement of solid particles suspended in a liquid or gas, caused by continual collisions between these particles and the **molecules** of the liquid or gas.

**bubble chamber**
In physics, a device for observing the movement of charged particles, which is observed as a string of

bubbles. The bubble chamber is regarded as more useful and reliable than the earlier **cloud chamber**.

**buckminsterfullerene**   A form of carbon with a molecule consisting of 60 carbon atoms arranged symmetrically to form a nearly spherical structure; also known by its familiar name buckyballs.

**buffer**   A substance added to a solution to maintain the level of its acidity when an **acid** or **base** is added to the solution.

**byte**   In computer science, a fixed number of **bits**, often eight, that correspond to a single letter or number and are operated on as a unit.

# C

**calculus**   The branch of mathematics that deals with very small or continuously varying quantities or functions. It can be used to calculate, for example, the area bounded by a curve. See **differentiation, integration**.

**carbohydrate**   Any of a large group of **organic** compounds of carbon, hydrogen and oxygen that are major sources of energy in the diets of humans and animals. Sugars, starches and cellulose are carbohydrates. See **Atoms, elements and molecules: Carbohydrates**.

**carbon dating**   see **radiocarbon dating**

**carcinogen**   A substance that can cause cancer, eg tobacco smoke or ionizing radiation.

**cardiology**   The branch of medical science that deals with the function and diseases of the heart.

**carnivore**   A flesh-eating creature; compare **herbivore, omnivore**.

**Cartesian coordinates**   see **coordinate geometry**

**catabolic**   Involving the breakdown of complex molecules into simpler ones, with the release of energy in the form of **ATP**. Such breakdown occurs when the body exerts itself and tissue is converted into energy. Compare **anabolic**.

**catalyst**   A substance that alters the rate of a chemical reaction but itself undergoes no permanent chemical change. In an organism, **enzymes** are biological catalysts.

**cathode**   The negative **electrode** in an **electrolytic cell** or **voltaic cell**; compare **anode**.

**cation**   An **ion** with a positive electrical **charge**.

**caudal**

If a body part is described as caudal, it is located towards an animal's tail or hindquarters; compare **rostral**.

**caustic**

Strongly alkaline and usually destructive or corrosive to living tissue.

**celestial sphere**

In astronomy, the imaginary sphere surrounding the Earth on which all planets, stars and other celestial bodies appear to lie.

**cell**

(1) In biology, the basic unit of matter of which all living things, with the exception of viruses, are composed. (2) In physical chemistry, a **voltaic cell** or an **electrolytic cell**; see **Electricity and magnets: Electricity**.

**cell division**

The division of a living cell into two or more cells, either as part of reproduction or in the process of tissue growth or repair; see **meiosis**, **mitosis**.

**cellulose**

A **carbohydrate** that is insoluble in water and is the main component of cell walls in plants. Its fibrous nature makes it an important ingredient in the manufacture of paper, textiles and other products. See **Materials: Bio-based materials**.

**Celsius scale**

The **SI** name for the temperature scale in which the freezing point of water is 0° and the boiling point is 100° under normal atmospheric pressure.

**centigrade scale**

Another name for the **Celsius scale**.

**centrifuge**

A machine that uses the force produced by rotation to separate molecules from solutions, particles and solids from liquids, and liquids that do not mix from each other.

**CFCs**

Chlorofluorocarbons, synthetic compounds that are chemically inert and were once widely used in industry, eg in aerosol propellants. When released into the atmosphere, they react with ozone and have resulted in damage to the **ozone layer**, contributing therefore to global warming; see also **greenhouse effect**.

**CGS system**

The Centimetre-Gram-Second system of units, based on the centimetre, the gram and the second as the fundamental units of length, mass and time. The system has, for most scientific purposes, been superseded by the **SI system**.

**chain reaction**

(1) In physics, a continuous cycle of nuclear **fission**, in which **neutrons** released from the splitting of **atoms** collide with other **nuclei** and induce further splitting, and so on. See **Energy, light and radioactivity: Nuclear reactions**. (2) In chemistry, a reaction in which

changes in one **molecule** induce changes in many other molecules, stopping only when a stable **compound** is formed.

**chaos theory**

The branch of mathematics that deals with describing systems that behave in unpredictable ways because slight changes in their **variables** produce significant changes in their results. The weather is a classic chaotic system. See **Key concepts: Chaos theory**.

**charge**

A property of some particles that causes them to be either attracted to or repelled by other particles. The property has two forms – positive and negative – and is responsible for all electrical phenomena. Particles of opposite charge attract each other and particles of like charge repel each other. See **Electricity and magnets: Electricity**.

**chemistry**

The study of the composition of substances and the changes they undergo.

**chlorofluorocarbons**

see **CFCs**

**chlorophyll**

Any of several green pigments involved in the process of **photosynthesis**. Chlorophyll A is the primary photosynthetic pigment in all organisms that release oxygen, ie all plants and algae.

**cholesterol**

A fatty molecule found in nerve tissues, gall stones and other tissues of the body. It is a main component of cell membranes and, in vertebrates, of blood, where increased levels are thought to cause diseases of the arteries.

**chromatography**

Any of various techniques used for analysing and separating mixtures of gases, liquids and dissolved substances. All techniques involve using a moving medium to transport the mixture through a stationary medium.

**chromosome**

A rod-like structure in the **nucleus** of a cell that carries the cell's **genes** and performs an important role in cell division and the transmission of hereditary features. See **Genetics: Chromosomes**.

**-cidal**

In science, the suffix -cidal relates to killing. For example, a *bacteriocidal* chemical kills bacteria.

**class**

In biological classification or **taxonomy**, a category of organisms that ranks above an **order** and below a **phylum**. See **Organisms: Levels of classification**.

**climatology**

The study of climate and its causes; compare **meteorology**.

**clone**
An organism, cell or group of cells produced asexually from a single ancestor. Clones can occur naturally, as when a plant produces a new and identical plant from a runner, or as the product of **genetic engineering**.

**cloud chamber**
In physics, a device for observing the movement of charged particles. Vapour inside the chamber is cooled, forming a cloud of droplets on the charged particles of the substance being observed. It has been largely superseded by the more useful and reliable **bubble chamber**.

**coefficient**
In **algebra**, a number or symbol that is multiplied by a **variable**, as the number 3 is in the term $3x$.

**colloid**
A substance consisting of particles between 1nm and 1μm in diameter, which forms a **suspension** in a liquid.

**commensalism**
A relationship between two different species in which one species, the commensal, benefits from the relationship and the other derives no benefit but is not harmed; compare **symbiosis**.

**commutative**
If a mathematical expression or operation is commutative, the result remains the same no matter what the order of the numbers, symbols or terms, as is the case in the operation $3 + 2$, which gives the same sum as $2 + 3$.

**compound**
In chemistry, a substance made up of two or more **elements** combined in fixed proportions. The **atoms** of the elements combine to form **molecules**. See **Atoms, elements and molecules: Chemical compounds**.

**condensation**
The process by which a gas or vapour becomes a liquid, either when it cools or when it is subjected to increased pressure.

**conductor**
A material that allows heat or electrical energy to pass through it. Metals are conductors. Compare **insulator**, **semiconductor**; see **Materials: Properties of materials**.

**congenital**
Congenital diseases or deformities are ones that are present at birth but are not passed on from a previous generation. See **Diseases and medicines: Congenital abnomalities**.

**congruent**
If two geometrical shapes are congruent, they have exactly the same size and shape as each other.

**constant**
(1) In mathematics, a quantity that has a fixed value; compare **variable**. (2) In physics, a quantity that is the same in all environments, eg the speed of light.

| | |
|---|---|
| **contagious** | A contagious disease is one that can be passed only through direct contact with an infected person or an infected object; compare **infectious**. |
| **continental drift** | The theory that the Earth's land surfaces were once one large mass that gradually broke apart to form separate continents; see also **plate tectonics**; **Key concepts: Continental drift**. |
| **convection** | The transfer of heat in a liquid or gas by means of a current that circulates as a result of temperature differences. For example, air heated by a radiator rises, to be replaced by cooler air at low levels. This in turn rises, to be replaced by the previously heated air that falls as it cools, and so on, creating a circulating current. |
| **coordinate geometry** | A system of geometry that represents points and lines in space as algebraic expressions. In two-dimensional coordinate geometry, the position of a point is defined by its distance along a horizontal $x$ axis and its distance along a vertical $y$ axis, from a point 0. |
| **Coriolis effect** | The effect whereby an object falling freely towards the Earth deviates slightly from a straight line and will fall to a point east of the point directly below its initial position, owing to the rotation of the Earth underneath as it falls. |
| **corona** | A ring of hot gas around the Sun or another celestial body, faintly visible through haze or thin cloud and more clearly visible at a solar eclipse. |
| **cosine** | In mathematics, the ratio, in a right-angled triangle, of the length of the side adjacent to an acute angle to the length of the **hypotenuse**; compare **sine, tangent**. |
| **cosmic rays** | High-energy particles from outer space that enter the Earth's atmosphere, often colliding with oxygen and nitrogen nuclei. See **Space: Cosmic rays**. |
| **cosmology** | The branch of astronomy that studies the universe on the largest scales of length and time, being concerned particularly with theories concerning its origin, nature, structure and evolution. |
| **cracking** | The process of breaking down chemical **compounds** using heat, especially the breaking down of heavier crude-oil **molecules** to form lighter molecules in the refining of petroleum products. |
| **cryo-** | In science, the prefix cryo- means 'extreme cold'. For example, *cryobiology* is the study of the effects of extreme cold on living organisms. |
| **cryogenics** | The branch of physics that studies materials at very low temperatures. |

| | |
|---|---|
| **crystal** | A solid substance with **atoms**, **molecules** or **ions** arranged in regular, repeated patterns that produce straight edges and flat surfaces of varying shape and size. |
| **crystalline** | Having the regular chemical structure that is typical of **crystals**, although not necessarily the physical form of a crystal. |
| **crystallography** | The study of the chemical structure of **crystals** and their classification into types. |
| **culture** | A growth of living cells or tissues produced in laboratory conditions. |
| **current** | A flow of electric **charge**; see **direct current**, **alternating current**; **Electricity and magnets: Electricity**. |
| **cybernetics** | The study of control and communications processes in complex electronic and mechanical systems, as well as in biological systems, especially humans. Cybernetic research often involves attempts to replicate human systems by artificial means. |
| **cytology** | The study of the structure and functions of cells. |

# D

| | |
|---|---|
| **Darwinian theory** | see **natural selection** |
| **DC** | see **direct current** |
| **decimal** | A decimal number system has 10 as its **base**. |
| **decimal places** | The number of figures written after a number's decimal point. For example, the number 6.53978 expressed to four decimal places is 6.5398. Compare **significant figures**. |
| **delocalized** | If an **electron** is delocalized, it is shared between several **atoms** in a **molecule** without being part of any single atom. |
| **dendrochronology** | The science of reconstructing past climate conditions by analysing the growth rings in tree trunks. |
| **density** | A measure of the compactness of a substance, equal to the amount of mass per unit of volume. |
| **deoxyribonucleic acid** | see **DNA** |
| **derivative** | In mathematics, the rate of change of a **function**, equivalent to the **gradient** of a curve. It can be determined by calculating the limit of the gradient of a line on the curve as the length of the line tends to zero; see **differentiation**. |

| | |
|---|---|
| **dermatology** | The branch of medical science that deals with the skin and its diseases. |
| **desertification** | The formation of deserts in zones that previously supported plant life, arising from the action of drought or from increased populations of humans and grass-eating animals. |
| **differentiation** | (1) In mathematics, the type of **calculus** that deals with finding the **derivative** of a given **function** in order to determine its rate of change; compare **integration**. (2) In biology, changes in cells, tissues or organs that take place to allow an organism to perform a specific function. |
| **diffraction** | The spreading of light or other waves passing through a narrow opening or by the edge of an opaque body. Diffraction patterns are useful for studying the minute structures of objects. See **Energy, light and radioactivity: Waves**. |
| **diffusion** | The movement of **molecules** or **ions** from an area of high concentration towards an area of low concentration, continuing until concentration is uniform. |
| **digital** | (1) Expressed in the form of numbers that can be processed by a computer or similar electronic device. (2) Able to process data represented in numerical form, as, for example, can a DVD player and a digital camera. Compare **analogue**. |
| **dimension** | (1) In mathematics, any of the physical properties of length, area and volume. A line has one dimension, a flat object has two dimensions, and a solid object has three dimensions. (2) In physics, any measurable physical quantity, eg time or mass. |
| **dimorphism** | (1) In chemistry, the existence of two distinct forms of an **element** or **compound**, eg diamond and graphite as forms of carbon. (2) In biology, the existence of two types of individual within a **species**, as frequently occurs in animals, many of which show marked differences between male and female. |
| **direct current (DC)** | An electric **current** which flows in one direction only; compare **alternating current**. |
| **dispersion** | The separation of visible light into its various colours when it passes between media of different density, eg air and glass. It occurs because light passing between the media deviates from a straight path by an amount that depends on the **wavelength**, ie the colour, and is observable, for example, when white light passes through a prism. |

| | |
|---|---|
| **distal** | In biology, the distal part of an organ or limb is the part that is furthest from the point of attachment to the body; compare **proximal**. |
| **diurnal** | (1) Occurring during, or once during, a period of twenty-four hours. The term is used, for example, in astronomy and meteorology to indicate the variations of an astronomical quantity or weather phenomenon during an average day. (2) Of animals, active during the day. (3) Of flowers, opening during the day and closing at night. |
| **DNA** | Deoxyribonucleic acid, the genetic material of organisms. Usually, two strands of DNA form a twisted spiral ladder shape known as a double helix. DNA is a major component of **chromosomes**. See **Genetics: DNA**. |
| **dominant** | If an **allele** of a gene is described as dominant, it produces a trait, eg the colour of eyes or hair, in an individual even when it is inherited from one parent only. The dominant allele overrides information carried by other alleles, which are known as **recessive**. See **Genetics: Genetic inheritance**. |
| **Doppler effect** | The apparent change of **frequency** of light or sound because of the relative motion of the source and the observer, eg the change in frequency of sound heard when an ambulance siren is moving towards or away from an observer. |
| **dorsal** | If a body part is described as dorsal, it is on an animal's back, or towards its back. |
| **dwarf star** | The name given to a small low-luminosity star; see **red dwarf**, **white dwarf**. |
| **dynamics** | The branch of applied mathematics that deals with the way in which force produces motion; also called kinetics. |

# E

| | |
|---|---|
| **echolocation** | A sensory system used by some animals, eg bats and dolphins, involving sending out a high-pitched sound and using its echo to locate an object. |
| **ecology** | The scientific study of the relationships between living organisms and their environment, including the distribution and abundance of living organisms (ie exactly where they occur and precisely how many there are). |

| | |
|---|---|
| **ecophysiology** | The branch of physiology that deals with how organisms are adapted to their natural environment. |
| **ecosystem** | A community consisting of animals, plants and their environment, often studied in terms of the interactions between living and non-living parts, and the flow of materials and energy between these parts. |
| **ecto-** | In science, the prefix ecto- means 'outside'. For example, an *ectoparasite* is a parasite that lives on the outside of its host's body. |
| **electric field** | A region in which there is an electrical **charge**. Any charged particle entering the region therefore experiences a **force**. See **Electricity and magnets: Electricity**. |
| **electrocardiography** | The study of electric **currents** produced by muscular activity in the heart. |
| **electrode** | Either of the conductors or terminals by which an electric **current** enters or leaves an **electrolytic cell**, **voltaic cell** or other conducting substance. The positive electrode is called the **anode** and the negative electrode is called the **cathode**. |
| **electrodynamics** | The branch of physics that deals with the phenomenon of electric charges that are flowing in a **current**; compare **electrostatics**. |
| **electrolysis** | Chemical change brought about by passing an electric **current** through a **solution**. |
| **electrolytic cell** | A device that uses a flow of electric **current** through a solution to bring about a chemical reaction. As with a **voltaic cell**, an electrolytic cell has two **electrodes**, one positive and one negative. Electrolytic cells have many industrial applications, including the electroplating of one metal with another. |
| **electromagnetic radiation** | A wave of energy that comprises interdependent electric and magnetic fields. The spectrum of electromagnetic radiation comprises **gamma radiation**, **X-rays**, **ultraviolet radiation**, visible light, **infrared radiation**, **microwaves** and **radio waves**. The speed in free space for all such waves is around 300 000 km (186 000 mi) per second. See **Energy, light and radioactivity: Electromagnetic radiation**. |
| **electromagnetism** | The science of the properties of, and relationships between, **magnetism** and electric **currents**. |
| **electromyography** | The study of electric currents set up in muscle fibres by bodily movement. |

| | |
|---|---|
| **electron** | A **subatomic particle** that is a basic constituent of the **atom**. Electrons have a negative electric **charge** and surround the **nucleus** of an atom. See **Atoms, elements and molecules: Atoms**. |
| **electrophoresis** | The movement of electrically charged particles in a liquid or gas that is under the influence of an **electric field**. It has many applications in biological science and industry. |
| **electrophysiology** | The study of electrical phenomena associated with living organisms. |
| **electrostatics** | The branch of physics that deals with the phenomenon of electric **charges** that are at rest rather than flowing in a **current**; compare **electrodynamics**. |
| **element** | A simple substance, composed of **atoms**, which cannot be resolved into simpler substances by normal chemical means. Elements can combine to form chemical **compounds**, the atoms of the elements often forming **molecules**. See **Atoms, elements and molecules: Elements**. |
| **embryo** | (1) An animal in its earliest stage of development, following fertilization of an egg cell or ovum. (2) A plant in its earliest stages of development, following fertilization of a seed. |
| **embryology** | The study of the formation and development of **embryos**. |
| **emulsion** | In chemistry, a **colloid** in which particles of one liquid are dispersed through another liquid, usually water in an oil or an oil in water. |
| **endo-** | In science, the prefix endo- means 'inside'. For example, an *endoparasite* is a parasite that lives inside its host's body. |
| **endocrinology** | The branch of biology or medicine that deals with the endocrine glands, which produce and secrete **hormones**. See **Human body: The endocrine system**. |
| **endothermic** | An endothermic chemical reaction is one that is accompanied by the absorption of heat; compare **exothermic**. |
| **energy** | The ability to do work, usually measured in joules. It exists in various forms, including electrical energy and chemical energy. The energy in a system, eg a chemical reaction, is never lost: it is merely transferred. See **Energy, light and radioactivity: Energy**. |

| | |
|---|---|
| **enthalpy** | The amount of **thermal energy** contained in a system. |
| **entomology** | The branch of zoology that deals with insects. |
| **entropy** | In thermal processes, a quantity that measures the extent to which the **energy** of a system is available for conversion to work. Entropy is a measure of the amount of disorder in the system. See **Key concepts: The laws of thermodynamics**. |
| **enzyme** | Any **protein** that acts as a **catalyst** in **metabolism**. For example, in the process of digestion, enzymes break down large molecules in food into smaller molecules that the body can process. See **Atoms, elements and molecules: Enzymes**. |
| **epicentre** | The point on the surface of the Earth that lies immediately above the point of origin of an earthquake or nuclear explosion. |
| **epidemiology** | The branch of medicine that deals with the causes and spread of diseases in the population, examining the role of external influences such as infection, diet or toxic substances, and devising appropriate preventive or curative measures. |
| **equation** | (1) In mathematics, a written statement showing that two **expressions** have equal value. (2) In chemistry, a written representation of a chemical reaction. |
| **equilibrium** | (1) In physics, a state of rest or unchanging motion in a body or system, in which any **forces** present cancel each other out. (2) In a reversible chemical reaction, a state in which forward and reverse reactions occur at equal rates. |
| **equinox** | Either of the two days of the year when the hours of daylight and hours of darkness are almost equal, around 21 March and 23 September. At a moment during these days, the Sun crosses a point in the sky known as the celestial equator. |
| **ergonomics** | The study of the relationships between people and the objects they interact with, including furniture, machinery and working tools, usually with the object of improving work performance and minimizing physical discomfort. |
| **ethanol** or **ethyl alcohol** | An alcohol that is the active substance in alcoholic drinks. It is produced naturally by the **fermentation** of sugars and starches and can also be made artificially. |
| **ethology** | An approach to the study of animal behaviour in which attempts to explain behaviour combine questions about its immediate causation, development, function and evolution. |

| | |
|---|---|
| **etiology** | see **aetiology** |
| **eugenics** | The study of the means whereby the characteristics of human populations might be improved by the application of **genetic engineering**. |
| **eukaryote** | An organism whose cells contain a **nucleus** surrounded by a **membrane**. All organisms are eukaryotes with the exception of bacteria and **archaea**. |
| **evaporation** | The process by which a liquid changes into a vapour at a temperature below its boiling point. |
| **evolution** | In biology, very gradual changes in the form of organisms owing both to genetic variations and to **natural selection**. Such changes are responsible for the development of modern complex organisms from earlier simpler ones. See **Organisms: Evolution**. |
| **exo-** | The prefix exo- means 'outside'. For example, *exobiology* is the monitoring of extraterrestrial environments for signs of living systems that might exist elsewhere in the universe. |
| **exothermic** | An exothermic chemical reaction is one that is accompanied by the release of **heat**; compare **endothermic**. |
| **exponent** | In mathematics, a number that indicates the number of times an **expression** is to be multiplied by itself, written above and to the right of the expression; also called an index. In the expression $3^2$, 2 is an exponent. |
| **expression** | In mathematics, a set of numbers and/or symbols that represent a quantity and operate as a unit, eg $a + b$ or $3x$. |
| **extra-** | In science, the prefix extra- means 'outside'. For example, an *extracellular* protein is a protein that is found outside cells. |

# F

| | |
|---|---|
| **factor** | A number by which another number can be divided exactly. For example, 8 is a factor of 32. |
| **Fahrenheit scale** | The temperature scale in which the freezing point of water is 32° and the boiling point is 212°. |
| **family** | In biological classification or **taxonomy**, a category of **organisms** that ranks above a **genus** and below an **order**. See **Organisms: Levels of classification**. |
| **fault** | A fracture in rocks along which some displacement has taken place. The displacement may vary from a few |

millimetres to thousands of metres. Movement along faults is the most common cause of earthquakes.

**fauna**
The animal life present in a particular region or at a particular period in history; compare **flora**.

**feedback**
A process in which part of the information that a system outputs is fed back into the input. Positive feedback enhances the output, as happens in an electrical circuit when a random amplified noise from a microphone is picked up by an amplifier and further amplified. In biological processes, negative feedback is often used to inhibit input and maintain an organism's equilibrium. For example, when the level of carbon dioxide in the human body rises, the high level triggers a signal to the lungs to make them expel more carbon dioxide.

**fermentation**
The process in which **organic** substances slowly decompose as a result of the action of **microorganisms** or **enzymes**. When fermentation takes place in yeast cells, the products of the breakdown of glucose are **ethanol** (ie alcohol) and carbon dioxide. Fermentation is the basis of wine and beer production.

**fibre optics**
see **optical fibre**

**field**
A region in which a physical **force** such as **magnetism** or **gravity** operates.

**fission**
(1) In biology, the reproduction of some single-cell organisms from a single parent by the division of the cell into two more or less equal parts. (2) In physics, the spontaneous or induced disintegration of a heavy atomic **nucleus** into two or more lighter fragments, with a release of **nuclear energy**. See **Energy, light and radioactivity: Nuclear reactions**.

**flora**
(1) The plant life of a particular region or a particular period in history; compare **fauna**. (2) Bacteria and other **microorganisms** that live in human and animal tissues.

**fluid**
A substance in which the **atoms** and **molecules** move freely past one another. All gases and liquids are fluids.

**force**
Any influence that changes the speed or direction of movement of a body.

**formula**
(1) In chemistry, a set of symbols that shows the chemical composition of a substance. (2) In mathematics, a set of symbols that expresses a mathematical rule.

**fossil**
The relic or trace of some plant or animal that has been preserved by natural processes in rocks. See **The Earth: Fossils**.

**fractal**
A geometric entity consisting of a basic pattern that is repeated at ever-decreasing sizes to produce structures that cannot be represented by standard **geometry**. See **Numbers and shapes: Fractals**.

**fraternal twins**
Twins that develop from two separately fertilized eggs and therefore have no more physical similarity to each other than brothers or sisters; compare **identical twins**.

**free radical**
An **atom** or **molecule** that is highly reactive because it has an unpaired **electron**. Free radicals are involved in chemical **chain reactions**.

**frequency**
(1) In physics, the number of cycles of a radio or other **wave** that occur per second, measured in hertz (Hz). (2) In statistics, the ratio of the number of times something happens or is true to the number of times it might have happened or might have been true.

**frequency modulation**
A method of radio broadcasting in which the **frequency** of the **wave** changes to reflect changes in the broadcast sounds, while the **amplitude** remains the same. Compare **amplitude modulation**.

**friendly numbers**
A pair of numbers each of which is the sum of the **factors** of the other.

**function**
(1) In mathematics, a relationship between one **variable** and one or more other variables. (2) A quantity with a value that depends on the value of one or more related quantities. For example, the volume of a cube is a function of the length of the sides of the cube.

**functional group**
In a chemical **compound** or type of compound, the group of **atoms** that is responsible for its typical chemical reactions.

**fusion**
(1) The process in which a new, heavy atomic **nucleus** is produced when two lighter nuclei combine with each other. The collision releases **nuclear energy**. See **Energy, light and radioactivity: Nuclear reactions**. (2) A synonym for melting, the conversion of a solid into a liquid.

**galaxy**
Any of the vast systems of stars and dust held together by gas that make up the universe. An average galaxy contains 100 billion stars. Galaxies exist in various shapes. Our own galaxy, the Milky Way, is a spiral galaxy with radiating arms, the Sun lying on one of these arms. See **Space: Galaxies**.

**game theory**
A set of mathematical theories about risk/benefit choices in human interactions, used to inform decision-making in political and economic contexts.

| | |
|---|---|
| **gamma radiation** | **Electromagnetic radiation** of high energy emitted by **radioactive** substances. Gamma radiation can damage the genetic material in living organisms. See **Radioactivity**. |
| **gas** | One of the three basic forms of matter, in which **atoms** or **molecules** are constantly moving in a random way. Gases expand to fill all the space available to them. |
| **-gen** or **-genic** | In science, the suffixes -gen or -genic mean 'producing' or 'generating'. For example, a *hallucinogen* is a drug or chemical that produces hallucinations. |
| **gene** | A segment of **DNA** that is the basic unit of heredity. Genes exist in different forms, known as **alleles**, and these are responsible for determining, for example, the colour of a person's hair or the shape of a plant leaf. See **Genetics: Genetic inheritance**. |
| **genetic code** | The system by which **genes** pass on instructions that ensure transmission of features inherited from previous generations. See **Genetics: Genetic code**. |
| **genetic engineering** | The techniques involved in artificially changing the **genes** of an **organism**, with the aim of producing or eliminating a trait in an organism, or of enabling an organism to produce a biological substance that it cannot normally produce. The techniques have numerous medical and commercial applications. |
| **genetics** | The study of the process by which differences between individuals are passed on from one generation to the next, and of how the information in the **genes** is used in the development and functioning of the adult organism. |
| **genome** | The full set of **chromosomes** of an individual, or the total number of **genes** in such a set. |
| **genotype** | (1) The genetic makeup of an individual **organism**. (2) A group that consists of all the individual organisms that have the same genetic constitution. |
| **genus** | In biological classification or **taxonomy**, a category of **organisms** that ranks above a **species** and below a **family**. See **Organisms: Levels of classification**. |
| **geo-** | In science, the prefix geo- means 'the Earth'. For example, *geology* is the study of the rocks, minerals and land forms of the Earth. |
| **geochronology** | The branch of geology in which the study of rocks and fossils is applied to dating the Earth. |
| **geometry** | The study of the properties of, and relationships between, points, lines, surfaces and angles. |

**geomorphology**  The branch of geology that deals with land forms such as mountains, valleys and plains, sometimes also encompassing the study of ocean basins and other underwater forms.

**geophysics**  The study of the physical properties of the Earth, including such disciplines as **seismology**.

**geostationary**  If an artificial satellite has a geostationary orbit, it moves at the same speed as the Earth rotates, thus maintaining its position above a fixed point on the Earth's surface. Such a satellite would have an altitude of 35 800km (22 200mi) above the Earth's surface.

**geothermal power**  Power generated using naturally occurring heat from rocks in the Earth's crust.

**gerontology**  The branch of medical science that deals with the processes of ageing.

**gestation**  In mammals, the period of time from the fertilization of an egg to the birth of an offspring.

**giant**  A large and luminous star with a low density; see also **red giant**, **supergiant**.

**global warming**  The slow increase in the Earth's surface air temperature, thought to be caused by the **greenhouse effect**. See **Climate and environment: Chemical imbalances**.

**gradient**  (1) The slope of a line, calculated by dividing the vertical distance by the horizontal distance. (2) The rate at which one physical quantity changes with time or with distance.

**gravitational field**  The area around a body within which any other body will experience a **force** of gravitational attraction.

**gravity**  The **force** of attraction that exists between objects because of their **masses**. The **weight** of a body is equal to the force of gravity acting on it.

**greenhouse effect**  The phenomenon by which **thermal energy** from the Sun, reflected by the Earth's surface, is trapped within the Earth's atmosphere by the presence of certain gases (known as greenhouse gases). The main greenhouse gases are carbon dioxide, methane, water vapour and nitrous oxide. See **Climate and environment: Chemical imbalances.**

**group**  (1) Two or more **atoms** within a **compound** that are bound together and act as a unit in chemical reactions. (2) A set of chemical **elements** that have similar properties, occupying a single vertical column in the **periodic table**.

| | |
|---|---|
| **gynaecology** or **gynecology** | The branch of medical science that deals with the functions and diseases of women's reproductive **organs**. |
| **gyroscope** or **gyro** | An apparatus in which a wheel spinning about an axis, moving freely within a ring-shaped frame, returns to its original level whenever the frame is displaced. Gyroscopes are essential components in modern navigation and stabilization equipment on ships. |

# H

| | |
|---|---|
| **habitat** | The natural environment in which an animal or plant lives. See **Climate and environment: Biomes, ecoregions and habitats**. |
| **heat** | (1) In strict usage, **energy** in the process of transfer between a system and its surroundings as a result of a difference in **temperature**. (2) Inaccurately, the same as **thermal energy**. |
| **herbaceous** | If a plant is classified as herbaceous, it has soft green **tissues** above ground. Herbaceous plants die back at the end of the summer, growing again the following spring if they are **perennials**. |
| **herbivore** | A grass-eating animal; compare **carnivore**, **omnivore**. |
| **hermaphrodite** | An **organism** that has both male and female reproductive **organs** in a single individual. Earthworms and some flowering plants are hermaphrodites. |
| **hetero-** | In science, the prefix hetero- means 'different'. For example, a *heterocyclic* molecule is a cyclic or ring molecule that contains different types of atom. |
| **histamine** | A substance that is present in all **tissues** of the body and is released into the blood under certain circumstances, eg when the skin is cut or burnt or during allergic reactions, eg hayfever. Large releases cause the contraction of nearly all smooth muscle, a fall of arterial blood pressure and shock. |
| **histology** | The study of the minute structure of **tissues** in **organisms**. |
| **HIV** | Human immunodeficiency virus, a virus that attacks the **immune system** and eventually causes the breakdown of immune function known as **AIDS**. |
| **homeostasis** | The maintenance of an **organism**'s internal state regardless of changes in external conditions. A mammal's ability to maintain a steady body temperature when external temperatures fluctuate is an example of homeostasis. |

| | |
|---|---|
| **homo-** | In science, the prefix homo- means 'the same'. For example, a *homograft* is a graft or transplant between individuals of the same species. |
| **homologous** | Homologous features are physical features that have a similar structure and the same evolutionary origin, but different functions. For example, a seal's flipper, a human's arm and a bat's wing are all modifications of one original type of structure. Compare **analogous**. |
| **hormone** | Any of various substances that regulate biological processes including growth and **metabolism**. Hormones are released by glands into the bloodstream. See **Human body: The endocrine system**. |
| **horology** | The science of time measurement, or of the construction of timepieces. |
| **host** | An **organism** that is exploited by a **parasite** living on or inside it. |
| **hybrid** | In biology, the offspring of parents from two different **species**. |
| **hydraulics** | The branch of physics that deals with the flow of **fluids** and the pressure they transmit, focusing on the applications of these properties in engineering. |
| **hydro-** | In science, the prefix hydro- means 'water'. For example, a *hydroelectric* power station produces electricity by using water to drive its turbines. |
| **hydrodynamics** | The branch of **dynamics** that studies the motion produced in **fluids** by applied forces. |
| **hydrology** | The study of water, including rain and snow as well as water on the Earth's surface, covering its properties, distribution and usage. |
| **hydroponics** | The technique of growing plants without soil, the roots of the plant being placed either in a **solution** of mineral salts or in an inert medium percolated by such a solution. |
| **hydrostatics** | The branch of **statics** that deals with the forces arising from the presence of fluids. |
| **hyper-** | In science, the prefix hyper- means 'over' or 'excessive'. For example, to *hyperextend* a limb is to extend it beyond its normal range, causing injury. |
| **hypo-** | In science, the prefix hypo- means 'under' or 'inadequate'. For example, *hypothyroidism* is a medical term meaning that the thyroid gland is underactive. |

| | |
|---|---|
| **hypotenuse** | The longest side of a right-angled triangle, opposite the right angle. See **Key concepts: Pythagoras's thereom**. |
| **hypothesis** | A statement that gives a possible explanation of a scientific event, and can be tested to determine if it is correct. |

# I

| | |
|---|---|
| **identical twins** | Twins that develop from a single fertilized egg and are therefore physically similar to each other; compare **fraternal twins**. |
| **igneous rock** | A rock mass that is formed by the solidification of **lava** or **magma**. Granite and basalt are igneous rocks. See **The Earth: Rocks**. |
| **immune system** | The system in humans and other **organisms** that protects the body from the action of disease-causing agents such as **bacteria** and **viruses**. The system is thought of as comprising **proteins**, including **antibodies**, various **cell** types, and physical barriers such as the skin and mucous membranes. See **Human body: Defense mechanisms**. |
| **immunity** | The state of having a high resistance to a disease due to the formation of **antibodies** in response to the presence of **antigens**. |
| **immunology** | The study of the biological responses of a living **organism** to its invasion by living **bacteria**, **viruses** or **parasites**, and its defence against these. |
| **imprinting** | In biology, an aspect of learning in which a young animal associates itself with the first moving object it sees after birth, usually its mother, and with the animals in its immediate environment, usually its own **species**. |
| **index** | see **exponent** |
| **indigenous** | Native to a particular region. |
| **induction** | Changes in the electrical or magnetic properties of a body under the influence of a **field**. See **Electricity and magnets: Electromagnetism**. |
| **inertia** | The tendency of a body to oppose a change in motion when an external **force** is applied to it. The tendency is proportional to the **mass** of the body. See **Key concepts: Newton's laws of motion**. |
| **infectious** | Infectious diseases are caused by agents such as **bacteria** and **viruses** that are not normally present in the body. Most diseases are infectious, but some are |

caused by injury and some by environmental or genetic factors. Compare **contagious**.

**infinity**

A number that is larger than any quantified concept. For many purposes it may be considered as one divided by zero.

**infrared radiation**

Electromagnetic waves in the **wavelength** range from about 750nm to 1mm, lying between the visible and **microwave** regions of the spectrum. See **Energy, light and radioactivity: Electromagnetic radiation**.

**infrasound**

The range of sound **frequencies** below the usual audible limit, ie of less than around 20 hertz.

**inorganic**

In chemistry, inorganic **compounds** are compounds that do not contain carbon and therefore generally occur outside living organisms. The branch of chemistry that deals with such compounds is called inorganic chemistry. Compare **organic**; see **Atoms, elements and molecules: Chemical compounds**.

**insulator**

A material that prevents the transfer of heat or electrical energy or conducts it very poorly. Glass and porcelain are electrical insulators. Compare **conductor**, **semiconductor**; see **Materials: Properties of materials**.

**integer**

Any whole number, including zero and negative numbers.

**integration**

In mathematics, the type of **calculus** that deals with finding the **function** whose **derivative** is known. It is often used to determine the area enclosed by a given curve. Compare **differentiation**.

**inter-**

In science, the prefix inter- means 'between'. For example, *interphase* is the time period between two **cell divisions**.

**intra-**

In science, the prefix intra- means 'inside'. For example, an *intracellular* protein is a protein that is found inside cells.

**invertebrate**

An animal that has no spine. Invertebrates include worms, jellyfish and insects. Compare **vertebrate**.

**in vitro fertilization (IVF)**

The process of fertilizing an egg outside the living body, in laboratory apparatus.

**ion**

Any **atom** or **molecule** that has an electrical **charge** owing to a loss or gain of **electrons** as a result of a chemical reaction; see also **anion**, **cation**.

**ionization**

The process of giving an **atom** or **molecule** an electrical **charge** by adding or subtracting **electrons**.

| | |
|---|---|
| **ionizing radiation** | see **radiation** |
| **irrational number** | A number that is neither an **integer** nor a ratio of two integers. The square roots of many integers are irrational numbers. Compare **rational number**. |
| **iso-** | In science, the prefix iso- means 'equal'. For example, an *isobar* is a line drawn through points of equal pressure on a graph or chart. |
| **isomer** | A chemical **compound** that has the same composition and **mass** as another but different chemical or physical properties because its **atoms** are arranged in a different structure. Lactose and sucrose are isomers. |
| **isotope** | One of a set of chemically identical species of **atom** that have the same number of **protons** but different numbers of **neutrons** and therefore different **relative atomic masses**. See **Atoms, elements and molecules: Elements**. |
| **-itis** | In science, the suffix -itis means 'inflammation'. For example, *tendonitis* is inflammation of a tendon. |
| **IVF** | see **in vitro fertilization** |

# J

| | |
|---|---|
| **jet stream** | A band of very strong wind occurring more than 7000m (20 000ft) above the Earth. The band is around 320–480km (200–300mi) wide with wind speeds up to around 320kph (200mph). |

# K

| | |
|---|---|
| **Kelvin scale** | A temperature scale in which **absolute zero** is assigned the value zero and the intervals between points on the scale are the same as on the **Celsius scale**. The freezing point of water on this scale is 273.15 Kelvin. |
| **kinematics** | The branch of applied mathematics that deals with the way in which **velocities** and accelerations of various parts of a moving system are related. |
| **kinetic energy** | The energy that a body possesses by virtue of its motion; compare **potential energy**. |
| **kinetics** | see **dynamics** |
| **kingdom** | In biological classification or **taxonomy**, the highest category of **organisms**, ranking above a **phylum**. See **Organisms: Levels of classification**. |

# L

**laser**
A source of intense light of a very narrow **wavelength** that can travel long distances without diffusing. Laser light is emitted when the **atoms** of a substance are excited by sending a light wave of a particular **frequency** through the substance.

**lateral**
If a body part is described as lateral, it is located towards an animal's side.

**lattice**
The regular arrangement of **atoms**, **molecules** or **ions** in a **crystal** or **crystalline** substance. see **Atoms, elements and molecules: Lattices**.

**lava**
Molten rock from underground that flows to the Earth's surface; see also **magma**.

**LED**
see **light-emitting diode**

**light-emitting diode (LED)**
A **semiconductor** device that emits light when an electric **current** is passed through it, used, for example, for displays in digital clocks and electronic calculators.

**light year**
A measure of astronomical distance, being the distance travelled by light in space during a year, which is approximately $9.46 \times 10^{12}$ km ($5.88 \times 10^{12}$ mi).

**lipid**
Any of various oils, fats, waxes and related products found in living tissues. Lipids are a component of cell membranes and are insoluble in water.

**liquid**
One of the three basic forms of matter, in which **atoms** or **molecules** do not have the fixed positions they have in a solid, but neither do they have the freedom of movement they have in a gas. Liquids flow and take on the shape of any container.

**lithology**
The systematic description of rocks, especially **sedimentary rocks**.

**litmus**
A powder obtained from certain lichens, useful in chemistry as an indicator as its colour changes to red in the presence of **acids**, and to blue in the presence of **alkalis**.

**logarithm** or **log**
The number that is the **exponent** of another number to a specified **base**. For example, the logarithm of 100 to the base 10 is 2, because $10^2 = 100$.

**longitudinal**
A longitudinal **wave** is one in which the displaced particles of the medium that the wave moves through move in the same direction as the wave travels. Sound waves are longitudinal. Compare **transverse**. See **Energy, light and radioactivity: Waves**.

**luminescence**     The emission of light by a substance that arises other than as a result of heating.

**lysis**     The destruction of a **cell**, which can occur beneficially, eg as part of **metabolism**, or harmfully, eg by a **toxin**.

# M

**Mach number**     The ratio of the speed of a body, or of the flow of a fluid, to the speed of sound in the same medium. At Mach 1, the speed of the body is that of sound; below Mach 1, it is subsonic; above Mach 1, it is supersonic.

**magma**     Molten rock when it is beneath the Earth's surface. When it rises to the Earth's surface, as can happen in a volcanic eruption, it becomes **lava**.

**magnetic field**     A field of **force** that exists around certain metal objects, allowing them to attract other metals. See **Electricity and magnets: Magnets**.

**magnetism**     The branch of physics that deals with **magnetic fields** and their effects on materials.

**magnitude**     (1) In mathematics and physics, the size of a property; see **scalar**, **vector**. (2) In astronomy, a measure of the apparent or absolute brightness of an astronomical object. The brightest stars visible to the naked eye are of around the first magnitude and the dimmest of around the sixth. See **Space: Stars**

**malacology**     The study of **molluscs**.

**mantle**     The rocky layer that lies between the Earth's core and its outer crust.

**mass**     A measure of the amount of matter contained in a body, considered in terms of both its resistance to acceleration and its gravitational attraction to other bodies. Mass is measured in kilograms and remains constant when **gravity** changes, which makes it distinct from **weight**.

**mathematics**     The study of the properties of numbers and quantities and the relationships between them. Pure mathematics comprises those branches studied for their own sake or their relation to other branches. The term applied mathematics is usually restricted to the application of mathematics to problems in physics.

**matrix**     In mathematics, a system of numbers arranged in a rectangular formation, representing information about a mathematical system and useful in solving some types of equation.

**mechanics**
The branch of physics that deals with forces acting on bodies and with the motions they produce. It is subdivided into **dynamics** and **statics**.

**meiosis**
A type of **cell division** that produces reproductive cells. Each complete division produces four daughter cells, each of which has only a single set of **chromosomes**, half the number of the parent cell. During reproduction, the full sets of chromosomes is restored. Compare **mitosis**; see **Cells: Cell division**.

**membrane**
A thin flexible layer of **lipid** and **protein** molecules that separates, connects or lines parts of a **cell** or **organ**. See **Cells: Cell structure**.

**meso-**
In science, the prefix meso- means 'in the middle'. For example, the *mesosternum* is the middle part of the sternum (breastbone).

**metabolism**
The set of chemical processes by which an organism's cells break down **organic** compounds to produce the substances and energy needed to sustain life.

**metallography**
The study of the structures of metals and their **alloys**.

**metamorphic rock**
A type of rock that is formed when existing rocks, which may be **igneous rocks**, **sedimentary rocks** or other metamorphic rocks, are changed under the influence of heat and pressure in the Earth's crust. Marble and slate are metamorphic rocks. See **The Earth: Rocks**.

**metastasis**
The spread of diseased **tissue**, especially cancerous **cells**, from one part of the body to another.

**meteor**
A small body that enters the Earth's atmosphere from the space between the planets and burns up due to friction, flashing across the sky and generally ceasing to be visible before it falls to Earth; also called a shooting star. Compare **meteorite**, **meteoroid**.

**meteorite**
A **meteoroid**, or fragment of a meteoroid, that reaches the Earth's surface.

**meteoroid**
A lump of metal or rock, smaller than an **asteroid**, that orginates from the asteroid belt or from a comet.

**meteorology**
The study of the Earth's atmosphere in its relation to weather and climate.

**metrology**
The science of measuring.

**microorganism**
An **organism** that is so small that it is visible only with the aid of a microscope. **Bacteria**, yeasts and some **algae** are microorganisms.

**microwave**
Electromagnetic **radiation** with a **wavelength** between 1mm and 30cm, lying between **radio waves** and

infrared radiation in the spectrum. See **Energy, light and radioactivity: Electromagnetic radiation**.

**microwave background**

A weak radio wave signal that is detectable in every direction in the sky with almost identical intensity. It is believed to be the relic of the early hot phase in the universe following the **Big Bang**.

**Milky Way**

The **galaxy** in which the planet Earth is located. See **Space: Galaxies**.

**mineralogy**

The study of the chemical composition, physical properties and occurrence of minerals.

**mitosis**

A type of **cell division** that occurs when **tissue** is growing or repairing itself. Each division produces two daughter cells, each with the same number of **chromosomes** as the parent cell. Compare **meiosis**; see **Cells: Cell division**.

**MKS system**

The Metre-Kilogram-Second system of units that replaced the **CGS system** and from which the **SI system** developed.

**modulation**

The process of impressing information (code, speech, video, data, etc) onto a higher-frequency carrier wave. See also **amplitude modulation, frequency modulation**.

**mole**

The **SI** unit of the amount of a substance, defined as the amount that contains as many entities (**atoms, molecules, ions,** etc) as there are atoms in twelve grams of carbon-12, an **isotope** of carbon. See **Key concepts: Avogadro's law**.

**molecule**

A group of two or more **atoms** bonded together by shared **electrons**. Molecules are capable of independent existence and have properties characteristic of the chemical **compound** of which they are the basic unit. See **Atoms, elements and molecules: Molecules**.

**mollusc**

A type of soft-bodied **invertebrate** animal. Most molluscs live in water and many have a hard outer shell and a muscular foot or tentacles. Snails, octopuses and oysters are molluscs.

**mono-**

In science, the prefix mono- means 'single'. For example, *monoculture* is the cultivation of a single type of crop.

**monomer**

see **polymer**

**morphology**

The study of the structure and forms of organisms, as opposed to the study of their functions.

| | |
|---|---|
| **multi-** | In science, the prefix multi- means 'many'. For example, a *multivitamin* supplement contains many different vitamins. |
| **mutation** | In biology, a sudden random change in the **genes** of an organism, resulting from a malfunction in the process by which **DNA** replicates itself. Mutations can cause the organism to differ in appearance or behaviour from the normal type. See **Genetics: Mutations**. |
| **mycology** | The study of fungi. |
| **myology** | The study of muscles. |

# N

| | |
|---|---|
| **nadir** | In astronomy, the point on the **celestial sphere** that is vertically below the observer; compare **zenith**. |
| **natural selection** | A theory of **evolution** stating that those **organisms** that are best adapted to their environment have the best chances of surviving and passing on their genetic information to their offspring. It is often referred to as the **Darwinian theory**; see **Key concepts: The theory of natural selection**. |
| **neap tide** | A tide in which the difference between water levels at high and low tide is relatively small. Neap tides occur when the Sun's tidal influence is working against that of the Moon. Compare **spring tide**. |
| **nebula** | (1) In strict usage, true clouds of interstellar dust and gas. (2) Loosely, any astronomical object that appears as a hazy smudge of light in an optical telescope; this usage predates modern astronomy. |
| **nervous system** | The system of nerves and **tissues** that regulates an **organism**'s actions and responses. In **vertebrates**, it consists mainly of the brain, the spinal cord and the nerves. See **Human body: The nervous system**. |
| **neurology** | The branch of medical science that deals with the **nervous system**. |
| **neuron** or **neurone** | A cell in the **nervous system**. Neurons transmit impulses that carry sensory information between the nervous system and the other parts of the body. See **Human body: The nervous system**. |
| **neuropathology** | The study of diseases of the **nervous system**. |
| **neutrino** | A **subatomic particle** with zero **charge** and zero **mass** that is thought to be responsible for carrying away the energy that is observed to be 'missing' in some forms of |

radioactivity. See **Atoms, elements and molecules: Subatomic particles**.

**neutron**
A **subatomic particle** that is part of the **nucleus** of an **atom**. Neutrons have no **charge**; their mass is approximately equal to that of a **proton**. See **Atoms, elements and molecules: Subatomic particles**.

**neutron star**
A very small dense star that results from the collapse of a massive star. **Electrons** and **protons** of atoms in the stellar material combine to form neutrons. See **Space: Stars**.

**noble gas**
Any of six **elements** (helium, neon, argon, krypton, xenon and radon) that, owing to their stable structures, are highly unreactive towards other elements and **compounds**; also known as inert gases and rare gases. See **Atoms, elements and molecules: Periodic table**.

**node**
(1) In physics, a point of minimum disturbance in a **wave**. (2) In botany, the point on a plant stem from which one or more leaves develop.

**nosology**
The branch of medical science that deals with the classification of diseases.

**nova**
A star that suddenly brightens by a factor of 10 000 or more, believed to occur when gas from a nearby star explodes on its surface. See **Space: Stars**.

**nuclear energy**
The energy released during a **nuclear reaction**; see **Energy, light and radioactivity: Energy**.

**nuclear fission**
The disintegration of the **nucleus** of a heavy **atom**, usually uranium but sometimes plutonium, into two lighter atoms. The process involves a loss of mass that is converted into **nuclear energy**. See **Energy, light and radioactivity: Nuclear reactions**.

**nuclear fusion**
The process of forming **atoms** of new elements by the **fusion** of atoms of lighter ones, usually the formation of helium from isotopes of hydrogen. The process involves a loss of mass which is converted into **nuclear energy**. See **Energy, light and radioactivity: Nuclear reactions**.

**nuclear reaction**
A process in which an atomic **nucleus** interacts with another nucleus or a **subatomic particle**, producing changes in energy and nuclear structure. See **Energy, light and radioactivity: Nuclear reactions**.

**nucleon**
A general name for a **neutron** or **proton**.

**nucleus**
(1) In biology, the central part of the **cells** in **eukaryotes**. The nucleus contains the **chromosomes**

and is enclosed in a double **membrane**. See **Cells: Cell structure**. (2) In physics, the central part of an **atom**. It is composed of **protons** and **neutrons**, has a positive **charge**, and constitutes almost all the mass of the atom. It is surrounded by **electrons**. See **Atoms, elements and molecules: Atoms**.

# O

**obstetrics**
The branch of medical science that deals with the problems and management of pregnancy and labour.

**odontology**
The study of the structure and diseases of teeth.

**oligo-**
In science, the prefix oligo- means 'few'. For example, an *oligomer* is a **polymer** that contains only a few **monomer** units.

**omnivore**
An animal that eats both plants and animals. Compare **carnivore**, **herbivore**.

**oncogene**
A **gene** that can become overactive and cause the development of cancer. See **Diseases and medicines: Cancer**.

**oncology**
The branch of medical science that deals with cancer.

**ontogeny**
The development of an **organism**, from fertilization of the egg until maturity.

**operon**
A group of **genes** that function as a unit and produce **enzymes** that control certain processes in **metabolism**.

**ophthalmology**
The study of the eye and its diseases.

**optical fibre**
A fibre of ultra-pure glass or plastic through which data can be transmitted as pulses of light, rather than as electric **currents**. The use of such fibres is commonly referred to as fibre optics and is steadily replacing the use of traditional cables in communications systems.

**optics**
The study of light. Physical optics deals with the nature of light and its **wave** properties, while geometrical optics looks at problems of **reflection** and **refraction**.

**order**
In biological classification or **taxonomy**, a category of **organisms** that ranks above a **family** and below a **class**. See **Organisms: Levels of classification**.

**order of magnitude**
In mathematics, a way of expressing numbers in terms of powers of ten. For example, if one number is less than ten times larger than another number, both numbers are of the same order of magnitude. It follows, then, that the numbers 10 and 100 differ by one order of magnitude, the numbers 10 and 1000 by two orders of magnitude, and so on.

| | |
|---|---|
| **ordinate** | In **coordinate geometry**, the *y*-coordinate of a point, corresponding to its distance along the vertical axis; compare **abscissa**. |
| **organ** | A part of an **organism** that carries out a specific function. Animal organs include the eyes, heart and lungs, while plant organs include leaves and roots. |
| **organelle** | In biology, a part of a **cell** that has its own **membrane** and has a specific function. The **nucleus** of a cell is an organelle. See **Cells: Cell structure**. |
| **organic** | In chemistry, organic **compounds** are compounds that contain carbon. Owing to the ability of carbon atoms to combine together in long chains, these compounds are far more numerous than those of other elements and are the basis of living matter. The branch of chemistry that deals with such compounds is called organic chemistry. Compare **inorganic**; see **Atoms, elements and molecules: Chemical compounds**. |
| **organism** | An individual form of life, capable of growing and reproducing. Organisms include animals, plants and **bacteria**. |
| **ornithology** | The study of birds. |
| **orogenesis** | The **tectonic** process in which mountain chains are formed through movement of the Earth's crust. |
| **orthopaedics** or **orthopedics** | The branch of surgery that deals with deformities arising from injury or disease of bones or joints. |
| **osmosis** | The movement of water or a solvent from an area of lower concentration to an area of higher concentration, through a semi-permeable membrane, which continues until the level of concentration is equal on both sides of the membrane. It is by this process that water is transmitted from the roots of a plant up through its stem. |
| **osteology** | The study of bones. |
| **otology** | The part of medical science that deals with the ear and its diseases. |
| **otorhinolaryngology** | The part of medical science that deals with diseases of the ear, nose and throat. |
| **oxidation** | (1) The addition of oxygen to a **compound**. (2) Any chemical reaction that involves the loss of **electrons** from an **atom**. |
| **ozone layer** | The region of the Earth's atmosphere, between about 20 and 40km (12.5 and 25mi) above the surface, where ozone, an **allotrope** of oxygen, makes up a greater |

proportion of the air than at any other height. This layer exerts a vital influence by absorbing much of the harmful ultraviolet **radiation** in sunlight and preventing it from reaching the Earth's surface. See **The Earth: The atmosphere**.

# P

**palaeoclimatology**  The study of climatic conditions in the earliest periods of history, using evidence from fossils, sediments and their structures.

**palaeoecology**  The study of creatures preserved as fossils in terms of their mode of life, their interrelationships and their environment.

**palaeogeography**  The study of the relative positions of land and water at particular periods in the geological past.

**palaeontology**  The study of **fossil** animals and plants.

**palynology**  The study of **fossil** spores and pollen. They are very resistant to destruction and in many **sedimentary rocks** they are the only fossils that can be used to determine the relationships of strata.

**parasite**  An **organism** that lives in or on another type of organism, called the **host**, and gets nourishment from it without rendering it any service in return. Most parasites are harmful to their hosts.

**parasitology**  The study of **parasites** and their habits.

**parsec**  The unit of length used for distances between objects beyond the **solar system**, approximately equal to 3.26 **light years**.

**parthenogenesis**  Reproduction that takes place without the fertilization of an egg, as is the case in bees, aphids and certain other insects.

**pasteurization**  Reduction of the number of **microorganisms** in a liquid, eg milk or beer, by heating it to a temperature of between 62.8° and 65.5°C (145° and 150°F) and maintaining that temperature for 30 minutes. Because the liquid is not heated to boiling point, its molecular structure does not change.

**pathogen**  An **organism** that causes disease. **Parasites, bacteria** and **viruses** are pathogens. See **Diseases and medicines: Infectious diseases**.

**pathology**  The branch of medical science that deals with the causes and nature of disease, and with the bodily changes brought about by disease.

**pedology**　　The study of soil.

**perennial**　　A plant that lives for more than two years.

**perfect number**　　A whole number that is the sum of all the numbers it can be divided by exactly, apart from itself. An example is 28, the sum of its divisors: 1, 2, 4, 7 and 14.

**perigee**　　The point in the orbit of a planet or other body at which it is nearest to the body it is orbiting; compare **apogee**.

**periodic table**　　A table in which all the chemical **elements** are arranged by **atomic number**. Elements in the same column have similar properties. See **Atoms, elements and molecules: Periodic table**.

**petrology**　　The study of the origin, structure and chemical and mineral composition of rocks.

**pH**　　A number used to show whether a substance is an **alkali** or an **acid** and the degree to which it is acid or alkaline, on a scale from 0 to 14. A pH above 7 indicates that a substance is alkaline, and below 7 that it is acid. A pH of 7 indicates that the substance is neutral. See **Measurement: Scales**.

**pharmacology**　　The scientific study of the action of chemical substances on living systems, especially in the treatment of disease.

**phenology**　　The study of plant development in relation to the seasons.

**-philic**　　In science, the suffix -philic means 'liking' or 'attracting'. For example, *hydrophilic* molecules are attracted to water.

**-phobic**　　In science, the suffix -phobic means 'disliking' or 'repelling'. For example, *hydrophobic* molecules repel water.

**phosphorescence**　　A type of **luminescence** that continues after the source of **radiation** that causes it is removed.

**photo-**　　In science, the prefix photo- relates to light or other **electromagnetic radiation**. For example, *photoemission* is the emission of **electrons** when a surface is exposed to light.

**photobiology**　　The study of light as it affects living **organisms**.

**photochemical reaction**　　A chemical reaction brought about by light or **ultraviolet radiation**.

**photoelectric effect**　　The emission of **electrons** from a substance that is struck by **photons**, usually photons from visible light or **ultraviolet radiation**.

| | |
|---|---|
| **photon** | The smallest unit of light or **electromagnetic** energy. Photons have no electrical **charge** and no **mass**. They travel at the speed of light. See **Energy, light and radioactivity: Electromagnetic radiation**. |
| **photosynthesis** | The process in which green plants, by means of **chlorophyll**, use energy from light to produce **carbohydrates** from carbon dioxide and water. See **Cells: Photosynthesis**. |
| **phycology** | The study of algae. |
| **phylum** | In biological classification or **taxonomy**, a category of **organisms** that ranks above a **class** and below a **kingdom**. See **Organisms: Levels of classification**. |
| **physical chemistry** | The branch of chemistry that deals with the physical structure of chemical **compounds** and the physical effects of chemical reactions. |
| **physics** | The study of the **forces** that exist between objects and the interrelationship between matter and **energy**. It encompasses electrical, mechanical, magnetic, radioactive and thermal phenomena. |
| **physiology** | The study of those functions of an **organism** that sustain life, eg **respiration**, digestion and circulation. |
| **pi** | An **irrational number** that expresses the ratio of the circumference of a circle to its diameter, represented by the symbol $\pi$ and, approximately, by the number $^{22}/_{7}$ or 3.142. See **Numbers and shapes: Types of numbers**. |
| **plane** | In **geometry**, a flat surface. |
| **plankton** | Minute animals and plants that drift in seas and rivers and constitute a major source of food for many larger animals. Plankton consists of, among other organisms, **bacteria**, certain **algae** and tiny crustaceans. |
| **plasma** | (1) In physics, a gaseous discharge that occurs naturally in the atmosphere of stars and in interstellar space. It has a balanced number of electrical **charges** and is a good conductor of electricity. (2) In biology, the watery fluid containing salts, protein and other **organic compounds**, in which the cells of the blood are suspended. |
| **plasmid** | A portion of **DNA** that can exist and replicate independently of its **chromosome**, usually found in bacteria. |
| **plate tectonics** | The theory that the Earth's crust and upper **mantle** is divided into plate-like sections that move as |

distinct masses. This movement is regarded as being responsible for the formation of the Earth's major physical features. See **The Earth: Plate tectonics**.

**polar coordinates**
A set of coordinates that represents a point in space in terms of its distance from a point 0 and its angle from that point; see **coordinate geometry**.

**polarization**
(1) In chemistry, the separation of the positive and negative **charges** of the **molecules** of a substance, typically done by placing the substance in an electric **field**. (2) In physics, the process of controlling the direction of the electric and magnetic fields of an **electromagnetic** wave.

**poly-**
In science, the prefix poly- means 'many'. For example, a *polygon* is a shape with many sides.

**polymer**
Any of various chemical compounds with very large **molecules** built up of many identical units called monomers. Cellulose is an example of a naturally occurring polymer, while nylon is a synthetic polymer. See **Materials: Polymers**.

**polymorphism**
(1) The presence in a population of two or more forms of a particular **gene**; see **Genetics: Genetic inheritance**. (2) The occurrence of different physical forms of the same **organism**, as in the case of bees, which exist as queens, workers and drones.

**polynomial**
In mathematics, an **expression** presented as the sum of two or more terms. The expression $3^2 + 4^3$ is a polynomial.

**positron**
A **subatomic particle** that has the same mass as an **electron** but the opposite (ie a positive) **charge**. Positrons are **antiparticles** to electrons. See **Atoms, elements and molecules: Subatomic particles**.

**potential difference**
A measure of the work involved in moving a **charge** between two points in an electric **field**. The **SI** unit of potential difference is the volt. Also called voltage; see **Electricity and magnets: Electricity**.

**potential energy**
The **energy** that a body possesses by virtue of its position or the positions of its atoms, rather than motion; compare **kinetic energy**.

**power**
(1) In physics, the rate at which work is done or **energy** is transferred, measured in watts. (2) In mathematics, an **exponent**.

**precession of the equinoxes**
Variation in the direction of the Earth's axis of rotation, caused mainly by the attraction of the Sun and Moon on the equatorial bulge of the Earth.

| | |
|---|---|
| **precipitate** | A solid substance separated from a **solution** by chemical means. |
| **primary colours** | Either of two sets of coloured light that can be combined in different proportions to produce all the colours of the **spectrum**. Red, green and blue are known as the additive primaries. When they are mixed in equal proportions, they produce white light. The additive primaries are combined to form the subtractive primaries cyan, magenta and yellow. When these are combined in equal proportions, they produce black. |
| **prime number** | A positive whole number that can be divided only by itself and 1. See **Numbers and shapes: Prime numbers**. |
| **prion** | A **protein** of unknown function that occurs in the brain. Defective prion protein is probably the transmittable agent responsible for diseases such as bovine spongiform encephalopathy (BSE) and Creutzfeldt-Jakob disease (CJD). |
| **prokaryote** | Any of a variety of **organisms** that have no distinct cell **nucleus** and have **DNA** that is not organized into **chromosomes**. **Bacteria** and certain **algae** are prokaryotes. |
| **promoter** | A substance added to a **catalyst** to make it more chemically active. |
| **prosthetics** | The branch of medical science involved in supplying artificial body parts. |
| **protein** | Any member of a group of complex **organic compounds** containing nitrogen that play an important role in the body's biological processes. They consist of smaller molecules called **amino acids**. **Enzymes** and **antibodies** are proteins. See **Atoms, elements and molecules: Proteins**. |
| **protist** | Any of various single-celled **organisms** that do not belong to the plant, animal, fungi, bacteria or **archaea** kingdoms. The majority of protists are **protozoa**. See **Organisms: Protista kingdom**. |
| **proton** | A **subatomic particle** that is part of the **nucleus** of an **atom**. Protons have a positive **charge** that is equal in magnitude to the negative charge of an **electron**. See **Atoms, elements and molecules: Atoms**. |
| **protozoa** | Single-celled **organisms** that live in water or as **parasites**. Protozoa do not have rigid cell walls. |
| **proximal** | In biology, the proximal part of an organ or limb is the part that is nearest to the point of attachment to the body; compare **distal**. |

# Q

**quantum mechanics**
A branch of **mechanics** that is based on the **quantum theory**, used in predicting the behaviour of elementary **subatomic particles**.

**quantum theory**
The theory that matter and energy are made up of tiny units called quanta that behave both as particles and as **waves**.

**quark**
A fundamental **subatomic particle**, currently seen as any of six types: bottom, top, up, down, charmed and strange. Although not yet observed directly, quarks are suggested to be the units out of which all other subatomic particles are formed. See **Atoms, elements and molecules: Subatomic particles**.

**quasar**
A distant, compact object far beyond our **galaxy**, which looks like a star on a photograph but appears to be much more distant than any star that we would be able to observe. Quasars emit very bright light, possibly due to the acceleration of matter towards **black holes**.

**radar**
A system that uses the reflection of pulsed **radio waves** to detect distant objects and measure their speed and direction of movement.

**radiation**
(1) Any energy in the form of **electromagnetic** waves or **photons**. Heat and light are forms of radiation.
(2) (also called ionizing radiation) Emissions of **subatomic particles** that arise when the **nuclei** of certain heavy elements, eg radium and uranium, disintegrate spontaneously. These emissions can cause considerable harm to **organisms** exposed to them.

**radioactivity**
The spontaneous disintegration of the **nuclei** of certain heavy elements, eg radium and uranium, which results in the emission of particles or gamma radiation; also called radioactive decay. **Energy, light and radioactivity: Ionizing radiation**.

**radiobiology**
The branch of biology that deals with the effect of radiation on living **organisms**.

**radiocarbon dating**
A technique for estimating the age of an organic material from the amount of a radioactive **isotope** of carbon in it. The quantity of the radioactive carbon naturally decreases with time once an organism has died. Also called carbon dating.

**radio galaxy**
A **galaxy** that emits large quantities of radio waves.

**radiology**

The science and application of X-rays, gamma-rays and other penetrating **radiation**.

**radio wave**

An electromagnetic wave of a **frequency** suitable for radio transmission, with a **wavelength** greater than around 10cm, ie with a longer wavelength than **microwaves. Energy, light and radioactivity: Electromagnetic radiation**.

**rational number**

A number that is either a whole number or can be expressed as a fraction; compare **irrational number**.

**receptor**

(1) In physiology, a **cell** or group of cells that can detect stimuli and initiate the transmission of sensory information. (2) In cell biology, a **protein** on the surface of a cell that can interact specifically with another molecule.

**recessive**

If an **allele** of a **gene** is described as recessive, it produces a trait, eg the colour of eyes or hair, in an individual only when it is inherited from both parents. Compare **dominant**; see **Genetics: Genetic inheritance**.

**recombination**

The rearrangement of **genes** that takes place naturally when **cells** divide during reproduction. It can also be induced by **genetic engineering** to alter the genetic makeup of a cell.

**rectify**

To change **alternating current** to **direct current** for use in a piece of electrical equipment.

**red dwarf**

A small cool star that is very faint, thought to be the most abundant type of star. See **Space: Stars**.

**red giant**

A large cool luminous star thought to be in a late stage of its evolution, when most of its hydrogen has been lost. See **Space: Stars**.

**red shift**

An increase in the **wavelength** of light, accompanied by a decrease in its **frequency**, as the source of light moves away from the observer. The phenomenon is observable in distant **galaxies** and is regarded as an indication that the universe is expanding. See **Key concepts: Hubble's law**.

**reduction**

Any process in which an **electron** is added to an **atom** or an **ion**. It is always accompanied by **oxidation**.

**reflection**

The process in which a **wave**, eg a light or sound wave, bounces back or is deflected when it strikes the surface of a new medium. See **Energy, light and radioactivity: Waves**.

**refraction**

The process in which a **wave**, eg a light or sound wave, bends as it passes from one medium to another of different density. Refraction explains why a straight object standing in a half-filled glass of water appears to bend at the surface of the water. See **Energy, light and radioactivity: Waves**.

**relative atomic mass**   The mass of an **atom** of an element in relation to the mass of an atom of the carbon-12 **isotope** of carbon. Sometimes shortened to atomic mass. See **Atoms, elements and molecules: Elements**.

**relativity**   The interdependence of matter, time and space as discussed in two theories developed by Albert Einstein. The theories state that qualities such as mass, length and time are not absolute but that they change in the case of objects moving at speeds approaching the speed of light. One consequence of the theories is the realization that very small amounts of matter contain enormous amounts of **energy**, a fact that paved the way for the discovery of **nuclear energy**. See **Key concepts: Special theory of relativity, Key concepts: General theory of relativity**.

**remote sensing**   Methods of gathering and recording information from distant objects, especially observation of the Earth's surface from the air or from space.

**renal**   Relating to the kidneys.

**replication**   The copying of **DNA** that occurs when cells divide. See **Cells: Cell division**.

**resistance**   (1) In physics, the difficulty experienced by an electric **current** when it flows through a material, leading to **energy** being wasted as **heat**. See **Electricity and magnets: Electricity**. (2) In biology, disease-causing organisms such as **bacteria** can develop resistance to antibiotics or other drugs through overuse, making these treatments ineffective.

**resonance**   In a vibrating or oscillating system, a rapid increase in the **amplitude** of the wave if a constant force is applied at regular intervals that match the **frequency** of the wave.

**respiration**   (1) Breathing, the process by which an **organism** exchanges gases, especially taking in oxygen and giving out carbon dioxide. (2) The process by which glucose and other food substances are broken down to release energy in the form of **ATP**, with carbon dioxide and water produced as waste products. See **Cells: Respiration**.

**ribonucleic acid**   see **RNA**

**Richter scale**

A scale of measurement from 1 to 10, used to indicate the magnitude of an earthquake.

**RNA**

Ribonucleic acid, a substance present in living **cells**, where it plays an important part in the production of **proteins**. It holds genetic information in some **viruses**. See **Genetics: RNA**.

**rostral**

If a body part is described as rostral, it is located towards an animal's mouth or nose; compare **caudal**.

# S

**salt**

Any of a class of chemical **compounds** formed when an **acid** reacts with a **base**. Most salts are **crystalline** and can conduct electricity when they are dissolved in water.

**saprobe**

An **organism** that gets nourishment from decaying **organic** matter. Fungi and some bacteria are saprobes. Saprobes are also called saprotrophs and used also to be known as saprophytes.

**saturated compound**

An **organic** compound in which all the carbon **atoms** are joined by single **bonds**, making it incapable of combining with any additional atoms.

**scalar**

A quantity that has **magnitude** but no direction. Mass, speed and temperature are scalar quantities. Compare **vector**.

**sedimentary rock**

A rock formed from sediments deposited by ice, water and wind. These sediments include fragments of fossils and shells, and pieces of **igneous**, **metamorphic** and other sedimentary rocks. Limestone and shale are sedimentary rocks. See **The Earth: Rocks**.

**seismology**

The study of earthquakes, particularly their shock waves. Studies of the speed and **refraction** of seismic waves enable the deeper structure of the Earth to be investigated.

**semiconductor**

A material that has a higher **resistance** to the flow of electricity than a **conductor**, but a lower resistance than an **insulator**. Semiconductors are used in a wide range of electronic devices. See **Materials: Electronic materials**.

**semiology**

The branch of medical science that deals with the symptoms of disease.

**sequencing**

The task of determining the sequence of the subunits of a large **molecule**, eg the sequence of **amino acids** in a **protein**, especially with a view to replicating it artificially.

| | |
|---|---|
| **sex determination** | The process by which the sex of an **organism** is determined. In **vertebrates** and many other organisms, sex is determined by the possession of a particular combination of **chromosomes**. In mammals, the female's chromosomes are designated X and X and the male's X and Y. See **Genetics: Chromosomes**. |
| **shooting star** | see **meteor** |
| **sidereal time** | Time measured by considering the rotation of the Earth relative to the distant stars, rather than to the Sun. A sidereal day is 4.09 minutes shorter than a solar day. |
| **significant figures** | The number of digits, not including leading zeros, in a number that are shown for a specified level of accuracy, the others being rounded up or rounded down. For example, the number 6.53978 expressed to four significant figures is 6.540. Compare **decimal places**. |
| **sine** | In mathematics, the ratio, in a right-angled triangle, of the length of the side opposite an acute angle to the length of the **hypotenuse**; compare **cosine**, **tangent**. |
| **SI system** | A system of coherent metric units proposed for international scientific use in 1960. It is based on seven units: the metre, kilogram, second, ampere, kelvin, mole and candela. It has replaced the **CGS** and **MKS** systems for most purposes. See **Measurement: SI units**. |
| **solar system** | The Sun and the bodies moving around it under **gravity**, bodies that comprise not only the nine major planets but also their moons and a vast number of asteroids, comets and meteors. See **Space: The solar system**. |
| **solid** | One of the three basic forms of matter, in which **atoms** or **molecules** vibrate around a fixed point. Unlike **liquids** and **gases**, solids have a fixed shape. |
| **solstice** | One of the two instants in the year when the Sun is furthest from a point in the sky known as the celestial equator. In the northern hemisphere, the summer solstice occurs around 21 June, on a day when the number of hours of daylight is greatest, and the winter solstice occurs around 21 December, on a day when the number of hours of daylight is smallest. |
| **solution** | A mixture in which one substance, the solute, is dissolved in another, the solvent. The particles in a solution are smaller than those in a **colloid** or a **suspension**. |
| **somatic** | The term somatic is used to describe all the **cells** of an **organism** that are not reproductive cells. |

| | |
|---|---|
| **sonic boom** | A noise that occurs when an accelerating object reaches the speed of sound, caused by shock waves from the object touching the ground. Shock waves from an aircraft travelling at supersonic speed create pressure that may be of sufficient intensity to cause damage to buildings. |
| **sonics** | The study of mechanical vibrations in matter. |
| **space-time** | The set of four dimensions in which all events occur. The theories of **relativity** link the three dimensions of space to time to form this single entity, usually called a continuum. |
| **species** | In biological classification or **taxonomy**, the lowest category, ranking below a **genus**. The **organisms** in a species have many characteristics in common and can breed with each other to produce fertile offspring, but cannot produce fertile offspring with members of other species. See **Organisms: Levels of classification**. |
| **spectrum** | The constituent parts of a type of energy arranged in order of **frequency** or **wavelength**. For example, the visible spectrum is a band of colours seen when white light is broken up into light of different wavelengths. |
| **spelaeology** or **speleology** | The study of the **fauna** and **flora** of caves. |
| **spore** | A small reproductive body consisting of a single **cell**, which can reproduce without fusing with another reproductive cell. Spores are produced by some simple plants, and by fungi and **bacteria**. |
| **spring tide** | A tide in which the difference between water levels at high and low tide is relatively great. Spring tides occur when the Sun's and Moon's tidal influences are working together. Compare **neap tide**. |
| **stalactite** | A deposit of calcium carbonate that hangs like an icicle from the roof of a limestone cavern. |
| **stalagmite** | An upward-growing conical formation of calcium carbonate on the floor and walls of a limestone cavern. |
| **star** | A celestial body consisting of a sphere of gas and dust held together by its own gravity. Stars generate energy by means of **nuclear fusion** reactions in their deep interiors. See **Space: Stars**. |
| **state** | One of the three conditions in which matter can exist: **solid**, **liquid** or **gas**. |
| **statics** | The branch of applied mathematics that deals with the way in which forces combine with each other to produce equilibria. |

**statistics**
The branch of mathematics that deals with the collection and analysis of numerical data.

**stellar evolution**
The sequence of events and changes covering the entire life-cycle of a star. See **Space: Stars**.

**stem cell**
A **cell** that has the potential to develop into more than one type of cell. The earliest stem cells from an **embryo** can produce any type of **tissue**. Stem cells can now be grown from embryos in the laboratory, making it likely that new **organs** may also be grown, for use in transplants. However, because it involves the use of human embryos, the technique is controversial. See **Cells: Gene expression**.

**stratigraphy**
The branch of geology that deals with the formation of **sedimentary rocks**.

**string theory**
In physics, the theory that **subatomic particles** have a string or loop structure, rather than being point-like. The theory has implications for **space-time**, where it increases the number of dimensions from four to as many as 26. See **Key concepts: String theory**.

**sub-**
In science, the prefix sub- means 'under' or 'less than'. For example, a *subspecies* is a division of living **organisms** that is smaller than a **species**.

**subatomic particle**
A basic unit of matter, from which **atoms** are made. **Electrons**, **neutrinos** and **quarks** are subatomic particles. See **Atoms, elements and molecules: Subatomic particles**.

**sublimation**
The process by which a **solid** becomes a **gas** without passing through the **liquid** state, under certain conditions of pressure and temperature. The sublimation of solid carbon dioxide ('dry ice') is used to produce 'smoke' effects in theatres.

**substrate**
A substance that is acted on by an **enzyme**.

**sunspot**
Any of various relatively cool dark spots on the surface of the Sun, thought to be caused by strong **magnetic fields** blocking the outward flow of heat. See **Space: The Sun**.

**super-**
In science, the prefix super- means 'over' or 'more than'. For example, an aeroplane flying at a *supersonic* speed is travelling at a speed greater than the speed of sound in air.

**superconductivity**
The property of some pure metals and metallic **alloys** at very low temperature of having negligible **resistance** to the flow of an electric **current**. See **Materials: Electronics materials**.

| | |
|---|---|
| **supergiant** | A star of enormous size, low density and very great luminosity. Supergiants are thousands of times brighter than the Sun. |
| **supernova** | A very bright **nova** resulting from an explosion that blows a star's material into space, leaving an expanding cloud of gas and sometimes a central compact object. See **Space: Stars**. |
| **suspension** | A mixture in which, as in a **solution** and a **colloid**, particles are dispersed through a liquid. In a suspension, the particles are larger than those in a colloid and those in a solution. |
| **symbiosis** | A mutually beneficial partnership between **organisms** of different kinds, especially such an association where one lives on or in the other; compare **commensalism**. |
| **symmetry** | The condition, in an object, of having the same form and arrangement of parts around a central axis, point or plane. Shapes are also said to possess symmetry when the arrangement is displaced by a **vector**. See **Numbers and shapes: Symmetry**. |
| **synecology** | The study of relationships between communities and their environment; compare **autecology**. |
| **system** | A group of parts that function as a whole. For example, the various bones and joints of a skeleton form a body's skeletal system. |
| **Système International d'Unités** | The full name of the **SI system**. |

# T

| | |
|---|---|
| **tangent** | (1) A line that touches a curve but does not intersect it. (2) The ratio, in a right-angled triangle, of the length of the side opposite an acute angle to the length of the side adjacent to it; compare **sine**, **cosine**. |
| **taxis** | The movement of a **cell** or **microorganism** in response to an external stimulus. |
| **taxonomy** | The classification of **organisms**. There are seven main levels of classification: **kingdom**, **phylum**, **class**, **order**, **family**, **genus** and **species**. See **Organisms: Classification of organisms**. |
| **tectonics** | The study of the movement of rocks on the Earth's surface and the formation of features such as folds and faults; see also **plate tectonics**. |
| **temperature** | A measure of the average **thermal energy** of the **molecules** or **atoms** of a substance. |

**teratology**
The study of biological malformations or abnormal growths, as an aid to the understanding of normal development.

**thermal energy**
The form of energy that a substance possesses by virtue of the movement of its **molecules** or **atoms**; compare **heat**.

**thermionics**
The branch of physics that deals with the processes involved in the emission of **electrons** from hot bodies.

**thermo-**
In science, the prefix thermo- means 'heat'. For example, a *thermostable* material is not damaged or broken down by heating.

**thermodynamics**
The branch of physics that deals with heat and heat-related phenomena. See **Key concepts: The laws of thermodynamics**

**thermonuclear energy**
Energy released by a **nuclear fusion** reaction that occurs because of the high **thermal energy** of the interacting particles.

**tissue**
A collection of similar **cells** that together form a particular type of fabric in an **organism**. In animals, for example, muscle and nerve are different types of tissue.

**titration**
In chemistry, a technique used to find the concentration of a substance in a solution by adding measured quantities of another substance that is known to react with it, until the reaction reaches a known end-point.

**topology**
The study of those properties of shapes and space that are independent of distance. See **Numbers and shapes: Topology**.

**toxicology**
The branch of medical science that deals with the nature and effects of poisons.

**toxin**
A harmful substance produced by an **organism**. Toxins produced by **bacteria** cause disease in humans and animals.

**trans-**
In science, the prefix trans- means 'across'. For example, a *transfusion* moves blood across from one patient to another.

**transcription**
In living **cells**, the process in which genetic material is copied from a strand of **DNA** to a strand of **RNA** as a first stage in the cell's production of **protein**. See **Cells: Gene expression**.

**transition metal**
Any of a group of metallic elements that form **alloys** easily and are excellent **conductors** of electricity. Copper, iron and cobalt are transition metals. See **Atoms, elements and molecules: Periodic table**.

**translation**

In living **cells**, the process in which **amino acids** are organized, using a strand of **RNA** as a template, into a sequence to form **proteins**. See **Cells: Gene expression**.

**transuranic element**

Any element with an **atomic number** greater than that of uranium, ie with 93 or more **protons** in the atomic **nucleus**. Neptunium and plutonium occur naturally, while others such as curium and lawrencium have been artificially produced.

**transverse**

A transverse **wave** is one in which the displaced particles of the medium that the wave moves through move perpendicular to the direction that the wave travels in. Compare **longitudinal**; see **Energy, light and radioactivity: Waves**.

**tsunami**

A series of very large waves produced in the ocean by an underwater earthquake or volcanic eruption.

**tundra**

In far northern regions of the world, a treeless lowland with subsoil that is permanently frozen. In summer, the soil can support some low-growing plants, eg lichens, mosses and heather. See **Climate and environment: Biomes, ecoregions and habitats**.

**turbulence**

The irregular flow of particles in a **liquid** or **gas**.

# U

**ultrasonic**

The term ultrasonic is used to describe sound **frequencies** above the upper limit of the normal range of hearing, at or about 20 kilohertz. Ultrasonic waves are used in medicine to produce images of the inside of the human body.

**ultraviolet radiation**

**Electromagnetic radiation** with a wavelength range between the visible and X-ray regions of the spectrum, from about 400nm to 10nm. Ultraviolet radiation is responsible for sunburn. See **Atoms, elements and molecules: Electromagnetic radiation**.

**uncertainty principle**

The principle that there is a limit to the precision with which the position and direction of a particle can be simultaneously known. See **Key concepts: Heisenberg's uncertainty principle**.

**uni-**

In science, the prefix uni- means 'one'. For example, a *unicellular* organism only has one cell.

**unified field theory**

In physics, a theory, as yet incomplete, that seeks to establish the existence of a single **force** from which all the basic forces of nature are derived, and seeks to

explain how these forces are related to each other. See
**Key concepts: Theory of everything.**

**unsaturated
compound**

An **organic** compound in which two or more of the
carbon **atoms** are joined by double or triple **bonds**,
making it capable of combining with additional atoms.

**urology**

The branch of medical science that deals with diseases
and abnormalities of the urinary tract.

# V

**vaccine**

A substance that provokes an **immune** response against
disease-causing agents such as **bacteria** and **viruses**.
Vaccines often contain a weakened form of the disease-
causing agent.

**vacuum**

(1) A space in which the air pressure is much lower than
atmospheric pressure. (2) A region that is completely
empty of matter.

**valency**

A measure of a chemical **element**'s ability to combine
with other elements, expressed as the number of
**electrons** it donates, accepts or shares when it forms a
**bond**.

**Van Allen radiation
belts**

Two bands of high-intensity **radiation** from the Sun
that encircle the Earth.

**variable**

In mathematics, a quantity that can be given any value;
compare **constant**.

**variation**

The differences between the individuals of a **species**.

**vector**

(1) In mathematics, a quantity that has both **magnitude**
and direction. **Force** and **velocity** are vector quantities.
Compare **scalar**. (2) In biology, an **organism** that can
transmit disease-causing **microorganisms** from one
**host** to another without being harmed itself. Mosquitoes
and ticks are vectors. (3) In genetics, a piece of DNA that
is used to transfer genes between cells or organisms.

**velocity**

The velocity of an object is a measure of its speed in a
stated direction. Velocity is a **vector** quantity.

**Venn diagram**

In mathematics, a diagram that uses circles to represent
sets and the relationships between them.

**ventral**

If a body part is described as ventral, it is on or towards
an animal's chest or abdomen.

**vertebrate**

An animal that has a spine. Vertebrates include mammals,
reptiles, birds and fish. Compare **invertebrate**.

**virology**

The study of **viruses**.

**virus**

A disease-causing agent that consists of a segment of **DNA** or **RNA** enclosed in a shell of **protein**, capable of reproducing rapidly inside a living **cell**. Because many viruses have a high rate of **mutation**, the host body has little chance of developing resistance to them. See **Organisms: Viruses**.

**viscosity**

The resistance of a **fluid** to flow, caused by its internal friction.

**vitamin**

Any of various **organic** compounds required in relatively small amounts in the diet for the proper functioning of an organism. See **Diseases and medicines: Dietary deficiencies**.

**voltage**

see **potential difference**.

**voltaic cell**

A device that produces an electric **current** by means of a chemical reaction. As with an **electrolytic cell**, a voltaic cell has two **electrodes**, one positive and one negative. The chemical reaction causes **ions** to form at one electrode and flow towards the other. Car batteries are voltaic cells.

# W

**wave**

A vibration that transfers **energy** from one place to another. Sound, light and X-rays are among the types of energy transmitted as waves. See also **amplitude**, **frequency**, **wavelength**; **Energy, light and radioactivity: Waves**.

**wavelength**

The distance between a point on one disturbance of a **wave** and the same point on the next disturbance.

**weight**

A measure of the force exerted on a body by a **gravitational field**. The weight of a body is measured in newtons and is distinguished from its **mass,** which is measured in kilograms and is unaffected by changes in gravity.

**white dwarf**

A small dim star in the final stages of its evolution. The masses of known white dwarfs do not exceed 1.4 times that of the Sun, and a typical diameter is about the same as that of the Earth. See **Space: Stars**.

# X

**X-chromosome**

see **sex determination**

| | |
|---|---|
| **xeno-** | In science, the prefix xeno- means 'foreign' or 'different'. For example, *xenotransplantation* is the transplantation of **organs** from an individual of one **species** into an individual of a different species. |
| **X-ray** | A form of **electromagnetic radiation** with a **wavelength** in the range between **ultraviolet radiation** and **gamma radiation**. X-rays can be used to produce images of the body's internal structures because they are absorbed by **tissues**, which makes their uncontrolled use dangerous. See **Energy, light and radioactivity: Waves**. |

# Y

| | |
|---|---|
| **Y-chromosome** | see **sex determination** |

# Z

| | |
|---|---|
| **zenith** | In astronomy, the point on the **celestial sphere** that is vertically above the observer's head; compare **nadir**. |
| **zodiac** | The name given to the belt of stars, about 18° wide, through which the Sun appears to pass during the year. |
| **zoology** | The scientific study of all aspects of animals. |
| **zygote** | A fertilized **cell** formed when two reproductive cells combine, before it divides to begin its development into an **embryo**. |

# CHRONOLOGY

The Earth is estimated to be 4.6 billion (4.6 × 10$^9$) years old. This estimate represents a compromise between the age of the oldest known terrestrial solid (a crystal found in the Jack Hills, Australia) and astronomers' theories about the age of the solar system. Primitive life, in the form of blue-green bacteria, is estimated to have originated more than 3.4 billion years ago (see **1977**).

> *To understand a science it is necessary to know its history.*
> —French philosopher Auguste Comte (1798–1857), *Système de Politique positive* (1851–4, 'Positive Philosophy').

## c.2700 BC

⊕ Acupuncture is first developed in China.

## c.2500 BC–c.2000 BC

◯ The stone circle now known as Stonehenge is constructed in present-day Wiltshire, England.

## 781 BC

◯ Chinese astronomers observe a solar eclipse.

## c.625 BC

◯ 🐚 🔺 Thales, the natural philosopher and pioneer of scientific thought, is born in Miletos, Greece (d.c.555 BC). He is credited with introducing basic geometry into Greece, and with accurately predicting a solar eclipse in May 585 BC.

## c.580 BC

◯ 🔺 The mathematician and philosopher Pythagoras is born in Samos, Greece (d.c.500 BC). He is associated with mathematical discoveries relating to the chief musical intervals, the relations of numbers, the theorem on right-angled triangles that bears his name, and more fundamental beliefs about the understanding and representation of the world of nature through numbers.

## c.540 BC

◯ 🐚 The Greek philosopher Xenophanes (c.570–c.480 BC) describes fossil fish and shells found in deposits on high mountains. Xenophanes is also remembered for developing several bizarre astronomical theories, including that a new Sun rises each day and that there is a different Moon for each region or zone of the (supposedly flat) Earth.

## c.475 BC

The first known eruption of the volcano Mount Etna, on the east coast of Sicily, was recorded by the Greek writers Aeschylus and Pindar.

## c.470 BC

The Greek philosopher Democritus is born in Abdera, Thrace (d.c.370 BC). He is best remembered for the atom theory he developed from Leucippus, whereby the world consists of an infinite number of everlasting atoms whose different characteristics and random combinations account for the different properties and qualities of everything in the world.

## c.460 BC

Hippocrates, the founding father of medicine, is born on the island of Cos, Greece (d.377/359 BC). In his writings, Hippocrates tried to separate medicine from religion by using rational and scientific explanations. His case histories were so accurate in detail that some are still valid today.

## 384 BC

The Greek philosopher and scientist Aristotle, a highly important and influential figure in the history of Western thought, is born (d.322 BC). His works include the classification of over 500 animals, achieved through methods of observation and deductive reasoning that are still being used in modern science. Aristotle proposed that the world consisted of four elements – earth, air, fire, water – and he realized that the Earth is spherical, although he wrongly believed it to be stationary.

### A Great Teacher

As well as being a scientist and philosopher, Aristotle was also a renowned teacher. In c.342 BC, he was appointed to be personal tutor to Alexander the Great in Macedonia, after having taught at Plato's Academy for 20 years. He founded his own school, the Lyceum, in 335 BC; his students became known as 'peripatetics' because of Aristotle's habit of walking around while lecturing.

## c.330 BC

Theophrastus (c.372–c.286 BC), a Greek philosopher and former pupil of Aristotle, begins recording his observations on plants. He classifies nearly 500 plants and is later acknowledged as an eminent figure in the development of botany.

## c.300 BC

The Greek mathematician Euclid (fl.300 BC) completes his *Elements,* a treatise on geometry in 13 books that covers the geometry of lines in the plane, including Pythagoras's theorem, and goes on to discuss circles, ratio, and the geometry of three dimensions.

### Euclid's Bestseller

Euclid's *Elements* was the first mathematical book to be printed and is the earliest surviving mathematical treatise. It served as the basic mathematics textbook for nearly 2000 years.

## c.287 BC

The Greek engineer and mathematician Archimedes is born in Syracuse (d.212 BC). He is remembered for his groundbreaking formulae in calculus and geometry, as well as for discovering the hydrostatic principle that bears his name (see **Key concepts: Archimedes' principle**).

## c.250 BC

The Greek mathematician, astronomer and geographer Eratosthenes (c.276–194 BC) measures the circumference of the Earth by calculating the difference in latitude between Alexandria and Syene (modern Aswan).

## 129 BC

The Greek astronomer and mathematician Hipparchus (c.180–125 BC) completes his detailed catalogue of 850 stars, giving their positions in celestial latitude and longitude. He classified the stars according to their 'magnitude' (luminosity), and a version of his scale is still used today.

## c.45 BC

The Alexandrian astronomer Sosigenes (fl.c.40 BC) assists the Roman ruler Julius Caesar in the development of the Julian calendar of 365.25 days. This calendar was eventually imposed throughout Europe, remaining in use until the introduction of the Gregorian calendar in 1582.

## c.40 BC

Asclepiades (b.124 BC), who introduced Greek medicine to the Romans, dies. He rejected the Hippocratic belief that disease was caused by an imbalance in the four humours of the body, believing instead that it resulted from discord in the corpuscles. He recommended good diet, baths, exercise and sometimes wine as a cure.

⊕ The Greek physician Pedanius Dioscorides is born in Anazarb, Cilicia (d.c.90 AD). He wrote *De materia medica* ('On the materials of medicine'), the standard work on substances used in medicine and the science of their properties for many centuries. In it, he recorded detailed information on the medicinal properties of over 500 plants including lavender, garlic, camomile and the opium poppy.

## AD 23

Pliny the Elder is born at Novum Comum (Como), Italy (d.79 AD). His universal encyclopedia in 37 volumes, *Historia Naturalis* ('Natural History'), is the only one of his many writings to have survived, and contains facts on astronomy, botany, geography, metallurgy, pharmacology and zoology. He was a commander of the Roman fleet, and was killed whilst attempting to witness the eruption of Mount Vesuvius at close hand in AD 79.

## c.30 AD

⊕ The Roman writer and physician Aulus Cornelius Celsus writes his *De Medicina* ('On Medicine'), a major medical treatise diagnosing many diseases with advice on their relevant treatments, surgical methods and medical history.

## c.100 AD

⊕ The Greek physician Aretaeus writes a great work in eight books, discussing the causes, symptoms and cure of diseases.

## c.130 AD

The Egyptian astronomer and geographer Ptolemy of Alexandria (c.90–168 AD) completes his *Almagest*, a 'great compendium of astronomy'. Although much of his work is based on the writings of Hipparchus, Ptolemy made a major and influential contribution to astronomy by introducing the mathematical theory of planetary motion. His Earth-centred view of the universe dominated cosmological thought until the work of Nicolaus Copernicus in the 16th century.

## c.201 AD

⊕ The Greek physician Galen (b.c.130 AD) dies. His prolific writings expanded on the theories of Hippocrates and Aristotle, and greatly influenced medicine for many centuries. By dissecting animals, Galen made remarkable observations on digestion, the spinal cord, heartbeat and blood formation.

## c.250 AD

🔢 The Greek mathematician Diophantus writes his *Arithmetica*, the earliest known treatise on algebra. In contrast to earlier Greek works, which used geometric notation, it uses algebraic symbols for solving equations and also examines number theory.

⊕ The Chinese physician Huang-Fu Mi writes the first textbook on acupuncture. Although acupuncture had been used in Chinese medicine since **c.2700 BC**, this work was unique as a systematic, step-by-step guide, and is still in use today.

## c.340 AD

🔢 The Greek mathematician Pappus of Alexandria writes his mathematical *Collection*, covering a wide range of geometrical problems. The work was of great importance for the historical understanding of Greek mathematics.

## AD 340

🪦 The Chinese alchemist Ge Hong (b.c.280 AD) dies. His most famous book, *Bao-pu zi* ('He Who Holds to Simplicity'), describes methods of producing solutions of minerals (including cinnabar and gold) in order to make immortality elixirs.

## AD 415

🔭 🔢 The Greek philosopher Hypatia (b.370 AD) is murdered by a Christian mob. Hypatia was the first notable female astronomer and mathematician, and head of the Neoplatonist school in Alexandria.

## AD 499

🔭 🔢 The Indian astronomer and mathematician Aryabhata (c.475–c.550) completes his *Aryabhatiya*, a treatise summarizing mathematical knowledge in his time.

## c.550

🔭 The astrolabe, a scientific instrument that shows the positions of the Sun and bright stars at any given time, is developed for use in astronomy and navigation.

## 628

🔭 🔢 The Indian astronomer and mathematician Brahmagupta (598–c.665) completes his *Brahmasphutasiddhanta* ('The Opening of the Universe') – an important text because, amongst other complex mathematical ideas, it displays an understanding of zero as a number in its own right.

## c.721

The Arab alchemist Abu Musa Jabir ibn Hayyan is born. He wrote a number of works on alchemy and metaphysics, and described accurate methods for distillation and crystallization.

## 787

The Arab astronomer and astrologer Albumazar is born (d.885). He was the leading astrologer of his day, and did valuable work on the nature of tides.

## c.800

The Arab mathematician Muhammad ibn Musa al-Khwarizmi is born (d.c.850). His writings were influential in the development of algebra, and in transmitting Indian and Arab mathematics to medieval Europe.

---

### The Language of Mathematics

Latin translations of al-Khwarizmi's writings were highly influential in transmitting Indian and Arab mathematics to medieval Europe, and they have also influenced the language of mathematics. The methods of arithmetic he described, based on the Hindu (or so-called Arabic) system of numeration, became known as algorismus, a medieval Latin corruption of his name, and this is the source of the English 'algorithm'. Al-Khwarizmi is also responsible for the word 'algebra', which comes from the term al-jabr in the title of his book *Hisab al-jabr w'al-muqabala* ('Calculation by completion and balancing').

---

## 808

The Arab scholar Hunayn ibn Ishaq is born near Baghdad (d.873). He accurately translated the medical treatises of Aristotle, Hippocrates and Galen, making Greek scientific knowledge readily available to the Islamic world.

## c.827

Ptolemy of Alexandria's (c.90–168 AD) *Almagest* (see c.130 AD) is translated from Greek into Arabic.

## c.865

The Persian physician and alchemist ar-Rāzī (known in Europe as Rhazes; d.c.923) is born in Baghdad. Some of his many medical works were translated into Latin and had considerable influence on medical science in the Middle Ages. He successfully distinguished smallpox from measles, and was considered the greatest physician of the Arab world.

## c.880

Arab alchemists distil alcohol (ethanol, the intoxicating ingredient) from wine. This alcoholic preparation of ethanol is later described in Spain by Arnau de Villanova (c.1300).

## 929

The Arab mathematician and astronomer al-Battani (b.c.858) dies. He wrote a collection of astronomical tables, and improved upon Ptolemy's calculations.

## 968

The Persian astronomer Abd Al-Rahman Al Sufi (b.903) dies. He translated and added to the work of Ptolemy, as well as writing the *Book of Fixed Stars*.

## 980

The philosopher and physician Avicenna is born near Bokhara, Persia (present-day Iran; d.1037). He was one of the main interpreters of Aristotle to the Islamic world, and was the author of some 200 works on science, religion and philosophy.

### Fossilized Thought

Avicenna carried out important geological research, studying erosion and rock formation. However, he reached the conclusion that fossils were not formed from living organisms but rather by the same forces that shaped rocks. This view dominated scientific thinking for several hundred years.

## 998

The Arab astronomer and mathematician Abu'l-Wafa' (b.940) dies. He had an important influence on the development of trigonometry.

## c.1040

The Arab mathematician Abu 'Ali al-Hasan ibn al-Haytham (known in Europe as Alhazen, b.c.965) dies. His work on optics gave the first accounts of atmospheric refraction and reflection from curved surfaces, and the construction of the eye.

## 1048

⌂ ⚛ ⚛ The Khwarezmian scientist al-Biruni (b.973) dies. Born in present-day Uzbekistan, he wrote widely on astronomy, mathematics, medicine and physics.

## c.1050

⚑ A Chinese alchemist, Pi Sheng, invents the first moveable type – created from a mixture of clay and glue, hardened by baking – for use in printing.

## 1054

⌂ Astronomers in China witness the explosion of a supernova, creating what is now known as the Crab Nebula.

## 1066

⌂ Halley's Comet is observed before the Battle of Hastings. The comet was later named after the English astronomer and mathematician Edmond Halley (1656–1742), who deduced that comets seen in 1531 and 1607 were the same object.

## c.1072

⊕ The Arab physician Ibn Zohr (known in Europe as Avenzoar; d.1162) is born in Seville, Spain. He published influential medical works describing conditions such as kidney stones and inflammation of the heart (pericarditis).

## 1087

⊕ Constantine the African, the first translator of Arabic medical texts into Latin, dies.

## c.1150

⊕ The Italian scholar Gerard of Cremona translates works by Galen, Rhazes and Avicenna into Latin.

## 1202

⚛ The Italian mathematician Leonardo Fibonacci (c.1170–c.1250) publishes *Liber abaci* ('The Book of Calculation'), illustrating the virtues of the modern Arabic system of numerals (which originated in India) and showing how it can be used to simplify highly complex calculations.

## c.1214

⚛ The English philosopher and scientist Roger Bacon is born, probably in Ilchester, Somerset (d.1292). He wrote many works on mathematics, philosophy and logic, emphasizing the primacy of mathematical proof and the importance of experiments.

### c.1252

◁ The Alfonsine Tables, astronomical tables adapted from Arabic models and used to calculate eclipses and planetary positions, are drawn up in Spain by order of King Alfonso X of Castile.

### c.1260

The German philosopher and cleric Albertus Magnus (c.1200–80) completes *De Mineralibus et Rebus Metallicis* ('On Minerals and Metallic Objects'), a work on geology noting his own observations and including Avicenna's account of fossils.

### c.1269

Petrus Peregrinus, a French scientist and soldier, is the first to describe the properties of magnets in his *Epistola de magnete* ('Letter on the magnet'). He is also remembered for inventing a compass with a graduated scale.

### c.1300

The French scholastic philosopher Jean Buridan (d.c.1358) is born. He published works on logic, mechanics and optics.

> ## Buridan's Ass
>
> Jean Buridan gave his name to a famous problem of decision-making called 'Buridan's Ass'. In this problem, an ass faced with two equidistant and equally desirable bales of hay starves to death because there are no grounds for preferring to go to one bale rather than the other.

### 1302

⊕ The first recorded post-mortem examination is carried out in Bologna, Italy, by the physician Bartolomeo de Varignana.

### 1304

After experimenting with a water-filled globe, the German monk Theodoric of Freibourg (c.1250–1310) writes his *De Ride* ('On the Rainbow'). The work correctly explains reflective aspects of rainbow formation.

## 1348

The Italian horologist and physician Giovanni de' Dondi (1318–89), begins work on an astronomical clock showing not only the usual planetary motions, but also the feasts of the Church calculated in accordance with a perpetual calendar. The clock was so far ahead of its time that only one replica is known to have been made until the 20th century.

## 1363

The French surgeon Guy de Chauliac (c.1300–68) publishes his *Chirurgia Magna* ('Great Treatise on Sugery') in Latin. This manual, translated into French more than 100 years later, was used by generations of European doctors.

## 1420

The Tatar prince and astronomer Ulugh-Beg (1394–1449) founds an observatory at Samarkand, where he takes part in preparing new planetary tables and a new star catalogue of unprecedented precision.

## 1423

The Austrian astronomer and mathematician Georg von Purbach is born (d.1461). His observational work resulted in the publication of a table of lunar eclipses, and he is considered to be the first great modern astronomer.

## 1472

The German mathematician and astronomer Regiomontanus (b.1436) dies. He worked on the *Alfonsine Tables* (**c.1252**) and on *Ephemerides*, a work used extensively by Christopher Columbus. He also established the study of algebra and trigonometry in Germany and wrote on waterworks, burning-glasses, weights and measures, and the quadrature of the circle.

## 1493

The German alchemist and physician Paracelsus (d.1541) is born in Einsieden, Switzerland. He rejected the theories of Hippocrates (**c.460 BC**), believing instead that diseases had external causes and that every disease had its unique symptoms. Many of his laboratory techniques became standard practice.

## c.1510

The surgeon Ambroise Paré is born near Laval, France (d.1590). His *Cinq Livres de chirurgie* (1562, 'Five books on sugery') and other writings exercised a great influence on surgery.

## c.1520

⊕ Smallpox is introduced to the Americas by the crew of a Spanish ship; the outbreak leads eventually to the destruction of the Aztec population.

## 1530

⬥ ⊕ The Italian scholar and physician Girolamo Fracastoro (1483–1553) publishes a poem about a 'new' venereal disease, *Syphilis sive morbus Gallicus* ('Syphilis, or the French disease') – the word syphilis is derived from its title.

## 1543

⬥ The Polish astronomer Nicolaus Copernicus (1473–1543) publishes his *De Revolutionibus Orbium Coelestium* ('The Revolutions of the Celestial Spheres'), detailing his theory of a Sun-centred solar system. This work, which fundamentally altered man's vision of the universe, was later banned by the Catholic Church and remained on the list of forbidden books until 1835.

⊕ The Belgian anatomist Andreas Vesalius (1514–64) publishes *De Humani Corporis Fabrica* ('On the Structure of the Human Body'). This large collection of detailed anatomical descriptions and illustrations set a completely new level of clarity and accuracy in anatomy, causing a movement away from the theories set forth by Galen (**c.201 AD**).

## 1562

⊕ The Italian anatomist Gabriele Falloppius (b.1523) dies. He particularly studied bones and the reproductive organs; the Fallopian tube, which connects the ovaries with the uterus, is named after him.

## 1565

The Swiss naturalist and physician Conrad Gesner (b.1516) dies. His *Historia Animalium* (1551–58, 'History of animals') attempted to describe all animals then known, and is thought to have introduced the concepts of species and genus in classification.

## 1572

⬥ The Danish astronomer Tycho Brahe (1546–1601) observes a new star (the supernova now known as Tycho's star) in the constellation Cassiopeia, interpreting this as evidence that the heavens are not without change.

## 1574

⊕ The Italian anatomist Hieronymus Fabricius ab Aquapendente (1537–1619) discovers that valves are distributed throughout veins. One of his pupils was

William Harvey, who later published a theory on the circulation of blood (see **1628**).

## 1576

◇ The Danish astronomer Tycho Brahe (1546–1601) establishes the Uraniborg (Castle of the Heavens) Observatory on the island of Ven (formerly Hven), in The Sound (between Zealand Island and Sweden).

## 1582

◇ In an attempt to correct the Julian calendar introduced **c.45 BC**, Pope Gregory XIII orders that ten days should be omitted from the month of October. The Gregorian calendar is adopted almost at once throughout Catholic Europe.

## 1590

The Italian astronomer, mathematician and natural philosopher Galileo Galilei (1564–1642) demonstrates that all bodies fall at the same rate if air resistance is not present, disproving Aristotle's theory that the rate at which a body falls is proportional to its weight.

## 1593

The Chinese pharmaceutical naturalist and biologist Li Shizen (b.1518) dies. His *Ben Cao Gang Mu* ('Great Pharmacopoeia') took 30 years to compile, and treats mineralogy, metallurgy, physiology, botany and zoology as sciences in their own right.

## 1595

The Dutch spectacle-maker Zacharias Janssen (1580–1638) produces an early compound microscope, possibly invented in collaboration with his father Hans Janssen.

## 1597

The German alchemist Andreas Libavius (c.1560–1616) publishes *Alchemia,* a richly illustrated book which has a claim to be the first chemical textbook; it gives accounts of a range of chemical methods and substances, and vigorously attacks the ideas of Paracelsus (see **1493**).

## 1600

The English physician William Gilbert (1544–1603) publishes *De Magnete* ('On the Magnet'), in which he establishes the magnetic nature of the Earth and conjectures that terrestrial magnetism and electricity are two allied emanations of a single force.

## 1604

The Italian anatomist Hieronymus Fabricius ab Aquapendente (1537–1619) publishes the first important study on embryology.

## 1608

The Dutch optician Hans Lippershey (c.1570–c.1619) applied for a patent for a type of telescope.

## 1609

The German astronomer Johannes Kepler (1571–1630) formulates his first two laws of planetary motion (see **1619**; **Key concepts: Kepler's laws of planetary motion**).

## 1610

Galileo perfects a refracting telescope, which he uses to discover the mountains of the Moon, the multitude of stars in the Milky Way, and the existence of Jupiter's four satellites.

## 1611

The German astronomer Johannes Kepler (1571–1630) publishes the earliest known work on the origins of snowflakes, correctly theorizing that their hexagonal nature was due to cold.

## 1614

The Scottish mathematician John Napier (1550–1617) describes his invention of logarithms in *Mirifici Logarithmorum Canonis Descriptio* ('Description of the Marvellous Canon of Logarithms'). Designed to simplify calculations, his system uses the natural logarithm base *e*, but is later modified by Henry Briggs (see **1617**).

## 1616

The English physician William Harvey (1578–1657) announces his discovery of the circulatory system of blood (see **1628**).

## 1617

The English mathematician Henry Briggs (1561–1630) suggests using 10 as the base in logarithms, instead of the base *e* as used by John Napier (see **1614**) – an important simplification for the practical use of logarithms in calculation.

## 1618

The Italian physicist Francesco Maria Grimaldi (1618–63) is born in Bologna. He discovered the diffraction of light and was one of the first to propose a wave theory of light.

## 1619

The German astronomer Johannes Kepler (1571–1630) formulates his third law of planetary motion (see **1609**; **Key concepts: Kepler's laws of planetary motion**).

## 1621

The Dutch mathematician Willebrod van Roijen Snell (1580–1626) discovers a law of refraction that relates the angles of incidence and refraction of a ray of light passing between two media of different refractive index. This becomes known as Snell's law.

The English mathematician William Oughtred (1575–1660) invents the earliest type of slide rule.

## 1624

The English physician Thomas Sydenham, known as 'the English Hippocrates', is born in Wynford Eagle, Dorset.

## 1625

The French astronomer Giovanni Domenico Cassini (d.1712) is born in Perinaldo, near Nice (then in Italy). He made many discoveries, including the polar ice caps of Mars, the rotational speed of Jupiter and the distance of all planets from the Sun. In 1675, Cassini also observed the division of Saturn's rings which still bears his name.

## 1628

The English physician William Harvey (1578–1657) publishes his celebrated treatise, *Exercitatio Anatomica de Motu Cordis et Sanguinis in Animalibus* ('An Anatomical Exercise on the Motion of the Heart and the Blood in Animals'), detailing the findings about the circulation of the blood that he announced in **1616**.

## 1637

The French philosopher and mathematician René Descartes (1596–1650) publishes his *Discours de la méthode* ('Discourse on Method'), which includes the famous quotation *'cogito ergo sum'* ('I think, therefore I am').

## 1642

The English scientist and mathematician Isaac Newton (d.1727) is born in Woolsthorpe, Lincolnshire.

## 1644

The Italian physicist and mathematician Evangelista Torricelli (1608–47) gives the first description of a mercury barometer or 'torricellian tube'.

## 1647

The Polish astronomer Johannes Hevelius (1611–87) publishes *Selenographica*, a description of the Moon with 133 copper plates of lunar features made by his own hand. He named many details on the Moon after features on Earth, and some of these names survive today.

The French mathematician, physicist and theologian Blaise Pascal (1623–62) patents a calculating machine, built to assist his father with accounts.

## 1648

The work of the Flemish chemist, physiologist and physician Johannes Baptista van Helmont (1579–1644) is posthumously published by his son, under the title *Ortus Medicinae vel Opera et Opuscula Omnia* ('On the development of medicine').

## 1651

The English physician William Harvey (1578–1657) publishes his *Exercitationes de Generatione Animalium* ('Essays on Generation in Animals'), confirming the theory that every living being has its origin in an egg.

## 1654

The German engineer and physicist Otto von Guericke (1602–86) gives a dramatic demonstration before the Emperor Ferdinand III of the powerful effects of atmospheric pressure on a near vacuum. Two large metal hemispheres were placed together, and the air within pumped out; they could not then be separated by two teams of eight horses, but fell apart when the air was allowed to re-enter.

🜨 Correspondence between the French mathematicians Pierre de Fermat (1601–65) and Blaise Pascal (1623–62) lays the foundations of probability theory.

## 1655

◁▷ The Dutch physicist Christiaan Huygens (1629–93) discovers the rings and fourth satellite of Saturn, using a refracting telescope that he constructed with his brother.

## 1656

◁▷ 🜨 The English astronomer and mathematician Edmond Halley (d.1742) is born in London.

🜨 The English mathematician John Wallis (1616–1703) publishes *Arithmetica infinitorum* ('The Arithmetic of Infinite Things'), in which he offers a remarkable method for finding areas under curves in terms of infinite sums. (This method was soon replaced by the more rigorous calculus.)

## 1657

🜨 The Dutch physicist Christiaan Huygens (1629–93) introduces the theory of mathematical expectation when he publishes the earliest known work on probability, *De ratiociniis in ludo aleae* ('On reasoning in games of chance').

## 1659

⊕ The English physician Thomas Willis (1621–73) gives the earliest known description of typhoid fever in his paper *De febribus* ('On fevers').

## 1660

🜨 The English scientist Robert Hooke (1635–1703) discovers the physical relationship between the stretch of a spring and its tension known as Hooke's law (see **Key concepts: Hooke's law**).

## 1662

🜨 The Irish physicist and chemist Robert Boyle (1627–91) discovers what is now known as Boyle's law, which states that the pressure and volume of gas are inversely proportional.

## 1665

🜨 The English scientist Robert Hooke (1635–1703), formerly an assistant to Robert Boyle (see **1662**), publishes his *Micrographia*, an impressive account of his microscopic investigations in botany, chemistry and other branches of science.

## 1669

The German alchemist Hennig Brand accidentally discovers phosphorus while experimenting with urine. As Brand did not publicize his discovery, phosphorus was discovered independently by Robert Boyle in 1680.

## 1674

The English scientist Robert Hooke (1635–1703) publishes *An Attempt to Prove the Motion of the Earth from Observations*.

The Dutch amateur scientist Antoni van Leeuwenhoek (1632–1723), an enthusiastic observer of life through a microscope, discovers the existence of blood corpuscles and of protozoa in water everywhere.

## 1675

The Royal Observatory is established at Greenwich, London, with the astronomer John Flamsteed (1646–1719) appointed as the first Astronomer Royal. Explorations of the skies using state-of-the-art telescopes and instruments put Britain ahead of France in trying to solve the problem of measuring longitude at sea. Among those closely associated with observing and charting the heavens were the English scientists Edmond Halley (see **1680**) and Isaac Newton (1642–1727).

The German philosopher and mathematician Gottfried Wilhelm Leibniz (1646–1716) made an important breakthrough in his work on integral calculus. He is jointly credited with the English scientist Isaac Newton (1642–1727) as the inventor of infinitesimal calculus.

---

### Calculus

Calculus is an important branch of mathematics dealing with the manipulation of continuously varying quantities. The many techniques of calculus arose from the study of natural phenomena, such as the changing speed of a falling object. Differential calculus is concerned with rate of change of a dependent variable, including the maximum and minimum points and the gradient of the graph of a given function, while integral calculus deals with areas and volumes, or methods of summation.

---

## 1680

The English astronomer and mathematician Edmond Halley (1656–1742), now the second Astronomer Royal, correctly predicts the return of a comet that had been observed in **1066**, 1531 and 1607 (Halley's comet).

## 1684

The English scientist and mathematician Isaac Newton (1642–1727) publishes his theory of gravitation in *De Motu Corporum* ('On the Movement of Bodies').

## 1686

The English naturalist John Ray (1627–1705) publishes his Historia Plantarum ('The History of Plants'), three volumes describing nearly 19000 species of plants. He had devised the basic principles of plant classification into cryptogams, monocotyledons and dicotyledons in his previous publications, *Catalogus Plantarum Angliae* (1670, 'Catalogue of English Plants') and *Methodus Plantarum Nova* (1682, 'A New Methodology of Plants'). Ray is credited with laying the groundwork for Linnaeus and his classification system (see **1735**).

## 1687

The English scientist and mathematician Isaac Newton (1642–1727) publishes his greatest work, *Philosophiae Naturalis Principia Mathematica* ('The Mathematical Principles of Natural Philosophy'), which includes his three laws of motion (see **Key concepts: Newton's laws of motion**). This work establishes the theory of universal gravitation, and is acknowledged as a revolutionary point in the history of science.

## 1690

The Dutch physicist Christiaan Huygens (1629–93) publishes his treatise on light.

## 1691

The English physician Clopton Havers (1655–1702) publishes *Osteologia Nova* ('Some New Observations about Bones'), the first complete and accurate textbook on the bones of the human body. He is regarded as a pioneer in osteology, and the Haversian canals in bones are named after him.

## 1694

The German physician and botanist Rudolph Jacob Camerarius (1665–1721) publishes *De Sexu Plantarum* ('On the sex of plants'), which describes his experimental proof of sexuality in plants.

The Italian anatomist and microscopist Marcello Malpighi (b.1628) dies. A pioneer of histology (the study of the microscopic structure of tissues and cells), Malpighi used a microscope to observe the minute links that connect blood from the arteries to the veins.

## 1701

◯ ▮ The Swedish astronomer Anders Celsius (d.1744) is born in Uppsala.

## 1702

⚛ ▮ The French instrument-maker and physicist Guillaume Amontons (1663–1705) invents an air thermometer and discovers the interdependence of volume, temperature and pressure of gases (see **Key concepts: The gas laws**).

## 1704

▲ ⚛ The English scientist and mathematician Isaac Newton (1642–1727) publishes his *Opticks*, an account of the nature and behaviour of light.

## 1707–10

✛ The English physician Sir John Floyer (1649–1734) publishes *The Physician's Pulse-watch*, a work recommending the accurate measurement of pulse rates in medical practice. Initially, Floyer used either the minute hand of a pendulum clock or a sea minute-glass as a timing device, but he later adapted a watch for measuring the pulse. This 'physician's pulse-watch' incorporated a second hand, as well as a special lever that stopped the mechanism.

## 1712

◯ The *Historia Coelestis* ('History of the Heavens'), a star catalogue based on observations made by John Flamsteed (1646–1719) at the Royal Greenwich Observatory, was printed under the editorship of Flamsteed's successor as Astronomer Royal, Edmond Halley (1656–1742). Flamsteed, who had not given permission for its publication, burned 300 of the 400 copies issued; an authorized version was published by his assistants in 1725, after his death.

## 1713

▲ *Ars conjectandi* ('The art of inference'), a treatise on probability theory by the Swiss mathematician Jacques Bernoulli (1654–1705), is published. It includes his 'law of large numbers', his permutation theory and the 'Bernoulli numbers', coefficients found in exponential series.

## 1714

▮ ⚛ The German instrument-maker and physicist (Gabriel) Daniel Fahrenheit (1686–1736) devises a commercially successful and accurate mercury thermometer.

## 1717

⊕ The Italian clinician and anatomist Giovanni Maria Lancisi (1654–1720) describes the characteristic black pigmentation of the brain and spleen of malaria victims in his monograph *On the Noxious Emanations of Swamps and their Cures*. Lancisi correctly suggests that malaria might be transmitted by the mosquito.

⊕ The English writer Lady Mary Wortley Montagu (1689–1762) sees inoculation successfully performed in Istanbul, Turkey, and has her son vaccinated against smallpox. She was instrumental in introducing vaccination to Great Britain when she returned in 1718.

### Bad Air

The name malaria originates from the Italian *mal aria* or 'bad air', a name which derives from early thoughts on the causes of the disease. Many other illnesses were also thought to result from foul-smelling air, which was known as miasma, until bacteria, viruses and other parasites were accepted as being responsible during the 19th century.

## 1720

▲ The Scottish mathematician Colin Maclaurin (1698–1746) publishes his first important work, *Geometrica organica* ('Organic Geometry'), on the subject of higher plane curves.

## 1724

▮ The Dutch physician and botanist Hermann Boerhaave (1668–1738) publishes his influential *Elementa Chemiae* ('Elements of Chemistry'), which treats heat as a fluid.

## 1729

❀ The English physicist Stephen Gray (1666–1736) experiments with static electricity on the surfaces of objects, and discovers that conductors can be used to transmit electricity over a distance between separate objects.

## 1730

◠ ▲ The English mathematician and astronomer John Hadley (1682–1744) invents the reflecting quadrant ('Hadley's quadrant'), an instrument used by navigators.

## 1733

◠ The Swedish astronomer Anders Celsius (1701–44) publishes his observations of the aurora borealis (northern lights).

The French mathematician Abraham de Moivre (1667–1754) describes the normal distribution curve (the normal curve of error in statistics).

## 1735

The Swedish naturalist and physician Carolus Linnaeus (1707–78) publishes his *Systemae Naturae* ('Systems of Nature'), setting out the classification of plants and animals which is still used in taxonomy today (see **Organisms: Classification of organisms**).

The German biologist, natural historian and geographer Johann Georg Gmelin (1709–55) discovers permafrost during a scientific expedition in Siberia.

## 1738

The Swiss mathematician Daniel Bernoulli (1700–82) publishes *Hydrodynamica*, a work examining the relationship between the velocity and pressure of flowing fluids (see **Key concepts: Bernoulli's principle**). Bernoulli also predicted the kinetic theory of gases by explaining that pressure would increase with increasing temperature (see **Key concepts: The gas laws**).

## 1740

Antonio Lazzaro Moro (1687–1764) publishes his treatise on marine fossils, *Dei crostacei e degli altri corpi marini che si trovano su' monti* ('On Shells and Other Marine Bodies which are Found on Mountains'). He proposed that fossils were the remains of organisms that had lived in other time periods and had been raised from the sea floor by the force of a volcanic eruption, rather than by biblical flooding of the world.

## 1744

The Swiss naturalist Abraham Trembley (1710–84) publishes *Memoires Concerning the Natural History of a Type of Freshwater Polyp with Arms Shaped Like Horns*, which describes his experiments on freshwater hydra.

The English botanist Sir Joseph Banks, remembered for his far-reaching influence on other scientists, is born in London (d.1820).

## 1746

The English inventor John Roebuck (1718–94), during his research in chemistry, devises the lead-chamber process for the production of sulphuric acid.

## 1748

The French physicist Jean Antoine Nollet (1700–70) discovers, and gives the first clear explanation of, the phenomenon of osmosis (the diffusion of molecules through a semi-permeable membrane from a place of higher concentration to a place of lower concentration, until the concentration on both sides is equal).

## 1749

The Swedish naturalist and physician Carolus Linnaeus (1707–78) introduces binomial nomenclature, giving each plant a Latin generic name with a specific adjective; this system leads to the hierarchical organization later known as taxonomy.

## 1750

The English astronomer and geologist John Michell (1724–93) publishes *A Treatise of Artificial Magnets,* which describes an easy method of making artificial magnets superior to naturally formed ones. This method of magnetization still bears his name. His treatise also contains an accurate explanation of magnetic induction.

## 1752

The Gregorian calendar, first decreed by Pope Gregory XIII in **1582**, is adopted throughout the British Empire.

The American inventor and scientist Benjamin Franklin (1706–90) demonstrates that lightning is electrical in a highly dangerous experiment, flying a kite during a thunderstorm.

## 1756

The Scottish chemist Joseph Black (1728–99) publishes *Experiments upon magnesia, quicklime and other alkaline substances*, a work investigating the causticity of alkalis. It is the first detailed examination of chemical actions, and his experimental method lays the foundations of quantitative analysis in chemistry.

## 1757

An English naval officer, John Campbell, invents the sextant, allowing mariners to use the angle of a celestial object above the horizon to determine latitude and longitude at sea.

## 1760

The Russian chemist Mikhail Lomonosov (1711–65) describes the formation of icebergs.

The English astronomer and geologist John Michell (1724–93) publishes his *Essay on the Causes and Phenomena of Earthquakes*, proposing a theory of earthquakes as wave motions in the interior of the Earth caused by one layer of rocks rubbing against another. Michell is remembered as the founder of seismology.

## 1761

⊕ The Italian physician Giovanni Morgagni (1682–1771) publishes *De Sedibus et Causis Morborum per Anatomen Indagatis* ('The Seats and Causes of Diseases Investigated by Anatomy'). This is the first major work to relate the symptoms of disease during a patient's life to post-mortem findings.

## 1765

The Italian biologist and naturalist Lazzaro Spallanzani (1729–99) disproves the theory of spontaneous generation by showing that broth, when boiled thoroughly and hermetically sealed, remains sterile.

The Scottish engineer James Watt (1736–1819) builds a model of his famous steam engine, which has a condenser that is separate from the cylinder. The condenser allows the steam to act directly on the piston.

## 1766

The English natural philosopher and chemist Henry Cavendish (1731–1810) isolates 'inflammable air' (hydrogen), demonstrating that it is at least seven times lighter than air.

The English chemist and natural philosopher John Dalton is born in Eaglesfield, Cumbria (d.1844). Although his greatest fame relates to his atomic theory (see **1808**), he also described colour-blindness (see **1794**). His important studies on gases led to Dalton's law of partial pressures.

## 1767

The English clergyman and chemist Joseph Priestley (1733–1804) publishes his first scientific work, the *History of Electricity*, describing his own experiments and Benjamin Franklin's famous kite experiment of 1752. Priestley is better known for his work on the nature and properties of gases (see **1775**).

## 1769

The Swiss naturalist and philosopher Charles Bonnet (1720–93) writes *Philosophical Palingenesis, or Ideas on the Past and Future States of Living Beings*, in which he proposes that the females of every species contain the egg or germ of all future generations.

## 1771

The Swedish chemist Carl Wilhelm Scheele (1742–86) discovers oxygen;

however, delays in publication mean that a later, independent discovery by the English chemist Joseph Priestley (1733–1804) in 1774 is more widely known.

## c.1772

⊕ The Austrian physician Franz Mesmer (1734–1815) introduces his theory of 'magnetism' (later known as mesmerism). A forerunner of hypnotism, his treatment, activated by a magnetized object, aimed to facilitate the flow of an invisible fluid around the body; it was eventually denounced as fraudulent.

## 1772

◁▷ The German astronomer Johann Elert Bode (1747–1826) publishes the empirical rule known as Bode's law, which expresses the proportionate distances of the planets from the Sun. The rule, alternatively called the Titius–Bode law, had been first discovered in 1766 by Johann Daniel Titius, but was brought into use by Bode. It does not hold for the most distant planet, Pluto, and has no theoretical foundation.

## 1773

▮ 🐚 The German mineralogist Friedrich Mohs is born in Gernrode, Sachsen–Anhalt (d.1839). He developed a mineralogical classification system based on a variety of mineral characters, rather than adopting the traditional purely chemical system. The Mohs scale of hardness, which he introduced, is still in use (see **Measurement: Scales**).

## 1774

⊕ The Scottish anatomist and obstetrician William Hunter (1718–83) publishes his chief work, *The Anatomy of the Human Gravid Uterus*, a masterpiece of anatomical illustrations.

## 1775

▮ The English clergyman and chemist Joseph Priestley (1733–1804) discovers hydrochloric and sulphuric acids. In total, Priestley isolated and characterized eight gases including oxygen, ammonia, nitrous oxide, sulphur dioxide and carbon monoxide.

## 1776

🪨 The Scottish chemist James Keir (1735–1820) proposes the theory that such rock formations as the Giant's Causeway in Ireland are a result of volcanic rock crystallizing as it cooled. His theory is based on observations of cooling glass at his glass-making business in Stourbridge.

## 1779

The Italian biologist and naturalist Lazzaro Spallanzani (1729–99) discovers that sperm must have physical contact with an egg for successful fertilization to occur. By artificially inseminating amphibians, silkworms and a dog, he provides further evidence to disprove the theory of spontaneous generation (see **1765**) and to support the theory of sexual reproduction.

The Dutch biologist and chemist Jan Ingenhousz (1730–1799) demonstrates that in plants, photosynthesis is the reverse process of respiration – respiration involves the combination of oxygen with carbon to form carbon dioxide, while photosynthesis breaks carbon dioxide back down into oxygen and carbon.

The French chemist Antoine Lavoisier (1743–94) names the element oxygen (see **1771**), and explains its role in combustion.

The Swiss geologist and physicist Horace de Saussure (1740–99) publishes the first volume of *Voyages dans les Alpes* ('Travels in the Alps'), which describes his observations on geology, mineralogy, botany and the movement of glaciers. The mineral saussurite is named after him.

## 1780

The Italian biologist and naturalist Lazzaro Spallanzani (1729–99) publishes his *Dissetazioni de fisica animale e vegetale* ('Dissertation on the physiology of animals and plants'), in which he states that gastric juice is the main digestive agent.

The giant skull of a prehistoric creature is discovered in a stone quarry near the Meuse River in the Netherlands. Bones from the same creature had been found in 1766, but the fossil would not be identified until **1795**.

## 1781

The British astronomer William Herschel (1738–1822) discovers the planet Uranus, which is later named by the German astronomer Johann Elert Bode (1747–1826). Herschel also discovered two satellites of Uranus in 1787, and two of Saturn in 1789.

The French chemist Antoine Lavoisier (1743–94) discovers the first version of the law of conservation – during his experiments, he observes that the total weight of material does not change during chemical reactions.

## 1783

The volcano Laki in Iceland erupts, killing thousands of islanders. This natural catastrophe contributes to the US scientist Benjamin Franklin's (1706–90) theory that the dust and gases from a volcanic eruption cause lower temperatures by blocking the Sun's radiation (see **1815**).

## 1785

The English natural philosopher and chemist Henry Cavendish (1731–1810) discovers the composition of normal atmospheric air – oxygen, nitrogen, hydrogen, carbon dioxide and an unknown gas (later identified as a mixture of argon, neon, krypton and xenon).

The Scottish geologist James Hutton (1726–97) publishes *A Theory of the Earth*, in which he demonstrated that the internal heat of the Earth caused intrusions of molten rock into the crust, and that granite was the product of the cooling of molten rock.

The French physicist Charles Augustin de Coulomb (1736–1806) establishes Coulomb's law, which states that the force between two small charged spheres is related to the charges and the distance between them.

## 1787

The publication of *Méthode de nomenclature chimique* ('Method of chemical nomenclature') by the French chemists Antoine Lavoisier (1743–94), Claude-Louis Berthollet (1749–1822), Antoine de Fourcroy (1755–1809) and Louis Bernard Guyton de Morveau (1737–1816), introduces revised scientific nomenclature for chemicals based on the origin or function of the elements.

The French physicist Jacques-Alexandre-César Charles (1746–1823) experiments with gas, temperature and pressure. His results become known as Charles' law (see **Key concepts: The gas laws**), and were published by Joseph Louis Gay-Lussac in **1802**.

## 1789

The English chemist James Marsh is born in London (d.1846). His work with poisons would result in the development of a sensitive test for arsenic (the Marsh Test), published in 1836.

## 1794

The English chemist and natural philosopher John Dalton (1766–1844) describes colour-blindness ('Daltonism'), using his own case as an example. Most colour perception defects relate to the colours green or red, or to both. Daltonism is associated with a recessive gene on the X-chromosome (see **Genetics: Genetic inheritance**).

The French mathematician Adrian Marie Legendre's (1752–1833) *Éléments de géométrie* ('Elements of geometry') refreshes the teaching of elementary geometry in France. Later, when it is translated into English by the Scottish historian Thomas Carlyle (1795–1881), it becomes the most widely used textbook on geometry in the US.

## 1795

The French anatomist and zoologist Georges Cuvier (1769–1832) identifies bones found between 1766 and **1780** in a quarry near the Meuse River in the Netherlands as belonging to a giant, prehistoric marine reptile, named the Mosasaur and measuring 14 m (46 ft) in length.

The Scottish physician Gilbert Blane (1749–1834) treats scurvy in British sailors by introducing lime juice to their diets. The original idea was suggested by the Scottish physician James Lind (1716–94) who correctly believed that eating citrus fruit prevented scurvy developing in people during long sea voyages. This is the origin of the nickname 'limey' for the British sailor. It is now known that a lack of vitamin C causes scurvy, thus eating citrus fruit prevents it.

## 1796

The English physician Edward Jenner (1749–1823) successfully inoculates eight-year-old James Phipps against smallpox, inaugurating vaccination. Centuries later, smallpox immunization would become the most successful vaccination programme in the world, eradicating the disease in 1980.

## 1798

The English economist and clergyman Thomas Malthus (1766–1834) anonymously publishes his *Essay on the Principle of Population*, in which he predicted that population growth, if left uncontrolled, would eventually outrun the means of subsistence. His recommendations for reducing the birth rate included sexual abstinence and birth control.

The English natural philosopher and chemist Henry Cavendish (1731–1810) carries out the famous 'Cavendish experiment', employing a torsion balance apparatus to estimate with great accuracy the mean density of the Earth and the universal gravitational constant.

## 1800

The English chemist Humphry Davy (1778–1829) discovers the anaesthetic effects of nitrous oxide ($N_2O$ or 'laughing gas').

The British astronomer William Herschel (1738–1822) discovers infrared radiation by noticing that the part of the spectrum beyond red light could heat a thermometer.

The Italian physicist and inventor Alessandro Volta (1745–1827) invents the electrochemical battery or 'voltaic pile', the first source of continuous or current electricity.

## 1801

The Italian astronomer Giuseppe Piazzi (1746–1826) becomes the first person to discover a minor planet, or asteroid, which he names Ceres.

While working with silver chloride, the German physicist Johann Wilhelm Ritter (1776–1810) discovers radiation beyond the spectrum of visible light (ultraviolet radiation).

The German astronomer, mathematician and physicist Carl Friedrich Gauss (1777–1855) publishes his textbook *Disquisitiones Arithmeticae* ('Arithmetic Investigations'), which contains new advances in number theory and introduces the concept of congruent integers (numbers that have the same remainder when divided by a particular number).

The English physicist and physician Thomas Young (1773–1829) discovers that the faulty vision caused by astigmatism is a result of an uneven curvature of the cornea of the eye. In the same year, Young also confirms Grimaldi's wave theory of light (see **1618**).

## 1802

The French chemist and physicist Joseph Louis Gay-Lussac (1778–1850) publishes *The Expansion of Gases by Heat*, in which he concludes that equal volumes of all gases expand equally with the same increase in temperature. This conclusion is usually called 'Charles's law' in honor of the French physicist Jacques-Alexandre-César Charles (see **1787**), who had reached the same conclusion nearly fifteen years earlier.

## 1803

The English physician and chemist William Henry's (1774–1836) experiments with pressure and temperature on the solubility of gases in water resulted in the generalization that has become known as Henry's law, that the solubility of a gas at a given temperature is proportional to its pressure.

## 1804

The French anatomist and zoologist Georges Cuvier (1769–1832) suggests that fossils found in the area around Paris are 'thousands of centuries' old. Cuvier also notes that the fossils he has studied show no resemblance to anything still living, which is good evidence to support the theory of extinction.

## 1805

The French chemist and physicist Joseph Louis Gay-Lussac (1778–1850) discovers that pure water has a ratio of two parts hydrogen to one part oxygen ($H_2O$).

The British naval officer Sir Francis Beaufort (1774–1857) creates an early version of his Beaufort scale of wind force (see **Measurement: Scales**).

## 1806

The French chemist Nicolas-Louis Vauquelin (1763–1829) becomes the first to isolate an amino acid (asparagine), obtained from asparagus.

The Swiss mathematician Jean-Robert Argand (1768–1822) publishes a pamphlet on what will become known as the Argand diagram, in which complex numbers are represented by points in the plane (see **Numbers and shapes: Types of numbers**).

## 1807

The Swedish chemist Jöns Jacob Berzelius (1779–1848) begins the work that will lead him to draw up a table of atomic weights using oxygen as a base, devising the modern system of chemical symbols.

The US geographer Arnold Guyot is born in Boudevilliers, Switzerland (d.1884). He is chiefly remembered for his study of glaciers. The flat-topped undersea mountains known as guyots, which were discovered in the 20th century, are named for him.

## 1808

The English chemist and natural philosopher John Dalton (1766–1844) publishes the first part of his *New System of Chemical Philosophy*, outlining his atomic theory. Although Dalton's theory was later refined, his thesis formed one of the fundamental stages in the development of chemistry.

## 1809

The English naturalist Charles Darwin is born in Shrewsbury, Shropshire (d.1882). Though not the sole originator of the evolution hypothesis, Darwin was the first thinker to supply to the idea a sufficient cause, which raised it at once from a hypothesis to a verifiable theory, thereby gaining it a wide acceptance among biological experts (see **Key concepts: The theory of natural selection**).

## 1811

The English fossil collector Mary Anning (1799–1847) finds the fossil skeleton of an ichthyosaur in a local cliff in Lyme Regis, Dorset – an area rich in aquatic fossils from the Jurassic period. Anning is regarded as one of the greatest fossil collectors, and did much to advance knowledge by her diligence and aptitude in collecting specimens.

The Italian physicist and chemist Amedeo Avogadro (1776–1856) formulated the famous hypothesis that equal volumes of all gases contain equal numbers of molecules when at the same temperature and pressure (see **Key concepts: Avogadro's law**).

## 1815

The English chemist Humphry Davy (1778–1829) invents the safety lamp for miners (the 'Davy lamp'), enabling deeper, more gaseous coal seams to be mined with less risk of explosion.

One of the most violent volcanic eruptions in recorded history takes place at Mount Tambora in Indonesia, sending so much dust into the atmosphere that weather patterns around the world are affected (the following year is, in consequence, nicknamed the 'year without a summer').

The English civil engineer and geologist William Smith (1769–1839) publishes his book *The Geological Map of England* – the first published geological map of any country.

## 1816

The French physician René Théophile Hyacinthe Laënnec (1781–1826) invents the stethoscope. He initially used a rolled-up sheet of paper, and then a wooden tube, similar to a candlestick, with adaptations at the end to help transmit sound more easily.

## 1817

The symptoms of paralysis agitans, or Parkinson's disease – previously known as the 'shaking palsy' – are described by London-based doctor James Parkinson (1755–1824).

## 1820

The Danish physicist Hans Christian Oersted (1777–1851) discovers electromagnetism during his experiments with a magnetic needle and an electric current.

After hearing of Oersted's discovery of electromagnetism, the French mathematician and physicist André Ampère (1775–1836) conducts theoretical and experimental work that lays the foundations of the science of electrodynamics.

## 1821

The English fossil collector Mary Anning (1799–1847) discovers the first complete example of the plesiosaur. Her other discoveries included an ichthyosaur (see **1811**), the pterodactyl, *Dimorphodon* (a flying reptile) and the squaloraja (type of fish).

⊕ The Scottish anatomist and surgeon Sir Charles Bell (1744–1842) is the first to describe the paralysis of muscles on one side of the face that will become known as Bell's palsy.

## 1822

The French chemist and bacteriologist Louis Pasteur – regarded as the founder of modern bacteriology – is born in Dôle.

## 1823

The Scottish industrial chemist Charles Macintosh (1766–1843) invents waterproof cloth by bonding two pieces of woollen cloth together with a solution of dissolved india-rubber. Patenting the process the same year, he joins forces with Thomas Hancock to begin making waterproof garments at a factory in Manchester.

The English chemist and meteorologist John Frederic Daniell (1790–1845) publishes *Meteorological Essays*, which includes his theory of trade winds and the atmosphere.

## 1825

The French anatomist and zoologist Georges Cuvier (1769–1832) posits his theory of 'catastrophism' – a series of extinctions due to periodic global floods, after which new forms of life supposedly appeared.

The English scientist William Sturgeon (1783–1850) constructs the first practical electromagnet.

## 1826

The German astronomer Heinrich Olbers (1758–1840) expresses the famous paradox that in a static infinite universe, the night sky should be bright – known as Olbers's paradox.

The French chemist Joseph Nicéphore Niepce (1765–1833) produces the world's first permanent photographic image on metal, using a bitumen-coated pewter plate. This historic negative is described as a 'heliograph' and takes eight hours to develop.

## 1827

The German naturalist and embryologist Karl Ernst von Baer (1792–1876) establishes through his research that offspring develop from eggs (ova) in all mammals, including humans.

The Scottish botanist Robert Brown (1773–1858) first observes the movement of fine particles in a liquid, subsequently named 'Brownian movement' or 'Brownian motion'. Brownian motion proves the existence of molecules and is also evidence to support the theory of kinetic energy as an inherent quality of all matter, as it is assumed that motion also occurs in other substances where it cannot be so readily observed.

The English physician Richard Bright (1789–1858) first describes the clinical symptoms of the kidney disorder that later becomes known as Bright's disease (glomerulonephritis).

The German physicist Georg Simon Ohm (1787–1854) publishes his 'Ohm's law', relating voltage, current and resistance in an electrical circuit (see **Key concepts: Ohm's law**).

## 1829

The Scottish chemist Thomas Graham (1805–69) conducts research on the diffusion of gases and related phenomena, leading eventually to the establishment of Graham's law, which states that the velocity of effusion of a gas is inversely proportional to the square root of its density.

## 1830

The Scottish geologist Charles Lyell (1797–1875) completes the first volume of his *Principles of Geology*, one of the most influential 19th-century works on geology.

## 1831

The English naturalist Charles Darwin (1809–82) is appointed official ship's naturalist to HMS *Beagle*, which is about to start for a scientific survey of South American waters.

The Scottish botanist Robert Brown (1773–1858) reports his discovery of the cell nucleus.

Chloroform is distilled for the first time by the US chemist and physician Samuel Guthrie (1782–1848), although it is not used as an anaesthetic until **1847**.

The English chemist and physicist Michael Faraday (1791–1867) discovers electromagnetic induction and demonstrates the 'dynamo' or electromagnetic motor, which becomes the basis of electrical engineering. The US physicist Joseph Henry (1797–1878) had constructed the first dynamo in 1829, but had not published his experimental observations.

## 1832

✚ A form of glandular disease, later known as Hodgkin's disease, is described for the first time by the English physician and pathologist Thomas Hodgkin (1798–1866).

✚ The act of parliament known as the Anatomy Act is passed in Britain, stating that anyone intending to practise anatomy must obtain a licence from the Home Secretary, and legalizing the use of unclaimed or donated corpses for dissection.

> ### Burke and Hare
>
> The Anatomy Act was prompted by the scandalous crimes of William Burke (1792–1829) and William Hare (1790–1860), who murdered visitors to their Edinburgh guest house in order to supply the Scottish anatomist Robert Knox (1791–1862) with bodies for dissection.

## 1833

The English chemist and physicist Michael Faraday (1791–1867) publishes a description of his quantitative laws of electrolysis, stating that the mass of a substance produced at an electrode is proportional to the quantity of electrical current used.

The English mathematician Charles Babbage (1791–1871) initiates a major step towards modern computers with his unrealized design for an 'analytical engine' intended to be programmable to carry out mathematical functions.

## 1834

The English mathematician John Venn is born near Hull, Humberside (d.1923). He is best remembered for devising 'Venn diagrams', pictorial representations of the relations between sets.

The German physicist Heinrich Lenz (1804–65) explains Lenz's law, which states that an induced current will flow in a direction opposing the change that induced the current.

## c.1835

The French physicist Gustave Coriolis (1792–1843) publishes a paper describing what later became known as the Coriolis force (the apparent force deflecting moving objects caused by the Earth's rotation).

## 1836

The English chemist and meteorologist John Frederic Daniell (1790–1845), after working with voltaic cells, invents a constant voltage (Daniell) cell, for which he is awarded the Royal Society's Copley medal in 1837.

## 1837

The US naturalist Louis Agassiz (1807–73) coins the term 'ice age' (die Eiszeit) in connection with his work on glaciers, their mobility, origin and past effects on habitats.

The English physicist Charles Wheatstone (1802–75), in conjunction with William Cooke (1806–79), takes out a patent on an electric telegraph.

## 1838

The German botanist Matthias Jakob Schleiden (1804–81) builds on Scottish botanist Robert Brown's discovery of the cell nucleus (see **1831**) to explain the role of the nucleus in cell formation.

The Welsh mineralogist and crystallographer William Hallowes Miller (1801–80) publishes his groundbreaking work *A Treatise on Crystallography*.

## 1839

The German physiologist Theodor Schwann's (1810–82) microscopic studies of animal tissue help to develop the cell theory of organisms. He contends that plants or animals are made entirely of cells and that cells have in some measure a life of their own, but that the life of the cells is also dependent on that of the whole organism.

The French photographic pioneer and painter Louis Daguerre (1789–1851) perfects his Daguerrotype process, in which a photographic image is obtained on a copper plate coated with a layer of metallic silver sensitized to light by iodine vapour.

The German chemist Christian Schönbein (1799–1868) discovers a denser form of oxygen called ozone. An ozone molecule contains three atoms of oxygen ($O_3$) per molecule, compared to the more common diatomic oxygen molecule ($O_2$).

The English mathematician and logician George Boole (1815–64) publishes his work on analytic transformations, the basis of Boolean algebra.

## 1840

The US author and scientist John William Draper (1811–82) is the first person to photograph the Moon, initiating astronomical photography.

The English physicist James Prescott Joule (1818–89) describes the 'Joule effect', which states that the heat produced in a wire by an electric current is proportional to the resistance and to the square of the current.

## 1842

The Austrian physicist Christian Doppler (1803–53) publishes a paper explaining the Doppler effect – the frequency variation observed when a vibrating source of waves and the observer approach or recede from one another.

The English zoologist and palaeontologist Richard Owen (1804–92) introduces the word 'dinosaur' ('terrible lizard') to classify the ancient reptiles whose fossils are increasingly being discovered.

## 1843

The English physicist James Prescott Joule (1818–89) demonstrates experimentally that heat is a form of energy, and establishes the mechanical equivalent of heat. The joule, a unit of work or energy, is named after him.

## 1844

The Italian cytologist Camillo Golgi is born in Corteno, Lombardy (d.1926). He discovered Golgi 'bodies' or 'apparatus' within cells; these bodies are essential for the assembly, sorting and modification of large molecules such as proteins (see **Cells: Cell structure, Gene expression**).

The US inventor Charles Goodyear (1800–60) receives a patent for his process of vulcanizing rubber (see **Materials: Polymers**).

The Scottish physician Patrick Manson is born in Oldmeldrum, Aberdeenshire (d.1922). Manson is remembered for discovering that the disease elephantiasis is caused by a parasite transmitted by mosquitos. He was also the first to argue that the mosquito is host to the malaria parasite (1877).

The US dentist Horace Wells (1815–1848) is the first to use nitrous oxide (laughing gas) as an anaesthetic on his patients, although it had been recommended for this purpose in **1800** by the English chemist Humphry Davy (1778–1829).

The US inventor Samuel Morse (1791–1872) demonstrates his experimental telegraph line on 24 May. Using a code of his own invention, he sends the historic message 'What hath God wrought?' over a line from Washington to Baltimore.

## c.1845

The Italian chemist Ascanio Sobrero (1812–88) creates nitroglycerine, describing both its explosive properties and possible use as a drug.

## 1845

The Polish apiculturist Jan Dzierzon (1811–1906) discovers parthenogenesis in bees.

⊕ The symptoms of leukaemia are first described by the German pathologist and politician Rudolph Virchow (1821–1902).

⚛ The English chemist and physicist Michael Faraday (1791–1867) publishes a description of his discovery of the rotation of polarized light by magnetism.

## 1846

◁▷ The German astronomer Johann Galle (1812–1910) becomes the first person to observe the planet Neptune.

⊕ The US dental surgeon William T G Morton (1819–68) uses ether ('letheon') as an anaesthetic for the excision of a vascular malformation from a patient, and patents the process.

## 1847

⊕ The Scottish obstetrician James Simpson (1811–70) originates the use of ether as an anaesthetic in childbirth and, experimenting on himself and his assistants in the search for a better anaesthetic, discovers the required properties in chloroform.

⚛ The German physiologist and physicist Hermann von Helmholtz (1821–94) publishes his paper on *Conservation of Energy*, which contains an equation expressing the most general form of the law that it is impossible to create or destroy energy within a system.

## 1848

🗲 ⚗ ⚛ The Scottish physicist and mathematician William Thomson, later Lord Kelvin (1824–1907), proposes the absolute, or Kelvin, temperature scale.

## 1849

⚛ The French physicist Armand Fizeau (1819–96) becomes the first to measure the velocity of light, by a laboratory experiment in which a ray of light is cut by a toothed wheel, producing intermittent flashes.

## 1850

◁▷ The French astronomer Édouard Roche (1820–83) calculates the theoretical 'Roche limit', the lowest orbit a satellite can maintain around its parent planet without being pulled apart by the tidal forces it creates.

⚛ The German physicist Rudolf Clausius (1822–88) postulates that heat cannot of itself pass from a colder body to a hotter one (the second law of thermodynamics) (see **Key concepts: The laws of thermodynamics**).

## 1851

The German botanist Hugo von Mohl (1805–72) publishes his observations on the structure of plant cells, describing the fibrous cell wall, nucleus, osmosis and cell membrane.

The French physicist Jean Foucault (1819–68) demonstrates the rotation of the Earth by use of a freely suspended pendulum.

## 1852

The Irish polymath Edward Sabine (1788–1883) discovers that there is a correlation between changes in the Earth's magnetic field and changes in sunspots.

The Irish mathematician and physicist George Gabriel Stokes (1819–1903) describes the phenomenon of fluorescence in a paper on his research into the wavelength of light.

The English chemist Edward Frankland (1825–99) introduces the theory of valency, which underlies all structural chemistry.

## 1853

The Scottish engineer and scientist William Rankine (1820–72) introduced the terms 'actual' (kinetic) and 'potential' energy.

## 1854

The German mathematician Bernhard Riemann (1826–66) gives a famous lecture, 'On the hypotheses that underlie geometry', in which he first presents his notion of an n-dimensional curved space. His work was important to the formulation of the German–Swiss–US mathematical physicist Albert Einstein's (1879–1955) theory of general relativity (see **Key concepts: General theory of relativity**).

The English nurse Florence Nightingale (1820–1910) takes a team of nurses to Scutari, where she introduces a regimen of cleanliness to the barracks hospital that dramatically reduces the death rate.

The English anaesthetist and epidemiologist John Snow (1813–58) demonstrates that cholera can be transmitted by water contaminated with raw sewage.

## 1855

The English metallurgist and inventor Henry Bessemer (1813–98) patents his process for converting pig iron into steel by blowing air through it in a 'Bessemer converter'.

The US hydrographer Matthew Maury (1806–73) publishes his important book *Physical Geography of the Sea*.

The German chemist August Wilhelm von Hofmann (1818–92) purifies and characterizes the aromatic chemical aniline (also called phenylamine and aminobenzene). The chemical forms the basis for the manufacture of various dyes (see **1856**), drugs (see **1932**) and plastics.

## 1856

The French chemist Louis Pasteur (1822–95) publishes his experiments on fermentation, demonstrating that it is caused by the growth of microorganisms and supporting germ theory.

In the Neander river valley in Germany, fossil remains of the species later known as Neanderthals are discovered, marking the beginning of paleoanthropology.

The German physiologist Karl Friedrich Wilhelm Ludwig (1816–95) is the first to keep animal organs alive outside the body, marking a significant step towards the possibility of organ transplantation.

The English chemist Sir William Henry Perkin (1838–1907) synthesizes a brilliant purple dye, which becomes known as mauveine, from aniline (see **1855**), while trying to produce the antimalarial drug quinine.

## 1857

The French physicist Jean Foucault (1819–68) constructs the Foucault prism to measure the speed of light.

## 1858

The Scottish organic chemist Archibald Scott Couper (1831–92) introduces the idea of bonds between atoms in chemistry in his paper *On a New Chemical Theory*.

The German mathematician August Ferdinand Möbius (1790–1868) discovers his 'Möbius strip' – a one-sided surface formed by giving a rectangular strip a half-twist and then joining the ends together.

## 1859

The English naturalist Charles Darwin (1809–82) publishes *The Origin of Species by Means of Natural Selection* (see **Key concepts: The theory of natural selection**).

Spectrum analysis, a method of identifying chemical elements, is discovered by the German scientists Robert Bunsen (1811–99) and Gustav Robert Kirchhoff (1824–87).

⊕ The psychoactive drug cocaine is extracted from the coca plant by the German student chemist Albert Niemann during research for his doctoral thesis, on a *New Organic Base in the Coca Leaves* (1860).

## 1861

The English naturalist Henry Walter Bates (1825–92) publishes his *Contributions to an Insect Fauna of the Amazon Valley*, describing the phenomenon (now known as Batesian mimicry) in which harmless, edible species of animal resemble others which are distasteful or poisonous, and thus gain protection from predators. This discovery provided strong evidence in favour of natural selection.

⊕ The French surgeon and anthropologist (Pierre) Paul Broca (1824–80) first locates the motor speech centre in the brain, since known as the convolution of Broca or Broca's gyrus.

## 1862

The Swedish physicist Anders Ångström (1814–74) predicts the presence of hydrogen in the Sun by analysing its spectrum. Ångström wrote on heat, magnetism, and especially optics; the angstrom unit, for measuring wavelengths of light, is named after him.

The French chemist Louis Pasteur (1822–95) develops the technique of 'pasteurization', a mild heat treatment to destroy disease-producing bacteria.

## 1863

The English chemist John Newlands (1837–98) devises a precursor to the periodic table by arranging the chemical elements into eight groups in ascending order of atomic masses.

⊕ The first slimming diet to prohibit specific foods, in this case anything containing starch, is devised by the English undertaker William Banting (1797–1878).

## 1864

The English astronomer William Huggins (1824–1910) discovers stellar spectra indicating that stars are composed of chemical elements that are also found on Earth. His pioneering work included spectroscopy of comets and observations of the Doppler shift in the spectra of stars as a means of measuring their radial motion (see **1868**).

📌 ⚛️ The Norwegian chemists Peter Waage (1833–1900) and Cato Maximilian Guldberg (1836–1902) propose the law of mass action, which says that the rate of a reaction is proportional to the concentrations of the reactants (see **Key concepts: Collision theory**).

⚛️ The Scottish physicist James Clerk Maxwell (1831–79) presents to the Royal Society a set of equations (now known as Maxwell's equations) that describe the behaviour of both the electric and magnetic fields, as well as their interactions with matter.

## 1865

🌿 The Austrian botanist Gregor Mendel (1822–84) presents his paper *Experiments on Plant Hybridization*, describing the research that led to the formulation of 'Mendel's law of segregation' and his 'law of independent assortment' (see **Key concepts: Mendel's laws of genetic inheritance**).

📌 The German chemist August Kekulé von Stradonitz (1829–96) announces that the structure of the benzene ring has been revealed to him in a dream involving serpents with their tails in their mouths. It is likely that this deduction in fact owed a great deal to his knowledge of earlier work by other scientists.

> **❝**
> Thought comes often clad in the strangest clothing:
> So Kekulé the chemist watched the weird rout
> Of eager atom-serpents writhing in and out
> And waltzing tail to mouth. In that absurd guise
> Appeared benzene and aniline, their drugs and their dyes.
>
> —English writer Robert Graves (1895–1985), *Difficult Questions, Easy Answers* (1972). Kekulé claimed that the dream about snakes with their tails in their mouths gave him the idea of the benzene molecule joining end to end.
> **❞**

📌 ⚛️ The US electrical engineer Charles Proteus Steinmetz is born in Breslau, Germany (d. 1923). After emigrating to the US in 1889, he was consulting engineer to General Electric from 1893 and is credited with numerous theories and discoveries. One of his earliest achievements was to work out in complete detail, using complex numbers, the mathematical theory of alternating currents. He discovered magnetic hysteresis, a simple notation for calculating alternating current circuits, and lightning arresters for high-power transmission lines.

## 1866

🪐 The Italian astronomer Giovanni Schiaparelli (1835–1910) observes meteors following the orbits of comets. He also achieves the first identification of a meteoroid stream with a specific comet, the pair being the Perseids and comet Swift–Tuttle (1862 III).

The Swedish chemist and industrialist Alfred Nobel (1833–96) invents a safe and manageable form of nitroglycerin, which he calls 'dynamite'.

## 1867

The English surgeon Joseph Lister (1827–1912) demonstrates antiseptic surgery using carbolic acid (phenol). His introduction of antiseptic techniques revolutionizes modern surgery, greatly improving survival rates.

## 1868

The English astronomer William Huggins (1824–1910) discovers the red shift emitted by receding stellar spectra.

The English astronomer Norman Lockyer (1836–1920) designs a spectroscope for observing solar prominences outside of a total eclipse (independently, the French astronomer Pierre Janssen (1824–1907) also advances spectrum analysis with his observation of the bright line spectrum of the solar atmosphere). In the same year, Lockyer postulated the existence of an unknown element, which he named helium (the 'Sun element') and which was not found on Earth until **1895**.

The Swiss biochemist Friedrich Miescher (1844–95) isolates a substance he calls 'nuclein' (nucleic acids) from the nuclei of white blood cells.

The French palaeontologist Louis Lartet (1840–99) discovers the fossil remains of Cro-Magnon Man in a cave in southern France.

The Russian chemist Dmitri Ivanovich Mendeleev (1834–1907) draws up the periodic table, tabulating the elements in ascending order of their atomic weight and finding that chemically similar elements tend to fall into the same columns (see **Atoms, elements and molecules: Periodic table**).

The Irish physicist John Tyndall (1820–93) discovers the 'Tyndall effect' (the scattering of light by particles in solution, which makes a light beam visible when viewed from the side) during his study of light beams.

## 1871

The Belgian electrical engineer Zénobe Théophile Gramme (1826–1901) begins manufacture of the first successful direct-current dynamo, incorporating a ring-wound armature (the 'Gramme ring').

## 1873

The English astronomer Richard Proctor (1837–88) suggests that craters on the Moon were formed by meteorites, rather than (as previously thought) by volcanoes.

The Dutch physicist Johannes Diderik van der Waals (1837–1923) derives his equation (the van der Waals equation) relating the pressure and volume of a gas. It is more accurate than previous gas laws, as it takes into account the weak attractive force between two neighbouring molecules.

The Scottish physicist James Clerk Maxwell (1831–79) publishes his *Treatise on Electricity and Magnetism*, providing the first conclusive evidence that light consists of electromagnetic waves.

## 1874

The German chemist Othmar Zeidler (1859–1911) synthesizes DDT, but is unaware of its insecticidal properties (see **1939**).

The Irish physicist George J Stoney (1826–1911) calculates an approximate value for the charge on the electron, a term he also introduces. His estimation of its charge is $10^{-20}$ coulombs, very near to the modern value of $1.6021892 \times 10^{-19}$ coulombs.

## 1876

The German bacteriologist Robert Koch (1843–1910) publishes his findings proving that the anthrax bacillus is the sole cause of the disease.

The German physicist Eugene Goldstein (1850–1930) describes the rays produced when an electric current is sent through a vacuum tube, naming them 'cathode rays'.

The US inventor Alexander Graham Bell (1847–1922) patents the telephone.

### For Whom The Bell Didn't Toll ...

Alexander Graham Bell died on 2 August, 1922. On the day of his burial, all telephone services in the USA were stopped for one minute in his honour.

## 1877

The Italian astronomer Giovanni Schiaparelli (1835–1910) detects linear markings on the surface of Mars that he terms *canali* (channels), and notices that they change as a function of the Martian season, sometimes splitting into two and sometimes disappearing altogether.

The US inventor and physicist Thomas Edison (1847–1931) patents the gramophone.

## 1878

⊕ The French physiologist Paul Bert (1833–86) published his *La Pression barométrique* ('Barometric Pressure'), which describes his investigation into the physiological effects of air-pressure both above and below the normal. His work would later (1943) be translated because of its continuing importance in aviation medicine.

## 1879

The US chemists Constantin Fahlberg (1850–1910) and Ira Remsen (1846–1927) discover saccharin, the first artificial sweetener, while working with coal tar derivatives.

The German mathematician Richard Dedekind (1831–1916) proposes the concept of an 'ideal' set of numbers in the third edition of his book *Über die Theorie der ganzen algebraischen Zahlen* ('On the theory of algebraic whole numbers').

The English chemist, inventor and industrialist Joseph Swan (1828–1914) and the US inventor and physicist Thomas Edison (1847–1931) develop the light bulb for commercial use.

The Austrian physicist Josef Stefan (1835–93) proposes Stefan's law (or the Stefan–Boltzmann law), that the amount of energy radiated from a black body is proportional to the absolute temperature.

## 1880

The US astronomer Samuel Langley (1834–1906) invents the bolometer, an instrument that records the infrared radiation of the Sun quantitatively in terms of an electric current.

The German botanist Andreas Schimper (1856–1901) proves that starch is the source of stored energy for plants.

## 1881

The US astronomer Henry Draper (1837–82) takes the first good photographs of a comet and gaseous nebula.

⊕ The French chemist Louis Pasteur (1822–95) successfully demonstrates a vaccine for the disease anthrax, injecting sheep and cattle with the live bacteria.

The US physicist and aeronautical engineer Theodore von Kármán is born in Budapest, Hungary (d.1963). Several theories bear his name, such as the Kármán 'vortex street' (1911), a double line of vortices formed when air flows over a cylindrical surface. He is considered a founder of modern aerodynamics.

## 1882

The German biologist Walther Flemming (1843–1905) provides an account of the process of cell division, which he names mitosis (see **Cells: Cell division**).

## 1883

The German bacteriologist Robert Koch (1843–1910) discovers the bacterium that causes cholera.

The Russian embryologist and immunologist Elie Metchnikoff (1845–1916) discovers phagocytes, cells that play a crucial role in the immune system as they fight invasion by bacteria.

## 1884

In an attempt to purify water, the French bacteriologist Charles Chamberland (1851–1908) invents unglazed porcelain bacterial filters, the use of which eventually leads to the discovery of viruses.

The Danish bacteriologist Hans Gram (1853–1938) devises the most important staining technique in microbiology, which is still in use today. The stain divides bacteria into two groups, Gram-positive or Gram-negative, depending on the structure of their cell walls.

The Swedish physical chemist Svante August Arrhenius (1859–1927) experiments with ionic compounds in dilute solution, and discovers their electrical conductivity as they dissociate into negatively and positively charged ions.

The French chemist and metallurgist Henri Louis Le Châtelier (1850–1936) formulates the principle named after him, which states that if a change is made in pressure, temperature or concentration of a system in chemical equilibrium, the equilibrium will be displaced in such a way as to oppose this change (see **Key concepts: Le Châtelier's principle**).

One of the pioneers of television, the German engineer Paul Nipkow (1860–1940), invents the 'Nipkow disc', a mechanical scanning device consisting of a revolving disc with a spiral pattern of apertures. It remained in use until electronic scanning superseded it in 1932.

## 1885

The German bacteriologist Paul Ehrlich (1854–1915) noted the existence of the blood–brain barrier, which effectively obstructs many substances, including drugs, dissolved in the blood from entering the brain.

The English physicist John William Strutt, Lord Rayleigh (1842–1919) conducts research into vibratory motion in both optics and acoustics, and predicts the existence of the earthquake waves now known as Rayleigh waves.

The Danish physicist Niels Henrik David Bohr is born in Copenhagen (d.1962). He greatly extended the theory of atomic structure when he explained the spectrum of hydrogen, and he was awarded the Nobel prize for physics in 1922.

The Swiss physicist Johann Jakob Balmer (1825–98) discovers an empirical formula for the relationship between the convergent lines in the visible spectrum of hydrogen.

## 1886

The German physician Adolf Weil (1848–1916) discovers an infectious disease transmitted to sewer workers by rats – initially called 'Weil's disease', it is now known as leptospirosis.

The soft drink Coca-Cola® is invented by US pharmacist John S Pemberton, initially as a medicinal beverage which he claims as a cure for various disorders including morphine addiction, dyspepsia and impotence.

The French physical chemist François Raoult (1830–1901) discovers Raoult's law, which states that the vapour pressure of solvent above a solution is proportional to the mole fraction of solvent in the solution.

## 1887

The German physicist Heinrich Hertz (1857–94) confirms James Clerk Maxwell's predictions with his fundamental discovery of 'Hertzian waves' (now known as radio waves) which, along with light, form part of the electromagnetic spectrum (see **Energy, light and radioactivity: Electromagnetic radiation**).

## 1888

The English scientist Francis Galton (1822–1911) devises the concept of 'correlation', a method for measuring the interdependence of two sets of variables. In the following year, he introduces the correlation coefficient and standard error formula in his research paper on genetics, *Natural Inheritance* (1889).

## 1889

The US surgeon William Stewart Halsted (1852–1922) pioneers the use of thin rubber gloves during surgery as a further aseptic technique to prevent infection and reduce mortality rates.

## 1890

The German bacteriologist Robert Koch (1843–1910) produces a drug named tuberculin to prevent the development of tuberculosis. It proves to be ineffective as a cure, but useful in diagnosis.

## 1891

The Dutch palaeontologist Marie Eugène François Thomas Dubois (1858–1940) discovers in Java the humanoid remains named as *Pithecanthropus erectus* (Java Man), which he claims to be the 'missing link'.

The Hungarian physicist Baron Roland von Eötvös (1848–1919) conclusively demonstrates Galileo's assertion that all bodies have the same acceleration in a gravitational field.

The French physicist Gabriel Lippmann (1845–1921) invents a technique of colour photography based on the interference phenomenon, for which he is eventually awarded the 1908 Nobel prize for physics.

## 1892

The English scientist Francis Galton (1822–1911) devises the system of fingerprint identification, published in *Finger Prints*.

The English bacteriologist Almroth Wright (1861–1947) develops a vaccine against typhoid fever.

The English seismologist John Milne (1859–1913), with colleagues, develops a seismometer to record horizontal components of ground motion that becomes used on a worldwide basis.

The Scottish chemist and physicist James Dewar (1842–1923) invents the vacuum flask, a vacuum bottle with a silver coating on its internal glass surfaces.

## 1893

The English physicist John Henry Poynting (1852–1914) calculates the gravitational constant (G).

## 1895

The English physicist Oliver Lodge (1851–1940) correctly suggests that radio waves are emitted by the Sun (see **1944**).

The Scottish chemist Sir William Ramsay (1852–1916) isolates a light inert gas resembling argon by boiling a mineral called cleivite. Spectroscopic analysis shows that the gas is helium, which had been discovered in the spectrum of the Sun nearly 30 years earlier (see **1868**).

The Scottish microbiologist and physician David Bruce (1855–1931) discovers while working in South Africa that the tsetse fly is the carrier of the protozoal parasite (*Trypanosoma brucei*) responsible for the cattle disease nagana, and for sleeping sickness in humans.

The German physicist Wilhelm Röntgen (1845–1923) discovers X-rays (known also as Röntgen rays), so called because of their unknown properties.

## 1896

The French physicist Antoine Henri Becquerel (1852–1908) discovers 'Becquerel rays' (radioactivity). His work led to the discovery of radium by Marie and Pierre Curie (**1898**), with whom he subsequently shared the Nobel prize for physics.

## 1897

The German chemist Felix Hoffmann (1868–1946) synthesizes the therapeutic drugs aspirin (acetylsalicylic acid) and heroin (diamorphine) during his work for the Bayer pharmaceutical company.

The German physicist Ferdinand Braun (1850–1918) invents the first cathode-ray oscilloscope (the 'Braun tube'), providing a basic component of the television.

The New Zealand physicist Ernest Rutherford (1871–1937) characterizes two distinct types of uranium radiations, known as alpha particles and beta particles.

The English physicist J J (Joseph John) Thomson (1856–1940) announces his discovery of the electron, revolutionizing the study of physics.

## 1898

The Dutch botanist Martinus Beijerinck (1851–1931) discovers the first known virus, the tobacco mosaic virus, which causes disease in plants.

Two French physicists, Marie Curie (1867–1934) and her husband Pierre Curie (1859–1906), begin the work of isolating the elements polonium and radium in the course of their investigations on magnetism and radioactivity (a term coined by Marie Curie).

## 1900

The French physicist Paul Villard (1860–1934) discovers that specific rays emitted from radioactive substances are not affected by electric or magnetic fields. These rays later become known as gamma rays.

The German physicist Max Planck (1858–1947) formulates the quantum theory, which relies on Austrian physicist Ludwig Boltzmann's (1844–1906) statistical interpretation of the second law of thermodynamics, and assumes energy changes to take place in small discrete instalments or quanta (see **Key concepts: Quantum theory**).

## 1901

The US pathologist Karl Landsteiner (1868–1943) discovers three of the major human blood groups (A, B, O).

The Russian embryologist and immunologist Elie Metchnikoff (1845–1916) discovers the important function of white blood cells (leucocytes) in fighting infections.

The Italian physicist Guglielmo Marconi (1847–1937) succeeds in sending signals in Morse code across the Atlantic, from Cornwall, England, to St John's, Newfoundland.

## 1902

The German physicist Philipp Lenard (1862–1947) observes the phenomenon known as the photoelectric effect, whereby light falling on a material can cause electrons to be released from its surface. The effect is later explained by Albert Einstein (see **1905**).

## c.1903

The German physician Georg Perthes (1869–1927) uses X-rays in the treatment of malignant tumours.

## 1903

The Dutch physiologist Willem Einthoven (1860–1927) invents the string galvanometer, prompting great advances in electrocardiography.

## 1904

The Russian physiologist Ivan Pavlov (1849–1936) is awarded the Nobel prize for physiology or medicine for his discovery of conditioned reflexes through his experiments on dogs.

The Danish physiologist Christian Bohr (1855–1911) describes the Bohr effect – an adaptation in which the pH of the body tissue determines whether oxygen will be released from, or taken up by, the haemoglobin in red blood cells.

The German chemist Richard Abegg (1869–1910) explains his 'rule of eight', stating that the outer atomic shell of an atom or ion tries to achieve optimum stability by containing eight electrons.

The US chemist Julius Nieuwland (1878–1936) develops the poisonous gas lewisite, discontinuing his research after its deadly nature became apparent. It was later used as a chemical weapon during World War I.

⚛ The German engineer Christian Hülsmeyer (1881–1957) patents and demonstrates his 'telemobiloscope', an anti-collision device for ships. It is a transmitter-receiver system for detecting distant metallic objects by means of electrical waves, and is an early form of what will become known as radar (Radio Detection And Ranging; see **1935**).

## 1905

⚛ German physical chemist Walther Nernst (1864–1941) develops the third law of thermodynamics, which relates to the thermal energy of substances at a temperature of absolute zero (see **Key concepts: The laws of thermodynamics**).

⚛ The German–Swiss–US mathematical physicist Albert Einstein (1879–1955) publishes his special theory of relativity (see **Key concepts: Special theory of relativity**) as well as work explaining the photoelectric effect (see **1902**).

> ## Recreational Relativity
>
> Einstein was not a full–time physicist until his thirties, having failed to get a job in a university. He worked out and published the special theory of relativity in his spare time while working in a patent office. He was finally appointed as a professor at the Karl–Ferdinand University in Prague in 1911.

## 1906

⚛ The US radio engineer and inventor Reginald Aubrey Fessenden (1866–1932) broadcasts what was probably the first US radio programme, from a transmitter he has built at Brant Rock, Massachusetts.

## c.1910

⬦ The Danish astronomer Ejnar Hertzsprung (1873–1967) and the US astronomer Henry Norris Russell (1877–1957) formulate the Hertzsprung-Russell diagram, which becomes the key to the theory of stellar evolution.

⚛ The US physicist Robert Millikan (1868–1953) measures the charge on an electron, using a 'falling drop' technique developed by the English physicist J J Thomson (1856–1940), whereby oil drops are balanced between gravitational and electromagnetic forces.

## 1910

▮ ⚛ The French chemist and physicist Georges Claude (1870–1960) is credited with the invention of neon lighting for signs.

## 1910–13

Two English philosophers and mathematicians, Bertrand Russell (1872–1970) and Alfred North Whitehead (1861–1947), produce their *Principia Mathematica*, a landmark in the history of logic and mathematics.

## 1911

The New Zealand physicist Ernest Rutherford (1871–1937) conceives the idea of the atom as a miniature universe in which the mass is concentrated in the nucleus surrounded by planetary electrons.

## 1911–12

The US physicist Victor Hess (1883–1964) initiates cosmic ray research by making a number of manned balloon flights carrying ionization chambers. He demonstrates that the radiation intensity in the atmosphere increases with height, and concludes that the high-energy cosmic radiation that was responsible must originate from outer space.

## 1912

The German geophysicist A L Wegener (1880–1930) proposes his theory of continental drift, which states that the continents were formed from one large land mass and have since drifted apart (see **Key concepts: Continental drift**).

## 1913

The English geologist Arthur Holmes (1890–1965), a pioneer of geochronology, publishes his book *The Age of the Earth*, a review of the history of attempts to ascertain the age of the Earth.

The English chemist Frederick Soddy (1877–1965) discovers isotopes during his investigation of radioactive substances.

The Danish physicist Niels Bohr (b.1922) produces a quantum model of the hydrogen atom known as the Bohr model (see **Key concepts: Quantum theory**).

## 1916

Albert Einstein (1879–1955) proposes his general theory of relativity, incorporating the effects of gravity (see **Key concepts: General theory of relativity**).

## 1919

The New Zealand physicist Ernest Rutherford (1871–1937), in a series of experiments, discovers that alpha-ray bombardment induce atomic transformation in atmospheric nitrogen, liberating hydrogen nuclei. This has become known as 'splitting the atom'.

## 1921

The Scottish physiologist John Macleod (1876–1935), with the Canadian physiologist Frederick Banting (1891–1941) and his research assistant Charles Best (1899–1978), discover the hormone insulin. Insulin is still the principal treatment in diabetes, and in 1923, Macleod and Banting were awarded the Nobel Prize for physiology or medicine for its discovery (Banting shared the award with Best).

The French bacteriologists Albert Calmette (1863–1933) and Camille Guérin (1872–1961) develop the BCG (Bacille Calmette–Guérin) vaccine, used in the inoculation against tuberculosis.

## 1924

The Austrian–Swiss theoretical physicist Wolfgang Pauli (1900–58) formulates his exclusion principle, which states that no two electrons in an atom can have identical properties (see **Key concepts: Pauli's exclusion principle**).

## 1925

The US biologist Ernest Just (1883–1941) discovers the carcinogenic effects of ultraviolet (UV) radiation.

The German physicist Hans Geiger (1882–1945), with the help of student Walther Müller, develops the Geiger tube, an instrument that can detect and measure radiation.

## 1926

The US astronomer Cecilia Payne-Gaposchkin (1900–79) publishes her doctoral thesis, *Stellar Atmospheres*, which leads to her pioneering work on determining the relative abundances of chemical elements in stars and in space.

The Scottish electrical engineer John Logie Baird (1888–1946) gives the first public demonstration of a television image.

## 1927

The Belgian astrophysicist and cosmologist Georges Lemaître (1894–1966) publishes his first major paper on the model of an expanding universe, laying the foundations of the 'Big Bang' theory that the universe began with an explosion of a small dense mass (see **Key concepts: Big Bang theory**).

The German theoretical physicist Werner Heisenberg (1901–76) develops his uncertainty principle, which says that certain properties of particles, such as location or velocity, cannot be accurately known simultaneously (see **Key concepts: Heisenberg's uncertainty principle**).

## 1928

The Scottish bacteriologist Alexander Fleming (1881–1955) accidentally discovers penicillin, which would become the first widely used antibiotic.

## 1929

The US astronomer Edwin Hubble (1889–1953) announces his experimental evidence that galaxies recede from us with speeds which increase with their distance, supporting the Big Bang theory (see **1927**; **Key concepts: Big Bang theory**).

A team of chemists at the DuPont company, led by Wallace Corothers (1896–1937), develops the first commercially successful synthetic rubber, known as neoprene. Corothers later develops nylon (see **1935**).

The US physicist Robert J Van de Graaff (1901–67) constructs the first working model of an improved type of electrostatic generator, which later becomes known as the Van de Graaff generator.

## 1930

The US astronomer Clyde Tombaugh (1906–97) discovers the planet Pluto.

## 1932

The US radio engineer Karl Jansky (1905–50) publishes his detection of radio waves originating from a stellar source in the constellation of Sagittarius (the direction towards the centre of the Milky Way). This helped to establish the science of radio astronomy during the 1950s.

The English physicist James Chadwick (1891–1974) discovers and names the neutron.

The US physicist Carl Anderson (1905–91) discovers the positron.

The German biochemist Gerhard Domagk (1895–1964) discovers the antibacterial action of prontosil, the first of the sulphonamide drugs. The active constituent of prontosil is later found to be sulphanilamide, a derivative of aniline (see **1855**).

## 1934

The Hungarian chemist George Charles de Hevesy (1885–1966) begins to use radioactive tracers to study chemical processes, particularly in living organisms.

## 1935

The US industrial chemist Wallace Carothers (1896–1937) develops nylon while working on polymer chemistry for DuPont (see **1929**), although commercial production of the material does not begin until 1939.

The US physical chemist Henry Eyring (1901–81) publishes his transition state theory, proposing that the reactants in a chemical reaction are converted to a transition state that then decomposes to form the products (see **Key concepts: Collision theory**).

The US seismologist Charles Richter (1900–85), with the US geophysicist Beno Gutenberg (1889–1960), completes the Richter scale of earthquake measurement.

The Scottish physicist Robert Watson-Watt (1892–1973) perfects a shortwave radio wave system called 'Radio Detection And Ranging', or radar, which is able to locate aeroplanes (see **1904**).

## 1936

The English mathematician Alan Turing (1912–54) outlines a theoretical 'universal' machine (later called a Turing machine) and gives a precise mathematical characterization of the concept of computability.

## 1939

The Swiss chemist Paul Müller (1899–1965), while researching chemical methods of pest control, produces from the German chemist Othmar Zeidler's (1859–1911) written instructions a compound that Zeidler had labelled dichlorodi-phenyltrichloroethane (see **1874**). Müller received the 1948 Nobel prize for physiology or medicine for discovering DDT's toxic effects.

## 1941

The US atomic scientist Glenn Seaborg (1912–99) produces plutonium while working at the University of California at Berkeley. The discovery is kept secret during the development of atomic bombs and the subsequent bombing of Hiroshima and Nagasaki in **1945**, and is finally publicized in 1946.

The German–Swiss–US mathematical physicist Albert Einstein (1879–1955) warns US President Franklin D Roosevelt of the possibility that Germany will try to make an atomic bomb, thus helping to initiate the Allied attempt to produce one (the Manhattan Project).

## 1942

The US nuclear physicist Enrico Fermi (1901–54) directs the construction of the first US nuclear reactor at the University of Chicago.

## 1944

The US radio engineer Grote Reber (b.1911) is the first to detect radio emission from the Andromeda galaxy and from the Sun.

## 1945

The first test explosion of a nuclear device is conducted by the USA in New Mexico. Three weeks later, atomic bombs are dropped on the Japanese cities of Hiroshima and Nagasaki, with devastating results.

## 1947

The US chemist Willard Frank Libby (1908–80) develops the carbon-14 method of determining the age of an object.

The US physicists John Bardeen (1908–91), Walter Brattain (1902–87) and William Shockley (1905–83) develop the point-contact transistor, using a thin germanium crystal.

## 1949

The American mathematician Claude Shannon (1916–2001) proposes a theorem of information entropy, thus approaching the problems of transmission and reception of information in a mathematical way (see **Key concepts: Shannon–Hartley theorem**).

## 1950

The medical statisticians Bradford Hill (1897–1991) and Richard Doll (1912–2005) carry out a case control study of patients with lung cancer, showing that smoking is one important cause of the disease. Hill's development of the randomized controlled clinical trial has transformed medical thinking.

The English mathematical physicist P A M Dirac (1902–84) proposes that particles are string-like in nature rather than being points (see **Key concepts: String theory**).

## 1952

The English X-ray crystallographer Rosalind Franklin (1920–58) produces X-ray diffraction pictures of DNA, which suggest that its sugar-phosphate backbone is on the outside of its structure (see **Genetics: DNA**).

The US biologists A D Hershey (1908–97) and Martha Chase (1930–2003) carry out experiments on viruses to show definitively that DNA, rather than protein, is the genetic material. Experiments by the US bacteriologist Oswald Avery (1877–1955) had suggested that this might be the case as early as 1944, but were not widely accepted.

The first test explosion of a hydrogen bomb is conducted by the USA at Enewetak Atoll in the South Pacific.

The US physicist Donald Glaser (b.1926) invents the 'bubble chamber' for observing the paths of elementary particles.

## 1953

The US chemists Harold Urey (1893–1981) and Stanley Miller (b.1930) create amino acids from a simulation of the Earth's early atmosphere. Their work provides clues as to how life could have arisen on Earth.

The double-helical model of DNA (see **Genetics: DNA**) is proposed in the journal *Nature* by James Watson (b.1928) and Francis Crick (1916–2004).

> *We have discovered the secret of life!*
>
> —Francis Crick, speaking to the patrons of The Eagle public house in Cambridge, on solving the structure of DNA while working there with James Watson (1953).

## 1954

Two US physiologists, Gregory Pincus (1903–67) and John Rock (1890–1984), conduct the first human trials of an oral contraceptive, which goes on sale in the USA in 1960 and quickly becomes known as 'the Pill'.

## 1956

The first public demonstration of a commercial videotape recorder takes place at the National Association of Radio and Television Broadcasters' convention in Chicago, Illinois.

## 1957

The USSR launches the world's first artificial satellite, *Sputnik 1*, into orbit.

A fire breaks out in one of the twin reactors at the Windscale nuclear site in Cumbria, England, causing what was then the world's worst nuclear accident (surpassed by the Chernobyl accident in **1986**).

## 1958

Francis Crick (1916–2004) publishes his 'Central Dogma', relating to the direction of flow of genetic information (see **Key concepts: Central dogma of molecular biology**).

The US electrical engineer Jack S Kilby (1923–2005) invents the first microchip.

## 1959

A Soviet space probe, *Luna 3*, successfully photographs the far side of the Moon.

## 1960

The English primatologist and conservationist Jane Goodall (b.1934) begins her study of the chimpanzees of Gombe National Park, Tanzania.

The US physicist Theodore Maiman (b.1927) constructs the first working laser (Light Amplification by Stimulated Emission of Radiation) at the Hughes Research Laboratories in Miami, Florida.

## 1961

The Soviet cosmonaut Yuri Gagarin (1934–68) becomes the first human being to travel in space, completing a circuit of the Earth in the *Vostok* spaceship satellite.

The US biochemist Marshall Nirenberg (b.1927) and his colleagues decipher the first codon of the genetic code, proving that a triplet of DNA bases encodes a single amino acid (see **Genetics: Genetic code**). Other biochemists, including Har Gobind Khorana (b.1922), later work out the rest of the code.

## 1962

In the USA, the National Aeronautics and Space Administration (NASA) launches *Telstar*, the first active communications satellite, which relays the first live transatlantic television signal.

## 1964

The US theoretical physicists Murray Gell-Mann (b.1929) and George Zweig (b.1937) propose the existence of the subatomic particles known as quarks (see **Atoms, elements and molecules: Subatomic particles**).

## 1965

Two US physicists, Arno Penzias (b.1933) and Robert Wilson (b.1936), detect a radio noise background that they suggest may be residual radiation from the Big Bang at the universe's creation (see **Key concepts: Big Bang theory**).

## 1967

The South African surgeon Christiaan Barnard (1922–2001) performs the first successful human heart transplant. The recipient, Louis Washkansky, died of pneumonia 18 days later, drugs given to prevent tissue rejection having heightened the risk of infection.

## 1969

The US astronaut Neil Armstrong (b.1930), as part of the *Apollo 11* mission, becomes the first person to set foot on the Moon.

## 1972

The English chemist James Lovelock (b.1919) proposes his Gaia hypothesis, suggesting that the Earth is self-regulating and in dynamic equilibrium, and can therefore be regarded as a 'super-organism' (see **Key concepts: The Gaia hypothesis**).

## 1974

The half-complete fossil remains of a female hominid, over 3 million years old, are discovered by the US palaeoanthropologist Donald Johanson (b.1943) at Hadar in the Afar Triangle of Ethiopia. The fossil specimen, later classified as *Australopithecus afarensis*, is nicknamed 'Lucy'.

## 1975

The US *Viking 1* and *Viking 2* spacecrafts land on Mars, and transmit the first photographs of its surface back to Earth.

The immunologists César Milstein (1927–2002) and Georges Köhler (1946–95) pioneer the production of monoclonal antibodies, thus allowing perpetual production of well-characterized antibodies that are widely used for medical, diagnostic and research purposes.

The term 'chaos' is first used with reference to mathematics by the US mathematical physicist James Yorke (b.1941) (see **Key concepts: Chaos theory**).

## 1976

The British ethologist Richard Dawkins (b.1941) publishes *The Selfish Gene*, in which he shows how natural selection acts on individual genes rather than at the individual or species level, and also describes how apparently altruistic behaviour in animals is designed to increase the probability of survival of genes.

## 1977

The US anthropologist and natural historian Elso Barghoorn (1915–84) discovers fossilized bacteria dating from an estimated 3.4 billion years ago during excavations in South Africa. This discovery, along with his earlier find of fossilized colonies of blue-green algae near Lake Superior in the 1950s, suggests an earlier date for the origins of life on Earth than had previously been estimated.

## 1978

Louise Brown, the world's first 'test-tube baby' (conceived using in vitro fertilization and implanted in her mother's uterus), is born in the UK under the supervision of the British physicians Patrick Steptoe (1913–88) and Robert Edwards (b.1925).

## 1980

The US experimental physicist Luis Walter Alvarez (1911–88), with his geologist son Walter Alvarez (b.1940), proposes that the catastrophe that killed the dinosaurs was caused by the impact on Earth of an asteroid or comet.

## 1983

The French molecular biologist Luc Montagnier (b.1932) leads a team of scientists in isolating the HIV virus.

## 1984

The English molecular biologist Alec Jeffreys (b.1950) develops the technique of 'DNA fingerprinting', in which DNA from an individual is broken down and the resultant DNA fragments separated.

## 1985

The English chemist Sir Harold Kroto (b.1939) and the US chemists Robert Curl (b.1933) and Richard Smalley (1943–2005) discover a new molecular form of carbon that is made up of 60 atoms. The chemists name it buckminsterfullerene, owing to the similarity between its 'football' shape and the buildings designed by the architect Buckminster Fuller (1895–1983).

A team of scientists at the British Antarctic Survey, led by Joseph Farman (b.1930), discover a hole in the atmospheric ozone layer over the Antarctic.

## 1986

◇ The USSR launches the first module of its Mir space station, the first inhabited long-term research station in space. Further modules are then launched throughout the following decade, allowing the station to be assembled while in orbit.

◇ Halley's Comet is observed. Its return had been correctly predicted by the English astronomer and mathematician Edmond Halley (1656–1742) (see **1066**, **1680**). It is next predicted to return in early 2062.

An explosion occurs in one of the reactors at the Chernobyl nuclear power plant in Ukraine, causing a fire and leading to nuclear meltdown – the most serious nuclear accident in the history of nuclear power.

## 1988

◇ The English theoretical physicist Stephen Hawking (b.1942) publishes his book *A Brief History of Time*, which explores the various concepts behind modern cosmology and raises the tantalizing prospect that humankind might one day discover 'the mind of God'.

## 1990

◇ The US space shuttle *Discovery* launches the Hubble space telescope.

## 1991

The US academic Phillip Johnson (b.1940) publishes his book *Darwin on Trial*, in which he proposes the theory of 'intelligent design' (ID).

## 1993

A proof of Fermat's last theorem is announced by the British mathematician Andrew Wiles (b.1953), thus solving a mystery that plagued mathematicians for nearly half a century (see **Key concepts: Fermat's last theorem**). Minor flaws in the proof are addressed by Wiles in 1994, with the help of Richard Taylor.

## 1994

◇ Data gathered by the Hubble space telescope appears to confirm the existence of black holes (regions of space-time from which matter and energy cannot escape).

## 1995

Scientists at the European Organization for Nuclear Research (CERN) laboratories in Geneva, Switzerland, manufacture atoms of anti-hydrogen, proving the existence of antimatter (matter which consists of particles similar to those of terrestrial matter, but of opposite electrical charge).

Scientists at the Fermi National Accelerator Laboratory (Fermilab) in Batavia, Illinois, discover the top quark, which they produce by using a powerful particle accelerator to collide protons and antiprotons. The top quark is thought to be the last of the predicted six quarks (see **Atoms, elements and molecules; Subatomic particles**).

## 1996

A meteorite from Mars, discovered in Antarctica in 1984, is found to contain organic compounds, suggesting the presence of single-cell life forms on the planet.

An international research team of approximately 600 scientists completes the genetic sequencing of *Saccharomyces cerevisiae* (baker's yeast), only the third species to have its genome completely sequenced.

The first successful cloning of a mammal from an adult cell takes place at the Roslin Institute near Edinburgh, Scotland. The birth of the cloned animal, Dolly the sheep, is announced in 1997, and she lives until 2003.

## 2000

The US space shuttle *Endeavour* uses the Shuttle Radar Topography system to map 123.3 million square kilometers (47.6 million square miles) of the Earth from space, obtaining topological data and images.

## 2001

Researchers working to sequence the human genome announce the first draft of their results, revealing how closely related the human species is to other life on Earth – humans not only share 98.4% of their genes with chimpanzees, but also have some genes that are found in fruit flies and yeast cells.

## 2002

The fossil remains of a hominid skull, approximately 7 million years old, are discovered in Chad, central Africa. The fossil specimen, classified as *Sahelanthropus tchadensis*, is nicknamed 'Toumaï', which means 'hope of life' in the language of the region.

US research scientists assemble the first synthetic virus, basing their work upon the genome sequence for polio.

## 2003

Two groups of researchers working to sequence the human genome announce that they have completed 99% of the sequencing with 99.99% accuracy, successfully completing the project.

Excavators working on the construction of the Channel Tunnel rail link in Stratford, East London, unearth fossils of shark teeth, oysters and palm trees, some approximately 55 million years old.

## 2004

The *Spirit* lander, described by the National Aeronautics and Space Administration (NASA) as a 'traveling robotic geologist', lands on Mars and sends back the most detailed pictures ever seen of the planet's surface.

## 2005

A team of US research scientists working in the mountains of southern Tanzania discovers a previously unknown species of monkey, the highland mangabey (*Lophocebus kipinji*).

A team of British researchers announces the first successful cloning of a human embryo in the UK.

# PEOPLE IN SCIENCE

## SOME IMPORTANT SCIENTISTS

### Niels Henrik Abel, 1802–29

Norwegian mathematician, born in Finnøy. By 1823 he had proved that there is no algebraic formula for the solution of a general polynomial equation of the 5th degree. Such a formula had been sought ever since the cubic and quartic equations had been solved in the 16th century. Abel developed the concept of elliptic functions independently of **Carl Gustav Jacobi**, and pioneered its extension to the theory of certain integrals and functions known as Abelian groups, which became a central theme of later 19th-century analysis. He died at the age of 26 from tuberculosis and never saw his work recognized during his lifetime.

### Abu 'Ali al-Hasan ibn al-Haytham **see Alhazen**

### John Couch Adams, 1819–92

English astronomer, born in Lidcot, Cornwall. By 1845 he had worked out mathematically the existence and position of Neptune. His prediction of Neptune occurred almost simultaneously with that of the French astronomer **Urbain Jean Joseph Leverrier**, while the German astronomer **Johann Galle**, working on Leverrier's calculations, actually observed Neptune in 1846. In 1858 Adams was appointed Lowndean Professor of Astronomy and Geometry at Cambridge, where he spent the rest of his life pursuing problems in mathematical astronomy.

> ## I Don't Believe It ...
>
> Adams sent his prediction to Sir George Biddell Airy, the Astronomer Royal, who was sceptical of its value and ignored it. Only when Leverrier in France announced similar results nine months later did Airy initiate a search at the Cambridge Observatory. Although a bitter controversy about the credit for the prediction developed, Adams's precedence was eventually recognized despite his taking no part in the debate. He turned down the subsequent offers of a knighthood and the post of Astronomer Royal.

### Thomas Addison, 1793–1860

English physician, born near Newcastle upon Tyne. He graduated in medicine at Edinburgh in 1815, moved to London, and eventually became physician to Guy's Hospital (1837). His chief researches were on pneumonia, tuberculosis and especially on the disease of the adrenal glands known as Addison's disease (first described in 1849). Addison's disease was the first to be correctly attributed to failure of the endocrine system, the glands that secrete hormones directly into the bloodstream.

## Alfred Adler, 1870–1937

Austrian psychiatrist, born in Vienna. He became a prominent member of the psychoanalytical group that formed around **Sigmund Freud** in 1900. His best-known work was *Studie über Minderwertigkeit von Organen* (1907, 'Study of Organ Inferiority and its Psychical Compensation'), which aroused great controversy. In 1911 he broke with Freud and developed his own 'Individual Psychology', investigating the psychology of the individual considered as different from others. His main contributions to psychology include the concept of the inferiority complex, and his special treatment of neurosis as the exploitation of shock.

## (Jean) Louis (Rodolphe) Agassiz, 1807–73

US naturalist and glaciologist, born in Môtier-en-Vully, Switzerland. His main interest was zoology and while still a student he published *The Fishes of Brazil* (1829) which brought him to the attention of **Georges Cuvier**. He examined evidence for the glacial transportation of rock material and proved that glaciers are mobile. Tracing their previous extents in the Alps, he developed the theory of ice ages, with global cooling and the past effects on flora and fauna. In 1859 Agassiz founded the Museum for Comparative Zoology at Harvard, to which he donated his collections. He became an oceanographer in 1851, taking an interest in coral reefs.

## Sir George Biddell Airy, 1802–92

English astronomer and geophysicist, born in Alnwick. Airy completely reorganized the Greenwich Observatory when he was Director there, transforming it into the finest meridian observatory in the world. He established magnetic and meteorological departments in Greenwich and used submarine telegraphy to determine the longitudes of various observatories internationally, in this way achieving worldwide acceptance of the Greenwich zero meridian. He pioneered the transmission of telegraphic time signals for the railways, determined the mass of the Earth from pendulum experiments in mines, and experimented with cylindrical lenses to correct astigmatism.

## Alhazen, Latinized name of Abu 'Ali al-Hasan ibn al-Haytham, c.965–c.1040

Arab mathematician, born in Basra, Iraq. He wrote a work on optics (known in Europe in Latin translation from the 13th century) giving the first account of atmospheric refraction and reflection from curved surfaces, and the construction of the eye. He constructed spherical and parabolic mirrors, and it was said that he spent a period of his life feigning madness to escape a boast he had made that he could prevent the flooding of the Nile. In later life he turned to mathematics and wrote on **Euclid**'s treatment of parallel lines and on Apollonius of Perga's theory of conic sections.

## Luis Walter Alvarez, 1911–88

American experimental physicist, born in San Francisco. He built one of the first Geiger counters in the USA and used it to study cosmic rays (see **Space: Cosmic rays**). Later he discovered electron capture by nuclei, tritium radioactivity and the magnetic moment of the neutron. During World War II he invented a radar guidance system for landing aircraft in conditions of poor visibility. After the war he developed **Donald Glaser**'s bubble chamber technique to carry out a range of experiments in which a large number of subatomic particles were identified.

These results ultimately led to the quark model of **Murray Gell-Mann** and **George Zweig** (see **Atoms, elements and molecules: Subatomic particles**). In 1968 Alvarez was awarded the Nobel prize for physics.

---

### From Pyramids to Presidents

Alvarez applied physics and ingenuity to a variety of problems, ranging from the use of cosmic X-rays to show that Chephren's Egyptian pyramid had no undiscovered chambers to showing that only one killer was involved in the assassination of President Kennedy. A man of varied interests, he founded two companies to make optical devices and, with his geologist son Walter, he concluded that a probable cause for the extinction of dinosaurs was the Earth's impact with an asteroid or comet.

---

### Alois Alzheimer, 1864–1915

German psychiatrist and neuropathologist, born in Markbreit. He studied medicine in Würzburg and Berlin and in 1912 became Professor of Psychiatry and Neurology at the University of Breslau. He made important contributions to the preparation of microscopical sections of brain tissue and left some clinical studies. He is best remembered for his full clinical and pathological description of pre-senile dementia (Alzheimer's disease) in 1907.

### André Marie Ampère, 1775–1836

French mathematician and physicist, born in Lyons. Self-taught, he gained a lectureship in mathematics at the École Polytechnique in Paris in 1803 and was elected to the Chair of Experimental Physics at the Collège de France in 1824. Although he contributed to a number of fields, he is best known for laying the foundations of the science of electrodynamics through his theoretical and experimental work, following **Hans Christian Oersted**'s discovery in 1820 of the magnetic effects of electric currents. His name is given to the basic SI unit of electric current (ampere, amp).

### Sir Edward Victor Appleton, 1892–1965

English physicist, born in Bradford. He researched propagation of radio waves, and discovered the existence of a layer of electrically-charged particles in the upper atmosphere (the Appleton layer) that plays an essential role in radio communication. This discovery was fundamental to the development of radar. He was elected FRS in 1927 and appointed President of the British Association for the Advancement of Science in 1953. He received the Nobel prize for physics in 1947 for studies of the Earth's ionosphere.

### Archimedes, c.287–212 BC

Greek mathematician, born in Syracuse. He discovered the formulae for the areas and volumes of spheres, cylinders, parabolas, and other plane and solid figures. The methods he used anticipated the theories of integration to be developed 1800 years later. He also founded the science of hydrostatics, studying the equilibrium positions of floating bodies of various shapes (see **Key concepts: Archimedes' principle**). He is remembered for the story that he discovered the principle of upthrust on a floating body or 'Archimedes' principle' whilst in the bath and subsequently ran into the street with a cry of 'Eureka!' ('I have found it!').

## Aristarchos or Aristarchus of Samos, fl.270 BC

Greek astronomer, probably born in Samos. He worked in Alexandria, Egypt, and is famous for his theory of the motion of the Earth, maintaining not only that the Earth revolves on its axis but that it travels in a circle around the Sun, anticipating the theory of Copernicus. He was also a practical astronomer and developed a method for determining the relative distances of the Sun and Moon. He inferred correctly that as the Sun and Moon are almost of the same apparent size, their dimensions are in proportion to their distances.

## Aristotle, 384–322 BC

Greek philosopher and scientist, born in Stagira. He wrote prolifically on biology, zoology, physics and psychology. He believed that sense perception is the only means of human knowledge. In natural philosophy, he saw the Earth as the centre of the eternal universe. He taught that everything beneath the orbit of the Moon was composed of earth, air, fire and water; everything above the orbit of the Moon was composed of ether. He believed that all material things could be analysed in terms of their matter and their form, and form constituted their essence. His work exerted an enormous influence on medieval philosophy, Islamic philosophy, and on the whole western intellectual and scientific tradition.

## Charlotte Auerbach, 1899–1994

German geneticist, born in Crefel. In 1933 anti-Semitism forced her to move from the Kaiser Wilhelm Institute to Edinburgh, where she completed her PhD thesis at the Institute of Animal Genetics. Her studies of the effects of nitrogen mustard and mustard gas on the fruit fly led her to discover chemical mutagenesis, which thereafter became her main research. She was one of the very first to work out how chemical compounds cause genetic mutations and to compare the differences between the actions of chemical mutagens and X-rays.

## (Lorenzo Romano) Amedeo Carlo Avogadro, 1776–1856

Italian physicist, born in Turin. He trained as a lawyer but from 1806 turned to science and soon became Professor of Mathematics and Physics at the College of Vercelli (1809). In 1811, seeking to explain **Joseph Gay-Lussac**'s law of combining gaseous volumes (1809), he formulated the famous hypothesis that equal volumes of all gases contain equal numbers of molecules at the same temperature and pressure (see **Key concepts: Avogadro's law**). The hypothesis was ignored for around 50 years, but became universally accepted by the 1880s. His name is given to the number of particles in a mole, Avogadro's number.

## Julius Axelrod, 1912–2004

US pharmacologist, born in New York City. His research focused on the chemistry and pharmacology of the nervous system, especially the role of the catecholamines adrenaline and noradrenaline. His work accelerated investigations into the links between brain chemistry and psychiatric disease, and the search for psychoactive drugs. He discovered an enzyme that inhibits neural impulses, laying the basis for significant advances in the treatment of disorders such as schizophrenia. He was a joint winner of the 1970 Nobel prize for physiology or medicine.

### Charles Babbage, 1791–1871

English mathematician, born in Teignmouth. He spent most of his life building two calculating machines. The first, the 'difference engine', was designed to calculate tables of logarithms and similar functions by repeated addition performed by trains of gear wheels. The second was for a much more ambitious machine, the 'analytical engine', which could be programmed by punched cards to perform many different computations. The cards would store the numbers as well as the sequence of operations to be performed. Babbage is regarded as the inventor of the programmable computer.

### Francis Bacon, Baron Verulam of Verulam and Viscount St Albans, 1561–1626

English statesman and natural philosopher, born in London. He studied at Trinity College, Cambridge, and at Gray's Inn, being called to the Bar in 1582. He became an MP in 1584. His greatness consists in his insistence on the facts, that man is the servant and interpreter of nature, that truth is not derived from authority, and that knowledge is the fruit of experience. Creator of the method of scientific induction, he stressed the importance of experiment in interpreting nature, which gave significant impetus to future scientific investigation.

### David Baltimore, 1938–

US microbiologist, born in New York City. In 1970 he discovered the 'reverse transcriptase' enzyme which can transcribe RNA into DNA, and which allows scientists to manipulate the genetic code. His research into the connection between viruses and cancer earned him the 1975 Nobel prize for physiology or medicine, jointly with **Renato Dulbecco** and **Howard Temin**. In the 1980s he chaired a US National Academy of Sciences committee on AIDS, and in 1997 was appointed as chairperson of the AIDS Vaccine Advisory Committee of the US National Institutes of Health.

### Stefan Banach, 1892–1945

Polish mathematician, born in Kraków. He is regarded as one of the founders of functional analysis, and his book *Théorie des opérations linéaires* (1932, 'Theory of linear operations') remains a classic. He founded an important school of Polish mathematicians which emphasized the importance of topology and real analysis, and his name is attached to a class of infinite-dimensional linear spaces which are important in the study of analysis, and are increasingly applied to problems in physics, especially in particle physics.

### Benjamin Banneker, 1731–1806

US mathematician and astronomer, born in Ellicott, Maryland. The son of a slave father and free mother, he was interested in mathematics and science, and as a young man constructed an entirely wooden clock that kept perfect time. He was recommended by Thomas Jefferson to assist with surveying the site of the District of Columbia and the city of Washington, and in his correspondence with Jefferson he defended the intellectual equality of African–Americans. He also published an almanac containing astronomical and tide calculations.

### Sir Frederick Grant Banting, 1891–1941

Canadian physiologist, born in Alliston, Ontario. He studied medicine at Toronto

University and later became professor there (1923). During World War I he served as a surgeon in the Canadian Army Medical Corps. Working under **John Macleod** on pancreatic secretions, in 1921 he discovered (with his assistant **Charles Herbert Best**) the hormone insulin, still the principal remedy for diabetes. For this discovery he was jointly awarded the Nobel prize for physiology or medicine in 1923 with Macleod, although Banting shared his part of the prize with Best. He was knighted in 1934.

### Robert Bárány, 1876–1936

Austrian physician and otologist, born in Vienna. He pioneered the study in humans of the inner ear's balancing apparatus, proving the connection between this apparatus and the brain, and thus making it possible for equilibrium disturbances and vertigo to be investigated systematically. In 1915, while in a Russian POW camp in Siberia, news reached him that he had been awarded the 1914 Nobel prize for physiology or medicine. He was released and in 1917 was appointed director of the otorhinolaryngology clinic at the University of Uppsala, Sweden.

### Christiaan Neethling Barnard, 1922–2001

South African surgeon, born in Beaufort West. He graduated from Cape Town Medical School, and after a period of research in the USA he returned to Cape Town in 1958 to work on open-heart surgery and organ transplantation. He performed the first successful heart transplant in December 1967 at Groote Schuur Hospital. Although the recipient, Louis Washkansky, died 18 days later from pneumonia, a second patient, Philip Blaiberg, survived for 594 days after his operation in January 1968. Barnard retired in 1983.

### Henry Walter Bates, 1825–92

English naturalist, born in Leicester. With his friend **Alfred Russel Wallace** he left to explore the Amazon in 1848, and returned in 1859 with 14700 specimens, including almost 8000 species of insect that were new to science. In 1861 his *Contributions to an Insect Fauna of the Amazon Valley* described the phenomenon now known as Batesian mimicry, in which harmless, edible species of animal resemble others which are distasteful or poisonous, and thus gain protection from predators. This discovery provided strong evidence in favour of natural selection.

### Gregory Bateson, 1904–80

US anthropologist, born in Grantchester, England. Based on fieldwork in New Guinea, his monograph *Naven* (1936) was an innovative work introducing many themes that have since become central to the anthropological study of ritual and symbolism. With **Margaret Mead** he was involved with the culture-and-personality movement. Influenced by the theory of cybernetics, he went on to study problems of communication and learning among aquatic mammals and human schizophrenics, and developed a distinctive interpretation of schizophrenia based on the notion of the 'double-bind'.

### William Bateson, 1861–1926

English geneticist, born in Whitby. He introduced the term 'genetics' in 1909, and became the UK's first Professor of Genetics at Cambridge (1908–10). He showed that some genes are inherited together, a process now known as 'linkage'. He played a dominant part in establishing Mendelian ideas but he was a major opponent of chromosome theory. Similarly, although an ardent evolutionist, he was opposed to **Charles Darwin**'s theory of natural selection, as the small changes demanded by the theory seemed insufficient to account for the evolutionary process.

### George Wells Beadle, 1903–89

US biochemical geneticist, born in Wahoo, Nebraska. He became interested in agricultural genetics, studying the genetics of maize, the fruit fly *Drosophila* and the bread mould *Neurospora*. At Stanford University (1937–46), in association with **Edward Tatum**, he developed the idea that specific genes control the production of specific enzymes. Beadle and Tatum shared the Nobel prize for physiology or medicine in 1958 with **Joshua Lederberg**. Beadle worked in the 1950s for more openness in scientific research.

### Antoine Henri Becquerel, 1852–1908

French physicist, born in Paris. During his study of fluorescent uranium salt, pitchblende, he accidentally left a sample that had not been exposed to light on top of a photographic plate, and noticed later that the plate had a faint image of the pitchblende. He concluded that these 'Becquerel rays' were a property of atoms, thus discovering radioactivity and prompting the beginning of the nuclear age. His work led to the discovery of radium by **Marie** and **Pierre Curie** and he subsequently shared with them the 1903 Nobel prize for physics. His name was given to the SI unit of radioactivity, the becquerel.

### Emil von Behring, 1854–1917

German bacteriologist, born in Hansdorf, West Prussia. His major contribution was the development of a serum therapy against tetanus and diphtheria (1890), which became instrumental in counteracting these diseases. Behring's recommendations for reducing the occurrence of tuberculosis in animals and for disinfecting milk were important public health measures. He was awarded the first Nobel prize for physiology or medicine in 1901. During World War I, the tetanus vaccine developed by him helped to save so many lives that he received the Iron Cross, very rarely awarded to a civilian.

### Georg von Békésy, 1899–1972

US physicist and physiologist, born in Budapest, Hungary. He studied chemistry and later optics, and worked as a telephone research engineer in Hungary (1924–46). Appointed Professor of Experimental Physics at Budapest University in 1940, he moved to Harvard in 1947. He won the 1961 Nobel prize for physiology or medicine for his discoveries concerning the physical mechanisms of the ear, which explained how people distinguished sounds. He was also interested in developing instrumentation, and his work contributed techniques for measuring deafness, improving surgery of the ear and restoring hearing.

### Alexander Graham Bell, 1847–1922

US inventor, born in Edinburgh. After experimenting with various acoustic devices, on 5 June 1875 he produced the first intelligible telephonic transmission, with the famous words to his assistant 'Mr Watson, come here – I want you'. He successfully defended three patents relating to his invention between 1875 and 1877, and formed the Bell Telephone Company in 1877. He established the Volta Laboratory

(1880) for research into deafness, and his work there resulted in the photophone (1880) and the graphophone (1887). He also founded the journal *Science* (1883) and invented the tetrahedral kite.

### (Susan) Jocelyn Bell Burnell, née Bell, 1943–

English astronomer, born in York. She was educated at the universities of Glasgow and Cambridge, where she received her PhD (1968). She was co-discoverer with Antony Hewish of the first pulsar in 1967 (see **Space: Stars**). She later joined the staff of the Royal Observatory, Edinburgh, and became the manager of their James Clerk Maxwell Telescope on Hawaii. She was awarded the Herschel Medal of the Royal Astronomical Society in 1989 and was appointed Professor of Physics at the Open University in 1991. She was awarded the CBE in 1999.

### Paul Berg, 1926–

US molecular biologist, born in New York City. In the 1960s, he purified several transfer RNA molecules (tRNAs) and, in the 1970s, he developed techniques to cut and splice genes from one organism into another. Concerned about the effects of mixing genes from different organisms, he organized a year-long moratorium on genetic engineering experiments, and in 1975 chaired an international committee to draft guidelines for such studies. These techniques are now widely used in biological research. In 1978 Berg enabled gene transfer between cells from different mammalian species for the first time. He shared the 1980 Nobel prize for chemistry.

### Daniel Bernoulli, 1700–82

Swiss mathematician, born in Groningen, the Netherlands. Born into a family of mathematicians, he worked on trigonometric series, mechanics and vibrating systems, and pioneered the modern field of hydrodynamics. His *Hydrodynamica* (1738, 'Hydrodynamics') explored the physical properties of flowing fluids (see **Key concepts: Bernoulli's principle**), and anticipated the kinetic theory of gases, pointing out that pressure would increase with increasing temperature. He solved a differential equation proposed by Jacopo Riccati, now known as Bernoulli's equation.

### Jöns Jacob Berzelius, 1779–1848

Swedish chemist, born in Väfversunda. Soon after Alessandro Volta's invention of the electric battery, Berzelius began in 1802 to experiment with the voltaic pile. He went on to suggest that all compounds are made up of positive and negative components, a theory which laid the foundations for our understanding of radicals. In 1803 he jointly discovered cerium, then single-handedly selenium and thorium, and was the first person to isolate silicon, zirconium and titanium. His greatest achievement, however, was his contribution to atomic theory. He drew up a table of atomic weights using oxygen as a base, devising the modern system of chemical symbols. He also made significant contributions to organic chemistry and pioneered gravimetric analysis.

### Charles Herbert Best, 1899–1978

Canadian physiologist, born in West Pembroke, Maine. When Best was still a research student in 1921, he helped **Sir Frederick Banting** to isolate the hormone insulin, used in the treatment of diabetes. They later shared the Nobel prize for physiology or medicine. He discovered choline (a vitamin that prevents liver damage) and histaminase (the enzyme that breaks down histamine), introduced the use of the anticoagulant heparin, and continued to work on insulin, showing in 1936 that the administration of zinc with insulin can prolong its activity.

### Hans Albrecht Bethe, 1906–2005

US physicist, born in Strassburg, Germany (now Strasbourg, France). During World War II he was director of theoretical physics for the Manhattan atomic bomb project based at Los Alamos. In 1939 he proposed the first detailed theory for the generation of energy by stars through a series of nuclear reactions. He also contributed to the 'alpha, beta, gamma' theory of the origin of the chemical elements during the early development of the universe. He was awarded the 1967 Nobel prize for physics.

### Homi Jehangir Bhabha, 1909–66

Indian physicist, born in Bombay. He derived a correct expression for the probability of scattering positrons by electrons, a process now known as Bhabha scattering. He co-authored a classic paper on cosmic ray showers (1937), which described how primary cosmic rays from space interact with the upper atmosphere to produce the particles observed at ground level; and demonstrated the existence of muons, fast, unstable cosmic ray particles. In 1938, he was the first to conclude that observations of the properties of such particles would provide experimental verification of **Albert Einstein**'s special relativity theory.

### Bhaskara II, 1114–c.1185

Indian mathematician, born in Biddur. Also known as Bhaskara The Learned, he was the leading mathematican of the 12th century, and was the first to write a book containing a full and systematic use of the decimal number system.

### Alfred Binet, 1857–1911

French psychologist, born in Nice. He abandoned his law studies to work at the Salpêtrière Hospital in Paris, and moved there (1878–91). He is known as the founder of 'Intelligence Tests'. Director of physiological psychology at the Sorbonne from 1892, his first tests were made on his children. Later, with Théodore Simon, he expanded the tests (1905) to encompass the measurement of relative intelligence amongst deprived children (the Binet–Simon tests). These were later developed further by **Lewis Terman**.

### Gerd Karl Binnig, 1947–

German physicist, born in Frankfurt am Main. With **Heinrich Rohrer**, he developed the scanning tunnelling electron microscope. For this work Binnig and Rohrer shared the 1986 Nobel prize for physics with **Ernst Ruska**, who had invented the electron microscope some 55 years earlier. The scanning tunnelling electron microscope, an important piece of research equipment, allows atom by atom inspection of surfaces and has been particularly useful in the development of electronic circuits.

### (John) Michael Bishop, 1936–

US molecular biologist and virologist, born in York, Pennsylvania. He was awarded the 1989 Nobel prize for physiology or medicine (jointly with **Harold Varmus**) for the discovery of oncogenes, which are normal cellular genes involved in the normal growth and development of all mammalian cells. Certain faults in oncogene regulation can severely damage the growth of the affected cell type and cause cancer (see **Diseases and medicines: Cancer**). An understanding of the function of oncogenes is therefore a crucial step in combating many types of cancer.

### Sir James Whyte Black, 1924–

Scottish pharmacologist, born in Uddingston. He is best known for the development of the first, and subsequently safer and more effective, beta-blocking drugs to control hypertension and certain types of heart disease (such as angina and tachycardia). He also developed new drugs, burimamide and cimetidine, to treat stomach ulcers. These worked by reducing the secretion of acids in the stomach. He shared with **Gertrude Elion** and **George Hitchings** the 1988 Nobel prize for physiology or medicine.

### Patrick Maynard Stuart, Baron Blackett, 1897–1974

English physicist, born in London. He was awarded the Nobel prize for physics in 1948 for developing the Wilson cloud chamber, using it to confirm the existence of the positron (the antiparticle of the electron). He pioneered research on cosmic radiation and, during World War II, the use of operational research to produce economies in military resources. He also contributed to the theories of particle pair production, and the discovery of 'strange' particles.

### Elizabeth Blackwell, 1821–1910

US physician, born in Bristol, England. Her family emigrated to the USA in 1832 and, after her father died, the teenage Elizabeth helped to support the family by teaching, devoting her leisure to the study of medical books. She was the first woman doctor in the USA. Despite encountering difficulty in being admitted to medical schools, she graduated from Geneva in New York State in 1849 and later was admitted into La Maternité in Paris, and St Bartholomew's Hospital in London. She was responsible for opening the field of medicine to women. Her sister, Emily, became the first woman doctor to undertake major surgery on a considerable scale.

### Colin Brian Blakemore, 1944–

British physiologist, born in Warwickshire. After a period at Cambridge (1968–79), he was appointed Waynflete Professor of Physiology at Oxford University in 1979. He has worked on the physiology of the brain, and published *Mechanics of the Mind* in 1977. He gave the BBC Reith Lectures in 1976, and received the Michael Faraday award of the Royal Society in 1989. A high-profile supporter of experiments on animals, he has become the object of fierce criticism by animal rights activists.

### Eugen Bleuler, 1857–1939

Swiss psychiatrist, born in Zollikon. He coined the word 'schizophrenia'. He studied medicine at the University of Bern, and became Professor of Psychiatry at Zurich (1898–1927). He carried out research on epilepsy and other physiological conditions, then turned to psychiatry, and in 1911 published an important study on what he called schizophrenia or 'splitting of the mind'. One of his pupils was **Carl Gustav Jung**.

### Konrad Emil Bloch, 1912–2000

US biochemist, born in Neisse, Germany (Nysa in Poland). His findings on glucose underlie our present-day understanding that, in animals, fatty acids cannot be converted into sugars. In 1943 he revealed the direct metabolic relationship between cholesterol and bile acids, and in the 1950s his discovery that the mould *Neurospora* required acetate for growth resulted in the recognition of mevalonic acid as the first-formed building block. For his work on cholesterol, Bloch shared the 1964 Nobel prize for physiology or medicine with Feodor Lynen.

### Baruch Samuel Blumberg, 1925–

US biochemist, born in New York City. He discovered the 'Australia antigen' in 1964 and reported its association with Hepatitis B (known as the HBV virus). The finding was very rapidly applied to screening blood donors. HBV is widespread in Vietnam, Thailand and elsewhere in south-east Asia, and further problems emerged over the adoption of Vietnamese children in America. In 1969 Blumberg developed a protective vaccine against Hepatitis B, now widely used. He shared the 1976 Nobel prize for physiology or medicine with **Daniel Gajdusek**.

### Aage Niels Bohr, 1922–

Danish physicist, born in Copenhagen. Together with **Benjamin Roy Mottelson**, he gathered experimental evidence for the collective model of the nucleus (proposed by **James Rainwater**), which combined the previous quantum-mechanical shell model of the nucleus and the classical liquid drop model. This led to the prediction of nuclei being deformed so that they were no longer spherical. This model has been developed and explains the properties of nuclei well. He shared the 1975 Nobel prize for physics with Mottelson and Rainwater for this work.

### Niels Henrik David Bohr, 1885–1962

Danish physicist, born in Copenhagen. In 1913 he greatly extended the theory of atomic structure when he explained the spectrum of hydrogen by means of **Ernest Rutherford**'s atomic model and the quantum theories of **Einstein** and **Max Planck**. His model was later shown to be a solution of **Erwin Schrödinger**'s equation. He was awarded the Nobel prize for physics in 1922. He later worked on nuclear physics and developed the liquid drop model of the nucleus. His son **Aage Niels Bohr** and others used this model to develop a new collective model of the nucleus.

### Ludwig Eduard Boltzmann, 1844–1906

Austrian physicist, born in Vienna. He is most celebrated for the application of statistical methods to physics and his work on the kinetic theory of gases. In 1868 he extended **James Clerk Maxwell**'s theory of the velocity distribution for colliding gas molecules to derive the 'Maxwell–Boltzmann distribution'. In 1877 he presented the famous 'Boltzmann equation' which showed how increasing entropy corresponded to increasing molecular randomness (see **Key concepts: The laws of thermodynamics**). He also worked on electromagnetism, viscosity and diffusion.

### Sir Jagadis Chandra Bose, 1858–1937

Indian physicist and botanist, born in Mymensingh, Bengal (now in Bangladesh). He became known for his study of electric waves, their polarization and reflection, and for his experiments demonstrating the sensitivity and growth of plants. In some of his ideas he foreshadowed **Norbert Wiener**'s cybernetics. He founded the Bose

Research Institute in Calcutta for physical and biological sciences in 1917, was knighted in the same year and became the first Indian physicist to be elected FRS (1920).

### Satyendra Nath Bose, 1894–1974

Indian physicist, born in Calcutta. In 1924 he discovered the quantum statistics of particles of integral spin. He succeeded in deriving the **Planck** black-body radiation law, without reference to classical electrodynamics. **Albert Einstein** generalized his method to develop a system of statistical quantum mechanics, now called Bose–Einstein statistics, for integral spin particles. **P A M Dirac** called these particles 'bosons' (see **Atoms, elements and molecules: Subatomic particles**). Bose also contributed to the studies of X-ray diffraction and the interaction of electromagnetic waves with the ionosphere.

### Jean Baptiste Joseph Dieudonné Boussingault, 1802–87

French agricultural chemist, born in Paris. Between 1834 and 1876, he demonstrated that legumes increase the nitrogen in the soil by fixing atmospheric nitrogen, but that all other plants – contrary to what was believed at the time – have to absorb nitrogen from the soil. He went on to suggest how nitrogen is recycled (see **Climate and enviroment: Cycles of life**). He further showed that all green plants absorb carbon from the atmosphere in the form of carbon dioxide. His work laid the basis for modern advances in microbiology. He was elected to the Academy of Sciences in 1839.

### (Edward) John (Mostyn) Bowlby, 1907–90

English psychiatrist. His early research concerned crime and juvenile delinquency, but he is best known for his work on the effects of maternal deprivation upon the mental health and emotional development of children. He argued that it was essential for the mother to be present during a critical formative period in order for emotional bonds to be formed. He was a consultant in mental health for the World Health Organization and honorary consultant psychiatrist to the Tavistock Clinic (1972–90).

### Robert Boyle, 1627–91

Anglo-Irish physicist and chemist, born in Munster. One of the first members of the Royal Society, he carried out experiments on air, vacuum, combustion and respiration. In 1662 he arrived at Boyle's law, which states that the pressure and volume of a gas are inversely proportional at constant temperature (see **Key concepts: The gas laws**). He also researched the calcination of metals, properties of acids and alkalis, specific gravity, crystallography and refraction, and was the first to prepare phosphorus.

### Sir (William) Lawrence Bragg, 1890–1971

British physicist, born in Adelaide, Australia. The son of **Sir William Henry Bragg**, he discovered the Bragg law (1912), which describes the conditions for X-ray diffraction by crystals. He later worked with his father to develop X-ray diffraction methods for determining crystal structures, which meant that for the first time the atomic interior of crystals could be studied. For their research, they shared the 1915 Nobel prize for physics. As head of the Cavendish Laboratory in Cambridge (1938–53), he supported **Francis Crick** and **James Watson** in their work.

### Sir William Henry Bragg, 1862–1942

English physicist, born in Westward, Cumberland. From 1912 he worked in conjunction with his son, **Sir Lawrence Bragg**, on determining the atomic structure of crystals from their X-ray diffraction patterns. Their efforts won them a joint Nobel prize for physics in 1915, the only father–son partnership to share this honour. During World War I he directed research on submarine detection for the Admiralty. He was knighted in 1920, probably as recognition for both his war work and his scientific eminence.

### Tycho or Tyge Brahe, 1546–1601

Danish astronomer, born in Knudstrup, Sweden. In 1563 he discovered serious errors in the existing astronomical tables, and in 1572 he carefully observed a new star in Cassiopeia (the supernova now known as Tycho's star), a significant observation which made his name. In 1576, with royal aid, he established his Uraniborg Observatory on the island of Ven (formerly Hven) between Zealand Island and Sweden. There, for 20 years, he successfully carried out his observations, measuring the positions of 777 stars and creating a catalogue of them with such accuracy that it provided a vital source of information for later astronomers. He is considered the greatest pre-telescope observer.

#### Tycho's Silver Nose

Gifted but hot-tempered, Brahe lost most of his nose in a duel at the age of 19 following an argument over a mathematical detail, and wore a false silver nose for the rest of his life. His tomb in Prague is marked by his effigy clad in armour with his right hand resting on his celestial globe.

### Henry Briggs, 1561–1630

English mathematician, born in Halifax. In 1596 he became the first Professor of Geometry at Gresham College, London, and in 1619 first Savilian Professor of Geometry at Oxford. With **John Napier**'s agreement, he proposed the use of base 10 for logarithms. This was an important simplification for the practical use of logarithms in calculation. He calculated and published logarithmic and trigonometric tables to 14 decimal places.

### Louis-Victor Pierre Raymond, 7th Duc de Broglie, 1892–1987

French physicist, born in Dieppe. Influenced by **Einstein**'s work on the photoelectric effect, which he interpreted as showing that waves can behave as particles, Broglie put forward the converse idea – that particles can behave as waves. The waves were detected experimentally by other scientists, and the idea of wave–particle duality was used by **Erwin Schrödinger** in his development of quantum mechanics (see **Key concepts: Quantum theory**). Broglie was awarded the Nobel prize for physics in 1929.

### Johannes Nicolaus Brønsted, 1879–1947

Danish physical chemist, born in Varde, Jutland. Most of Brønsted's contributions to physical chemistry concerned the behaviour of solutions. He is best known for the new and very useful definition of acids and bases, which he developed at the same time as, but quite separately from, **Martin Lowry**. The Brønsted–Lowry definition defines an acid as a substance with a tendency to lose a proton, and a base as a substance that tends to gain a proton. Brønsted's definition is still in use today.

### Rachel Fuller Brown, 1898–1980

US biochemist, born in Springfield, Massachusetts. Educated at the University of Chicago, she made important studies of the causes of pneumonia and the bacteria involved. Shortly after the end of World War II, by which time some methods of controlling bacterial forms of disease had been introduced, Brown isolated the first antifungal antibiotic, nystatin (1949). She was awarded the Pioneer Chemist Award of the American Institute of Chemists in 1975.

### Robert Brown, 1773–1858

Scottish botanist, born in Montrose. He was appointed naturalist to Matthew Flinders's coastal survey of Australia in 1801–05, and brought back nearly 4000 species of plants for classification. He is well known for his investigation into the reproduction of plants and for being the first to note that, in general, living cells contain a nucleus. Also in 1827, he first observed the movement of fine particles in a liquid. This movement is still called 'Brownian motion' after the Scotsman who discovered it as he studied pollen grains under a microscope.

### Denis Parsons Burkitt, 1911–93

British surgeon and nutritionist, born in Enniskillen, Northern Ireland. From around 1957, he began a series of clinical and epidemiological observations on a common childhood cancer found in Uganda. The cancer – now known as Burkitt's lymphoma – behaved as if it were infectious and subsequent research showed that it was caused by a virus. He also related the low African incidence of coronary heart disease, bowel cancer and other diseases to the high unrefined fibre in the native diet. He was nicknamed 'the bran man' for advocating a high fibre content in Western diets. He was elected FRS in 1976, a rare honour for a surgeon.

### Sir (Frank) Macfarlane Burnet, 1899–1985

Australian immunologist and virologist, born in Traralgon, Victoria. His work on culturing viruses in living chick embryos led him to the view that an animal's ability to produce antibodies against foreign cells is not inherited but is developed in foetal life. **Peter Medawar**'s experimental work with mouse skin grafts supported Burnet's idea that immunological tolerance was achievable. The successful human organ transplants that began in the 1960s stemmed from this work. Burnet and Medawar shared the 1960 Nobel prize for physiology or medicine.

### (Léon Charles) Albert Calmette, 1863–1933

French bacteriologist, born in Nice. He is best known for the BCG vaccine (Bacille Calmette–Guérin), used in the inoculation against tuberculosis, which he discovered jointly with Camille Guérin (1908). They recognized that a virulent strain of tuberculosis could be weakened by using bile, but would still convey a certain amount of immunity to protect against infection. This attenuated strain was used to produce BCG which was introduced in continental Europe around 15 years after the discovery, and later in the UK and the USA. Calmette also discovered an anti-snakebite serum.

## Melvin Calvin, 1911–97

US chemist, born in Minnesota. In 1948 Calvin helped to work out the Thunberg–Wieland cycle by which some bacteria, unlike animals, can make glucose from ethanoate. This work led him on to investigate photosynthesis, and he set up a team using many different types of scientists to try to sort out exactly what went on as plants made their own food. The outcome was the Calvin cycle, the biological pathway by which plants fix carbon dioxide from the air and use it to make glucose (see **Cells: Photosynthesis**). Calvin was awarded the Nobel prize for chemistry in 1961.

## (Nicolas Léonard) Sadi Carnot, 1796–1832

French physicist, born in Paris. After studying at the École Polytechnique and the École de l'Artillerie, he became a captain of engineers, but from 1819 concentrated on scientific research. In his sole published work, *Réflexions sur la puissance motrice du feu* (1824, Eng trans *Reflections on the Motive Power of Fire*, 1890), he applied for the first time scientific principles to an analysis of the working cycle and efficiency of the steam engine, thus arriving at an early form of the second law of thermodynamics (see **Key concepts: The laws of thermodynamics**) and the concept of reversibility in the form of the ideal Carnot cycle.

## Rachel Louise Carson, 1907–64

US naturalist and pioneer conservationist, born in Springdale, Pennsylvania. She worked as a marine biologist for the US Fish and Wildlife Service (1936–49). She became well known with *The Sea Around Us* (1951), which warned of the increasing danger of large-scale marine pollution, and the hard-hitting *Silent Spring* (1962), which directed public concern to the problems caused by synthetic pesticides and their effect on food chains. The resulting controls on their use owe much to her work, which also contributed to the growing conservationist movement from the 1960s onwards.

## Giovanni Domenico Cassini, 1625–1712

French astronomer, born in Perinaldo (then in Italy). His determinations of the rotation periods of the planets and his tables of the motions of Jupiter's satellites (1668) brought him fame. In 1669 he became the first director of the new Paris Observatory, where he made a host of observations of Mars, Jupiter and Saturn, and discovered the division of Saturn's rings which still bears his name (1675). He also discovered four satellites of Saturn. One of Cassini's great achievements was his determination of the distance of the planet Mars, and thereby of the distance of the Sun, from observations made simultaneously in Paris and in the French colony of Cayenne.

## Henry Cavendish, 1731–1810

English natural philosopher and chemist, born in Nice, France. He isolated 'fixed air' (carbon dioxide) and 'inflammable air' (hydrogen). In 1784 he ascertained that hydrogen and oxygen, when caused to explode by an electric spark, combined to produce water, which could not therefore be an element. Similarly, in 1795 he showed nitric acid to be a combination of atmospheric gases. The famous 'Cavendish experiment' (1798) employed a torsion balance apparatus to estimate with great accuracy the mean density of the Earth and the universal gravitational constant.

### Anders Celsius, 1701–44

Swedish astronomer, born in Uppsala. He taught mathematics and became Professor of Astronomy at the University of Uppsala (1730). He devised the Celsius temperature scale, described by him in 1742 before the Swedish Academy of Sciences. Two fixed points had been chosen: one (0 degrees) at the boiling point of water, the other (100 degrees) at the melting point of ice. A few years after his death, colleagues at the University began to use the familiar inverted version of this centigrade scale. He published an aurora borealis compendium (1733) and also advocated the introduction of the Gregorian calendar.

### Sir James Chadwick, 1891–1974

English physicist, born near Macclesfield. He worked on radioactivity with **Ernest Rutherford**. In 1932 he repeated the experiment previously performed by other scientists in which a neutral penetrating radiation was released from the bombardment of beryllium by alpha particles. He suggested that the radiation was due to a neutral particle whose mass was close to that of the proton. Chadwick named the particle the neutron and was awarded the 1935 Nobel prize for physics for this discovery. He built Britain's first cyclotron (a type of particle accelerator) in 1935, and during World War II he worked on the Manhattan Project to develop the atomic bomb in the USA.

### Carlos Ribeiro Justiniano Chagas, 1879–1934

Brazilian physician and microbiologist, born in Oliveira, Minás Gerais. He studied at the Medical School of Rio de Janeiro. Much of Chagas's early work was concerned with malaria prevention and control. During one of his field missions, in Lassance, a village in the interior of Brazil, he first described a disease (Chagas' disease) caused by a trypanosome. Chagas elucidated its mode of spread through an insect vector, established the trypanosome's virulence in laboratory animals and described its acute and chronic course in human beings.

### Sir Ernst Boris Chain, 1906–79

British biochemist, born in Berlin, Germany. Of Russian–Jewish extraction, he studied physiology and chemistry at Berlin. At Cambridge (1933–5), he identified an enzyme in snake venom which caused paralysis of the nervous system. Later with **Sir Howard Florey** at Oxford, he characterized lysozyme and determined its mode of action on bacteria. He encountered **Sir Alexander Fleming**'s paper on penicillin (1929), discovered that penicillin was not an enzyme but a new small molecule, and greatly improved its purification. Fleming, Chain and Florey shared the 1945 Nobel prize for physiology or medicine.

### Subrahmanyan Chandrasekhar, 1910–95

US astrophysicist, born in Lahore (now in Pakistan). He showed that at the end of their lives, stars of less than a certain critical mass will collapse to form white dwarfs, and that the fate of a star depends on its mass (see **Space: Stars**). He also concluded that stars with masses greater than about 1.4 solar masses will be unable to evolve into white dwarfs, and this limiting stellar mass, confirmed by observation, is known as the Chandrasekhar limit. He also suggested that if the mass of a star is greater than this, it can become a white dwarf star only if it ejects its excess mass in a supernova explosion before collapse. He was awarded the 1983 Nobel prize for physics, jointly with William Fowler.

### Jean Martin Charcot, 1825–93

French pathologist and neurologist, born in Paris. He turned the Salpêtrière Hospital in Paris into an international centre for the investigation of neurological diseases, himself making important observations on multiple sclerosis, amyotrophic sclerosis and familial muscular atrophy. During the last twenty years of his life, he began using hypnosis in the diagnosis and treatment of functional disorders. His lectures stimulated the young **Sigmund Freud**, who developed Charcot's special interest in hysteria and also translated some of his work into German.

### Jacques-Alexandre-César Charles, 1746–1823

French experimental physicist, born in Beaugency. He made himself an expert in popular scientific display, taking part in the first manned ascent by hydrogen balloon in Paris in December 1783. He invented a megascope, a hydrometer and a goniometer (for measuring angles of crystals). He formulated Charles's Law, which relates the volume of a gas at constant pressure to its absolute temperature (see **Key concepts: The gas laws**). Charles's Law is sometimes called Gay-Lussac's Law; **Gay-Lussac** published his general law, extended to soluble gases, in 1802.

### Dame Harriette Chick, 1875–1977

English nutritionist, born in London. She was educated in West London and at University College London (1894–6). In 1905 she gained a position at the Lister Institute, despite calls by some staff to prevent the appointment of a woman. She remained at the Institute for the rest of her long working life, retiring aged 95. With her colleagues Elsie Dalyell and Margaret Hume, she established that sunlight and dietary cod-liver oil, rich in vitamin D, could eliminate childhood rickets. From 1922 onwards she made extensive studies into the role of vitamins. She became a DBE in 1949.

### Albert Claude, 1899–1983

Belgian biologist, born in Longlier. He developed cell fractionation using a high-powered centrifuge, isolating a tumour agent from cancerous cells, and applied the technique to the study of normal cells, separating various 'organelles' (see **Cells: Cell structure**) such as the nucleus, mitochondria and microsomes (later known as ribosomes). In 1942 he began applying electron microscopy to biology, which led to important advances in understanding the structure of cells. He shared the 1974 Nobel prize for physiology or medicine with **George Palade** and **Christian de Duve.**

### Rudolf Julius Emmanuel Clausius, 1822–88

German physicist, born in Köslin, Prussia. In 1850 he postulated that heat cannot of itself pass from a colder body to a hotter one (the second law of thermodynamics). He introduced the term 'entropy' (1865) in such a way that dissipation of energy was equivalent to entropy increase, thus enabling the two laws of thermodynamics to be stated succinctly (see **Key concepts: The laws of thermodynamics**). He studied electrolysis, calculated the mean speed of gas molecules, ignoring collisions (1857), and introduced the concepts of mean free path and effective radius (1858). He is regarded as the founder of thermodynamics.

### Ferdinand Julius Cohn, 1828–98

German botanist and bacteriologist, born in Breslau (now in Poland). Although as a Jew he was barred from taking the degree examinations, he obtained his doctorate in botany in Berlin at the age of 19. He is regarded as the father of bacteriology because he was the first to regard it as a separate science, to define bacteria and to designate the group as plants. He did important research in plant pathology, and worked with **Robert Koch** on anthrax. Through his experiments on the effects of heat on bacteria, he identified bacterial spores. His work was a major factor in the overthrow of the theory of spontaneous generation.

### Nicolaus Copernicus, 1473–1543

Polish astronomer, born in Torún. He had a varied career involving law, medicine and astronomy. He considered the description of the world by Ptolemy, which had the Earth as the stationary centre of the universe, as unsatisfactory and became converted to the idea of a Sun-centred universe. He set out to describe this mathematically in 1512. Copernicus published his complete work, *De Revolutionibus Orbium Coelestium* (1543, 'The Revolutions of the Celestial Spheres'), which he dedicated to Pope Paul III. In the new system, the Earth is merely one of the planets, revolving around the Sun and rotating on its axis. His work was later banned by the Catholic Church, and remained on the list of forbidden books until 1835.

### Charles Augustin de Coulomb, 1736–1806

French physicist, born in Angoulême. His experiments on mechanical resistance resulted in 'Coulomb's law' concerning the relationship between friction and normal pressure (1779). He also became known for the torsion balance for measuring the force of magnetic and electrical attraction (1784–85). With 'Coulomb's law' he observed that the force between two small charged spheres is related to the charges and the distance between them. The unit of electric charge (coulomb) is named after him.

### Francis Harry Compton Crick, 1916–2004

English biologist, born in Northampton. In the early 1950s, in Cambridge, he and **James Watson** worked on the structure of DNA, publishing in 1953 their model of a double-helical molecule, consisting of two chains of nucleotide bases wound round a common axis in opposite directions (see **Genetics: DNA**). This structure suggested a mechanism for the reproduction of the genetic code. With Watson and **Maurice Wilkins** he was awarded the Nobel prize for physiology or medicine in 1962. He also carried out research into the visual systems of mammals, and the connections between brain and mind.

### Paul Josef Crutzen, 1933–

Dutch chemist, born in Amsterdam. He was educated in Amsterdam and at Stockholm University, where he joined the department of meteorology and helped to run barotropic weather prediction models. He has done pioneering work on the photochemistry of atmospheric ozone and conducted research into stratospheric chemistry. For work on the role of chloroflurocarbons (CFCs) in the catalytic destruction of atmospheric ozone, he shared the 1995 Nobel prize for chemistry with F Sherwood Rowland and Mario J Molina. In 1980 he was appointed director of research at the Max Planck Institute for Chemistry in Mainz, Germany.

### Marie, originally Maria, Curie, née Skłodowska, 1867–1934

Polish–French physicist, born in Warsaw. She graduated in physics from the Sorbonne (1893), taking first place, and went on to study mathematics. In 1898 Marie, together with her husband **Pierre Curie,** discovered radium and polonium, which she named after her native Poland. For the discovery of radioactivity, they were awarded the Nobel prize for physics in 1903, with **Antoine Henri Becquerel** (who had discovered the radioactive properties of uranium in 1896). In 1911 she received a second Nobel prize for chemistry for her work on radium and its compounds. During World War I she developed X-radiography. She died of leukaemia, probably caused by her long exposure to radioactivity.

### Pierre Curie, 1859–1906

French chemist and physicist, born in Paris. With his brother Jacques, he discovered piezoelectricity in 1880 and used a piezoelectric crystal to construct an electrometer. In studies of magnetism, Pierre showed that a ferromagnetic material loses this property at a certain temperature – the 'Curie point'. He also established 'Curie's law', which relates the magnetic susceptibility of a paramagnetic material to the absolute temperature. With his wife **Marie Curie**, he showed that the rays emitted by radium contained electrically positive, negative and neutral particles. For this discovery, with his wife and **Antoine Henri Becquerel**, he was awarded the Nobel prize for physics in 1903. Element 96 is named curium after the Curies.

### Robert Floyd Curl, Jnr, 1933–

US chemist, born in Alice, Texas. He was educated at the William Marsh Rice University and the University of California at Berkeley. His research with **Harold Kroto** and **Richard Smalley** at Rice University led to the discovery of carbon $C_{60}$ molecules named 'buckminsterfullerene' (known as 'buckyballs') resulting in much further research. For this work Curl, with Kroto and Smalley, was awarded the 1996 Nobel prize for chemistry. In 1996 he was also appointed professor of Natural Sciences at Rice University.

### Georges Léopold Chrétien Frédéric Dagobert, Baron Cuvier, 1769–1832

French anatomist, born in Montbéliard. In his scientific work he originated the natural system of animal classification which anticipated the modern division of the animal kingdom into phyla. His studies of animal and fish fossils, through his reconstructions of the extinct giant vertebrates of the Paris basin, linked palaeontology to comparative anatomy. He was a militant anti-evolutionist, and accounted for the fossil record by positing 'catastrophism' – a series of extinctions due to periodic global floods after which new forms of life appeared. He is known as the father of comparative anatomy and palaeontology.

### John Dalton, 1766–1844

English chemist, born in Eaglesfield. He carried out a wide range of research (including describing colour blindness, from which he suffered). He showed that in a mixture of gases each gas exerts the same pressure as it would if it were the only gas present in the given volume (Dalton's law). This led to the interpretation of chemical analyses in terms of the relative atomic weights of the elements involved and to the laws of chemical combination. He is famous for his atomic theory, which recognized that all matter is made up of combinations of atoms, the atoms of each element being identical. He concluded that atoms could be neither created nor destroyed, and that chemical reactions take place through the rearrangement of atoms.

### Charles Robert Darwin, 1809–82

English naturalist, born in Shrewsbury. His studies abroad (he went on a scientific survey of South American waters between 1831 and 1836) and at home led him to speculate on the origin of species. The result was the theory of evolution by natural selection, which **Alfred Wallace** was also putting forward at the time (see **Key concepts: The theory of natural selection**). In 1859 Darwin published his theory of evolution in the now famous work *The Origin of Species by Means of Natural Selection.* He argued that each organism has a unique combination of heritable variations and that the variations crucial to survival are passed down to the offspring of survivors. Though not the sole originator of the evolution hypothesis, Darwin was the first thinker to supply to the idea a sufficient cause, which raised it at once from a hypothesis to a verifiable theory, thereby gaining it a wide acceptance among biological experts.

### Erasmus Darwin, 1731–1802

English physician and poet, born in Elton. He studied medicine at Cambridge and Edinburgh. Many of his ideas on evolution, outlined in *Zoonomia, or The Laws of Organic Life* (1794–96), anticipated later theories such as that of **Jean-Baptiste Lamarck** and those of his own grandson, **Charles Darwin**. He edited translations of **Carolus Linnaeus**'s work and wrote a long verse work, *The Botanic Garden* (1789), as well as prose works.

### Clinton Joseph Davisson, 1881–1958

US physicist, born in Bloomington, Illinois. In 1927, with Lester Germer, Davisson was observing electron scattering from a block of nickel when their vacuum system broke down. Upon continuing the experiment the results were completely different, as they found the familiar peaks and troughs of a diffraction pattern. They had observed the diffraction of electrons, confirming **Louis de Broglie**'s theory of the wave nature of particles. This accidental discovery was crucial to the development of the quantum theory of matter (see **Key concepts: Quantum theory**). Davisson was joint winner of the 1937 Nobel prize for physics.

### Sir Humphry Davy, 1778–1829

English chemist, born in Penzance. He experimented with newly discovered gases, and discovered the anaesthetic effect of laughing gas. He also discovered the new metals potassium, sodium, barium, strontium and magnesium and the metallic element calcium; and proved that diamond is a form of carbon. His *Elements of Agricultural Chemistry* (1813) was the first book to apply chemical principles systematically to farming. He invented the safety lamp (1815, the 'Davy lamp'), which enabled greater coal production as deeper, more gaseous seams could be mined with less risk of explosion. Davy popularized science and interested industrialists in scientific research.

### Richard (Clinton) Dawkins, 1941–

British ethologist, born in Nairobi, Kenya. His major contribution to date is his ability to expound complex evolutionary ideas so as to make them explicable to fellow biologists and laypersons alike. In *The Selfish Gene* (1976), he shows how natural selection can act on individual genes rather than at the individual or species level. He also describes how apparently altruistic behaviour in animals can be of selective advantage by increasing the probability of survival of genes controlling this behaviour. He introduced the concept of the 'meme', a unit of cultural transmission.

### Christian René de Duve, 1917–

Belgian biochemist, born in Thames Ditton, England. He explored the new technique of differential centrifugation, separating a tissue into its separate constituents by centrifugation at different speeds. However, he is best known as the discoverer of lysosomes, small organelles within cells that contain enzymes, whose malfunction causes some metabolic diseases, such as cystinosis. For this and other discoveries on the structure and biochemistry of cells he shared the 1974 Nobel prize for physiology or medicine with **Albert Claude** and **George Palade**.

### Max Delbrück, 1906–81

German biophysicist, born in Berlin. He studied atomic physics at the University of Göttingen, where he received his PhD in 1930. In the 1940s Delbrück began working on the genetics of viruses known as bacteriophage or phage, which consist of a protein coat surrounding a coil of DNA. Independently of A D Hershey, he discovered in 1946 that viruses can exchange genetic material to create new types of virus, and together with Salvador Luria they set up the Phage Group, to encourage the use of phage as an experimental tool. The three were awarded the 1969 Nobel prize for physiology or medicine for their work in viral genetics.

### René Descartes, 1596–1650

French philosopher and mathematician, born near Tours. Usually regarded as the father of modern philosophy, he was educated at the Jesuit College at La Flèche. His theory of astronomy, which explained planetary motion by means of vortices surrounding the Sun, was eventually refuted by **Isaac Newton**. In mathematics he made his most lasting contribution by reforming algebraic notation and establishing coordinate geometry. This allows geometrical problems to be reformulated and even solved algebraically.

### Jared Mason Diamond, 1937–

US physiologist and ecologist, born in Boston. He has contributed significantly to the study of ecological diversity through his studies on islands, particularly on their bird faunas, following up the theory of island biogeography proposed by Robert MacArthur and Edward Wilson. He distinguished organisms that spread readily and easily ('super-tramps') from those that are less mobile, and calculated the turnover of species on a number of Pacific islands. His *Rise and Fall of the Third Chimpanzee* (1991) is an influential work of popular biology.

### Diophantus, fl.3rd century AD

Greek mathematician. He lived in Alexandria, and his largest surviving work is the *Arithmetica*, which deals with the solution of algebraic equations. In contrast to earlier Greek works, it uses a rudimentary algebraic notation instead of a purely geometric one. In many problems there is no uniquely determined solution, and these have become known as Diophantine problems. The study of Diophantus's work inspired **Pierre de Fermat** to take up number theory in the 17th century with remarkable results.

### P(aul) A(drien) M(aurice) Dirac, 1902–84

English mathematical physicist, born in Bristol. He worked on his own interpretation of quantum mechanics, and in 1928 he produced his relativistic wave equation which explained the electron spin. He was awarded the Nobel prize for physics in 1933 with **Erwin Schrödinger** for their work on quantum theory. His work on quantum electrodynamics predicted the existence of the magnetic monopole (not yet discovered), and in 1950 he proposed the idea of particles being not point-like, but string-like, an idea now gaining support following the work of **Green,** Schwarz and Witten (see **Key concepts: String theory**). He was elected FRS in 1930.

### Carl Djerassi, 1923–

US chemist, born in Vienna. He became well known for his studies in organic molecular structure, which included research into the chemistry of steroids and antibiotics. Most influential of all were the breakthroughs that led to the development of the contraceptive pill, antihistamines and anti-inflammatory agents.

### Johann Wolfgang Döbereiner, 1780–1849

German chemist, born in Bug bei Hof, Bavaria. He is remembered as the inventor of 'Döbereiner's lamp', in which hydrogen, produced in the lamp by the action of sulphuric acid on zinc, burns on contact with a platinum sponge. He was also one of the first chemists to begin to see the patterns in the behaviour of the elements which led eventually to the development of the periodic table (see **Atoms, elements and molecules: Periodic table**). In 1829 he showed that many of the elements known at the time could be arranged into groups of three, with all three showing similar properties.

### Sir Richard Doll, 1912–2005

British physician and epidemiologist, born in Hampton. He developed the science of epidemiology – the study of the impact of disease on populations – throughout his working life. In 1950 Doll, with his colleague **Austin Bradford Hill** (1897–1991), demonstrated the clear link between smoking and lung cancer at the end of an extensive study of people suffering from the disease. They showed that the huge increase in lung cancers in the 1940s was a direct result of the large increase in smoking that had begun 40 years before that.

### Gerhard Johannes Paul Domagk, 1895–1964

German biochemist, born in Lagow (now in Poland). In 1932 he discovered a dye that could be used as a drug to successfully treat streptococcal infection, which caused widespread and generally lethal infections. In 1936 a French group found that the dye, prontosil, is converted in the body into the simple compound sulfanilamide, which is the effective agent. Domagk used it to cure his own small daughter who was dying of a streptococcal infection. He received the Nobel prize for physiology or medicine in 1947, having been prevented from accepting it in 1939 by the Nazi regime.

### Christian Johann Doppler, 1803–53

Austrian physicist, born in Salzburg. He is well-known for the 'Doppler effect' (1842). This effect explains the frequency variation observed when a vibrating source of waves and the observer approach or recede from one another. The first experimental verification was performed in the Netherlands in 1845. The Doppler effect applies not only to sound but to all forms of electromagnetic radiation. In astronomy, the changes of the spectral wavelengths of approaching or receding celestial bodies provide important evidence for the concept of an expanding universe (see **Key concepts: Hubble's law**).

### Charles Richard Drew, 1904–50

US physician, born in Washington, DC. He developed a method of preserving blood plasma for transfusion and, as the leading expert in the field, he organized and directed blood-plasma programmes in Great Britain and the USA in the early years of World War II, becoming head of the first American Red Cross Blood Bank in 1941. Ironically, the Red Cross would not accept donations of his own blood because he was an African–American. He lobbied to change their policy, but when they responded only by establishing a separate supply of blood donated and used by African–Americans, he resigned in protest (1942). The policy was eventually changed.

### Marie Eugène François Thomas Dubois, 1858–1940

Dutch palaeontologist, born in Eijsden. He studied medicine in Amsterdam and taught there from 1899. His interest in the 'missing link' between the apes and humans took him to Java in 1887, where in the 1890s he found the humanoid remains named as *Pithecanthropus erectus* (Java Man) and which he claimed to be the missing link. His view was contested and even ridiculed. When in the 1920s it eventually became widely accepted, Dubois began to insist that the fossil bones were those of a giant gibbon, and maintained this view until his death.

### Guillaume Benjamin Amand Duchenne, 1806–75

French physician, born in Boulogne. A pioneer of electrophysiology and electrotherapeutics, he carried out important work on poliomyelitis, locomotor ataxia and a common form of muscular ('Duchenne's') dystrophy. He also developed a method of taking small pieces of muscle (biopsy) from patients for microscopical examination. Although he never held a formal hospital appointment, he worked at the Salpêtrière Hospital where his patron was **Jean Martin Charcot**, a pathologist and one of the founders of neurology.

### Renato Dulbecco, 1914–

Italian virologist, born in Catanzaro. From 1972 to 1977 he was assistant director of research at the Imperial Cancer Research Fund in London. In 1977 he became Research Professor at the Salk Institute, La Jolla, and president emeritus from 1993. Dulbecco demonstrated how certain viruses can transform some cells into a cancerous state, such that those cells grow continuously, unlike normal cells. For this discovery he was awarded the 1975 Nobel prize for physiology or medicine, jointly with his former students, **David Baltimore** and **Howard Temin**.

### Sir Arthur Stanley Eddington, 1882–1944

English astronomer, born in Kendal. He pioneered the study of the internal structure of stars and discovered the mass–luminosity relationship, which shows that the more massive a star the greater its luminosity, and which allows the mass of a star to be determined from its intrinsic brightness. His observation that light from stars near to the Sun's rim during the total solar eclipse of 1919 was slightly deflected by the Sun's gravitational field was the most powerful evidence of support for **Einstein**'s theory of relativity (see **Key concepts: General theory of relativity**). Eddington tried to popularize science by writing books for the layman.

## Thomas Alva Edison, 1847–1931

US inventor and physicist, born in Milan, Ohio. He took out more than 1000 patents including the gramophone (1877), the incandescent light bulb (1879), and the carbon granule microphone as an improvement for **Alexander Graham Bell**'s telephone. He invented a system for generating and distributing electricity and designed the first power plant (1881–82). Amongst his other inventions were a megaphone, a storage battery, the electric valve (1883) and the kinetoscope (1891). In 1912 he produced the first talking motion pictures. He also discovered thermionic emission, formerly called the 'Edison Effect'. Tireless at experimentation but always practical and commercial in his goals, he was the most prolific inventor the world has ever seen.

## Robert Geoffrey Edwards, 1925–

British physiologist, born in Batley. In collaboration with **Patrick Steptoe** he contributed substantially to the successful development of the *in vitro* fertilization ('test-tube babies') programme. He discovered ways of encouraging immature eggs to ripen in a woman, and he provided the right artificial conditions to ensure successful fertilization and early development of the embryo outside the woman's body. In July 1978 Louise Brown, the first healthy 'test-tube baby', was born as a result of the work of Edwards and Steptoe. They established the Bourne Hall Clinics, of which Edwards became scientific director (1988–91).

## Paul Ehrlich, 1854–1915

German bacteriologist, born in Strzelin, Poland. He discovered a cure for syphilis (synthesizing salvarsan as a treatment in 1910) and propounded the side-chain theory in immunology. Ehrlich's unique contribution was to conceptualize the interactions between cells, antibodies and antigens as essentially chemical responses. He recognized the need to look systematically for chemicals which attack and destroy disease-causing microorganisms, without harming human cells. For his contributions to research on immunity and serum therapy, he won with Elie Metchnikoff the Nobel prize for physiology or medicine in 1908.

## Christiaan Eijkman, 1858–1930

Dutch physician and pathologist, born in Nijkerk. He investigated beriberi disease in the Dutch East Indies (Indonesia). He was the first to produce a dietary deficiency disease experimentally (in chickens) and to propose the concept of 'essential food factors', later called vitamins. He showed that the substance (now known as thiamine, a B-complex vitamin) which protects against beriberi is contained in the husks of grains of rice, and carried out clinical studies on prisoners in Java to show that unpolished rice could cure the disease. He shared the 1929 Nobel prize for physiology or medicine with **Sir Frederick Gowland Hopkins**.

## Albert Einstein, 1879–1955

German–Swiss–US mathematical physicist, born in Ulm, Bavaria. With **Galileo Galilei** and **Sir Isaac Newton**, he is ranked as one of the great contributors to the understanding of the universe. Of Jewish parentage, he achieved world fame through his special and general theories of relativity (1905 and 1916). The special theory of relativity provided a new system of mechanics which accommodated **James Clerk Maxwell**'s electromagnetic field theory, as well as the previously inexplicable results of the experiments carried out by **Albert Michelson** and **Edward Morley** on the speed of light (see **Key concepts: Special theory of relativity**). His general theory accounted for the slow rotation of the elliptical path of the planet Mercury, which Newtonian gravitational theory had failed to do (see **Key concepts: General theory of relativity**). He won the 1921 Nobel prize for physics for his work. Element 99 was named einsteinium after him. In September 1939 he wrote to President Roosevelt warning him of the possibility that Germany would try to make an atomic bomb, thus helping to initiate the Allied attempt to produce one (called the Manhattan Project). After World War II Einstein urged international control of atomic weapons and protested against the proceedings of the un-American Activities Senate Subcommittee, which had arraigned many scientists.

> 66
>
> *If only I had known, I would have become a watchmaker.*
>
> —Albert Einstein on his part in developing the atom bomb, in the *New Statesman* (16 April 1955).
>
> 99

### Professor, Not President

Einstein was a supporter of the foundation of the State of Israel. After the death of Israel's first president Chaim Weizman in 1952, Einstein was offered the presidency of the state but decided to decline. He instead continued being a professor at the Institute of Advanced Study in Princeton, New Jersey.

## Gertrude Belle Elion, 1918–99

US biochemist, born in New York City. With **George Hitchings**, she worked extensively on drug development, succeeding in producing drugs that were active against leukaemia and malaria, drugs for the treatment of gout and kidney stones, and those that suppressed the normal immune reactions of the body, proving vital in transplant surgery. In the 1970s they produced an anti-viral compound active against the herpes virus, which preceded the successful development of AZT, the anti-AIDS compound. In 1988 they shared the Nobel prize for physiology or medicine with **Sir James Whyte Black**.

## Charles Sutherland Elton, 1900–91

English ecologist, born in Liverpool. He was the first biologist to develop the concepts of 'food chain', 'niche' and 'food web', which are now such an important part of any study of ecology. His four Arctic expeditions in the 1920s and his use of trappers' records for fur-bearing animals led to his classic books on animal ecology. Elton's work on animal communities led to the recognition of the ability of many animals to counter environmental disadvantage by change of habitats. He was elected FRS in 1953.

### Sir (Michael) Anthony Epstein, 1921–

English microbiologist, born in London. He was educated at Trinity College, Cambridge, and worked initially at Middlesex Hospital Medical School. In 1964 he discovered a new human herpes virus, known as the Epstein–Barr virus, which has been implicated in some forms of human cancer, notably Burkitt's lymphoma. This was the first virus to be associated with cancer in man, and its discovery stimulated the current vast research on the viral origins of human tumours. He has received many national and international awards: elected FRS in 1979, knighted in 1991 and awarded the Royal Society's Royal Medal in 1992.

### Richard Robert Ernst, 1933–

Swiss physical chemist, born in Winterthur. He was awarded the Nobel prize for chemistry in 1991 for innovations in nuclear magnetic resonance (NMR) spectroscopy, which has been an important tool for the determination of molecular structure in organic chemistry. During the first 20 years its applications were based on a restricted range of nuclei, which Ernst sought to extend after 1966 by increasing enormously the sensitivity of the instrumentation and developing his 'Fourier transform NMR'. His work is of particular value in probing very large molecules, such as are often involved in biology and medicine.

### Euclid, fl.300 BC

Greek mathematician. His *Elements* of geometry, in 13 books, is the earliest substantial Greek mathematical treatise to have survived. It is probably better known than any other mathematical book, still being used as the basis of school textbooks in the earlier part of the 20th century. It covers the geometry of lines in the plane, including **Pythagoras**'s theorem, and goes on to discuss circles, ratios, and the geometry of three dimensions. He wrote other works on geometry including the theory of conic sections and also wrote on astronomy, optics and music.

### Leonhard Euler, 1707–83

Swiss mathematician, born in Basel. He studied infinite series and differential equations, introduced or established many new functions, including the gamma function and elliptic integrals, and created the calculus of variations. His *Introductio in analysin infinitorum* (1748, 'Introduction to the analysis of the infinite') and later treatises on differential and integral calculus and algebra became standard textbooks, and his notations such as $e$ and $i$ (the square root of $-1$) have been used ever since (see **Numbers and shapes: Types of numbers**). In mechanics Euler studied the motion of rigid bodies in three dimensions, the construction and control of ships, and celestial mechanics.

### Alice Evans, 1881–1975

US microbiologist, born in Neath, Pennsylvania. She received little formal education, but won a scholarship to study science at Cornell University. Her investigations into the dangers of non-pasteurized cows' milk, and her assertion that cattle brucellosis and human Malta fever had a common origin, were strongly resisted by veterinarians, dairymen and many physicians. Compelling confirmation during the late 1920s and 1930s led to the recognition of Evans's achievements and she received several honours, including that of being the first woman president of the Society of American Bacteriologists (1928).

## Hans Jürgen Eysenck, 1916–97

British psychologist, born in Berlin. He began his career in the field of clinical psychology, which led to psychometric research into the normal variations of human personality and intelligence. He frequently championed the view that genetic factors play a large part in determining the psychological differences between people, and often held controversial views, particularly with his study of racial differences in intelligence in *Race, Intelligence and Education* (1971). In 1962 he published *Know Your Own IQ*.

## Johann Christian Fabricius, 1745–1808

Danish entomologist, born in Tondern. He studied at Copenhagen and Uppsala, Sweden, becoming Professor of Natural History at Kiel University in 1775. He was a student of **Linnaeus** and was himself one of the founders of entomological taxonomy, using the mouthparts of insects as the basis of his classification. He developed some advanced ideas concerning evolution. For example, he suggested that new species might arise through hybridization. Although pre-dating **Lamarck**, he believed that inherited change could result from environmental effects.

## (Gabriel) Daniel Fahrenheit, 1686–1736

German physicist, born in Danzig (now Gdansk, Poland). He produced high-quality meteorological instruments, devising an accurate alcohol thermometer (1709) and a commercially successful mercury thermometer (1714). Adopting what he believed to be Olaus Roemer's practice of taking thermometric fixed points as the temperatures of melting ice and of the human body, Fahrenheit eventually devised a temperature scale with these points calibrated at 32 and 96 degrees, and zero fixed at the freezing point of ice and salt. He was the first to show that the boiling point of liquids varies at different atmospheric pressures, and suggested this as a principle for the construction of barometers.

## Michael Faraday, 1791–1867

English chemist and physicist, born in Newington Butts near London. He was the first to isolate benzene and he synthesized the first chlorocarbons. Faraday discovered the process of electrolysis (1832) and formulated the laws that control it. He also formulated the laws of induction to explain the relationship between electricity and magnetism (see **Electricity and magnets: Electromagnetism**). The first to build an electrical generator and transformer, his name was given to the unit of capacitance, the farad. Greatly influential on later physics, he nevertheless had no pupils and worked with only one assistant. He is generally considered the greatest of all experimental physicists.

## Pierre de Fermat, 1601–65

French mathematician, born in Beaumont. His correspondence with **Blaise Pascal** marks the foundation of probability theory. He studied maximum and minimum values of functions in advance of the differential calculus, but is best known for his work in number theory, the proofs of many of his discoveries being first published by **Leonhard Euler** a hundred years later. His 'last theorem' was the most famous unsolved problem in mathematics, stating that it is impossible to find an integer solution to the equation $x^n + y^n = z^n$ if $n$ is greater than 2. Its solution was finally published in 1995 (see **Key concepts: Fermat's last theorem**). In optics

Fermat's principle was the first statement of a variational principle in physics, saying that the path taken by a ray of light between two given points is the one in which the light takes the least time (see **Key concepts: The principle of least action**).

### Enrico Fermi, 1901–54

US nuclear physicist, born in Rome. Between 1927 and 1933 he expanded upon the work of **Wolfgang Pauli**, published his semiquantitative method of calculating atomic particles, and in 1934 he and his colleagues split the nuclei of uranium atoms by bombarding them with neutrons, thus producing artificial radioactive substances. This was an important step in the development of nuclear power and weapons. He was awarded the 1938 Nobel prize for physics. He played a prominent part in interesting the US Government in atomic energy, constructed the first US nuclear reactor at Chicago (1942), and produced the first controlled chain reaction. Element 100 was named fermium after him.

### Richard Phillips Feynman, 1918–88

US physicist, born in New York City. He devised his own pictorial way of describing quantum processes, the 'path integral approach', which has proved to be a very powerful calculational tool. Using this he further developed quantum electrodynamics and introduced 'Feynman diagrams' (1949) which provide a pictorial representation of particle interactions. In 1957, together with **Murray Gell-Mann**, he developed the theory of weak nuclear force. For his important contribution to the work on quantum electrodynamics, he was awarded the Nobel prize for physics in 1965 together with **Sin-Itiro Tomonaga** and **Julian Schwinger**. He was also involved in building the first atomic bomb during World War II.

### Leonardo Fibonacci, also called Leonardo of Pisa, c.1170–c.1250

Italian mathematician, probably born in Pisa. He popularized the modern Arabic system of numerals, which originated in India. His main work *Liber abaci* (1202, 'The Book of Calculation') illustrated the virtues of the new numeric system, showing how it can be used to simplify highly complex calculations. The book also includes work on geometry, the theory of proportion and techniques for determining the roots of equations. He also made remarkably advanced contributions to number theory. He discovered the 'Fibonacci sequence' of integers (see **Numbers and shapes: Fibonacci numbers**) in which each number is equal to the sum of the preceding two (1,1,2,3,5,8,...). He was the first outstanding mathematician of the Middle Ages.

### Edmond Henri Fischer, 1920–

US biochemist, born in Shanghai, China. He was educated at the universities of Geneva, Montpellier and Basel, and moved to the USA in 1953. He studied the enzyme phosphorylase and, with **Edwin Krebs**, he showed in 1955 that the reversible addition of phosphate groups is involved in activating glycogen phosphorylase. This fundamental mechanism controls a wide variety of processes from muscle contraction to the expression of genes, and for this work they were jointly awarded the 1992 Nobel prize for physiology or medicine.

### Sir Alexander Fleming, 1881–1955

Scottish bacteriologist, born in Loudoun, Ayrshire. He became the first to use antityphoid vaccines on human beings, and pioneered the use of salvarsan, a treatment that **Paul Ehrlich** had synthesized, against syphilis. He also discovered the enzyme lysozyme that kills some bacteria without harming normal tissue. In 1928 by chance exposure of a culture of staphylococci, he noticed a curious mould, penicillin, which he found to have unsurpassed antibiotic powers. For this discovery of penicillin, he was awarded the 1945 Nobel prize for physiology or medicine, which he shared with **Howard Florey** and **Ernst Chain**, who had perfected a method of producing the volatile drug.

### Howard Walter, Baron Florey, 1898–1968

Australian pathologist, born in Adelaide. In 1935, as Professor of Pathology at Oxford, he worked with the biochemist **Sir Ernst Chain** in purifying the antibiotic penicillin, which had been discovered in 1928 by **Alexander Fleming**. He supervised clinical testing of the drug in the USA where it was put into mass production; by 1943 it was readily available, and by the end of World War II had already saved many lives. Florey, Chain and Fleming were jointly awarded the Nobel prize for physiology or medicine in 1945. Florey became the first Australian President of the Royal Society in 1960, and was awarded a life peerage in 1965.

### Jean Bernard Léon Foucault, 1819–68

French physicist, born in Paris. He began his career as a physician but gave this up, as he detested the sight of blood, turning instead to experimental physics. He determined the velocity of light by the revolving mirror method originally proposed by François Arago, and proved that light travels more slowly in water than in air (1850). In 1851, by means of a freely suspended pendulum, he proved that the Earth rotates. In 1852 he constructed the first gyroscope and in 1857 the Foucault prism. By 1858 he had improved the mirrors of reflecting telescopes.

### (Jean Baptiste) Joseph, Baron de Fourier, 1768–1830

French mathematician, born in Auxerre. He introduced the expansion of functions in trigonometric series, now known as Fourier series, which proposed that almost any function of a real variable can be expressed as a sum of the sines and cosines of integral multiples of the variable. This method has become an essential tool in mathematical physics and a major theme of analysis. His *Théorie analytique de la chaleur* (1822, 'Analytical Theory of Heat') applied the technique to the solution of partial differential equations to describe heat conduction in a solid body. He also discovered an important theorem on the roots of algebraic equations.

### Rosalind Elsie Franklin, 1920–58

English X-ray crystallographer, born in London. Educated at Cambridge, she became experienced in X-ray diffraction techniques while working in Paris, and returned to London in 1951 to work on DNA at King's College. Extending the X-ray diffraction studies of **Maurice Wilkins,** she produced X-ray diffraction pictures of DNA, thereby providing crucial information that led to the discovery of its structure as a double helix (see **Genetics: DNA**). These were published in the same issue of *Nature* (1953) in which **James Watson** and **Francis Crick** proposed their double-helical model of DNA. Franklin died four years before she could be awarded the 1962 Nobel prize for physiology or medicine jointly with Watson, Crick and Wilkins for the determination of the structure of DNA.

### Sigmund Freud, 1856–1939

Austrian neurologist and founder of psychoanalysis, born in Freiberg (now in the Czech Republic). He developed the technique of conversational 'free association' in place of hypnosis, and refined psychoanalysis as a method of treatment. He argued that dreams are disguised manifestations of repressed sexual desires, and propounded theories of infantile sexuality and the division of the unconscious mind into the 'Id', the 'Ego' and the 'Super-Ego'. Although his scientific methods were questionable and some of his ideas now lack favour with psychologists and psychiatrists, he inspired modern psychiatry by his study of mental illness and also introduced the subject of sexuality into the scientific arena.

### Charlotte Friend, 1921–87

US oncologist and medical microbiologist, born in New York City. She discovered that a fatal leukaemia could be induced in experimental animals by a virus, now known as the Friend Leukaemia Virus (FLV). Her findings were initially received with hostility, but colleagues soon recognized that some viruses were able to produce cancers. She received numerous honours worldwide and was elected to the National Academy of Sciences in 1976. She was appointed professor at the Mount Sinai School of Medicine in 1966 where she remained until her death.

### Karl von Frisch, 1886–1982

Austrian ethologist and zoologist, born in Vienna. His early work showed that fish perceive colours and that their visual acuity is superior to that of humans, but he is mainly remembered for his later work on honey bees. He demonstrated that bees are able to distinguish odours, tastes and colours, and that the honey bee's visual spectrum allows it to see ultraviolet light. He also described how hive bees communicate the location of a source of food by means of coded dances ('waggle dances'). In 1949 he further showed that bees can navigate even on cloudy days by making use of the pattern of polarized light in the sky. One of the pioneers of ethology, he was joint winner of the Nobel prize for physiology or medicine in 1973.

### Otto Robert Frisch, 1904–79

British physicist, born in Vienna, Austria. In 1939, with **Lise Meitner** (his aunt), he correctly interpreted and later confirmed that **Otto Hahn**'s observation of uranium splitting was due to nuclear fission. He studied the possibility of nuclear chain reactions, which led to his involvement in the British and US atom bomb projects. He received an OBE in 1948 and was elected FRS in the same year.

### Johan Gadolin, 1760–1852

Finnish chemist, born in Turku. He is remembered for his investigations of the rare earth elements, analysing a new black mineral from Ytterby, Sweden, and isolating from it a rare earth mineral, yttria, in 1794. This was an important step towards identifying the remaining undiscovered elements. Over the next century yttria was found to contain the oxides of nine new rare earth elements, leading eventually to the establishment of the whole series. Around 30 years after Gadolin's death, one of these was discovered by Jean Charles Galissard de Marignac and Paul Emile Lecoq de Boisbaudran, who named it gadolinium in his honour.

## Daniel Carleton Gajdusek, 1923–

US virologist and paediatrician, born in Yonkers, New York. He spent much time in Papua New Guinea, studying the origin and dissemination of infectious diseases amongst the Fore people, especially a slowly developing lethal disease called kuru. He worked out that the disease is caused by an infectious agent that was unlike any other that had previously been described, and that may take years to induce symptoms. He shared the 1976 Nobel prize for physiology or medicine with **Baruch Blumberg** for his work on what are now known to be prions, which cause such diseases as Creutzfeldt–Jakob disease (CJD).

## Galen, c.130–c.201

Greek physician, born in Pergamum. He was a voluminous writer on medical and philosophical subjects, and collated all the medical knowledge of his time, especially promoting the work of **Hippocrates**. An active experimentalist, and dissector of animals, he elaborated a physiological system whereby the body's three principal organs – heart, liver and brain – were central to living processes, and he was the first to use the pulse as a diagnostic aid. He was venerated for many centuries as the standard authority on medical matters.

## Galileo, properly Galileo Galilei, 1564–1642

Italian astronomer, mathematician and natural philosopher, born in Pisa. He realized the value of a pendulum as a timekeeper and proved that all falling bodies, great or small, descend due to gravity at the same rate. He also showed that a body moving along an inclined plane has a constant acceleration, and demonstrated the parabolic trajectories of projectiles. He perfected the refracting telescope and pursued astronomical observations which revealed mountains and valleys on the Moon, four satellites of Jupiter, the phases of Venus, sunspots on the Sun's disc, the Sun's rotation and Saturn's appendages. These brilliant researches convinced him of the correctness of **Copernicus**'s theory. His advocacy of this heliocentric system, that the Earth moves around the Sun, led to his imprisonment by the Inquisition. He was eventually allowed to live under house arrest in his own home, where he continued his researches until his death. The sentence of heresy passed on him by the Inquisition was formally retracted by Pope John Paul II on 31 October 1992.

## Johann Gottfried Galle, 1812–1910

German astronomer, born in Pabsthaus. Educated at Berlin University, he graduated in mathematics and physics in 1833. His most dramatic discovery, made in Berlin, was of the planet Neptune, whose existence had been theoretically predicted and whose expected position had been calculated by **Urbain Leverrier**. In 1872 he proposed the use of asteroids rather than regular planets for determinations of the solar parallax, a suggestion which bore fruit in a successful international campaign (1888–9). The method was last used during the closest approach of the minor planet Eros in 1930–31.

## Sir Francis Galton, 1822–1911

English scientist, born in Birmingham. Galton's investigations covered many domains. His investigations in meteorology were the basis for modern weather maps, and he pioneered the system of fingerprint identification as a means of identifying individuals in criminal investigations. He conducted research into colour blindness and mental imagery and he trailblazed the use of statistical techniques, in 1888 presenting to the Royal Society a method for calculating correlation coefficients. A supporter of his cousin **Charles Darwin**'s evolutionary thinking, he is also remembered as the founder of eugenics (the science of creating superior offspring).

### Luigi Galvani, 1737–98

Italian physiologist, born in Bologna. He became a lecturer in anatomy in 1768, and from 1782 was Professor of Obstetrics. He is famous for the discovery of animal electricity, inspired by his observation that dead frogs suffered convulsions when fixed to an iron fence to dry. He then showed that paroxysms followed if a frog was part of a circuit involving metals, wrongly believing the current source to be in the material of muscle and nerve. Galvani's name lives on in the word 'galvanized', meaning stimulated as if by electricity, and in the galvanometer, used from 1820 to detect electric current.

### (Johann) Carl Friedrich Gauss, 1777–1855

German mathematician, astronomer and physicist, born in Brunswick. By the age of 15, through a notebook he kept in Latin, it appeared that he had conjectured and often proved many remarkable results, including the prime number theorem. He made significant new advances in number theory, studied errors of observation and devised the method of least squares for fitting a curve to a data set. He also carried out much work on pure mathematics, studied the Earth's magnetism and was involved in the development of the magnetometer, as well as giving a mathematical theory of optical systems of lenses. He made many other discoveries with which he was not credited, including the theory of elliptic functions and the possibility of a non-Euclidean geometry of space.

### Joseph Louis Gay-Lussac, 1778–1850

French chemist and physicist, born in Saint-Léonard. A brilliant student, he studied engineering before becoming interested in physics and chemistry. He established the law of gas expansion (1802) independently of **Jacques Charles**, and formulated the law of combining volumes of gases (1808). The two laws regarding gases formed the basis for Avogadro's law of 1811. He also isolated and investigated a variety of elements such as boron, potassium, sodium and silicon, and improved methods of organic analysis. During the later part of his career, he did much work as a technical adviser to industry. He was elected an honorary Fellow of the Chemical Society in 1849.

### Hans Wilhelm Geiger, 1882–1945

German physicist, born in Neustadt-an-der-Haart. With **Ernest Rutherford**, he devised a means of detecting alpha particles (1908), and subsequently showed that two alpha particles are emitted in the radioactive decay of uranium. With J M Nuttall he demonstrated the linear relationship between the logarithm of the range of alpha particles and the radioactive time constant of the emitting nucleus, now called the Geiger–Nuttall rule. Together with Walther Müller, he made improvements to the particle counter, resulting in the modern form of the Geiger–Müller counter, which also detects electrons and ionizing radiation.

## Murray Gell-Mann, 1929–

US theoretical physicist, born in New York City. At the age of 24 he made a major contribution to the theory of elementary particles by introducing the concept of 'strangeness', a new quantum number which must be conserved in any so-called 'strong' nuclear interaction event. Gell-Mann and Yuval Ne'eman (independently) used 'strangeness' to group elementary particles such as mesons, nucleons (neutrons and protons) and hyperons, and thus they were able to form predictions about chemical elements. The omega-minus particle was predicted by this theory and observed in 1964. With **George Zweig**, he also introduced the concept of quarks, a set of hypothetical elementary particles (see **Atoms, elements and molecules: Subatomic particles**). ('Quark' is an invented word, said to be taken from James Joyce's *Finnegans Wake*.) He was awarded the Nobel prize for physics in 1969.

## Sophie Germain, 1776–1831

French mathematician, born in Paris. As a woman, she was not admitted to the newly established École Polytechnique, but in the guise of a male student she submitted a paper which so impressed one of the leading mathematicans, Joseph de Lagrange, that he became her personal tutor. She gave a more generalized, although still incomplete, proof of **Pierre de Fermat**'s 'last theorem' than had previously been available, developed a mathematical explanation of the figures of Ernst Chladni and went on to derive a general mathematical description of the vibrations of curved as well as plane elastic surfaces. Her *Recherches sur la théorie des surfaces élastiques* ('Research on the Theory of Elastic Surfaces') was published in 1821.

## Walter Gilbert, 1932–

US molecular biologist, born in Boston, MA. He studied physics and mathematics at Harvard and Cambridge. During the 1960s he isolated a bacterial repressor molecule, which **Jacques Monod** and **François Jacob** had suggested to be centrally involved in controlling gene action. Using methods developed by **Frederick Sanger**, he described the nucleotide sequence of DNA to which the repressor molecule binds. For this work he shared the 1980 Nobel prize for chemistry with Sanger and **Paul Berg**. Since the late 1980s he has been a vigorous supporter of the Human Genome Initiative, a project to map and sequence all genes in the human body.

## Donald Arthur Glaser, 1926–

US physicist, born in Cleveland, Ohio. He was awarded the 1960 Nobel prize for physics for inventing the 'bubble chamber' for observing the paths of elementary particles. Bubble chambers were used to discover many subatomic particles and reached their pinnacle in 1971 with the construction of 'Gargamelle', a thousand-tonne detector, but have now largely been superseded by electronic or gas detectors capable of providing data immediately.

## Sheldon Lee Glashow, 1932–

US physicist, born in New York City. He shared the 1979 Nobel prize for physics with Pakistani scientist **Abdus Salam** and fellow American **Steven Weinberg** for 'the standard model' of all particle interactions. Weinberg and Salam had independently produced a single unifying theory of both the weak and electromagnetic interactions between elementary particles. Glashow had developed one of the first models to simultaneously describe the electromagnetic and weak forces (see **Key concepts: The theory of everything**). The predictions of the 'electroweak' theory were confirmed experimentally in the 1970s and 1980s. He subsequently extended the theory (now called the Weinberg–Salam theory) to apply to other particles by introducing a new particle property known as 'charm'. He was also a major contributor to the theory of quantum chromodynamics.

## Kurt Gödel, 1906–78

US logician and mathematician, born in Brünn, Moravia (now Brno, Czech Republic). He studied and taught in Vienna, then emigrated to the USA in 1940 and joined the Institute for Advanced Study at Princeton University. He stimulated a great deal of significant work in mathematical logic and propounded one of the most important proofs in modern mathematics, namely Gödel's theorem, published in 1931, which demonstrated the existence of formally undecidable elements within any formal system of arithmetic. His contact with **Einstein** led him to discover novel solutions to Einstein's field equations which seem to impy the physical possibility of time travel.

## Jane Goodall, 1934–

English primatologist and conservationist, born in London. She worked in Kenya with the anthropologist **Louis Leakey** and obtained her PhD from Cambridge in 1965. She has carried out a study of the behaviour and ecology of chimpanzees that has transformed the understanding of primate behaviour by demonstrating its complexity. She discovered that chimpanzees modify a variety of natural objects to use as tools and weapons, and showed that they hunt animals for meat. A recipient of many awards, she is active in chimpanzee conservation in Africa and became scientific director of the Gombe Wildlife Research Institute in 1967.

## Stephen Jay Gould, 1941–2002

US palaeontologist, born in New York City. With palaeontologist Niles Eldgredge, he put forward the theory of 'punctuated equilibrium' or rapid evolutionary change followed by stasis (1972). He has also championed the idea of 'hierarchical evolution'. This suggests that natural selection operates at many levels, including genes and species as well as at the traditional level of individuals. He popularized his ideas in a series of collected essays and his books have won many awards. Influenced by Marxist ideas in his scientific work, he has been a forceful speaker against pseudo-scientific racism and biological determinism. His book *The Mismeasure of Man* (1981) is a critique of intelligence testing.

## Michael Boris Green, 1946–

English theoretical physicist, born in London. He was co-founder of the superstring theory (see **Key concepts: String theory**). This is based on the idea that the ultimate constituents of nature, when inspected at very small scales, do not exist as point-like particles but as 'strings' in more than three dimensions. String theories are now considered very good candidates for the actual laws of physics at the ultimate small scale.

### Alexandre Grothendieck, 1928–

French mathematician, born in Berlin. After early important work on infinite-dimensional vector spaces, he switched to algebraic geometry, where he revolutionized the subject. His work led to a unification of geometry, number theory, topology and complex analysis, and helped to resolve the important conjectures of **André Weil**. His work has also had profound implications for the theory of logic. His remarkably powerful introduction of the ideas at the very basis of algebraic geometry have extended the language of geometry from fields to rings. He was awarded the Fields Medal (the mathematical equivalent of the Nobel prize) in 1966.

### Beno Gutenberg, 1889–1960

US geophysicist, born in Darmstadt, Germany. He made two important contributions: he deduced in 1913 from earthquake shock waves the existence of a zone in the mantle where seismic waves travel with low velocities, and in 1914 he made the first correct determination of the depth to the Earth's core, which he concluded is liquid. He also helped **Charles Richter** to devise the Richter scale for measuring earthquakes.

### Fritz Haber, 1868–1934

German physical chemist, born in Breslau. In 1904 he began to study the direct synthesis of ammonia from nitrogen and hydrogen gases, which, in association with Carl Bosch, led to the large-scale production of ammonia. This was important in maintaining an explosives supply for the German war effort from 1914 to 1918. It also led to Haber receiving the Nobel prize for chemistry in 1918. This occasioned some criticism because he had been involved in the organization of gas warfare. In 1933 he resigned as director of the Kaiser Wilhelm Institute for Physical Chemistry and Electrochemistry in protest at the anti-Jewish policies of the Nazi regime.

### Otto Hahn, 1879–1968

German radiochemist, born in Frankfurt. He was involved in the discovery of several new radioactive elements, among them radiothorium, radioactinium and mesothorium, but his best-known research was on the irradiation of uranium and thorium with neutrons. This work, initially in association with **Lise Meitner** and later with Fritz Strassmann, led to the discovery of nuclear fission (1938). For this Hahn received the Nobel prize for chemistry in 1944. Greatly upset that his discovery led to the horror of Hiroshima and Nagasaki, he became a staunch opponent of nuclear weapons.

### Edmond Halley, 1656–1742

English astronomer and mathematician, born in London. He studied the solar system and correctly predicted the return (in 1758, 1835 and 1910) of a comet that had been observed in 1583, and is now named after him (see **Space: Comets**). His prodigious output includes being the first to produce a catalogue of the stars in the southern hemisphere (*Catalogus Stellarum Australium*, 1679); the first to make a complete observation of the transit of Mercury; and the first to recommend the observation of the transits of Venus in order to determine the Sun's parallax. He also established the mathematical law connecting barometric pressure with heights above sea level (on the basis of Boyle's law) and was the first to use an isometrical representation in map-making. He became Astronomer Royal of England in 1720.

## William Donald Hamilton, 1936–2000

English zoologist, born in Cairo, Egypt. In 1964 he proposed his theory of 'kin selection', which accounted for the altruistic behaviour observed in animal societies by demonstrating that an individual may influence the survival and successful breeding of a relative, thus increasing the probability of survival of shared genes, even though the individual may be sterile. He subsequently developed the concept of 'reciprocal altruism', arguing that natural selection favours such behaviour in social animals. More recent research has demonstrated that choice of a sexual partner is affected by parasite load.

## Godfrey Harold Hardy, 1877–1947

English mathematician, born in Cranleigh. An internationally important figure in mathematical analysis, he was chiefly responsible for introducing English mathematicians to the great advances in function theory that had been made abroad. He brought the self-taught Indian genius **Srinivasa Ramanujan** to Cambridge, and with Ramanujan he found an exact formula for the partition function, which expresses the number of ways a number can be written as a sum of smaller numbers. In his one venture into applied mathematics, he developed (concurrently with, but independently of, William Weinberg) the Hardy–Weinberg law, which is fundamental to population genetics.

## Lee Hartwell, 1939–

US biologist, born in Los Angeles. He studied at the California Institute of Technology and the Massachusetts Institute of Technology. He was professor at the University of California (1965–68) and University of Washington (1968– ) before becoming president and director of the Fred Hutchinson Cancer Research Center, Seattle (1998– ). In 2001 he shared the Nobel prize for physiology or medicine with **Paul M Nurse** and **Tim Hunt** for their discoveries of key regulators of the cell cycle, allowing for more accurate cancer diagnostics (see **Cells: Cell cycle**).

## William Harvey, 1578–1657

English physician, born in Folkestone. He discovered the circulation of the blood. His key claim concerning the cardiovascular system was that the heart was a muscle functioning as a pump, and that it effected the movement of the blood through the body via the lungs by means of the arteries, the blood then returning through the veins to the heart. He was not able to show how blood passed from the arterial to the venous system, there being no connections visible to the naked eye. His views contradicted ideas central to medicine since **Galen**, and were widely ridiculed at the time by traditionalists, notably in France.

## Stephen William Hawking, 1942–

English theoretical physicist, born in Oxford. His early research on relativity led him to study gravitational singularities (such as the Big Bang theory of the origin of the universe; see **Key concepts: Big Bang theory**) and black holes (where space–time is curved due to enormous gravitational fields; see **Space: Black holes**). The theory of black holes, which result when massive stars collapse under their own gravity at the end of their lives, owes much to his mathematical work. Since 1974 he has shown that a black hole could actually evaporate through loss of thermal radiation, and predicted that mass can escape entirely from its gravitational pull.

This loss of mass is known as the Hawking process. He became Lucasian Professor of Mathematics at Cambridge in 1980, a post famously held by **Newton** and **Dirac**. Since the 1960s, he has suffered from a disabling and progressive neuromotor disease, amyotrophic lateral sclerosis, which has made it impossible for him to speak or write except through an electronic interface.

> 66
>
> *One could still imagine that God created the universe at the instant of the Big Bang, or even afterwards in just such a way as to make it look as though there had been a Big Bang, but it would be meaningless to suppose that it was created before the Big Bang. An expanding universe does not preclude a creator, but it does place limits on when he might have carried out his job!*
>
> —Stephen Hawking, in *A Brief History of Time* (1988).
>
> 99

### Sir Henry Head, 1861–1940

English neurologist, born in London. His famous observations on the sensory changes in his own arm after cutting some nerve fibres provided important information about the physiology of sensation, and reinforced his reputation as a leading scientifically-inclined neurologist. He wrote widely on aphasia (disorders of speech), summarizing many of his ideas in *Aphasia and Kindred Disorders of Speech* (1926) which reported on the clinical disturbances of speech that he observed in a large number of men suffering from gunshot wounds. He edited the influential neurological journal *Brain* (1905–21) and also published poetry. He was knighted in 1927.

### Werner Karl Heisenberg, 1901–76

German theoretical physicist, born in Würzburg. In 1925 he reinterpreted classical mechanics with a matrix-based quantum mechanics where phenomena must be describable both in terms of wave theory and quanta. For this theory and its applications he was awarded the Nobel prize for physics in 1932. In his revolutionary principle of indeterminacy or uncertainty principle (1927), he showed that there is a fundamental limit to the accuracy to which certain pairs of variables (such as position and momentum) can be determined (see **Key concepts: Heisenberg's uncertainty principle**).

### Hermann (Ludwig Ferdinand) von Helmholtz, 1821–94

German physiologist and physicist, born in Potsdam. His physiological works are principally connected with the eye, the ear, and the nervous system, with his work on vision regarded as fundamental to modern visual science. He made important contributions in fluid dynamics, studies of vibrations and the spectrum, and studies of the development of the electric current within a galvanic battery. He was elected a Foreign Member of the Royal Society and in 1873 was awarded the Society's Copley Medal.

### Caroline Lucretia Herschel, 1750–1848

British astronomer, born in Hanover, Germany. Between 1786 and 1797 she discovered eight comets, and in 1783 discovered the companion of the Andromeda nebula. Her *Index to Flamsteed's Observations of the Fixed Stars* and a list of errata were published by the Royal Society (1798). At the age of 72 she worked on the reorganization of the catalogue of nebulae compiled by her brother, **William Herschel**. For this unpublished work she was awarded the gold medal of the Royal Astronomical Society (1828). She was elected (with **Mary Somerville**) an honorary member of the Royal Astronomical Society (1835).

### Sir John Frederick William Herschel, 1792–1871

English astronomer, born in Slough. The son of the astronomer **Sir William Herschel**, he re-examined his father's double stars to produce a catalogue, and also reviewed his father's great catalogue of nebulae and discovered 525 new nebulae. He completed a survey of nebulae and clusters in the southern skies, observing 1708 of them, the majority previously unseen. His southern observations, published as *Cape Observations* (1847) earned him the Copley Medal of the Royal Society (1847). He also pioneered celestial photography and researched photoactive chemicals and the wave theory of light. A recipient of many prestigious awards, he never occupied an academic post, supporting his research from his private means.

### Sir (Frederick) William Herschel, originally Friedrich Wilhelm Herschel, 1738–1822

British astronomer, born in Hanover, Germany. He made a reflecting telescope (1773–4) with which he discovered the planet Uranus in 1781. He also discovered satellites of Uranus and Saturn, the rotation of Saturn's rings and Saturn's rotation period. He researched binary stars and nebulae, and produced a model of the Milky Way as a non-uniform aggregation of stars. Following the publication of Charles Messier's catalogue of nebulae and star clusters (1781), he began a systematic search for such non-stellar objects which revealed a total of 2500; these were published in three catalogues (1786, 1789, 1802). Herschel was knighted in 1816. The epitaph on his tomb reflects his influence on the course of astronomy: *Coelorum perrupit claustra*, 'he broke the barriers of the heavens'.

### Gustav Ludwig Hertz, 1887–1975

German physicist, born in Hamburg. The nephew of **Heinrich Hertz**, he showed, with James Franck, that atoms would only absorb a fixed amount of energy, thus demonstrating the quantized nature of the atom's electron energy levels. For this work they shared the 1925 Nobel prize for physics. The results provided data for **Niels Bohr** to develop his theory of atomic structure, and for **Max Planck** to develop his ideas on quantum theory. After World War II Hertz went to the USSR to become head of a research laboratory (1945–54), then returned to Germany to become director of the Physics Institute in Leipzig (1954–61).

### Heinrich Rudolf Hertz, 1857–94

German physicist, born in Hamburg. In 1887 Hertz confirmed **James Clerk Maxwell**'s predictions by his fundamental discovery of 'Hertzian waves', now known as radio waves, which, like light waves, are examples of electromagnetic radiation. Later he explored the general theoretical implications of Maxwell's electrodynamics, was widely honoured for his work on electric waves, and in 1890 was awarded the Rumford Medal of the Royal Society.

## Antony Hewish, 1924–

English radio astronomer, born in Fowey. He studied at Cambridge and spent his career there, becoming Professor of Radio Astronomy (1971–89), then Emeritus Professor. In 1967 he began studying the scintillation ('twinkling') of astronomical radio sources. This led him and his student **Jocelyn Bell Burnell** to discover the first radio sources emitting radio signals in regular pulses now known as pulsars; many others have since been discovered. They are believed to be very small and dense rotating neutron stars (see **Space: Stars**). He shared the Nobel prize for physics in 1974 with his former teacher **Sir Martin Ryle**.

## Sir (Austin) Bradford Hill, 1897–1991

English medical statistician, born in London. He studied occupational hazards, the value of immunization against whooping cough and poliomyelitis, and the effects of smoking. This was set out in *Principles of Medical Statistics* (1937). Together with **Richard Doll** he designed a case control study of patients with lung cancer (1950), which enabled him to conclude that smoking was one important cause of the disease. Hill devised and established the randomized controlled clinical trial, which has transformed medical thinking. He was Professor of Epidemiology and Medical Statistics at the London School of Hygiene and Tropical Medicine, and later its Dean.

## Hipparchus or Hipparchos, c.180–125 BC

Greek astronomer and mathematician, born in Nicaea, Bithynia. He was the first to compile a catalogue of 850 stars (completed in 129 BC) giving their positions in celestial latitude and longitude, and this catalogue remained of primary importance up to the time of **Edmond Halley**. He observed the annual motion of the Sun, developed a theory of its eccentric motion and measured the unequal durations of the four seasons. He made similar observations of the Moon's more complex motion. Following the method of eclipse observations used by **Aristarchos**, he estimated the relative distances of the Sun and Moon and improved calculations for the prediction of eclipses. He developed the mathematical science of plane and spherical trigonometry required for his astronomical work. Hipparchus was the first to fix places on the Earth by latitude and longitude.

## Hippocrates, c.460–c.377/359 BC

Greek physician, born in Cos. Known as the 'father of medicine', he is associated with the medical profession's Hippocratic oath. Skilled in diagnosis and prognosis, he gathered together all the work of his predecessors which he believed to be sound, and laid the early foundations of scientific medicine. His followers developed the theories that the four fluids or humours of the body (blood, phlegm, yellow bile and black bile) are the primary seats of disease. They conceived that excesses or deficiencies of the humours caused diseases, which were to be treated by measures (such as drugs, diet, change of life, blood letting) which countered them. The Hippocratic writings contain many treatises which long exerted great influence.

## George Herbert Hitchings, 1905–98

US biochemist, born in Hoquiam, Washington State. In 1948 his investigations produced a folic acid antagonist which paved the way for the discovery of drugs to alleviate gout and combat cancer and malaria. In 1954 his team synthesized the very successful anti-leukaemia drug, 6-mercaptopurine, followed by azathioprine, which suppresses the body's immune system to enable organ transplantation from an unrelated donor. His laboratory also produced the antiviral drug aciclovir, active against herpes, and the anti-AIDS drug zidovudine. Hitchings shared with **Gertrude Elion** and **James Black** the 1988 Nobel prize for physiology or medicine for these achievements.

### Dorothy Mary Hodgkin, née Crowfoot, 1910–94

British crystallographer, born in Cairo, Egypt. Her detailed X-ray analysis of cholesterol was a milestone in crystallography, but an even greater achievement was the determination of the structure of penicillin (1942–45), especially since some of the best chemists in the UK and USA had been unable to find its constitution using chemical rather than physical techniques. Even with increased computational facilities after World War II, it took Hodgkin eight years to determine the structure of vitamin B12e (used to fight pernicious anaemia). She was awarded the Nobel prize for chemistry in 1964.

### Robert William Holley, 1922–93

US biochemist, born in Urbana, Illinois. He was a member of the team that first synthesized penicillin in the 1940s. In 1962 he identified two distinct transfer RNAs, and later secured the first pure transfer RNA (tRNA) sample (see **Genetics: RNA**). In 1965 he published the full molecular structure of this nucleic acid, which fulfils the role of Crick's proposed 'adaptor molecule' in the cellular synthesis of proteins. He shared the 1968 Nobel prize for physiology or medicine with **Har Gobind Khorana** and **Marshall Nirenberg**. He became a resident Fellow at the Salk Institute for Biological Studies in La Jolla, California, where he remained until his death.

### Robert Hooke, 1635–1703

English chemist, physicist and architect, born in Freshwater, Isle of Wight. He anticipated the development of the steam engine, discovered the relationship between the force applied to a spring and the resultant extension of the spring (see **Key concepts: Hooke's law**) and formulated the simplest theory of the arch, the balance-spring of watches, and the anchor escapement of clocks. He also anticipated **Newton**'s law of the inverse square in gravitation (1678), and constructed the first Gregorian or reflecting telescope, with which he discovered the fifth star in Orion and inferred the rotation of Jupiter. He materially improved or invented the compound microscope, the quadrant, a marine barometer, and the universal joint.

### Sir Frederick Gowland Hopkins, 1861–1947

English biochemist, born in Eastbourne. He learned chemistry in a pharmaceutical firm before commencing a brilliant career at Guy's Hospital, where he received the University of London gold medal in chemistry and qualified in medicine. He discovered accessory food factors, now called vitamins (see **Diseases and medicines: Dietary deficiencies**), associated lactate production in muscle with muscle contraction (1907), and discovered glutathione (1921). Knighted in 1925, he shared with **Christiaan Eijkman** the 1929 Nobel prize for physiology or medicine.

### Sir Fred Hoyle, 1915–2001

English astronomer and mathematician, born in Bingley. In 1948, with Hermann Bondi and Thomas Gold, he propounded the influential but now discredited 'steady state' theory of the universe, which proposed that the universe is uniform in space and unchanging in time. He also suggested the currently accepted scenario of the build-up to supernovae, in which a chain of nuclear reactions in a star is followed by a massive explosion, in which matter is ejected into space, and recycled in second-generation stars that form from the remnants. He was the Honorary Research Professor at both Manchester University (1972–2001) and University College, Cardiff (1975–2001).

### Edwin Powell Hubble, 1889–1953

US astronomer, born in Marshfield, Missouri. He found that spiral nebulae are independent stellar systems and that the Andromeda nebula in particular is very similar to our own Milky Way galaxy. In 1929 he announced his discovery that galaxies recede from us with speeds that increase with their distance. This was the phenomenon of the expansion of the universe, the observational basis of modern cosmology. The linear relation between speed of recession and distance is known as Hubble's law (see **Key concepts: Hubble's law**). The 2.4m (7.9ft) aperture Hubble Space Telescope, launched in 1990 in the space shuttle *Discovery*, was named in his honour.

### (Richard) Tim(othy) Hunt, 1943–

English biologist, born in Neston. He studied at Clare College, Cambridge. In 1991 he became principal scientist at the Imperial Cancer Research Fund's Clare Hall Laboratories, Hertfordshire. In 2001 he shared the Nobel prize for physiology or medicine with **Lee Hartwell** and **Paul M Nurse** for their discoveries of key regulators of the cell cycle, allowing more accurate cancer diagnostics (see **Cells: Cell cycle**).

### James Hutton, 1726–97

Scottish geologist, born in Edinburgh. Hutton's ideas form the basis of modern geology. In *A Theory of the Earth* (1785; expanded, Vols I and II 1795, Vol III 1799), he demonstrated that the internal heat of the Earth caused intrusions of molten rock into the crust, and that granite was the product of the cooling of molten rock and not the earliest chemical precipitate of the primeval ocean as advocated by Abraham Werner and others. His system of the Earth recognized that most rocks were detrital in origin, having been produced by erosion from the continents, deposited on the seafloor, lithified by heat from below and then uplifted to form new continents (see **Key concepts: Uniformitarianism**). The cyclicity of such processes led him to envisage an Earth with 'no vestige of a beginning and no prospect of an end'.

### T(homas) H(enry) Huxley, 1825–95

English biologist, born in Ealing. From 1854 to 1885 he made significant contributions to palaeontology and comparative anatomy, including studies of dinosaurs, coelenterates, and the relationship between birds and reptiles. He was best known as the foremost scientific supporter of **Charles Darwin**'s theory of evolution by natural selection during the heated debates which followed its publication, tackling Bishop Samuel Wilberforce in a celebrated exchange in Oxford (1860), when he is alleged to have declared that he would rather be descended from an ape than a bishop. Later he turned to theology and philosophy, and coined the term 'agnostic' for his views.

## Christiaan Huygens, 1629–93

Dutch physicist, born in The Hague. In 1655 he discovered the rings and fourth satellite of Saturn, using a refracting telescope he constructed with his brother. He later constructed the pendulum clock, based on the suggestion of **Galileo** (1657), and developed the latter's doctrine of accelerated motion under gravity. He discovered the laws of collision of elastic bodies at the same time as John Wallis and Sir Christopher Wren, and improved the air-pump. In optics he first put forward the wave theory of light, and discovered polarization. The 'principle of Huygens' is a part of the wave theory. He was, after **Isaac Newton**, the greatest scientist of the second half of the 17th century.

## Ibn-El-Nafis, 1208–88

Arab doctor and scholar. Ibn-El-Nafis was a physician, a linguist, a philosopher, and a historian. He was the first chief of Al-Mansuri Hospital in Cairo and the dean of the School of Medicine in AD 1284. He worked out the correct anatomy of the heart and the way the blood flowed through it. Ibn-El-Nafis also worked out the correct anatomy of the lungs and was the first person known to record the coronary circulation – the vessels supplying blood to the heart itself. Shortly after his work had been translated into Latin in the 16th century, European scientists began to 'discover' the same things.

## François Jacob, 1920–

French biochemist, born in Nancy. During the 1950s, he worked on the bacterium *Escherichia coli*, and suggested that genes are controlled by a system of other genes that regulate certain enzymes. He formulated the 'operon system', in which a regulator gene controls structural genes by manipulating sections of DNA. With **André Lwoff** and **Jacques Monod**, Jacob was awarded the 1965 Nobel prize for physiology or medicine for research into cell physiology and the structure of genes.

## Carl Gustav Jacob Jacobi, 1804–51

German mathematician, born in Potsdam. He was educated at Berlin University, and became a lecturer at the University of Königsberg, where he was appointed Extraordinary Professor in 1827 and Ordinary Professor of Mathematics in 1829. His *Fundamenta nova theoriae functionum ellipticarum* (1829, 'New principles of the theory of elliptic functions') was the first definitive book on elliptic functions, which he and **Niels Henrik Abel** had independently discovered. He discovered many remarkable infinite series connected to elliptic functions, and made important advances in the study of differential equations, the theory of numbers, and determinants.

## Karl Guthe Jansky, 1905–50

US radio engineer, born in Norman, Oklahoma. He built a high-quality receiver and aerial system, with which he investigated the sources of interference on short-wave radio telephone transmissions. Using this system, he noticed that the background hiss maximized every 23 hours 56 minutes. Aware that this is the period of rotation of the Earth, he concluded that the radiation originated from a stellar source. By 1932 he had pinpointed the source as being in the constellation of Sagittarius – the direction towards the centre of the Milky Way. His findings (1932) led to the development of radio astronomy during the 1950s. In 1973 the unit of radio emission strength, the jansky, was named after him.

### Sir James Hopwood Jeans, 1877–1946

English physicist and astronomer, born in Ormskirk. He developed a formula to describe the distribution of energy of enclosed radiation at long wavelength, now known as the Rayleigh–Jeans law. He also carried out important work on the kinetic theory of gases, and made significant advances in the theory of stellar dynamics by applying mathematics to problems. His wide-ranging research included studies of the formation of binary stars, stellar evolution, the nature of spiral nebulae and the origin of stellar energy, which he believed to be associated with radioactivity. He is best known for his role in popularizing physics and astronomy.

### Sir Alec John Jeffreys, 1950–

English molecular biologist, born in Oxford. He developed the technique of 'DNA fingerprinting', in which DNA from an individual is broken down and the resultant DNA fragments separated. Each individual has a unique pattern of DNA fragments, and thus samples of blood or semen can conclusively identify an individual in much the same way as a fingerprint. This technology is now used widely in forensic work. He was knighted in 1994. He moved to the department of genetics at the University of Leicester, where he has remained throughout his career, becoming Professor of Genetics in 1987.

### Edward Jenner, 1749–1823

English physician, born in Berkeley. He began to examine the truth of the traditions relating to cowpox (1775), and became convinced that it was efficacious as a protection against smallpox. In 1796 he vaccinated James Phipps, an eight-year-old boy, with cowpox matter from the hands of Sarah Nelmes, a milkmaid, and soon afterwards inoculated him with smallpox, and showed that the boy was protected. The practice of vaccination met with brief opposition, until over 70 principal physicians and surgeons in London signed a declaration of their entire confidence in it, and within five years vaccination was being practised in many parts of the world.

### Niels Kai Jerne, 1911–94

British immunologist, born in London. Jerne's research into the immune system examined the creation of antibodies, explained the development of T lymphocytes, and formulated the network theory, which views the immune system as a network of interacting lymphocytes and antibodies. He proposed in 1955 the first selection theory of antibody formation, and shared the 1984 Nobel prize for physiology or medicine with **Cesar Milstein** and **Georges Köhler**.

### Donald Carl Johanson, 1943–

US palaeoanthropologist, born in Chicago. His spectacular finds of fossil hominids 3–4 million years old at Hadar in the Afar Triangle of Ethiopia (1972–77) generated worldwide interest. They include 'Lucy', a unique female specimen that is half complete, and the so-called 'first family', a scattered group containing the remains of 13 individuals. He suggested that these remains belong to a previously undiscovered species, which he named *Australopithecus afarensis* ('southern ape of Afar'). He founded the Institute of Human Origins in California (1981), which later moved to Arizona and became associated with Arizona State University (1997).

### Frédéric Joliot-Curie, originally Jean-Frédéric Joliot, 1900–58

French physicist, born in Paris. In 1925 he joined the Radium Institute under **Marie Curie**, where he studied the electrochemical properties of polonium. He married Marie's daughter **Irène Joliot-Curie** in 1926, and in 1935 he shared with his wife the Nobel prize for chemistry for making the first artificial radioisotope. He succeeded his wife as head of the Radium Institute, and as president of the Communist-sponsored World Peace Council, he was awarded the Stalin Peace Prize (1951). He was given a state funeral by the Gaullist government when he died from cancer, caused by lifelong exposure to radioactivity.

### Irène Joliot-Curie, née Curie, 1897–1956

French physicist, born in Paris. The daughter of **Pierre** and **Marie Curie**, she worked with her husband **Frédéric Joliot-Curie** in studies of radioactivity from 1931. Their work on the emissions of polonium was built on by **Sir James Chadwick** in his discovery of the neutron. Between 1933 and 1934 the Joliot-Curies made the first artificial radioisotope, and it was for this work that they were jointly awarded the Nobel prize for chemistry in 1935. Similar methods led them to make a range of radioisotopes, some of which have proved indispensable in medicine, scientific research and industry. Irène Joliot-Curie became director of the Radium Institute in 1946 and a director of the French Atomic Energy Commission. She died from leukaemia due to long periods of exposure to radioactivity.

### James Prescott Joule, 1818–89

English physicist, born in Salford. The 'Joule effect' (1840) asserted that the heat produced in a wire by an electric current was proportional to the resistance and to the square of the current. In a series of notable researches (1843–78) he showed experimentally that heat is a form of energy, determined quantitatively the amount of mechanical (and later electrical) energy to be expended in the propagation of heat energy, and established the mechanical equivalent of heat. Between 1853 and 1862 he collaborated with **Lord Kelvin** on the 'porous plug' experiments, showing that when a gas expands without doing external work its temperature falls (the Joule–Thomson effect). The joule, a unit of work or energy, is named after him.

### Carl Gustav Jung, 1875–1961

Swiss psychiatrist, born in Kesswil. After collaborating with **Sigmund Freud**, he went on to develop his own theories of 'analytical psychology'. He introduced the concepts of 'introvert' and 'extrovert' personalities, and developed the theory of the 'collective unconscious' with its archetypes of man's basic psychic nature as a 'self-regulating' system. He held professorships at Zurich (1933–41) and Basel (1944–61). He was regarded by many as a religious leader and is seen as the founder of a new humanism.

### Immanuel Kant, 1724–1804

German philosopher, born in Königsberg, Prussia (now Kaliningrad, Russia). His early publications were in the natural sciences, particularly geophysics and astronomy, and in an essay on Newtonian cosmology he anticipated the nebular theory of **Pierre Laplace** and predicted the existence of the planet Uranus before its actual discovery in 1781. In his major philosophical work *Critique of Pure Reason* (1781), he likened his conclusions to a Copernican revolution in philosophy, whereby some of the properties we observe in objects are due to the nature of the observer, rather than the objects themselves. There exist basic concepts (or 'categories'), such as cause and effect, which are not learned from experience but constitute our basic conceptual apparatus for making sense of experience and the world.

## Sir Bernard Katz, 1911–2003

British biophysicist, born in Leipzig, Germany. After leaving Nazi Germany in 1935, he began physiological research at University College London. From the 1950s to the 1970s his research focused on the mechanisms of neural transmission, showing that chemical neurotransmitters are stored in nerve terminals and released in specific portions called quanta when stimulated by the arrival of the neural impulse. For this work he shared the 1970 Nobel prize for physiology or medicine with **Julius Axelrod** and Ulf von Euler. He was elected FRS in 1952, and knighted in 1969.

## William Thomson, 1st Baron Kelvin (of Largs), 1824–1907

Scottish physicist and mathematician, born in Belfast. He entered Glasgow University at the age of 10 and went to Cambridge at 16. At the age of 22, he was appointed Professor of Mathematics and Natural Philosophy (1846–99). In a career of astonishing versatility, he brilliantly combined pure and applied science. He solved important problems in electrostatics, proposed the absolute, or Kelvin, temperature scale (1848) and established the second law of thermodynamics simultaneously with **Rudolf Clausius** (see **Key concepts: The laws of thermodynamics**). He also investigated geomagnetism and hydrodynamics, and invented innumerable instruments (his house in Glasgow was the first to be lit by electric light). He is buried in Westminster Abbey, beside **Sir Isaac Newton**.

## Sir John Cowdery Kendrew, 1917–97

English molecular biologist, born in Oxford. He carried out research into the chemistry of the blood and used X-ray crystallography to determine the structure of the muscle protein, myoglobin. He was awarded the 1962 Nobel prize for chemistry jointly with **Max Perutz**. He was elected FRS in 1960 and knighted in 1974.

## Johannes Kepler, 1571–1630

German astronomer, born in Weil der Stadt, Württemberg. He demonstrated that the planets do not move uniformly in circles, but in ellipses with the Sun at one focus and with the radius vector of each planet describing equal areas of the ellipse in equal times (Kepler's first and second laws). He completed his researches in dynamical astronomy 10 years later by formulating his third law, which connects the periods of revolution of the planets with their mean distances from the Sun (see **Key concepts: Kepler's laws of planetary motion**). In 1627 he published the *Tabulae Rudolphinae* ('Rudolphine tables'), which contained the predicted positions of the planets according to the new laws, and also an extended catalogue of 1005 stars based on **Tycho Brahe**'s observations. Kepler also made discoveries in optics, general physics and geometry.

## Har Gobind Khorana, 1922–

US molecular chemist, born in Raipur, India (now in Pakistan). He determined the sequence of the nucleic acids, also known as 'bases', for each of the 20 amino acids in the human body. His work on nucleotide synthesis at Wisconsin was a major contribution to the elucidation of the genetic code (see **Genetics: Genetic code**). In the early 1970s he was one of the first to artificially synthesize a gene, initially from yeast, then later from the bacterium *Escherichia coli*. He shared the 1968 Nobel prize for physiology or medicine with **Marshall Nirenberg** and **Robert Holley**.

### Muhammad ibn Musa al Khwarizmi, c.800–c.850

Arab mathematician, born in Baghdad. He wrote an early Arabic treatise on the solution of quadratic equations, synthesizing Babylonian solution methods with Greek-style proofs of their correctness for the first time. His writings in Latin translation were influential in transmitting Indian and Arab mathematics to medieval Europe. This resulted in methods of arithmetic based on the Hindu (or so-called Arabic) number system becoming known in medieval Latin as algorismus, which was a corruption of his name, and from which comes the English 'algorithm'. The word algebra is derived from the word al-jabr in the title of his book on the subject.

### Alfred Charles Kinsey, 1894–1956

US sexologist and zoologist, born in Hoboken, New Jersey. He was Professor of Zoology at Indiana University from 1920, and in 1942 was the founder director of the Institute for Sex Research there. He published in 1948 *Sexual Behavior in the Human Male: The Kinsey Report*, which was based upon 18500 interviews and attracted much attention from the general public as well as from fellow scientists. It appeared to show a greater variety of sexual behaviour than had previously been suspected, although the report was much criticized for the interviewing techniques used. *Sexual Behavior in the Human Female* followed in 1953.

### Gustav Robert Kirchhoff, 1824–87

German physicist, born in Königsberg. He distinguished himself in electricity, heat, optics and especially (with Robert Bunsen) spectrum analysis, which led to the discovery of caesium and rubidium (1859). More importantly it resulted in his explanation of the Fraunhofer lines in the solar spectrum as the absorption of the corresponding spectral wavelengths in the Sun's atmosphere. He formulated Kirchoff's law of radiation, the key to the whole thermodynamics of radiation which, in the hands of his successor **Max Planck**, would later be developed into the concept of quanta (see **Key concepts: Quantum theory**). His electromagnetic theory of diffraction is still the most commonly used in optics.

### Baron Shibasaburo Kitasato, 1852–1931

Japanese bacteriologist, born in Oguni. After graduating from the Imperial University of Tokyo (1883), he moved to Berlin, and later founded in Japan an institute for infectious diseases. Kitasato succeeded in isolating the first pure culture of tetanus (1889), and he made the invaluable discovery of antitoxic immunity (1890), which led to the development of treatments and immunization for both tetanus and diphtheria. He also discovered the bacillus of bubonic plague (1894) and isolated the bacilli of symptomatic anthrax (1889) and dysentery (1898).

### Sir Aaron Klug, 1926–

English biophysicist, born in Zelva (now in Belarus). He moved to South Africa as a young child and studied physics at the universities there. Moving to England, he worked at Cambridge, and later at Birkbeck College (Nuffield Research Fellow, 1954–

57) with **Rosalind Franklin,** where he became particularly interested in viruses and their structure. His studies employed a wide variety of techniques to elucidate the structure of viruses. From the 1970s he applied these methods to the study of chromosomes and other biological macromolecules such as muscle filaments. He was awarded the Nobel prize for chemistry in 1982.

### Robert Koch, 1843–1910

German physician and pioneer bacteriologist, born in Klausthal in the Harz. He proved that the anthrax bacterium was the sole cause of the disease, and in 1882 he discovered the bacterium that causes tuberculosis. In 1883 he led a German expedition to Egypt and India, where he discovered the cholera bacterium, and in 1890 he produced a drug named tuberculin to prevent the development of tuberculosis. It proved to be ineffective as a cure, but useful in diagnosis. He was awarded the Nobel prize for physiology or medicine in 1905 for his work on tuberculosis. His formulation of essential scientific principles, known as 'Koch's postulates', established clinical bacteriology as a medical science in the 1890s.

### Georges Jean Franz Köhler, 1946–95

German immunochemist, born in Munich. In 1975 he and **Cesar Milstein** discovered how to produce hybridomas – hybrid cells created by fusing an antibody-generating cell with a cancer cell. Hybridomas are used to produce a single type of antibody against a specific antigen (foreign body). Their use opened the way to a precise examination of antibody structure. The commercial production of monoclonal antibodies, resulting from the hybridoma research, has led to their use in pregnancy and drug testing, and in the diagnosis and treatment of cancer and other diseases. For this work, Köhler shared with Milstein and **Niels Jerne** the 1984 Nobel prize for physiology or medicine.

### Arthur Kornberg, 1918–

US biochemist, born in Brooklyn, New York City. In studies of the bacterium *Escherichia coli*, Kornberg discovered DNA polymerase, the enzyme that synthesizes new DNA (see **Cells: Replication**). For this work he was awarded the 1959 Nobel prize for physiology or medicine jointly with **Severo Ochoa**. He was appointed professor at Stanford University in 1959. Kornberg became the first to synthesize viral DNA (1967) and wrote *DNA Replication* (1980).

### Sir Edwin Gerhard Krebs, 1918–

US biochemist, born in Lansing, Iowa. Krebs and **Edmond Fischer** built on Carl Cori's work on the activation of glycogen enzymes to show that the reversible addition of phosphate groups is involved, catalysed by two enzymes. These initial findings led to the discovery of the cascade of enzymes that switches on glycogen phosphorylase and other enzymes under the influence of hormones such as glucagon and adrenaline (epinephrine). Similar systems controlled by other activators were also subsequently discovered. With Fischer, Krebs was awarded the 1992 Nobel prize for physiology or medicine.

### Sir Hans Adolf Krebs, 1900–81

British biochemist, born in Hildesheim, Germany. In 1932 he described the urea cycle whereby carbon dioxide and ammonia form urea in the presence of liver slices. Leading on from his earlier work, he elucidated the citric acid cycle (Krebs' cycle) of energy production (see **Cells: Respiration**). He also carried out studies on acid oxidase, L-glutamine synthetase, purine synthesis in birds, and ketone bodies. In 1953 he shared with Fritz Lipmann the Nobel prize for physiology or medicine for his discovery of the citric acid cycle.

### Sir Harold Walter Kroto, 1939–

English chemist, born in Wisbech. He is noted for his work in detecting unstable molecules through the use of methods such as microwave and photoelectron spectroscopy, including the study of molecules which exist in space. However, he is best known for his 1985 discovery of the third allotrope of carbon $C_{60}$, known as 'buckminsterfullerene' (familiarly 'buckyballs'), because its 'football' shape resembles the buildings designed by the architect Buckminster Fuller. Kroto worked with **Robert Curl** and **Richard Smalley** on buckyballs, and in 1996 they shared the Nobel prize for chemistry.

### Jean-Baptiste Pierre Antoine de Monet Chevalier de Lamarck, 1744–1829

French naturalist and evolutionist, born in Bazentin. He lectured on zoology, originating the taxonomic distinction between vertebrates and invertebrates, and proposed early ideas on evolution and variation. In *Philosophie zoologique* (1809, 'Zoological philosophy') he suggested that characters acquired during the lifetime of one organism can be inherited by its offspring and later generations. Although this view was disproved by **Darwin**, Lamarck's ideas are considered to be the precursor to the theory of evolution by natural selection, as he recognized that species need to adapt to survive environmental changes.

### Hubert Horace Lamb, 1913–97

English climatologist, born in Bedford. Throughout World War II he produced weather forecasts for transatlantic flights. His expertise in analysing weather charts led to two major achievements: the production of a daily weather classification for Great Britain for each day from 1861, and a study of major volcanic eruptions since 1500. This work has been invaluable in climate change studies. He helped to establish the Climatic Research Unit at the University of East Anglia in 1973, which uncovered much detail about past climates and the way people lived in those times. His major publication has been *Climate, Present, Past and Future* (2 Vols, 1972, 1977).

### Karl Landsteiner, 1868–1943

US pathologist, born in Vienna, Austria. Landsteiner showed that all human blood groups can be grouped in terms of the presence or absence of antigens (A and B) in the red cells, and the corresponding antibodies in the serum (see **Human body: Blood**). He won the 1930 Nobel prize for physiology or medicine for his valuable discovery of the four major human blood groups (A, B, AB, O) which he discovered in 1901, and the M and N groups (discovered in 1927). In 1940 he also discovered the rhesus (Rh) factor. Other blood group systems have since been found.

### Pierre Simon, Marquis de Laplace, 1749–1827

French mathematician and astronomer, born in Beaumont-en-Auge. His astronomical work culminated in the publication of the five monumental volumes of *Mécanique céleste* (1799–1825, 'Celestial mechanics'), the greatest work on celestial mechanics since **Newton**'s *Principia*. He proposed in his famous nebular hypothesis of planetary origin that the solar system originated as a massive cloud of gas, and that the centre collapsed to form the Sun, leaving outer remnants which condensed to form the planets. He also formulated the fundamental differential equation in physics that bears his name, and made important contributions to the theory of probability.

### Antoine Laurent Lavoisier, 1743–94

French chemist, born in Paris. Following up work by **Joseph Priestley**, he showed that air is a mixture of gases, identifying both oxygen and nitrogen, and deduced the importance of oxygen in respiration, combustion and in compounds with metals. He devised the modern method of naming chemical compounds, and helped to introduce the metric system. Lavoisier's genius for meticulous experiment distinguished all his work, and his influence on quantitative chemical method was as far reaching as his actual discoveries. Despite a lifetime of work for the state, inquiring into the problems of taxation (which he helped to reform), hospitals and prisons, he was guillotined as a government tax-collector during the French Revolution.

### Ernest Orlando Lawrence, 1901–58

US physicist, born in Canton, South Dakota. In 1929 he constructed the first cyclotron particle accelerator for the production of artificial radioactivity, which was fundamental to the development of the atomic bomb. He was professor at Berkeley, California, from 1930, and in 1936 was appointed as the first Director of the Berkeley Radiation Laboratory (later renamed the Lawrence Berkeley Radiation Laboratory). He received the Nobel prize for physics in 1939. Element 103 was named lawrencium after him.

### Louis Seymour Bazett Leakey, 1903–72

English archaeologist and physical anthropologist, born in Kabete, Kenya. His great discoveries of early hominid fossils took place at Olduvai Gorge in East Africa. He and his wife, **Mary Leakey**, discovered the remains of many hominids, including the skull of *Zinjanthropus* (later reclassified as a form of *Australopithecus*) and the remains of *Homo habilis*, a smaller species some 2 million years old. The latter led him to postulate the simultaneous evolution of two different species, of which *Homo habilis* was the true ancestor of man, while *Australopithecus* became extinct. Leakey's findings established East Africa as the possible birthplace of man, and traced human ancestry further back than had been possible previously. His son Richard is a noted East African palaeoanthropologist.

### Mary Douglas Leakey, née Nicol, 1913–96

English archaeologist, born in London. Her interest in prehistory was roused during childhood trips to south-western France, where she collected stone tools and visited the painted caves around Les Eyzies. She and her husband, **Louis Leakey**, made major archaeological discoveries in Kenya. These included finding *Proconsul africanus* (1948), a 1.7 million-year-old dryopithecine (primitive ape), and the 1.75 million-year-old hominid *Zinjanthropus* (later reclassified as a form of *Australopithecus*), which was filmed as it happened. In 1976 at Laetoli, 30 miles (48.3km) south of Olduvai, she made the remarkable discovery of three trails of fossilized hominid footprints. These demonstrated unequivocally that our ancestors already walked upright 3.6 million years ago.

### Henrietta Swan Leavitt, 1868–1921

US astronomer, born in Lancaster, Massachusetts. She was a volunteer research assistant at Harvard College Observatory and joined the staff there in 1902, quickly becoming head of the department of photographic photometry. Whilst studying Cepheid variable stars, she noticed that the brighter they were, the longer their period of light variation. By 1912 she had succeeded in showing that the apparent magnitude decreased linearly with the logarithm of the period. This simple relationship proved invaluable as the basis for a method of measuring the distance of stars.

### Joshua Lederberg, 1925–

US biologist and geneticist, born in Montclair, New Jersey. With **Edward Tatum**, he showed that bacteria can reproduce by a sexual process known as conjugation, in which a new strain has the characteristics of both parents. He made a further fundamental contribution with his description of 'transduction' in bacteria, whereby a virus transfers small amounts of DNA from one host bacterium into another. This study led to the development of techniques for manipulation of genes. In 1958 he was awarded the Nobel prize for physiology or medicine, jointly with Tatum and **George Beadle**.

### Tsung-Dao Lee, 1926–

US physicist, born in Shanghai, China. He was educated at Jiangxi (Kiangsi) and at Zhejiang (Chekiang) University. He won a scholarship to Chicago in 1946, became a lecturer at the University of California, and from 1956 was professor at Columbia University, as well as a member of the Institute for Advanced Study (1960–63). With **Chen Ning Yang** he disproved the parity principle of the symmetry of subatomic particles, until then considered a fundamental physical law, and they were awarded the Nobel prize for physics in 1957.

### Antoni van Leeuwenhoek, 1632–1723

Dutch amateur scientist, born in Delft. He was educated as a businessman, and became skilled in grinding and polishing lenses to inspect cloth fibres. With his microscopes, each made for a specific investigation, he discovered the existence of protozoa in water everywhere (1674) and bacteria in the tartar of teeth (1676). Independently, he discovered blood corpuscles (1674), blood capillaries (1683), striations in skeletal muscle (1682), the structure of nerves (1717) and plant microstructures, among many other observations. He was elected FRS in 1680.

### Gottfried Wilhelm Leibniz, 1646–1716

German mathematician and philosopher, born in Leipzig. He discovered calculus around the same time as **Isaac Newton**. He made original contributions to optics, mechanics, statistics, logic and probability theory; he built calculating machines, and contemplated a universal language; he wrote on history, law and political theory; and his philosophy was the foundation of 18th-century rationalism. A genius, he was remarkable for his encyclopedic knowledge and diverse accomplishments outside the fields of philosophy and mathematics. He died in Hanover without real recognition and with almost all of his work unpublished.

## Sir William Boog Leishman, 1865–1926

Scottish bacteriologist, born in Glasgow. In 1900 he discovered the protozoan parasite (*Leishmania*) responsible for the disease known variously as kala-azar and leishmaniasis. He went on to develop the widely used 'Leishman's stain' for the detection of parasites in the blood. He also made major contributions to the development of various vaccines, particularly those used against typhoid, and it was as a result of his work that mass vaccination was introduced in 1914 for the British army. He was knighted in 1909, and elected FRS in 1910.

## Urbain Jean Joseph Leverrier or Le Verrier, 1811–77

French astronomer, born in St Lô, Normandy. He became teacher of astronomy at the Polytechnique in 1836. His *Tables de Mercure* ('Tables of Mercury') and several memoirs gained him admission to the Academy in 1846. From disturbances in the motions of planets he inferred the existence of an undiscovered planet and calculated the point in the heavens where, a few days afterwards, Neptune was actually discovered by **Johann Gottfried Galle** at Berlin (1846). In 1852 Louis Napoleon (Napoleon III) made him a senator, and in 1854 he became director of the observatory of Paris.

## Rita Levi-Montalcini, 1909–

Italian neuroscientist, born in Turin. Her research has primarily been on chemical factors that control the growth and development of cells. She isolated, from mouse salivary glands, a substance now called nerve growth factor that promotes the development of sympathetic nerves. This work has provided powerful new insights into processes of some neurological diseases and possible repair therapies, into tissue regeneration, and into cancer mechanisms. In 1986 she shared the Nobel prize for physiology or medicine with Stanley Cohen.

## Richard Charles Lewontin, 1929–

US geneticist, born in New York City. His empirical work has involved detailed studies of the genetics of natural populations of the fruit fly species, and has been dominated by what he has termed 'the struggle to measure variation'. The widespread application of his 1966 gel electrophoresis technique resulted in the discovery of large amounts of variation, and indirectly led to the neutral theory of molecular evolution – that at the molecular level, most evolutionary changes result from mutations with no selective advantages. A major figure in the development of population genetics, he has continued to apply technological developments to population genetics problems, carrying out the first study of nucleotide sequence polymorphism in 1983.

## Willard Frank Libby, 1908–80

US chemist, born in Grand Valley, Colorado. He studied and lectured at the University of California at Berkeley, where he became associate professor in 1945. He carried out atom-bomb research (1941–45) on the separation of the isotopes of uranium at Columbia, and was awarded the 1960 Nobel prize for chemistry for his part in the invention of the carbon-14 method of determining the age of an object. He was Professor of Chemistry at California University from 1959 to 1976.

### Carolus Linnaeus, originally Carl von Linné, 1707–78

Swedish naturalist and physician, born in Raceshult. He studied botany at Uppsala University, where he was appointed lecturer in 1730. His major contribution was the introduction of binomial nomenclature of generic and specific names for animals and plants, which permitted the hierarchical organization later known as systematics. His manuscripts and collections are kept at the Linnaean Society in London, established in his honour in 1788. As the founder of modern scientific nomenclature for plants and animals, in his time he had a uniquely influential position in natural history.

### Li Shizen (Li Shih-chen), 1518–93

Chinese pharmaceutical naturalist and biologist. Regarded as the father of herbal medicine, he produced an encyclopedia of pharmaceutical natural history. The *Ben Cao Gang Mu* (1596, 'Great Pharmacopoeia') took 30 years to complete. It gives an exhaustive description of 1000 plants and 1000 animals, and includes more than 11 000 prescriptions. It is much more than a pharmacopoeia, however, as it treats mineralogy, metallurgy, physiology, botany and zoology as sciences in their own right. He also recorded many instances of the sophistication of Chinese medicine, for example the use of mercury-silver amalgam for tooth fillings, not introduced to Europe until the 19th century; and adopted a system of priority in naming plants and animals.

### Joseph, 1st Baron Lister, 1827–1912

English surgeon, born in Upton. The introduction of Lister's antiseptic system (1867) revolutionized modern surgery. Inspired by **Louis Pasteur**'s work on microorganisms, Lister began soaking his instruments and surgical gauzes in carbolic acid, a well-known disinfectant. His early antiseptic work was primarily concerned with the operative reduction of compound fractures and the excision of tuberculous joints. Both conditions would previously have been treated with amputation, since the operation mortality for conservative surgical treatment would have been very high. Surgical mortality was greatly reduced when Listerian procedures were employed during surgery. He was the first medical man to be elevated to the peerage.

### Sir (Joseph) Norman Lockyer, 1836–1920

English astronomer, born in Rugby. In 1868 he designed a spectroscope for observing solar prominences outside a total eclipse, and in the same year he postulated the existence of an unknown element which he named helium (the 'Sun element'), an element not found on Earth until 1895 by **William Ramsay**. He also discovered and named the solar chromosphere. His research gave rise to unconventional ideas such as his theory of dissociation, whereby atoms were believed to be capable of further subdivision, and his meteoritic hypothesis which postulated the formation of stars out of meteoric material. The founder (1869) and first editor of the scientific periodical *Nature*, he was knighted in 1897.

### Hendrik Antoon Lorentz, 1853–1928

Dutch physicist, born in Arnhem. He contributed greatly to the theory of the electron and of electromagnetism. His derivation in 1904 of a mathematical transformation, the 'Fitzgerald–Lorentz contraction', explained the apparent absence of relative motion between the Earth and the (supposed) ether, and prepared the way for **Albert Einstein**'s theories of relativity. He explained, with **Pieter Zeeman**, the Zeeman effect, whereby atomic spectral lines are split in the presence of magnetic fields (1896). For this research Lorentz and Zeeman were awarded the 1902 Nobel prize for physics.

### Konrad Zacharias Lorenz, 1903–89

Austrian zoologist and ethologist, born in Vienna. He founded with **Nikolaas Tinbergen** the science of ethology in the 1930s. Rather than studying animal learning in laboratories, Lorenz and his colleagues made a point of investigating the behaviour of animals in the wild. They mainly studied the behaviour of birds, fish and some insects, and made comparisons between the species. His studies have led to a deeper understanding of behaviour patterns. In 1935 he published his observations on imprinting in young birds (the discovery for which he is chiefly known), by which hatchlings 'learn' to recognize substitute parents at the earliest stages in life. He shared the 1973 Nobel prize for physiology or medicine with Tinbergen and **Karl von Frisch**.

### (Augusta) Ada, Countess of Lovelace, née Byron, 1815–52

English writer and mathematician, born in London. The daughter of Lord Byron, she taught herself geometry, and was educated in astronomy and mathematics. She translated and annotated an article on **Charles Babbage**'s analytical engine written by an Italian mathematician, L F Menabrea, adding many explanatory notes of her own. The 'Sketch of the Analytical Engine' (1843) is an important source on Babbage's work. The high-level universal computer programming language, ADA, was named in her honour, and is said to realize several of her insights into the working of a computer system.

### Sir (Alfred Charles) Bernard Lovell, 1913–

English astronomer, born in Oldham Common. He was a pioneer in the use of radar to detect meteors and day-time meteor showers. In 1950 he discovered that the rapid oscillations in the detected intensity (or 'scintillations') of signals from galactic radio sources were produced by the Earth's ionosphere, and were not intrinsic to the sources. From 1958 Lovell collaborated with Fred Whipple in the study of flare stars. He has written several books on radio astronomy and on its relevance to life and civilization today. Elected FRS in 1955, he was knighted in 1961.

### James Ephraim Lovelock, 1919–

English chemist, born in Letchworth. He invented the 'electron capture detector' (1958), a high-sensitivity device which was used in the first, and most subsequent, measurements of the accumulation of CFCs (or chlorofluorocarbons) in the atmosphere. In 1972 he put forward his controversial 'Gaia' hypothesis, which proposes that the Earth's climate is constantly regulated by plants and animals, to maintain a life-sustaining balance of organic substances in the atmosphere (see **Key concepts: The Gaia hypothesis**). Gaia is now regarded as an evolving system comprising the atmosphere, oceans, surface rocks and living organisms, which behaves as a superorganism. He was awarded the CBE in 1990.

### Percival Lowell, 1855–1916

US astronomer, born in Boston. He established the Flagstaff (Lowell) Observatory in Arizona (1894) and is best known for his observations of Mars, which resulted in a series of maps showing linear features crossing the surface. He popularized his ideas in a series of books which include *Mars and its Canals* (1906). He is known for his prediction of the brightness and position of a planet that was supposedly responsible for the orbital perturbation of Neptune and Uranus. This he called planet X. In 1930, 14 years after his death, Pluto was found (discovered by **Clyde William Tombaugh**).

## (Thomas) Martin Lowry, 1874–1936

English chemist, born in Bradford. In 1920 he was the first chair of physical chemistry at Cambridge. His earliest researches were on the changes in optical rotation (mutarotation) which occur when camphor derivatives are treated with acids or bases, leading ultimately to his redefinition of the terms acid and base (1923). He also worked extensively on optical rotatory dispersion, foreshadowing its importance many years later as a structural tool in organic chemistry. He was elected FRS in 1914, and from 1928 to 1930 was president of the Faraday Society.

## André Michel Lwoff, 1902–94

French microbiologist, born in Ainy-le-Château. Of Russian–Polish extraction, he researched the genetics of bacterial viruses (phage), studying their behaviour in a bacterial cell. His findings have had important implications for the development of drug resistance and for cancer research. In 1965 Lwoff was awarded the Nobel prize for physiology or medicine jointly with **François Jacob** and **Jacques Monod**, for their discoveries concerning genetic control of enzyme and virus synthesis.

## Sir Charles Lyell, 1797–1875

Scottish geologist, born in Kinnordy. He established the fundamental principle of uniformitarianism in geology, which is the view that geological changes have been gradual and produced by forces still at work, not by catastrophic changes (see **Key concepts: Uniformitarianism**). His work significantly influenced **Charles Darwin**, although Lyell never accepted the theory of evolution by natural selection. Lyell's publications include *The Elements of Geology* (1838) and *The Geological Evidence of the Antiquity of Man* (1863). He was knighted in 1848.

## Donald Lynden-Bell, 1935–

English astrophysicist, born in Dover. In 1962 Lynden-Bell identified the Population II stars, which contain few metals and have little net motion around the centre of our galaxy. He pioneered the study of the dynamic evolution of the centres of globular clusters, and in 1969 was the first to propose that the cores of galaxies might contain supermassive black holes. His 1985 review of galactic structure meant that the distance to the centre of the galaxy was changed from 100 000 to 85 000 parsecs. He received the Royal Astronomical Society's Eddington Medal in 1984, was elected Fellow of the Royal Society in 1978 and awarded its gold medal in 1993.

## Mary Frances Lyon, 1925–

English biologist, born in Norwich. Her name is particularly associated with the 'Lyon hypothesis' (1961). She suggested that one of the two X chromosomes in female mammals is inactivated in early development, so that females are in effect mosaics of different genetic cell lines (characterized by which of the X chromosomes is switched off). This idea, widely confirmed, has greatly helped studies on clinical genetics and imprinting. Through her work on mouse genetic compilations, she demonstrated the immense value of mouse genetics in helping us to understand the mammalian genome and to tackle the problems of hereditary disease. She was elected a Fellow of the Royal Society in 1973 and was awarded its Royal Medal in 1984.

### Trofim Denisovich Lysenko, 1898–1976

Soviet geneticist and agricultural biologist, born in Karlovka. During the famines of the early 1930s, he promoted 'vernalization', suggesting that plant growth could be accelerated by short exposures to low temperatures. His techniques seemed to offer a rapid way of overcoming the food shortages then prevailing, and gained him political support. In 1935 he developed a theory of genetics which suggested that environment can alter the hereditary material. He pronounced the Mendelian theory of heredity to be wrong, ruthlessly silencing scientists who opposed him. After Stalin's death in 1956, Lysenko increasingly lost support and was forced to resign in 1965.

### Ernst Mach, 1838–1916

Austrian physicist and philosopher, born in Turas, Moravia. His findings on supersonic projectiles and on the flow of gases have proved to be of great importance in aeronautical design and the science of projectiles. His name has been given to the ratio of the speed of flow of a gas to the speed of sound (Mach number) and to the angle of a shock wave to the direction of motion (Mach angle). His writings greatly influenced **Einstein** and laid the foundations of logical positivism.

### Barbara McClintock, 1902–92

US geneticist, born in Hartford, Connecticut. Her work on the chromosomes of maize provided the ultimate proof of the chromosome theory of heredity. In the 1940s she showed how genes can control other genes, and can be copied from chromosome to chromosome. It was not until the 1970s that her work began to be appreciated, and finally in 1983 she was awarded the Nobel prize for physiology or medicine. Her work on promoter and suppressor genes was extended by **Jacques Monod** in the 1960s.

### John James Rickard Macleod, 1876–1935

Scottish physiologist, born in Cluny. He published many papers on the control of respiration, and on aspects of carbohydrate metabolism, but his fame rests upon his involvement with the discovery of insulin. With **Sir Frederick Grant Banting** and a student, **Charles Best**, they succeeded in purifying a pancreatic extract that lowered blood sugar levels. The extract was insulin, and insulin therapy soon became the main treatment for diabetes. In 1923 Macleod and Banting were awarded the Nobel prize for physiology or medicine.

### Edwin Mattison McMillan, 1907–91

US atomic scientist, born in Redondo Beach, California. In 1940, with the help of his assistant Philip Hauge Abelson, he synthesized an element heavier than uranium by bombarding uranium with neutrons. They called this new silvery metal 'neptunium'. McMillan obtained evidence that the radioactive neptunium decayed to form a new element, plutonium. However, it was **Glenn Theodore Seaborg** who synthesized plutonium, which facilitated the development of the atomic bomb. McMillan was awarded the Nobel prize for chemistry, jointly with Seaborg, in 1951.

### Marcello Malpighi, 1628–94

Italian anatomist, born near Bologna. An early pioneer of animal and plant histology, he conducted microscopic studies of the structure of the liver, lungs, skin, spleen, glands and brain. He showed that the lung was linked to the venous system on one side and to the arterial system on the other, corroborating the insights of **William Harvey**. He also discovered capillary blood vessels, gave the first full account of an insect, the silkworm moth, and investigated muscular cells. In plant anatomy, he discovered stomata in leaves and delineated the formation of the plant embryo.

### Gideon Algernon Mantell, 1790–1852

English palaeontologist, born in Lewes. A practising surgeon, he studied the local geology and collected many fossils which were put on show to the public. His collection was sold to the British Museum in 1838. He discovered several dinosaur types, including the first to be fully described; noting the similarity between the fossil teeth and those of the living iguana, he named it 'Iguanodon'. In 1831 he introduced the notion of the 'age of reptiles', one of the earliest pictorial representations of which was produced by the celebrated artist John Martin (1789–1819) for Mantell's *The Wonders of Geology* (1838).

### Guglielmo, Marchese Marconi, 1874–1937

Italian physicist and inventor, born in Bologna. He was educated for a short time at the Technical Institute of Livorno, but mainly by private tutors, and started experimenting with a device to convert electromagnetic waves (recently discovered by **Heinrich Hertz**) into electricity. His first successful experiments in wireless telegraphy were made at Bologna in 1895, and in 1898 he transmitted signals across the English Channel. In 1899 he erected a wireless station at La Spezia, but failed to win the support of the Italian government and decided to establish the Marconi Telegraph Company in London. He succeeded in sending Morse code signals across the Atlantic in 1901. He also developed short-wave radio equipment and established a worldwide radio telegraph network for the British government. For the development of wireless telegraphy, Marconi was joint winner of the 1909 Nobel prize for physics.

### Lynn Margulis, née Alexander, 1938–

US biologist, born in Chicago. Her most important work deals with the origin of eukaryotic cells (cells with nuclei) and the role of symbiosis in cell evolution. She has written numerous popular science books on the origin of life, the development of sex, and global ecology, many with her son Dorion Sagan. She collaborated with **James Lovelock** on the Gaia hypothesis (see **Key concepts: The Gaia hypothesis**). In 1999 she was awarded the US National Medal of Science.

### Andrei Andreyevich Markov, 1856–1922

Russian mathematician, born in Ryazan. He worked on number theory, continued fractions, the moment problem, and the law of large numbers in probability theory. He is best known for originating the process called the Markov chain where, in a sequence of events, the probability of a given event occurring depends only on the immediately previous event. He applied this idea to a text by the Russian writer

Alexander Pushkin but his method has since found many applications in physics and biology.

## O(thniel) C(harles) Marsh, 1831–99

US palaeontologist, born in Lockport, New York. Marsh discovered (mainly in the Rocky Mountains) over a thousand species of extinct American vertebrates, including dinosaurs and the mammals known as uintatheres and brontotheres. By 1874 he was able to establish an evolutionary lineage for horses, using the fossil remains which he had assembled. He also contributed to the documentation of evolutionary changes with his discovery of Cretaceous birds with teeth. His major contribution to stratigraphic palaeontology was an early discussion of the Miocene–Pliocene boundary.

## James Clerk Maxwell, 1831–79

Scottish physicist, born in Edinburgh. At the age of 15 he devised a method for drawing oval curves which was published by the Royal Society of Edinburgh. His *Treatise on Electricity and Magnetism* (1873) treated mathematically **Michael Faraday**'s theory of electrical and magnetic forces and provided the first conclusive evidence that light consisted of electromagnetic waves, which he suggested could be generated in a laboratory (see **Energy, light and radioactivity: Electromagnetic radiation**). He also worked on the kinetic theory of gases, theoretically established the nature of Saturn's rings, investigated colour perception and demonstrated colour photography with a picture of tartan ribbon. In the field of mechanics, his theory of electromagnetism stands alongside the achievements of **Newton** and **Einstein**.

## John Maynard Smith, 1920–2004

English geneticist and evolutionary biologist, born in London. He developed a new phase of the mathematical understanding of evolutionary processes. In particular, he extended **William Donald Hamilton**'s inclusive fitness concept through the application of game theory to behavioural ecology. His later research has focused on mutations and recombination in human mitochondrial DNA. His popular book, the *Theory of Evolution* (1958), was widely influential. He was elected FRS in 1977.

## Margaret Mead, 1901–78

US anthropologist, born in Philadelphia. She studied sexual behaviour and the rites of adolescence in traditional communities in Samoa and New Guinea. In her later work, she argued that personality characteristics, especially as they differ between men and women, are shaped by cultural conditioning rather than heredity. Her work often focused on the relativity of values from culture to culture and implicitly suggested the need to question social standards in the USA and other 'civilized' nations. Her work was criticized by Derek Freeman in *Margaret Mead and Samoa, The Making and Unmaking of an Anthropological Myth* (1983).

## Sir Peter Brian Medawar, 1915–87

British zoologist and immunologist, born in Rio de Janeiro, Brazil. Of English–Lebanese parents, he studied zoology at Magdalen College, Oxford. He pioneered experiments in skin grafting and investigated the problems of tissue rejection in transplant operations. In 1960 he shared the Nobel prize for physiology or medicine with **Sir Macfarlane Burnet** for research into immunological tolerance. They showed that prenatal injection of tissues from one individual to another resulted in the acceptance of the donor's tissues. He was elected FRS in 1949 and knighted in 1965.

## Lise Meitner, 1878–1968

Austrian physicist, born in Vienna. She discovered the radioactive element protactinium in 1917 with **Otto Hahn**. In 1938 she fled to Sweden to escape the Nazis, and shortly afterwards Hahn wrote to her concerning his discovery of radioactive barium. With her nephew **Otto Frisch**, she proposed that the production of barium was the result of nuclear fission, later verified by Frisch. She declined to work on the atomic bomb, hoping that the project would prove impossible. Nuclear physicists recently named the element of atomic number 109 after her.

## Gregor Johann Mendel, 1822–84

Austrian biologist and botanist, born near Udrau. He was appointed abbot in 1868. In the experimental garden of the monastery, he researched the inheritance characteristics of plants. He crossed species that produced tall and short plants, and the resulting numbers of tall and short plants in subsequent generations led him to suggest that each plant received one character from each of its parents, tallness being 'dominant', and shortness being 'recessive' or hidden, appearing only in later generations. His experiments led to the formulation of 'Mendel's law of segregation' and his 'law of independent assortment' (see **Key concepts: Mendel's laws of genetic inheritance**). His concepts have become the basis of modern genetics.

## Dmitri Ivanovich Mendeleev, 1834–1907

Russian chemist, born in Tobolsk. He drew up the periodic table (see **Atoms, elements and molecules: Periodic table**). In 1869 he tabulated the elements in ascending order of their atomic weight and found that chemically similar elements tended to fall into the same columns. Mendeleev's great achievement was to realize that certain elements still had to be discovered and to leave gaps in the table where he predicted they would fall. Later he noted that the 63 known elements exhibited a striking pattern (or 'periodicity' as Mendeleev termed it), with families of elements all having atomic weights which varied by integer multiples of eight times the atomic weight of hydrogen. (The underlying reason would not become clear until the structure of the atom was discovered.) Element 101 was named mendelevium after him.

## Albert Abraham Michelson, 1852–1931

US physicist, born in Strelno (now Strzelno, Poland). He developed optical devices and measurement methods of great accuracy that were useful for a variety of purposes in physics. He invented the interferometer to carry out the famous Michelson–Morley experiment (with **Edward Morley**) which confirmed the non-existence of 'ether', a result which set **Einstein** on the road to the theory of relativity. In 1898 he invented the echelon grating, an ultra-high-resolution device for the study and measurement of hyperfine spectra. He became the first US scientist to win a Nobel prize in 1907 (for physics).

## Robert Andrews Millikan, 1868–1953

US physicist, born in Illinois. He refined **J J Thomson**'s oil drop technique, and was able to show that the charge on each droplet was always a multiple of the same basic unit – the charge on the electron – which he measured very precisely. In studies of the photoelectric effect he confirmed **Einstein**'s theoretical equations and gave an accurate value for **Planck**'s constant. For determining the charge on the electron, he was awarded the 1923 Nobel prize for physics. He also investigated cosmic rays, a term that he coined in 1925.

### Cesar Milstein, 1927–2002

British molecular biologist and immunologist, born in Bahía Blanca, Argentina. With **Georges Köhler**, he devised the hybridoma technique for the production of monoclonal antibodies. This technique has become widespread in the commercial development of new drugs and diagnostic tests, and in 1984 it won Milstein, Köhler and **Niels Jerne** the Nobel prize for physiology or medicine.

### Maria Mitchell, 1818–89

US astronomer, born in Nantucket, Massachusetts. She worked as a librarian on the island while observing the skies at night. Upon discovering a new comet in 1847, she became the first woman to be elected to the American Academy of Arts and Sciences. Her first professional commission was the computing of tables of the planet Venus for the *American Ephemerides and Nautical Almanac*, a duty she performed for 20 years.

### August Ferdinand Möbius, 1790–1868

German mathematician, born in Schulpforta. He extended Cartesian coordinate methods to projective geometry, and gave a straightforward algebraic account of statics, using vectorial quantities before vectors as such entered mathematics. In topology he investigated which surfaces can exist, and became one of the discoverers of the 'Möbius strip' (a one-sided surface formed by giving a rectangular strip a half-twist and then joining the ends together).

### Jacques Lucien Monod, 1910–76

French biochemist, born in Paris. He worked closely with **François Jacob** on genetic control mechanisms, developing the theory of the operon system, whereby a regulator gene controls other genes by binding to a specific section of the DNA strand. In 1965 they shared the Nobel prize for physiology or medicine with **André Lwoff**. Monod published *Chance and Necessity* in 1970, a biologically-based philosophy of life.

### Luc Montagnier, 1932–

French molecular biologist, born in Chabris. He has published widely in molecular biology and virology, and is now credited with the discovery of the HIV virus. He and his team first isolated it from a Frenchman with AIDS in 1983. Montagnier holds the controversial view that mycoplasms (bacteria-like organisms) might play a crucial part in the progression from HIV infection to symptomatic AIDS.

### Edward Williams Morley, 1838–1923

US chemist and physicist, born in Newark, New Jersey. He had a passionate concern for precise measurement, and worked on measuring the oxygen content of the atmosphere. His later research interests involved collaborative studies with physicists, notably with **Albert Michelson** on the velocity of light and the 'ether drift' problem. Their experiment on velocity showed that the hypothetical medium in space, 'ether', did not exist.

### Ben(jamin) Roy Mottelson, 1926–

Danish physicist, born in Chicago, USA. He worked with **Aage Bohr** on the problem of combining the two models of the atomic nucleus, and they secured experimental evidence in support of **James Rainwater**'s collective model. From 1953 to 1957 Mottelson held a research position in CERN (Conseil Européen pour la Recherche Nucléaire) before returning to Copenhagen where he became professor at NORDITA (Nordic Institute for Theoretical Atomic Physics). Bohr, Mottelson and Rainwater shared the 1975 Nobel prize for physics.

### Kary Banks Mullis, 1944–

US biochemist, born in Lenoir, North Carolina. He developed a technique known as the 'polymerase chain reaction' (PCR), which allows tiny quantities of DNA to be copied millions of times to make analysis practical. It is now used in a multitude of applications, including tests for the HIV virus and the bacteria that cause tuberculosis, in forensic science and in evolutionary studies of the genetic material in fossils. For this work Mullis was awarded the 1993 Nobel prize for chemistry (with **Michael Smith**).

### John Napier, 1550–1617

Scottish mathematician, born in Edinburgh. He is famous for the invention of logarithms to simplify computation. His system used the natural logarithm base e, but was modified soon after by **Henry Briggs** to use base 10. He is also famous for devising a calculating machine using a set of rods, known as 'Napier's Bones'. A strict Presbyterian, he published religious works and believed in astrology and divination, and for defence against Philip II of Spain he devised warlike machines (including primitive tanks).

### Walther Hermann Nernst, 1864–1941

German physical chemist, born in Briesen, West Prussia. He was a pioneer of chemical thermodynamics, developing the important theory of electrode potential and the concept of solubility product. He devised experimental methods for measuring the dielectric constant, pH, and other physico-chemical quantities. In 1906 he enunciated his heat theorem, which has come to be regarded as a statement of the third law of thermodynamics (see **Key concepts: The laws of thermodynamics**). This enables equilibrium constants for chemical reactions to be calculated from heat data. He received the Nobel prize for chemistry in 1920.

### Sir Isaac Newton, 1642–1727

English scientist and mathematician, born in Woolsthorpe. In 1665 or 1666 he contemplated the fall of an apple in his mother's garden, which led him to begin formulating the law of gravitation. By 1684 he had demonstrated the whole gravitation theory, which he expounded first in *De Motu Corporum in Gyrum* (1684, 'On the motion of bodies in an orbit'). Newton showed that the force of gravity between two bodies, such as the Sun and the Earth, is directly proportional to the product of the masses of the bodies and inversely proportional to the square of the distance between them. He described this more completely in his greatest work, the *Philosophiae Naturalis Principia Mathematica* (1687, 'Mathematical

Principles of Natural Philosophy'), in which he stated his three laws of motion (see **Key concepts: Newton's laws of motion**). He also discovered the binomial theorem, carried out important work in optics, concluding that the different colours of light making up white light have different refrangibility, developed the reflecting telescope, and invented differential calculus and the method of fluxions. His work gave mathematical expression to physical phenomena and permanently altered modern thought.

### Charles Jules Henri Nicolle, 1866–1936

French physician and microbiologist, born in Rouen. He and his colleagues worked on the spread, prevention and treatment of a number of diseases, including leishmaniasis, toxoplasmosis, Malta fever and typhus. His discovery that typhus is spread by lice (1909) had important implications during World War I and led to his award, in 1928, of the Nobel prize for physiology or medicine.

### Marshall Warren Nirenberg, 1927–

US biochemist, born in New York City. He deciphered the 'code dictionary', or the genetic code (see **Genetics: Genetic code**), of DNA and RNA by utilizing an approach which involved synthesizing a nucleic acid with a known base sequence, and then finding which amino acid it converted to protein. With his success, **Har Gobind Khorana** and others soon completed the task of deciphering the full code. In 1968 Nirenberg, Khorana and **Robert Holley** shared the Nobel prize for physiology or medicine for this work.

### (Amalie) Emmy Noether, 1882–1935

German mathematician, born in Erlangen. Expelled by the Nazi regime from working at the university of Göttingen for being Jewish (and where as a woman she could only work in a semi-honorary capacity), she emigrated to the USA in 1933. She was one of the leading figures in the development of abstract algebra, working in ring theory and the theory of ideals. The theory of Noetherian rings has been an important subject of later research, and she developed it to provide a neutral setting for problems in algebraic geometry and number theory.

### Hideyo Noguchi, 1876–1928

US bacteriologist, born in Inawashiro, Japan. At the Rockefeller Institute in New York City he successfully cultured the bacterium which causes syphilis, and devised a diagnostic skin test for the disease using an emulsion of this culture. This earned him the Order of the Rising Sun in his home country in 1915. He went on to show the bacterial cause of Oroya fever, and proved yellow fever to be a disease of viral origin. He contracted yellow fever during his researches in West Africa and died shortly afterwards.

### Sir Paul Maxime Nurse, 1949–

English biologist, born in Norwich. He studied at the universities of Birmingham and East Anglia, with post-doctoral work at Bern, Edinburgh and Sussex. He was knighted in 1999, and in 2001 he shared the Nobel prize for physiology or medicine with **Lee Hartwell** and **Tim Hunt** for their discoveries of key regulators of the cell cycle (see **Cells: Cell cycle**). These discoveries have been impotant in the development of cancer diagnostics .

### Severo Ochoa, 1905–93

US geneticist, born in Luarca, Spain. He studied the enzyme later used for the first synthesis of artificial RNA, and in 1961 adopted **Marshall Nirenberg**'s approach to solving the amino acid genetic code, determining a number of base triplets (see **Genetics: Genetic code**). He also studied the direction of protein synthesis along DNA (1965), and the first amino acid in a peptide sequence (1967). For his contributions to the elucidation of the genetic code he was awarded the 1959 Nobel prize for physiology or medicine, jointly with **Arthur Kornberg**.

### Hans Christian Oersted, 1777–1851

Danish physicist, born in Rudkøbing, Langeland. He discovered in 1820 the magnetic effect produced by an electric current. This paved the way for the electromagnetic discoveries of **André Ampère** and **Michael Faraday**, and the development of the galvanometer, in which Oersted also played a part. He made an extremely accurate measurement of the compressibility of water, and succeeded in isolating aluminium for the first time in 1825.

### Georg Simon Ohm, 1787–1854

German physicist, born in Erlangen, Bavaria. In 1827 he published 'Ohm's law', relating voltage, current and resistance in an electrical circuit (see **Key concepts: Ohm's law**). Neither this nor his work on the recognition of sinusoidal sound waves by the human ear (1843) received immediate recognition. He was awarded the Royal Society's Copley Medal (1841) and was elected a foreign member of the Society in 1842. The SI unit of electrical resistance is named after him.

### Jan Hendrik Oort, 1900–92

Dutch astronomer, born in Franeker. He proved (1927) by observation that our galaxy is rotating, and calculated the distance of the Sun from the centre of the galaxy, initially locating it 300 000 light years away. He also made the first calculation of the mass of galactic material interior to the Sun's orbit. In 1932 he made the first measurement that indicated that there is dark matter in the galaxy. In 1950 he extended Ernst Öpik's suggestion concerning the huge circular reservoir of comets surrounding the solar system. This 'Oort cloud' was the suggested source of long-period comets (see **Space: Comets**).

### (Julius) Robert Oppenheimer, 1904–67

US nuclear physicist, born in New York City. During World War II he led the atomic bomb development project at Los Alamos, and after the war continued to play an important role in US atomic energy policy. From 1947 he promoted peaceful uses of atomic energy and opposed the development of the hydrogen bomb. Considered a security risk by the US government, he was suspended from secret nuclear research in 1953. His work included studies of electron–positron pairs, cosmic ray theory and deuteron reactions. He received the Enrico Fermi award in 1963.

### Sir Richard Owen, 1804–92

English zoologist and palaeontologist, born in Lancaster. He named and reconstructed numerous celebrated fossils, including the giant moa bird *Deinornis* and the earliest bird, *Archaeopteryx*. He coined the term 'dinosaur' ('terrible lizard'). He studied in detail the homologies between apparently dissimilar structures in organisms and drew the crucial distinction between homologous and analogous organs. However, he remained implacably opposed to evolution; for him, homologies were variants on a divine plan or 'archetype', not evidence of common descent. Owen accepted a knighthood in 1884, having previously declined the honour in 1842.

### Sir James Paget, 1814–99

English physician and pathologist, born in Great Yarmouth. One of the founders of modern pathology, he discovered the cause of trichinosis as being a parasitic worm, *Trichina spiralis*. He described 'Paget's disease' (an early indication of breast cancer) and 'Paget's disease of bone' (*osteitis deformans*, a bone inflammation). He was among the first to advocate surgical removal of bone marrow tumours in place of amputation of the affected limb. A hospital in his birthplace was named in his honour.

### George Emil Palade, 1912–

US cell biologist, born in Iassy, Romania. In the 1950s Palade developed a method of separating cell components, known as 'cell fractionation'. He identified the cell components as the mitochondria, the endoplasmic reticulum, the Golgi apparatus and the ribosomes (see **Cells: Cell structure**), and showed that protein synthesis occurs on strands of RNA in the ribosomes (see **Cells: Gene expression**). For his work in cell biology he shared the 1974 Nobel prize for physiology or medicine with **Albert Claude** and **Christian de Duve**.

### George Nicholas Papanicolaou, 1883–1962

US physiologist and microscopic anatomist, born in Kimi, Greece. He discovered that the cells lining the wall of the guinea pig vagina change with the oestrus cycle. Similar changes take place in women but, more importantly, he noticed that he could identify cancer cells from scrapings from the cervixes of women with cervical cancer. He subsequently pioneered the technique, now known as the 'pap smear', of microscopical examination of exfoliated cells for the early detection of cervical and other forms of cancer.

### Paracelsus, real name Philippus Aureolus Theophrastus Bombastus von Hohenheim, 1493–1541

German-Swiss alchemist and physician, born in Einsieden, Switzerland. His name referred to the celebrated Roman physician Celsus and meant 'beyond' or 'better than' Celsus. His work became enormously influential, particularly through the emphasis he laid on observation and experiment and the need to assist – rather than hinder – natural processes. He stated that diseases had external causes and that every disease had its own characteristics, thus reversing the traditional view that disease was generated within the patient and followed an unpredictable course. He discovered many techniques which became standard laboratory practice, prepared drugs with due regard to their purity, and advocated carefully measured doses, all important steps forward in medicine.

### James Parkinson, 1755–1824

English physician and amateur palaeontologist, born in London. In 1817 he gave the first description of *paralysis agitans*, or 'Parkinson's disease' (shaking palsy, a disease characterized by shaking hands and rigidity of muscles). He had already

(1812) described appendicitis and perforation, and was the first to recognize the latter condition as a cause of death.

## Blaise Pascal, 1623–62

French mathematician, physicist, theologian and man of letters, born in Clermont-Ferrand. A young genius, by the age of 11 he had worked out for himself in secret the first 23 propositions of **Euclid**, calling straight lines 'bars' and circles 'rounds'. At the age of 16 he published an essay on conic sections which **René Descartes** refused to believe was the work of a youth; it contains his famous theorem on a hexagram inscribed in a conic section. He later carried out important work in geometry, invented a calculating machine, demonstrated that air pressure decreases with altitude as previously predicted and developed probability theory. The SI unit of pressure (pascal) and the modern computer programming language, *Pascal*, are named after him. After 1654 he gave up mathematics and society to devote himself to religious and philosophical writing.

## Louis Pasteur, 1822–95

French chemist, born in Dôle. He discovered that fermentations are essentially due to organisms, not spontaneous generation. He greatly extended **Theodor Schwann**'s researches on putrefaction, and gave valuable rules for making vinegar and preventing wine disease, introducing in this work the technique of 'pasteurization', a mild and short heat treatment to destroy pathogenic bacteria. His 'germ theory of disease' maintained that disease was communicable through the spread of microorganisms, and he demonstrated that sheep and cows 'vaccinated' with the weakened bacteria of anthrax were protected from the harmful results of subsequent inoculation with the virulent form. He also made possible the prophylactic treatment of diphtheria, tubercular disease, cholera, yellow fever, plague and hydrophobia (rabies). He is regarded as the father of modern bacteriology.

## Wolfgang Pauli, 1900–58

Austrian-Swiss theoretical physicist, born in Vienna. Pauli demonstrated that a fourth 'spin' quantum number was required to describe the state of an atomic electron, and went on to formulate the 'Pauli exclusion principle' (1924), which states that no two electrons in an atom can exist in exactly the same state, with the same quantum numbers (see **Key concepts: Pauli's exclusion principle**). This gave a clear quantum description of electron distribution within different atomic energy states, and earned him the 1945 Nobel prize for physics. He suggested the existence of a low-mass neutral particle (1931), later discovered as the neutrino, and his studies in the early 1950s of quantum interactions paved the way for **Tsung-Dao Lee** and **Chen Ning Yang**'s discovery of parity non-conservation in 1956.

## Linus Pauling, 1901–94

US chemist, born in Portland, Oregon. He greatly illuminated mineral chemistry with his early work on crystal structures (1928). He then turned to the quantum-mechanical treatment of the chemical bond and made many important contributions, including the concept of the 'hybridization of orbitals', central to understanding the shapes of molecules. His contribution to science was exceptional in its range, covering inorganic and organic chemistry, theoretical chemistry and practical devices, work on minerals and in biology. He was awarded the Nobel prize for chemistry in 1954 for his work on molecular structure. A supporter of the peace movement and critic of US nuclear deterrence policy, he also won the Nobel peace prize in 1962.

### Ivan Petrovich Pavlov, 1849–1936

Russian physiologist, born near Ryazan. He studied the physiology of circulation, digestion and 'conditioned' or acquired reflexes, believing that the brain's only function is to couple neurones to produce reflexes. His most famous research showed that if a bell is sounded whenever food is presented to a dog, the dog will eventually begin to salivate when the bell is sounded without food being presented. This he termed a 'conditioned' or acquired reflex. He was awarded the Nobel prize for physiology or medicine in 1904.

### Cecilia Helena Payne-Gaposchkin, née Payne, 1900–79

US astronomer, born in Buckinghamshire, England. Her doctoral thesis, *Stellar Atmospheres* (1925), led to her pioneering work on determining the relative abundances of chemical elements in stars and in space. With her husband and colleague Sergei I Gaposchkin, she identified and measured variable stars on photographic plates, an immense programme which resulted in a catalogue of variable stars published in 1938. They later carried out a similar project on variable stars in the Magellanic Clouds (1971).

### Sir Rudolf Ernst Peierls, 1907–95

British theoretical physicist, born in Berlin, Germany. In 1963 he moved to Oxford University, where he was Wykeham Professor of Physics. He studied the theory of solids and analysed electron motion in them, developed the theory of diamagnetism in metals (see **Electricity and magnets: Magnets**), and in nuclear physics studied the interactions of protons and neutrons. During World War II, Peierls and **Otto Frisch** studied uranium fission, publishing a report in 1940 that showed the possibility of producing an atomic bomb. The British Government appointed Peierls to lead a group in developing ways of separating uranium isotopes and calculating the efficiency of the chain reaction. The work was moved to the USA as part of the combined Manhattan Project (1943).

### Sir Roger Penrose, 1931–

English mathematical astronomer, born in Colchester. He is known for his work on black holes, showing (jointly with **Stephen Hawking**) that, once collapse of a very massive star at the end of its life has started, the formation of a black hole – a point of zero volume and infinite density – is inevitable (see **Space: Black holes**). Penrose also put forward the hypothesis of 'cosmic censorship', proposing that there must be an 'event horizon' around a black hole, isolating its physically unlawful behaviour from the rest of the universe. At Oxford Penrose has been working on 'twistor theory', in which the four dimensions of space-time are quantized by imaginary numbers as opposed to real numbers. He received the Einstein Medal in 1990 and was knighted in 1994.

### Max Ferdinand Perutz, 1914–2002

British biochemist, born in Vienna, Austria. Using the technique of X-ray diffraction, he determined the structure of haemoglobin, showing that it is composed of four chains of molecules. He was joint winner of the 1962 Nobel prize for chemistry. In further studies he predicted the detailed distribution of amino acids in haemoglobin (1964). Following this, Perutz studied the effects of genetic variants, the evolutionary development, and numerous other aspects of haemoglobin.

### Jean Piaget, 1896–1980

Swiss psychologist, born in Neuchâtel. He was a pioneer in the study of child intelligence. He is best known for his research on the development of cognitive functions (perception, intelligence, logic), for his intensive case-study methods of research (using his own children), and for postulating 'stages' of cognitive development. His books include *The Child's Conception of the World* (1926), *The Origin of Intelligence in Children* (1936), and *The Early Growth of Logic in the Child* (1958).

### Gregory Goodwin Pincus, 1903–67

US physiologist, born in Woodbine, New Jersey. In 1951 he began work on developing a contraceptive pill, studying the antifertility effect of those steroid hormones which inhibit ovulation in mammals. Synthetic hormones became available in the 1950s and Pincus organized field trials of their antifertility effects in Haiti and Puerto Rico in 1954. The results were successful, and oral contraceptives ('the pill') have since been widely used, despite concern over some side effects. Their success is a pharmaceutical rarity, showing nearly 100 per cent effectiveness in a specific physiological action, and having remarkable social effects.

### Steven Pinker, 1954–

US psychologist, born in Montreal, Canada. He established his reputation in experimental psychology through his exploration of language, as discussed in such books as *The Language Instinct* (1994), *How the Mind Works* (1997) and *Words and Rules: The Ingredients of Language* (1999). Throughout his work he adopts a strictly evolutionary approach to human behaviour and the development of the brain, inevitably provoking religious and philosophical objections.

### Max Karl Ernst Ludwig Planck, 1858–1947

German theoretical physicist, born in Kiel. His work on the law of thermodynamics and black body radiation led him to abandon classical dynamical principles and formulate the quantum theory (1900), which relied on **Ludwig Boltzmann**'s statistical interpretation of the second law of thermodynamics, and assumed energy changes to take place in small discrete instalments or quanta (see **Key concepts: Quantum theory**). This successfully accounted for and predicted certain phenomena inexplicable in the classical Newtonian theory. **Einstein**'s application of the quantum theory to light (1905) led to the theories of relativity, and in 1913 **Niels Bohr** successfully applied it to the problems of subatomic physics. He was awarded the Nobel prize for physics in 1918.

### (Jules) Henri Poincaré, 1854–1912

French mathematician, born in Nancy. He created the theory of automorphic functions, non-Euclidean geometry and complex functions, and showed the importance of topological considerations in differential equations. Many of the basic ideas in modern topology – such as triangulation, homology, the Euler–Poincaré formula and the fundamental group – are due to him. In a paper on the three-body problem (1889) he opened up new directions in celestial mechanics, and began the study of dynamic systems in the modern sense.

## Joseph Priestley, 1733–1804

English clergyman and chemist, born in Fieldhead. Priestley was a pioneer in the chemistry of gases, and one of the discoverers of oxygen (with **Carl Wilhelm Scheele**). He discovered another ten gases, including hydrogen chloride, sulphur dioxide, ammonia and nitrous oxide (laughing gas). He supported the later discredited phlogiston theory, that substances contain a vital essence which they lose when they burn. His reply to Edmund Burke's *Reflections on the French Revolution* led a Birmingham mob to break into his house and destroy its contents (1791). He then settled in Hackney, London, and moved to the USA in 1794.

## Ptolemy, Latin name Claudius Ptolemaeus, c.90–168 AD

Egyptian astronomer and geographer who lived and worked in Alexandria. He corrected and improved the astronomical work of his predecessors to form the Ptolemaic System, with the Earth at the centre of the Universe and heavenly bodies revolving round it; beyond this lay the sphere of the fixed stars. He also compiled geographical catalogues and maps. His Earth-centred view of the universe dominated cosmological thought until swept aside by **Copernicus** in the 16th century.

## Pythagoras, c.580–c.500 BC

Greek mathematician and philosopher, probably born in Samos. He is associated with mathematical discoveries involving the chief musical intervals, the relations of numbers and the relations between the lengths of sides of right-angled triangles (See **Key concepts: Pythagoras's theorem**). He was founder of the Pythagorean school, whose main belief was in the immortality and transmigration (reincarnation) of the soul. It is impossible to disentangle Pythagoras's own views from the later accretions of mysticism and neoplatonism, but he had a profound influence on Plato and on later philosophers, astronomers and mathematicians.

## (Leo) James Rainwater, 1917–86

US physicist, born in Council, Idaho. He unified two theoretical models of the atomic nucleus. One theory held that the nuclear particles were arranged in concentric shells, while in the other, the nucleus was described as analogous to a liquid drop. He developed the collective model theory together with **Aage Bohr** and **Ben Roy Mottelson** who provided experimental evidence in its support. The three shared the Nobel prize for physics in 1975 for this work. Rainwater also worked on studies of muonic X-rays, and developed an improved theory of high-energy particle scattering.

## Sir Chandrasekhara Venkata Raman, 1888–1970

Indian physicist, born in Trichinopoly, Tamil Nadu. In 1930 he was awarded the Nobel prize for physics for demonstrating that light scattered by molecules will show lower and higher frequency components (the 'Raman effect'). His discovery led to one of the earliest confirmations of quantum theory, and also gave a powerful method of analysing molecular structure ('Raman spectroscopy'). He also researched the vibration of musical instruments and the physiology of vision. He was knighted in 1929 and was influential in building up the study of physics in India.

### Srinivasa Ramanujan, 1887–1920

Indian mathematician, born in Eroda, Madras. A self-taught mathematician, he devised over 100 remarkable theorems which included results on elliptic integrals, partitions and analytic number theory. His most remarkable publication was an exact formula for the number of ways an integer can be written as a sum of positive integers. He arrived at his results by an uncanny form of intuition, often having no idea of how they could be proved or even what the form of an orthodox proof might be.

### Santiago Ramón y Cajal, 1852–1934

Spanish physician and histologist, born in Petilla de Aragon. He carried out important work on the brain and nerves, isolated the neuron and discovered how nerve impulses are transmitted to brain cells. He also worked on the problem of the degeneration and regeneration of nerve cells, on the neuroglia, and on the retina. He was joint winner of the 1906 Nobel prize for physiology or medicine.

### Sir William Ramsay, 1852–1916

Scottish chemist, born in Glasgow. In 1894, he co-discovered argon with **John William Strutt, 3rd Baron Rayleigh**. He also isolated helium, neon, krypton and xenon. Further research confirmed the inert nature of these gases and their atomic weights. In 1908 Ramsay obtained radon in sufficient quantities to show that it belonged to the same family as helium and the other inert gases. In 1904, he was both knighted and awarded the Nobel prize for chemistry.

### John William Strutt, 3rd Baron Rayleigh, 1842–1919

English physicist, born near Maldon. He carried out valuable research on vibratory motion in optics and acoustics, the theory of sound and the wave theory of light. With **Sir William Ramsay** he discovered argon (1894), for which they were both awarded the Nobel prize, Rayleigh for physics and Ramsay for chemistry (1904). Rayleigh's research on radiation led to the Rayleigh–Jeans formula, which accurately predicts the long-wavelength radiation emitted by hot bodies.

### René Antoine Ferchault de Réaumur, 1683–1757

French natural philosopher, born in La Rochelle. He developed improved methods for producing iron and steel, and became one of the greatest naturalists of his age, publishing the first serious and comprehensive work of entomology. His thermometer of 1731 used a mixture of alcohol and water instead of mercury, and was calibrated with a scale (the Réaumur scale) of 80 degrees between the freezing and boiling points of water.

### Walter Reed, 1851–1902

US army surgeon, born in Belroi, Virginia. Much of his work was on epidemic diseases. He was appointed head of a commission to study the cause and transmission of yellow fever in Cuba (1899). His investigations proved that yellow fever in Cuba was transmitted by the female *Aedes aegypti* mosquito. The research led to the eventual eradication of yellow fever from Cuba through the destruction of mosquito breeding grounds.

### Sir Martin John Rees, 1942–

English astrophysicist, born in York. Rees has made important contributions to the study of stellar systems and 'dark matter', and his best-known work is in the study of active galactic nuclei. He demonstrated that the variations in brightness observed in quasars and active galaxies could be best understood if the nuclei contained gas which is outflowing at almost the speed of light. Observational evidence for this appeared in the 1970s. Rees also showed that the strong radio-emitting regions of some galaxies could be produced by beams of particles moving outwards from the nuclei at almost the speed of light. In 1995 he became Astronomer Royal.

### Charles Francis Richter, 1900–85

US seismologist, born near Hamilton, Ohio. In 1932, with **Beno Gutenberg**, he devised the famous Richter scale, the original instrumental scale for determining the energy released by an earthquake. He played a key role in establishing the southern California seismic array and published *Seismicity of the Earth* (1954, with Gutenberg) and *Elementary Seismology* (1958).

### Richard Roberts, 1943–

English molecular biologist, born in Derby. In 1977 he announced his intriguing discovery that genes contain sections of DNA (now known as 'introns') which carry no genetic information. He shared the 1993 Nobel prize for physiology or medicine with **Phillip Sharp**, who had independently come to the same conclusions at about the same time.

### Wilhelm Konrad von Roentgen

see **Wilhelm Konrad von Röntgen or Roentgen**

### Heinrich Rohrer, 1933–

Swiss physicist, born in Buchs. By 1981, he and **Gerd Binnig** had completed making the scanning tunnelling microscope which won them the 1986 Nobel prize for physics (jointly with **Ernst Ruska**). The scanning tunnelling microscope is now found in laboratories around the world, and is especially used in the development of small solid-state electronic devices.

### Wilhelm Konrad von Röntgen or Roentgen, 1845–1923

German physicist, born in Lennep, Prussia (now Remscheid, Germany). In 1895 he discovered the electromagnetic rays which he called X-rays (known also as Röntgen rays), so called because of their unknown properties (see **Energy, light and radioactivity: Electromagnetic radiation**). He was joint winner of the first 1901 Nobel prize for physics for his work on X-rays. He also achieved important results on the heat conductivity of crystals, the specific heat of gases and the magnetic effects produced in dielectrics.

### Sir Ronald Ross, 1857–1932

British physician, born in Almara, Nepal. He discovered the malaria parasite in the stomachs of mosquitoes that had bitten patients suffering from the disease, and by 1898 had worked out the life cycle of the malaria parasite for birds. He was a gifted if eccentric mathematician who also wrote poetry and romances. His award of the 1902 Nobel prize for physiology or medicine was contested by Giovanni

Grassi (1854–1925), an Italian parasitologist who had independently and almost simultaneously worked out the life cycle of the human malaria parasite. Ross was knighted in 1911.

### Dame Miriam Louisa Rothschild, 1908–2005

English naturalist and entomologist, born in Ashton Wold. A world authority on fleas, she worked on the flea jumping mechanism, and discovered that the life and breeding cycle of the rabbit flea is controlled by the sex hormone cycle of its host (1964). In her later years, she turned to the biochemistry of insect communication, being particularly fascinated by the range of highly aromatic pyrazines employed for this purpose. She decoded German wireless messages during World War II, and later became entomological adviser to royalty. Lacking a formal education, her 8 university doctorates were all honorary. She produced over 300 scientific papers, was elected FRS in 1985 and made a Dame in 2000.

### (Francis) Peyton Rous, 1879–1970

US pathologist, born in Baltimore, Maryland. From 1909 he began studying a sarcoma in chickens, which he demonstrated to have been caused by a virus. In the 1930s he discovered a rabbit tumour which was also caused by a virus, and found that coal tar and the virus could stimulate each other in making the tumour malignant. This was the first time that a virus was implicated in cancer, and the discovery of many other oncogenic (cancer-causing) viruses from the 1950s made his early work more widely appreciated. He was joint winner of the 1966 Nobel prize for physiology or medicine.

### (Pierre Paul) Émile Roux, 1853–1933

French bacteriologist, born in Confolens. With **Pasteur** he tested the anthrax vaccine, and contributed much of the early work on the rabies vaccine. He showed that the symptoms of diphtheria are caused by a lethal toxin produced by the diphtheria bacillus; and, following the principles of **Emil von Behring** and **Baron Shibasaburo Kitasato**, he tested on patients large quantities of blood serum containing the antitoxin from horses. As a result the mortality rate fell dramatically. He also made important contributions to research into syphilis.

### Ernst August Friedrich Ruska, 1906–88

German electrical engineer, born in Heidelberg. In 1931 he developed the world's first electron microscope, which he continued to improve in subsequent work. In 1986 he received a share of the Nobel prize for physics, along with the inventors of the scanning tunnelling electron microscope, **Gerd Binnig** and **Heinrich Rohrer**.

### Ernest Rutherford, 1st Baron Rutherford (of Nelson), 1871–1937

New Zealand physicist, born in Brightwater, South Island. He made the first successful wireless transmissions over two miles, discovered three types of uranium radiations, formulated a theory of atomic disintegration and determined the nature of alpha particles; this led to a new atomic model in which the mass is concentrated in the nucleus (see **Atoms, elements and molecules: Atoms**). Rutherford's assistant, **Niels Bohr**, applied to this the quantum theory (1913), and the concept of the 'Rutherford–Bohr atom' of nuclear physics was born. Rutherford also discovered that alpha-ray bombardment could produce atomic transformation, and predicted the existence of the neutron. Regarded as the 'father of nuclear physics', he was awarded the Nobel prize for chemistry in 1908.

### Sir Martin Ryle, 1918–84

English physicist, born in Brighton. He investigated the emission of radio waves from the Sun and improved the low resolving power of radio telescopes. He then turned to studies of radio waves from the universe and found that the numbers of radio sources increased as their intensities decreased (1955), a result which pointed to an evolving universe starting with a Big Bang (see **Key concepts: Big Bang theory**). He mapped radio sources by his ingenious method of 'aperture synthesis'. Knighted in 1966, he received the 1974 Nobel prize for physics with his colleague **Antony Hewish**.

### Albert Bruce Sabin, 1906–93

US microbiologist, born in Bialystok, Russia (now in Poland). After working on developing vaccines against dengue fever and Japanese B encephalitis, he became interested in the polio vaccine and attempted to develop a live attenuated vaccine (as opposed to **Jonas Salk**'s killed vaccine). In 1959, as the result of 4.5 million vaccinations, his vaccine was found to be completely safe; it presented a number of advantages over that of Salk, especially in affording a stronger and longer-lasting immunity and in being suitable for oral administration.

### Carl Edward Sagan, 1934–96

US astronomer, born in New York City. He worked on the physics and chemistry of planetary atmospheres and surfaces. He also investigated the origin of life on Earth and the possibility of extraterrestrial life. He was an active member of the imaging team associated with the *Voyager* space mission to the outer planets, was interested in the concept of the nuclear winter, and had worked on the theoretical calculation of the Venus greenhouse effect. His books helped to popularize astronomy, evolutionary theory and neurophysiology. He was a strong proponent of SETI, the search for extraterrestrial intelligence.

### Andrei Dimitriyevich Sakharov, 1921–89

Soviet physicist, born in Moscow. He took a leading part in the development of the Soviet hydrogen bomb, but during the early 1960s he became increasingly estranged from the Soviet authorities when he campaigned for a nuclear test-ban treaty, peaceful international co-existence and improved civil rights. In 1975 he was awarded the Nobel peace prize, and in 1980 he was sent into internal exile in the 'closed city' of Gorky (now Nizhny Novgorod). Here he undertook a series of hunger strikes in an effort to secure permission for his wife, Yelena Bonner, to receive medical treatment overseas. He was eventually released in 1986 under the personal orders of Mikhail Gorbachev. In 1989 he was elected to the Congress of the USSR People's Deputies.

### Abdus Salam, 1926–96

Pakistani theoretical physicist, born in Jhang, Punjab. In 1979 he was awarded the Nobel prize for physics, with **Steven Weinberg** and **Sheldon Glashow**. Independently each had produced a single unifying theory of both the weak and electromagnetic interactions between elementary particles (see **Key concepts: Theory of everything**). The predictions of the 'electroweak' theory were confirmed experimentally in the 1970s and 1980s. Salam was made an honorary KBE in 1989. His concern for the study of physics in developing countries led to his setting up the International Centre of Theoretical Physics in Trieste in 1964.

### Jonas Edward Salk, 1914–95

US virologist, born in New York City. Some of his early research was on the influenza virus, and in 1954 he became known worldwide for his work on the 'Salk vaccine' against poliomyelitis. His killed virus vaccine had to overcome initial opposition arising from 1935, when killed and attenuated vaccines given to over 10 000 children proved ineffective and unsafe. However, a trial in 1954 showed that Salk's vaccination was 80–90 per cent effective, and by the end of 1955 over 7 million doses had been administered. Later the vaccine was superseded by that developed by **Albert Bruce Sabin**, which used a live attenuated strain and could be given orally instead of by injection. Salk spent the last years of his life researching the HIV virus.

### Frederick Sanger, 1918–

English biochemist, born in Rendcombe. He won the Nobel prize for chemistry in 1958 for deducing the sequence of amino acids in insulin by novel methods. In 1980 (with **Walter Gilbert and Paul Berg**) he won his second Nobel prize in chemistry when he developed a method for sequencing nucleic acids. He was the first scientist to twice win the Nobel prize in the same field. His highly ingenious methods of unravelling the secrets of molecular structures led to the full base sequence of the Epstein–Barr virus in 1984.

### Carl Wilhelm Scheele, 1742–86

Swedish chemist, born in Stralsund (now in Germany). He discovered oxygen, although credit for this went to **Joseph Priestley** because of a delay in publication. He also discovered hydrofluoric acid, chlorine, copper arsenite (known as 'Scheele's green'), hydrogen sulphide, and many important organic acids. In 1781 he distinguished between two very similar minerals, plumbago (graphite) and molybdena, discovering the metal molybdenum in the process. His investigations of plant and animal material were fundamental to the development of organic chemistry.

### Erwin Schrödinger, 1887–1961

Austrian physicist, born in Vienna. He originated the study of wave mechanics as part of the quantum theory with the celebrated Schrödinger wave equation (see **Key concepts: Quantum theory**). P A M Dirac soon developed a more complete theory of quantum mechanics from these foundations, and for this work both Dirac and Schrödinger were awarded the 1933 Nobel prize for physics. Schrödinger also made contributions to field theory. He wrote *What is Life?* (1946) and *Science and Man* (1958).

### Theodor Schwann, 1810–82

German physiologist, born in Neuss. He discovered the enzyme pepsin, investigated muscle contraction, demonstrated the role of microorganisms in putrefaction and extended the cell theory from plants to animal tissues. He also discovered the 'Schwann cells' which lay down the sheath around peripheral nerve axons (see **Human body: The nervous system**). He is famous for his cell theory, proposing that the entire plant or animal is composed of cells, that cells carry out independently the reactions of life, but that the life of the cells is also adapted to benefit and make possible the whole organism.

### Karl Schwarzschild, 1873–1916

German astronomer, born in Frankfurt am Main. He was the first to predict the existence of black holes (see **Space: Black holes**). In 1916, while serving on the Russian front, he wrote two papers on **Einstein**'s general theory of relativity, giving the first solution to the complex partial differential equations of the theory. He also introduced the idea that, when a star contracts under gravity, there will come a point at which the gravitational field is so intense that nothing, not even light, can escape. The radius to which a star of given mass must contract to reach this stage is known as the Schwarzschild radius. Stars that have contracted below this limit are now known as black holes.

### Julian Schwinger, 1918–94

US physicist, born in New York City. Independently of **Richard Feynman** and **Sin-Itiro Tomonaga,** he developed a theory of quantum electrodynamics describing the interaction of light and matter. He was awarded the 1965 Nobel prize for physics jointly with Feynman and Tomonaga for the development of quantum electrodynamics. He went on to study synchrotron radiation.

### Glenn Theodore Seaborg, 1912–99

US atomic scientist, born in Ishpeming, Michigan. It was his laboratory that, in 1945, produced enough plutonium for the first atomic bomb. Seaborg and his team continued research on further transuranic elements and in 1944 synthesized americium and curium. In 1950, by bombarding these with alpha rays, they produced berkelium and californium. They later produced einsteinium, fermium, mendelevium and unnilhexium. In 1951 Seaborg shared the Nobel prize for chemistry with **Edwin McMillan** for discovering plutonium.

### Phillip Allen Sharp, 1944–

US molecular biologist, born in Kentucky. He invented the mapping technique used in the analysis of RNA molecules. This led to the discovery that genes are split into several sections, separated by stretches of DNA ('introns') that appear to carry no genetic information. He was jointly awarded the 1993 Nobel prize for physiology or medicine with **Richard Roberts**.

### Burrhus Frederic Skinner, 1904–90

US psychologist, born in Susquehanna, Pennsylvania. He is famous for his work on animal behaviour, and invented the 'Skinner Box', a chamber containing mechanisms for an animal to operate and an automatic device for presenting rewards. In education, his ideas led to the development of 'programmed learning', a technique which tries to direct teaching to the needs of each individual and to reinforce learning by regular and immediate feedback.

### Richard Errett Smalley, 1943–2005

US chemist, born in Akron, Ohio. He was educated at the University of Michigan and Princeton University, and became director of the Rice Center for Nanoscale Science and Technology in 1996. That same year, he was awarded the Nobel prize for chemistry (with **Robert Curl** and **Harold Kroto**) for his role in the discovery of the carbon $C_{60}$ molecules named 'buckminsterfullerene' (also known as 'buckyballs').

### Michael Smith, 1932–2000

Canadian biochemist, born in Blackpool, England. In 1978 he published his discovery of 'site-specific mutagenesis', a technique which allows scientists to alter the genetic code through mutations induced at specific locations, whereas all previous methods of mutation had produced only random mutations. This new method has allowed the production of a whole new range of proteins with diverse functions. Smith was awarded the 1993 Nobel prize for chemistry jointly with **Kary Mullis**.

### Mary Somerville, née Fairfax, 1780–1872

Scottish mathematician and astronomer, born in Jedburgh. She presented a paper on *The Magnetic Properties of the Violet Rays in the Solar Spectrum* (1826) to the Royal Society. She published *The Mechanism of the Heavens,* which was her account for the general reader of **Pierre Simon Laplace**'s *Mécanique Céleste*. The latter was a great success and she wrote several further expository works on physics, physical geography and microscopic science. She supported the emancipation and education of women, and Somerville College (1879) at Oxford is named after her.

### Sören Peter Lauritz Sörensen, 1868–1939

Danish biochemist, born in Havrabjerg, Slagelsi. In 1909 he described the effects of hydrogen ion concentration on enzyme activity, and introduced the term pH to represent the negative logarithm of the hydrogen ion concentration. By 1923, after several years' research in enzyme activity, he devised the pH scale, arguably the most important single contribution ever made to the life sciences (see **Measurement: Scales**).

### Roger Wolcott Sperry, 1913–44

US neuroscientist, born in Hartford, Connecticut. His experiments helped to establish the means by which nerve cells come to be connected in particular ways in the central nervous system. He established that each hemisphere in the brain possessed specific higher functions, the left side controlling verbal activity and processes such as writing, reasoning, etc, whereas the right side is more responsive to music, face and voice recognition, etc. He was jointly awarded the Nobel prize for physiology or medicine in 1981.

### Patrick Christopher Steptoe, 1913–88

English gynaecologist and reproduction biologist, born in Witney. He worked with **Robert Edwards** in 1968 on the problem of *in vitro* fertilization of human embryos. This resulted ten years later in the birth of a baby (Louise Brown) after *in vitro* fertilization and implantation of the embryo in her mother's uterus. His later work consisted of refining and developing infertility treatments.

### Nettie Maria Stevens, 1861–1912

US biologist, born in Cavendish, Vermont. She studied physiology at Stanford University, received a PhD from Bryn Mawr College, Pennsylvania (1903), and was later appointed to research posts there. She was one of the first to explain the principle that sex is determined by particular chromosomes (see **Genetics: Chromosomes**). She also studied sex determination in various plants and insects, demonstrating unusually large numbers of chromosomes in certain insects and the paired nature of chromosomes in mosquitoes and flies.

### Eduard Suess, 1831–1914

Austrian geologist, born in London, England. The greater part of his life was devoted to the study of the evolution of the features of the Earth's surface, particularly the problem of mountain building. His theory that there had once been a great supercontinent made up of the present southern continents was a forerunner of modern theories of continental drift. His four-volume book *Das Antlitz der Erde* (1885–1909, Eng trans 'The Face of the Earth', 1904–25) was his most important contribution, ranking alongside **Sir Charles Lyell**'s *Principles of Geology* and **Charles Darwin**'s *Origin of Species*.

### Albert von Nagyrapolt Szent-Györgyi 1893–1986

US biochemist, born in Budapest, Hungary. He became professor at Szeged (1931–45), where he crystallized vitamin C from paprika and, in consequence, vitamin B2 (riboflavin). He also discovered the reducing system involved in the Krebs cycle (see **Cells: Respiration**), and made important contributions towards understanding glycerinated fibres and muscular contraction and relaxation. He was awarded the Nobel prize for physiology or medicine in 1937.

### Leo Szilard, 1898–1964

US physicist, born in Budapest, Hungary. In 1934 he had taken a patent on nuclear fission as an energy source, and on hearing of **Otto Hahn** and **Lise Meitner**'s fission of uranium (1938), he immediately approached **Albert Einstein** in order to write together to warn President Franklin D Roosevelt of the possibility of Germany creating an atomic bomb. Together with **Enrico Fermi**, Szilard organized work on the first fission reactor, which operated in Chicago in 1942. He was a central figure in the Manhattan Project leading to the atomic bomb, and after World War II he did experimental work on bacterial mutations and theoretical work on ageing and memory.

### Edward Lawrie Tatum, 1909–75

US biochemist, born in Boulder, Colorado. With **George Beadle** he demonstrated the role of genes in biochemical processes by growing bread mould spores on a variety of nutritional media. They suggested that each spore had one or more blocks in the metabolic pathway for particular nutrients, which led to the 'one gene, one enzyme' hypothesis, that a single gene codes for the synthesis of one protein. Tatum also collaborated with **Joshua Lederberg** to show that bacteria can reproduce by the sexual process of conjugation. All three shared the 1958 Nobel prize for physiology or medicine.

### Edward Teller, 1908–2003

US physicist, born in Budapest, Hungary. He worked on the Manhattan atomic bomb project (1941–6), and joined **Robert Oppenheimer**'s theoretical study group at Berkeley, California, where he was director of the new nuclear laboratories at Livermore (1958–60). He repudiated any moral implications of his work, stating that, but for Oppenheimer's moral qualms, the USA might have had hydrogen bombs in 1947. After Russia's first atomic test (1949) he was one of the architects of President Harry S Truman's crash programme to build and test (1952) the world's first hydrogen bomb.

## Howard Martin Temin, 1934–94

US virologist, born in Philadelphia. He formulated the 'provirus' hypothesis, that the genetic material of an invading virus is copied into the host cell DNA. In 1970 he isolated the enzyme 'reverse transcriptase' (independently of **David Baltimore**), which enables DNA to be made using an RNA template. Viruses which contain this enzyme are retroviruses. Reverse transcriptase can be used to make copies of specific genes, and is widely used for genetic engineering. Temin shared the 1975 Nobel prize for physiology or medicine with **Renato Dulbecco** and Baltimore.

## Lewis Madison Terman, 1877–1956

US psychologist, born in Johnson County, Indiana. At Stanford University he developed an English version of the Binet–Simon intelligence test and introduced Terman Group Intelligence Tests into the US army in 1920. He pioneered the use of the term IQ (Intelligence Quotient) in his *The Measurement of Intelligence* (1916), and launched the five-volume *Genetic Studies of Genius* (1926–59).

## Thales, c.620–c.555 BC

Greek natural philosopher, astronomer and geometer, probably born in Miletus on mainland Ionia. He is important for having proposed the first natural cosmology, identifying water as the original substance and (literally) the basis of the universe. He is supposed to have visited Egypt and developed his interest in land-surveying and astronomical techniques there, to have predicted accurately a solar eclipse in 585 BC, and to have proposed a federation of the Ionian cities of the Aegean.

## Sir J(oseph) J(ohn) Thomson, also called J J, 1856–1940

English physicist, born in Cheetham Hill. The son of a bookseller, he won a scholarship to Trinity College, Cambridge. Thomson's early theoretical work was concerned with the extension of **James Clerk Maxwell**'s electromagnetic theories. This led to the study of gaseous conductors of electricity and in particular the nature of cathode rays. Using X-rays, he showed that cathode rays were rapidly-moving particles and, by measuring their speed and specific charge, he deduced that these 'corpuscles' (electrons) must be nearly 2000 times smaller in mass than the lightest known atomic particle, the hydrogen ion. This discovery of the electron was the greatest revolution in physics since **Sir Isaac Newton**. He also pioneered mass spectrometry and discovered the existence of isotopes of elements. Seven of his research assistants subsequently won the Nobel prize, including **Niels Bohr** and **Ernest Rutherford**. One of the greatest pioneers of nuclear physics, he was awarded the Nobel prize for physics in 1906.

## Nikolaas Tinbergen, 1907–88

Dutch ethologist, born in The Hague. With **Konrad Lorenz**, he is considered the co-founder of the science of ethology (the study of animal behaviour in natural surroundings). He analysed social behaviour of certain animals and insects as an evolutionary process with considerable relevance to human behaviour, especially courtship and aggression. He was the joint winner of the 1973 Nobel prize for physiology or medicine, with **Karl von Frisch** and Lorenz.

### Alexander Robertus Todd, Baron Todd (of Trumpington), 1907–97

Scottish chemist, born in Glasgow. His work on the structure and synthesis of nucleotides was a necessary preliminary to **Francis Crick** and **James Watson**'s proposal of the double helix as the structure of DNA. For his work he was awarded the Nobel prize for chemistry in 1957. As a trustee of various charities and a member of many government committees, he played a substantial part in promoting scientific activity both in Great Britain and abroad.

### Clyde William Tombaugh, 1906–97

US astronomer, born in Streator, Illinois. Too poor to attend college, he built his own telescope, and in 1929 became an assistant at the Lowell Observatory. Tombaugh devised the blink comparator, which enabled him to detect if anything had moved in the sky between the taking of two celestial photographs a few days apart. In 1930, he discovered Pluto in the constellation of Gemini.

### Sin-Itiro Tomonaga, 1906–79

Japanese physicist, born in Kyoto. His most important work was a relativistic quantum description of the interaction between a photon and an electron, producing the theory of quantum electrodynamics. For this work, he shared the 1965 Nobel prize for physics with **Richard Feynman** and **Julian Schwinger**. He was president of the Science Council of Japan (1951) and of Tokyo University (1956).

### Evangelista Torricelli, 1608–47

Italian physicist and mathematician, born probably in Faenza. His *Trattato del Moto* (1641, 'Treatise on Motion') led **Galileo** to invite him to become his literary assistant, and on Galileo's death he was appointed mathematician to the grand-duke and Galileo's successor as professor to the Florentine Academy. He discovered that, because of atmospheric pressure, water will not rise above 33 feet in a suction pump. To him are owed the fundamental principles of hydromechanics, and he gave the first description of a mercury barometer or 'torricellian tube'. He greatly improved both telescopes and microscopes, and published a large number of mathematical papers.

### Alan Mathison Turing, 1912–54

English mathematician, born in London. In 1936 he made an outstanding contribution to the development of computer science, outlining a theoretical 'universal' machine (later called a Turing machine) and giving a precise mathematical characterization of the concept of computability. In World War II he worked in cryptography and on Colossus (a forerunner of the modern computer). Later he put into practice his theoretical ideas on computing, with his brilliant design for the Automatic Computing Engine (ACE). He made contributions to the programming of early computers (such as the Manchester Mark I computer) and explored the problem of machine intelligence. He committed suicide after being prosecuted for homosexuality.

### James Alfred Van Allen, 1914–2006

US physicist, born in Mount Pleasant, Iowa. He is best known for his investigations into the properties of the Earth's upper atmosphere, particularly the measurement of cosmic-ray intensity at high altitudes. He was involved in the launching of the USA's first satellite, *Explorer I* (1958), which was carrying his cosmic ray detector. Such detectors later revealed the startling result that above a certain altitude there was much more high-energy radiation than previously expected, and satellite observations showed that the Earth's magnetic field traps high-speed charged particles in two zones known as the Van Allen belts.

### Robert Jemison Van de Graaff, 1901–67

US physicist, born in Tuscaloosa, Alabama. He constructed the first working model of an electrostatic generator (later to be known as the Van de Graaff generator), in which electric charge could be built up on a hollow metal sphere. The generator was used as a particle accelerator for atomic and nuclear physics, and to produce high-energy X-rays for cancer treatment. He was also involved in the development of X-ray sources for the examination of the interior structure of heavy artillery.

### Harold Varmus, 1939–

US molecular biologist, born in New York. In 1989 he was awarded the Nobel prize for physiology or medicine (jointly with **Michael Bishop**) for his contribution to the discovery of oncogenes, normal cellular genes which control cellular growth. If their production is altered in some way, the faulty protein gives rise to cancer in the cell, and the discovery of these genes has been of vital importance in understanding cancer mechanisms (see **Diseases and medicines: Cancer**).

### Andreas Vesalius, 1514–64

Belgian anatomist, born in Brussels. His greatest work, the *De Humani Corporis Fabrica* (1543, 'On the Structure of the Human Body'), was enriched by magnificent illustrations. With both its excellent descriptions and drawings of bones and the nervous system, the book set a completely new level of clarity and accuracy in anatomy.

### Alessandro Giuseppe Anastasio, Count Volta, 1745–1827

Italian physicist, born in Como. He invented the electrophorus (1775, the precursor of the induction machine), the condenser (1778), the candle flame collector of atmospheric electricity (1787) and the electrochemical battery, or 'voltaic pile' (1800), which was the first source of continuous or current electricity. It was inspired by a controversy he had with **Luigi Galvani** concerning the nature of animal electricity. He also invented an 'inflammable air' (hydrogen) electric pistol (1777). His name is given to the SI unit of electric potential difference, the volt.

### John (Johann) Von Neumann, 1903–57

US mathematician, born in Budapest, Hungary. His best-known mathematical work was on the theory of linear operators, but he also redefined the set of axioms behind set theory and formulated a precise description of quantum theory (1932). He designed some of the earliest computers. His work *The Theory of Games and Economic Behavior* (1944) contained a theory applicable both to games of chance and to games of pure skill, such as chess. These ideas have since become important in mathematical economics and operational research. He went on to invent the idea of self-replicating machines and cellular automata.

### Johannes Diderik van der Waals, 1837–1923

Dutch physicist, born in Leiden. He formulated the van der Waals equation, which defined the physical state of a gas or liquid, and investigated the weak attractive forces (van der Waals forces) between molecules. The van der Waals equation was a guide for the future liquefaction of permanent gases such as hydrogen and helium. He was awarded the Nobel prize for physics in 1910.

### Selman Abraham Waksman, 1888–1973

US biochemist, born in Priluka, Ukraine. From 1915 he worked on the microbial breakdown of organic substances in the soil, work which led to a new classification of microbes and methods for their scientific cultivation. From 1939 he discovered the anti-cancer drug actinomycin, the first anti-tuberculosis drug streptomycin and several other antibacterial agents. For these important discoveries he was awarded the Nobel prize for physiology or medicine in 1952.

### Alfred Russel Wallace, 1823–1913

Welsh naturalist, born in Usk. He is remembered for 'Wallace's line', the division in the Malay Archipelago between the Asian and Australian floras and faunas. He conceived the idea of the 'survival of the fittest' as the key to evolution, independently of **Darwin** (see **Key concepts: The theory of natural selection**). He sent an article (1858) outlining his theory to Darwin, who had not published his ideas. This led to the joint Darwin–Wallace paper at the Linnaean Society in 1858, which first promulgated the theory of evolution by means of natural selection, and hastened the publication of Darwin's *Origin of Species*. Wallace generously allowed Darwin the credit, and even entitled his own book on evolution *Darwinism* (1889). He was an outspoken advocate of socialism, pacifism, women's rights and other causes, and encapsulated his views in *Social Environment and Moral Progress* (1913).

### James Dewey Watson, 1928–

US biologist, born in Chicago. In 1951, he worked with **Francis Crick** on the structure of DNA, the biological molecule contained in cells which carries the genetic information. In 1953, they proposed a two-stranded helical molecule, showing each strand consisting of a series of nucleotide bases wound around a common centre, with the strands linked together by hydrogen bonds (see **Genetics: DNA**). The 1962 Nobel prize for physiology or medicine was awarded to Watson, Crick and **Maurice Wilkins**. Watson has been an active supporter of the Human Genome Initiative.

### James Watt, 1736–1819

Scottish engineer and inventor, born in Greenock, Strathclyde. In 1763–4 a model of Thomas Newcomen's steam engine was sent to his workshop for repair. He easily put it into order and, seeing the defects in the working of the machine, hit upon the idea of the separate condenser. This was probably the greatest single improvement ever made to the steam engine, which Watt manufactured from 1774. The modern scientific unit of power, the watt, is named after him, and horse-power, the original unit of power, was first experimentally determined and used by him in 1783. In 1785 he was elected FRS.

### Alfred Lothar Wegener, 1880–1930

German meteorologist and geophysicist, born in Berlin. *Die Entstehung der Kontinente und Ozeane* ('The Origin of Continents and Oceans') was first published in 1915, based on his observations that the continents may once have been joined into one supercontinent (Pangaea), which later broke up, the fragments drifting apart to form the continents as they are today (see **Key concepts: Continental drift**). Wegener provided historical, geological, geomorphological, climatic and palaeontological evidence, but at that time no logical mechanism was known by which continents could drift and the hypothesis remained controversial until the 1960s, when the structure of oceans became understood.

### André Weil, 1906–98

French mathematician, born in Paris. He worked in number theory, algebraic geometry and topological group theory. He was one of the founders of the Bourbaki group, who worked on set theory, and he wrote on the history of mathematics. Weil did much to extend the theory of algebraic geometry to varieties of any dimension, and to define them over fields of arbitrary characteristics. He was one of the most brilliant mathematicians of the 20th century.

### Steven Weinberg, 1933–

US physicist, born in New York City. Independently of **Abdus Salam**, he unified the electromagnetic and weak nuclear forces, and predicted a new interaction due to 'neutral currents' whereby a chargeless particle is exchanged, giving rise to a force between particles (see **Key concepts: The theory of everything**). This was duly observed in 1973, giving strong support to the theory (now called the Weinberg–Salam theory). Weinberg, Salam, and **Sheldon Glashow** (who extended the work) shared the 1979 Nobel prize for physics. The combined theory has recently been precisely tested by experiments at the European nuclear research centre, CERN (Conseil Européen pour la Recherche Nucléaire), in Geneva.

### Wilhelm Wien, 1864–1928

German physicist, born in Gaffken, East Prussia. Working on black-body radiation, he showed that the wavelength at which maximum energy is radiated is inversely proportional to the absolute temperature of the body (1893). He cleared the way for **Max Planck** to resolve the observed distribution of all frequencies with the quantum theory (1900), and in 1911 was awarded the Nobel prize for physics for his work on black-body radiation. His subsequent research covered hydrodynamics, X-rays and cathode rays.

### Norbert Wiener, 1894–1964

US mathematician, born in Columbia, Missouri. He worked on stochastic processes and harmonic analysis, inventing the concepts later called the Wiener integral and Wiener measure. During World War II he studied mathematical communication theory applied to predictors and guided missiles. His study of feedback in the handling of information by electronic devices led him to compare this with analogous mental processes in animals in *Cybernetics* (1948) and other works.

## Maurice Hugh Frederick Wilkins, 1916–2004

British physicist, born in New Zealand. He worked initially on the separation of uranium isotopes during World War II. After the war, opposing the use of the atomic bomb, he turned to the application of physical techniques to biological research. He applied the techniques of X-ray crystallography specifically to biological molecules, most famously on DNA. Wilkins and **Rosalind Franklin**'s X-ray data of DNA fibres were instrumental in allowing **James Watson** and **Francis Crick** to deduce the double helix structure of DNA (see **Genetics: DNA**). Wilkins, Watson and Crick were awarded the 1962 Nobel prize for physiology or medicine for this work.

## Edward Osborne Wilson, 1929–

US biologist, born in Birmingham, Alabama. He has been a major figure in the development of sociobiology, the investigation into the biological basis of social behaviour. His early researches into the social behaviour, communication and evolution of ants resulted in the publication of *The Insect Societies* (1971), in which he outlines his belief that the same evolutionary forces have shaped the behaviours of insects and other animals including human beings. Later works include *On Human Nature* (1978) and *The Diversity of Life* (1992).

## Chen Ning Yang, 1922–

US physicist, born in Hefei, China. In 1956 with **Tsung-Dao Lee** he concluded that the quantum property known as parity, which relates to the symmetry of subatomic particles, was unlikely to be conserved in weak interactions, a finding that was later confirmed. For this prediction, Lee and Yang were awarded the 1957 Nobel prize for physics.

## Thomas Young, 1773–1829

English physicist, physician and Egyptologist, born in Milverton. He became best known in the 19th century for his wave theory of light, and combined the wave theory of **Christiaan Huygens** with **Newton**'s theory of colours to explain the interference phenomenon produced by ruled gratings, thin plates, and the colours of the rainbow. He generalized **Hooke**'s law, relating stress and strain of materials; the constant that relates these properties (Young's modulus) is named after him (see **Materials: Properties of materials**). He also did valuable work in insurance, haemodynamics and Egyptology, and made a fundamental contribution to the deciphering of the inscriptions on the Rosetta Stone.

## Hideki Yukawa, originally Hideki Ogawi, 1907–81

Japanese physicist, born in Tokyo. In 1935 he suggested that a strong short-range attractive interaction between neutrons and protons would overcome the electrical repulsion between protons. The existence of the intermediate particles which propagate the interaction was confirmed in 1947. Yukawa also predicted the capture of atomic electrons by the nucleus, which was soon observed. For his work on quantum theory and nuclear physics, he was awarded the Nobel prize for physics in 1949, the first Japanese to be so honoured.

## Pieter Zeeman, 1865–1943

Dutch physicist, born in Zonnemaire. In 1896 he studied light sources in a magnetic field, and deduced that the resultant broadening of spectral emission lines was due to the splitting of spectrum lines into two or three components. This phenomenon became known as the Zeeman effect. He also investigated the absorption and motion of electricity in fluids, magnetic fields on the solar surface, the Doppler effect and the effect of nuclear magnetic moments on spectral lines. In 1902 he and **Hendrik Antoon Lorentz** won the Nobel prize for physics for the discovery and explanation of the Zeeman effect.

### George Zweig, 1937–

US physicist, born in Moscow. Independently of **Murray Gell-Mann**, he developed the theory of quarks as the fundamental building blocks of hadrons, the particles that experience strong nuclear forces. They suggested that three types exist, giving rise to the three different observed properties associated with new particles that were being discovered at that time. It is now believed that there are six types of quark.

## NOBEL PRIZES

Nobel prizes were established by a bequest in the will of Alfred Nobel (1833–96) to honour 'those who, during the preceding year, shall have conferred the greatest benefit on mankind'. They were first awarded in 1901.

### Nobel prize for physics

The Nobel prize for physics is awarded annually to whoever has 'made the most important discovery or invention within the field of physics.'

| 1901 | Wilhelm Conrad Röntgen |
|------|------------------------|
| 1902 | Hendrik A Lorentz, Pieter Zeeman |
| 1903 | Henri Becquerel, Pierre Curie, Marie Curie |
| 1904 | Lord Rayleigh |
| 1905 | Philipp Lenard |
| 1906 | J J Thomson |
| 1907 | Albert A Michelson |
| 1908 | Gabriel Lippmann |
| 1909 | Guglielmo Marconi, Ferdinand Braun |
| 1910 | Johannes Diderik van der Waals |
| 1911 | Wilhelm Wien |
| 1912 | Gustaf Dalén |
| 1913 | Heike Kamerlingh Onnes |
| 1914 | Max von Laue |
| 1915 | William Bragg, Lawrence Bragg |

| 1916 | *no award* |
|------|------------|
| 1917 | Charles Glover Barkla |
| 1918 | Max Planck |
| 1919 | Johannes Stark |
| 1920 | Charles Edouard Guillaume |
| 1921 | Albert Einstein |
| 1922 | Niels Bohr |
| 1923 | Robert A Millikan |
| 1924 | Manne Siegbahn |
| 1925 | James Franck, Gustav Hertz |
| 1926 | Jean Baptiste Perrin |
| 1927 | Arthur H Compton, C T R Wilson |
| 1928 | Owen Willans Richardson |
| 1929 | Louis de Broglie |
| 1930 | Venkata Raman |
| 1931 | *no award* |
| 1932 | Werner Heisenberg |
| 1933 | Erwin Schrödinger, P A M Dirac |
| 1934 | *no award* |
| 1935 | James Chadwick |
| 1936 | Victor F Hess, Carl D Anderson |
| 1937 | Clinton Davisson, George Paget Thomson |
| 1938 | Enrico Fermi |
| 1939 | Ernest Lawrence |
| 1940 | *no award* |
| 1941 | *no award* |
| 1942 | *no award* |
| 1943 | Otto Stern |
| 1944 | Isidor Isaac Rabi |
| 1945 | Wolfgang Pauli |
| 1946 | Percy W Bridgman |

| | |
|---|---|
| 1947 | Edward V Appleton |
| 1948 | Patrick M S Blackett |
| 1949 | Hideki Yukawa |
| 1950 | Cecil Powell |
| 1951 | John Cockcroft, Ernest T S Walton |
| 1952 | Felix Bloch, E M Purcell |
| 1953 | Frits Zernike |
| 1954 | Max Born, Walther Bothe |
| 1955 | Willis E Lamb, Polykarp Kusch |
| 1956 | William B Shockley, John Bardeen, Walter H Brattain |
| 1957 | Chen Ning Yang, Tsung-Dao Lee |
| 1958 | Pavel A Cherenkov, Il´ja M Frank, Igor Y Tamm |
| 1959 | Emilio Segrè, Owen Chamberlain |
| 1960 | Donald A Glaser |
| 1961 | Robert Hofstadter, Rudolf Mössbauer |
| 1962 | Lev Landau |
| 1963 | Eugene Wigner, Maria Goeppert-Mayer, J Hans D Jensen |
| 1964 | Charles H Townes, Nicolay G Basov, Aleksandr M Prokhorov |
| 1965 | Sin-Itiro Tomonaga, Julian Schwinger, Richard P Feynman |
| 1966 | Alfred Kastler |
| 1967 | Hans Bethe |
| 1968 | Luis Alvarez |
| 1969 | Murray Gell-Mann |
| 1970 | Hannes Alfvén, Louis Néel |
| 1971 | Dennis Gabor |
| 1972 | John Bardeen, Leon N Cooper, Robert Schrieffer |
| 1973 | Leo Esaki, Ivar Giaever, Brian D Josephson |
| 1974 | Martin Ryle, Antony Hewish |
| 1975 | Aage N Bohr, Ben R Mottelson, James Rainwater |
| 1976 | Burton Richter, Samuel C C Ting |
| 1977 | Philip W Anderson, Sir Nevill F Mott, John H van Vleck |

| | |
|---|---|
| 1978 | Pyotr Kapitsa, Arno Penzias, Robert Woodrow Wilson |
| 1979 | Sheldon Glashow, Abdus Salam, Steven Weinberg |
| 1980 | James Cronin, Val Fitch |
| 1981 | Nicolaas Bloembergen, Arthur L Schawlow, Kai M Siegbahn |
| 1982 | Kenneth G Wilson |
| 1983 | Subramanyan Chandrasekhar, William A Fowler |
| 1984 | Carlo Rubbia, Simon van der Meer |
| 1985 | Klaus von Klitzing |
| 1986 | Ernst Ruska, Gerd Binnig, Heinrich Rohrer |
| 1987 | J Georg Bednorz, K Alex Müller |
| 1988 | Leon M Lederman, Melvin Schwartz, Jack Steinberger |
| 1989 | Norman F Ramsey, Hans G Dehmelt, Wolfgang Paul |
| 1990 | Jerome I Friedman, Henry W Kendall, Richard E Taylor |
| 1991 | Pierre-Gilles de Gennes |
| 1992 | Georges Charpak |
| 1993 | Russell A Hulse, Joseph H Taylor Jr |
| 1994 | Bertram N Brockhouse, Clifford G Shull |
| 1995 | Martin L Perl, Frederick Reines |
| 1996 | David M Lee, Douglas D Osheroff, Robert C Richardson |
| 1997 | Steven Chu, Claude Cohen-Tannoudji, William D Phillips |
| 1998 | Robert B Laughlin, Horst L Störmer, Daniel C Tsui |
| 1999 | Gerardus 't Hooft, Martinus JG Veltman |
| 2000 | Zhores I Alferov, Herbert Kroemer, Jack S Kilby |
| 2001 | Eric A Cornell, Wolfgang Ketterle, Carl E Wieman |
| 2002 | Raymond Davis Jr, Masatoshi Koshiba, Riccardo Giacconi |
| 2003 | Alexei A Abrikosov, Vitaly L Ginzburg, Anthony J Leggett |
| 2004 | David J Gross, H David Politzer, Frank Wikzek |
| 2005 | Roy J Glauber, John L Hall, Theodor W Hänsch |

## Nobel prize for chemistry

The Nobel prize for chemistry is awarded annually to whoever has 'made the most important chemical discovery or improvement.'

| 1901 | Jacobus H van 't Hoff |
|------|------------------------|
| 1902 | Emil Fischer |
| 1903 | Svante Arrhenius |
| 1904 | Sir William Ramsay |
| 1905 | Adolf von Baeyer |
| 1906 | Henri Moissan |
| 1907 | Eduard Buchner |
| 1908 | Ernest Rutherford |
| 1909 | Wilhelm Ostwald |
| 1910 | Otto Wallach |
| 1911 | Marie Curie |
| 1912 | Victor Grignard, Paul Sabatier |
| 1913 | Alfred Werner |
| 1914 | Theodore W Richards |
| 1915 | Richard Willstätter |
| 1916 | *no award* |
| 1917 | *no award* |
| 1918 | Fritz Haber |
| 1919 | *no award* |
| 1920 | Walther Nernst |
| 1921 | Frederick Soddy |
| 1922 | Francis W Aston |
| 1923 | Fritz Pregl |
| 1924 | *no award* |
| 1925 | Richard Zsigmondy |
| 1926 | The Svedberg |
| 1927 | Heinrich Wieland |
| 1928 | Adolf Windaus |

| | |
|---|---|
| 1929 | Arthur Harden, Hans von Euler-Chelpin |
| 1930 | Hans Fischer |
| 1931 | Carl Bosch, Friedrich Bergius |
| 1932 | Irving Langmuir |
| 1933 | *no award* |
| 1934 | Harold C Urey |
| 1935 | Frédéric Joliot, Irène Joliot-Curie |
| 1936 | Peter Debye |
| 1937 | Norman Haworth, Paul Karrer |
| 1938 | Richard Kuhn |
| 1939 | Adolf Butenandt, Leopold Ruzicka |
| 1940 | *no award* |
| 1941 | *no award* |
| 1942 | *no award* |
| 1943 | George de Hevesy |
| 1944 | Otto Hahn |
| 1945 | Artturi Virtanen |
| 1946 | James B Sumner, John H Northrop, Wendell M Stanley |
| 1947 | Sir Robert Robinson |
| 1948 | Arne Tiselius |
| 1949 | William F Giauque |
| 1950 | Otto Diels, Kurt Alder |
| 1951 | Edwin M McMillan, Glenn T Seaborg |
| 1952 | Archer J P Martin, Richard L M Synge |
| 1953 | Hermann Staudinger |
| 1954 | Linus Pauling |
| 1955 | Vincent du Vigneaud |
| 1956 | Sir Cyril Hinshelwood, Nikolay Semenov |
| 1957 | Lord Todd |
| 1958 | Frederick Sanger |
| 1959 | Jaroslav Heyrovsky |

| 1960 | Willard F Libby |
|------|-----------------|
| 1961 | Melvin Calvin |
| 1962 | Max F Perutz, John C Kendrew |
| 1963 | Karl Ziegler, Giulio Natta |
| 1964 | Dorothy Crowfoot Hodgkin |
| 1965 | Robert B Woodward |
| 1966 | Robert S Mulliken |
| 1967 | Manfred Eigen, Ronald G W Norrish, George Porter |
| 1968 | Lars Onsager |
| 1969 | Derek Barton, Odd Hassel |
| 1970 | Luis Leloir |
| 1971 | Gerhard Herzberg |
| 1972 | Christian Anfinsen, Stanford Moore, William H Stein |
| 1973 | Ernst Otto Fischer, Geoffrey Wilkinson |
| 1974 | Paul J Flory |
| 1975 | John Cornforth, Vladimir Prelog |
| 1976 | William Lipscomb |
| 1977 | Ilya Prigogine |
| 1978 | Peter Mitchell |
| 1979 | Herbert C Brown, Georg Wittig |
| 1980 | Paul Berg, Walter Gilbert, Frederick Sanger |
| 1981 | Kenichi Fukui, Roald Hoffmann |
| 1982 | Aaron Klug |
| 1983 | Henry Taube |
| 1984 | Bruce Merrifield |
| 1985 | Herbert A Hauptman, Jerome Karle |
| 1986 | Dudley R Herschbach, Yuan T Lee, John C Polanyi |
| 1987 | Donald J Cram, Jean-Marie Lehn, Charles J Pedersen |
| 1988 | Johann Deisenhofer, Robert Huber, Hartmut Michel |
| 1989 | Sidney Altman, Thomas R Cech |
| 1990 | Elias James Corey |

| 1991 | Richard R Ernst |
|------|-----------------|
| 1992 | Rudolph A Marcus |
| 1993 | Kary B Mullis, Michael Smith |
| 1994 | George A Olah |
| 1995 | Paul J Crutzen, Mario J Molina, F Sherwood Rowland |
| 1996 | Robert F Curl Jr, Sir Harold Kroto, Richard E Smalley |
| 1997 | Paul D Boyer, John E Walker, Jens C Skou |
| 1998 | Walter Kohn, John Pople |
| 1999 | Ahmed Zewail |
| 2000 | Alan Heeger, Alan G MacDiarmid, Hideki Shirakawa |
| 2001 | William S Knowles, Ryoji Noyori, K Barry Sharpless |
| 2002 | John B Fenn, Koichi Tanaka, Kurt Wüthrich |
| 2003 | Peter Agre, Roderick MacKinnon |
| 2004 | Aaron Ciechanover, Avram Hershko, Irwin Rose |
| 2005 | Yves Chauvin, Robert H Grubbs, Richard R Schrock |

### *Strange Science*

The Ig Nobel prizes were established in 1991 by a scientific humour journal, the *Annals of Improbable Research*, as a means of increasing interest in science. The awards, in varying categories, recognize 'achievements that cannot or should not be reproduced'. The annual Ig Nobel awards ceremony, which is held at Harvard University in Boston, Massachusetts, has been described by the journal *Nature as* 'arguably the highlight of the scientific calendar'.
Previous Ig Nobel laureates include:

| Year | Category | Winner |
|------|----------|--------|
| 1993 | Biology | Paul Williams Jr and Kenneth W Newell, for their study 'Salmonella excretion in joy-riding pigs' |
| 1997 | Meteorology | Bernard Vonnegut, for his report 'Chicken plucking as a measure of tornado wind speed' |
| 2001 | Astrophysics | Dr Jack and Rexella Van Impe, for discovering that black holes fulfil all the technical requirements to be the location of Hell |
| 2002 | Physics | Arnd Leike, for demonstrating that beer froth obeys the mathematical Law of Exponential Decay |
| 2004 | Biology | Ben Wilson, Lawrence Dill, Robert Batty, Magnus Whalberg and Hakan Westerberg, for showing that herrings apparently communicate by farting |

## Nobel prize for physiology or medicine

The Nobel prize for physiology or medicine is awarded annually to whoever has 'made the most important discovery within the domain of physiology or medicine.'

| | |
|---|---|
| 1901 | Emil von Behring |
| 1902 | Ronald Ross |
| 1903 | Niels Ryberg Finsen |
| 1904 | Ivan Pavlov |
| 1905 | Robert Koch |
| 1906 | Camillo Golgi, Santiago Ramón y Cajal |
| 1907 | Alphonse Laveran |
| 1908 | Ilya Mechnikov, Paul Ehrlich |
| 1909 | Theodor Kocher |
| 1910 | Albrecht Kossel |
| 1911 | Allvar Gullstrand |
| 1912 | Alexis Carrel |
| 1913 | Charles Richet |
| 1914 | Robert Bárány |
| 1915 | *no award* |
| 1916 | *no award* |
| 1917 | *no award* |
| 1918 | *no award* |
| 1919 | Jules Bordet |
| 1920 | August Krogh |
| 1921 | *no award* |
| 1922 | Archibald V Hill, Otto Meyerhof |
| 1923 | Frederick G Banting, John Macleod |
| 1924 | Willem Einthoven |
| 1925 | *no award* |
| 1926 | Johannes Fibiger |
| 1927 | Julius Wagner-Jauregg |

| 1928 | Charles Nicolle |
| 1929 | Christiaan Eijkman, Sir Frederick Hopkins |
| 1930 | Karl Landsteiner |
| 1931 | Otto Warburg |
| 1932 | Sir Charles Sherrington, Edgar Adrian |
| 1933 | Thomas H Morgan |
| 1934 | George H Whipple, George R Minot, William P Murphy |
| 1935 | Hans Spemann |
| 1936 | Sir Henry Dale, Otto Loewi |
| 1937 | Albert Szent-Györgyi |
| 1938 | Corneille Heymans |
| 1939 | Gerhard Domagk |
| 1940 | *no award* |
| 1941 | *no award* |
| 1942 | *no award* |
| 1943 | Henrik Dam, Edward A Doisy |
| 1944 | Joseph Erlanger, Herbert S Gasser |
| 1945 | Sir Alexander Fleming, Ernst B Chain, Sir Howard Florey |
| 1946 | Hermann J Muller |
| 1947 | Carl Cori, Gerty Cori, Bernardo Houssay |
| 1948 | Paul Müller |
| 1949 | Walter Hess, Egas Moniz |
| 1950 | Edward C Kendall, Tadeus Reichstein, Philip S Hench |
| 1951 | Max Theiler |
| 1952 | Selman A Waksman |
| 1953 | Hans Krebs, Fritz Lipmann |
| 1954 | John F Enders, Thomas H Weller, Frederick C Robbins |
| 1955 | Hugo Theorell |
| 1956 | André F Cournand, Werner Forssmann, Dickinson W Richards |
| 1957 | Daniel Bovet |
| 1958 | George Beadle, Edward Tatum, Joshua Lederberg |

| 1959 | Severo Ochoa, Arthur Kornberg |
| 1960 | Sir Frank Macfarlane Burnet, Peter Medawar |
| 1961 | Georg von Békésy |
| 1962 | Francis Crick, James Watson, Maurice Wilkins |
| 1963 | Sir John Eccles, Alan L Hodgkin, Andrew F Huxley |
| 1964 | Konrad Bloch, Feodor Lynen |
| 1965 | François Jacob, André Lwoff, Jacques Monod |
| 1966 | Peyton Rous, Charles B Huggins |
| 1967 | Ragnar Granit, Haldan K Hartline, George Wald |
| 1968 | Robert W Holley, H Gobind Khorana, Marshall W Nirenberg |
| 1969 | Max Delbrück, Alfred D Hershey, Salvador E Luria |
| 1970 | Sir Bernard Katz, Ulf von Euler, Julius Axelrod |
| 1971 | Earl W Sutherland Jr |
| 1972 | Gerald M Edelman, Rodney R Porter |
| 1973 | Karl von Frisch, Konrad Lorenz, Nikolaas Tinbergen |
| 1974 | Albert Claude, Christian de Duve, George E Palade |
| 1975 | David Baltimore, Renato Dulbecco, Howard M Temin |
| 1976 | Baruch S Blumberg, D Carleton Gajdusek |
| 1977 | Roger Guillemin, Andrew V Schally, Rosalyn Yalow |
| 1978 | Werner Arber, Daniel Nathans, Hamilton O Smith |
| 1979 | Allan M Cormack, Godfrey N Hounsfield |
| 1980 | Baruj Benacerraf, Jean Dausset, George D Snell |
| 1981 | Roger W Sperry, David H Hubel, Torsten N Wiesel |
| 1982 | Sune K Bergström, Bengt I Samuelsson, John R Vane |
| 1983 | Barbara McClintock |
| 1984 | Niels K Jerne, Georges JF Köhler, César Milstein |
| 1985 | Michael S Brown, Joseph L Goldstein |
| 1986 | Stanley Cohen, Rita Levi-Montalcini |
| 1987 | Susumu Tonegawa |
| 1988 | Sir James W Black, Gertrude B Elion, George H Hitchings |
| 1989 | J Michael Bishop, Harold E Varmus |

| 1990 | Joseph E Murray, E Donnall Thomas |
| 1991 | Erwin Neher, Bert Sakmann |
| 1992 | Edmond H Fischer, Edwin G Krebs |
| 1993 | Richard J Roberts, Phillip A Sharp |
| 1994 | Alfred G Gilman, Martin Rodbell |
| 1995 | Edward B Lewis, Christiane Nüsslein-Volhard, Eric F Wieschaus |
| 1996 | Peter C Doherty, Rolf M Zinkernagel |
| 1997 | Stanley B Prusiner |
| 1998 | Robert F Furchgott, Louis J Ignarro, Ferid Murad |
| 1999 | Günter Blobel |
| 2000 | Arvid Carlsson, Paul Greengard, Eric R Kandel |
| 2001 | Leland H Hartwell, Tim Hunt, Sir Paul Nurse |
| 2002 | Sydney Brenner, H Robert Horvitz, John E Sulston |
| 2003 | Paul C Lauterbur, Sir Peter Mansfield |
| 2004 | Richard Axel, Linda B Buck |
| 2005 | Barry J Marshall, J Robin Warren |

## FIELDS MEDAL

The Fields Medal is the world's highest award for achievement in mathematics. Named after a Canadian mathematician, Professor J C Fields (1863–1932), the medals are awarded at the International Congress of Mathematicians (ICM) to 'recognize outstanding mathematical achievement' by a mathematician of no older than 40 years. Up to four medals may be awarded at each ICM.

| 1936 | Lars Valerian Ahlfors, Jesse Douglas |
| 1950 | Laurent Schwartz, Atle Selberg |
| 1954 | Kunihiko Kodaira, Jean-Pierre Serre |
| 1958 | Klaus Friedrich Roth, René Thom |
| 1962 | Lars Hörmander, John Willard Milnor |
| 1966 | Michael Francis Atiyah, Paul Joseph Cohen, Alexander Grothendieck, Stephen Smale |
| 1970 | Alan Baker, Heisuke Hironaka, Serge Novikov, John Griggs Thompson |
| 1974 | Enrico Bombieri, David Bryant Mumford |
| 1978 | Pierre René Deligne, Charles Louis Fefferman, Gregori Alexandrovitch Margulis, Daniel G Quillen |

| 1982 | Alain Connes, William P Thurston, Shing-Tung Yau |
|------|--------------------------------------------------|
| 1986 | Simon K Donaldson, Gerd Faltings, Michael H Freedman |
| 1990 | Vladimir Drinfeld, Vaughan FR Jones, Shigefumi Mori, Edward Witten |
| 1994 | Jean Bourgain, Pierre-Louis Lions, Jean-Christophe Yoccoz, Efim Zelmanov |
| 1998 | Richard E Borcherds, W Timothy Gowers, Maxim Kontsevich, Curtis T McMullen |
| 2002 | Laurent Lafforgue, Vladimir Voevodsky |

# KEY CONCEPTS

## Occam's Razor

### What is it?

Occam's (or Ockham's) Razor is a philosophical principle that can be used as a guide to choosing between different explanations for observed facts. It says that 'entities are not to be multiplied beyond necessity', meaning that a theory should not propose the existence of anything more than is needed for its explanation. It is sometimes called the principle of parsimony or the principle of economy.

### Who proposed it?

Occam's razor is named after William of Occam, a 14th-century English philosopher who used it extensively, although other philosophers including Aristotle had made similar suggestions much earlier. It became known as a 'razor' because it 'cuts' away unnecessary parts of a theory, leaving only what is essential.

### Why is it important?

The principle of Occam's Razor is still used by scientists when they are thinking about possible explanations for a finding. It can also sometimes be useful when designing computer programs that model processes or make predictions.

### Is it really true?

It is not true that things are always as simple as they could be in the natural world, as T H Huxley summed up beautifully in the quotation included here. However, the principle of not making more assumptions than necessary is a useful one when trying to solve scientific problems.

> **"**
> *The great tragedy of Science – the slaying of a beautiful hypothesis by an ugly fact.*
>
> —English biologist T H Huxley, *'Biogenesis and Abiogenesis', British Association Annual Report* (1870).
> **"**

If there are two possible explanations for a finding and one requires fewer assumptions than the other, the former is more likely to be correct but is not necessarily so, meaning that Occam's Razor can only be used as a guide. For example, if a dog owner finds that a plate of mince pies left out one evening are no longer there in the morning, either her pet dog or Santa Claus could have eaten them. But we know that the dog exists, whereas we would have to assume that Santa Claus exists. Occam's Razor would therefore tell us that we should blame the dog.

If two completely different explanations require the same number of assumptions, the Razor is not helpful. For example, if the dog owner described above owns two dogs, Occam's Razor does not tell us anything about which dog might have eaten the mince pies.

## Central Dogma of Molecular Biology

### What is it?

The central dogma of molecular biology is the statement that genetic information resides in the nucleic acid (DNA and RNA) and passes to the protein sequence, but cannot flow from protein to protein or back to nucleic acid.

The central dogma is often oversimplified to 'DNA makes RNA makes protein'. However, this is inaccurate (see below).

> *The central dogma of molecular biology deals with the detailed residue-by-residue transfer of sequential information. It states that such information cannot be transferred from protein to either protein or nucleic acid.*
>
> —Francis Crick, in *Nature* (1958).

### Who worked it out?

The English molecular biologist Francis Crick published the central dogma in 1958. He had earlier published the double-helix model of DNA with the American molecular biologist James Watson in 1953, and Crick continued to work on the genetic code, and the production of DNA and proteins, for around ten more years.

### Is it really true?

The central dogma, as stated in its original form, is still thought to be correct. However, two processes are often claimed to disprove it.

The first of these processes is the production of DNA from RNA by retroviruses such as the HIV virus. This contravenes the oversimplified version of the dogma, which says that RNA should be produced from DNA, not the other way round. However, the original form of the dogma does not rule out the transfer of genetic information between different types of nucleic acid; rather, it only rules out the transfer from protein to nucleic acid.

The other process that can appear to contradict the dogma is the replication of brain proteins called prions, which cause the transmissible spongiform encephalopathy group of diseases including bovine spongiform encephalopathy (BSE) and Creutzfeldt-Jakob disease (CJD). Disease-causing versions of these proteins are able to confer their structure on the normal version, making the spongiform encephalopathies the first known diseases that can be transmitted by proteins. However, it is the incorrect folding of prions that is passed from protein to protein, not the actual sequence of the protein as determined by the genetic code.

To date, therefore, the central dogma has not been disproved.

## Mendel's Laws of Genetic Inheritance

### What are they?

Mendel's laws describe the way in which genes are passed from parents to their offspring (see also **Genetics: Genetic inheritance**). There are two laws: the law of segregation and the law of recombination.

### The law of segregation

Mendel's first law, the law of segregation, says that the transfer of observable inherited characteristics, such as colour, from parents to their offspring is determined by the segregation of the parents' genes into gametes (eggs and sperm). This means that each gamete receives one gene allele or the other with equal probability. The segregation results in various notable ratios in the characteristics of the offspring, who receive one allele from each parent. Also, alleles can be dominant or recessive – if the offspring have one dominant allele and one recessive one, their appearance will be dictated by the dominant one.

The diagram below shows the offspring that would be produced by two flowers of different colours, when the dark allele (D) is dominant and the light (L) allele is recessive. All of the first generation offspring inherit the D allele from one parent and the L allele from the other. Because D is dominant, the flowers are all dark in colour. If two of the first generation offspring produce offspring themselves, the resultant second generation offspring show a ratio of 3 dark flowers to every 1 light flower, due to the four possible combinations of alleles they can inherit.

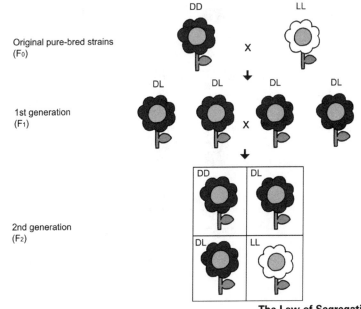

Original pure-bred strains ($F_0$)

1st generation ($F_1$)

2nd generation ($F_2$)

**The Law of Segregation**

# KEY CONCEPTS

## The law of recombination

Mendel's second law, which is known as the law of recombination or the law of independent assortment, says that two characteristics determined by two unlinked genes are recombined at random in gamete formation. They therefore segregate independently of each other, each according to the first law. This results in various notable ratios when individuals that differ in two different characteristics produce offspring.

The diagram shows the offspring that would be produced by two insects that have either coloured (C) or colourless (c) eyes, and wings (W) or no wings (w). The alleles in capital letters are dominant and those in small letters are recessive – this is a convention used by geneticists. As with the flowers, all the first generation offspring show the character of the dominant alleles, so they have wings and coloured eyes. When the first generation insects breed together, a ratio of 9 coloured/winged to 3 colourless/winged to 3 coloured/wingless to 1 colourless/wingless is observed in the second generation offspring.

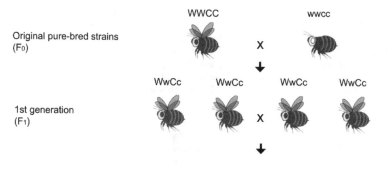

Original pure-bred strains (F$_0$)

1st generation (F$_1$)

2nd generation (F$_2$)

**The Law of Recombination**

## Who worked them out?

An Austrian monk, Gregor Mendel, worked out these laws of inheritance in the 19th century by studying plants in the garden of the monastery where he was abbot. He observed the segregation of characteristics in peas, including whether they were round or wrinkled, and whether they were green or yellow.

The importance of Mendel's laws was not realized during his lifetime. His work was discovered in the early 20th century by the German botanist Carl Correns, the Dutch botanist Hugo de Vries and the Austrian botanist Erich von Tschermak-Seysenegg.

## Why are they important?

Before Mendel's work, people thought that the characteristics seen in offspring were a blend of those from both parents. For example, it was thought that the offspring of a red flower and a white flower would always be pink, whereas in fact they can all be red. The concept of recessive alleles explains why characteristics can seem to 'skip' a generation, so that sometimes people have characteristics that seem to come from their grandparents rather than their parents. The concept of inheriting genetic information in discrete units (genes) underpins much of modern genetics.

## Are they really true?

Mendel's laws apply only to organisms that reproduce sexually. The laws assume that each characteristic is determined by one gene. In fact, some characteristics are more complex, with several genes being involved. The clear ratios of offspring are not seen when this is the case.

It is not always the case that one allele is completely dominant over another – some red and white flowers do produce pink offspring. This effect is called codominance.

If genes are very close together on a chromosome, they show a phenomenon called linkage, where they tend to be inherited together rather than independently. This means that the second law only holds true when the genes are on different chromosomes, or are far apart on the same chromosome.

Genetic characteristics that obey Mendel's laws are known as Mendelian traits.

---

*Teaching Troubles*

Despite being a gifted teacher, Mendel twice failed his teaching accreditation examinations. Ironically, his failures were at least partially due to disputes with the biology examiners.

## The Theory of Natural Selection

### What is it?

Natural selection is an evolutionary theory which proposes that the organisms best suited to their environment are the most likely to survive. It is based on the fact that sexually-reproducing organisms pass characteristics down to their offspring in their genes. The genes can be inherited in different combinations, and mutations (changes) can also occur. This means that a diverse collection of offspring are produced.

The random nature of the genetic changes means that some offspring will be better suited to the environment than their parents, while others are worse off. The offspring that are more likely to survive and reproduce are those who gained helpful characteristics, so the beneficial genetic changes are the ones that tend to persist in the genetic make-up of the species. This phenomenon is often referred to as 'survival of the fittest'.

At the time the theory of natural selection was proposed, the exact genetic mechanisms involved were not understood. The current view of natural selection in the context of our knowledge about genetics is often referred to as neo-Darwinism.

> *How extremely stupid not to have thought of that!*
> —English biologist T H Huxley, on reading Darwin's *Origin of Species*.

### Who worked it out?

Prior to the theory of natural selection, the best model for evolution was that of a French naturalist, Jean-Baptiste Lamarck. Lamarck realised that characteristics were passed from parents to offspring, but thought that the characteristics were acquired during an organism's life. An example often used to illustrate this idea is that a giraffe's neck would get longer because it stretches up to eat leaves from tall trees.

The alternative theory, natural selection, was proposed by the English naturalist Charles Darwin. He devised the theory during his travels to the Galápagos islands, where he noticed that one species of finch found on mainland South America had given rise to many species on the islands, a procees now known as adaptive radiation (see **Organisms: Evolution**). Each species was particularly well adapted to the habitat on its island. He published his findings in his work *The Origin of Species by Means of Natural Selection* (1859). The theory is therefore often referred to as Darwinism or the Darwinian Theory.

### Captain Fitzroy

The meteorologist Robert Fitzroy, for whom the shipping forecast area known as Fitzroy is named, was the captain of HMS *Beagle*, the ship on which Darwin travelled whilst conducting his research.

**Darwin's Sketch of Galápagos Finches**

Although Darwin is usually regarded as the originator of the theory of natural selection, the publication of Darwin's work was prompted by his receipt of an unpublished paper by the Welsh naturalist Alfred Russel Wallace in 1858, which suggested a similar mechanism for evolution based on Wallace's research in the Malay Archipelago. A joint paper by Darwin and Wallace was read before the Linnaean Society, an important biological society, in 1858.

> *I see no good reasons why the views given in this volume should shock the religious feelings of anyone.*
>
> —Charles Darwin, *The Origin of Species by Means of Natural Selection* (1859).

### Is it really true?

Neo-Darwinism, which places natural selection on evolving organisms in the context of modern genetics, is the explanation for the diversity of life that best fits the available evidence. As such, it is accepted by the majority of scientists.

## Le Châtelier's Principle 🜹

### What is it?

Le Châtelier's principle concerns chemical equilibrium, a state that occurs when a reversible chemical reaction takes place. The reaction reaches chemical equilibrium when the rates of the forward and reverse reactions are equal, so that the system has no further tendency to change. Le Châtelier's principle states that if a change is made in the pressure, temperature or concentration of a system in chemical equilibrium, the equilibrium will be displaced in such a way as to oppose this change. For example, if the reaction tends to give out heat in the forward direction but absorb heat in the reverse direction, lowering the reaction temperature would favour the forward reaction.

### Who worked it out?

The French chemist Henri Louis Le Châtelier gave his name to this principle, which he formulated in 1884. He worked it out after his earlier research on the nature and setting of cements led him to consider the fundamental laws of chemical equilibrium.

### Why is it important?

Le Châtelier's principle is very important in many industrial chemical processes involving reversible reactions. It allows the optimum pressure and temperature to be calculated to ensure the best yield of the desired product. It also demonstrates that removing the product from the reaction, and therefore lowering its concentration, will help the reaction to take place in the correct direction.

The general principle of change in a system provoking an opposite reaction has also influenced other fields, including the social sciences.

---

### Egg Science

Boiling an egg involves a chemical reaction, although it is not reversible. Dr Charles Williams of the School of Physics at the University of Exeter has worked out a scientific formula to calculate the exact cooking time needed to produce a perfect soft-boiled egg. He concluded that the equation is:

$$t = aM^{2/3} \ln \left[ \frac{2 \times (T_{egg} - T_{water})}{(T_{yolk} - T_{water})} \right]$$

where:

$t$ is the total cooking time in minutes;

$a$ is a constant which depends on the egg's specific heat capacity and thermal conductivity (use $a = 16$ s g$^{-2/3}$ for eggs that are a week or two old – very fresh eggs will need a higher value, old eggs may need a lower value);

$M$ is the mass of the egg in grams;

ln is the natural logarithm of the bracketed expression;

$T_{egg}$ is the temperature in °C of the egg at the beginning;

$T_{yolk}$ is the temperature in °C at which the egg is ready to be eaten (for soft-boiled eggs use 45°C);

$T_{water}$ is the temperature in °C of the boiling water.

## Collision Theory ⚗

### What is it?

Collision theory is an important part of chemical kinetics – the study of how particles such as atoms, molecules or ions react with one another and the rate at which they do so. The theory is based on the idea that, in order for a reaction to occur, particles must collide with each other in the correct orientation and with a minimum energy called the activation energy. The activation energy is required to break chemical bonds so that new ones can be made; even if the overall reaction gives out energy, this activation energy 'barrier' still applies. The energy is used to produce an unstable transition state during the reaction, which then breaks down to form the reaction products.

### Who worked it out?

The Norwegian chemists Peter Waage and Cato Maximilian Guldberg, who were brothers-in-law, established the law of mass action in 1864. This says that the rate of a reaction is proportional to the concentrations of the reactants. Twenty-five years later, the Swedish physical chemist Svante Arrhenius showed that the rate of a reaction depends on temperature in a more complex manner.

The Danish physical chemist Jens Christiansen's doctoral thesis (1921) contained a collision theory and a rate theory of chemical reactions that could explain the earlier findings of Waage, Guldberg and Arrhenius. Both of Christiansen's theories have provided the basis for later, more sophisticated treatments, but his contributions have not been widely recognized because his thesis was in Danish.

The US physical chemist Henry Eyring published his transition state theory, involving conversion of the reactants to a transition state that then decomposed to form the products, in 1935. The British physical chemists Michael Polanyi and Sir Cyril Hinshelwood, as well as the Soviet physical chemist Nikolai Semenov, also carried out research relating to this theory.

### Why is it important?

Collision theory explains the effects of the temperature and concentration of the reacting chemicals on the rate of a chemical reaction. When the temperature is increased, the particles have more energy so more of the collisions will break the activation energy 'barrier'. When the concentration of one or more of the chemicals is increased, the chances of an appropriate collision occurring also rise, allowing more particles to react. Increasing the pressure of gases has the same effect.

Reactions can often be speeded up by using a catalyst. Catalysts do not take part in the reaction, but they lower the activation energy so that collisions between particles are more likely to make those particles react. Living organisms use protein catalysts to control the rates of biochemical reactions (see **Atoms, elements and molecules: Enzymes**).

An increased understanding of all of these properties of reactions has allowed commercial production of chemicals and materials to be carried out more efficiently.

# KEY CONCEPTS

## The Gas Laws 🔔 ⚛

### What are they?

The gas laws are a set of relationships between the pressure, volume and temperature of a gas. They are based on the kinetic theory of gases, which accounts for the properties of gases in terms of the motion of the molecules of the gas. In its simplest form, the gas molecules are treated as elastic spheres that move around randomly and collide with each other. These spheres also bombard the walls of the vessel in which the gas is contained, and this causes the pressure exerted by the gas. The temperature of the gas is proportional to the average kinetic (movement) energy of the gas molecules – the more the molecules move around, the warmer the gas.

### Boyle's law

Boyle's law says that the volume of a fixed mass of gas is inversely proportional to its pressure, providing that the temperature remains constant. This means that, as the volume of the gas is decreased, the pressure rises. The law can be explained by the fact that the gas molecules are more likely to bounce off the walls of a smaller container. Boyle's law is also known as Mariotte's law.

### The pressure law

The pressure law says that the pressure of a fixed mass of gas is directly proportional to its temperature, providing that the volume remains constant. This can be explained by the fact that the gas molecules move around faster as the temperature rises, so they bounce off the walls of the container more often. The pressure law is also known as Amontons's law.

### Charles's law

Charles's law says that the volume of a fixed mass of gas is directly proportional to the absolute temperature, providing that the pressure remains constant. This means that the gas expands as it heats up. The law can be explained by the fact that, in order to keep the pressure constant, the bouncing of the molecules off the wall of the container must be kept the same. However, increasing the temperature makes the molecules move around more, so the volume must increase to stop this increasing the pressure. Charles's Law is also known as Gay-Lussac's law.

### La Charlière

The French physicist Jacques Charles is today best known for developing Charles's law. In his lifetime, however, he was more famous for making the first ascent in a hydrogen balloon, known as *La Charlière*. The flight took place on 1 December 1783, just weeks after the Montgolfier brothers' first manned hot-air balloon ascent.

### The ideal gas law

The three laws can also be combined into a single law known as the ideal gas law. This law relies on **Avogadro's law** and his concept of moles to bring the three laws together. The law is written as $PV = nRT$, where $P$ is pressure, $V$ is volume, $n$ is the amount of gas in moles, $R$ is a constant called the gas constant and $T$ is absolute temperature.

## Who worked them out?

The 18th-century Swiss mathematician Daniel Bernoulli anticipated the kinetic theory of gases by pointing out that the pressure of a gas would increase with its temperature. Work by the Scottish natural philosopher John Waterston, published in 1845, contained the basis of the kinetic theory. Later in the 19th century, the Scottish physicist James Clerk Maxwell further developed the theory, and the English physicist Sir James Hopwood Jeans provided a mathematical proof. The German physicist Rudolf Clausius also contributed. At the same time, the Russian physicist Konstantin Tsiolkovsky independently developed the theory.

The French physicist Guillaume Amontons worked out the pressure law at the beginning of the 18th century. Boyle's law is named after the Anglo-Irish physicist and chemist Robert Boyle, who described the law in 1662; the French physicist Edmé Mariotte restated the law in 1679. Charles's law was worked out by the French physicist Jacques Charles between 1786 and 1787, but was published by another French scientist, Joseph Gay-Lussac, who referred to Charles's work as well as his own findings. The combination of the laws into the ideal gas law depended on work by the Austrian physicist Ludwig Boltzmann and the Italian physicist Amedeo Avogadro.

## Are they really true?

The kinetic theory of gases, which is behind the gas laws, assumes that the size of the molecules is very small compared with the amount of space between them, and that the molecules do not attract each other. A theoretical gas that behaves in exactly this way, and therefore fully obeys the gas laws, is known as an ideal gas. In practice, real gases do not exactly meet these requirements, but the laws can be used as an approximation.

## The Laws of Thermodynamics ⚛

### What are they?

The laws of thermodynamics are a set of three laws that describe the relationships between thermal ('heat') energy and other forms of energy such as mechanical energy.

### First law

Energy exists in many different forms, including thermal energy, electrical energy and mechanical energy (see **Energy, light and radioactivity: Energy**). The first law says that energy can be transferred from one form to another but it cannot be created or destroyed.

### Second law

An important concept in thermodynamics is entropy. This is a measure of the amount of disorder in a system, and determines how much energy is actually available to do useful work. Entropy increases as the temperature of a system goes up, because the molecules have more energy and move around more quickly (thermal energy), so they are more likely to become disordered.

There are several ways of expressing the second law; one of them is to say that the entropy of a closed system, where energy cannot be transferred in or out, tends to increase. This means that the system becomes more disordered and less energy is available to do useful work.

The second law means that heat will tend to be transferred from a hot object to a cold one, because the heat transfer spreads out thermal energy and makes the system more disordered. If you leave an ice-cube in a warm room, the heat will tend to move from the air to the ice, making it melt. The highest amount of entropy is present when both objects are at the same temperature; a state known as thermal equilibrium. Overcoming this effect requires additional energy from outside. For example, a freezer is colder than the room it is in because energy from electricity is supplied to it. However, the system is no longer closed, so the second law has not been broken. If there is a long power cut, the freezer will gradually warm up to room temperature. This shows that energy must be put in to keep the system from returning to thermal equilibrium.

### Third law

The third law says that, at a temperature of absolute zero, the entropy of a perfect crystal of a substance is zero. Atoms at this temperature don't have any thermal energy and therefore do not move around according to classical physics. However, quantum physics requires that they still have a very small amount of motion due to energy known as zero-point energy, in order to prevent their momentum being completely certain (see **Heisenberg's uncertainty principle**).

### How Low Can You Go?

Although scientists have cooled various substances down to within a degree of absolute zero, no-one has ever reached it. Even in outer space the temperature is about three Kelvin, which is equivalent to three degrees above absolute zero on the Celsius scale.

## Who worked them out?

It took many different people to work out the principles of thermodynamics over the years, so only a few are mentioned here. The English natural philosopher James Joule and the French physicist Sadi Carnot both played an important part in the early work on thermodynamics during the 19th century. The German physicist Rudolf Clausius and the Scottish physicist William Lord Kelvin simultaneously worked out the First and Second Laws, while the Third Law was developed by the German physical chemist Walther Nernst.

The Austrian physicist Ludwig Boltzmann showed that the entropy of a system could be described statistically in terms of the number of 'microstates' it could be in. The microstates give each atom a particular location and energy. For example, if a jar of gas is at a particular temperature, the locations of all the atoms in the gas have to be inside the jar, and the total energies of the atoms must combine to give the observed temperature. The more disordered a system, the more possible microstates it has, and the higher its entropy.

### Physics from Beyond the Grave

Boltzmann's entropy equation, $S = k \ln W$, is carved on his tombstone in Vienna. It shows that the entropy $S$ of a system is proportional to $\ln W$, the natural logarithm of the number of possible microstates. $k$ is a constant, and is known as the Boltzmann constant.

## Why are they important?

The Second Law is important because it explains why many processes only happen in one direction. If you spray water from a hosepipe, the water droplets travel in different directions and the water ends up all over the garden. There are many places in which the water droplets can end up, so the amount of disorder, ie the entropy, is higher than when the water was in the hose. It is not impossible for the water molecules to move back into the hose but it is *extremely* unlikely, because there are many other directions in which each water molecule could move.

# KEY CONCEPTS

## Avogadro's Law

### What is it?

Avogadro's law says that equal volumes of gases, at the same temperature and pressure, contain the same number of molecules. The mass of the molecules will vary between gases, as some have bigger and more complicated molecules than others, so equal volumes of different gases will not weigh the same.

### Who worked it out?

Joseph Gay-Lussac, a French chemist and physicist, worked out in 1809 that the volume of a mixture of gases is equal to the sum of the volumes of the different gases at the same temperature and pressure. An Italian physicist and chemist, Amedeo Avogadro, developed Gay-Lussac's findings whilst working in Vercelli, resulting in the publication of Avogadro's law in 1811.

### Why is it important?

Avogadro's Law has been fundamental to the development of chemistry. For example, the combination of three separate gas laws into the ideal gas law relies on it (see **The gas laws**).

The concept of considering substances in terms of numbers of molecules makes it easier to study chemical reactions. Chemists now use a term known as a mole to relate equivalent quantities of different substances. A mole is defined as the number of atoms contained in twelve grams of carbon-12, the most common form of carbon. It can be thought of as the quantity of a substance that contains a number of grams equal to the atomic mass of the substance. Both atoms and molecules can be counted in terms of moles, as can other particles such as electrons.

The number of particles in a mole was renamed Avogadro's number in his honour, even though it was actually calculated by Josef Loschmidt in 1865.

---

### National Mole Day

National Mole Day, celebrated in the USA, is not a festival for small furry animals but a celebration of the measuring unit in chemistry. It is celebrated from 6.02am to 6.02pm on 23 October, which is 6.02 10/23 in the American style of writing dates – a play on Avogadro's number, which is $6.02 \times 10^{23}$.

## Heisenberg's Uncertainty Principle 🍶⚛

### What is it?

Heisenberg's uncertainty principle concerns the position and momentum of subatomic particles (see **Atoms, elements and molecules: Subatomic particles**). Momentum is a property that depends on both the mass of the particle and its speed in a particular direction. The uncertainty principle says that we can never know both the precise location of a particle and its precise momentum. The more accurately we know one of these properties, the more uncertain the other becomes. One of the implications of the principle is that we can never know both the precise energy of a particle and the precise time over which the energy is measured.

These phenomena are often attributed to our inability to measure one property without influencing the other. However, poor measuring instruments are not the problem – the uncertainty is a fundamental property.

In both statements, the product of the uncertainties in the measurements of the two quantities involved must be greater than $h/2$, where $h$ is a number known as Planck's constant.

### Who worked it out?

Heisenberg's uncertainty principle is named after Werner Heisenberg, a German theoretical physicist. Heisenberg developed the principle in 1927, by considering subatomic particles to be wave-like in nature.

The Austrian physicist Erwin Schrödinger and the American mathematician Howard Percy Robertson later developed more general versions of the principle.

### Why is it important?

Heisenberg's uncertainty principle showed modern physicists that it is necessary to study the probabilities of particle properties such as location and momentum, and to look at average values, because precise, definite values for these properties do not exist.

### Is it really true?

Heisenberg's uncertainty principle has so far been found to hold for all situations. It even applies to objects that are larger than subatomic particles, but the uncertainty becomes so small that it is insignificant compared with the scale of the object. So it is only really necessary to take the principle into account at the subatomic level.

# KEY CONCEPTS

## Pauli's Exclusion Principle ⚛

### What is it?

Pauli's exclusion principle is a fundamental law of quantum mechanics (see **Quantum theory**), and relates to certain properties of electrons called quantum numbers. An electron in an atom has four of these properties, known as principal quantum number, azimuthal quantum number, magnetic quantum number and spin quantum number. The principle says that no two electrons in an atom can exist in exactly the same state, with all four quantum numbers being the same. Each quantum number can only take certain values, which restricts the numbers and arrangements of electrons within atoms.

### Who worked it out?

The principle is named after the Austrian–Swiss theoretical physicist Wolfgang Pauli. Pauli demonstrated that, in addition to the principal, azimuthal and magnetic quantum numbers, a fourth 'spin' quantum number was required to describe the state of an atomic electron. He went on to formulate the exclusion principle in 1924.

### Why is it important?

Pauli's exclusion principle explains the arrangement of electrons in atoms. This in turn determines the properties of chemical elements and their arrangement in the periodic table. The principle therefore lies at the heart of our understanding of the properties of materials and how chemical reactions occur.

> ## The Pauli Effect
>
> Pauli was undoubtedly extremely talented as a theoretical physicist. His practical skills, however, apparently left something to be desired. The correlation between his presence in the laboratory and the breakdown of the scientific equipment was so strong that it became known as the Pauli Effect.

## Hooke's Law

### What is it?

Hooke's law describes the behaviour of elastic materials. In its original form, it describes a coiled spring, and says that the length to which the spring is stretched is directly proportional to the force applied to the spring. This means that pulling twice as hard on a spring will stretch it to twice the length.

A more general version of the law says that the amount by which any elastic material is stretched, known as the strain, is directly proportional to the tensile stress on the material. Tensile stress is the force pulling on a particular area of a material, so this still means that the amount of stretch is proportional to the force. The constant that relates tensile stress to strain is called Young's modulus (see **Materials: Properties of materials**). This can be written as $\sigma = E\varepsilon$, where $\sigma$ represents tensile stress, $\varepsilon$ is strain and E is Young's modulus.

### Who worked it out?

The basic statement of linear elasticity relating to springs was published fully by the English scientist Robert Hooke in 1676, and resulted from his attempts to make a clock that was controlled by a spring rather than a pendulum. The English physicist Thomas Young realized over 100 years later that the proportionality was between tensile stress and strain; the constant that relates the two properties is named after him.

### Why is it important?

An understanding of the general form of Hooke's law has been important in learning about the properties of materials. Equations similar to the one used for tensile stress can be used to relate other forms of stress, such as compression, to their resultant strains.

### Is it really true?

Hooke's original version of the law holds true for springs as long as they are not stretched too far. Beyond a certain point, the spring does not return to its original shape and the law no longer applies. Young's general version of the law is a good approximation of the behaviour of most types of material – these are known as linear-elastic materials. Again, the law applies within a certain range of strain and stress, but not if these become too great. The two main types of materials that do not behave in a linear-elastic way are polymers and elastomers such as rubber.

> ### Puzzling Publication
>
> Robert Hooke actually worked out his law in 1670 but was worried that his rival, Isaac Newton, would steal his ideas. He therefore decided to publish his findings firstly as the anagram 'ceiiinosssttuv', which rearranges to the Latin phrase *ut tensio, sic vis*. The English meaning of the phrase is 'as the extension, so the force'.

## Continental Drift

### What is it?

Continental drift is the theory that all the Earth's continents were originally one vast land mass, and that it has broken up and drifted apart into separate continents over time. The land mass is often referred to as Pangaea, from the Greek for 'all Earth'.

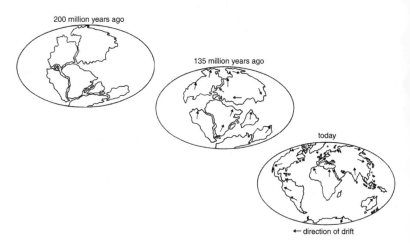

200 million years ago

135 million years ago

today

← direction of drift

### Who worked it out?

Many people, including the English philosopher Francis Bacon and the US statesman and scientist Benjamin Franklin, noticed that the shapes of the continents on either side of the Atlantic ocean would fit together. Inspired by this observation, the German geophysicist A L Wegener proposed the theory of continental drift in 1912 to explain the structural, geological and physical similarities that exist between continents. However, lack of an obvious mechanism for the continents to travel through an apparently solid sea floor meant that his theory was ignored for many years.

In the 1960s, the US marine geophysicist Harry Hess proposed a model for the formation of flat-topped seamounts called guyots, which involved the continual flow of magma into the mid-ocean ridges. This was based on the idea of convection currents in the Earth's mantle, as proposed by the English geologist Arthur Holmes in 1929. Hess's model provided a mechanism for the spreading of the sea-floor, which could carry the continents apart (see also **The Earth: Plate tectonics**).

### Is it really true?

There is a lot of evidence for continental drift. For example, fossil records show that the same organisms lived in continents that are now separate. For example, the US palaeontologist Edwin Colbert discovered fossils of the reptile *Lystrosaurus* in Africa, India and Antarctica. Other evidence includes the measurement of heat from the sea floor, which supports the idea that it spreads due to magma flow.

## Uniformitarianism

### What is it?

Uniformitarianism is a theory about how the Earth's rocks were formed. Its main concept is that the processes that operate to modify the Earth today also operated in the geological past. The theory suggests that even the greatest geological changes might have been produced by these processes, given sufficient time. In its more extreme form it also says that the rates at which these processes occur remain constant.

### Who worked it out?

Prior to the development of the uniformitarian theory, the predominant theory about the formation of rocks was catastrophism. This was the theory that the Earth's geological history has been fashioned by infrequent violent events, and was championed by the German geologist Abraham Werner. Werner advocated that crystalline igneous rocks such as granite were formed by direct precipitation from sea water during a great flood, and that they formed part of an overall system of layers of rock, each laid down at a different time.

The 18th-century Scottish geologist James Hutton then proposed that the internal heat of the Earth caused intrusions of molten rock into the crust, and that granite was the product of the cooling of molten rock. He realized that most rocks were produced by erosion from the continents and deposition of the eroded material on the seafloor, followed by heating from below to form new rock. The new rock would then be uplifted to form new continents. The fact that these processes operated in a cycle led Hutton to propose somewhat drastically that the Earth had 'no vestige of a beginning and no prospect of an end'. Hutton's ideas and research were published in *A Theory of the Earth* in 1785.

Uniformitarianism was brought to people's attention by two other Scottish geologists. John Playfair's work *Illustrations of the Huttonian Theory* (1802) and the later *Principles of Geology* (1830–3) by Sir Charles Lyell were both instrumental in raising awareness of Hutton's work.

### Why is it important?

As well as being important for our understanding of geology, the general concept of gradual change that is at the core of uniformitarianism has also influenced other areas of science. In particular, Charles Darwin's work on the evolution of living organisms was inspired in part by reading Lyell's work (see **The theory of natural selection**).

### Is it really true?

Uniformitarianism is certainly at the core of modern thinking about geology. However, it is now accepted that catastrophic events have also occurred throughout the Earth's history, such as volcanic eruptions and asteroid impacts. The current picture is therefore one of a continuous, gradual process of rock formation, punctuated by occasional sudden events.

# KEY CONCEPTS

## The Gaia Hypothesis

### What is it?

The Gaia hypothesis proposes that the Earth's climate is constantly regulated by plants and animals, to maintain a life-sustaining balance of organic substances in the atmosphere. This phenomenon is known as homeostasis. Gaia is now regarded as an evolving system comprising the atmosphere, oceans, surface rocks and living organisms. This system is in dynamic equilibrium; small changes in conditions affect the relative populations of different organisms in such a way that the system tends to return to its original state. The hypothesis says that the whole system can be regarded as itself behaving as a living 'superorganism'.

### Earthly Goddess

The name 'Gaia' was suggested by the author William Golding, who was James Lovelock's neighbour, and is the name of the Greek goddess of the Earth. The prefix 'geo-', meaning 'related to the Earth', derives from the same name.

### Who worked it out?

The Scottish geologist James Hutton proposed the idea of 'planetary physiology' in the late 18th century, but he had little evidence for the concept. The English chemist James Lovelock constructed the Gaia hypothesis in 1972 after studying the atmospheres of different planets while working for NASA. Lovelock noticed that the Earth's atmosphere was unusual because the different gases were held in proportions that should not be stable. For example, oxygen is a reactive gas and yet is present in the Earth's atmosphere at a stable, relatively high concentration, whereas the neighbouring planets Mars and Venus have much less oxygen and more carbon dioxide. The difference is that the Earth has organisms such as plants that turn carbon dioxide into oxygen.

Work by Lovelock and the American biologist Lynn Margulis demonstrated the importance of bacteria in regulating the climate and chemical composition of the Earth. The Russian geochemist Vladimir Vernadsky showed that living organisms can transfer energy and matter between different parts of the planetary system, and proposed the term 'biosphere' to encompass the whole system of Earth's surface, atmosphere, oceans and living creatures.

### Why is it important?

The Gaia hypothesis suggests that any changes we cause to the planet, such as global warming, may not actually destroy the Earth, but that they would alter the balance of creatures living on it, both ourselves and others, thus maintaining homeostasis.

## Is it really true?

The Gaia hypothesis is highly controversial. Some people argue that it is teleological (it presumes that events have a purpose), saying it requires that the biosphere is somehow capable of consciously regulating itself. Lovelock argues that the self-regulation is an emergent property – it can take place without any sense of purpose or overall organization. He carried out a computer simulation called Daisy World to show this, where a planet populated by black and white daisies, which absorb the Sun's heat differently, was able to regulate its own atmospheric temperature to be optimal for daisy growth even when the Sun's temperature increased.

Part of the problem with the Gaia hypothesis is that it is open to various different interpretations, including what being 'alive' actually means. However, living organisms and the environment certainly affect each other, and this forms a central principle of the discipline known as Earth systems science.

# KEY CONCEPTS

## Milankovitch Theory

### What is it?

The Milankovitch theory, also known as orbital forcing, relates to climate change. It says that large changes to the Earth's climate, such as ice ages, have been caused by variations in the Earth's orbit around the Sun, which alter the distribution and timing of solar radiation received by the Earth. These variations take the form of repeating cycles known as Milankovitch cycles. The cycle of ice ages and interglacial periods is currently around 100 000 years. The theory proposes that this cycle results from a combination of three main sources of orbital variation: eccentricity, axial tilt and precession.

### Eccentricity

The Earth's orbit is not precisely circular, but actually takes the form of an ellipse (see **Kepler's laws of planetary motion**). This means that the Earth's distance from the Sun varies – its closest point is called the perihelion, while the furthest point is called the aphelion. The eccentricity is a measure of how far away the orbit is from being circular. The eccentricity effects approximately fall into two cycles, a major one of 400 000 years and a smaller one of 100 000 years.

### Axial tilt

The axis around which the Earth spins is not 'upright' in relation to its orbit around the Sun, but is tilted. The amount of axial tilt varies between approximately 22° and 24°, following a cycle of around 40 000 years.

### Precession

An effect of the axis being tilted is that it rotates, so that each pole appears to move through a circle. This affects the severity of the seasons in the northern and southern hemispheres, depending on which pole is pointing towards the Sun and whether this happens when the Earth is close to the Sun or far away. This effect is called precession of the equinoxes. (The equinoxes are the two days of the year on which day and night are of equal length; the position of the Earth in relation to the Sun on these dates varies due to precession.) Precession has a cycle of around 25 000 years; various smaller effects give an overall cycle length closer to 20 000 years.

### Who worked it out?

The French mathematician Joseph Adhemar first proposed that precession could affect climate, in his 1842 publication *Révolutions de la mer* ('Revolutions of the Sea'). A quarter of a century later, the Scottish geologist James Croll suggested in his work *Climate and Time in their Geological Relations* that precession and eccentricity could together cause the cycle of ice ages, but his theory still didn't fit the data.

The Yugoslav geophysicist Milutin Milankovitch realised that eccentricity, axial tilt and precession might all act together to affect climate, and he gave his name to the complete theory. In the first half of the 19th century he constructed graphs showing how much energy from the Sun should have reached the Earth for the past 650 000 years, and compared them with the occurrence of ice ages and interglacial periods, worked out from measuring the levels of normal and radioactive oxygen in samples taken from deep ocean beds and polar ice caps.

**Milankovitch Cycles**

## Why is it important?

An understanding of how and when ice ages and accompanying climate change occur would allow scientists to make future predictions about the Earth's climate.

## Is it really true?

It is likely that eccentricity, axial tilt and precession all affect climate and glaciation. However, the climate changes that the theory predicts are smaller than those that were measured. It may be that orbital forcing can trigger larger changes to occur by other mechanisms (see **The Gaia hypothesis**). Another problem is that, if the minor eccentricity cycle of 100 000 years is responsible for the ice age cycle of the same length, then it would be expected that the major cycle of 400 000 years would also affect the ice ages. It therefore seems that Milankovitch theory is an important factor in climate change, but is not the whole story.

The ice age cycle has not always been 100 000 years; in previous times in the Earth's history it has been 23 000 and 41 000 years. Although these cycles could be explained by axial tilt and precession respectively, it is not clear what could have caused the change in cycle length.

# Key Concepts

## Big Bang Theory

### What is it?

Big Bang theory says that the universe, with all its matter and energy, was once concentrated into an unimaginably small, extremely dense state called a singularity. The name refers to the explosive and extremely hot event that is thought to have occurred about 13 billion years ago to produce this concentrated matter and energy.

Big Bang theory suggests that quarks and leptons, together with their antiparticles, dominated the universe less than a second after its beginning. A slight imbalance between quarks and antiquarks then resulted in the annihilation of most antiparticles, creating an immense amount of electromagnetic radiation. After a microsecond the universe cooled sufficiently for the quarks to combine to form protons and neutrons.

After about one second, electromagnetic radiation dominated the universe for the next million years. However, in the first few minutes of this phase, interactions between protons and electrons led to the formation of helium nuclei. (More complex nuclei were formed much later in stars, and were distributed throughout space when stars exploded.) After this period of a million years, the universe cooled down enough to allow electrons to combine with nuclei, forming stable atoms.

### Who worked it out?

Before Big Bang theory was proposed, the widely-accepted model of the universe was that the universe is infinitely old and will continue into the infinite future. This is known as steady-state theory. Albert Einstein's **General theory of relativity** predicted that the universe was dynamic rather than in a steady state, but he didn't accept this as being the case. Instead, he included a completely arbitrary 'cosmological repulsion' factor into his equations in order to stabilize the universe.

In 1929, the US astronomers Edwin Hubble and Milton Humason showed that the universe is expanding (see **Hubble's law**). This is consistent with the idea of galaxies continuing to rush away from the explosion. However, supporters of steady-state theory, including Fred Hoyle, Hermann Bondi and Thomas Gold, got around this by proposing that matter is continually being created to fill the gaps left by expansion.

In the 1960s, the US physicists Robert Wilson and Arno Penzias detected microwave background radiation coming from all directions. This is thought to be the residual energy from the Big Bang.

### Is it really true?

The Big Bang model cannot explain why the universe has the density we observe, nor can it explain how galaxies were formed. Also, it does not account for the extraordinarily uniform level of background radiation throughout the universe. However, these difficulties have been resolved by a more sophisticated version of Big Bang theory known as the inflationary universe model, which has been developed since 1980. This proposes that the universe momentarily expanded much faster than the speed of light, just a tiny fraction of a second after the Big Bang. (Although objects cannot *travel* faster than the speed of light according to relativity, the expansion of space would still be permissible.) Currently almost all astrophysicists choose the Big Bang picture to interpret their results.

## Hubble's Law

### What is it?

Hubble's Law describes the rate at which galaxies move apart. It states that the recession speed of a distant galaxy is directly proportional to the distance of the galaxy from the observer.

The recession speed and distance of a galaxy are related by a property known as the Hubble parameter. It was originally called the Hubble constant, but it is now known that the value is changing as the universe gets older. Astrophysicists are still unagreed as to the current value of the parameter, but it is probably about 70 kilometres (45 miles) per second per megaparsec, or about 20 kilometres (12 miles) per second per million light years. This means that, for every million light years away a galaxy is located, its recession speed increases by 20 kilometres (12 miles) per second.

The first indication that galaxies are moving apart came from atomic spectroscopy studies on galaxies. These showed that most of the galaxies had spectra that were shifted, so that the wavelengths of the lines were longer than expected. This effect is known as red shift, because all the colours shift towards the red end of the spectrum. Red shift is an example of the phenomenon called Doppler shift, which occurs when the distance between an object and its observer increases so that waves are stretched out. (Doppler shift is also responsible for the way that an ambulance siren seems to drop in pitch as the ambulance drives away from you.) The atomic spectroscopy results therefore indicated that the distance between the galaxies was increasing.

---

**Atomic spectroscopy**

Atomic spectroscopy involves splitting the light from glowing objects, such as stars or galaxies, into all its different colours, producing bands of colour known as spectral lines. Each chemical element present in a glowing object gives a different pattern of these lines. The light from the distant object is focused to a parallel beam by a lens called the collimator. The first experiments used glass prisms to split the light (see **Energy, light and radioactivity: Waves**) but nowadays a device called a diffraction grating is used instead. The spectral pattern is detected by photographic film or light sensors.

---

The data showed that the galaxies appeared to be moving apart at speeds of up to 2000 kilometres (1200 miles) per second. The widely accepted explanation for this result is that the universe is expanding, just as dots drawn on a balloon move apart from each other as the balloon is inflated.

### Who worked it out?

The effect of Doppler shift was discovered by the Austrian physicist Christian Johann Doppler in 1842. Early atomic spectroscopy studies on red shift in stars were conducted by the English astronomer Sir William Huggins in 1864. The atomic spectroscopy studies showing red shift in galaxies were carried out by the US astronomer V M Slipher in the early 1920s.

# KEY CONCEPTS

The US astronomers Edwin Hubble and Milton Humason carried out further observations, studying the spectra of galaxies that are different distances from the Earth, and then published the relationship now known as Hubble's law in 1929.

## Why is it important?

Hubble's law has played a significant part in the debate as to whether the universe is in a steady state or whether it began as an immeasurably small, dense singularity (see **Big Bang theory**). The law has also enabled astronomers to estimate the distances to other remote galaxies.

## Is it really true?

The recession speeds of extremely distant galaxies deviate from those predicted by Hubble's law. This deviation may hold the key to establishing whether the universe will continue to expand infinitely, or whether it will eventually collapse back to a singularity referred to as the Big Crunch.

### The Hubble Space Telescope

The Hubble space telescope is an optical telescope, 4.2m (14ft) in diameter, that was launched into space in 1990. It made measurements to determine the Hubble parameter and to examine how recession speeds of distant galaxies start to wander. The main mirror was manufactured to the wrong shape, so corrective optics had to be installed to allow sharp images to be transmitted back to Earth.

## Kepler's Laws of Planetary Motion

### What are they?

Kepler's laws describe the movement of planets around the Sun in our solar system.

**The first law**

The first law says that the orbit of a planet around the Sun has the shape of an ellipse ('flattened' circle), with the Sun at a focus of the ellipse. (An ellipse has two foci; in the special case of a circle, both of these lie at a single point in the centre.)

**The second law**

The second law says that a line drawn from the Sun to a planet sweeps across equal areas in equal times: on the diagram, the area between the Sun and points 1 and 2 is the same as the area between the Sun and points 3 and 4. The planets move most slowly when they are at a point furthest from the Sun, called the aphelion, and most quickly when they are at a point closest to the Sun, called the perihelion.

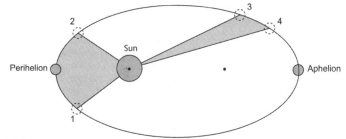

**The third law**

The third law says that the squares of the periodic times of the planets are proportional to the cubes of their mean distances from the Sun.

### Who worked them out?

The Polish astronomer Nicolaus Copernicus was unconvinced by the generally-held view that the Earth was the stationary centre of the universe, and instead proposed a Sun-centred universe. His work was published in 1543, in *De Revolutionibus Orbium Coelestium* ('The Revolutions of the Celestial Spheres').

The Italian astronomer Galileo Galilei studied the phases of Venus, the Sun's rotation, and Saturn's rings. His work, which supported that of Copernicus, was published in *Dialogue on the Two Principal Systems of the World* (1632).

Tycho Brahe, a Danish astronomer, made many observations of the stars over the course of 20 years. After his death, his assistant Johannes Kepler used Brahe's data to work out his laws, which he published in *New Astronomy* (1609).

### Why are they important?

Kepler's laws inspired Isaac Newton to formulate his laws of motion (see **Newton's laws of motion**). They also apply to systems other than the solar system, such as the orbit of artificial satellites.

## Newton's Laws of Motion

### What are they?

Newton's laws of motion are three laws that are fundamental to classical physics.

### Newton's first law

The first law states that a body will continue in a state of rest, or constant motion in a straight line, unless an external force acts upon it. This phenomenon is called inertia.

### Newton's second law

The second law relates to a property known as momentum, which depends on the mass of an object and its velocity (its speed in a particular direction). The law states that the rate of change of momentum of an object is proportional to the force applied to it, and that the change takes place in the direction of the applied force. This law gives rise to the rule that the force applied (in newtons) is equal to the mass of the object (in kilograms) multiplied by the object's acceleration (in metres per square second) – this rule is stated as $F = ma$.

### Newton's third law

The third law states that every action (every force that is applied) has a reaction, and that the action and reaction are equal and opposite. This means that, when two bodies interact, the force exerted by the first body on the second body is equal and opposite to the force exerted by the second body on the first. This gives rise to effects like the recoil of a gun when it is fired.

gun recoils backward due to force of bullet acting on gun

bullet travels forward due to force of gun acting on bullet

**Recoil of a Gun**

### Who worked them out?

This set of laws was first stated by the English physicist Isaac Newton in his 1687 work *Philosophiae Naturalis Principia Mathematica* ('The Mathematical Principles of Natural Philosophy'). This work is often known simply as the *Principia*. However, Newton's first law is basically a restatement of a principle of inertia that was devised by the Italian natural philosopher Galileo Galilei.

### Why are they important?

Newton's laws are able to explain the motion of everyday objects and phenomena, such as pendulums, projectiles and tides. The second law shows that objects can have different weights when they are on different planets, even though their masses remain the same. The weight of an object (the force) is greater on planets where gravity (acceleration) is higher.

## Are they really true?

Newton's laws fail when objects are travelling at speeds close to the speed of light, when physicists must turn to more complex explanations (see **General theory of relativity** and **Special theory of relativity**). They also don't work properly in systems at the subatomic scale (see **Quantum theory**). However, they are a good model for many everyday situations.

> 66
>
> *When Newton saw an apple fall, he found,*
> *In that slight startle from his contemplation, ...*
> *A mode of proving that the Earth turned round*
> *In a most natural whirl, called 'gravitation';*
> *And this is the sole mortal who could grapple,*
> *Since Adam, with a fall or with an apple.*
>
> —English poet Lord Byron (1788–1824), *Don Juan*, canto 10, stanza 1 (1819–24). It is said that Newton developed his theory of gravitation, which also was published in the *Principia*, after watching an apple fall in his mother's garden at Woolsthorpe Manor in Lincolnshire.
>
> 99

## Special Theory of Relativity

### What is it?

Special relativity is the collective name for two important principles about the universe: the principle of relativity and the constancy of the speed of light.

### The principle of relativity

The principle of relativity says that movement is relative to the frame of reference (the place from which you are watching) and that no one place is absolutely still, or any more important than another place. So, a man travelling at a steady speed in spaceship A can see spaceship B going past, but a woman travelling at a steady speed in the opposite direction in spaceship B can also watch spaceship A going past. Each person thinks they are sitting 'still' in their spaceship, but in fact they are moving relative to each other. The principle also says that the same laws of physics always apply, no matter where you are observing from.

### The constancy of the speed of light

The constancy of the speed of light in a vacuum says that light always travels through empty space at the same speed – around 300 000 kilometres (186 0000 miles) per second – no matter where it is being watched from.

### The mass-energy relation

When the principle of relativity is combined with the principle that momentum, energy and mass are conserved, another relationship can be deduced: the equivalence of mass and energy. This can be expressed in the form of the mass-energy equation, better known as $E = mc^2$, where $E$ is energy, $m$ is mass and $c$ is the speed of light. If a body gains energy $E$, its inertia is increased by the amount of mass equal to $m = E/c^2$.

### Effects of special relativity

Special relativity has some counterintuitive consequences. It turns out that motion distorts time and space in unexpected ways. To a person on Earth, a clock travelling in a spaceship at a speed close to that of light would appear to run more slowly than the person's own clock. An astronaut on the spaceship, meanwhile, would think the clock on Earth was running more slowly than the one on the spaceship! This effect is called time dilation. Similarly, distances would appear to shrink, a phenomenon known as Lorentz contraction. However, these effects would only be noticeable at extremely high speeds, close to the speed of light, so we do not notice them in everyday life.

### Who worked it out?

The special theory of relativity was proposed by the German physicist Albert Einstein in 1905. He realized that work by the Scottish physicist James Clerk Maxwell, showing that light consisted of electromagnetic radiation, conflicted with **Newton's laws of motion**, and devised special relativity to overcome these problems. Einstein worked out his theory by doing Gedanken experiments ('thought experiments') in his head and reasoning what must happen. The Dutch physicist Hendrik Lorentz proposed the relativistic contraction of distances and dilation of time.

## Why is it important?

The mass-energy relation tells us that nothing can travel at or beyond the speed of light; as an object gets close to that speed, its mass and inertia increase more and more. It would take an infinite amount of energy to accelerate the object to exactly the speed of light.

The mass-energy relation is also the key to nuclear power and atomic weapons. The extremely small mass that is 'lost' when an atomic nucleus is split, or when nuclei are fused together, is converted to a large amount of energy.

## Is it really true?

Special relativity works as long as you do not have to take gravity into account. When gravity must be considered, a related theory called the **General theory of relativity** is used instead.

### A Head Start

Neuroscientists at McMaster University in Canada think they may have found an anatomical reason for Einstein's mathematical brilliance. They studied Einstein's brain, which had been retained and preserved during his post-mortem examination over 40 years previously, and found that a sulcus (fissure) called the parietal operculum was missing. Their results, which were published in 1999, showed that the lack of this fissure had allowed a part of the brain called the inferior parietal lobe to grow 15 per cent wider than average. Among other things, the inferior parietal lobe is involved in mathematical thought and visuo-spatial awareness.

# Key Concepts

## General Theory of Relativity

### What is it?

The general theory of relativity is a generalization of the **Special theory of relativity**. Whereas special relativity can only be applied to objects that are stationary or moving at constant speed, general relativity takes into account accelerating frames of reference and can incorporate gravity.

General relativity is needed because Einstein's special theory of relativity conflicts with Newton's law of gravitation. This law says that objects are attracted to each other due to a gravitational force (which increases in proportion to the masses of the objects, but decreases in proportion to the square of the distance between them). Einstein realized that this force would have to be transmitted instantaneously in order for both objects to experience it at the same time. However, special relativity tells us that nothing can travel faster than the speed of light, and even light cannot travel from one place to another instantaneously.

The general theory of relativity proposes that time and three-dimensional space are fundamentally interwoven to form a four-dimensional continuum known as space-time. It says that gravity is actually a distortion of space-time itself. Heavy objects cause space-time to warp; an analogy in fewer dimensions is the warping of a flat rubber sheet when a heavy ball is placed on it. The distortion of space-time then causes other objects to be drawn towards it, rather like the way that a marble placed on the curved rubber sheet would tend to roll down the dip in the sheet.

The properties of Newton's law are still fulfilled by the model of gravity as a curvature of space-time, because heavier objects cause more distortion, and the distortion is less noticeable at greater distances. However, calculations based on the model show that the rate of transmission of gravity would not be instantaneous, but instead that gravitational 'ripples' would travel through space-time at the speed of light. This allows gravity and relativity to be compatible.

> "
> Space grips mass, telling it how to move, and mass grips space, telling it how to curve.
> —US theoretical physicist John Archibald Wheeler (b.1911).
> "

### Who worked it out?

The general theory of relativity was proposed by the German physicist Albert Einstein in 1916. Various experiments, including those by the English astronomer Sir Arthur Stanley Eddington and the US astronomer Walter Adams, verified the bending of star light that was predicted by general relativity due to the presence of the Sun's mass. These types of experiment were often carried out during solar eclipses.

> " 
> *Revolution in science – New theory of the Universe
> – Newtonian ideas overthrown*
>
> —Headline in *The Times* newspaper (7th November 1919), after Sir Arthur Stanley Eddington made his observations supporting the general theory of relativity during the solar eclipse.
> "

The Italian mathematician Tullio Levi-Civita worked on a mathematical topic known as tensor calculus, and the German mathematician Bernhard Riemann developed the concepts of a multi-dimensional curved space and complex mathematical planes known as Riemann surfaces. These ideas were extremely important in the formulation of general relativity.

## Why is it important?

General relativity resolves the conflict between the constancy of the speed of light and the transmission of gravitational force. It also provides the underlying explanation for the possibility of black holes, saying that these are stars with such high mass that the warp of space-time prevents even light from escaping (see **Space: Black holes**).

## Is it really true?

General relativity is an extremely good model for predicting the behaviour of the universe at a large scale, and no observations have yet been made that contradict it. However, the theory is incompatible with the mathematics behind **Quantum theory**, which is currently the best model for the behaviour of subatomic particles. Physicists are therefore seeking to use **String theory** to produce a **Theory of everything** in order to reconcile the different models.

> " 
> *If my theory of relativity is proven successful, Germany will claim me as a German and France will declare that I am a citizen of the world. Should my theory prove untrue, France will say I am a German and Germany will declare that I am a Jew.*
>
> —Albert Einstein (1879–1955), in an address at the Sorbonne in Paris (1929).
> "

# KEY CONCEPTS

## Quantum Theory ⚛

### What is it?

Quantum theory is part of a model of the universe that says that everything is made up of small fundamental particles that cannot be subdivided. These particles form the building blocks of everything else – not just matter, but also light and other forms of energy. Modern physics uses quantum theory to describe the behaviour of atoms and subatomic particles.

### Planck's law

The basis of quantum theory is a law known as Planck's law, which says that the energy of electromagnetic waves (light, radio waves etc) is confined in indivisible packets or quanta, each of which has to be radiated or absorbed as a whole. The size of these packets is proportional to the frequency of the wave, so that higher frequency waves have more energetic quanta. Planck's law can be written as $E = hf$, where $E$ is the energy, $h$ is a constant called Planck's constant and $f$ is the frequency of the wave.

### Wave-particle duality

The quantum theory of light contrasts with classical optics, which assumes a wave-like nature of light resulting in, among other things, refraction of light and interference patterns (see **Energy, light and radioactivity: Waves**). The fact that some properties of light fit with it being a wave while others require it to be a particle is called wave-particle duality. Electrons, which were traditionally thought of as particles, also have wave-particle duality, as do any particles small enough to experience strong quantum effects.

### The quantum atom

Quantum theory refines the model of the atom as a nucleus surrounded by electrons. A consequence of the theory is that each electron can only occupy discrete (quantized) energy levels, and an electron jumping between levels results in the emission of a light quantum (photon) with a frequency corresponding to the energy difference.

### Quantum mechanics

Quantum mechanics uses quantum theory as the basis of its laws of motion and energy. Whereas classical mechanics (see **Newton's laws of motion**) is deterministic – that is, the speeds and positions of objects can be predicted – it has turned out that quantum mechanics gives only probabilities for these types of property. Quantum theory therefore introduces chance as a fundamental property of physics.

### The correspondence principle

As a quantum mechanical system is made larger and larger, the effects of quantum theory become smaller and smaller, so that for large systems, quantum theory and classical theory agree with each other. This is called the correspondence principle.

## Who worked it out?

In 1900, the German theoretical physicist Max Planck proposed that energy must exist only in quanta. The idea arose as a result of Planck trying to explain the findings of the German physicist Gustav Kirchhoff relating to 'black body radiation', the emission of heat from objects that absorb radiation perfectly. Planck's law was a development of work by the Austrian physicist Ludwig Boltzmann (see **The laws of thermodynamics**); the Indian physicist Satyendra Bose also played an important role. In 1905, Albert Einstein realized that the quantum nature of light could explain the photoelectric effect, which involves the emission of electrons from certain materials when they absorb light.

In 1913, the Danish physicist Niels Bohr combined the traditional model of the hydrogen atom, developed by the New Zealand physicist Ernest Rutherford, with quantum theory, thus producing the quantum model of the atom known as the Bohr model. The German physicist Arnold Sommerfeld then generalized the theory to heavier atoms.

Influenced by Einstein's work showing that waves can behave as particles, the French physicist Louis de Broglie put forward the converse idea that particles can behave as waves, thus extending wave-particle duality to electrons and other particles. The waves were detected experimentally by US physicists Clinton Davisson and Lester Germer in 1927, and also by the English physicist Sir George Thomson. The idea of wave-particle duality was used by Erwin Schrödinger to develop quantum mechanics.

> 66
>
> *I am going to tell you what nature behaves like. If you will simply admit that maybe she does behave like this, you will find her a delightful, entrancing thing. Do not keep saying to yourself 'But how can it be like that?' because you will get ... into a blind alley from which nobody has yet escaped. Nobody knows how it can be like that.*
>
> —US physicist Richard Feynman, during the Messenger Lectures, MIT, 1964.
>
> 99

**Heisenberg's uncertainty principle** and **Pauli's exclusion principle** arose from developments in quantum theory.

The English mathematician P A M Dirac and the US mathematician John von Neumann provided mathematical proofs of important aspects of quantum theory.

## Why is it important?

All modern physics describing events at an atomic or subatomic level is based on quantum theory. As well as being extremely important in theoretical physics, quantum theory has many practical applications. It lies at the heart of our understanding of the electronic behaviour of matter, and is therefore fundamental to microelectronics. Recently, progress has been made towards developing quantum computers.

## Divine Dice?

Although he was heavily involved in its emergence, Albert Einstein's initial reaction to quantum theory was not very enthusiastic. In a letter to his fellow physicist Max Born in 1926, he wrote:

*'Anyway, I am sure that he [God] does not play dice.'*

Around 50 years later, Stephen Hawking responded in the journal *Nature*:

*'God not only plays dice. He also sometimes throws the dice where they cannot be seen.'*

### Is it really true?

Quantum theory can seem completely counterintuitive. Nonetheless, it fits the detailed observations at the atomic scale made by many scientists, and does so far better than any other model. However, it conflicts with the **General theory of relativity**, which is the current best model for large-scale physics (see **The theory of everything**).

## Quantum Quotes

When quantum theory was first developed, it was very controversial. The only thing about which everyone seemed to agree was that it was extremely confusing, with its ideas that energy has to exist in 'packets' and that light can behave like waves and particles. Niels Bohr, the Danish physicist who played a part in developing the theory, suggested:

*'If quantum mechanics hasn't profoundly shocked you, you haven't understood it yet.'*

The US physicist Richard Feynman went further, saying:

*'I think I can safely say that nobody understands quantum mechanics.'*

## String Theory ⊛

### What is it?

String theory is a theory in fundamental physics that attempts to reconcile **Quantum theory** with gravity and **General relativity**, so that one model of the universe can be applied to all situations. The model is based on the assumption that elementary particles, such as quarks, are one-dimensional 'strings', with measurable length but infinitely small thickness, rather than the zero-dimensional immeasurable 'points' of conventional particle physics. These strings are thought to be around $10^{20}$, or a hundred billion billion, times smaller than an atom; they could be closed in a loop like an elastic band, or open-ended. The strings are predicted to vibrate in different patterns known as resonances. These resonances would produce different masses as well as different amounts of force of various kinds.

There are a number of different forms of string theory. The basic string theory only allows for the subatomic particles called bosons, and is called bosonic string theory. It requires that there are 26 dimensions and would provide a mechanism for forces such as gravity and electromagnetic force. Superstring theory, on the other hand, allows for both bosons and fermions, so that matter as well as forces could be produced. It requires a property called supersymmetry where every boson has a corresponding fermion (see **Atoms, elements and molecules: Subatomic particles**). These extra particles could possibly make up 'dark matter', believed by some physicists to be necessary to explain the observed properties of galaxies. There are currently five interrelated versions of superstring theory, requiring ten dimensions.

We only experience a maximum of four dimensions, consisting of three spatial dimensions and time. String theory says that the extra dimensions are 'curled in on themselves' so that we are unaware of them.

### Who worked it out?

The English mathematical physicist P A M Dirac proposed the idea of particles being not point-like, but string-like, in 1950. The English theoretical physicist Michael Green, along with the American physicists John H Schwarz and Edward Witten, founded superstring theory.

### Why is it important?

Because superstring theory proposes that all matter and all forces could arise from strings, it provides a possible basis for a **Theory of everything**.

### Is it really true?

String theories are now considered very good candidates for the actual laws of physics at the ultimate small scale.

# KEY CONCEPTS

## The Theory of Everything ⚛

### What is it?

The theory of everything, or TOE, is an as yet non-existent theory that would simultaneously describe all four forces of nature that affect matter: the electromagnetic interaction, the strong and weak interactions affecting particles and nuclei, and the gravitational interaction.

---

**The electromagnetic interaction**

The electromagnetic interaction occurs between charged subatomic particles, and is carried by packets of energy called photons. It is intermediate in strength between strong and weak interactions.

**The strong interaction**

The strong interaction occurs between the types of subatomic particles that are made up of quarks; these include baryons and mesons (see **Atoms, elements and molecules: Subatomic particles**). This interaction binds protons and neutrons together in the nuclei of atoms. The strong interaction is carried by gluons; these are particles with no mass.

**The weak interaction**

The weak interaction affects quarks and leptons. It acts through their property of weak charge, causing changes in the quark flavours, and can transform neutrons into protons and vice versa. The weak interaction is transmitted by particles called intermediate vector bosons.

**Gravitation**

Gravitation is by far the weakest of the forces, but it acts over immense distances so it is very important in cosmology. It is carried by particles called gravitons.

---

Each of these interactions has its own theoretical formalism. Gravitation is now described through the **General theory of relativity**. Electromagnetic, weak and strong interactions are described through different theories known as gauge theories. (Gauge group theory is a powerful branch of mathematics.)

Although a TOE has not yet been reached, the electroweak theory (also known as the Weinberg–Salam theory) has successfully unified the electromagnetic and weak interactions. A theory known as quantum chromodynamics describes the interactions between quarks, which make up heavy particles such as protons and neutrons, and allows the weak and strong forces to be considered together. These unified theories achieved well-publicized successes by predicting new elementary particles that were eventually found using the particle accelerator at CERN.

Currently, the most progress is being made on linking the strong and electroweak forces into a Grand Unified Theory, or GUT. The existence of an additional particle called the Higgs boson is predicted by some versions of GUT, but it has not yet been observed.

The incorporation of gravitation into unified theories with the other forces poses the greatest challenge to modern physicists. **String theory** may provide a mechanism of uniting the large-scale gravitational mechanisms with the other small-scale interactions (see **Quantum theory**).

### Who worked it out?

In the 1960s and 1970s, the US physicist Steven Weinberg and the Pakistani theoretical physicist Abdus Salam worked out the electroweak theory. The theory was further developed by the US physicist Sheldon Glashow, who also contributed to the development of quantum chromodynamics. The US physicist Carlo Rubbia led the team that discovered the W and Z bosons which mediate the weak nuclear force, thus putting the electroweak theory on a firm experimental footing.

The US physicist Howard Georgi pioneered the research for a GUT to combine the strong and electroweak theories. The existence of the Higgs boson is predicted by the British theoretical physicist Peter Higgs.

### Why is it important?

Modern theoretical physics aims to describe the nature of the physical universe with as few assumptions and laws as possible. In a complete framework of physical theory, those parameters that we now measure experimentally, such as the speed of light, would emerge naturally from the equations. Just as Newton was able to explain Kepler's laws of planetary motion through his more powerful theory of gravitation, so in modern physics there is a desire to find all-embracing physical laws.

> 66
>
> *I know not what I may appear to the world, but to myself I seem to have been only like a boy playing on the sea shore, and diverting myself in now and then finding a smoother pebble or a prettier shell than ordinary, whilst the great ocean of truth lay all undiscovered before me.*
>
> —Sir Isaac Newton (1642–1727), quoted in *Memoirs of Newton* (edited by D Brewster, 1855).
>
> 99

# KEY CONCEPTS

## The Principle of Least Action

### What is it?

In mechanics, 'action' is a property that determines how things move. It depends on the kinetic (movement) energy and the potential energy of the object, and on the time for which it is moving. The principle of least action states that the motion between two points takes place in such a way that the action has a minimum value with reference to all other paths between the points which correspond to the same energy. That is, if there is a choice of routes, the route taken will be the most 'economical'.

### Who worked it out?

The 17th-century French mathematician Pierre de Fermat developed a 'principle of least time', saying that the path taken by a ray of light between two given points is the one in which the light takes the least time. This work was a precursor to the principle of least action.

The principle itself was developed in the 18th century by the French mathematician Pierre-Louis Moreau de Maupertuis, who worked out that a mechanical system evolves in such a way that its action is as small as possible. He is often quoted as saying that 'Nature is thrifty in all actions'. His work was supported by the German philosopher and mathematician Gottfried Leibniz and the Swiss mathematician Leonhard Euler. The Irish mathematician Sir William Hamilton and the French mathematician Joseph Lagrange also worked on the theory.

> ### Sums and Sonnets
>
> Sir William Hamilton had a strong interest in writing poetry as well as working on mathematics, and he believed that poetry and mathematical language were equally artistic. He was great friends with the English poet William Wordsworth, with whom he discussed both subjects. Unfortunately, Wordsworth didn't rate Hamilton's poems very highly, and suggested that he should focus his efforts exclusively on scientific matters:
>
> *'You send me showers of verses which I receive with much pleasure...yet have we fears that this employment may seduce you from the path of science.'*

### Why is it important?

The idea of action being minimized lies at the heart of mechanics, as well as electricity and magnetism. Both classical and quantum mechanics can be derived from it (see **Newton's laws of motion** and **Quantum theory**).

# KEY CONCEPTS

## The Principle of Work 🔅

### What is it?

Work is a particular form of energy. It is defined as the kinetic (movement) energy that is transferred to an object as a result of a force being applied to that object. When a force acts on an object, making it move in the same direction as the force, the work done is equal to the force multiplied by the distance. This is often stated as 'work done equals force times distance', and can be written as $W = Fd$, where $W$ is work, $F$ is the force and $d$ is distance.

Direction is important in work: if the force is applied at a right angle to the intended direction of movement, no work is done. For instance, pressing down on a toy car does not make it move along.

### Who worked it out?

The Greek mathematician Archimedes discovered that the relationship between force and distance could be used to move heavy objects in the 3rd century BC, thus inventing the lever (see below). Three French scientists formalized the concept of work at the beginning of the 19th century: the civil engineer Claude Navier, the engineer and geometrician Jean Victor Poncelet and the physicist Gustave Coriolis.

> *Give me a firm spot on which to stand, and I will move the Earth.*
> —Traditionally attributed to Archimedes.

### Why is it important?

The concept of work explains the operation of one of the simplest, but most useful, machines in existence: the lever. A lever is a rigid beam that is pivoted at a point called the fulcrum. A load that is to be moved is applied at one point on the beam. An effort is then applied at a different point on the beam, to move the load. When the load and effort are balanced, the work theorem tells us that 'force times distance' is the same for both load and effort. If the effort is applied further from the fulcrum than the load, a smaller force can be applied because the beam moves further. The three classes of levers are shown below.

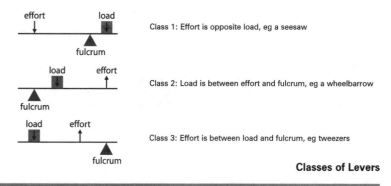

Class 1: Effort is opposite load, eg a seesaw

Class 2: Load is between effort and fulcrum, eg a wheelbarrow

Class 3: Effort is between load and fulcrum, eg tweezers

**Classes of Levers**

# KEY CONCEPTS

## Archimedes' Principle

### What is it?

Archimedes' principle, also called the hydrostatic principle, describes what happens when objects are immersed in a fluid. It says that when an object is wholly or partly immersed, it experiences an upward force equal to the weight of the fluid it displaces. This force is called the buoyancy force.

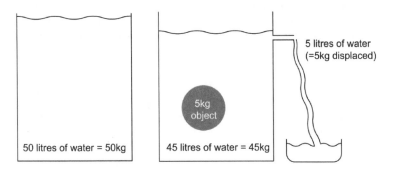

50 litres of water = 50kg

45 litres of water = 45kg

5 litres of water (=5kg displaced)

5kg object

### Who worked it out?

The Greek mathematician Archimedes worked out the principle, in the 3rd century BC. According to legend, the hydrostatic principle occurred to him while he was in the bath, leading him to jump out and run stark naked around the town. Another legend says that he used the principle to determine whether a crown made for King Heiron II of Syracuse was made of pure gold, by working out the crown's density.

> **"**
>
> *Eureka! ('I have found it!')*
>
> —Archimedes is alleged to have shouted this whilst running naked through the streets of Syracuse, on becoming aware of the hydrostatic principle.
>
> **"**

### Why is it important?

Archimedes' principle determines whether an object will float or sink in a particular fluid. If the weight of the object is less than the buoyancy force, it will float, whereas an object whose weight is more than the buoyancy force will sink. This is equivalent to saying that an object whose average density is lower than that of the fluid will float. Engineers can therefore design ships that will float in water, even though they are made out of dense, 'heavy' materials such as concrete or steel, as long as they have enough air inside that their average density is kept to below that of water.

## Bernoulli's Principle ⚛

### What is it?

Bernoulli's principle is an important principle in aerodynamics and hydrodynamics, and relates to a horizontal flow of air or another fluid. It says that an increase in the speed of the flow leads to a drop in pressure. The principle comes from a law called Bernoulli's law, which states that the sum of the pressure, kinetic energy per unit volume and potential energy per unit volume must always remain constant. Therefore, if the speed goes up, the kinetic energy goes up, so the pressure must drop in order to maintain a balance.

### Who worked it out?

The principle is named after the Swiss mathematician Daniel Bernoulli, who published a rudimentary form of the principle in 1738, in a work entitled *Hydrodynamica*. The modern form of the Bernoulli equation was published 50 years later by the French mathematician Joseph-Louis Lagrange in his work *Traité de mécanique analytique* ('Treatise on analytical mechanics'). Lagrange also drew upon the work of the Swiss mathematician Leonhard Euler.

### *Family Feuds*

It isn't surprising that Daniel Bernoulli became interested in mathematics, as his father, brothers and uncle were all mathematicians, but following in their footsteps proved to be unexpectedly difficult. Daniel's father Johann Bernoulli wanted his son to become a businessman and was determined that he should not study mathematics, even though Johann's own father had tried to stop Johann becoming a mathematician.

Daniel studied medicine for a while, but he was eventually drawn back to mathematics and physics. He entered some of his work for the 1734 Grand Prize of the Académie des Sciences in Paris; unfortunately his father had also entered and the two were named joint winners of the prize. This enraged Johann so much that he banned Daniel from his house.

### Why is it important?

The Bernoulli principle is fundamental to the design of aircraft wings. When an aircraft flies, it has to push air out of the way, so the air has to travel backwards over the wings. Each wing is shaped so that the upper surface is longer than the lower surface. This means that the air moving over the wing has to travel faster than the air moving below the wing. According to Bernoulli's principle, the air pressure above the wing is therefore lower than the air pressure below it, causing an upward force known as lift. In order for an aeroplane to fly, the air must be travelling quickly enough over the wings that the lift force is greater than the weight of the aeroplane, which is why aircraft have to reach high speeds on a runway before taking off.

In the diagram of an aeroplane shown below, L is the lift force, which supports the aircraft in flight. It acts at right angles to the direction of the undisturbed airflow relative to the aircraft. D is the drag force caused by air resistance, which is measured parallel to the direction of motion. The air resistance is low along the laminar boundary layer at the front of the aircraft, but is much higher along the turbulent boundary layer at the rear. R is the overall combination of the lift and drag forces.

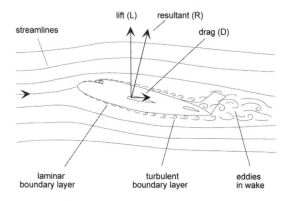

**Forces Acting on an Aircraft**

The special shape of an aeroplane wing is called an aerofoil. Aerofoils are also used for propeller blades and helicopter rotors, and sails take the shape of an aerofoil when filled with wind. An upside-down aerofoil creates a downward force – this effect is used for car spoilers, to stop the rear of the car from tending to rise up from the road.

### Is it really true?

Bernoulli's law is only actually true for fluids that cannot be compressed and that are non-viscous. However, it is a good approximation for many other fluids, such as air.

## Ohm's Law ⚛

### What is it?

Ohm's law is the relationship between electric current, voltage and resistance (see **Electricity and magnets: Electricity**). It states that, in conducting materials, the current flowing through a component is proportional to the voltage (potential difference) between its ends, and inversely proportional to the resistance of the component. This can be stated as $I = V/R$ or, more commonly, $V = IR$, where $V$ is the voltage in volts, $I$ is the current in amps and $R$ is the resistance in ohms. So, increasing the current through a component, or its resistance, also increases the voltage across it.

### Who worked it out?

Ohm's law is named after a German physicist, Georg Ohm, who published the work describing the law in 1827. He worked it out by looking for patterns in his data rather than by deriving it mathematically.

> *All Play, No Work ...*
>
> Georg Ohm started studying at Erlangen University in Bavaria in 1805. However, he apparently spent more time enjoying sports and dancing than he spent studying. This approach led to his having to leave the university little more than a year later. He had to work as a mathematics teacher while studying on his own, and did not return to university until 1811.

### Why is it important?

As well as explaining the relationship between some important concepts in electricity, Ohm's law can be extended by analogy to any situation where a pressure difference (potential difference in the case of electricity) causes a flow (current) through an impedance (resistance). Examples of other situations where it can be used include heat passing through walls, or water flowing through pipes.

### Is it really true?

Ohm's law is only true when a component is at a constant temperature. In practice, real components tend to heat up when a current flows through them, so Ohm's law only applies over a certain range. The law also only holds when there is no magnetic field acting on the component.

Strictly speaking, Ohm's law is only applicable to circuits carrying direct current (DC), but in practice it can be applied to some alternating current (AC) circuits.

## Chaos Theory ⚛ π

### What is it?

Chaos theory relates to processes that are highly sensitive to their initial conditions. A small variation in these initial conditions will produce wildly different results, so that long-term behaviour of chaotic systems cannot be predicted. For a system to be chaotic, it must be non-linear – the output of the system is not directly proportional to the input. Chaos is a form of dynamical instability, and chaos theory is technically called non-linear dynamics.

In traditional (linear) mechanics, precise knowledge of the initial conditions of a system allows accurate prediction of the system's future behaviour. We can never measure the initial conditions with absolute accuracy but small uncertainties here create only small errors in the predictions. However, the behaviour of a chaotic system can vary dramatically even when the differences between sets of initial conditions are tiny. This phenomenon is sometimes called the butterfly effect, in reference to the idea that even the flap of a butterfly's wings in one part of the world could have a huge impact on the weather somewhere else.

The behaviour of systems can be represented graphically by using phase space, where each factor that influences the state of the system is given a different axis on a graph so that all the different states can be plotted. For a so-called deterministic system, the way its state evolves over time can be described by equations that relate the state of the system at the present time to the states at earlier times.

Non-chaotic systems tend to settle into either a constant, unchanging state (represented by a single point on the graph) or a periodic (repeating) pattern of states, giving a simple loop on the graph. However, chaotic systems tend to show more complex patterns such as scatterings of dots confined within fairly clear boundaries. Some of these patterns look like loops, but the positions of the loops do not repeat exactly. These chaotic states are known as attractors. They are not periodic – they do not repeat – but they are still highly ordered, and can appear very beautiful. The description 'chaotic' thus applies to the unpredictability of the observed states of the system, rather than to the underlying patterns.

Chaotic systems often show self-similarity on different scales; measuring a system over a short or a long period of time produces the same pattern in phase space. In this respect, they show a form of fractal behaviour (see **Numbers and shapes: Fractals**).

### Who worked it out?

The French mathematician Henri Poincaré first realized that systems could be chaotic in 1889, while studying the interactions between the Sun, the Moon and the Earth, known as the three-body problem. (Isaac Newton realized that he was unable to solve his equations of motion for this problem.) The Russian mathematician Aleksandr Lyapunov also carried out related work.

The next advance in chaos theory occurred in the early 1960s, when the US mathematician and meteorologist Edward Lorenz worked on the circulation of the atmosphere. He demonstrated that weather systems produced from slightly different initial conditions diverge with time, and proved the limit of predictability of useful forecasts to be about 10–14 days.

The Australian physicist and ecologist Sir Robert May applied chaos theory to biology, using it to study the dynamics of animal populations.

The French mathematician Benoît Mandelbrot noticed the self-similarity properties of chaotic systems while studying the prices of stocks and shares, and discovered the link between chaotic systems and fractals.

The term 'chaos' as applied to mathematics was coined by the US mathematical physicist James Yorke in 1975.

## Why is it important?

It has become apparent during the past hundred years that many natural systems show chaotic behaviour. These include the weather, population size, dripping taps and the flow of blood through blood vessels. Chaos theory also affects artificial systems such as the stock market and the behaviour of lasers. The nature of these systems warns us to be cautious about trying to predict future states by studying past behaviours.

---

### Computer modelling

It is important to verify scientific theories by making predictions and testing them experimentally. However, it is not always practical or possible to do this. For example, the experiment might need to run for thousands of years or use millions of samples in order to detect a very small effect, or it might require extremely dangerous procedures to be carried out.

For these reasons, computer models are often used to work out the probable outcomes of experiments. These models consist of computer programs that simulate a real-life situation as closely as possible. The starting conditions of the simulation can be altered, and the resulting outcomes studied. This approach is often used in the examination of chaotic systems, for example in weather forecasting. Computer models can also be used by mathematicians, to simulate complicated equations that cannot be solved analytically.

Computer modelling has its drawbacks. Often, many assumptions must be made about a system in order to model it on a computer, and important factors may be unwittingly omitted. This can lead to a model that is overly simplistic. It is therefore important to test a computer model, ensuring that its results match previously obtained experimental results for simpler problems, before relying on it to provide answers to complex problems. Despite this, computer modelling provides a useful additional tool in scientific investigations.

---

# KEY CONCEPTS

## Shannon–Hartley Theorem $\pi$

### What is it?

The Shannon–Hartley theorem relates to information theory – the mathematical study of factors affecting the transmission and reception of information.

#### Information entropy

Information can be defined as data of some kind (such as letters, words, numbers or pictures) that are passed from one person or machine to another, so that the recipient knows something that was previously unknown to them. If someone sends a transmission consisting of an eight-digit number, each digit could be any in the range zero to nine. This means that there are many possibilities for the total value of the number. The longer the number, the less chance the recipient has of guessing what the number might be before receiving it. This uncertainty is called information entropy, a name taken from the concept of thermodynamic entropy (see **The laws of thermodynamics**), and it can be overcome by transmitting information, in much the same way that thermodynamic entropy can be overcome by an input of energy. The reduction in information entropy when information is received is sometimes known as negentropy.

#### Signal-to-noise ratio

The Shannon–Hartley theorem says that there is always 'noise' getting in the way of accurate transmission of information. This can mean actual noise (eg during a telephone call), or it can be interference of other kinds, such as smudged printing in a book, electrical noise in computer components, or mutations in DNA sequences. The aim is to keep the noise in a transmission to a minimum, maintaining a high signal-to-noise ratio.

#### Bits and bandwidth

The total amount of data that is transmitted over a given time period, including both information and noise, is called the bandwidth. It is often measured in bits per second. A bit is the amount of information that cuts uncertainty by half; in computing, each of the eight bits that make up a byte can be in one of two states, often represented by the values 1 ('on') and 0 ('off').

#### Maximum transmission rate

The Shannon–Hartley theorem defines the ultimate capacity of a communication channel in terms of its bandwidth and its signal-to-noise ratio. The maximum transmission rate in bits per second is given by the formula $W \log_2(1 + S{:}N)$, where $W$ is the bandwidth and $S{:}N$ is the signal-to-noise ratio.

### Who worked it out?

The American mathematician Claude Shannon proposed the theorem in *The Mathematical Theory of Communications* (1949, with Warren Weaver), while working at the Bell Telephone Laboratories. He drew upon the work of a US electronics researcher, Ralph Hartley.

## A Bicycle Made For Two

Claude Shannon was as well-known for his eccentric modes of transport as he was for his work on information theory. His colleagues at the Massachusetts Institute of Technology, where he worked from 1957 onwards, used to warn each other of his approach as he travelled through the corridors on his unicycle, especially if he happened to be juggling at the time. He tried to invent a motorized pogo stick and also produced a two-seater unicycle, although he apparently had difficulty finding someone to join him in trying it out.

The English mathematician Alan Turing independently worked on similar ideas while attempting to break the German Enigma cipher at Bletchley Park during World War II. Rather than using the bit as his unit of information, Turing used the ban – the quantity of information that reduces uncertainty by a factor of ten. The deciban and centiban were used for smaller quantities of information.

## Bans and Banburismus

Turing's unit of information, the ban, was named after Banburismus, a technique for working out which of many combinations of letter wheels were being used in Enigma machines on a particular day. Banburismus was itself named after the town of Banbury, near Bletchley Park, because special grids that were used for the technique were manufactured there.

### Why is it important?

The Shannon–Hartley theorem, and information theory in general, have given an insight into how best to code and transmit information, and the limitations involved. These issues affect everything from burning and reading CDs, to sending data back to Earth from space probes.

Even genetic information is affected by information entropy. Geneticists have noted that the mutation rate of DNA is very low, compared with the disorder that should arise. It turns out that organisms use 'proofreading' enzymes to check the sequence as DNA is made, thus expending energy to overcome the information entropy.

# KEY CONCEPTS

## Pythagoras's Theorem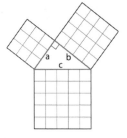

### What is it?

Pythagoras's theorem describes the relationship of the lengths of the sides of a right-angled triangle. It is stated as:

'The square of the hypotenuse is equal to the sum of the squares of the other two sides.'

(The hypotenuse is the longest side of the triangle, opposite the right angle.)

The theorem can be written as an equation:

$$a^2 + b^2 = c^2$$

where the hypotenuse is $c$ and the other two sides are $a$ and $b$.

This means that, if you square the length of each of the shorter sides (multiply each length by itself) and add these numbers together, you will get the same result as if you square the length of the longest side. The diagram below shows a triangle with sides of length 3, 4 and 5 units; this size of triangle is right-angled. The squares attached to the shorter sides have areas of 9 square units and 16 square units; these add up to the same area as the square on the longest side (25 square units).

### Who worked it out?

As its name suggests, this theorem is often attributed to the Greek mathematician Pythagoras, who lived in the 6th century BC. In fact, he was actually beaten to it by other people, including Indian and Babylonian mathematicians. The first proof of the theorem is thought to have been written down by Euclid, another Greek mathematician, in around 300 BC.

### Is it really true?

Pythagoras's theorem works as long as the triangle is right-angled and is on a flat surface (this is called Euclidean geometry). Triangles on curved surfaces behave differently – so the equation would not work for a right-angled triangle drawn on the surface of a beach ball, for example.

## Fermat's Last Theorem 🔺

### What is it?

Fermat's last theorem is probably the most famous problem in mathematics. It states that it is impossible to find an integer solution to the equation

$$x^n + y^n = z^n$$

if $n$ is greater than 2 and $x$, $y$ and $z$ are not zero. (When $n$ is equal to 2, this equation is the same as **Pythagoras's theorem** and can be solved.)

### Who worked it out?

The theorem was written by the French mathematician Pierre de Fermat (1601–65). Most of Fermat's work was sent in letters to friends, containing results without proof. His 'last' theorem was found scrawled in the margin of a page of a Greek text called *Arithmetica* by Diophantus.

> *I have a truly marvellous demonstration of this proposition which this margin is too narrow to contain.*
>
> —This tantalizing comment was written alongside Fermat's last theorem in Diophantus's *Arithmetica*.

Fermat's 'truly marvellous' proof was never found. The puzzle to find a proof went on to baffle and outwit mathematicians for almost 350 years. The proof was finally announced in 1993 by the British mathematician Andrew Wiles, and revised by him in 1994 with the help of Richard Taylor. Wiles was just too old to qualify for the Fields Medal, a major prize awarded to outstanding young mathematicians by the International Mathematical Union. Instead, they honoured him with a silver plaque as a special tribute.

### Has it really been proved?

Wiles's initial proof of the theorem was found to have some holes in it, but his revised version is widely accepted. The proof is so complicated, and relies on so many new mathematical discoveries, that it seems unlikely that Fermat did ever prove the theorem.

## HUMAN BODY DATA

| | |
|---|---|
| Number of bones | 206 |
| Number of muscles | approximately 650 |
| Number of cell types | approximately 220 |
| Number of protein types | approximately 100 000 |
| Average body temperature | 37°C (98.6°F) |
| Average pulse rate | 72 beats per minute (men), 80 beats per minute (women) |
| Average weight of brain | 1.4 kg (3 lb) |
| Number of nerve cells in the brain | more than 10 billion |
| Speed of fastest nerve impulses | approximately 120 m s$^{-1}$ (390 ft/s) |
| Total surface area of the skin of an adult | approximately 1.86 m$^2$ (20 sq ft) |
| Total dead skin cells shed per person in a lifetime | approximately 18 kg (40 lb) |
| Average total surface area of the alveoli in the lungs | 70 m$^2$ (753 sq ft) |
| Average total blood volume | 5 litres (8 pints) |
| Volume of blood filtered by the kidneys each day | approximately 150 litres (264 pints) |
| Volume of urine produced each day | approximately 1.5 litres (2.6 pints) |
| Number of sperm produced by an adult man each day | approximately 50 million–500 million |

> *Man is only man at the surface. Remove his skin, dissect, and immediately you come to the machinery.*
>
> —French poet and writer Paul Valéry (1871–1945).

# THE SKELETON

Humans have an internal skeleton, or endoskeleton, made of bone or cartilage. It supports the tissues and organs of the body, and protects soft internal organs such as the lungs.

## Bones

Adjective: **osteal**          Prefix: **osteo-**

In total, the adult human skeleton has 206 bones; some are illustrated below.

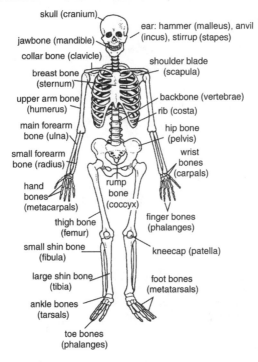

skull (cranium)

ear: hammer (malleus), anvil (incus), stirrup (stapes)

jawbone (mandible)

collar bone (clavicle)

shoulder blade (scapula)

breast bone (sternum)

upper arm bone (humerus)

backbone (vertebrae)

rib (costa)

main forearm bone (ulna)

hip bone (pelvis)

small forearm bone (radius)

wrist bones (carpals)

hand bones (metacarpals)

rump bone (coccyx)

finger bones (phalanges)

thigh bone (femur)

small shin bone (fibula)

kneecap (patella)

large shin bone (tibia)

foot bones (metatarsals)

ankle bones (tarsals)

toe bones (phalanges)

## Tendons

The muscles are attached to the bones of the skeleton by means of tendons, which pull against the bones when the muscles contract, causing them to move.

## Ligaments and joints

Bones are connected to each other by means of ligaments. The point of articulation or contact between two or more bones of the skeleton is known as a joint. Different types of joint allow varying degrees of movement.

## MUSCLES

Adjective: **muscular**          Prefix: **myo-**

Muscles consist of bundles of small fibres, each of which is in turn composed of many protein myofibrils. These myofibrils contain polymers of the proteins actin and myosin, which attach and slide past one another using energy from a chemical called adenosine triphosphate (ATP). This movement, which occurs in response to a stimulus from the nervous system, or a hormonal signal, causes contraction of the whole muscle. There are three types of muscle: skeletal, involuntary and cardiac.

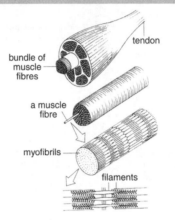

tendon

bundle of muscle fibres

a muscle fibre

myofibrils

filaments

**Muscle Structure**

### Skeletal muscle

Skeletal muscle is under conscious control. It produces voluntary movements by pulling against the bones of the skeleton, to which it is attached by means of tendons, so that contractions of such muscles cause the bones to move. Skeletal muscle is striated (striped) in appearance; it has light and dark bands of fibres.

#### Limb movement

Movement of a limb requires the combined action of a pair of muscles which can pull in opposite directions and are said to be antagonistic. For example, when the biceps muscle at the front of the upper arm contracts, and the triceps muscle at the back of the arm relaxes, the arm bends at the elbow. When the triceps contracts and the biceps relaxes, the arm is straightened again.

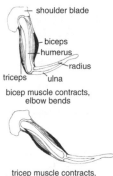

shoulder blade

biceps
humerus
radius
triceps    ulna

bicep muscle contracts,
elbow bends

tricep muscle contracts,
arm straightens

**Muscle Contraction**

### Types of skeletal muscle

Different types of skeletal muscle fibres are used for sudden movement and
sustained effort. Muscles are found near to the surface of the body and also deeper
down. Some of the body's major superficial muscles, important in moving the
body, are illustrated below. Deeper muscles, such as the transversus abdominus
and the pelvic floor muscles, are important for posture and supporting the organs.

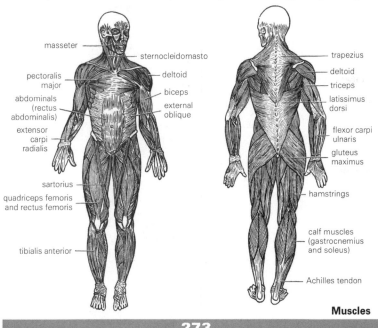

masseter

sternocleidomasto

pectoralis
major

abdominals
(rectus
abdominalis)

extensor
carpi
radialis

sartorius

quadriceps femoris
and rectus femoris

tibialis anterior

deltoid

biceps

external
oblique

trapezius

deltoid

triceps

latissimus
dorsi

flexor carpi
ulnaris

gluteus
maximus

hamstrings

calf muscles
(gastrocnemius
and soleus)

Achilles tendon

**Muscles**

## Involuntary muscle

Involuntary, or smooth, muscle maintains the movements of the internal body systems, and forms part of internal organs such as the intestines, bladder and uterus.

## Cardiac muscle

Cardiac muscle, found only in the heart, does not become fatigued, and continues to contract rhythmically even when it is disconnected from the nervous system. Like skeletal muscle, cardiac muscle is striped in appearance.

## THE NERVOUS SYSTEM

| | |
|---|---|
| Adjective: **neural** | Prefix: **neuro-** |

The central nervous system consists of the brain and spinal cord, while the remainder of the nervous system is known as the peripheral nervous system. Signals are carried between the two halves of the nervous system by means of electrical impulses, controlled by sodium and potassium levels in the neurons (nerve cells).

### Peripheral nervous system

Some neurons in the peripheral nervous system carry sensory signals to the central nervous system. Others carry motor (movement) signals back to muscles and organs to make them respond. The peripheral nervous system can be divided into two parts: somatic and autonomic. Both of these parts can generate reflex responses.

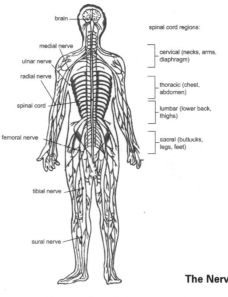

brain

spinal cord regions:

medial nerve

ulnar nerve

radial nerve

cervical (necks, arms, diaphragm)

thoracic (chest, abdomen)

spinal cord

lumbar (lower back, thighs)

femoral nerve

sacral (buttocks, legs, feet)

tibial nerve

sural nerve

**The Nervous System**

### Somatic nervous system

The somatic nervous system controls skeletal muscle and external sensory organs; it is also known as the voluntary system because an individual can control these responses.

### Autonomic nervous system

The autonomic nervous system controls vital body functions that are not under conscious control, such as breathing and heartbeat. It is responsible for controlling the sympathetic responses, which occur in times of stress or danger and are often known as 'fight or flight' responses because they increase activity and heart rate. It also contols the parasympathetic responses, which are known as 'rest and digest' responses because they slow down heart rate and promote digestion, and the enteric (gut) innervation.

### Reflexes

Some nerves operate by means of reflexes (to produce rapid withdrawal of the hand from a hot object, for example). These involve the transmission of sensory information only as far as the spinal cord, which then sends a response directly to the muscles, without the need for processing of information in the brain.

## Central nervous system

The central nervous system receives sensory information relayed via the peripheral sensory neurons. The central nervous system then processes the information it has received, and relays a suitable motor response, again in the form of a nerve impulse, along motor neurons to muscles or glands (often referred to as effectors).

## Neurons

Neurons, or nerve cells, have a cell body, which contains a nucleus just like all other cells. A long process called an axon allows the neuron to carry the nerve impulse a long way.

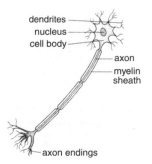

**Structure of a Neuron**

### Nerve impulses

The axon is covered in an insulating myelin sheath, which is in short lengths with gaps in between. The electrical nerve impulse jumps between the gaps; this is called saltatory conduction.

### Synapses

Axon endings reach out to pass the impulse to another neuron or to a muscle at a meeting point called a synapse. The signal is passed on by means of an electrical impulse or by chemicals called neurotransmitters.

## THE BRAIN

| Adjective: **cranial** | Prefix: **cranio-** |
| --- | --- |

The human brain is part of the central nervous system. It contains more than ten billion nerve cells, and on average weighs about 1.4kg (3lb). The brain receives sensory information via spinal nerves from the spinal cord and cranial nerves from sense organs such as the eye and the ear. When this information has been processed within the brain, appropriate instructions are sent out along motor neurons to effector organs such as muscles.

### Grey matter and white matter

Areas of the brain that contain mainly the cell bodies of neurons appear dense and grey; these areas are known as grey matter. White matter consists of areas containing mainly axons rather than cell bodies.

### Structure of the brain

The brain is enclosed within three membranes, the meninges, and is protected by the rigid bones of the skull. It can be divided into three parts: forebrain, midbrain and hindbrain.

#### Forebrain

The forebrain consists of the cerebral hemispheres, the thalamus and the hypothalamus. The outermost layer of the cerebral hemispheres, which are deeply folded and cover most of the surface of the human brain, is known as the cerebral cortex. It is involved in the integration of all sensory input to the brain, including memory and learning, enabling behaviour to be based on past experience.

#### Midbrain

The midbrain connects the forebrain to the hindbrain and spinal cord. It contains a region of neurons called the substantia nigra, which is affected in Parkinson's disease.

#### Hindbrain

The hindbrain comprises the cerebellum, the medulla oblongata and the pons. The cerebellum co-ordinates complex muscular processes such as maintaining posture. The medulla oblongata contains centres that regulate breathing, heartbeat and blood pressure.

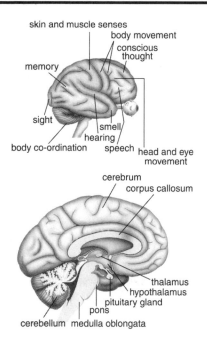

The Brain

## THE ENDOCRINE SYSTEM

The hormonal, or endocrine, system works in tandem with the nervous system to control body activities.

### Endocrine glands

The hormonal communications system that exerts this control consists of a network of endocrine glands. These glands release many different hormones, or chemical messengers, each of which affects particular glands or tissues in other parts of the body.

### Hormones

Hormones are carried to their target tissues by the bloodstream. By attaching themselves to receptors on the cell membranes in the target tissues, the hormones pass on their instructions.

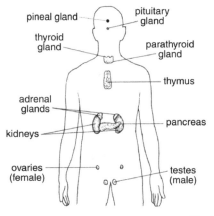

pineal gland

thyroid gland

adrenal glands

kidneys

ovaries (female)

pituitary gland

parathyroid gland

thymus

pancreas

testes (male)

**The Endocrine System**

## Hormone functions

Some important hormones are listed, together with their functions and the glands that produce them.

| Gland | Hormone | Function |
|---|---|---|
| Pituitary | Thyroid-stimulating hormone (thyrotropin) | Control of thyroxine release |
| | Gonadotropic hormones: follicle-stimulating hormone; luteinizing hormone | Control of sex organ development |
| | Prolactin | Stimulation of milk production |
| | Oxytocin | Contractions during labour; bonding between mother and child |
| | Anti-diuretic hormone | Control of water conservation |
| Pineal | Melatonin | Day/night (circadian) rhythm |
| Thyroid | Thyroxine | Control of metabolism |
| | Calcitonin | Controls blood calcium levels |
| Parathyroid | Parathyroid hormone | Controls blood calcium levels |

| Gland | Hormone | Function |
|---|---|---|
| Adrenal | Mineralocorticoids, eg aldosterone | Control of blood pressure via water and sodium levels |
| | Glucocorticoids, eg hydrocortisone | Control of blood sugar; regulation of the immune response |
| | Gonadocorticoids | Control of sex organ development |
| | Adrenaline | Stress response; increases blood pressure and heart rate |
| | Noradrenaline | Stress response; increases blood pressure and heart rate |
| Pancreas | Insulin | Control of blood sugar |
| | Glucagon | Control of blood sugar |
| Kidneys | Erythropoietin | Regulation of red blood cell production |
| | Renin | Control of blood pressure |
| Testes | Testosterone | Development of male characteristics; sex drive |
| Ovaries | Oestrogen | Development of female characteristics including breast development; control of menstruation |
| | Progesterone | Control of menstruation |

## THE DIGESTIVE SYSTEM

The body uses the food we eat to provide energy for growth and repair; however, the food cannot be used until it has been processed by the digestive system.

### The alimentary canal

Processing of food is carried out along the alimentary canal, a tubular organ that extends from the mouth, where the food is ingested, to the anus, where waste material is eliminated. A wave of muscle contractions moves the food along the canal; this is called peristalsis. The alimentary canal consists of the mouth cavity, pharynx, oesophagus, stomach, small intestine, large intestine and rectum.

### The teeth

| Adjective: **dental** | Prefix: **dent-** |
|---|---|

Teeth assist digestion by grinding, chewing and cutting food into small particles that can be further broken down by the chemicals and enzymes of the digestive system.

In humans, the first set of teeth, consisting of 20 deciduous or milk teeth, is gradually replaced from about six years of age by 32 permanent teeth. These consist of chisel-shaped incisors for cutting, situated at the front of each jaw, and behind them the pointed canine teeth, for tearing food. Behind the canines are the molars and premolars, which have uneven surfaces for grinding and chewing food.

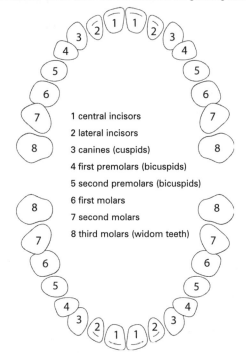

1 central incisors
2 lateral incisors
3 canines (cuspids)
4 first premolars (bicuspids)
5 second premolars (bicuspids)
6 first molars
7 second molars
8 third molars (widom teeth)

**The Teeth**

### The stomach

| Adjective: **gastric** | Prefix: **gastro-** |
|---|---|

The stomach stores food, mixes it with acid and other secretions, and slowly passes it on to the small intestine.

## The small intestine

> Adjective: **enteric**          Prefix: **entero-**

Most of the absorption of the products of digestion takes place in the small intestine. It is divided into three sections: duodenum, jejunum and ileum.

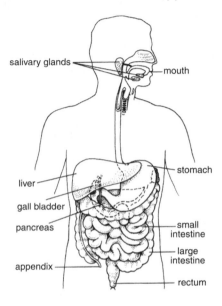

salivary glands — mouth

liver

gall bladder

pancreas

appendix

stomach

small intestine

large intestine

rectum

**The Digestive System**

## Digestive enzymes

Specialized regions of the digestive system secrete different enzymes and chemicals to break down food. For example, the stomach secretes hydrochloric acid, while the small intestine contains enzymes secreted by the pancreas and the intestinal lining.

## THE LIVER

> Adjective: **hepatic**          Prefix: **hepato-**

The liver has several important functions. It stores and cleanses blood, produces bile to aid the digestive system, and regulates metabolic processes. The liver also stores vitamins and iron, and is important in removing drugs and other substances from the body.

## Storage and cleansing of blood

The liver can expand, so it acts as a blood reservoir to help regulate the volume of blood in circulation. Special cells called Kupffer cells clean the blood as it passes through, by removing bacteria.

## Bile production

The liver produces around a litre of bile every day. It is stored and concentrated in a structure called the gallbladder, and then secreted into the small intestine. Bile contains bile salts that act as a detergent to assist with the processing of fat. It also contains leftover cholesterol and products from the breakdown of red blood cells.

## Metabolic processes

The liver plays an important part in the production and breakdown of sugars, fat and protein.

### Sugar metabolism

When blood sugar levels are high, for example after a meal, the liver converts glucose from the blood into a storage material called glycogen. As blood sugar falls again, the liver converts glycogen back into glucose to maintain appropriate levels. These processes are regulated by hormones from the pancreas: insulin drives the storage of glucose, while glucagon drives the breakdown of glycogen.

### Fat metabolism

The liver produces cholesterol, which is a constituent of bile, as well as fatty substances called phospholipids that are needed to make cell membranes. It can break down fat to produce energy, and it can also convert sugars and proteins into fat, which is then stored elsewhere in the body.

### Protein metabolism

Protein metabolism is one of the liver's most important functions. It can break down proteins from food into amino acids (see **Atoms, elements and molecules: Amino acids**). As the liver breaks down the amino acids, nitrogen-containing compounds are released, which the liver converts to a substance called urea for removal by the kidneys. The liver can also convert amino acids from one form to another, and make new proteins from them.

## THE KIDNEYS

Adjectives: **renal, nephric**      Prefixes: **reni-, nephro-**

The kidneys eliminate waste products from the body, as well as regulating other functions.

## Urine production

The kidneys contain approximately a million nephrons, which produce urine in order to eliminate waste products such as urea. Each nephron contains a structure called a glomerulus, which filters fluid from the blood, and a tubule that converts the filtered fluid into urine. The urine travels down structures called ureters and is stored in the bladder.

## Regulatory functions

The kidneys maintain the levels of salts and water in the body and the acidity of the body's fluids. They also regulate blood volume, which affects blood pressure. A long loop in the nephron tubule, known as the loop of Henle, is involved in these functions, as it controls how dilute or concentrated the urine will be through a mechanism called counter-current multiplication. The kidneys also control the production of new red blood cells through the release of the hormone erythropoeitin.

## THE HEART

Adjective: **cardiac**          Prefix: **cardio-**

The heart is responsible for pumping blood around the circulation, so that oxygen is supplied to the tissues and waste carbon dioxide is removed.

### Chambers of the heart

The heart is divided into four chambers, namely the right and left atria (sometimes called auricles), and the right and left ventricles. The presence of several valves within the heart ensures that the blood can only flow between these chambers in one direction.

### Oxygenated blood

Blood that has been oxygenated in the lungs enters the left atrium of the heart and passes to the left ventricle. Contraction of the left ventricle passes oxygenated blood into the aorta, a major blood vessel that leads to the arteries and thence to all the tissues of the body.

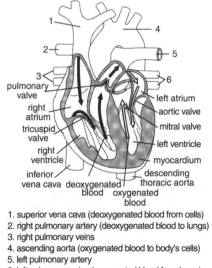

1. superior vena cava (deoxygenated blood from cells)
2. right pulmonary artery (deoxygenated blood to lungs)
3. right pulmonary veins
4. ascending aorta (oxygenated blood to body's cells)
5. left pulmonary artery
6. left pulmonary veins (oxygenated blood from lungs)

**The Heart**

## Deoxygenated blood

Deoxygenated blood from the body tissues is returned to the heart via the veins, which lead into the superior vena cava and inferior vena cava, two major blood vessels. These carry the blood to the right atrium of the heart, and from there to the right ventricle, which pumps blood on to the lungs. The blood is oxygenated in the lungs and then returned to the heart so that the cycle can begin again.

## Heart beat

The muscular contractions of the heart are self-sustaining. This is a property of the cardiac muscle that makes up the heart (see **Muscles**). The average rate of contraction, measured as the pulse rate, is about 72 beats per minute in men and about 80 beats per minute in women.

## THE CIRCULATORY SYSTEM

The process by which blood is continuously moved throughout the body is shown in diagrammatic form below. The arteries carry oxygenated blood from the lungs to the other organs. Veins return oxygen-depleted blood to the lungs. Fine capillaries in the tissues ensure that oxygen reaches all the cells.

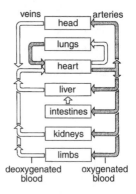

**The Circulation**

### One-Way System

Human leg veins have a special system of 'non-return' valves to cope with the fact that the blood has to travel upwards from the legs back to the lungs against the effects of gravity. However, humans don't have valves to help get the blood up from the brain to the lungs, because we don't spend much time upside down. Bats, which hang upside down for long periods, have special adaptations in their circulatory systems.

## THE LUNGS

Adjective: **pulmonary, pneumonic**    Prefix: **pneumo-**

The lungs are large spongy respiratory organs that remove carbon dioxide from the blood and replace it with oxygen.

### Breathing

Air is forced in and out of the lungs as a result of movements of the diaphragm, a sheet of muscle that separates the thorax from the abdomen. During inhalation the diaphragm is lowered and the lungs expand to fill with air. During exhalation the diaphragm is raised and air is forcibly expelled from the lungs.

### The trachea, bronchi and bronchioles

Air containing oxygen is drawn into the lungs through the trachea (windpipe), which divides at its lower end to form two bronchi. These in turn divide into many fine tubes known as bronchioles.

### Alveoli

The surface area of the lungs is greatly increased by the presence of millions of tiny air sacs, known as alveoli. Each bronchiole terminates in a cluster of alveoli, which are lined with a thin moist membrane richly supplied with capillaries. Oxygen from the air on one side of the membrane passes through the thin walls of the alveoli into the capillaries, while carbon dioxide passes out of the capillaries into the lungs in the same way. In humans, the total surface area of the alveoli is about 70m$^2$.

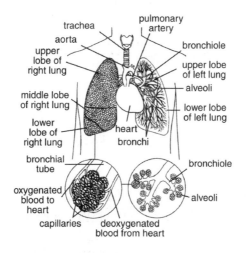

**The Lungs**

## THE LYMPHATIC SYSTEM

Lymph is a colourless fluid, derived from blood, that bathes all the tissues, cleansing them of cellular debris and infectious agents such as bacteria.

Lymph leaks out from capillaries into the tissues, and then drains into a network of vessels known as the lymphatic system. The fluid travels from the tissues to the nearest site of lymphoid tissue, such as lymph nodes, spleen or tonsils. Lymph contains lymphocytes and antibodies that fight infections, and the lymphoid tissue is where the body's response to a new infection starts (see **Defence Mechanisms**).

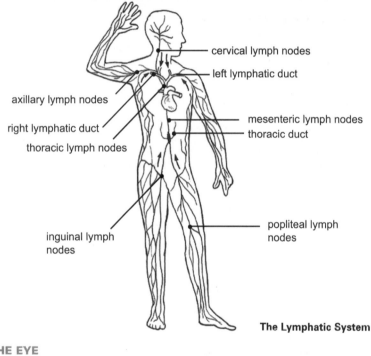

cervical lymph nodes

left lymphatic duct

axillary lymph nodes

right lymphatic duct

thoracic lymph nodes

mesenteric lymph nodes

thoracic duct

inguinal lymph nodes

popliteal lymph nodes

**The Lymphatic System**

## THE EYE

| Adjective: **optic** | Prefix: **opto-** |

The eye processes light into nerve impulses that can be interpreted by the brain.

### Structure of the eye

The eye is surrounded by a white fibrous outer layer, the sclera, which is modified at the front of the eye to form the transparent cornea. The sclera is lined by a vascular layer, the choroid, which is in turn lined at the back of the eye by the retina.

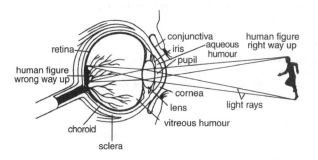

| | conjunctiva | human figure |
|retina| iris — aqueous | right way up |
| | pupil | humour |
|human figure | | |
|wrong way up | cornea | |
| | lens | light rays |
| | vitreous humour | |
|choroid | | |
|sclera | | |

**The Eye**

## Rods and cones

The retina contains millions of light-sensitive cells of two types, rods and cones. The rods function at low light levels, and are responsible for black and white vision, while the cones are responsible for colour vision when more light is available.

## Entry of light into the eye

Light enters the eye through the cornea, and passes through a watery medium (the aqueous humour) and then through the pupil, a small circular aperture in the iris. The iris is an adjustable ring of muscle that forms the coloured part of the eye, and controls the size of the pupil and thus the amount of light entering the eye.

## Focusing and processing the light

Behind the iris lies the transparent lens, whose curvature is regulated by means of ciliary muscles. These contract to make the lens thin, for viewing distant objects, or relax to make it thicker, for viewing nearby objects. The shape of the lens is adjusted in this way so that light is directed through the jelly-like vitreous humour lying between the lens and the retina, and is focused on to the retina. The light-sensitive rods and cones of the retina then transmit nerve impulses via the optic nerve to the brain, where they are interpreted as vision.

## THE EAR

| Adjective: **otic** | Prefix: **oto-** |

The ear converts vibrations caused by sound waves into nerve impulses that can be interpreted by the brain. It is also important in maintaining balance. The ear consists of three parts: the outer ear, the middle ear and the inner ear.

## The outer ear

The outer ear transmits sound waves from outside the ear to the tympanic membrane (eardrum), and consists of a pinna (commonly referred to as the 'ear') that projects from the head and is made of a thin layer of cartilage covered with skin. It funnels sound into a channel that leads to the tympanic membrane. In some other mammals, eg dogs, the pinna can be moved independently in order to detect the direction of sounds.

## The middle ear

The middle ear is an air-filled cavity containing three small bones or ossicles, known as the malleus (hammer), incus (anvil) and stapes (stirrup). A structure called the Eustachian tube links the middle ear to the pharynx at the back of the throat, ensuring that the air pressure remains the same on both sides of the tympanic membrane. The ossicles transmit vibrations from the tympanic membrane to the fenestra ovalis (oval window), the upper of two membrane-covered openings that separate the middle ear from the fluid-filled inner ear.

## The inner ear

Vibrations from the fenestra ovalis are finally transmitted to the spiral-shaped cochlea in the inner ear. The cochlea is filled with fluid and lined with sensory cells (hair cells) that detect vibrations as movements of fluid, and relay them as nerve impulses via the auditory nerve to the brain, where they are interpreted as the tone and pitch of the original sound.

## Balance

The inner ear also contains three fluid-filled semicircular tubes, known as semicircular canals, which can detect movements of the head and are concerned with the maintenance of balance.

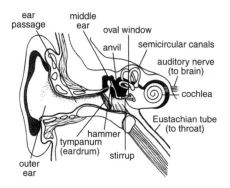

**The Ear**

## THE SKIN

| Adjective: **dermal** | Prefix: **dermato-** |
|---|---|

The skin is an important sense organ. It also acts as a barrier and helps to regulate body temperature.

## Structure of the skin

The skin consists of two main layers. The epidermis is a thin outer layer, which is continually being renewed as dead cells are shed from its surface. The thicker underlying layer is called the dermis and is composed of a network of collagen and elastic fibres. The dermis contains blood and lymph vessels, sensory nerve endings, hair follicles, sweat and sebaceous glands, and smooth muscle.

## Temperature regulation

In humans, as well as other warm-blooded animals, the skin has an important role in temperature regulation. Heat loss is achieved by sweating and by dilation of the skin capillaries. In order to conserve heat, the skin capillaries contract and the hairs on the surface are raised, trapping a layer of warm air next to the skin.

## Other functions

The skin is an important sense organ, sensitive to touch, pressure, changes in temperature, and painful stimuli. It prevents fluid loss and dehydration, and protects the body from invasion by microorganisms and parasites.

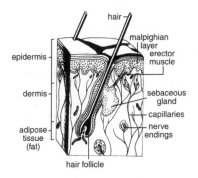

The Skin

## DEFENCE MECHANISMS

The body has many ways to defend itself against disease, which are collectively known as the immune system. This system includes innate immune responses that act rapidly, and adaptive immune responses that are more specific but take several days to work effectively.

### Innate immunity

| Mechanism | Action |
| --- | --- |
| Skin | Acts as a protective layer to prevent entry of pathogens (disease-causing agents) |
| Lysozyme | Destroys bacteria in saliva, tears, mucus, blood |

| Hydrochloric acid | Destroys pathogens in the stomach |
|---|---|
| Phagocytosis | Pathogens or infected cells are 'eaten' by cells of the immune system |
| Complement system | Proteins destroy bacteria in the blood |

### Cells of the adaptive immune system

| Cell | Function |
|---|---|
| Helper T lymphocytes | Needed for activating killer T and B lymphocytes |
| Killer T lymphocytes | Kill infected cells |
| B lymphocytes | Respond to pathogens outside the cell; some become plasma cells |
| Plasma cells | Produce antibodies |
| Natural killer cells | Kill cells that try to evade other immune cells |
| Dendritic cells | Act as 'sentinels', displaying material from pathogens to T lymphocytes |
| Follicular dendritic cells | Display material from pathogens to B lymphocytes |

*One Step Ahead*

Some viruses have evolved to infect the very cells that are supposed to protect us. The HIV virus, which causes AIDS, hijacks T cells and is also thought to cling on to follicular dendritic cells. Similarly the virus that causes glandular fever, Epstein-Barr virus, invades B cells.

### Antibodies

Antibodies are proteins that play an important role in the immune system (see **Atoms, elements and molecules: Proteins**).

### Antibody structure

Antibodies have a constant region and two variable regions. The variable regions bind to pathogens or material from pathogens. Sometimes this binding 'neutralizes' harmful effects of toxins released by bacteria. In other cases, the constant region needs bind to cells of the immune system; this triggers the cells to clear up the infection.

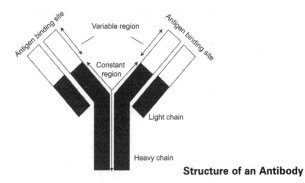

**Structure of an Antibody**

## Antibody diversity

Each person makes a diverse collection of antibodies because each B cell has its antibody genes jumbled up in a different order. The antibody response is called an 'adaptive' or 'acquired' response because it is also tailor-made to each infection. When an infection starts, any B cells that produce slightly effective antibodies are mutated, and the best ones selected.

---

### Immunoassays

Immunoassays can be used to detect proteins in blood or other fluids, and are often used in diagnosing diseases. They make use of antibodies that bind the protein of interest; usually, monoclonal antibodies are used, which are antibodies that can be produced in the lab and will always bind in the same place. One way in which immunoassays can be performed is to coat an antibody on to a plate or tube. A sample is added so that the protein of interest can bind. Unbound sample is washed away and a second (different) antibody that also binds to the protein is added. This second antibody is tagged with a fluorescent or radioactive molecule. The level of fluorescence or radioactivity is measured to show how much protein was in the sample.

---

## THE REPRODUCTIVE SYSTEM

Human reproduction involves the fertilization of an egg from a woman by a sperm from a man. Each of these sex cells, or gametes, contains half the genetic information of a normal cell. This means that the resultant cell, or zygote, contains the correct amount of genetic information, half of which comes from each parent.

### Male reproductive organs

The male reproductive system is closely associated with the urinary system. The bladder stores urine, releasing it to the outside along a tube inside the penis called the urethra. The urethra also carries sperm during ejaculation. Sperm are made inside the testis and stored in coiled tubes called the epididymis until, during ejaculation, they are carried to the penis along the sperm duct or vas deferens. The prostate gland, which is located where the sperm ducts and urethra join, releases semen, the milky medium in which sperm are ejaculated from the penis.

## Female reproductive organs

Within the female reproductive system, a single egg, or ovum, is released each month from one of the ovaries. It travels along the Fallopian tube to the uterus. The neck of the uterus, or cervix, forms a narrow opening between the uterus and the vagina.

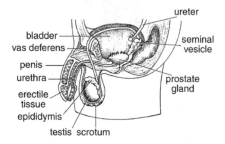

**The Male Reproductive System**

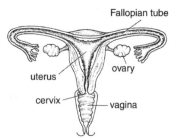

**The Female Reproductive System**

## The female sexual cycle

Ovulation occurs in a cycle known as the female sexual cycle (also called the oestrus cycle or the menstrual cycle). Hormones from the pituitary gland control levels of the sex hormones oestrogen and progesterone in the ovaries, which in turn affect the lining of the uterus (womb) and maturation of the ova (eggs). A 'typical' cycle lasts for 28 days, with ovulation occuring at around day 14, although the length can vary considerably.

### The follicular phase and ovulation

The first part of the cycle is known as the follicular phase, and involves maturation of an ovarian follicle containing an egg. The sex hormone oestrogen is important during this phase. Ovulation (release of the egg from the follicle) occurs half-way through the cycle.

### The luteal phase

The second half of the cycle is known as the luteal phase, because the leftover follicle cells form a structure called the corpus luteum, which is important in the production of the sex hormone progesterone.

### Fertilization

If the egg is fertilized, the level of progesterone remains high. The fertilized egg becomes embedded in the womb lining and begins to divide and grow.

### Menstruation

If the egg is not fertilized, the level of progesterone drops. Menstruation occurs at the end of the cycle, and involves the shedding of the womb lining and the unfertilized egg.

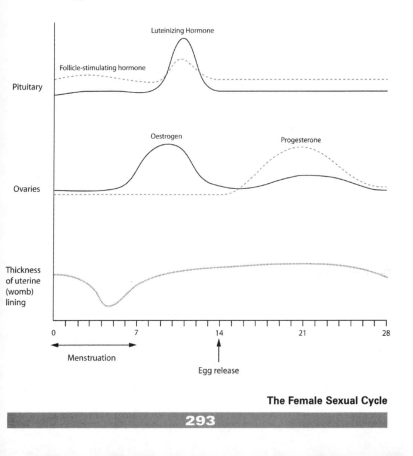

**The Female Sexual Cycle**

## BLOOD

> Adjective: **haematic**     Prefix: **haemo-**

Blood performs many important functions as it circulates through the tissues of the body. It transports oxygen, nutrients and hormones, and carries waste products to the organs of excretion. It also helps to maintain a uniform temperature in humans and other warm-blooded organisms.

### Blood composition

| Component | Function |
|---|---|
| Red blood cells | Carry oxygen, by means of haemoglobin |
| White blood cells | Defend the body against infection; include lymphocytes, plasma cells, monocytes, macrophages, natural killer cells, neutrophils, eosinophils and basophils |
| Platelets | Needed for blood clotting |
| Plasma | Distribution of nutrients, salts, hormones, clotting factors and proteins needed for defence |

### ABO blood group system

Every person has a particular blood group, determined by genes inherited from their parents. The red blood cells of the A, B, AB and O groups carry, respectively, the A antigen, B antigen, both antigens and neither. The blood contains natural antibodies against the blood group antigens that are absent from the red blood cells. Before a transfusion, the blood of the recipient and donor is cross-matched to ensure that red blood cells from the donor are not given to a person possessing antibodies against them, as this could have fatal consequences.

| Blood group | Genes carried | Antigens on red cells | Antibodies in plasma | Can receive blood type |
|---|---|---|---|---|
| A | AA or OA | A | anti-B | A and O |
| B | BB or OB | B | anti-A | B and O |
| AB | AB | A and B | none | A, B, AB, O |
| O | OO | none | anti-A and anti-B | O |

### Rhesus factor

There are actually several Rhesus antigens, so called because they were first characterized in Rhesus monkeys. The one called Rhesus D is particularly common and is also much more likely to cause a blood transfusion reaction. Rhesus D is known as the 'Rhesus factor', and people are told whether they are positive or negative for it when they are told their ABO blood group. The Rhesus factor is not connected with the ABO blood group, so a person can be O RhD$^+$ or O RhD$^-$, for example.

## Haemolytic Disease of the Newborn

If a mother is negative for Rhesus factor but a father is positive, there can be problems when it comes to having children. The father sometimes passes the gene on to the developing child, and the Rhesus factor can pass between the mother and the foetus. The mother's immune system can react against the foetus's blood cells and destroy them because they seem foreign. Although the first child is usually unaffected, the mother must be treated with antibodies to prevent any subsequent children being affected.

### Universal donors and recipients

The blood type O RhD$^-$ is known as the 'universal donor' because it does not carry the A antigen, the B antigen or Rhesus D. It can therefore be given safely to anyone, although it is a rare blood type so it is often saved for emergencies. The blood type AB RhD$^+$ is called the universal recipient, as someone with this blood group carries all the antigens and will not react to any other blood type.

# DISEASES AND MEDICINES

## INFECTIOUS DISEASES

Many illnesses are caused by infectious agents (pathogens). Viruses infect cells and replicate themselves by hijacking the cell's own processes (see **Organisms: Eubacteria kingdom**), while bacteria are single-celled microorganisms that can live and reproduce independently (see **Organisms: Viruses**). Other, generally larger, infectious agents of various types are known as parasites; they are often carried and transmitted to humans by other animals. Some of the diseases caused by these pathogens are listed below.

| Disease | Type | Transmission | Pathogen |
|---------|------|--------------|----------|
| AIDS (Acquired Immune Deficiency Syndrome) | Viral | Infected blood; sexual transmission | Human immuno-deficiency virus (HIV) (retrovirus family) |
| Amoebiasis | Bacterial | Contaminated food | *Entamoeba histolytica* |
| Anthrax | Bacterial | Animal hair | *Bacillus anthracis* |
| Bilharziasis | Parasitic | Certain snails | *Schistosoma haematobium* (also called Bilharzia), *Schistosoma mansoni* or *Schistosoma japonicum* |
| Bronchiolitis | Viral | Droplet infection | Respiratory syncytical virus (RSV) (paramyxovirus family) |
| Brucellosis | Bacterial | Cattle or goats | *Brucella abortus* or *Brucella meliteusis* |
| Bubonic plague | Bacterial | Fleas | *Yersinia pestis* |
| Chickenpox | Viral | Droplet infection | Varicella-zoster virus |
| Cholera | Bacterial | Contaminated water | *Vibrio cholerae* |
| Common cold | Viral | Droplet infection | Rhinoviruses (picornavirus family) |
| Dengue fever | Viral | Mosquitos | Dengue virus (flavivirus family) |
| Diphtheria | Bacterial | Droplet infection | *Corynebacterium diphtheriae* |

| Disease | Type | Transmission | Pathogen |
|---|---|---|---|
| Dysentery | Bacterial | Contaminated food or water | *Shigella* genus |
| German measles | Viral | Droplet infection | Rubella virus (togavirus family) |
| Glandular fever | Viral | Infected saliva | Epstein-Barr virus (EBV) (herpesvirus family) |
| Gonorrhoea | Bacterial | Sexual transmission | *Neisseria gonorrhoeae* |
| Hepatitis A | Viral | Contaminated food or water | Hepatitis A virus (picornavirus family) |
| Hepatitis B | Viral | Infected blood; sexual transmission | Hepatitis B virus (hepadnavirus family) |
| Hepatitis C | Viral | Infected blood | Hepatitis C virus (flavivirus family) |
| Influenza (flu) | Viral | Droplet infection | Influenza A, B or C (all orthomyxovirus family) |
| Kala-azar (leishmaniasis) | Parasitic | Sandfly | Genus *leishmania* |
| lassa fever | Viral | infected urine | Lassa virus (arenavirus family) |
| Legionnaire's disease | Bacterial | Infected water | *Legionella pneumophila* |
| Leprosy | Bacterial | Droplet infection; minimally contagious | *Mycobacterium leprae* |
| Malaria | Parasitic | *Anopheles* mosquitos | *Plasmodium falciparium*, *Plasmodium ovale*, *Plasmodium malariae* |
| Measles | Viral | Droplet infection | Measles virus (paramyxovirus family) |
| MRSA (Methicillin-Resistant *Staphylococcus aureus*) | Bacterial | Droplet contact | Specific strains of *Staphylococcus aureus* |

| Disease | Type | Transmission | Pathogen |
|---------|------|--------------|----------|
| Mumps | Viral | Droplet infection | Mumps virus (paramyxovirus family) |
| Poliomyelitis | Viral | Droplet infection; infected faeces | Three strains of poliovirus (picornavirus family) |
| Psittacosis | Bacterial | Birds, eg parrots | *Chlamydia psittaci* |
| Rabies | Viral | Animal bite | Rabies virus (rhabdovirus family) |
| River blindness | Parasitic | *Simulium* flies | *Onchocerca volvulus* worm |
| SARS (Severe Acute Respiratory Syndrome) | Viral | Droplet infection; possibly direct contact | SARS coronavirus |
| Scarlet fever | Bacterial | Droplet infection; infected dairy products | *Streptococcus pyogenes* |
| Shingles | Viral | Reactivation of dormant virus; see chickenpox | Varicella-zoster virus |
| Sleeping sickness | Parasitic | Tsetse fly | Trypanosoma brucei gambiense or Trypanosoma rhodesiense |
| Smallpox | Viral | Droplet infection | major or minor variants of variola virus (poxvirus family) |
| Syphilis | Bacterial | Sexual transmission | *Treponema pallidum* |
| Tetanus | Bacterial | Infected soil | *Clostridium tetani* |
| Thrush | Yeast | Rapid multiplication of yeast already present on skin | *Candida albicans* |
| Trachoma | Bacterial | Eye-to-eye, often via flies | *Chlamydia trachomatis* |
| Tuberculosis | Bacterial | Droplet infection | *Mycobacterium tuberculosis* |
| Typhoid (fever) | Bacterial | Contaminated food or water | *Salmonella typhi* |

| Disease | Type | Transmission | Pathogen |
| --- | --- | --- | --- |
| Typhus | Parasitic | Fleas, ticks, mites or lice | Various *Rickettsia* species |
| Whooping cough | Bacterial | Droplet infection | *Bordetella pertussis* |
| Yellow fever | Viral | Mosquitos infected by monkeys | Yellow fever virus (flavivirus family) |

## Mutant Proteins

The Transmissible Spongiform Encephalopathies (TSEs) are unusual diseases in that the infectious agents are probably folded proteins called prions. Certain brain cells have normal prions in their membranes but, in these diseases, mutant versions of prions form. These mutant prions then force the surrounding normal prions to become mutants. Examples of TSEs are Creutzfeldt-Jakob Disease (CJD), Bovine Spongiform Encephalopathy (BSE) and scrapie.

66

*You will find that fatigue has a larger share in the promotion and transmission of disease than any other single condition you can name.*

—English physician and pathologist Sir James Paget (1814–99), *Science in War* (1940).

99

## AUTOIMMUNE DISEASES

Autoimmune diseases are conditions caused by the immune system attacking its own tissues. Some examples are described below.

| Disease | Description |
| --- | --- |
| Type 1 (insulin-dependent) diabetes mellitus | Destruction of insulin-producing islet cells in the pancreas |
| Hashimoto's thyroiditis | Destruction of thyroid cells that produce thyroxine hormone |
| Multiple sclerosis | Destruction of the myelin sheath of nerve cells, inhibiting nerve impulses |
| Rheumatoid arthritis | Inflammation of the joint linings |

## Cloning

The term 'cloning' strictly means creating a whole organism that is genetically identical to the donor cells from which it is produced. However, as the term has taken on other meanings, this procedure tends to be known specifically as reproductive cloning. A famous example of successful reproductive cloning was the birth of Dolly the sheep, who was the first true example of cloning from an adult mammal, in 1997 at the Roslin Institute near Edinburgh. This was carried out by injecting the genetic material from an adult cell into an egg from which the genetic material had been removed. The egg was implanted into a parent animal and Dolly was born. Plants have been cloned much further back in history by taking cuttings and growing them into new plants.

The procedure known as therapeutic cloning is properly called somatic cell nuclear transfer. It involves replacing the genetic material in an egg with the genetic material from a normal (somatic) cell, as with reproductive cloning, but then using the resultant embryo as a source of stem cells (see **Cells: Gene expression**). The purpose of this technique would be to produce cells identical to a patient's own, to replace those destroyed in disease. Examples would include insulin-producing cells in people with diabetes, or brain cells in people with Parkinson's disease. However, there is controversy over the use of embryos for this purpose.

Molecular biologists often use the terms 'cloning' or 'gene cloning' to refer to genetic manipulation procedures in which a gene or other piece of DNA is inserted into a carrier DNA molecule known as a vector. Special bacterial enzymes called restriction enzymes are used to cut pieces of DNA in particular places so that they can be joined together. Bacteria or yeasts can make copies of the vectors, meaning that the DNA of interest can be copied many times.

## CANCER

Cancer occurs when the normal controls of cell division and organization fail. This happens when genetic mutations occur that disrupt these controls. The mutant cells grow and divide more quickly than the normal ones.

### Metastasis

In solid tissues, a tumour forms and invades the surrounding tissues; once the cancer cells reach the bloodstream they can seed tumours elsewhere in the body. This invasion and spreading is called metastasis.

### Genes and cancer

Mutations in genes that control cell division can lead to the development or progression of cancer. The genes can be tumour suppressor genes or oncogenes.

## Tumour suppressor genes

Tumour suppressor genes tend to be ones that prevent growth and cell division, and the mutations stop them working properly. Both copies of a gene must be damaged in order for the cancer to occur. In these cases, it is very unlikely that something will randomly go wrong twice in the same cell. However, if one mutant copy of the gene is already present in every cell, only one more mutation needs to occur in any cell in order to cause cancer. This is called the 'two-hit hypothesis', and means that people who inherit one faulty copy of a tumour suppressor gene are at increased risk of cancer. Some tumour suppressor genes are described below.

| Gene | Cancer | Organ affected |
|---|---|---|
| Rb | Retinoblastoma | Eye |
| BRCA1 and 2 | Carcinoma | Breast and ovary |
| FAP (Familial Adenomatous Polyposis) | Colorectal cancer | Bowel |
| HNPCC (Heriditary Non-Polyposis Colon Cancer) | Colorectal cancer | Bowel |

## Oncogenes

Oncogenes can cause cancer even if only one copy is mutated. These genes tend to be ones that promote growth, and the mutations make them overactive. The normal form of an oncogene is called a proto-oncogene.

### X-ray machine

An X-ray machine fires electrons at a positively-charged solid target in a glass tube containing a vacuum. Electrons passing near an atomic nucleus in the target decelerate and 'lose' energy, which is emitted as X-rays (see **Energy, light and radioactivity: Electromagnetic radiation**). The target is placed diagonally across the end of the glass tube; this means that lots of the X-rays travel across the tube and can be directed at a patient.

Soft tissues do not absorb X-rays well, whereas hard or dense tissues absorb them much more efficiently. Bone absorbs X-rays extremely well because of their high calcium content. Capture of the exiting rays on photographic film produces a picture of the body, in which tumours, bone fractures and other medical conditions can be visualized.

## Environment and cancer

Environmental factors can increase the risk of some cancers, because of the increased likelihood of genetic mutations occurring. Substances that increase the risk of cancer are called carcinogens. Some risk factors, and examples of the cancers to which they can contribute, are given below.

| Risk factor | Cancer | Organ affected |
| --- | --- | --- |
| Sunburn | Malignant melanoma | Skin |
| Tobacco smoke | Carcinoma | Lung, pancreas |
| Asbestos exposure | Mesothelioma | Lung |
| Poor diet | Colorectal cancer | Bowel |

## CONGENITAL ABNORMALITIES

A congenital abnormality is one that is present at birth. Causes or contributing factors can include genetic mutations, as well as environmental factors such as the mother's diet or any drugs taken during pregnancy. Many congenital abnormalities have no apparent cause – the development of a human being is a complex process and, as such, sometimes goes wrong by chance. Some congenital abnormalities are described below.

> " 
> *Men that look no further than their outsides, think health an appurtenance unto life, and quarrel with their constitutions for being sick; but I that have examined the parts of man, and know upon what tender filaments that fabric hangs, do wonder that we are not always so; and considering the thousand doors that lead to death, do thank my God that we can die but once.*
>
> —English writer and physician Sir Thomas Browne (1605–82), in *Religio Medici* (c. 1635).
> "

### Cleft lip and palate

The terms 'cleft lip' and 'cleft palate' describe a gap in the upper lip or roof of the mouth respectively. Babies can be born with one or both of these conditions. The structures in the middle of the face develop from tissues that migrate from either side of the face and fuse in the middle. Cleft lip and palate occur when the tissues do not join up, and can lead to problems with feeding and learning to talk. Both conditions can usually be corrected by surgery.

### Spina bifida

Spina bifida, or 'split spine', occurs when the vertebrae of the backbone do not encase the spinal cord properly. In its more severe forms, where the nerves bulge out, they are damaged. This can lead to difficulty with activities such as walking or going to the toilet. Problems with the production of the cerebro-spinal fluid that bathes the brain and spinal cord mean that most babies born with spina bifida also have a condition called hydrocephalus, where the head fills with fluid and squashes the brain. Taking folic acid supplements before conceiving a baby can help to prevent spina bifida.

## Sirenomelia

Sirenomelia is also known as 'mermaid syndrome', because babies born with the condition have legs that are fused together in a tail-like structure, and their feet are splayed out. This condition is extremely rare, and the cause is unknown.

## Thalidomide syndrome

Thalidomide is a drug that was used to treat morning sickness in pregnant women during the late 1950s and early 1960s. An unknown side effect of the drug affected the development of blood vessels, leading to many of the babies being born without some or all of their limbs. In some cases, the hands or feet developed on the ends of extremely short limbs. The development of internal organs was also sometimes affected.

### A Silver Lining?

The ability of thalidomide to block blood vessel formation means that it may be useful in treating cancer, by preventing tumours from forming a blood supply. The clinical trials taking place to study this possibility have extremely strict regulations to ensure that women do not become pregnant while taking the drug.

### CT scanner

A CT scanner is used to build up three-dimensional pictures of tissues and organs inside the body. It is circular in shape, with an X-ray source and an X-ray detector positioned at opposite sides of the circle. The patient lies through the ring, and the source and detector slowly move around the ring so that X-rays are taken from every angle. The detector is used in place of photographic film, and sends information about the different X-ray 'pictures' to a computer. The computer calculates the only original three-dimensional shape that could give rise to exactly the pictures that were taken from all directions.

CT stands for 'computed tomography' or 'computerized tomography'. Another name for the same technique is CAT scanning ('computer-aided tomography').

## GENETIC DISEASES

Many diseases and medical conditions are passed from parents to children rather than arising spontaneously. Faulty genes can be passed down on the sex chromosomes or the autosomes, and can be dominant or recessive (see **Genetics: Genetic inheritance**). Some genetic diseases are described below.

## Autosomal recessive disorders

Autosomal recessive genetic disorders affect, on average, one in four children if each parent is an unaffected carrier. Affected children inherit one faulty copy from each of their healthy carrier parents (see **Genetics: Genetic inheritance**).

### Cystic fibrosis

The gene responsible for cystic fibrosis encodes a protein called CFTR, which controls the amount of salt and water transported in and out of cells. The faulty protein keeps too much salt and too little water in the cells lining the lungs. Abnormal, sticky mucus is produced in the lungs, leading to recurrent severe chest infections.

### Sickle-cell anaemia

The gene responsible for sickle-cell anaemia encodes a protein called beta-globin. This protein is an important part of a substance called haemoglobin, which is found in red blood cells and carries oxygen from the lungs to the tissues of the body. The faulty protein causes the haemoglobin of affected people to clump together and distort the shape of the red blood cells, which then get stuck in small blood vessels, causing a great deal of pain. Sickle-cell anaemia can lead to strokes and internal organ damage.

*Better by Half*

Carriers who have one faulty and one normal copy of the beta-globin gene do not get sickle-cell anaemia, and are resistant to getting malaria. This is known as heterozygote advantage, and may explain why sickle-cell anaemia is more common amongst people who are descended from the populations of countries where malaria is widespread.

## Marfan syndrome

Marfan syndrome is an autosomal dominant disease (see **Genetics: Genetic inheritance**). If either of the parents have the disease, half of all their children are likely to inherit a faulty copy of the gene, whereas if both parents have the disease, all their children will inherit it. The gene responsible for Marfan syndrome encodes a protein called fibrillin, which is is found in connective tissue. People who develop the syndrome often grow very tall and have long, thin hands and feet. They usually also have heart problems.

*The Doctors behind the Diseases*

Marfan syndrome and Duchenne muscular dystrophy are both named after notable 19th-century French physicians. Marfan syndrome is named after Antoine Marfan, who first described the condition in 1896. Marfan's other work included observation on tuberculosis, which contributed to the development of the BCG vaccine. Duchenne muscular dystrophy is named after Guillaume Duchenne, who described the disease in the 1860s, despite never having held a formal hospital appointment.

## Duchenne muscular dystrophy

Duchenne muscular dystrophy is an X-linked recessive genetic disorder (see **Genetics: Genetic inheritance**). If a mother is a carrier of the disease, on average half of her sons, but none of her daughters, will have the disease. The gene responsible for Duchenne muscular dystrophy encodes a protein called dystrophin, which is found in muscle tissue. The faulty protein leads to muscle wasting, causing mobility and breathing difficulties.

## HYPERSENSITIVITY DISORDERS

Also known as allergic disorders, hypersensitivity disorders involve an overreaction to otherwise harmless substances by the immune system.

| Disorder | Description |
| --- | --- |
| Anaphylaxis | Extreme widespread allergic reaction in response to specific triggers such as foods and bee or wasp stings. |
| Asthma | Allergic response in the lungs to inhaled pollen, dust mite particles, etc. |
| Atopic eczema | Allergic response by cells under the skin. |
| Hayfever | Allergic response in the upper respiratory tract to inhaled pollen, dust mite particles, etc. |

## MENTAL HEALTH DISORDERS

There are many types of mental health disorders. Some tend to run in families, suggesting that they are partly caused by faulty genes, and the fact that many of these disorders can be treated with medication suggests that they have a physical component. Environment and lifestyle may also be important, as life events can sometimes trigger mental health disorders; treatments such as counselling and exercise can therefore be helpful. Some mental health disorders are described below.

## Eating disorders

People with eating disorders often have a distorted view of their own body image, which leads them to develop an inappropriate pattern of eating. People with anorexia nervosa eat too little and can become dangerously underweight, while those with bulimia nervosa tend to alternate between eating too much and trying to get rid of what they have eaten by vomiting or taking laxatives.

## Depression

People with depression experience periods of abnormally low mood, even when there is no obvious cause.

## Bipolar disorder

Bipolar disorder is also known as manic depression. People with this condition experience periods of both very low mood (depression) and very high mood (mania).

## Schizophrenia

Schizophrenia is a name given to a group of mental health problems. These involve disturbances in the way sufferers think about, and interact with, the outside world. People with schizophrenia often experience delusions and hallucinations.

## DIETARY DEFICIENCIES

### Fat-soluble vitamins

| Vitamin | Chemical name | Deficiency symptoms | Source |
|---|---|---|---|
| A | Retinol (carotene) | Night blindness; rough skin; impaired bone growth | Dairy foods, egg yolk liver, oily fish, dark green vegetables, carrots |
| D | Cholecalciferol | Rickets; osteomalacia | Egg yolk, liver, oily fish; made on skin in sunlight |
| E | Tocopherols | Multiple symptoms follow impaired fat absorption | Vegetable oils |
| K | Phytomenadione | Haemorrhagic problems | Green leafy vegetables, beef, liver |

### Water-soluble vitamins

| Vitamin | Chemical name | Deficiency symptoms | Source |
|---|---|---|---|
| $B_1$ | Thiamin | Beri-beri (nerve lesions, heart failure) | Germ and bran of seeds, grains, yeast |
| $B_2$ | Riboflavin | Skin disorders; failure to thrive | Liver, milk, cheese, eggs, green leafy vegetables, pulses, yeast |
| $B_3$ | Niacin | Pellagra (gastrointestinal problems, skin problems, depression, paralysis) | Dairy products, eggs, poultry, fish, meat, nuts, breads, cereals |

| Vitamin | Chemical name | Deficiency symptoms | Source |
|---------|---------------|---------------------|--------|
| B$_6$ | Pyridoxine | Dermatitis; neurological disorders | Liver, meats, fruits, cereals, leafy vegetables |
| | Pantothenic acid | Dermatitis; neurological disorders | Widespread in plants and animals; destroyed in heavily-processed food |
| | Biotin | Dermatitis | Liver, kidney, yeast extract; made by microorganisms in large intestine |
| B$_{12}$ | Cyanocobalamin | Anaemia; neurological disturbance | Liver, kidney, dairy products, eggs; none found in plants or yeast |
| | Folic acid | Anaemia | Liver, green leafy vegetables, peanuts; cooking and processing can cause serious losses in food |
| C | Ascorbic acid | Scurvy (anaemia, ulcers, haemorrhage) | Blackcurrants, citrus fruits, other fruits, green leafy vegetables, potatoes; losses occur during storage and cooking |

## Minerals

| Mineral | Deficiency symptom | Source |
|---------|--------------------|--------|
| Calcium | Rickets in children; osteoporosis in adults | Milk, butter, cheese, sardines, green leafy vegetables, citrus fruits |
| Chromium | Adult-onset diabetes | Brewer's yeast, black pepper, liver, wholemeal bread, beer |
| Copper | Anaemia; heart problems | Green vegetables, fish, oysters, liver |

| Mineral | Deficiency symptom | Source |
|---------|-------------------|--------|
| Fluoride | Tooth decay; possibly osteoporosis | Fluoridated drinking water, seafood, tea |
| Iodine | Goitre; cretinism in new-born children | Seafood, salt water fish, seaweed, iodized salt, table salt |
| Iron | Anaemia | Liver, kidney, green leafy vegetables, egg yolk, dried fruit, potatoes, molasses |
| Magnesium | Irregular heartbeat; muscular weakness; insomnia | Green leafy vegetables (eaten raw), nuts, whole grains |
| Phosphorus | Muscular weakness; bone pain; loss of appetite | Meat, poultry, fish, eggs, dried beans and peas, milk products |
| Potassium | Irregular heartbeat; muscular weakness; fatigue; kidney and lung failure | Fresh vegetables, meat, orange juice, bananas, bran |
| Sodium | Impaired acid-base balance in body fluids (very rare) | Table salt, other naturally occurring salts |
| Zinc | Impaired wound healing; loss of appetite; impaired sexual development | Meat, whole grains, legumes, oysters, milk |

## MEDICINES

This section includes drugs that are commonly prescribed in the UK, the USA and other countries of the developed world. They are grouped according to their usage, and listed by their generic names, not by brand names. Names follow the rINNs system (recommended International Nonproprietary Names).

### Anabolic steroids

These are used to help muscle repair following injury, and can be abused by body-builders and athletes to improve their physique.

Nandrolone
Stanozolol

### Antacid drugs

These are used to neutralize stomach acids, thus relieving heartburn, peptic ulcers and other gastric complaints.

| | |
|---|---|
| Aluminium hydroxide | Magnesium trisilicate |
| Magnesium carbonate | Sodium bicarbonate |

## Antianxiety drugs

These are used to reduce feelings of tension, nervousness and anxiety that interfere with a person's ability to cope with everyday life. Benzodiazepines depress the action of the central nervous system, promoting drowsiness and relaxation. Beta-blockers block nerve endings, stopping release of neurotransmitters, so reducing tremors, palpitations and sweating.

### Benzodiazepines include:

| | |
|---|---|
| Alprazolam | Diazepam |
| Chlordiazepoxide | Oxazepam |

### Beta-blockers include:

| | |
|---|---|
| Nadolol | Propranolol |
| Oxprenolol | Atenolol |
| Pindolol | |

## Antibiotics

These are used to treat bacterial infections.

| | |
|---|---|
| Amoxicillin | Minocycline |
| Gentamicin | Cefaclor |
| Ampicillin | Cefradine |

| | |
|---|---|
| Oxytetracycline | Erythromycin |
| Cephalexin | Streptomycin |
| Phenoxymethyl penicillin | Flucloxacillin |
| Doxycycline | Tetracycline |
| Benzylpenicillin | |

## Anticancer drugs

These are used to treat certain cancers. Some are cytotoxic, which means they kill cancer cells, while others are similar to sex hormones or act as hormone antagonists.

### Cytotoxic drugs include:

| | |
|---|---|
| Lomustine | Methotrexate |
| Chlorambucil | Etoposide |
| Medroxy-cyclophosphamide | Procarbazine |
| Doxorubicin | Fluorouracil |

### Sex hormone-based drugs include:

| | |
|---|---|
| Diethylstilbestrol | Megestrol |
| Aminoglutethimide | Progesterone |
| Ethinylestradiol | Tamoxifen |

## Anticoagulant drugs

These are used both to prevent and to treat strokes or heart attacks by stopping the abnormal formation of blood clots.

Heparin
Warfarin
Phenindione

## Antidepressant drugs

These are used to treat serious depression by stimulating the nervous system to elevate the mood of the depressed individual. Selective serotonin re-uptake inhibitors (SSRIs) elevate levels of the neurotransmitter serotonin, so stimulating brain cell activity, and are also used in the treatment of the eating disorder bulimia nervosa. Both tricyclics and monoamine oxidase inhibitors (MAOIs) elevate the levels of two neurotransmitters – serotonin and noradrenaline – in the brain, stimulating brain cell activity.

### SSRIs include:

| | |
|---|---|
| Fluoxetine | Citalopram |
| Paroxetine | Fluroamine |

### Tricyclics include:

| | |
|---|---|
| Amitriptyline | Imipramine |
| Clomipramine | Mianserin |
| Dosulepin | Trazodone |

### MAOIs include:

Isocarboxazid
Phenelzine
Tranylcypromine

## Antidiarrhoeal drugs

These are used to make faeces more bulky, or to slow down gut motility.

| | |
|---|---|
| Codeine | Co-phenotrope |
| Kaolin | Loperamide |

## Antiemetic drugs

These are used to treat vomiting and nausea.

| | |
|---|---|
| Chlorpromazine | Dimenhydrinate |
| Metoclopramide | Promethazine |
| Cinnarizine | Hyoscine |
| Prochlorperazine | Thiethylperazine |

## Antifungal drugs

These are used to treat fungal and yeast infections including thrush, ringworm and athlete's foot.

| | |
|---|---|
| Amphotericin b | Nystatin |
| Ketoconazole | Flucytosine |
| Clotrimazole | Tolnaftate |
| Miconazole | Griseofulvin |
| Econazole | |

## Antihelminthic drugs

These are used to kill parasitic worms such as tapeworms, threadworms and roundworms.

| | |
|---|---|
| Bephenium | Pyrantel |
| Piperazine | Niclosamide |
| Mebendazole | Tiabendazole |

## Antihistamine drugs

These are used to treat allergic reactions such as hayfever and urticaria.

### Sedating (older) drugs include:

Chlorphenamine
Azatadine
Promethazine

### Non-sedating (newer) drugs include:

Terfenadine
Cetirizine
Loratadine

## Antihypertensive drugs

These are used to treat high blood pressure to reduce the risk of heart failure or stroke. They include thiazides (diuretics), beta-blockers, calcium channel blockers, ACE inhibitors and other drugs.

### Thiazides (diuretics) used in hypertension include:

| | |
|---|---|
| Bendrofluazide | Chlortalidone |
| Hydrochlorothiazide | Cyclopenthiazide |

### Beta-blockers include:

Atenolol
Propanolol
Oxprenolol

**Calcium channel blockers include:**

Verapamil
Diltiazem
Nifedipine

**ACE inhibitors include:**

Captopril
Enalapril

**Other antihypertensives include:**

| | |
|---|---|
| Clonidine | Hydralazine |
| Minoxidil | Prazosin |
| Methyldopa | |

## Antimuscarinic drugs

These block the transmission of impulses along parts of the nervous system. They are used to treat asthma, irritable bowel syndrome, Parkinson's disease and other conditions.

| | |
|---|---|
| Atropine | Trihexyphenidyl |
| Hyoscine | Orphenadrine |
| Ipratropium | Dicyclomine |

## Antipsychotic drugs (major tranquillizers)

These are used to treat abnormal behaviour shown by patients with psychotic disorders involving loss of contact with reality, particularly schizophrenia. They block the action of the neurotransmitter dopamine, so inhibiting nerve activity in the brain.

**Phenothiazines include:**

| | |
|---|---|
| Chlorpromazine | Thioridazine |
| Fluophenazine | Trifluoperazine |
| Perphenazine | |

**Butyrophenones include:**

Haloperidol
Droperidol

## Antirheumatic drugs

These are used to treat rheumatoid arthritis. They include immunosuppressants, corticosteroids and other drugs.

**Immunosuppressants used as antirheumatics include:**

Azathioprine
Chlorambucil

**Corticosteroids used as antirheumatics include:**

Prednisolone
Dexamethasone

**Other antirheumatic drugs include:**

Gold
Penicillamine
Chloroquine

## Antispasmodic drugs

These are used to control spasms in the wall of the bladder (causing irritable bladder) or intestine (causing irritable bowel syndrome).

Dicyclomine
Peppermint oil
Hyoscine

## Antiviral drugs

These are used to treat infections caused by viruses.

| | |
|---|---|
| Aciclovir | Zidovudine |
| Inosine pranobex | Idoxuridine |
| Amantadine | Zanamivir |

## Beta-blocker drugs

These are used to reduce heart rate in treating anxiety, high blood pressure and angina.

| | |
|---|---|
| Acebutolol | Metoprolol |
| Oxprenolol | Propanolol |
| Atenolol | Nadolol |
| Pindolol | |

## Bronchodilator drugs

These are used to treat asthma and bronchitis; they widen the airways to the lungs, making breathing easier.

| | |
|---|---|
| Aminophylline | Terbutaline |
| Rimiterol | Pirbuterol |
| Fenoterol | Theophylline |
| Salbutamol | Reproterol |

### Calcium channel blocker drugs

These are used to treat irregular heartbeat, high blood pressure and angina by reducing the workload of the heart.

Diltiazem
Verapamil
Nifedipine

### Cholesterol-lowering drugs

These are used to lower levels of cholesterol in the blood in patients with heart disease; most common are those in the statin group.

| | |
|---|---|
| Atorvastatin | Pravastatin |
| Fluvastatin | Simvastatin |
| Lovastatin | |

### Corticosteroid drugs

These are used to treat a wide range of conditions, including rheumatoid arthritis, eczema, asthma and Crohn's disease.

| | |
|---|---|
| Beclometasone | Cortisone |
| Fludrocortisone | Prednisolone |
| Betamethasone | Dexamethasone |
| Hydrocortisone | Prednisone |

### Diuretic drugs

These are used to treat high blood pressure and oedema (fluid retention) by increasing the amount of water lost from the body in urine.

| | |
|---|---|
| Amiloride | Spironolactone |
| Cyclopenthiazide | Chlorothiazide |
| Bendroflumethiazide | Triamterene |
| Furosemide | Chlortalidone |
| Bumetanide | |

### Hypoglycaemic drugs (oral)

These are used to lower levels of glucose in the blood to normal levels in patients with type 2 (non-insulin dependent) diabetes.

| | |
|---|---|
| Chlorpropamide | Tolazamide |
| Glipizide | Gliclazide |
| Glibenclamide | Tolbutamide |

### Immunosuppressant drugs

These are used to suppress activity of the immune system so that it does not cause the rejection of a recently transplanted organ.

| Cyclosporin | Chlorambucil |
| Methotrexate | Cyclophosphamide |
| Azathioprine | Tacrolimus |

## Mood-stabilizing drugs

These are used to treat bipolar disorder. They act on brain neurotransmitters to reduce extreme mood swings.

| Lithium |
| Sodium valproate |

## Non-opioid analgesics

These are used for the relief of mild or moderate pain.

| Aspirin | Benorilate |
| Ibuprofen | Nefopam |
| Paracetamol | Sodium salicylate |

## NSAIDs (non-steroidal anti-inflammatory drugs)

These are used to relieve pain and inflammation in a range of conditions, including arthritis, menstrual pain and headaches. Some are also used to reduce fever.

| Diclofenac | Fenoprofen |
| Indometacin | Naproxen |
| Diflunisal | Flurbiprofen |
| Ketoprofen | Piroxicam |
| Fenbufen | Ibuprofen |
| Mefenamic acid | |

## Opioid analgesics

These are used to relieve severe pain.

| Buprenorphine | Dextropropoxyphene |
| Dihydrocodeine | Pentazocine |
| Codeine | Diamorphine |
| Morphine | Pethidine |

## Oral contraceptive drugs

These are used by women to prevent conception by stopping the release of eggs from the ovaries, or by thickening the mucus to block entry of sperm into the uterus. They consist of synthetic analogues of progesterone and oestrogen. 'Combined' pills contain both types of hormone; progesterone-only pills are also used.

| Ethinylestradiol | Norethisterone |
| Mestranol | Levonorgestrel |
| Gestodene | |

## Thrombolytic drugs

These are used to dissolve blood clots in cases of heart attack or stroke.

| Anistreplase |
| Streptokinase |

## DRUGS DERIVED FROM PLANTS

Many drugs are purified or modified versions of chemicals originally extracted from plants. A selection of these is given below.

| Drug | Plant | Effect |
| --- | --- | --- |
| Aspirin | White willow | Pain relief |
| Atropine | Deadly nightshade (belladonna) | Anticholinergic (blocks nerve impulses) |
| Cocaine | Coca | Local anaesthetic/central nervous system stimulant |
| Codeine | Opium poppy | Pain relief |
| Curare | Various tropical American plants | Muscle relaxant |
| Digitalis | Foxglove | Heart stimulant |
| L-dopa | Velvet bean | Mitigation of Parkinson's disease |
| Morphine | Opium poppy | Pain relief/narcotic |
| Penicillin | *Penicillium notatum* fungus | Antibiotic |
| Quinine | Yellow cinchona | Antimalarial |
| Strychnine | *Nux vomica (strychnos nux-vomica)* | Central nervous system stimulant |

## *Two Sides to Every Story*

Not everything extracted from plants is beneficial to humans. Ricin, a deadly poison, is made from castor bean plants (*Ricinus communis*), and *Cerbera odollam* is nicknamed the 'suicide tree' because its kernels are so toxic to the heart.

# GENETICS

## DNA

DNA (deoxyribonucleic acid) is the genetic material of most organisms and organelles, and is copied when cells divide. Different stretches of DNA, known as genes, act as instructions for making different proteins, which then carry out the functions of the cell. Generally, every cell in an organism contains the same DNA, but the genes are regulated differently so that cells can do different jobs. Some genes, known as 'housekeeping genes', are switched on in every cell.

> *Shall we conjecture that one and the same kind of living filaments is and has been the cause of all organic life?*
>
> —Erasmus Darwin (1731–1802), English physician and poet and grandfather to Charles Darwin, in *Zoonomia* (1794).

## Double helix

The DNA inside cells is made up of two strands joined together in a double helix. The bases project towards each other and pair up, forming links across the double helix like the rungs of a ladder. The filled circles in the diagram are carbon atoms, the open are nitrogen (large) and hydrogen (small) and the double circles are oxygen. T, A, C and G are the base abbreviations.

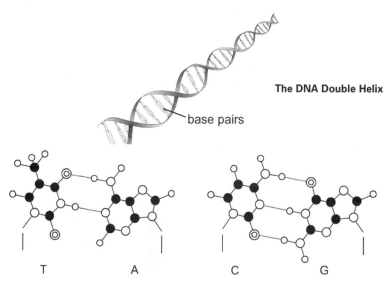

**The DNA Double Helix**

base pairs

T          A          C          G

**Base Pairs**

## As Dull as DNA?

For a long time, it was thought that DNA was a very dull, uniform molecule that existed simply for structural purposes, and that proteins were the genetic material of cells. In 1944, the US bacteriologists Oswald Avery, Colin MacLeod and Maclyn McCarty produced evidence that DNA might actually be the genetic material by transferring genetic characteristics between bacteria. The definitive experiment, involving transferring characteristics between viruses, was carried out by US biologists A D Hershey and Martha Chase in the early 1950s.

### PCR

PCR, or polymerase chain reaction, is a method for amplifying a small amount of DNA. It makes use of the fact that DNA consists of two strands, which can be separated and copied.

PCR involves three steps. The first step is to separate the DNA strands; this is done by heating to around 95°C (200°F). The second step involves binding short pieces of DNA, called primers, to the ends of the separated strands. This step takes place at around 35–65°C (95–150°F). The third step is to use an enzyme called DNA polymerase to extend the primers, creating matching strands for the separated strands of DNA. This produces two double-stranded DNA molecules where originally there was only one. The enzyme works at around 72°C (160°F). These steps are repeated many times, with the DNA doubling each time. Twenty-five cycles increase the amount of DNA by a factor of over 30 million. The first PCR experiments needed fresh enzyme to be added during each cycle, because it was destroyed at the high temperatures in the first step. However, enzymes from bacteria that live in hot springs are now used, and these are able to last throughout a PCR procedure.

PCR is used for many purposes, including diagnosis of, and screening for, genetic disease, 'DNA fingerprinting' in forensic science, and in manipulating DNA for cloning and other laboratory experiments.

### Nucleotides

A strand of DNA consists of a series of molecules called nucleotides. Each nucleotide contains a sugar – deoxyribose – and one of four bases, as well as phosphate groups containing the chemical elements phosphorus and oxygen. The sugar and phosphate parts link up between the nucleotides to form a 'backbone' and the bases stick out from the backbone. Two of the bases are structures called pyrimidines, while the other two are purines. Each base has a unique partner.

| Letter | Name | Type | Pairs with |
|--------|----------|------------|------------|
| A | Adenine | Purine | T |
| T | Thymine | Pyrimidine | A |
| G | Guanine | Purine | C |
| C | Cytosine | Pyrimidine | G |

## RNA

RNA (ribonucleic acid) acts as a 'middleman' between the DNA instructions and the proteins that are made. It is similar in structure to DNA, but there are some important differences.

| DNA | RNA |
|-----|-----|
| **Double**-stranded | **Single**-stranded |
| Contains **deoxyribose** sugar | Contains **ribose** sugar |
| Contains A, **T**, G and C bases | Contains A, **U**, G and C bases |

The base abbreviated as U in RNA is called uracil. It takes the place of T (thymine), so it pairs with A (adenine).

**RNA Structure**

### Messenger RNA

Messenger RNA is made as a long strand that pairs with one of the strands of DNA. It carries the genetic information to the protein-making machinery, where it is 'read' to indicate the order in which amino acid 'building blocks' should be joined together to make proteins (see **Atoms, elements and molecules: Amino acids**).

### Transfer RNA

Transfer RNA exists as short pieces, each of which attaches to a particular amino acid. The pieces of transfer RNA bind to the messenger RNA in the correct order; the amino acids that they bring are joined together to make a protein.

## GENETIC CODE

The four bases of DNA or RNA are like letters of the alphabet that are grouped together in 'words' of 3 'letters'. Each group of three bases, called a triplet or codon, encodes for one of 20 different amino acids. There are 64 possible different triplets using all possible combinations and arrangements of the four bases. One codon uniquely specifies one amino acid, but each amino acid can be coded by up to six different triplet sequences.

### Start and stop codons

Start codons specify where the cell's machinery should start to 'read' the DNA (see **Cells: Replication**). In humans and other animals, the start codon is the same one that encodes the amino acid methionine. There are also three stop codons known as Ochre, Amber and Opal; these signal that DNA replication should end.

### Genetic code table

The genetic code is shown for messenger RNA. The codons are the same for DNA except that U is replaced by T. Transfer RNA has 'anti-codons' that fit on to the codons; for example, the tryptophan codon is UGG and the anti-codon of its transfer RNA is therefore ACC.

| Amino acid | Three-letter symbol | One-letter symbol | Codons |
|---|---|---|---|
| Alanine | Ala | A | GCU, GCC, GCA, GCG |
| Arginine | Arg | R | CGU, CGC, CGA, CGG, AGA, AGG |
| Asparagine | Asn | N | AAU, AAC |
| Aspartate | Asp | D | GAU, GAC |
| Cysteine | Cys | C | UGU, UGC |
| Glutamic acid | Glu | E | GAA, GAG |
| Glutamine | Gln | Q | CAA, CAG |
| Glycine | Gly | G | GGU, GGC, GGA, GGG |
| Histidine | His | H | CAU, CAC |
| Isoleucine | Ile | I | AUU, AUC, AUA |
| Leucine | Leu | L | UUA, UUG, CUU, CUC, CUA, CUG |
| Lysine | Lys | K | AAA, AAG |
| Methionine | Met | M | AUG |
| Phenylalanine | Phe | F | UUU, UUC |
| Proline | Pro | P | CCU, CCC, CCA, CCG |
| Serine | Ser | S | UCU, UCC, UCA, UCG, AGU, AGC |
| Threonine | Thr | T | ACU, ACC, ACA, ACG |
| Tryptophan | Trp | W | UGG |

| Amino acid | Three-letter symbol | One-letter symbol | Codons |
|---|---|---|---|
| Tyrosine | Tyr | Y | UAU, UAC |
| Valine | Val | V | GUU, GUC, GUA, GUG |
| Stop (ochre) | | | UAA |
| Stop (amber) | | | UAG |
| Stop (opal) | | | UGA |

## MUTATIONS

When something goes wrong in the process of interpreting genetic information, or if the information itself is faulty, mutations can occur. Sometimes mutations do not have a significant effect on the function of proteins, and occasionally a mutant protein may be better than the original. In other cases, mutations have a bad effect, leading to genetic disorders (see **Diseases and medicines: Genetic diseases**). Some different types of mutation are explained below, using the following sentence as an analogy:

**'This sentence shows important genetic mutations.'**

### Substitution

If the wrong base appears in a gene, it may not always alter the amino acid. This is because of the redundancy of the genetic code: if ACU is altered to ACG, the amino acid threonine is still encoded. These 'silent' mutations often occur if the third base of a codon is altered.

In other cases, the alteration of a base changes the amino acid, which can mess up a protein in the same way as changing a word in a sentence:

**'This sentence strawberries important genetic mutations.'**

### Deletion

If three bases are deleted from a gene, a whole amino acid will be missing from the protein. The protein may still have some function, like this sentence:

**'This sentence shows genetic mutations.'**

Alternatively, the missing amino acid may turn the protein into nonsense:

**'This sentence important genetic mutations.'**

### Insertion

Sometimes a whole codon can be inserted:

**'This sentence shows banana important genetic mutations.'**

A common way in which an insertion can happen is if there is a duplication of existing material:

**'This sentence sentence shows important genetic mutations.'**

### Frame shift

DNA bases are always read in threes. If one or two bases are inserted or deleted, this leads to frame shift, an alteration in the reading pattern. This often turns a protein into complete nonsense:

**'This xxsenten cesho wsimporta ntgenet icmutatio ns.'**

## CHROMOSOMES

Genetic information in the form of DNA is stored inside the animal and plant cells in structures called chromosomes. The DNA is packaged with proteins called histones to form compact structures called nucleosomes. Each chromosome has a centromere in the middle and a telomere at each end.

### Human chromosomes

Most human cells are in a state known as diploid. They have 46 chromosomes; 44 of these, known as the autosomes, consist of 22 matched pairs. The remaining two chromosomes, X and Y, are the sex chromosomes. Women have two large X chromosomes in each cell, whereas men have one large X and one small Y. Eggs and sperm are haploid: they only contain one set of autosomes and one sex chromosome.

### The Birds and the Bees

In birds, the males have the identical pair of sex chromosomes, ZZ, and the females have the unmatched pair, ZW. The duck-billed platypus was recently discovered to have five pairs of sex chromosomes. Some creatures don't even use pairs of chromosomes for sex determination. Reptiles use temperature rather than chromosomes to determine sex, with warm incubation of the eggs producing males and cooler incubation producing females. Some fish can change from one sex to the other, while honey bees produce females from fertilized eggs and males from unfertilized ones.

### Sex determination

Humans are female by default. In males, genes on the Y chromosome control the production of hormones that switch development of the reproductive organs from female to male. This happens at two stages in development: in the embryo and at puberty.

### Eggs at Twelve

In a remote village in the Dominican Republic, parents are used to giving birth to three, not two, types of babies: girls, boys and *guevedoces*. The name 'guevedoce' ('eggs at twelve' in Spanish) refers to the fact that these babies, who are genetically male, are born looking like girls but develop testes (i.e. 'eggs') and other male characteristics in their early teens. This type of abnormality is extremely rare in most places, but is common enough in the village that it is accepted as normal. It occurs because of a genetic abnormality that prevents the male hormone from taking effect at the embryonic stage but not at puberty.

## Visualizing chromosomes

Chromosomes can be stained to give a pattern of bands when the cells are in a state called metaphase (see **Cells: Cell division**). The combination of size, shape and banding pattern gives each chromosome a unique appearance.

## Telomeres

Telomeres contain a small number of certain short DNA sequences, which have been shown to be progressively lost as the nucleus divides during life. This is thought to be a way of limiting the age of each cell.

> *Colourful Chromosomes*
>
> The word chromosome comes from the Greek for 'coloured body', because they take up a lot of dye when cells are stained during laboratory experiments.

## GENETIC INHERITANCE

For a long time, it was thought that features were passed from parents to children by blending or mingling of the parents' genetic information. The concept of genes – discrete units of inherited information – was first proposed by the Austrian monk and botanist Gregor Mendel in the 19th century (see **Key concepts: Mendel's laws**). However, the term 'gene' was coined later, in the early 20th century, by the Danish biologist Wilhelm Johannsen.

## Polymorphism and alleles

Some genes have more than one version; they are said to be polymorphic. Different versions of the same gene are called alleles. Mendel studied alleles of peas, such as green or yellow colour and smooth or wrinkled skin. These types of characteristics are known as traits. An example of a human trait is that some people can roll up their tongues while others cannot; this ability is determined by two different alleles of the same gene.

## Wild type and mutant alleles

The most common allele of a gene is often known as the wild type allele. Rare alleles, caused by small changes in the DNA, are known as mutant alleles, especially if they have a harmful effect. However, if there are several common alleles, all of which are considered 'normal', then these terms would not be used. For example, geneticists would talk about wild type and mutant alleles for a genetic disease, whereas they would not for a trait such as eye or hair colour.

## Genotype and phenotype

An individual's genotype describes which alleles of a gene they have. The observable characteristics of the individual are called the phenotype.

Genotype plays a large part in determining phenotype. For example, a person's genotype includes alleles for different pigments that are found in eyes. Their eye colour phenotype depends on their genotype for the eye pigment genes. The environment can also influence phenotype. For example, how tall a plant grows can

be influenced by its genes but also by the amount of sunlight, food and water it can obtain.

## Autosomal and sex chromosome inheritance

### Autosomes

Most genes are on the chromosomes known as autosomes, of which there are two in each cell. Therefore, an individual has two copies of each of these genes. If both copies are the same allele, the individual is said to be homozygous for that gene, while someone with two different alleles is said to be heterozygous.

### Sex chromosomes

A slightly different situation occurs with the sex chromosomes. In humans, males have one X and one Y sex chromosome. They only have one copy of any genes that are on one sex chromosome but not the other; they are said to be hemizygous for those genes. Genes that are on the X and Y chromosomes are known as X-linked and Y-linked genes.

## Dominant and recessive alleles

If two versions of a gene are present in the same cell, one of them may be dominant over the other one. This means that the observed phenotype will be based on that version. The other allele is said to be recessive, and will only show up in the phenotype if both copies of the gene are the recessive allele. Individuals with one copy of a recessive allele that causes a genetic disease are called carriers of the disease.

## Genetically inherited diseases

Described below are some of the main ways in which genetic diseases are inherited. A disease allele can be dominant or recessive, and it can be on a sex chromosome or an autosome.

| Type | Sex affected | Usual transmission | Likelihood of transmission |
|------|--------------|--------------------|-----------------------------|
| Autosomal dominant | Either sex | Affected mother or father | 50% of offspring |
| Autosomal recessive | Either sex | Two carrier parents | 25% of offspring |
| X-linked recessive | Usually males | Carrier mother (for males) | 50% of sons (so 25% of all offspring) |
| X-linked dominant | More females than males | Affected mother | 50% of all offspring |
| | | Affected father | 100% of daughters; 0% of sons |
| Y-linked | Only males | Always affected father | 100% of sons; 0% of daughters |

## DNA sequencing

DNA sequencing is often used in the diagnosis of genetic diseases, as well as being an important research tool. It is usually carried out using a modified version of a method named Sanger sequencing, after the English biologist Fred Sanger. A single strand of DNA is used, and an additional short piece of DNA called a primer is added, which binds to one end. (This means that the sequence of the first short section must be known; the unknown DNA is often taken from a standard carrier called a vector, so this is not usually a problem.) The sample also contains the four bases needed to make DNA, and the enzyme (DNA polymerase) that can add them on to the primer to make the second strand of the DNA. However, the sample also contains a small quantity of a 'fake' version of each of the four bases, which can substitute for one of the four real bases but then stops any more bases being added. These 'fake' bases are tagged with a fluorescent marker, each one being a different colour. When the enzyme tries to extend the DNA strand, sometimes it will pick up a 'fake' base instead of a real one. Because it is random whether a 'real' or 'fake' base will be picked up, strands of all possible lengths are generated. The strands are separated by gel electrophoresis (see **Atoms, elements and molecules: Proteins**). A computer connected to a fluorescence detector uses the fluorescent tags to work out which lengths of strand end in each of the four bases. In this way, the sequence of the bases can be worked out.

The Human Genome Project, which relied on public funding, used highly automated versions of this method to sequence the set of genes found in humans (known as the human genome). A commercial venture run by Celera Genomics also sequenced the human genome, using related techniques that were riskier but faster. The complete data from both ventures were published in 2003.

## Pedigrees

The pedigree of a family is a chart showing how the people in the family are affected by a genetic disease. Studying pedigrees of families with a particular rare disease can be a useful way to work out how the disease is inherited. Different symbols are used to represent males and females, affected and unaffected individuals, and unaffected carriers; these are illustrated overleaf.

### Crane's Foot

The word 'pedigree' comes from the French expression *pied de grue*, meaning 'crane's foot'. This unusual description relates to the claw-like branched lines that are used to connect parents to multiple offspring in a pedigree chart.

**Symbols used in a Pedigree**

☐ Males

◯ Females

Vertical lines connect children to their parents

● or ■ A solid square or circle indicates that the person has a certain trait

◨ or ◑ A half-filled square or circle indicates that the person is a carrier of the trait

**Generation**

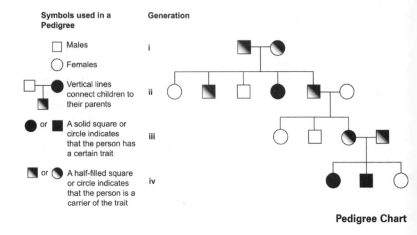

i

ii

iii

iv

**Pedigree Chart**

# CELLS

Cells are the basic structural unit of living things. Some organisms, such as bacteria and amoebae, have only one cell. Other larger organisms have many different cells that take on specialized functions as part of different tissues.

## PROKARYOTES AND EUKARYOTES

Cells fall into two main groups, prokaryotes and eukaryotes, based on whether they have a proper nucleus or not.

Bacteria are single cells without a proper nucleus and are called prokaryotes. The cells in plants, animals and fungi have their genetic material inside a nucleus and are called eukaryotes.

### Light microscopy

Light microscopes are used for looking at very small objects such as cells. A condenser, consisting of a series of lenses, focuses light on the object of interest. Because the object is very close to the microscope, the light rays travel away from it in all directions. A very powerful lens called the objective lens bends the diverging rays to come together and form an image of the object. The image is magnified by another lens in the eyepiece of the microscope. Light microscopes can resolve images of objects down to about half the size of the wavelength of the light; this means that they can be used to study cells but they can't show details of the structures within cells.

## CELL STRUCTURE

The diagram shows a generalized cell from a eukaryote such as a plant or animal. All eukaryotic cells have these features and share the same basic structure.

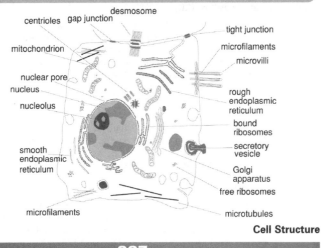

**Cell Structure**

### Cell membrane

Cells are surrounded by a membrane made up of two fluid layers of lipid (fatty) molecules. The membrane keeps the contents of the cell, known as the cytoplasm, separate from its surroundings. Proteins in the membrane can form channels to allow certain substances to move in and out of the cell in various ways.

### Cytoplasm and cytosol

The cytoplasm comprises the total cell contents, including the sub-cellular structures, or organelles, as well as the fluid that bathes them. The fluid itself is called the cytosol.

### Organelles

Individual compartments inside the cell are collectively known as organelles. Each is surrounded by its own membrane. Like the cell membrane, proteins in the membrane allow transport of substances into and out of organelles. The inside of an organelle is called the lumen.

### Nucleus

The nucleus contains the cell's genetic information, in the form of DNA organized into chromosomes (see **Genetics: Chromosomes**). Most cells contain just one nucleus, although some, such as skeletal muscle cells, can have multiple nuclei.

### Mitochondria

Mitochondria provide energy in a useful form for the cell, by carrying out respiration. As well as the outer membrane, they have a folded inner membrane that is important in the later stages of respiration. Another function of mitochondria is to trigger a cell to destroy itself (apoptosis) if something goes very wrong with the cell's functions such as DNA replication. This is important in helping to prevent cancer.

### Endoplasmic reticulum (ER)

The ER is the site of protein and lipid production. It consists of stacked sheets of membrane. Proteins are made in small bead-like structures called ribosomes on the surface of parts of the ER. These regions of ER are called rough ER because the ribosomes stick out of the ER membrane, giving it a rough appearance. Other regions do not have ribosomes on them. These areas are called smooth ER and are important for lipid manufacture.

### Golgi apparatus

The Golgi apparatus is named after the Italian cell biologist Camillo Golgi. It consists of flattened compartments of membrane, and is often located close to the nucleus. It modifies proteins and lipids, and distributes them to the rest of the cell. The modifications often include the addition of sugar-type structures.

### Evolution of organelles

Some organelles, including mitochondria and chloroplasts, probably evolved a long time ago as a result of cells engulfing bacteria and using them as energy producers. The evidence for this hypothesis includes the fact that mitochondria and chloroplasts have two membrane layers, the idea being that the inner membranes originated from the bacteria. These organelles also contain their own DNA.

## Electron microscopy

Electron microscopes are used for studying objects that are too small for light microscopy to resolve, such as organelles within a cell. A condenser lens, consisting of a series of magnets, focuses a beam of electrons on the object of interest. In the traditional form, transmission electron microscopy (TEM), the electrons pass through the object and move apart. Another magnetic lens, the objective, focuses the beam to produce an image. Unlike light microscopes, the final image can't be viewed by eye. Instead, a final magnetic lens, the projection lens, projects the electron image on to photographic film or on to a screen that glows when the electrons strike it. The wavelength of an electron is much shorter than that of light, so much more detail can be resolved. A slightly different technique called scanning electron microscopy (SEM) also allows three-dimensional images to be built up by reflecting a beam of electrons from a sample. However, electron microscopes have to operate in a vacuum to prevent the electrons from hitting other atoms and molecules. This means that electron microscopy can't be performed on living organisms or cells.

## Cytoskeleton

The cytoskeleton gives the cell its shape, just as a person's skeleton and muscles give shape to the whole body. Two important components of the cytoskeleton, microfilaments and microtubules, are shown on the diagram.

### Microfilaments

Microfilaments are strands of actin that are flexible and kept taut like a stretched elastic band. They tend to stretch around the edge of the cell, just underneath the cell membrane.

### Microtubules

Microtubules are more rigid and are compressed like wooden roof beams. They run from the centre of the cell out towards the edge.

## Junctions

Some cells, like red blood cells, function independently. However, other cells are found joined together to form tissues such as skin or muscle. Sheets of cells are also held down on to a basement membrane. Junctions enable cells to hold on to one another and to the basement membrane. Some examples are described in the table below and are marked on the Cell Structure diagram.

| Type of junction | Function |
| --- | --- |
| Tight junctions | Limit movement of substances between cells |
| Gap junctions | Allow small molecules to move between cells |
| Desmosomes | Act as rivets to hold cells together at their strongest points |

### Cellular transport

Cells can take up material of various kinds into membrane 'bubbles' called vesicles, a process known as endocytosis (cell internalization). Additionally, specific molecules can bind to protein receptors on the outside of the cell and be taken inside. The vesicles include endosomes, into which material is taken, and lysosomes, in which the material is broken down. Molecules made by the cell can be transported outside; this is called exocytosis.

---
### *Wining and Dining*

Cells can engulf and swallow large particles. This is called phagocytosis, meaning 'cell eating'. They can also take up fluid by pinocytosis ('cell drinking').

---

## PLANT CELL FEATURES

As well as having the general cell features described above, plant cells have some additional features that animal cells don't possess.

### Cell wall

As well as being contained by a membrane, plant cells have a cell wall around the outside. In many plants this wall contains a lot of cellulose fibres embedded in a matrix, in the same way that glass fibres are used to reinforce plastic, making it strong. The way that the fibres are laid down in plant cells helps to determine the shape of the cells and ultimately, in bigger plants, the shape of the whole plant.

#### Non-woody plants

Having a strong wall allows the contents of cells to be at a high pressure without the cell bursting. This helps non-woody plants to maintain their structure, in the same way that a tyre filled with air keeps its shape much better than a flat tyre. This is why a leafy plant that is short of water, and doesn't have enough fluid to keep its cells at high pressure, tends to wilt.

#### Wood

In wood, the cell wall is bonded with a glue-like substance called lignin, which keeps it stiff even when water is in short supply.

### Vacuole

Plant cells often have a vacuole, which is a large fluid-filled bubble taking up much of the space inside the cell.

### Plastids

Plastids are organelles that have a separate inner membrane as well as the outer membrane.

#### Chloroplasts

Plants use chloroplasts to make their own food in the form of sugars, by using energy from sunlight in a process called photosynthesis. Chloroplasts also accumulate nitrogen for protein manufacture, and to make molecules such as amino acids. They are mainly found in specialized cells in plant leaves, in a tissue called mesophyll.

### Amyloplasts

Amyloplasts are used to store starch inside the cell.

---

### Centrifugation

A centrifuge is a piece of equipment that can be used for separating materials or objects based on their density and particle size. Samples are placed in tubes and held in a rotor that is spun at high speed. The forces acting on the tubes make bigger or denser particles move to the bottom of the tube, while lighter or less dense material moves to the top. Centrifugation can be used to separate cells from liquid, to separate different types of cell or, at really high speeds, to separate out the organelles from within a cell.

---

## CELLULAR ENERGY

A chemical called adenosine triphosphate, or ATP, is an important way of storing energy in cells.

### ATP and ADP

ATP can be converted into a similar chemical called adenosine diphosphate, or ADP. The difference between ATP and ADP is in the number of phosphorus- and oxygen-containing phosphate groups they have: ATP has three, while ADP only has two.

### Energy release

Energy is released to be used in a reaction by breaking down ATP into ADP. A spare phosphate group is also released.

### Energy storage

Energy produced by reactions can be stored by adding a phosphate group on to an ADP molecule, turning it into ATP.

## PHOTOSYNTHESIS

Photosynthesis is the process by which plants, algae and some bacteria convert carbon dioxide and water into sugars and oxygen. This requires the input of energy, which comes from sunlight. The process that takes place in many plants is described; some other organisms have slightly different systems.

### Chlorophylls

The chloroplasts contain special pigments called chlorophylls, which act like solar panels, absorbing light and producing an electrical charge releasing electrons. Chlorophylls are usually green, giving rise to the green colour of many plants.

## The light reaction

The part of photosynthesis driven by chlorophylls is called the light reaction, and produces oxygen from water. This is because hydrogen is removed from water molecules and added to a chemical called NADP to make NADPH, leaving oxygen behind. The electrons released from the chlorophyll are needed for this reaction. Energy is also stored by converting ADP into ATP.

## The dark reaction

The dark reaction is also known as the Calvin cycle. It uses NADPH and ATP from the light reaction to produce sugars from carbon dioxide. This involves a complex series of reactions that use energy from ATP as well as hydrogen ions and electrons from NADPH.

## RESPIRATION

Respiration involves processes that degrade sugars in order to release energy. The energy is stored by converting ADP into ATP. There are two main types of respiration, aerobic and anaerobic, both of which start with a step called glycolysis.

## Glycolysis

Glycolysis is the initial breakdown of glucose sugar into a smaller molecule called pyruvate, and takes place in the cytoplasm of cells. Electrons and hydrogen ions are produced and stored by converting a chemical called NAD into NADH, and by producing water. A small amount of energy is released, which is stored by converting ADP into ATP.

## Anaerobic respiration

Anaerobic respiration takes place without the need for oxygen. However, it doesn't produce as much energy as aerobic respiration, as no additional energy is released. Yeasts convert the pyruvate produced by glycolysis into alcohol – this is the basis for beer and wine production. Certain bacteria break down the pyruvate to produce lactic acid – this reaction is important in the production of cheese and yogurt from milk. The lactic acid reaction also occurs in human muscles that are starved of oxygen, and leads to cramp.

## Aerobic respiration

Aerobic respiration begins with the conversion of pyruvate from glycolysis into a substance called acetyl coenzyme A. The acetyl coenzyme A enters a cycle called the citric acid cycle, TCA (tricarboxylic acid) cycle or Krebs cycle. The final stage of aerobic respiration is called oxidative phosphorylation, and requires the presence of oxygen.

### Citric acid cycle

The citric acid cycle takes place in the mitochondria. It consists of a complex series of reactions to break down acetyl coenzyme A into carbon dioxide. Electrons and hydrogen ions released by the reactions are stored by converting a chemical called NAD into NADH – these chemicals are similar to the NADP and NADPH used in

photosynthesis. Citric acid is broken down during the first part of the cycle and
regenerated during the second part.

### Oxidative phosphorylation

Oxidative phosphorylation involves the transfer of electrons from NADH along
a series of proteins called the electron transport chain. They are eventually
transferred to oxygen molecules, along with some of the hydrogen ions from the
NADH, to make water. The remaining hydrogen ions from the NADH are pumped
across the inner membrane of the mitochondria. This creates an electrochemical
gradient, in a similar way to charging up a rechargeable battery. When the
hydrogen ions flow back, they release energy that is used to convert ADP into ATP.
The stored energy can then be used to power the cell's activities.

## CELL CYCLE

Cells grow and divide in a strictly regulated way, with a series of events
occuring in a set order. There are four main phases: $G_1$, S, $G_2$ and M. An
additional phase, $G_0$, is used to describe cells that are in a resting state and are
not dividing. The growth and DNA synthesis phases are collectively known as
interphase, as they are between rounds of cell division.

| Name of stage | Event |
| --- | --- |
| $G_1$ | First growth phase of cell |
| S | Synthesis of DNA (= DNA replication) |
| $G_2$ | Second growth phase of cell |
| M | Mitosis (normal cell division) |

### Checkpoints

Checkpoints between the events prevent a cell from moving to the next stage
until the previous stage is properly completed. If something goes wrong, safety
mechanisms normally cause the cell to pause in the cycle, or even to destroy
itself (apoptosis). A lack of these 'fail-safe' mechanisms is one of the things that
tend to go wrong in cancer cells.

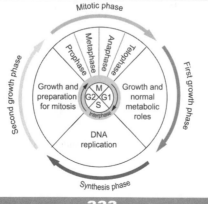

**Cell Cycle**

| Time of checkpoint | Checks made |
|---|---|
| Late $G_1$ | Is cell big enough? Is it in the right environment? |
| $G_1 \to S$ | Is DNA undamaged? |
| $G_2 \to M$ | Has DNA all been replicated properly? |
| Mid-M | Are chromosomes in the correct place for cell division? |

## REPLICATION

DNA replication occurs during the S phase of the cell cycle. S stands for synthesis, because this phase is where a new matching strand of DNA is synthesized for each of the two existing strands.

The double-stranded DNA within each chromosome unzips, a section at a time, to expose the bases on each strand that are normally paired up. New bases are added to partner the exposed ones, and joined up to make a new strand of DNA. In this way, each of the single strands of DNA now forms a new double helix. Each of the four bases has a specific partner, which explains how the polymerase is able to add the correct new bases on and maintain the genetic code (see **Genetics: Genetic Code**). The process of replication can only happen once in each cell cycle; the cell must grow and divide before more DNA can be made. This ensures that each cell keeps the correct amount of DNA.

## CELL DIVISION

### Mitosis

The purpose of mitosis is to divide the duplicated chromosomes between the two halves of each cell so that, when the cell divides, each of the resulting cells (known as daughter cells) will receive an identical set of chromosomes. There are four main stages of mitosis.

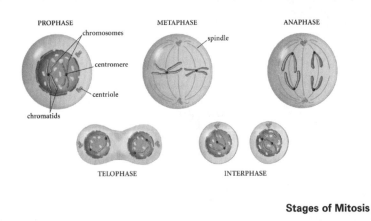

**Stages of Mitosis**

### Prophase

Two structures in the cell, called centrioles, move to opposite ends of the cell. The chromosomes get shorter and thicker. In some cells, including human cells, the membrane surrounding the nucleus breaks down.

### Metaphase

Microtubules form a scaffold called the spindle. The spindle is attached to the centriole at either end of the cell. The chromatids attach to the spindle and line up across the middle of the spindle. The chromatids being lined up correctly is the mid-M phase checkpoint.

### Anaphase

The chromatids separate and move to opposite ends of the cell, becoming chromosomes in their own right. They aren't hauled in by the spindle; they move under their own power.

### Telophase

The nuclear membrane re-forms around each set of chromosomes. The cell is now ready to divide into two by a process called cytokinesis. A contractile ring of microfilaments begins to tighten around the cell and new membrane is formed to complete the separation.

## Meiosis

Meiosis is a form of cell division that creates cells with only one set of chromosomes.

### Haploid cells

Most cells in humans are diploid: they have two sets of chromosomes. However, eggs and sperm have just one set, a state known as haploid (see **Genetics: Chromosomes**). This means that an egg and a sperm, and therefore the father and mother, each contribute one set of chromosomes to an embryo at fertilization.

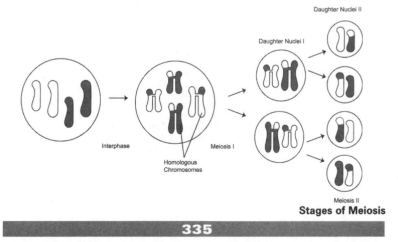

**Stages of Meiosis**

### Genetic recombination

Meiosis produces genetic differences in the daughter cells due to genetic recombination. One way in which this happens is a process called crossing over, involving swapping of sections of DNA between sister chromatids.

### Differences between meiosis and mitosis

Haploid cells are formed by meiosis, a process that is similar in some ways to mitosis. There are, however, some important differences.

| Mitosis | Meiosis |
|---|---|
| **One** cell division | **Two** cell divisions |
| Produces **diploid** cells | Produces **haploid** cells |
| Daughter cells are genetically **similar** | Daughter cells are genetically **different** |

## GENE EXPRESSION

Gene expression is the process that makes a protein from the template provided by a gene. The sequence of DNA in the gene encodes the composition of the protein; see **Genetics: Genetic code**. The processes of transcription and translation carry out the manufacture of proteins.

### Housekeeping genes

Every cell in an organism's body has the same set of genes. Some of these are 'housekeeping' genes that are switched on in every cell type. The proteins encoded by these genes perform basic functions that are needed by every cell, such as maintenance of the cell's structure.

### Stem cells

Cells that have not yet become specialists are known as stem cells. Stem cells in the embryo can become every other cell type in the body. Stem cells in the bone marrow can become different types of blood cell but can no longer become brain cells or kidney cells. This process of specialization is called differentiation.

---
*Ethical Dilemmas*
---

Therapeutic cloning, the process of making embryonic stem cells to treat disease, is widely believed to have great potential for the treatment of conditions such as diabetes or Parkinson's disease. However, the ethics of research involving embryos are hotly debated. In addition to the question of whether or not an embryo should be granted the status of a human being, there is concern in some quarters about the ethics of using therapeutic cloning. As a result, legislation to regulate this type of research has been passed in many countries.

## Specialized genes

Some cells are highly differentiated, and can perform a particular set of specialized functions. For example, a liver cell is different from a muscle cell – the two cells look different and can each perform their own functions but not each other's. This happens because different sets of genes are switched on in the two cell types, in a similar way to two artists having the same set of paints but using a subset of the colours to paint different pictures.

## Transcription

Transcription involves the DNA from the gene being used as a template to make a strand of RNA. Only one strand of the DNA double helix, known as the coding strand, is used. An enzyme called RNA polymerase builds up bases by fitting them against the bases from the DNA, as though doing a jigsaw.

## Translation

Translation is a process in which the RNA from transcription is used as a template to assemble amino acids, in an order corresponding to the original gene sequence. A chemical reaction takes place between the amino acids, so that they end up joined together by peptide bonds to form a protein (see **Atoms, elements and molecules: Proteins**). The protein may then need to be modified, for example by adding sugars to it; this takes place in the Golgi apparatus.

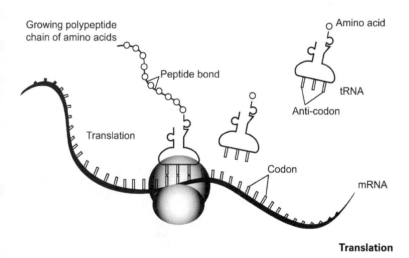

**Translation**

## EVOLUTION

The widely-accepted explanation among scientists for the huge diversity of organisms is called evolution. This theory proposes that a small number of simple organisms have given rise to a large number of other organisms, some of which are more complex, over time.

### The beginning of life

The earliest life forms are thought to have arisen during a time when the Earth was very different from now. Before life began, the atmosphere contained gases such as methane, ammonia and hydrogen sulphide rather than oxygen, and the oceans contained very simple chemicals.

### Formation of organic compounds

All living creatures contain more complex types of chemicals known as organic compounds, which contain carbon and hydrogen. The American scientists Stanley Miller and Harold Urey set up a model of the conditions on Earth at the time of the beginning of life, and showed that passing electrical sparks through the model could cause the formation of organic compounds. This suggested that lightning storms could have caused similar events on Earth.

### Primordial soup

The early oceans, with their newly-formed organic compounds, are often referred to as 'primordial soup'. It is thought that the organic compounds may have reacted together to form even more complex molecules. These probably came together to form droplet structures, from which proper cells eventually arose.

### Comets as a source of organic material

Another theory for the beginning of life is that organic compounds may have been brought to Earth by comets. These types of compounds are certainly found in comets, and many comets would have collided with the Earth in its early years, as much debris would have remained from the formation of the solar system.

### Evidence for evolution

There are two main types of evidence for evolution. The first involves various types of comparative biology, in which different organisms are studied at various levels to look for similarities and differences between them. The second involves studying the fossil record, which shows that changes have taken place over time.

### Comparative anatomy

Comparative anatomy shows that there are surprising similarities within groups of creatures that differ greatly in appearance and lifestyle. For example, the skeletons of different mammals are modifications of the same basic form; the front limbs can take the form of bat wings, human arms or the legs of a horse. This suggests that they derive from a common ancestor rather than arising separately.

### Comparative biochemistry

The cellular machinery of apparently dissimilar organisms is remarkably similar. These mechanisms are so conserved that animal cells can interpret plant genes and make their proteins. This suggests common ancestry.

### Comparative genetics

Some genes are highly conserved between different organisms. An example of this is a set of genes called the Hox, or homeobox, genes. These are turned on in different combinations along a developing embryo from head to tail. Cells use the combination of these genes at a particular place to sense their location in the body. Similar Hox genes are found in a huge variety of animals, from the most primitive to the most complex.

#### Freaky Flies

Mutations in the Hox genes can lead to bizarre mistakes in an organism's body plan. Fruit flies with a Hox gene mutation called *antennapedia* have legs growing out of their heads where their antennae should be.

#### Well Eye Never ...

A gene called Pax-6 is involved in making eyes in creatures as different as mammals and fruit flies. When geneticists from the University of Basel in Switzerland put the mouse Pax-6 gene into the leg joints of fruit flies, tiny fruit fly eyes were made on the joints. These eyes were even able to detect light – shining light on them made the flies jump.

### Fossil record

Studying fossils allows palaeontologists to work out the types of organisms that existed during different periods in the Earth's history. They have found that the earliest organisms were very simple, and that more complex organisms have appeared more recently. Whereas comparative biology only shows that different creatures are related, the fossil record demonstrates that they have come into being at different times.

## Natural selection

The widely-accepted mechanism for evolution is known as natural selection.

### Survival of the fittest

In order for natural selection to work, small changes must occur within individuals of a particular type of organism. These changes occur at random, so some are helpful and some are harmful. The individuals that gain helpful characteristics are more likely to survive and reproduce, so the beneficial changes are passed to their offspring; this phenomenon is often referred to as 'survival of the fittest'. (See also **Key concepts: The theory of natural selection.**)

### Genetic changes

Small inherited changes, which are needed in order to allow natural selection to take place, arise at the genetic level. They can occur due to mutations (changes) within genes (see **Genetics: Mutations**), and also by mixing of parents' genes in their offspring (see **Cells: Meiosis**).

## Sexual reproduction

Some organisms reproduce by combining the genetic material of two individuals; this is known as sexual reproduction. The vast majority of organisms can reproduce sexually.

### Sexes and hermaphrodites

Sexual reproduction requires that a species produces haploid cells, which contain only one of each chromosome rather than two (see **Genetics: Chromosomes**). These haploid cells are called gametes. Some types of organism, such as mammals, have two separate sexes, each of which produces a different type of gamete (sperm and eggs). Other types of organism have individuals that produce both types of gamete; these individuals are called hermaphrodites.

### Gene rearrangements

Meiosis, the cellular process that forms gametes, includes swapping of different versions, or alleles, of genes between a pair of chromosomes before they are separated into the gametes (see **Cells: Meiosis**). The joining of two gametes to make a new individual leads to further mixing up of gene alleles.

> *A hen is only an egg's way of making another egg.*
> —English author Samuel Butler (1835–1902),
> *Life and Habit* (1878).

## Asexual reproduction

Asexual reproduction involves making exact copies of an individual, with no shuffling of genetic material. The copy will therefore be the same as the original, unless the genes spontaneously mutate. Many plants and bacteria can reproduce asexually as well as sexually.

## Costs and benefits of sex

Sexual reproduction has many benefits, but also has costs that are not present in asexual reproduction.

### Changing environments

Sexual reproduction leads to increased mixing of genetic material, meaning that there are more possibilities to undergo natural selection. This is an overall advantage for a species when the environment is changing, because it is more likely that adaptations will arise that will be suited to the new conditions.

## The Red Queen hypothesis

Environments can alter due to sudden changes in climate or habitat. However, constant smaller changes take place in the circumstances of a species because other species that cause diseases are constantly evolving. Many evolutionary biologists support the theory that every species therefore ends up having to evolve in order to survive; this is known as the Red Queen hypothesis.

> *Now, here, you see, it takes all the running you can do, to keep in the same place.*
>
> —The Red Queen to Alice, in *Through the Looking-Glass* by Lewis Carroll (1871).

## Individuals versus species

Genetic changes are random, and many of them may turn out to be unhelpful or even harmful. Sexual reproduction can therefore be disadvantageous for individuals if they do not inherit the desireable characteristics of their parents. However, the benefits for the species as a whole often outweigh the disadvantages for individuals.

> *I'd lay down my life for two brothers or eight cousins.*
>
> —Indian biologist J B S Haldane (1892–1964), quoted in *New Scientist* (8 August 1974).

## Speciation

Speciation is the formation of new species. A species is often defined as a group of organisms that can breed together to produce fertile offspring. Horses and donkeys are not part of the same species because, although they can breed with each other, the mules they produce as offspring are infertile.

### Evolution and speciation

It is thought that new species arise when small changes accumulate within a group of organisms to such an extent that two separate groups arise and breeding can only take place within, and not between, the groups. They may become unable to mate to produce fertile offspring due to differences in breeding season, mating rituals, or physical or genetic incompatibilities.

### Isolation

The accumulation of changes needed for speciation can't take place while organisms are still breeding with each other. A period of geographical isolation, where a species is physically separated into two or more groups, is one way in which interbreeding can be prevented. This allows each group to evolve independently; if they do so for long enough, then they will have diverged too much to breed together even if they meet again.

### Gene pool

The gene pool of a species is the variety of versions of different genes. Species with a large gene pool have more chance of surviving a sudden change in their environment such as disease or climate, because it is more likely that a few individuals will have appropriate features for coping with the new conditions.

### Founder effect

If a very few unusual individuals from a species are isolated from the main population, the new population experiences a phenomenon known as a founder effect. The whole new population is based on a set of characteristics that were extremely rare in the original population. Some genetic diseases that are rare amongst most humans are much more common on certain remote islands because one of the first few people to live there carried the faulty gene.

## CLASSIFICATION OF ORGANISMS

Living organisms are problematic to categorize – the more information that is obtained, the more complex the relationships appear to be. However, it is useful to have a system that indicates how 'similar' one organism is to another.

### Taxonomy

The most widely-used system of classification involves grouping organisms with similar characteristics into a group called a taxon (plural 'taxa'). This system, known as taxonomy, was originally developed by a Swedish botanist, Carolus Linnaeus, in the 18th century. The classifications have become more sophisticated over time, as various types of extra information have become available, and there are still controversies within the system.

### Cladistics

A useful method of working out the relationships between organisms involves devising 'evolutionary trees' to show the likely descent of particular groups. Organisms are placed in groups known as clades, based on shared features. This technique is called cladistics.

### Homology and analogy

Similar features can indicate shared ancestry, in which case they are often decribed as homologous. For example, various mammals share a five-fingered hand structure. However, some features with similar functions are stucturally dissimilar and are thought to have arisen independently; these are called analogous features. For example, bird wings and insect wings are described as analogous because they both allow flight but operate in different ways.

### Genetics

An important technique in recent years has been the sequencing of genes from different organisms; the degree to which genes are shared can indicate the closeness of the relationship. However, the neat distinction between homologous and analogous structures can break down at the genetic level. For example, as discussed above, many scientists think that human eyes and insect eyes arose independently, yet the Pax-6 gene is important in both.

## LEVELS OF CLASSIFICATION

There are seven major levels of classification in taxonomy: kingdom, phylum (plural 'phyla'), class, order, family, genus (plural 'genera') and species.

> *Nail those Names*
>
> A well-known mnemonic, or memory aid, for
> remembering the order of the classification levels is:
>
> <u>K</u>ing <u>P</u>hilip <u>C</u>ame <u>O</u>ver <u>F</u>or <u>G</u>ood <u>S</u>paghetti

The genus and species of an organism are always written in italics; the genus starts with a capital, but the species does not. As well as these major levels, 'super-' (higher) and 'sub-' (lower) versions of the levels can also be used, such as 'superphylum' or 'subspecies'.

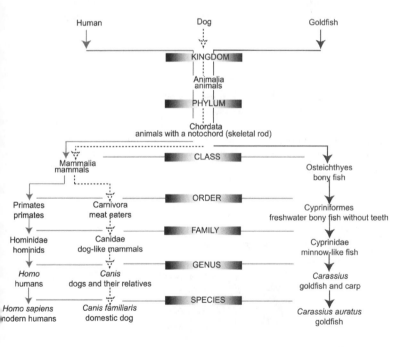

**Taxonomy**

## KINGDOM NAMES

Linnaeus's system included only two kingdoms: Plants and Animals. Nowadays, three or four additional kingdoms are generally recognized: Eubacteria and Archaea (sometimes grouped together as Monera), Fungi and Protista. The kingdoms can be broadly grouped in two ways: two empires or three domains.

**Two-empire system:** distinguishes between organisms on the basis of whether their cells have a proper nucleus (Eukaryotes) or not (Prokaryotes).

**Three-domain system:** considers that Eubacteria and Archaea are separate groups.

| Name | Empire | Domain |
|------|--------|--------|
| Eubacteria (bacteria) | Prokaryota | Eubacteria |
| Archaea (archaeans) | Prokaryota | Archaea |
| Protista or protoctista (protists) | Eukaryota | Eukaryota |
| Fungi | Eukaryota | Eukaryota |
| Plantae (plants) | Eukaryota | Eukaryota |
| Animalia (animals) | Eukaryota | Eukaryota |

### EUBACTERIA KINGDOM (BACTERIA)

Bacteria are single-celled organisms that can have many different features. However, all bacteria have in common the fact that their genetic material is not enclosed in a nucleus.

Some bacteria live inside other cells, while others are free-living. Some need oxygen but others can only live in an oxygen-free environment. Some are rod-shaped (bacilli) while others are round (cocci). Some can carry out photosynthesis to make sugars and oxygen from water and carbon dioxide. Some have a cell wall surrounding the membrane, with or without an additional outer membrane, and a few don't have a wall at all. As well as their main genome, bacteria often have circular pieces of DNA called plasmids; these can be transferred between bacteria to increase genetic diversity.

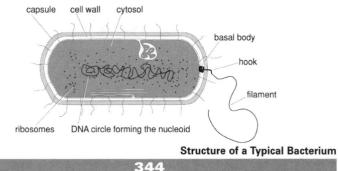

**Structure of a Typical Bacterium**

---

*Bacteria: Bad and Brilliant*

Some bacteria are harmful to other living organisms, including humans, and cause a variety of different diseases. However, others can aid digestion in the gut, turn milk into yoghurt, make soil fertile or even help to clean up oil spills.

---

## ARCHAEA KINGDOM (ARCHAEANS)

Archaeans are similar in form to bacteria. They even used to be called Archaebacteria ('old bacteria'), but it is now known that they are not closely related to the Eubacteria ('true bacteria').

Archaeans often metabolize hydrogen or sulphur, and usually cannot tolerate oxygen. This is probably because they evolved before the Earth had an oxygen-based atmosphere. They are less common today than the Eubacteria, and tend to inhabit environments that are hostile to other organisms.

## PROTISTA KINGDOM (PROTISTS)

Protists include amoebae, slime moulds, protozoa and some algae. They are the oldest eukaryotic organisms; they have a proper nucleus and their DNA is arranged into chromosomes.

Protists live in water or damp environments. They probably came into existence as a result of different bacteria and archaea combining to share their abilities, a mutually beneficial process known as endosymbiosis. In protists, metabolic processes such as photosynthesis and respiration take place inside compartments within the cell, called chloroplasts and mitochondria; each of these organelles probably derives from a different bacterium (see **Cells: Cell structure**). The nucleus probably comes from an archaean.

## FUNGI KINGDOM

Fungi tend to live on dry land, and are non-motile (they cannot move around actively). Fungi are not plants – in fact, it is likely that they are more closely related to animals than they are to plants. Most, but not all, can reproduce sexually. Their cell division differs from that of other eukaryotes; for example, the membrane surrounding the nucleus stays intact rather than dissociating.

Some fungi spend a lot of their time as filaments called hyphae. The mushrooms or toadstools that spring to mind when thinking about fungi are a short part of the reproductive cycle of some of these species. Other fungi are single-celled; these are called yeasts. The phyla of fungi are listed overleaf.

---

*Fungal Friends and Foes*

Some fungi are very helpful: they can recycle plant waste in the soil, make bread rise and beer ferment, and provide antibiotics. However, others cause diseases in humans and other animals. Plants can also fall prey to harmful fungi; Dutch elm disease wiped out elm trees across Britain and northern Europe, while other fungal diseases can ruin food crops.

---

| Zygomycota | Fungae that mate by growing towards each other and fusing. Many of them live in soil; others are moulds. |
| Ascomycota | Sac fungae, including yeasts, truffles and the fungi found in lichens. |
| Basidiomycota | Club fungae, including most mushrooms and toadstools. |
| Chytridiomycota | Primitive fungae that do not release spores. They mainly live in wet environments or as parasites. |

## Humongous Fungus

The largest single living organism ever found on Earth is an underground fungus, *Armillaria ostoyae*, also known as the honey mushroom or 'humongous fungus'. The fungus is thought to be several thousand years old and, when it was discovered by Canadian researchers, it covered an area of 9.65 square kilometres (3.73 square miles).

## PLANTAE KINGDOM (PLANTS)

Plants are multicellular organisms that can make their own carbohydrates (starch) from carbon dioxide and light energy by photosynthesis (see **Cells: Photosynthesis**). Their cells have a wall that is made out of cellulose; this wall can sometimes become hardened with lignin to form wood. Plants are non-motile; they therefore react more slowly to external factors, such as light and food, than do organisms such as animals and bacteria.

Whereas most animal cells (except reproductive cells such as eggs and sperm) have two sets of chromosomes, plants have just one set of chromosomes in each cell for part of their life cycle. Plants alternate between these two phases, which are known as generations.

| Generation | Sets of chromosomes | Description |
|---|---|---|
| Gametophyte | 1 | Haploid phase |
| Sporophyte | 2 | Diploid phase |

### Bryophyta phylum

Plants in the Bryophyta phylum spend the majority of their life cycle in the haploid gametophyte phase, with only one set of chromosomes in each cell. They include liverworts (Marchantiopsida), hornworts (Anthocerotopsida), and true mosses

(Bryopsida), all of which prefer to grow in damp environments. These plants are very old in evolutionary terms.

## Tracheophyta phylum

Plants in the Tracheophyta phylum spend the majority of their time in the diploid sporophyte phase. Tracheophytes can be divided into three subphyla: Pteridophytina, Coniferophytina (gymnosperms) and Magnoliophytina (angiosperms). They all form separate leaves and roots, and their stems contain separate tissues called xylem and phloem.

| Xylem | Carries water and supports the plant. |
| --- | --- |
| Phloem | Carries sugars. |

### Pteridophytina subphylum

The Pteridophytina plants have gametophytes (haploid stages) that can live independently. They include clubmosses (Lycopodiopsida), horsetails (Equisetopsida) and ferns (Polypodiopsida).

*Scouring Rushes*

Horsetails have small crystals of silica (silicon dioxide) on the surfaces of their stems. The resulting abrasive texture gives rise to their other common name – scouring rushes.

### Coniferophytina subphylum

Plants in the Coniferophytina subphylum are often called gymnosperms. They have two sexes; the female makes ovules that become seeds when fertilized by the male's pollen. The male and female sex organs are often found in cones. The gymnosperms include conifers (Pinopsida), the Gingko or maiden-hair tree (Gingkoopsida), cycads (Cycadopsida) and certain woody plants (Gnetopsida).

*Starkers Seeds*

Gymnosperm means 'naked seed', a name given because gymnosperms don't have their seeds encased inside a carpel or fruit. Angiosperms are more decent, being 'encased seeds'.

### Magnoliophytina subphylum

Plants in the Magnoliophytina subphylum are known as angiosperms. They make seeds that are enclosed inside a structure called a carpel. Angiosperms are flowering plants – the ones with large, colourful flowers tend to be those pollinated by bees, butterflies and other insects, while plants whose pollen is dispersed by the wind usually have more subtle flowers.

┌─ *Appetizing Angiosperms* ─────────┐
│ Most of the fruits we eat are the carpels of │
│ angiosperms. Examples include apples and oranges. │
└──────────────────────────────────┘

## Monocotyledons and dicotyledons

There are two very distinct groups of angiosperms or flowering plants: the Liliopsida or monocotyledons, and the Magnoliopsida or dicotyledons. They are divided by how many seed-leaves, or cotyledons, they have.

### Monocotyledons

The Liliopsida are known as monocotyledons or 'monocots' because they only produce one seed-leaf when they germinate (sprout from seed). Their leaves tend to be long and thin; they appear striped because of their parallel leaf veins. Their flowers tend to be divided into three or six petals, or multiples of these numbers. The subclasses of Liliopsida are listed below.

| | |
|---|---|
| **Alismatidae** | Aquatic plants. |
| **Commelinidae** | Grasses and cereals. |
| **Liliidae** | Lilies, orchids, asparagus, onions. |

┌─ *Monocots on the Menu* ─────────┐
│ Most edible cereal crops come from the │
│ Commelinidae group of monocotyledons, including │
│ wheat, oats and barley. These descended from │
│ grasses, whose modern relatives are still munched │
│ by livestock. Rice, maize and sugar cane are also in │
│ the Commelinidae subclass. │
└──────────────────────────────────┘

### Dicotyledons

The Magnoliopsida are known as dicotyledons or 'dicots' because they produce two seed-leaves. Their leaves tend to be broad with branched veins, often described as 'pinnate', and their flowers are usually divided into two or five petals, or multiples of these numbers. The subclasses of Magnoliopsida are listed below.

| | |
|---|---|
| **Magnoliidae** | Primitive flowering plants, including magnolias. |
| **Hamamelidae** | Woody plants, often have seeds in catkins. |
| **Caryophyllidae** | Leafy plants, including spinach and beetroot. |
| **Dillenidae** | Diverse group of trees and shrubs, including tea and cotton. |
| **Rosidae** | Shrubs and plants including roses, berry fruits, and legumes such as peas and beans. |

## ANIMALIA KINGDOM (ANIMALS)

Animals are multicellular organisms. They can move around, either by rearranging their cells to change their outline, or by having muscle cells and truly being able to move themselves. They go through a development stage known as a blastula, involving cleavage of a fertilized egg to form a fluid-filled spherical layer of cells. As well as being grouped into phyla, many of them can be divided into 'superphyla' that share broad characteristics.

### Parazoa superphylum

The Parazoa superphylum contains two phyla of tubular sponges.

| | |
|---|---|
| **Porifera** | Sponges made up of separate cells. |
| **Symplasma** | Sponges made up of sheets of cells called syncytia. |

### Phagocytellozoa superphylum

The Phagocytellozoa superphylum contains just one phylum, the Placozoa. These creatures are made up of a flat, solid mass of cells. At present, the only known species is *Trichoplax adhaerens*.

### Radiata superphylum

The Radiata superphylum contains radially symmetrical creatures with nerve and muscle cells. There are two phyla in this superphylum.

| | |
|---|---|
| **Cnidaria** | Aquatic creatures with tentacles and a blind-ended gut, such as jellyfish. |
| **Ctenophora** | Luminescent marine plankton. |

### Mesozoa superphylum

The Mesozoa superphylum contains a single phylum of worm-like creatures with solid bodies and only a few cells. These creatures, Rhombozoa, live inside molluscs either as commensals or parasites.

### Acoelomata superphylum

The Acoelomata superphylum contains flat worms without a body cavity. The phyla in the Acoelomata superphylum are listed below.

| | |
|---|---|
| **Platyhelminthes** | Microscopic flatworms, such as liver flukes. |
| **Gnathostomula** | Marine worms that are similar to Platyhelminthes but have hair-like structures called cilia and rudimentary jaws. |
| **Orthonecta** | Parasitic worms that reproduce sexually. |

## Aschelminthes superphylum

Aschelminthes are worms that have a body cavity called a coelom; this superphylum contains several phyla.

| | |
|---|---|
| **Nematoda** | Roundworms that live in water or inside other organisms. |
| **Nematomorpha** | Long aquatic worms similar to nematodes. |
| **Kinorhyncha** | Marine 'mud-dragons' that have an introvert (an organ for burrowing and food-collection). |
| **Loricifera** | Short stubby marine creatures that also have an introvert. |
| **Priapula** | Sausage-shaped worms that live on the ocean floor. |
| **Rotifera** | Small aquatic creatures that don't look very 'worm-like', although they are part of the Aschelminthes phylum. |
| **Acanthocephala** | Parasitic worms. |

## Panarthropoda superphylum (arthropods)

Panarthropoda are creatures that have segmented bodies and pairs of legs. The word 'arthropod' means 'jointed leg' and these creatures do indeed have jointed appendages. In some cases, one or more of these pairs of legs is modified, forming structures such as antennae and mouth parts. There are several phyla in the Panarthropoda superphylum; the animals contained within these phyla represent around three-quarters of all the animals on Earth.

| | |
|---|---|
| **Onychophora** | Cylindrical 'velvet worms' that live in tropical climates. |
| **Uniramia** | Creatures with jointed limbs, a hard exoskeleton, antennae and jaws. |
| **Chelicerata** | Creatures with jointed limbs and a hard external 'skeleton' (exoskeleton) but no antennae or jaws. They include the arachnids such as spiders and scorpions. |
| **Crustacea** | Creatures with jointed limbs and a hard exoskeleton. They include crabs. |

### Myriapoda class (myriapods)

Myriapods belong to the Uniramia phylum, and include centipedes and millipedes. True centipedes are collectively known as Chilopoda, while Symphyla and Pauropoda are very small creatures that resemble centipedes. Centipedes have one pair of legs attached to each of their body segments. Millipedes, however, have two pairs of legs per body segment, hence their collective name: Diplopoda.

> ### Pulling Your Leg
> Centipedes and millipedes don't really have a hundred or a thousand legs, despite their names. Myriapods can actually have between ten and two hundred pairs of legs.

### Hexapoda class (insects)

Insects belong to the Uniramia phylum, and are called Hexapoda because they have six legs. Their bodies are made up of three body segments: head, thorax and abdomen. The legs are attached to the thorax. Some of the diverse orders of insects are listed below.

| Name | Meaning | Common name |
|------|---------|-------------|
| Coleoptera | 'sheath-winged' | Beetles |
| Diptera | 'two pairs of wings' | Flies |
| Lepidoptera | 'scale-winged' | Moths and butterflies |
| Hymenoptera | 'membrane-winged' | Wasps, bees and ants |
| Orthoptera | 'straight-winged' | Grasshoppers and crickets |
| Neuroptera | 'nerve-winged' | Lacewings, antlions, owlflies |

### Eutrochozoa superphylum

The Eutrochozoa superphylum contains a wide variety of creatures, all of which have in common their spiral blastula division, presence of a blood circulation and separate sexes. The phyla in the Eutrochozoa superphylum are listed below.

| | |
|---|---|
| **Mollusca (molluscs)** | A diverse collection of creatures including squid, clams, slugs and snails. |
| **Sipunculida** | Creatures known as 'peanut worms' that have tentacles around the mouth and live on the ocean floor. |
| **Echiura** | Worms similar to Sipunculida but with a proboscis. |
| **Annelida** | Round worms with a body cavity and organs, such as earthworms. |

| | |
|---|---|
| **Pogonophora** | Ocean floor dwelling segmented 'beard worms'. |
| **Nemertea** | Worm-like creatures with a two-ended gut, which mostly live on the ocean floor. |
| **Cycliphora** | Minute creatures that live attached to the mouths of crustaceans. |

## Mollusca phylum (molluscs)

The Mollusca phylum contains a diverse collection of creatures, and it can be difficult to see the relationships between them. They are basically solid-bodied, although they do have a two-chambered heart set inside a cavity. They have a double-ended gut, a blood circulation and a nervous system. Most molluscs have some or all of these features: a feeding organ covered in tiny teeth, known as a radula; a calcium-containing shell; and a muscular foot that may or may not be modified into tentacles. Molluscs are divided into several classes, a few of which are listed here.

| | |
|---|---|
| **Gastropoda** | Creatures including slugs, snails and limpets. |
| **Bivalves** | Creatures with paired shell valves, including oysters, mussels and clams. |
| **Cephalopods** | Creatures with tentacles surrounding the mouth, which derive from the original muscular foot. Examples are cuttlefish, squid and octopus. |

### *Head-footed and Stomach-footed*

'Gastropod' means 'stomach-foot', and comes from the muscular foot attached to the underside of slugs and snails. 'Cephalopod', on the other hand, means 'head-foot', from the tentacles surrounding the head.

## Lophophorata superphylum

Lophophorata are creatures with a ring of tentacles around the mouth and more than one body compartment. The phyla in the Lophophorata superphylum are listed.

| | |
|---|---|
| **Entoprocta** | Marine worms that live inside their own shell-like tube. |
| **Brachiopoda** | Creatures with a shell in two parts, one ventral (at the front) and one dorsal (at the back). |
| **Bryozoa** | Small aquatic creatures that live in colonies. |

## Deuterostoma superphylum

The Deuterostoma superphylum contains animals in which, unlike other creatures, the anus is formed first and the mouth second, giving the name 'deuterostome' meaning 'mouth second'. The deuterostome phyla are listed below.

| | |
|---|---|
| **Hermichordata** | Marine creatures with a nerve cord running dorsally (along the back). |
| **Echinodermata** | Creatures with five-fold radial symmetry, including sea stars (starfish), sea urchins and sea cucumbers. |
| **Chaetognatha** | Marine 'arrow-worms' with spiny mouths and three body compartments. |
| **Chordata** | Creatures that have, during some stage of development, features including a notochord (skeletal rod), a dorsal nerve cord and a muscular tail. |

### Notable Notochords

Although the name 'chordate' sounds as though it should mean animals with a spinal cord, and does include the vertebrate class, some chordates are in fact invertebrates. The word 'chordate' actually refers to the presence of a notochord, a skeletal rod running internally along the creature's back, at some stage during development.

## Other phyla

Some phyla do not fit neatly into one superphylum. They are described here.

| | |
|---|---|
| **Gastrotricha** | Small worms with a two-ended gut and a rudimentary brain. They may be related to the Acoelomata. |
| **Pentastoma** | 'Tongue worms' that have claws near the mouth. They could possibly be grouped with the panarthropods but are not very similar to them. They may actually be modified crustaceans. |
| **Tardigrada** | Minute aquatic 'water bears'. They are probably panarthropods but could possibly be grouped with the Aschelminthes. |

| Chaetognatha | Marine 'arrow-worms' that have spiny mouths and three body compartments. They could possibly be grouped with the deuterostomes or the aschelminthes. |

## VERTEBRATA SUBPHYLUM (VERTEBRATES)

The Chordata phylum can be split into three sub-phyla, one of which is the vertebrata or vertebrates. The key feature of vertebrates is that they have a backbone; they also have a head and brain, eyes, a sense of smell, a pair of jaws and two pairs of limbs. The classes of vertebrates are listed.

| Agnatha | Jawless fish (eg lampreys). |
| Chondrichthyes | Cartilaginous fish (eg sharks). |
| Osteichthyes | Bony fish. |
| Amphibia | Amphibians. |
| Reptilia | Reptiles. |
| Aves | Birds. |
| Mammalia | Mammals. |

### Agnatha class (jawless fish)

The Agnatha are salt-water fish that lack jaws and generally don't have paired fins. Their skeletons are normally made out of cartilage rather than bone. They include lampreys and hagfish.

### Chondrichthyes class (cartilaginous fish)

The Condrichthyes are fish that have a skeleton made out of cartilage rather than bone. They have jaws and paired fins but don't have lungs or a swim bladder. They include sharks and rays. Cartilaginous fish are also sometimes called Elasmobranchs.

### Osteichthyes class (bony fish)

The Osteichthyes are fish that have a skeleton made out of bone. They have jaws and paired fins, and also have either lungs or a swim bladder. Bony fish are also sometimes called Teleosts.

### Amphibia class (amphibians)

Amphibians are a class of cold-blooded vertebrates including frogs, toads, newts and salamanders. There are approximately 4000 species.

Amphibians have a moist, thin skin without scales. The adults live partly or entirely on land, but can usually only survive in damp habitats. They return to water to lay their eggs, which hatch to form fish-like larvae or tadpoles that breathe by means of gills but gradually develop lungs as they approach adulthood.

## Reptilia class (reptiles)

Reptiles evolved from primitive amphibians. They can be divided into several orders, including Squamata (snakes and lizards), Chelonia (tortoises and turtles), Crocodylia (crocodiles and alligators) and Rhynocephalia (the tuatara). There are over 6500 living species; extinct reptiles include dinosaurs and pterodactyls.

Most reptiles live on the land, breathe with lungs, and have horny or plated skins. Reptiles are cold-blooded (ectothermic or poikilothermic), so they require the rays of the sun to maintain their body temperature. This means that they are often found in warm, tropical and subtropical regions, but does allow some species to exist in particularly hot desert environments in which mammals and birds would find it impossible to sustain life.

## Aves class (birds)

Birds are warm-blooded, egg-laying, and, in the case of adults, feathered vertebrates. There are approximately 8600 species, most of which have evolved for flight. The body of a bird is streamlined to reduce air resistance, the fore-limbs are modified as feathered wings, and the skeletal structure, heart and wing muscles, centre of gravity, and lung capacity are designed for the act of flying.

### Flightless birds

Two groups of birds have evolved to become flightless. The ratites, such as the ostrich, kiwi and emu, have become too large to be capable of sustained flight. Penguins have evolved into highly aquatic creatures, using their streamlining for swimming rather than flight.

> ### Reptilian Relatives
> Birds are thought to have evolved from reptiles, their closest living relative being the crocodile.

## Mammalia class (mammals)

Mammals are the group of animals to which humans belong. They can be distinguished by the presence of mammary (milk-producing) glands in the female and the fact that they are covered by hair. There are over 4000 species of mammals.

### Mammalian habitats

Mammals' hair and skin glands allow them to regulate their temperature from within; that is, they are warm-blooded (endothermic or homothermic). This gives them a greater adaptability to more varied environments than that of cold-blooded animals. Most mammals are terrestrial; however, bats have developed the ability to fly and whales lead an aquatic existence.

### Types of mammal

There are three different types of mammals, which produce their young in different ways.

| Monotremes | Mammals that lay eggs, eg echidnas. |
|---|---|
| Marsupials | Mammals that give birth to their young at an early developmental stage and nurture them outside the womb, often in a pouch, eg kangaroos. |
| Eutherian or placental mammals | Mammals that nourish their young in the womb and give birth to them at a late stage of development, eg humans. |

## Gestation periods

The gestation period of placental mammals, during which the foetus develops in the womb, varies hugely.

| Mammal | Gestation period (days) | Mammal | Gestation period (days) |
|---|---|---|---|
| Camel | 406 | Kangaroo | 40 |
| Cat | 62 | Lion | 108 |
| Chimpanzee | 237 | Mink | 50 |
| Cow | 280 | Monkey, Rhesus | 164 |
| Dog | 62 | Mouse | 21 |
| Dolphin | 276 | Opossum | 13 |
| Elephant, African | 640 | Orang-utan | 246–275 |
| Ferret | 42 | Pig | 113 |
| Fox | 52 | Rabbit | 32 |
| Giraffe | 395–425 | Rat | 21 |
| Goat | 151 | Reindeer | 215–245 |
| Guinea Pig | 68 | Seal, Northern Fur | 350 |
| Hamster | 16 | Sheep | 148 |
| Hedgehog | 35–40 | Skunk | 62 |
| Horse | 337 | Squirrel, Grey | 44 |
| Human | 266 | Tiger | 105–109 |
| Hyena | 110 | Whale | 365 |

## VIRUSES

Viruses are extremely small infectious agents, all of which are less than one thousandth of a millimetre in diameter.

There is debate as to whether viruses should be classed as living organisms, because they do not have their machinery to reproduce and can only multiply inside cells. Their hijacking of cells' functions means that viruses often cause disease in their hosts. They contain genetic material in the form of one or two strands of DNA or RNA (see **Genetics: DNA, RNA**), surrounded by a protein coat and sometimes a lipid membrane.

### Double-stranded DNA viruses

Several families of viruses have double-stranded DNA as their genetic material. The major double-stranded DNA virus families are listed.

| Family name | Examples |
| --- | --- |
| Papillomaviridae | Papillomaviruses (warts; cervical cancer) |
| Polyomaviridae | SV40 virus (HIV-like virus in monkeys) |
| Adenoviridae | Adenovirus (acute respiratory disease) |
| Herpesviridae | Herpes simplex viruses (cold sores), Epstein-Barr virus (glandular fever), Varicella Zoster virus (chickenpox) |
| Poxviridae | Variola virus (smallpox) |
| Hepadnaviridae[1] | Hepatitis B virus |

[1] Hepadnaviruses also have an RNA intermediate as part of their replication.

### Single-stranded DNA viruses

The Parvoviridae family are an example of viruses that have single-stranded DNA as their genetic material. Parvoviruses can cause diseases in cats and dogs.

### Double-stranded RNA viruses

The Reoviridae family are an example of viruses that have double-stranded RNA as their genetic material. They include human rotavirus, which causes acute infantile gastroenteritis.

### Single-stranded RNA viruses

Several families of viruses have a single strand of RNA as their genetic material.

The RNA can either be the positive form, which can be translated directly into proteins, or the negative form, which is a mirror image and must be used as a template to make a positive version before proteins can be made. The form of RNA is indicated in brackets.

| Family name | Examples |
| --- | --- |
| Picornaviridae (+) | Polio virus, rhinoviruses (colds), foot and mouth disease virus |
| Togaviridae (+) | Rubella virus |
| Flaviviridae (–) | Yellow fever virus |
| Orthomyxoviridae (–) | Influenza viruses |
| Filoviridae (–) | Ebola virus |
| Arenaviridae (–) | Lassa fever virus |
| Paramyxoviridae (–) | Measles virus, canine distemper virus |
| Rhabdoviridae (–) | Rabies virus |
| Retroviridae[1] | HIV virus (AIDS) |

[1] Retroviruses have a positive strand of RNA, which undergoes 'reverse transcription' to produce a DNA strand.

### *Bacteria-eaters*

Some viruses can live inside bacteria. A virus that can do this is called a bacteriophage, from the Latin for 'bacteria-eater'. As the English mathematician Augustus De Morgan wrote in his 1866 work *A Budget of Paradoxes*:

*'Great fleas have little fleas upon their backs to bite 'em,*
*And little fleas have lesser fleas, and so ad infinitum.'*

# ATOMS, ELEMENTS AND MOLECULES

## ATOMS

All ordinary matter in the universe is made up of atoms – they are the smallest unit of any substance. The word 'atom' comes from the Greek word *atomos*, meaning 'indivisible'. An atom consists of a positively-charged nucleus orbited by one or more negatively-charged electrons.

> *Sooner or later every one of us breathes an atom*
> *that has been breathed before by anyone you can*
> *think of who has lived before us – Michelangelo or*
> *George Washington or Moses.*
>
> —Polish mathematician Jacob Bronowski (1908–74)
> made this remark in 1966, and was quoted in the
> *New York Times* (13 Oct 1969).

### Empty Atoms

Most of an atom is empty space – the nucleus is
very small compared with the total size of the atom.
This was worked out by the British physicist Ernest
Rutherford, who bombarded a very thin sheet of
gold with alpha particles from radioactive substances
and found that most of them could pass straight
through the gold atoms.

## The nucleus

The nucleus contains one or more protons, which give it its positive charge. Most nuclei also contain neutrons, which are very similar to protons in terms of size and mass, but are not charged. The simplest atom, a hydrogen atom, contains only one proton and no neutrons.

## Electrons

> *I believe that there are 15 747 724 136 275 002 577 6*
> *05 653 961 181 555 468 044 717 914 527 116 709 366*
> *231 425 076 185 631 031 296 protons in the universe,*
> *and the same number of electrons.*
>
> —English astronomer Sir Arthur Stanley Eddington
> (1882–1944), during his Tarner Lecture (1938).

Electrons are much smaller (1836 times smaller, to be exact) than protons. They have the same amount of charge as protons, but their charge is negative rather than positive. This means that the electrons are attracted to the positively-charged nucleus, and this attraction keeps the electrons in the atom. The number of electrons is always equal to the number of protons so that the atom has no overall charge.

> 66
> *The electron is not as simple as it looks.*
> —British physicist Sir Lawrence Bragg (1890–1971). 99

## Describing electrons

Electrons have been described using various models. Like other subatomic particles, they can also be thought of as waves. They can therefore be considered as particles orbiting the nucleus as planets orbit the sun, or as spread-out waves that surround the nucleus in predictable zones called orbitals. (See **Key concepts: Quantum theory**.)

## Electron shells

Electrons can be thought of as filling up energy levels or 'shells'. All the electrons in the same shell have very similar energies, and the shells furthest from the nucleus have the most energy. Atoms are most stable when their energy is lowest, so the shells near to the nucleus tend to fill up with electrons first.

## Orbitals

We can never know exactly where an electron is as well as knowing the speed at which it is travelling (see **Key concepts: Heisenberg's uncertainty principle**). Also, it isn't possible to have electrons that share all the same values for a special set of properties (see **Key concepts: Pauli's exclusion principle**). These problems are avoided by considering the electron shells as having sub-shells made up of orbitals of varying shapes. Each orbital can contain two electrons, which have opposite values for a property called spin (see **Subatomic particles**) so they don't violate the exclusion principle. The orbital shapes represent the zones in which the electrons are most likely to be found.

| Sub-shell | Number of electrons | Description |
|-----------|---------------------|-------------|
| *s* | 2 | 1 spherical orbital |
| *p* | 6 | 3 lobed orbitals |
| *d* | 10 | 5 lobed orbitals |
| *f* | 14 | 7 lobed orbitals |

## SUBATOMIC PARTICLES

Subatomic particles make up atoms and carry forces. Protons, neutrons and electrons are examples of subatomic particles; there are also many others.

## Bosons and fermions

Subatomic particles have a property called spin, which can be in half- or whole units. If a particle has a whole number for its overall spin, it is called a boson, after the Indian physicist Satyendra Nath Bose. Particles that have an overall spin that is not a whole number are called fermions, after the Italian physicist Enrico Fermi.

## Gauge bosons

Gauge bosons are fundamental particles; that is, they are not made up of any other type of particle. As they are bosons, their spin property has a whole-number value.

Gauge bosons carry the fundamental interactions of nature (see **Key concepts: The theory of everything**).

| Gauge boson | Force |
|---|---|
| Photon | Electromagnetic force |
| W boson | Weak nuclear force |
| Z boson | Weak nuclear force |
| Gluon | Strong nuclear force |
| Gravitron | Gravity |

## The God Particle

The existence of other gauge bosons has been predicted. One of these is the Higgs boson, predicted by the British theoretical physicist Peter Higgs. This boson would have a spin of zero and would explain how particles get their mass. This would be so important to our understanding of the universe that the Higgs boson is also known as the 'God particle'.

### Leptons

Leptons are fundamental particles and include electrons. They have a value of ½ for their spin property and therefore belong to the fermion family. They do not use the strong nuclear force in their interactions (see **Hadrons**). Each lepton has a corresponding antilepton. The muon and tau seem to be higher-mass versions of the electron, and can be seen in particle accelerators.

| Lepton | Charge | Antilepton | Charge |
|---|---|---|---|
| Electron | −1 | Positron | +1 |
| Muon | −1 | Positive Muon | +1 |
| Tau | −1 | Tau-plus | +1 |
| Electron neutrino | 0 | Electron antineutrino | 0 |
| Muon neutrino | 0 | Muon antineutrino | 0 |
| Tau neutrino | 0 | Tau antineutrino | 0 |

### Quarks

Quarks are fundamental particles that have a spin of $+\frac{1}{2}$ or $-\frac{1}{2}$ and therefore belong to the fermion family. They have a charge of $\frac{1}{3}$ or $\frac{2}{3}$. Quarks also have a property known as 'colour', which is variable rather than fixed and is mediated by gluons. There are six 'flavours' of quark, each of which also has a corresponding antiquark. It seems that the top, bottom, charmed and strange quarks are higher-mass versions of the up and down quarks.

| Quark | Charge |
|---|---|
| Up | $+\frac{2}{3}$ |
| Down | $-\frac{1}{3}$ |

| | |
|---|---|
| Top | $+2/3$ |
| Bottom | $-1/3$ |
| Charmed | $+2/3$ |
| Strange | $-1/3$ |

### The Naming of Quarks

The name 'quark' was chosen by the US theoretical physicist Murray Gell-Mann. Some people believe that he was inspired by the line 'Three quarks for Mister Mark' in *Finnegans Wake* by James Joyce (there were originally only believed to be three types of quark). The top and bottom quarks were at one time called truth and beauty. The strange quark was given its name because physicists hadn't expected it to exist; there weren't any logical reasons for the other names.

### Particle accelerators

A particle accelerator is a machine used to accelerate charged particles to very high energies and speeds. A type of particle accelerator called a synchotron is often used to accelerate subatomic particles to speeds close to that of light. A synchotron consists of a tube that can be many kilometres in length and that contains a vacuum. An electric field is initially used to accelerate subatomic particles and to send them into the tube. Sources of electromagnetic radiation at points around the tube are then used to continue the acceleration. Cavities in the wall of the tube help the electromagnetic waves to travel between the radiation sources. Special electromagnets are used to bend the path of the charged subatomic particles into the appropriate circular path so that they can travel around the accelerator – as the particles speed up, the strength of the magnets must be increased to maintain the same circular orbit. If one of the electromagnets is switched off, the subatomic particles fly out of the tube and can be collected for an experiment, which often involves colliding them with atoms.

### Hadrons

Hadrons are made up of quarks. There are two main types of hadrons, known as baryons and mesons. Much of the mass of hadrons comes from their energy, rather than from their consituent quarks.

### Baryons

Baryons are made up of three quarks, one each of the 'red', 'green' and 'blue' colour property. They include the protons and neutrons found in the nucleus of an atom.

| Baryon | Constituent quarks |
|---|---|
| Proton | Up, Up, Down |
| Neutron | Up, Down, Down |

### Mesons

Mesons usually contain one quark and one anti-quark and are very unstable. They are bosons; that is, they have a whole number for their spin property. Mesons are involved in holding the atomic nucleus together.

| | |
|---|---|
| Pion | J/psi |
| Kaon | Upsilon |

## ELEMENTS

An element is a pure substance that is made up of only one type of atom. Some notable properties of elements are described below.

### Atomic number

Each element has a different number of protons in its nucleus; this is called the atomic number and has the symbol $Z$. The number of protons in a particular element is always the same.

### Isotopes

The number of neutrons in the nucleus of each atom of a given element can vary. These forms are called isotopes, from the Greek *isos* ('equal') and *topos* ('place'). The number of protons remains the same. An isotope can be either stable or unstable; if it is unstable then it tends to undergo radioactive decay (see **Energy, light and radioactivity: Radioactive decay**). For example, the most common form of carbon, known as carbon-12 ($^{12}C$), is stable, but there is also another stable isotope known as carbon-13 ($^{13}C$) and a radioactive isotope known as carbon-14 ($^{14}C$). The numbers refer to the differing atomic masses of the isotopes.

### Carbon dating

One carbon atom in every trillion is a radioactive carbon-14 atom. A small proportion of the carbon contained in living things is therefore radioactive. The carbon-14 decays at a fixed rate but, as long as the organism is alive, it is replenished from the environment, where it is constantly being produced. When the organism dies, however, the decay continues but the carbon-14 is no longer replenished. Carbon-14 levels can therefore be used to work out how long ago an organism died. The level of carbon-14 radioactivity halves every 5568 years.

### Mass number

The mass number of an isotope is based on the number of protons and neutrons in the nucleus. For example, an atom of carbon-12 contains six protons and six neutrons, giving it a mass number of twelve. An atom of carbon-13, however, contains six protons and seven neutrons, giving it a mass number of thirteen. The atomic mass of an isotope corresponds to its mass number, measured in units called 'atomic mass units' or 'amu'.

## Relative atomic mass

The relative atomic mass of an element takes an average of the atomic masses of each isotope of the element, taking into account the relative abundance of each isotope. For example, chlorine has two isotopes. The chlorine-35 isotope ($^{35}Cl$) accounts for 75% of chlorine but the remaining 25% is in the chlorine-37 ($^{37}Cl$) form. This gives a relative atomic mass of 35.5.

The relative atomic mass of an element is also sometimes called its atomic weight, and has the symbol $A_r$.

## Element names and numbers

Relative atomic masses are taken from the 2001 list of the International Union of Pure and Applied Chemistry. For radioactive elements, the relative atomic mass of the most stable isotope is given in square brackets.

| Symbol | Element | Derived from | Atomic number | Relative atomic mass |
|--------|---------|--------------|---------------|----------------------|
| Ac | Actinium | Greek, *aktis* = ray | 89 | [227] |
| Ag | Silver | Anglo-Saxon, *seolfor* | 47 | 107.8682 |
| Al | Aluminium | Latin, *alumen* = alum | 13 | 26.98154 |
| Am | Americium | America | 95 | [243] |
| Ar | Argon | Greek, *argos* = inactive | 18 | 39.948 |
| As | Arsenic | Greek, *arsenikon* = yellow or piment | 33 | 74.9216 |
| At | Astatine | Greek, *astatos* = unstable | 85 | [210] |
| Au | Gold | Anglo-Saxon, gold | 79 | 196.9665 |
| B | Boron | Arabic, *buraq* = borax | 5 | 10.811 |
| Ba | Barium | Greek, *barys* = heavy | 56 | 137.33 |
| Be | Beryllium | Greek, *beryllion* = beryl | 4 | 9.01218 |
| Bh | Bohrium | Niels Bohr, Danish physicist | 107 | [262] |
| Bi | Bismuth | German (origin unknown) | 83 | 208.9804 |
| Bk | Berkelium | Berkeley, California | 97 | [247] |
| Br | Bromine | Greek, *bromos* = stench | 35 | 79.904 |
| C | Carbon | Latin, *carbo* = charcoal | 6 | 12.011 |
| Ca | Calcium | Latin, *calx* = lime | 20 | 40.078 |
| Cd | Cadmium | Greek, *kadmeia* = calamine | 48 | 112.41 |
| Ce | Cerium | Asteroid Ceres | 58 | 140.12 |
| Cf | Californium | California | 98 | [251] |

| Symbol | Element | Derived from | Atomic number | Relative atomic mass |
|--------|---------|-------------|--------------|---------------------|
| Cl | Chlorine | Greek, *chloros* = green | 17 | 35.453 |
| Cm | Curium | Pierre and Marie Curie, French physicists | 96 | [249] |
| Co | Cobalt | German, *Kobold* = goblin | 27 | 58.9332 |
| Cr | Chromium | Greek, *chroma* = colour | 24 | 51.9961 |
| Cs | Caesium or Cesium | Latin, *caesium* = bluish-grey | 55 | 132.9054 |

## Atomic clock

An atomic clock is a device that uses the frequency of an atomic or molecular process as its counter. The caesium atomic clock is used to define standard time: the second is defined as 9 192 631 770 vibrations of a caesium-133 atom between two energy states. The clock consists of a chamber containing ionized caesium gas. A radio transmitter sends microwaves into the chamber and the frequency is adjusted until it is exactly correct to make the electrons bounce up to the higher energy level. As they fall back down, they emit light. A light meter is used to monitor the light levels and keep on fine-tuning the microwaves to maintain the excitation of the electrons at a maximum. The waves are counted and analysed by a computer so that the timing can be used by other clocks and equipment. Radio signals are often broadcast so that other clocks can be calibrated remotely.

| Symbol | Element | Derived from | Atomic number | Relative atomic mass |
|--------|---------|-------------|--------------|---------------------|
| Cu | Copper | Cyprus | 29 | 63.546 |
| Db | Dubnium | Dubna, Russia | 105 | [261] |
| Ds | Darmstadtium | Darmstadt, Germany | 110 | [281] |
| Dy | Dysprosium | Greek, *dysprositos* = difficult to reach | 66 | 162.500 |
| Er | Erbium | Ytterby, Sweden | 68 | 167.26 |
| Es | Einsteinium | Albert Einstein, US physicist | 99 | [252] |
| Eu | Europium | Europe | 63 | 151.96 |
| F | Fluorine | Latin, *fluo* = flow | 9 | 18.998403 |
| Fe | Iron | Anglo-Saxon, *iren* | 26 | 55.845 |

| Symbol | Element | Derived from | Atomic number | Relative atomic mass |
|--------|---------|--------------|---------------|----------------------|
| Fm | Fermium | Enrico Fermi, Italian physicist | 100 | [257] |
| Fr | Francium | France | 87 | [223] |
| Ga | Gallium | Latin, *Gallia* = France, or *gallus* = cock | 31 | 69.723 |
| Gd | Gadolinium | Johan Gadolin, Finnish chemist | 64 | 157.25 |
| Ge | Germanium | Latin, *Germania* = Germany | 32 | 72.64 |
| H | Hydrogen | Greek, *hydor* = water + *gennaein* = to produce | 1 | 1.00794 |
| He | Helium | Greek, *helios* = sun | 2 | 4.002602 |
| Hf | Hafnium | Latin, *Hafnia* = Copenhagen | 72 | 178.49 |
| Hg | Mercury | Mercury (myth) | 80 | 200.59 |
| Ho | Holmium | Latin, *Holmia* = Stockholm | 67 | 164.9304 |
| Hs | Hassium | Latin, *Hassias* = Hesse, state in Germany | 108 | [265] |
| I | Iodine | Greek, *iodes* = violet | 53 | 126.90447 |
| In | Indium | Indigo lines in the spectrum | 49 | 114.82 |
| Ir | Iridium | Latin, *iris* = rainbow | 77 | 192.22 |
| K | Potassium | English, potash | 19 | 39.0983 |
| Kr | Krypton | Greek, *kryptos* = hidden | 36 | 83.798 |
| La | Lanthanum | Greek, *lanthanein* = to escape notice | 57 | 138.9055 |
| Li | Lithium | Greek, *lithos* = stone | 3 | 6.941 |
| Lr | Lawrencium | Ernest Lawrence, US physicist | 103 | [260] |
| Lu | Lutetium | Latin, *Lutetia* = Paris | 71 | 174.967 |
| Md | Mendelevium | Dmitri Mendeleev, Russian scientist | 101 | [258] |
| Mg | Magnesium | Magnesia, Thessaly, Greece | 12 | 24.305 |
| Mn | Manganese | Latin, *magnes* = magnet | 25 | 54.9380 |
| Mo | Molybdenum | Greek, *molybdos* = lead | 42 | 95.94 |
| Mt | Meitnerium | Lise Meitner, Austrian physicist | 109 | [266] |
| N | Nitrogen | Greek, *nitron* = saltpetre (sodium carbonate) + *gennaein* = to produce | 7 | 14.0067 |

| Symbol | Element | Derived from | Atomic number | Relative atomic mass |
|--------|---------|--------------|---------------|----------------------|
| Na | Sodium | English, soda | 11 | 22.98977 |
| Nb | Niobium | Niobe (Greek myth) | 41 | 92.9064 |
| Nd | Neodymium | Greek, *neos* = new and *didymos* = twin | 60 | 144.24 |
| Ne | Neon | Greek, *neos* = new | 10 | 20.179 |
| Ni | Nickel | German, *Kupfernickel* = niccolite | 28 | 58.69 |
| No | Nobelium | Nobel Institute | 102 | [259] |
| Np | Neptunium | Planet Neptune | 93 | [237] |
| O | Oxygen | Greek, *oxys* = acid + *gennaein* = to produce | 8 | 15.9994 |
| Os | Osmium | Greek, *osme* = odour | 76 | 190.23 |
| P | Phosphorus | Greek, *phosphoros* = light-bearer | 15 | 30.97376 |
| Pa | Protactinium | Greek, *protos* = first + actinium | 91 | [231] |
| Pb | Lead | Anglo-Saxon, lead | 82 | 207.2 |
| Pd | Palladium | Minor planet Pallas | 46 | 106.42 |
| Pm | Promethium | Prometheus (Greek myth) | 61 | [145] |
| Po | Polonium | Poland | 84 | [209] |
| Pr | Praseodymium | Greek, *prasios* = green and *didymos* = twin | 59 | 140.9077 |
| Pt | Platinum | Spanish, *plata* = silver | 78 | 195.08 |
| Pu | Plutonium | Planet Pluto | 94 | [244] |
| Ra | Radium | Latin, *radius* = ray | 88 | [226] |
| Rg | Roentgenium | Wilhelm Konrad von Röntgen (Roentgen), German physicist | 111 | [272] |
| Rb | Rubidium | Latin, *rubidus* = red | 37 | 85.4678 |
| Re | Rhenium | Latin *Rhenus* = the Rhine | 75 | 186.207 |
| Rf | Rutherfordium | Ernest Rutherford, British physicist | 104 | [262] |
| Rh | Rhodium | Greek, *rhodon* = rose | 45 | 102.9055 |
| Rn | Radon | Radium emanation | 86 | [222] |

| Symbol | Element | Derived from | Atomic number | Relative atomic mass |
|--------|---------|--------------|---------------|----------------------|
| Ru | Ruthenium | Latin, *Ruthenia* = Russia | 44 | 101.07 |
| S | Sulphur or sulfur | Latin, *sulfur* | 16 | 32.065 |
| Sb | Antimony | Latin, *antimonium* | 51 | 121.76 |
| Sc | Scandium | Scandinavia | 21 | 44.95591 |
| Se | Selenium | Greek, *selene* = moon | 34 | 78.96 |
| Sg | Seaborgium | Glenn Seaborg, US physicist | 106 | [263] |
| Si | Silicon | Latin, *silex* = flint | 14 | 28.0855 |
| Sm | Samarium | Colonel M Samarski, Russian engineer | 62 | 150.36 |
| Sn | Tin | Anglo-Saxon, *tin* | 50 | 118.710 |
| Sr | Strontium | Strontian, Scotland | 38 | 87.62 |
| Ta | Tantalum | Tantalus (Greek myth) | 73 | 180.9479 |
| Tb | Terbium | Ytterby, Sweden | 65 | 158.9254 |
| Tc | Technetium | Greek, *technetos* = artificial | 43 | [99] |
| Te | Tellurium | Latin, *tellus* = earth | 52 | 127.60 |
| Th | Thorium | Scandinavian god Thor | 90 | 232.0381 |
| Ti | Titanium | Greek, *Titan* = Titan | 22 | 47.867 |
| Tl | Thallium | Greek, *thallos* = a young shoot | 81 | 204.3833 |
| Tm | Thulium | Greek and Roman, *Thule* = Northland | 69 | 168.9342 |
| U | Uranium | Planet Uranus | 92 | 238.0289 |
| Uub | Ununbium | Systematic name, 'one hundred and twelve' | 112 | [285] |
| Uun | Ununnilium | see Ds – darmstadtium | | |
| Uuu | Unununium | see Rg – roentgenium | | |
| V | Vanadium | Old Norse, *Vanadis* = goddess Freya | 23 | 50.9415 |
| W | Tungsten | Swedish, *tungsten* = heavy stone | 74 | 183.84 |
| Xe | Xenon | Greek, *xenos* = stranger | 54 | 131.29 |
| Y | Yttrium | Ytterby, Sweden | 39 | 88.9059 |

| Symbol | Element | Derived from | Atomic number | Relative atomic mass |
|---|---|---|---|---|
| Yb | Ytterbium | Ytterby, Sweden | 70 | 173.04 |
| Zn | Zinc | German, *zink* | 30 | 65.409 |
| Zr | Zirconium | Persian, *zargun* = gold-coloured | 40 | 91.224 |

## PERIODIC TABLE

> The periodic table arranges the elements by atomic number.

### Periods

The horizontal rows, or periods, represent the filling of the electron shells (see **Atoms**). The period number indicates how many electron shells the elements in that period have.

### Groups

The vertical columns, or groups, tend to contain elements with similar chemical and physical properties, because they have the same number of electrons in their outermost shell. This number is equal to the group number.

**— *Metal or Non-Metal?* —**

Hydrogen has one electron in a shell that can contain a maximum of two electrons. It can therefore show both metal and non-metal properties – it can lose its 'spare' electron to become a metal-like positive ion, or it can gain an electron to fill its shell, becoming a negative ion like many non-metals.

### Electron configurations

The electron shells are numbered from the innermost shell outwards (see **Atoms**). The first three shells are shown; the total number of electrons possible in each period include those from previous periods, as these shells remain filled.

| Period | Sub-shells filled | Electrons added | Total number possible |
|---|---|---|---|
| 1 | 1$s$ | 2 | 2 |
| 2 | 2$s$, 2$p$ | 8 | 10 |
| 3 | 3$s$, 3$p$ | 8 | 18 |
| 4 | 4$s$, 3$d$, 4$p$ | 18 | 36 |
| 5 | 5$s$, 4$d$, 5$p$ | 18 | 54 |
| 6 | 6$s$, 4$f$, 5$d$, 6$p$ | 32 | 86 |
| 7 | 7$s$, 5$f$, 6$d$, 7$p$ | 32 | 118 |

| | | | | | | | | | | | | | | | | | 8 |
|---|---|---|---|---|---|---|---|---|---|---|---|---|---|---|---|---|---|
| 1 | 2 | | | | | | | | | | | 3 | 4 | 5 | 6 | 7 | He 2 — helium |
| H 1 — hydrogen | | | | | | | | | | | | | | | | | |
| Li 3 — lithium | Be 4 — beryllium | | | | | | | | | | | B 5 — boron | C 6 — carbon | N 7 — nitrogen | O 8 — oxygen | F 9 — fluorine | Ne 10 — neon |
| Na 11 — sodium | Mg 12 — magnesium | | | | | | | | | | | Al 13 — aluminium | Si 14 — silicon | P 15 — phosphorus | S 16 — sulphur | Cl 17 — chlorine | Ar 18 — argon |
| K 19 — potassium | Ca 20 — calcium | Sc 21 — scandium | Ti 22 — titanium | V 23 — vanadium | Cr 24 — chromium | Mn 25 — manganese | Fe 26 — iron | Co 27 — cobalt | Ni 28 — nickel | Cu 29 — copper | Zn 30 — zinc | Ga 31 — gallium | Ge 32 — germanium | As 33 — arsenic | Se 34 — selenium | Br 35 — bromine | Kr 36 — krypton |
| Rb 37 — rubidium | Sr 38 — strontium | Y 39 — yttrium | Zr 40 — zirconium | Nb 41 — niobium | Mo 42 — molybdenum | Tc 43 — technetium | Ru 44 — ruthenium | Rh 45 — rhodium | Pd 46 — palladium | Ag 47 — silver | Cd 48 — cadmium | In 49 — indium | Sn 50 — tin | Sb 51 — antimony | Te 52 — tellurium | I 53 — iodine | Xe 54 — xenon |
| Cs 55 — caesium | Ba 56 — barium | 57–71 * | Hf 72 — hafnium | Ta 73 — tantalum | W 74 — tungsten | Re 75 — rhenium | Os 76 — osmium | Ir 77 — iridium | Pt 78 — platinum | Au 79 — gold | Hg 80 — mercury | Tl 81 — thallium | Pb 82 — lead | Bi 83 — bismuth | Po 84 — polonium | At 85 — astatine | Rn 86 — radon |
| Fr 87 — francium | Ra 88 — radium | 89–103 ** | Rf 104 — rutherfordium | Db 105 — dubnium | Sg 106 — seaborgium | Bh 107 — bohrium | Hs 108 — hassium | Mt 109 — meitnerium | Ds 110 — darmstadtium | Rg 111 — röntgenium | Uub 112 — ununbium | | | | | | |

Transition metals

element symbol / atomic number / element name

* Lanthanide series

| La 57 — lanthanum | Ce 58 — cerium | Pr 59 — praseodymium | Nd 60 — neodymium | Pm 61 — promethium | Sm 62 — samarium | Eu 63 — europium | Gd 64 — gadolinium | Tb 65 — terbium | Dy 66 — dysprosium | Ho 67 — holmium | Er 68 — erbium | Tm 69 — thulium | Yb 70 — ytterbium | Lu 71 — lutetium |
|---|---|---|---|---|---|---|---|---|---|---|---|---|---|---|

** Actinide series

| Ac 89 — actinium | Th 90 — thorium | Pa 91 — protactinium | U 92 — uranium | Np 93 — neptunium | Pu 94 — plutonium | Am 95 — americium | Cm 96 — curium | Bk 97 — berkelium | Cf 98 — californium | Es 99 — einsteinium | Fm 100 — fermium | Md 101 — mendelevium | No 102 — nobelium | Lr 103 — lawrencium |
|---|---|---|---|---|---|---|---|---|---|---|---|---|---|---|

**Periodic Table**

### Transition metal configurations

The 4s sub-shell is at a slightly lower energy level than the 3d sub-shell, so 4s fills up first. The 5s then fills before the 4d, and so on. This gives rise to the phenomenon of the transition metals.

### Lanthanide and actinide configurations

In a similar way, the 5p and 6s sub-shells fill before the 4f sub-shell, and the 6p and 7s fill before the 5f sub-shell. This gives rise to the lanthanides and actinides.

## Group 1: Alkali metals

The alkali metals are soft metals that have a single electron in their outermost shell, making them very reactive. They react readily with the halogens from group 7, forming ionic compounds such as sodium fluoride (an ingredient in toothpaste). They take their name from their ability to form very strongly alkaline solutions when they dissolve in water (see **Acids, alkalis and bases**). An example is sodium hydroxide (caustic soda).

## Group 2: Alkaline earth metals

The alkaline earth metals are similar in their properties to the group 1 alkali metals, although they are somewhat less reactive. They are named because their oxides, compounds formed when they react with oxygen, used to be called the 'alkaline earths'. Examples of alkaline earth metals are magnesium and calcium.

## Groups 3, 4 and 5

The elements in these groups have an outer electron shell that is approximately half-full. Their atoms tend to share electrons with other atoms to form covalent bonds (see **Chemical bonds**). The elements towards the left of groups 3, 4 and 5 are metals, while the ones towards the right are non-metals. The divide between metals and non-metals lies on a diagonal line. Aluminium, germanium, antimony and polonium are classed as metals, while boron, silicon, arsenic, tellurium and astatine are classed as non-metals. These borderline elements have characteristics intermediate between metals and non-metals, and some of them can act as semiconductors (see **Materials: Electronics materials**).

## Group 6

The group 6 elements are non-metals and are very reactive. They include oxygen and sulphur.

## Group 7: Halogens

Halogens are also reactive non-metals; the outermost electron shell is one electron short of being full, so they readily become negatively-charged ions in order to gain an electron. Their name comes from the Greek words *hals*, meaning 'salt', and *gennaein*, meaning 'to produce'. Several of the halogens are coloured.

| Halogen | Colour |
| --- | --- |
| Fluorine | Yellow |
| Chlorine | Green |

| Halogen | Colour |
|---------|--------|
| Bromine | Red/brown |
| Iodine | Purple/black |

### Group 8: Noble gases

The noble gases are sometimes known as the inert gases, as they are very unreactive. This is because their outermost electron shell is full. The group can be also be numbered zero. Helium, neon and argon are all examples of noble gases.

### Transition metals

The collection of metals known as the transition metals lies between groups 2 and 3. The transition metals represent the filling of the *d* sub-shells with electrons, moving from left to right across the periodic table, and are therefore also known as 'd-block elements'. They often form coloured salts; for example, copper sulphate solution is blue.

### Lanthanide and actinide series

The elements that represent the filling of the *f* electron sub-shells belong between group 2 and the transition metals. However, they are conventionally written underneath the main periodic table to avoid it becoming very long. The two rows of these elements are called the lanthanide series and the actinide series, after their first elements. Many of them are unstable and radioactive; some of them do not occur naturally and have only been made in laboratories. They are also known as 'inner transition elements' or 'f-block elements'.

## CHEMICAL BONDS

Chemical bonds are the basis of interactions between atoms, and involve the sharing or trading of electrons. Atoms are most stable when a complete electron shell is filled. Elements with atoms containing partially-filled shells tend to share or trade electrons to become more stable, thus forming chemical bonds.

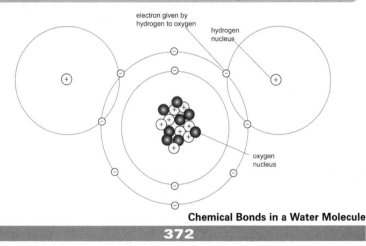

**Chemical Bonds in a Water Molecule**

## Covalent bonds

Bonds are said to be covalent when electrons are shared between atoms. Covalent bonds are strong and have a particular direction. They can be described using hybrid orbitals that derive from the electron orbitals of the atoms; this is called molecular orbital theory.

Covalent bonds commonly involve one pair of electrons (single bond), two pairs (double bond), or three pairs (triple bond). The number of pairs of electrons is called the bond order.

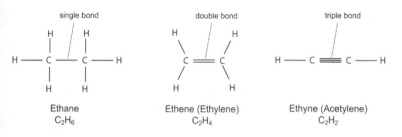

| single bond | double bond | triple bond |
| --- | --- | --- |
| Ethane | Ethene (Ethylene) | Ethyne (Acetylene) |
| $C_2H_6$ | $C_2H_4$ | $C_2H_2$ |

## Ionic bonds

Bonds are said to be ionic when one atom donates one or more 'spare' electrons to another atom that is 'missing' one or more electrons in its outer shell. These bonds are based on the imbalance in electrical charge that this creates – the atom that donates electrons is left positively charged, while the atom that accepts electrons becomes negatively charged. These charged atoms are called ions. Like covalent bonds, ionic bonds can be very strong.

## Polar bonds

Bonds that are intermediate between covalent and ionic bonds are known as polar bonds. The electrons are not shared equally but neither are they entirely 'possessed' by one or other of the atoms. Instead, they are shared unequally and are nearer to one atom than the other. This creates a slight charge difference between the atoms but they are not entirely ionized.

## MOLECULES

Molecules contain two or more atoms joined together by covalent or polar chemical bonds.

> *Almost all aspects of life are engineered at the molecular level, and without understanding molecules we can only have a very sketchy understanding of life itself.*
>
> —English biologist Francis Crick (1916–2004), *What Mad Pursuit* (1988).

Molecules are discrete (separate from one another) and every molecule of a pure substance contains the same number of atoms. The atoms can be of the same element; for example, an oxygen molecule contains two oxygen atoms. Alternatively, a molecule can contain atoms of different elements; for example, a water molecule contains one oxygen atom and two hydrogen atoms.

### Oranges and Lemons

Molecules can have two chiral forms. *Cheir* is the Greek word for 'hand', and 'chiral' means that these forms are 'handed' – they are mirror images of one another. The two chiral forms of a molecule called limonene are found in oranges and lemons respectively, and give these fruits their different smells and tastes.

## LATTICES

**Atoms linked by ionic bonds form lattice structures.**

Unlike molecules, lattice structures contain a large uncountable array of ions, rather than discrete units of set numbers of atoms. Because of this, lattices are described by the proportion of each type of ion they contain, rather than the actual numbers of ions. An example of a lattice structure is sodium chloride (salt), where equal numbers of positively-charged sodium ions ($Na^+$) and negatively-charged choride ions ($Cl^-$) are present. Sodium chloride is therefore described as NaCl. In magnesium chloride, however, the ratio is two chloride ions for every magnesium ion, so it is described as $MgCl_2$.

### Buckyballs

Carbon exists in more than one form. Graphite (pencil lead) is very soft because it contains sheets of carbon atoms that can slide over one another. Diamond is much harder because its atoms are arranged in a very strong lattice-type structure. A molecular form of carbon was discovered much more recently. Buckminsterfullerene molecules, or 'buckyballs', contain 60 carbon atoms arranged in a structure resembling a football. This form of carbon is named after the US engineer and architect Richard Buckminster Fuller, who designed domes with similar structures.

## METALS

In pure metals, the outer electrons are very loosely held by the atomic nuclei. These electrons can form a mobile 'sea' of electrons between a closely packed array of nuclei, a phenomenon called delocalization. This makes metals good at conducting electricity, as the electrons can move around easily. The bonds between metal atoms are relatively weak. See also **Materials: Metals**.

## CHEMICAL COMPOUNDS

Substances that contain atoms from more than one element are known as compounds.

### Ionic compounds

Ionic compounds contain ionized atoms (ions). They can be formed from a metal, whose atoms lose one or more electrons to become positively-charged ions, and a non-metal element, whose atoms gain one or more electrons to become negatively-charged ions. Alternatively, either or both of the ions can be formed from molecules rather than elements. Ionic compounds are often called salts; 'salt' is also used as a common name for one particular salt, sodium chloride (table salt).

### Organic compounds

Compounds that contain both carbon and hydrogen are members of a group known as the organic compounds. These compounds, which can also contain other elements such as sulphur, nitrogen and oxygen, are the basis of living organisms.

> 66
> *Organic chemistry just now is enough to drive one mad. It gives one the impression of a primeval, tropical forest full of the most remarkable things, a monstrous and boundless thicket, with no way of escape, into which one may well dread to enter.*
> —German chemist Friedrich Wöhler (1800–82).
> 99

### Aliphatic compounds

Aliphatic compounds contain atoms bonded together by covalent bonds. The compounds ethane, ethene and ethyne (shown above) are all examples of aliphatic compounds.

### Aromatic compounds

Aromatic compounds are based on a structure called a benzene ring. Benzene contains six carbon and six hydrogen atoms. The carbon atoms form a ring and one hydrogen atom is attached to each carbon atom. Two doughnut-shaped zones, containing delocalized electrons, form above and below the carbon ring. The bonds formed have properties that are half-way between those of single and double bonds.

Benzene can be drawn as a 'resonance structure', which represents bonds hovering between single and double, or with a circle to represent the delocalized electron 'doughnuts'.

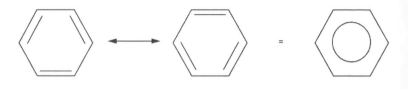

resonance structures                    delocalized structure

**Benzene Structures**

Aromatic compounds can contain a single benzene ring, or multiple rings joined together. The rings can be modified in various ways but still contain delocalized electrons. Not all ring structures are aromatic; the ring-shaped compound cyclohexane contains six carbon atoms and twelve hydrogen atoms, allowing normal single bonds to be formed, so there is no delocalization and cyclohexane is therefore aliphatic.

*Oily and Smelly*

Aliphatic compounds get their name from the Greek word *aleiphatos*, meaning oil, while aromatic compounds are so-called because they often have distinctive smells.

## STRUCTURES OF ORGANIC COMPOUNDS

Organic compounds can be represented on paper in a number of ways. These include displayed formulae, molecular formulae, skeletal formulae and three-dimensional structures, as shown below for butane (LPG, Calor Gas®, $C_4H_{10}$).

### Displayed formula

The displayed formula shows each atom and each bond.

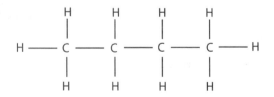

### Molecular formula

The molecular formula describes the atoms that are attached to each carbon atom;

if the structure is branched, the formula is based on the longest chain of carbon atoms with side-chains given in brackets.

$$CH_3CH_2CH_2CH_3$$

## Skeletal formula

The skeletal formula shows all the bonds; the meeting points of bonds are assumed to be carbon atoms with an appropriate number of hydrogen atoms attached to them.

## Three-dimensional structure

The three-dimensional structure shows the directions of the bonds.

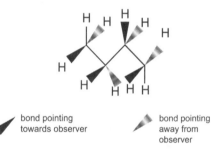

◤ bond pointing towards observer        ◢ bond pointing away from observer

## CARBOHYDRATES

Carbohydrates are a particular group of organic compounds that contain oxygen as well as carbon and hydrogen. Pure carbohydrates contain equal proportions of carbon and oxygen atoms, and twice as many hydrogen atoms. Other similar compounds are also classed as carbohydrates; these include deoxyribose, which forms the 'backbone' of the DNA double helix (see **Genetics: DNA**).

## Sugars

Water-soluble carbohydrates that form crystals are called sugars. These include sucrose (often known simply as 'sugar'), glucose and fructose.

## Polysaccharides

Polysaccharides are are made from long chains of sugars by removing water, and include starch and cellulose. They are examples of naturally-occurring polymers (see **Materials: Polymers**).

## AMINO ACIDS

Amino acids are a particular set of nitrogen-containing organic molecules that form the basis of proteins.

### Carboxyl groups and amino groups

Amino acids have a negatively-charged carboxyl group, which contains carbon and oxygen. A positively-charged amino group is also present, which contains nitrogen and hydrogen. Molecules that contain both a positive and a negative charge in this manner are called zwitterions, from the German word *zwittter*, meaning 'hybrid'. The carboxyl and amino groups are separated by a carbon atom.

### Side chains

The carbon atom between the amino and carboxyl groups carries a side chain. In the simplest amino acid, glycine, this side chain is simply a hydrogen atom. Other amino acids have much more complicated side chains, which can have a positive or negative charge, a short aliphatic chain or an aromatic group. The side chains on the 20 amino acids found in proteins are shown below.

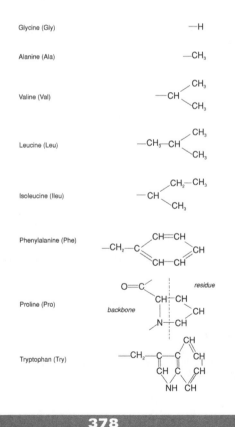

Serine (Ser)  —$CH_2$—OH

Threonine (Thr)  —CH$\begin{smallmatrix}OH\\CH_3\end{smallmatrix}$

Cysteine (Cys)  —$CH_2$—SH

Methionine (Met)  —$CH_2$—$CH_2$—S—$CH_3$

Aspartic acid (Asp)  —$CH_2$—C$\begin{smallmatrix}O\\O^-\end{smallmatrix}$

Glutamic acid (Glu)  —$CH_2$—$CH_2$—C$\begin{smallmatrix}O\\O^-\end{smallmatrix}$

Asparagine (AspNH$_2$)  —$CH_2$—C$\begin{smallmatrix}O\\NH_2\end{smallmatrix}$

Glutamine (GluNH$_2$)  —$CH_2$—$CH_2$—C$\begin{smallmatrix}O\\NH_2\end{smallmatrix}$

Tyrosine (Tyr)  —$CH_2$—C(CH=CH)(CH=CH)C—OH

Histidine (His)  —$CH_2$—C=CH / NH—N / CH

Lysine (Lys)  —$CH_2$—$CH_2$—$CH_2$—$CH_2$—$NH_3^+$

Arginine (Arg)  —$CH_2$—$CH_2$—$CH_2$—NH—C$\begin{smallmatrix}NH_3\\NH_2^+\end{smallmatrix}$

**Amino Acid Side Chains**

## PROTEINS

Protein molecules consist of one or more polypeptide chains.

### Structure of proteins

Each polypeptide chain is a linear chain formed from up to several hundred amino acids. These are bonded through their amino and carboxyl groups, eliminating water molecules and leaving amino acid 'residues'. Proteins are naturally-occurring polymers (see **Materials: Polymers**).

### Diversity of proteins

Because the 20 amino acids can be arranged in nearly any sequence, the potential diversity of protein structure and function is enormous. The properties of each polypeptide depend on the amino acid sequence, which itself determines the correct folding of the chain in three dimensions and gives its specific biological activity.

### Gel electrophoresis

Gel electrophoresis is a method for separating molecules of DNA or protein, usually based on their size. Samples are loaded into a slab of gel, which is placed in a tank filled with a solution that can conduct electricity, with electrodes at both ends. An electric current is passed through the apparatus, which makes the molecules travel through the gel towards the opposite electrode. DNA is negatively charged, so the current is applied to make the opposite electrode positively charged. Proteins vary in charge, so they are mixed with a loading solution that gives them a uniform negative charge.

An interesting property of the gels used is that the pore size in the gel follows a fractal pattern, with lots of small spaces but only a few large ones (see **Numbers and shapes: Fractals**). This means that smaller molecules move quickly and easily through the gel, because they can fit into lots of the pores, but larger molecules move more slowly because they only fit into a few pores. The size of the molecules can therefore be worked out by using standard size markers alongside the samples.

## ENZYMES

Enzymes are proteins that speed up or catalyse chemical reactions in living organisms. These reactions can be for making (synthesis) or breaking down (decomposition) of organic molecules.

### Active site

The catalytic effect depends on a restricted region of the protein molecule, known as the active site of the enzyme, which consists of a specific and unique configuration of a few amino acid side chains brought together by the way the polypeptide chains are folded. The molecule to be acted on, known as the substrate, binds to the active site. Enzymes are highly specific for particular substrates and reactions. Their names often end in –ase, –zyme or -in.

## Types of enzyme

| Enzyme | Reaction catalysed | Where found |
| --- | --- | --- |
| Amylase | Breakdown of starch | Saliva and pancreatic juice |
| DNA polymerase | Formation of DNA from nucleotides | Cell nuclei |
| Invertase | Conversion of sucrose into glucose and fructose | Bees, for honey production from nectar |
| Lysozyme | Breakdown of bacterial cell wall | Saliva; egg white |
| Pepsin | Breakdown of proteins | Stomach juices |
| Plasmin or fibrinolysin | Breakdown of blood clots | Blood |
| Thrombin | Formation of blood clots | Blood |

> *Chemistry without catalysis, would be a sword without a handle, a light without brilliance, a bell without sound.*
>
> —German chemist Alwin Mittasch (1869–1953), in *Journal of Chemical Education* (1948).

## CHEMICAL REACTIONS

Chemical reactions allow different atoms to combine to form molecules or ionic compounds. The substances taking part in the reaction are known as reactants, and the substances that are formed are known as products. There are four basic types of reaction: combination, decomposition, displacement and substitution.

### Combination reactions

Combination reactions, also called synthesis reactions, occur when two reactants combine to form a single product. For example, carbon and oxygen can react to form carbon dioxide. They can be represented as:

$$A + B \rightarrow AB$$

### Decomposition reactions

Decomposition reactions occur when a complex substance is broken down into two or more elements or smaller molecules. These reactions are often endothermic; they require energy to be put in. Sodium chloride (table salt) can be broken down into sodium metal and chlorine gas by passing an electric current through a solution of the salt (electrolysis), while calcium hydroxide decomposes to calcium oxide and water when heated. Decomposition reactions can be represented as:

$$AB \rightarrow A + B$$

## Single displacement reactions

Single displacement reactions are also called single substitution reactions. They involve an element being displaced out of a substance and replaced by a more reactive element. For example, if magnesium chloride reacts with sodium metal, it forms sodium chloride and magnesium metal because sodium is more reactive than magnesium. They can be represented as:

$$A + BX \rightarrow AX + B$$

## Double displacement reactions

Double displacement reactions are also known as double substitution reactions. They involve swapping ions or chemical groups between substances. For example, sodium chloride and copper sulphate can react to form copper chloride and sodium sulphate. Double displacement reactions can be represented as:

$$AX + BY \rightarrow BX + AY$$

## Exothermic reactions

Reactions that give out heat are called exothermic reactions. These reactions often occur spontaneously between reactive substances. The products of the reaction have less energy in their chemical bonds than the reactants, and the excess energy is transferred to the surroundings as heat.

## Endothermic reactions

Endothermic reactions can't take place unless energy is put into them by heating the reactants, exposing them to light or passing an electric current through them (electrolysis). The reason for this is that the chemical bonds in the products contain more energy than those in the reactants, and this additional energy must be supplied externally.

## ACIDS, ALKALIS AND BASES

Water is made up of two hydrogen atoms and one oxygen atom. These can dissociate (come apart) to form equal numbers of positively-charged hydrogen ions ($H^+$) and negatively-charged hydroxyl ions ($OH^-$). Substances that disturb this balance when added to water are called acids and alkalis respectively. Alkalis belong to a category of substances called bases, which react with acids to form salts.

## Acids

An acid is a substance that causes an excess of hydrogen ions to be formed when it is dissolved in water. Acids can dissolve metals, producing hydrogen gas, and they can react with a base or alkali to form a salt.

## Alkalis

An alkali is a substance that causes an excess of hydroxyl ions to be formed when it is dissolved in water. Alkalis can react with acids to form a salt.

## Bases

A base is any substance that can react with an acid to form a salt. Bases include the alkalis, as well as other substances that do not dissolve in water.

# MATERIALS

Materials have many measurable properties that are important in determining their suitability of use for different purposes. Some of these properties are described below.

### Density

Density is a measure of how compact a material is, and is the ratio of the mass of a material to its volume. Fixed-size blocks of material are heavier for denser materials.

### Isotropic and anisotropic materials

Some materials have the same physical properties in all directions. These are said to be isotropic. Materials whose properties vary with direction are anisotropic.

### Stress and strain

Stress is the amount of force acting on a particular area of a material. When stress causes a material to be deformed, the material is said to be under strain. Stress and strain can be due to tensile (pulling) or compressive (pressing) forces. They can also be caused by shear forces, which try to make adjacent layers of a material slide past each other.

### Strength

Strength is a measure of a material's resistance to failure such as breakage or deformation. Different modes of strength can be meaured, including tensile strength, compressive strength and shear strength.

### Brittle, tough and soft materials

Brittle materials tend to break straight away, without being deformed, if a sudden stress is applied to them. Tougher materials are better at resisting being broken when sudden stresses are applied, and can absorb energy before breaking. Soft materials tend to deform rather than breaking.

### Hardness

The hardness of a material is really a combination of other properties such as elasticity and toughness. The hardnesses of materials can be compared by dropping 'indenters' of a particular shape on to the material and studying the dent left, or by testing which materials will scratch others (see **Measurement: Scales**).

### Ductility and malleability

Ductility is the ability of a material to retain strength and freedom from cracks when its shape is altered, especially when it is drawn out into thin strands. Malleability is a measure of how easily a material can be beaten or hammered into a new shape. These terms are most often used to describe metals or alloys.

## Elasticity

A material is said to be elastic if returns to its original shape after being stretched, compressed or otherwise deformed. The amount of energy that a certain volume of an elastic material can absorb when it is deformed is called the resilience of the material (see **Key concepts: Hooke's law**).

### Young's modulus

Young's modulus is one of the most important elastic constants of materials. It is the ratio of the tensile stress to the tensile strain in a material. Elastic materials have a lower Young's modulus than stiff materials.

## Conductivity

Conductivity is a measure of how efficiently a material transmits something. Electrical conductivity concerns the transmission of electric charge, while thermal conductivity is a measure of how well a substance can transmit thermal energy and give out heat. Materials with high electrical conductivities tend also to have high thermal conductivities.

## Melting point

The melting point of a material is the temperature at which it begins to change state from a solid to a liquid.

## Chemical stability

Some materials are very unreactive, while others tend to take part in chemical reactions. Oxidation, a reaction with oxygen from the atmosphere, is a significant problem with some materials.

## Porosity

Materials that contain numerous small cavities tend to absorb water easily, and are described as porous.

## Magnetization

Some materials can become magnetic, either temporarily or permanently, when placed in a magnetic field, while others are spontaneously magnetic (see **Electricity and Magnets: Magnets**).

### ▬ *Magnetic Mapping* ▬

The beak of the homing pigeon, *Columba livia*, contains a magnetic material called magnetite. Biologists at the University of Auckland in New Zealand have shown that homing pigeons can detect magnetic fields, but that this ability is disrupted when small magnets are taped to their beaks. This evidence supports the idea that pigeons use an 'internal compass' to navigate using the Earth's magnetic field.

## METALS

Pure metals are used for many purposes, both decorative and practical. They tend to be dense and shiny, and they conduct heat and electricity efficiently. Most have a high melting temperature, although mercury is a liquid at room temperature. They are ductile and malleable; most are quite hard, though gold is very soft. Many metals oxidize easily, a process better known as rusting, but gold and platinum are unreactive. Iron, nickel and cobalt can become magnetic easily.

## ALLOYS

Alloys are a mixture of metals, or of metals with non-metals. They are usually made by adding other metals or non-metals to a liquid metal, which acts as a solvent. Alloys are stronger than their pure components; they usually have lower electrical conductivity and reduced ductility compared with their constituents. They melt over a temperature range rather than having a single melting point.

| Alloy | Composition | Uses and properties |
|-------|-------------|---------------------|
| Alnico® | Iron, nickel, aluminium, cobalt and copper | Magnets |
| Amalgam | Mercury and other metal | Dental fillings |
| Brass | Copper and zinc | Attractive appearance; musical instruments |
| Brazing solder | Copper, silver and zinc | Joining metal |
| Bronze | Copper and tin (now also other copper alloys) | |
| Cast iron | Iron, carbon (>2%) and cementite or graphite | Brittle and rusts easily; heavy saucepans and engine cylinder blocks |
| Chromel | Nickel and chromium | Heating elements |
| Constantan | Nickel and copper | Strain gauges |
| Cupronickel | Copper and nickel | Resistant to corrosion |
| Duralumin® | Aluminium and copper | |
| Ferro-alloy | Iron and another metal | |
| Gunmetal | Copper and tin or zinc | Resistant to corrosion and wear; gears, bearings etc |
| Invar® | Iron, nickel and carbon (heated) | Minimal temperature expansion; scientific instruments |
| Iridosmine | Iridium and osmium | Pen nib tips |
| Magnalium | Magnesium and aluminium | Aircraft construction |

| Alloy | Composition | Uses and properties |
|---|---|---|
| Manganin® | Copper, manganese and nickel | Resistors |
| Mischmetal | Cerium, rare-earth metals and iron | Sparking devices |
| Mumetal® | Nickel and other metals | Can be magnetized; transformer cores |
| Nichrome® | Nickel and chromium | High electrical resistance; heating elements |
| Pewter | Tin, copper, antimony and/or bismuth (formerly tin with lead) | Eating and drinking ware eg tankards |
| Phosphor-bronze | Copper, tin and phosphorus | Resists corrosion and wear; cast objects eg gears, bearings |
| Soft solder | Lead and tin | Joining metal |
| Speculum | Copper and tin | Mirrors and reflectors |
| White gold | Gold and nickel or palladium | Jewellery |
| Zircaloy | Zirconium, tin, iron and chromium | Cladding of nuclear reactors |

## International Alloys

Some alloys are named after places. Dutch gold contains copper and zinc, and is used as a substitute for gold leaf. German silver contains nickel as well as copper and zinc, and is whitish in colour. Corinthian bronze was said to be made from gold, silver and copper, and was much prized.

## STEEL

Steels are made from iron with a small proportion of carbon, and usually traces of other elements. The carbon hardens the steel by reducing the movement of iron atoms past one another. Varieties of steel include plain carbon steels, which contain traces of other elements despite their name, low-alloy steels and high-alloy steels. Stainless steel contains a relatively high proportion of chromium. Steels can be described by their carbon content.

### Mild steel

Mild steel contains less than 0.25% carbon. Low carbon steels are strengthened by deformation at relatively low temperatures, a process known as work-hardening.

### Medium-carbon steel

Medium-carbon steels contain 0.3–0.7% carbon. They can be strengthened by heat treatment; rapidly-cooled steel is stronger but more brittle than slowly-cooled steel.

A process called tempering or drawing can then be carried out, involving reheating to a lower temperature to reduce internal strain.

## High-carbon steel

High-carbon steel contains 0.8–2% carbon. Higher carbon steels are strengthened by heat treatment. They contain cementite, which makes them less ductile and more brittle. However, they retain sharp edges well, making them a good choice for the manufacture of cutting tools.

## CERAMICS

The term 'ceramics' originally referred to clay, but is now used to describe a wider range of materials that are neither metal nor organic. Ceramics are generally hard but are brittle rather than tough. Some have a regular, crystalline structure; the ones that do not are described as amorphous. Some important ceramics are described.

## Corundum

Corundum consists of aluminium oxide in a crystalline form. It is almost as hard as diamond while being much cheaper, so it is used as an abrasive.

### Costly Corundum

Sapphires, which can be blue, violet or even yellow, are clear forms of corundum, while rubies are clear red corundum.

## Boron nitride

Boron nitride is used in two forms. Borazon consists of a crystalline form of boron nitride, which is similar to diamond in terms of structure and hardness. It can withstand higher temperatures than diamond, so it is used for shaping tools as well as cutting diamonds. The other form of boron nitride is similar to the other form of carbon, graphite, and is used as a lubricant.

## Silicon-based ceramics

### Clay

Clay is made from granular deposits or sediments of hydrated aluminium silicates. The silicates can be amorphous or in crystalline form. Clay is sufficiently plastic to be moulded when wet but retains its shape when dried. When it is heated, it comes together to form a hard coherent mass without losing its shape, a process known as firing. Clay is used for making bricks, tiles and pots but must be glazed if it is to hold liquids, as it is porous.

### Glass

Glass is normally based on silicon dioxide, also known as silica, which is the main component of sand. The main characteristics of glasses are that they are amorphous, rather than crystalline, and that they have a property known as the glass transition temperature. Below this temperature they are hard, rigid and brittle, but above it they become softer and can be deformed. Glass can be made by cooling liquid silica so quickly that there is no opportunity for crystals to form, so that it retains the structural disorder of the liquid and remains amorphous.

## Precious Gems

Quartz is a crystalline form of silica. Many coloured varieties of quartz are used as gemstones, including amethyst (purple), cairngorm (brownish-yellow), citrine (yellow) and rose quartz (pink). The clear variety of quartz is known as rock crystal. Opal is a hydrated form of silica, and is much prized in its precious varieties as a gemstone.

## Structural Silica

Silica is important in biological structures. The cell walls of certain algae called diatoms are made of it, as are the skeletons of certain sponges and a type of plankton called radiolara. Silica is also found in the stems of horsetail plants.

## Portland cement

Portland cement is made from a mixture of about 75% limestone (calcium carbonate) and 25% clay (mostly aluminium silicate), which is fired and ground to produce a gravel containing various oxides. Water is added to make the cement. During the setting reaction, silica polymerizes to form an interlocking network of silica gel fibres around each cement particle. Various other minerals crystallize and interlock. The initial setting reaction is very rapid and is dependent on the particle size – the smaller the particles, the faster the cement sets. Cement has a high compressive strength, but it is porous and its tensile strength is low.

## Slow to Set

The setting reaction of cement is exothermic – it gives out a great deal of heat. Cement continues to harden at an increasingly slow rate for a long time after it is poured, and heat from the reaction can still be detected after 30 years.

## Sialons

Sialons are ceramics based on silicon nitride, in which a proportion of the silicon is replaced by aluminium and a proportion of the nitrogen by oxygen, to give a range of compositions. They are hard, tough and able to withstand high temperatures, so they are used for high-performance cutting tools, bearings, and internal combustion engines.

## Carbides

### Carborundum

Carborundum consists of silicon carbide, and is formed by fusing a mixture of carbon and sand or silica at high temperatures. It is very hard and can withstand high temperatures, so it is used as an abrasive and for lining furnaces. It can also act as a semiconductor (see **Electronics materials**).

### Boron carbide

Boron carbide is made by heating boron oxide and carbon at high temperatures. It is an extremely hard material; for this reason it is used as an abrasive in specialist cutting tools. It is also used in bullet-proof vests and tank armour.

## POLYMERS

Polymers are materials comprising long-chain molecules built up from a series of smaller molecules called monomers. Many polymers are made up of a single type of monomer; these are known as homopolymers, while those with more than one type are called co-polymers. Most polymers are organic, having a carbon backbone, but some are silicon-based and therefore inorganic.

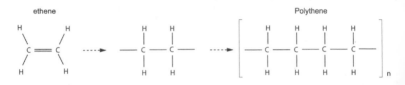

**Formation of Polythene from Ethene Monomers**

### Polymer properties

| | |
|---|---|
| **Conformation** | The alterable shape of the monomer, determined by rotations of the bonds. |
| **Configuration** | The fixed shape of the monomer, determined by the arrangement of the atoms. |
| **Branching** | The presence of side chains joined on to the main polymer chain. |
| **Degree of polymerization** | The number of monomers in one polymer chain. |
| **Cross-linking** | The joining of two polymer chains. |

### Types of polymer

#### Plastics

Plastics can be moulded or shaped at particular temperatures and pressures. They have low elasticity. Some plastics, called thermoplastics, can be reheated and reshaped many times. Others are treated to prevent this, and are known as thermosets or thermosetting plastics.

**Elastomers**

Elastomers have high elasticity and return to their original shape after being stretched. They are not as strong as plastics but some elastomers, notably natural and synthetic rubbers, can be strengthened by cross-linking with sulphur compounds, a process known as vulcanization.

**Fibres**

Fibres can be formed from plastics or elastomers, and are used as textiles. They have high tensile strength.

| Polymer | Monomer | Type | Example of use |
|---------|---------|------|----------------|
| Latex rubber | Isoprene | Elastomer | Car tyres, rubber gloves |
| Polythene (polyethylene)[1] | Ethene (ethylene) | Plastic | Packaging, insulation |
| Nylon (polyamide) | A diamine and a dicarboxylic acid | Plastic fibre | Textiles |
| Polystyrene | Styrene | Plastic | Packaging (expanded polystyrene), disposable foodware |
| PVC (polyvinyl chloride) | Vinyl | Plastic | Construction, packaging |
| Saran® (polyvinylidine chloride | Vinylidene chloride and vinyl chloride | Plastic | Food wrap |
| Polyurethane | Molecules containing urethane groups | Elastomer or plastic | Foam rubber; car body parts |

[1] Polythene is made in low density (LDPE) and high density (HDPE) forms. The former is used for thin sheets and films, while the latter is used where rigidity is important.

**Natural polymers**

Proteins are naturally occurring co-polymers. They are formed from the polymerization of 20 different monomers, known as amino acids (see **Atoms, elements and molecules: Amino acids**). Starch and cellulose are two polymers of glucose that have very different properties due to their different structures. Cellulose has long, unbranched chains that form strong fibres, and is insoluble in water and indigestible by humans. Starch has chains that can branch; it is water soluble, and is an important food source for humans.

## COMPOSITES

> Composite materials are made by combining two or more materials in order to utilize the desirable properties of each material.

### Glass-fibre reinforced plastic

Glass-fibre reinforced plastic (GFRP) consists of a plastic polymer matrix reinforced with fibres of glass, which are made by melting glass and drawing it out. Both the glass fibres and GFRP itself are referred to as fibreglass. GFRP is light, because the plastic matrix has low density, but the glass fibres give it additional strength.

### Concrete

Concrete is made from cement and aggregate, by adding water so that they set together. The aggregate contains sand and gravel. The most frequently used cement, especially in the UK, is Portland cement. The great advantage of concrete as an engineering material is that it remains pourable and workable during the first few hours of setting. It is widely used in civil engineering.

### Reinforced concrete

Reinforced concrete is made by pouring concrete around mild steel reinforcing bars, held together with links made from a soft mild steel. The steel bars are positioned to resist the tensile stresses in the structure, some of which can be the result of shear and bending, while the concrete resists loads in compression. In this way, reinforced concrete makes use of both the high tensile strength of steel and the high compressive strength of concrete.

### Cermets

Cermets are ceramics bonded with metal. They combine the hardness and high temperature characteristics of ceramics with the mechanical properties of metal. They are used to make electronics components, nuclear-reactor fuel rods and cutting blades.

## BIO-BASED MATERIALS

> Many materials are produced by, or made from, living organisms, both plants and animals.

| Plant-derived materials | Animal-derived materials |
| --- | --- |
| Cotton | Silk |
| Wood | Wool |
| Paper | Leather |
| | Bone |

### Cotton

Cotton fibre is almost entirely made out of cellulose. The cellulose polymer chains in cotton are highly crystalline, and are organized in fibrils. These line up along the fibres, giving them high tensile strength. Cotton fibres are short, so they must be spun into yarn before being woven into cloth. Both spinning and weaving increase the flexibility of the product, modifying a very stiff fibre for practical use.

# Wood

Wood is a cellular composite material that has a complex cellular structure and is highly anisotropic.

The cell wall structure of wood shares common features with cotton, but there are significant differences. Although a large proportion of the cell wall is made up of cellulose, the wall also contains significant amounts of a simpler polymer called hemicellulose and a tarry, aromatic compound called lignin. The hemicellulose mainly acts as the cement for the cellulose, while the lignin forms a hard layer around the outside of the cell wall. The high stiffness of wood relative to cotton is due to the higher content of hemicellulose and the presence of lignin.

### Hardwood

Hardwoods are close-grained woods that come from broad-leafed trees. They are generally dense and hard, but balsa is a relatively soft 'hardwood'. They are often used for furniture and flooring due to the fine appearance of the grain, but are generally slower-growing than softwood trees.

### Softwood

Softwoods come from conifers. Despite their name, they are not necessarily softer than hardwoods, as the categorization is on the basis of the source tree rather than physical properties of the wood (for example, yew is harder than most 'hardwoods'). Softwoods are often used for construction because they are easier to saw than hardwoods. They also grow more quickly, so large quantities can be used and replaced.

# Paper

Paper consists of a mat of cellulose fibres. Cellulose is a fibrous polymer made up of glucose units linked together through oxygen atoms. The source for paper-making is usually wood pulp, which is beaten in water to break down the cellulose fibres so that small fibrils splay out. The beaten material is spread out and drained. The properties of the resulting paper are determined by the beating stage, which controls the extent to which the cellulose fibres are broken down, as well as additives and coatings. The density, elasticity and strength of paper can all vary, as well as its colour, gloss, liquid absorbency and suitability for printing.

# Silk

Silk is a protein-based material obtained from the cocoon of silkworms, especially those of the moth *Bombyx mori*.

Silk fibres are composed of fibroin protein, which contains a regular pattern of the amino acids glycine, serine and alanine and forms into a long, continuous fibre with high tensile strength. The fibroin is surrounded by another protein, sericin, which forms a gum that is removed during wet processing.

## Sericulture

The breeding of silkworms for production of raw silk is called sericulture, named after the Chinese people known as the Seres, who produced silk in ancient times. The silk protein sericin and the amino acid serine are also named after the Seres.

### Wool

Wool is made up of fibres that are similar to hair, but are crinkled and have small scales covering their surfaces. Wool fibres contain a high proportion of keratin, a tough, fibrous protein that is also found in skin and nails. In wool, the keratin strands coil round each other to produce strong filaments, which are in turn linked together by bonds between sulphur atoms in the protein. The resultant fibres have high tensile strength, while the coils allow wool to stretch out because they can unwind. The crinkles in the wool, as well as the small scales covering the surface, help the fibres to latch on to one another when wool is spun. Wool is naturally surrounded by a waxy coating called lanolin, which makes it water-repellent.

### Leather

Leather is a material made by tanning and other treatment of hides or skins. The layer of the hide used for leather production is called the dermis, and lies underneath the outer surface or epidermis. The dermis contains densely interwoven fibres of a protein called collagen, which give leather both strength and flexibility. Other proteins such as keratin, as well as hair and other structures within the hide, are removed during the treatment process. The hide must undergo a process known as tanning, to prevent degradation of the collagen network while maintaining flexibility.

### Bone

Bone is a composite material, made up of inorganic material embedded in protein fibres. Most of the inorganic part of bone consists of a form of calcium phosphate called hydroxyapatite, but carbonate, citrate and fluoride compounds are also present. Hydroxyapatite has high compressive strength, although its tensile strength is low. The protein fibres in which these inorganic materials are embedded are made of collagen. These help to make bone less brittle. Long bones like the femur (thigh bone) are composed of a hard, compact composite outer layer surrounding a spongy interior called cancellous bone, which makes them lighter while maintaining strength.

## ELECTRONICS MATERIALS

### Semiconductors

Semiconductors can conduct electricity, but do so less efficiently than conductors such as metals. Their ability to conduct increases with temperature. Semiconductor materials are the basis of electronics components, including diodes, transistors, thyristors, photodiodes and all integrated circuits (see **Electricity and magnets: Electricity**).

## Silicon

Pure silicon acts as an inefficient semiconductor at room temperature. A small proportion of its electrons are able to move around, allowing transmission of negative charge. As the electrons move, they leave positively-charged 'holes' where electrons are missing.

## Doped semiconductors

The ability of silicon to act as a semiconductor can be greatly increased by a process called doping. This involves adding a small amount of a material, known as a dopant, that has either more or fewer electrons in its outside shell than silicon, which has four outer electrons (see **Atoms, elements and molecules: Atoms**). The two types of doping are n-doping and p-doping. Junctions between these types of semiconductor allow current to flow only in one direction, and form the basis of diodes and transistors.

| Type | Example of dopant | Outer electrons | Effect |
|------|-------------------|-----------------|--------|
| n-doping | Arsenic | 5 | Extra electrons |
| p-doping | Boron | 3 | Extra 'holes' |

silicon lattice     shared electrons        silicon lattice     shared electrons

Boron dopant nuclei     positive charges or holes       Arsenic dopant nuclei     free electrons

*p-type*                   *n-type*

## Superconductors

Superconductors are materials that are able to conduct electricity extremely well at very low temperatures, due to the effects of quantum mechanics (see **Key concepts: Quantum mechanics**). Some metals are superconductors, as well as many chemical compounds.

## Electric current

The resistance of a superconductor to the flow of electric current drops to zero below a critical temperature. In normal superconductors this temperature is very close to absolute zero, but some ceramics can act as superconductors at higher temperatures. Vibrations in the lattice structure of the superconductor, which normally interfere with current flow, cause electrons to pair up in an ordered

fashion. The electron pairs are then able to move around the whole material in an efficient, delocalized way, without losing any energy.

### Meissner effect

When a superconductor is placed in a magnetic field, an opposite magnetic field of the same strength is generated inside the superconductor. This is called the Meissner effect, after the German physicist Walter Meissner. This effect can be used to make a small magnet 'float' above a superconducting material under cold conditions.

# THE EARTH

## EARTH FACTS

### Time facts

| | |
|---|---|
| Age | 4.6 billion years |
| Period of axial rotation | 23 hours 56 minutes 4.0966 seconds |

### Distance facts

| | |
|---|---|
| Distance from Sun (mean) | 150 million km (93 million mi) |
| Aphelion: greatest distance from Sun | 152.1 million km (94.5 million mi) |
| Perihelion: smallest distance from Sun | 147.1 million km (91.4 million mi) |

### Size facts

| | |
|---|---|
| Surface area | 510 million km$^2$ (196 million sq mi) |
| Mass | 5 976 × 10$^{24}$ kg (13 175 × 10$^{24}$ lb) |
| Land surface (approximate) | 148 million km$^2$ (57 million sq mi) (approx 29% of total area) |
| Water surface (approximate) | 361.6 million km$^2$ (140 million sq mi) (approx 71% of total area) |
| Circumference (equator) | 40 076 km (24 902 mi) |
| Circumference (meridian) | 40 000 km (24 860 mi) |
| Diameter (equator) | 12 757 km (7927 mi) |
| Diameter (meridian) | 12 714 km (7900 mi) |

### Other facts

| | |
|---|---|
| Temperature at core | 4500°C (8100°F) |
| Surface gravity | 9.81 m s$^{-2}$ (32 ft/s$^2$) |

> *The only truly alien planet is Earth.*
> —British writer J G Ballard (b. 1930), 'Which Way to Inner Space?', in *New Worlds* (May 1962).

## THE EARTH'S HISTORY

The Earth was formed at the same time as the other planets of our solar system and the Sun from a condensing cloud of gas and dust called the solar nebula.

The matter in the solar nebula was drawn together by its own gravitational attraction. The most dense matter in the centre formed the Sun, while slowly rotating matter around the Sun accumulated to form the Earth and the other planets. The solar nebula was disc-shaped, which is why the planets now orbit the Sun more or less on the same plane.

### Hell on Earth

The first billion years of the Earth's existence is known as the Hadean ('hellish') period, because the planet was still hot and molten, and was bombarded with the remnants of the material that swirled around the Sun. Only after this time did it solidify and settle into a stable orbit around the Sun.

## GEOLOGICAL TIMESCALE

The various stages of the history of life on Earth are divided into aeons, based on fossil evidence and changes in climate. The aeons are further divided into eras, periods, series and sometimes stages. Three eras make up the most recent aeon, known as the Phanerozoic aeon. The most recent of these is the Cenozoic; further back in time are the eras known as Mesozoic and Palaeozoic. The period of time before the Phanerozoic aeon is called the Precambrian aeon, so named because it occurred before the earliest (Cambrian) period of the Palaeozoic era.

### Ages of Life

The names for the geological time periods come from ancient Greek. Phanerozoic means 'visible life', while Cenozoic, Mesozoic and Palaeozoic mean 'recent life', 'middle life' and 'old life'.

### Cenozoic era

The Cenozoic era (also Cainozoic or Kainozoic) is divided into two sub-eras, Tertiary and Quaternary. In the early part of the Tertiary sub-era, the plants and animals of the Cretaceous (see **Mesozoic era**) gave way to more modern forms, with mammals replacing reptiles as the dominant animals. Later, in the Miocene, large-scale earth movements built many of the mountain ranges of the world, followed by wide-scale volcanic activity. In the much shorter Quaternary, modern landscape and geography were laid down, and humans appeared and developed.

| Sub-era[1] | Period[2] | Series | Age[3] |
|---|---|---|---|
| Quaternary | | Holocene (recent) | 10 000 years ago to present day |
| | | Pleistocene | 1.64 Mya to 10 000 years ago |
| Tertiary | Neogene | Pliocene | 5.2–1.64 Mya |
| | | Miocene | 23.3–5.2 Mya |
| | Palaeogene | Oligocene | 35.4–23.3 Mya |
| | | Eocene | 56.5–35.4 Mya |
| | | Palaeocene | 65–56.5 Mya |

[1] Also known as Period

[2] Also known as Epoch

[3] Mya = million years ago

### Quaternary sub-era

The Quaternary sub-era was completely different from any previous period. It had a much shorter time span than any earlier period – less than two million years – but the period has exerted a profound influence on life: its processes and deposits have moulded the modern landscape and geography.

#### Climate of the Quaternary

Much of Britain and Europe were affected by glaciation, which also markedly influenced sea levels. Fluctuations in climate were used to sub-divide the Quaternary into many stages, which differ in name and typical climate around the world.

#### Animals of the Quaternary

Large mammals such as mastodons and woolly mammoths were present at the start of the Quaternary but became extinct during the late Pleistocene and early Holocene. The start of the Holocene marks the transition between the palaeolithic and mesolithic periods in the development of humans.

### Tertiary sub-era

The Tertiary sub-era derives its name from an old and disused division of all geological time into three parts. It forms the lower (older) part of the Cenozoic era and consists of five series or epochs: Palaeocene, Eocene, Oligocene, Miocene and Pliocene. The latter two form the Neogene period, while the first three form the Palaeogene period.

#### Neogene period

In the Neogene, the climate was generally temperate and warm, although it was

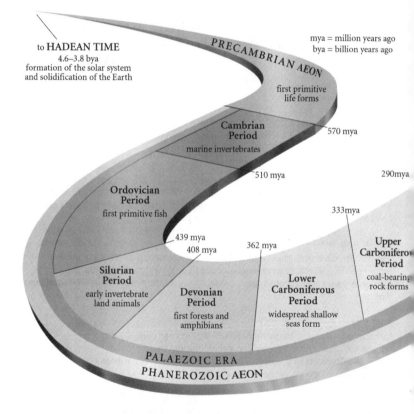

mya = million years ago
bya = billion years ago

PRECAMBRIAN AEON

to **HADEAN TIME**
4.6–3.8 bya
formation of the solar system
and solidification of the Earth

first primitive
life forms

**Cambrian
Period**

marine invertebrates

570 mya

510 mya

290mya

**Ordovician
Period**

first primitive fish

333mya

439 mya
408 mya

362 mya

**Upper
Carboniferous
Period**

coal-bearing
rock forms

**Silurian
Period**

early invertebrate
land animals

**Devonian
Period**

first forests and
amphibians

**Lower
Carboniferous
Period**

widespread shallow
seas form

PALAEZOIC ERA
PHANEROZOIC AEON

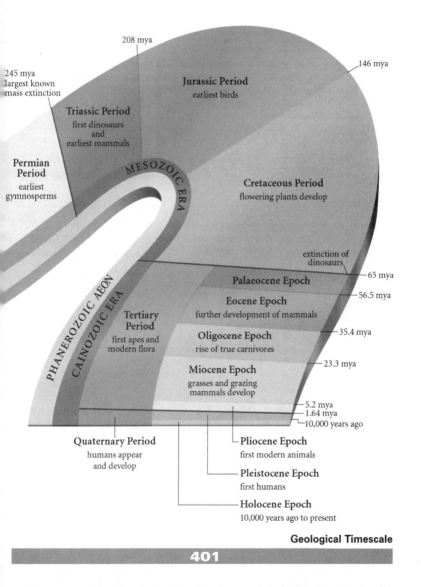

208 mya

245 mya
largest known
mass extinction

146 mya

**Jurassic Period**
earliest birds

**Triassic Period**
first dinosaurs
and
earliest mammals

**Permian
Period**
earliest
gymnosperms

MESOZOIC ERA

**Cretaceous Period**
flowering plants develop

PHANEROZOIC AEON

CAINOZOIC ERA

extinction of
dinosaurs

**Palaeocene Epoch** — 65 mya

— 56.5 mya

**Tertiary
Period**
first apes and
modern flora

**Eocene Epoch**
further development of mammals

**Oligocene Epoch**
rise of true carnivores

— 35.4 mya

— 23.3 mya

**Miocene Epoch**
grasses and grazing
mammals develop

— 5.2 mya
— 1.64 mya
— 10,000 years ago

**Quaternary Period**
humans appear
and develop

┘ **Pliocene Epoch**
first modern animals

— **Pleistocene Epoch**
first humans

— **Holocene Epoch**
10,000 years ago to present

**Geological Timescale**

cooler in the Pliocene of more northern latitudes. Earth movements, particularly during the Miocene, built many of the mountain ranges of the world including the Himalayas, Rockies and Alps.

## Palaeogene period

The Palaeogene had a temperate to warm climate and forests became widespread. There were many tremors and lava flows, especially during the Eocene, causing the formation of extensive series of dykes – vertical lava deposits rising up through rock.

## Plants and animals of the Tertiary

During the Tertiary, there was a very marked change from the flora (plant life) and fauna (animal life) of the earlier Cretaceous period to plants and animals with a closer resemblance to those of modern times. This was influenced by the mass extinction at the end of the Cretaceous. The first grasses appeared in the Eocene, and trees also thrived.

## Mesozoic era

Animals present during the Mesozoic era included spiral-shaped molluscs called ammonites, as well as reptiles and corals.

| Period | Series | Age[1] |
| --- | --- | --- |
| Cretaceous | Upper | 97–65 Mya |
| | Lower | 146–97 Mya |
| Jurassic | Upper (Malm) | 161–146 Mya |
| | Middle (Dogger) | 178–161 Mya |
| | Lower (Lias) | 208–178 Mya |
| Triassic | Upper | 210–208 Mya |
| | Middle | 241–210 Mya |
| | Lower | 245–241 Mya |

[1] Mya = million years ago

## Cretaceous period

The first flowering plants developed and spread during the Cretaceous period. A mass extinction occurred at the end of the Cretaceous, which marked the extinction of most birds, a large proportion of marine life and all remaining dinosaurs.

## Jurassic period

During the middle period, the Jurassic, there was diverse plant life in the warm climate, when reptiles, notably dinosaurs, were dominant on land.

## Triassic period

The earliest period, the Triassic, had an impoverished range of animals and plants that followed the extinctions at the end of the Palaeozoic era.

## Palaeozoic era

The Palaeozoic is the oldest of the Phanerozoic eras, stretching from the Cambrian to the present. Until this time, only primitive life forms such as bacteria, algae and sponges existed.

| Period | Age[1] |
| --- | --- |
| Permian | 290–245 |
| Upper Carboniferous | 333–290 |
| Lower Carboniferous | 362–333 |
| Devonian | 408–362 |
| Silurian | 439–408 |
| Ordovician | 510–439 |
| Cambrian | 570–510 |

[1] Mya = million years ago

### Permian and Carboniferous periods

The trilobites died out in the Permian, a period of desert conditions in Britain. During the Carboniferous there was rich plant life in parts of the world, but a glacial climate existed in other regions known as the Gondwana continents.

### Devonian and Ordovician periods

Amphibians evolved by the end of the Devonian. The Ordovician was a time of diverse sea life, including the first coral reefs.

### Cambrian period

The era began with the Cambrian period, when there was a sudden great expansion of animal life known as the 'Cambrian explosion'. Types of creature included small marine arthropods called trilobites, and molluscs; early plant life was also present.

## Precambrian aeon

The Precambrian is also known as the Cryptozoic, meaning 'hidden life'. The rocks that were formed during this time consisted of two divisions: the Archaean and the Proterozoic. There is still confusion about the naming of this period in time, but radio-carbon dating is now being used to determine the ages of rocks more accurately (see **Atoms, elements and molecules: Elements**).

| Division | Era | Age[1] |
| --- | --- | --- |
| Proterozoic | Vendian | 610–570 |
| | Riphean | 1650–610 |
| | Aphebian | 2500–1650 |
| Archaean | | 4600–2500 |

[1] Mya = million years ago

### Proterozoic division

The newer rocks formed during the Proterozoic age are sediments. In the most recent Proterozoic rocks there are impressions of soft-bodied animals and trace fossils (burrows and tracks) indicating a long period of earlier evolution. The algae are the only fossil group to have had a widespread development in the Precambrian.

### Archaean division

The older rocks of the Archaean age are a series of highly metamorphosed rocks, crystalline schists and gneisses (see **Rocks**). Primitive plant life existed well back into the Archaean, and bacteria may have existed as early as 3800 million years ago.

## FOSSILS

Fossils are produced when animals and plants decompose and become preserved within sedimentary rock.

Echinoderms
Marsupites

Trilobites
Ogygiocaris

Ammonites
Echioceras

Corals
Syringopora

**Examples of Fossils**

| Period | Fossil type |
| --- | --- |
| Cenozoic | Foraminifera (plankton) |
| Upper Cretaceous | Foraminifera, echinoderms, bivalves and belemnites |
| Lower Cretaceous | Ammonites |
| Jurassic | Ammonites plus ostracods (tiny crustacea) and bivalves |
| Triassic | Ammonites |
| Permian | Foraminifera, ammonites and goniatites (ammonite ancestors) |

| Period | Fossil type |
|--------|-------------|
| Carboniferous | Foraminifera, goniatites, fresh-water bivalves and plants |
| Lower Carboniferous | Corals and brachiopods |
| Devonian | Goniatites, fish and plants |
| Silurian | Graptolites (thin, branching, free-swimming, coral-like) |
| Ordovician | Graptolites, trilobites (small crustacea) |
| Cambrian | Trilobites and brachiopods |

## ICE AGES

At certain times during the Earth's history, a large proportion of the planet has been covered in ice. The major ice ages are listed below.

| Era | Part of Era |
|-----|-------------|
| Cenozoic era | Pleistocene (and Holocene?) |
| Palaeozoic era | Upper Carboniferous |
| Precambrian era | Upper Proterozoic |
| Precambrian era | Early Proterozoic |

### 'The Ice Age'

The most recent ice age, occurring during the Pleistocene in the Cenozoic era, is generally known as 'the Ice Age'. There is some controversy as to whether we are still at the very tail end of the Ice Age, as around a tenth of the planet is still covered in ice (mostly at the South Pole). Cycles of glaciation have occurred during this time, with glacial periods being interspersed with slightly warmer interglacial periods. Some of the most recent glacial periods of the Ice Age are given below.

| European Name | American Name | Time period |
|---------------|---------------|-------------|
| Würm | Wisconsinian | 40 000–18 000 years ago |
| Riss | Illinoian | 130 000–100 000 years ago |
| Mindel | Kansan | 430 000–370 000 years ago |
| Günz | Nebraskan | 520 000–490 000 years ago |

### Field Events

The Earth's magnetic field has reversed many times during the course of history. It is produced by electrical currents caused by movements of the molten metallic core. Studies on the solidified lava from past volcanic eruptions reveal this, because the magnetic constituents line up with the Earth's magnetic field at that time. These studies have shown that the average time between reversals of the magnetic field is 200 000 years, but the intervals have varied from only tens of thousands of years to as high as 30 million years.

## STRUCTURE OF THE EARTH

### Layers of the Earth's structure

The Earth is made up of a number of different layers. Seismic waves, such as are generated during earthquakes, have been used to study the internal structure of the Earth; the waves are bent and reflected differently according to the materials they pass through.

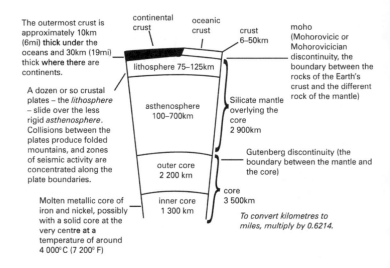

The outermost crust is approximately 10km (6mi) thick under the oceans and 30km (19mi) thick where there are continents.

A dozen or so crustal plates – the *lithosphere* – slide over the less rigid *asthenosphere*. Collisions between the plates produce folded mountains, and zones of seismic activity are concentrated along the plate boundaries.

Molten metallic core of iron and nickel, possibly with a solid core at the very centre at a temperature of around 4 000°C (7 200° F)

continental crust

oceanic crust

lithosphere 75–125km

asthenosphere 100–700km

outer core 2 200 km

inner core 1 300 km

crust 6–50km

Silicate mantle overlying the core 2 900km

core 3 500km

moho (Mohorovicic or Mohorovicician discontinuity, the boundary between the rocks of the Earth's crust and the different rock of the mantle)

Gutenberg discontinuity (the boundary between the mantle and the core)

*To convert kilometres to miles, multiply by 0.6214.*

The Earth's Structure

### The Earth's crust

In planetary terms, the surface rocks of the Earth are very young, with the basaltic rocks forming the ocean floors being among the youngest. The Precambrian shields, which occupy about 10% of the surface, are the oldest and the nearest approximation to the cratered terrain that forms a large part of other planetary surfaces. Weathering and erosion have removed all but a few traces of any impact craters that now remain. The Earth's crust is largely composed of silicon and oxygen, combined in the form of minerals called silicates. Other elements are also present – the varying quantities of these in the minerals gives them their different characteristics.

| Element | % weight |
|---------|----------|
| Oxygen | 46.60 |
| Silicon | 27.72 |
| Aluminium | 8.13 |
| Iron | 5.00 |
| Calcium | 3.63 |
| Sodium | 2.83 |
| Potassium | 2.59 |
| Magnesium | 2.09 |
| Others | 1.41 |

## THE ATMOSPHERE

### Layers of the atmosphere

The atmosphere is divided into several layers. The temperature varies through the different layers of the atmosphere. It is affected by convection (the flow of warm air upwards and cold air downwards) and also by the radiation of heat into the atmosphere from the Sun. The amount of thermal energy contained at any level depends on the pressure or density as well as the temperature; atmospheric pressure decreases with height.

### False Dawn

The ionosphere is formed from a layer of electrically charged particles from the Sun, at a height of 200–300km (120–190mi). The Earth's magnetic field guides these particles towards the polar regions, causing the luminous effects in the sky known as the *aurora*, named after the Latin word for 'dawn'. In the northern hemisphere, they are called *aurora borealis* (Northern lights), while in the southern hemisphere they are known as *aurora australis* (Southern lights). The aurora is strongest when the sun's activity is highest, when more charged particles are produced.

### Unsavoury Atmosphere

The Earth hasn't always had an oxygen-rich atmosphere; the first creatures that could produce oxygen and release it into the atmosphere appeared only approximately 1.5 million years after the Earth was formed. It is thought that the early atmosphere contained gases such as methane, carbon monoxide, ammonia and sulphur compounds, which are toxic to many of today's creatures.

### Thermosphere

Uppermost layer, in which the air is very 'thin' (at low density) and atmospheric pressure is only a millionth of a billionth of that at sea level. Temperature increases with height, and may reach 2000°C (3600°F).

Composed of the *ionosphere*, which reflects radio waves back to Earth enabling signals to be transmitted around the curved surface of the Earth, the *ionopause* transitional layer, and the *exosphere*, the outermost layer of the Earth's atmosphere, approximately 500km (300mi) above the surface, from which light gases can escape into space.

### Mesopause

Transitional layer between the mesosphere and the thermosphere, approximately 80–85km (50–55mi) above the surface. The minimum atmospheric temperature of approximately –100°C (–150°F) occurs in this layer, and atmospheric pressure is a hundred thousand times lower than at sea level.

### Mesosphere

Middle atmosphere, up to approximately 85km (55mi) above the surface. Temperature decreases with height.

### Stratopause

Transitional layer, approximately 50–55km (30–35mi) above the surface. The temperature is approximately 0°C (32°F).

### Stratosphere

Contains very few clouds. Aircraft usually fly in this layer above the weather disturbances in the troposphere. Temperatures increase with height, and typical pressure is only a hundredth of that on the surface. Also includes the ozone layer, approximately 20–40km (12–25mi) above the surface.

### Tropopause

Transitional layer, approximately 10km (6mi) above the surface. The temperature is approximately –60°C (–80°F).

### Troposphere

Lower part of the atmosphere, from the surface up to a height varying from approximately 9km (5mi) at the poles to 17km (10mi) at the equator. Contains almost all of the clouds. Temperature decreases with height.

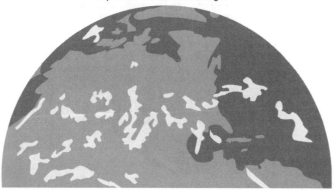

Note: diagram is not to scale

## Composition of the atmosphere

The Earth's atmosphere is composed of air, generally containing 78% nitrogen, 21% oxygen and 1% argon together with carbon dioxide, hydrogen, ozone and methane, and traces of the other rare gases. A variable amount of water vapour is present, depending on the temperature and humidity.

| Gas | % volume |
| --- | --- |
| Nitrogen | 78.1 |
| Oxygen | 20.95 |
| Argon | 0.934 |
| Carbon dioxide | 0.031 |
| Neon | 0.00182 |
| Helium | 0.00052 |
| Methane | 0.0002 |
| Krypton | 0.00011 |
| Hydrogen | 0.00005 |
| Nitrous oxide | 0.00005 |
| Ozone | 0.00004 |
| Xenon | 0.000009 |

## PLATE TECTONICS

### Mechanisms of plate tectonics

Plate tectonics is a widely accepted geological theory, developed in the late 1960s, according to which the Earth's crust is composed of a small number of large plates of solid rock, whose movements in relation to one another are responsible for continental drift (see **Key concepts: Continental drift**).

### Plate movements

According to the theory, the plates of the Earth's crust, which comprise the lithosphere, are floating on the moving molten rock (asthenosphere) that lies beneath. The plates move as a result of convection currents which occur deep within the mantle. New crust is formed at the edges of the plates where rising convection currents bring up new material from the mantle. Plate movements can cause earthquakes, as well as changes to the Earth's surface.

### Mountain ranges

Mountain ranges, eg the Himalayas, are formed when one crustal plate pushes into another, forcing the land upwards under great pressure.

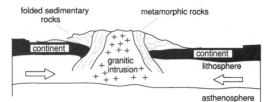

## Ocean floor

The ocean floor is extended when plates move apart.

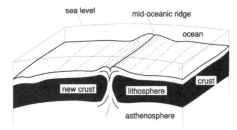

## Ocean trenches and island chains

Deep ocean trenches and volcanic island chains are formed by plate collisions when one plate pushes underneath the other.

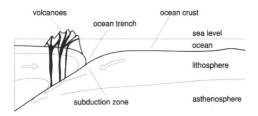

## Faults

Some plates are 'sliding' in relation to one another, causing huge fault systems, eg the San Andreas fault system in California. These are called transform faults.

## Distribution of plates

The major plates of the Earth and some of these associated features are shown below. The plates move away from the mid-oceanic ridges at divergent plate boundaries. The space between the separating plates is filled by volcanic rock, welling up from below to form new crust (new sea floor). While the sea-floor crust has been moving away from the mid-oceanic ridges, the polarity of the Earth's magnetic field has reversed many times, resulting in magnetic anomaly patterns in the new crust. There are also many transform faults across the axes of spreading.

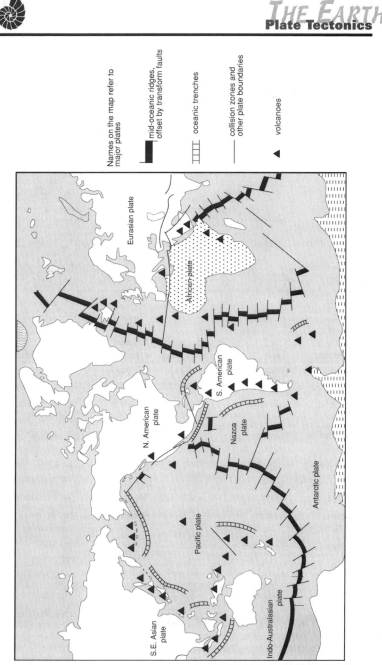

Names on the map refer to major plates

▬ mid-oceanic ridges, offset by transform faults

▭ oceanic trenches

— collision zones and other plate boundaries

▲ volcanoes

Eurasian plate

African plate

S. American plate

N. American plate

Nazca plate

Antarctic plate

Pacific plate

S.E. Asian plate

Indo-Australasian plate

**Plates of the Earth's Crust**

## MINERALS

Minerals are substances that occur naturally in the Earth's surface. Some are elements, while others are inorganic compounds. They exist in a number of crystal forms, which fit into the following crystal structures.

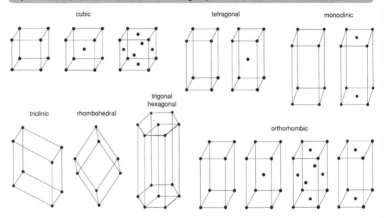

cubic    tetragonal    monoclinic

trigonal hexagonal

triclinic    rhombohedral

orthorhombic

| Mineral | Type | Mohs of hardness | Crystal structure | Appearance |
|---------|------|------------------|-------------------|------------|
| Talc | Silicate | 1 | Monoclinic | Pale green or grey, pearly lustre |
| Graphite | Element | 1–2 | Trigonal/ hexagonal | Grey metallic lustre |
| Glauconite | Silicate | 2 | Monoclinic | Shades of green |
| Gypsum | Sulphate | 2 | Monoclinic | White to transparent |
| Biotite | Silicate | 2.5–3 | Monoclinic | Dark colours |
| Mica | Silicate | 2.5–3 | Monoclinic | Brown or colourless |
| Calcite | Carbonate | 3 | Trigonal/ hexagonal | Double refraction |
| Barytes | Sulphate | 3–3.5 | Orthorhombic | Pale, translucent |
| Aragonite | Carbonate | 3.5–4 | Orthorhombic | Translucent white |
| Dolomite | Carbonate | 3.5–4 | Trigonal/ hexagonal | Pale, translucent |
| Fluorite | Halide | 4 | Cubic | Many colours, fluorescent |

| Mineral | Type | Mohs of hardness | Crystal structure | Appearance |
|---------|------|------------------|-------------------|------------|
| Apatite | Phosphate | 5 | Trigonal/ hexagonal | Usually green |
| Hornblende | Silicate | 5–6 | Monoclinic | Greens or browns |
| Pyroxene | Silicate | 5–6.5 | Various | Many colours |
| Sodalite | Silicate | 5.5–6 | Cubic | Blue |
| Plagioclase | Silicate | 6–6.5 | Triclinic | Very pale colours, vitreous lustre |
| Pyrite | Sulphide | 6–6.5 | Cubic | 'Fool's Gold' |
| Olivine | Silicate | 6.5–7 | Orthorhombic | Greens and browns |
| Quartz | Oxide | 7 | Trigonal/ hexagonal | Translucent, also microcrystalline |
| Garnet | Silicate | 7 | Cubic | Various forms, often plum red |
| Tourmaline | Silicate | 7–7.5 | Trigonal/ hexagonal | Often pink or green |
| Zircon | Silicate | 7.5 | Tetragonal | Often brown |
| Beryl | Silicate | 7–8 | Trigonal/ hexagonal | Many colours, emerald green |
| Spinel | Oxide | 7.5–8 | Cubic | Many colours, vitreous lustre |
| Corundum | Oxide | 9 | Trigonal/ hexagonal | Various forms including ruby and sapphire |
| Diamond | Element | 10 | Cubic | Transparent, sparkles if cut |

## ROCKS

### Sedimentary rocks

Sedimentary rocks result from the deposition of materials transported by water, wind or ice. Clastic rocks are the eroded remnants of earlier rocks; chemical sediments are formed from precipitation out of solution; organic sediments are formed from living material.

## Clastic rocks

| Rock | Description |
| --- | --- |
| Conglomerate | Large, rounded, cemented |
| Breccia | Coarse, angular, cemented |
| Gritstone | Coarse |
| Sandstone | Medium |
| Greensand | Greenish, due to glauconite content |
| Greywacke | Deep ocean sediments |
| Siltstone | Fine, with more quartz than shale |
| Loess | Fine, angular particles |
| Marl | Fine silt or clay with limestone cement |
| Shale | Very fine laminated clay and detritus |
| Mudstone | Clay and very fine grains cemented with iron or calcite |
| Clay | Very fine; absorbs water |

## Chemical sediments

| Sediment | Composition |
| --- | --- |
| Limestone | Calcium carbonate |
| Chalk | Soft white limestone, mostly microfossils |
| Tufa | Calcium carbonate; precipitated from fresh water |
| Dolomite | Calcium and magnesium carbonate |
| Ironstone | Limestone or chert enriched in iron, often Precambrian |
| Chert and flint | Hard silicon-containing nodules or sheets in chalk or limestone |

## Organic sediments

| Sediment | Composition |
| --- | --- |
| Peat | Plant material |
| Lignite | Soft, made up of carbon |
| Coal | Hard, brittle, made up of carbon |
| Jet | Hard, black, coal-like |

## Metamorphic rocks

Metamorphic rocks are produced when pressure and heat cause changes in existing rocks. Some principal metamorphic rocks are described below.

| Name | Texture | Origin |
|------|---------|--------|
| Slate | Aligned minerals produce perfect cleavage; not necessarily aligned with bedding | Sedimentary shale and clay |
| Phyllite | As slate, but coarser, with small-scale folding | Medium grain sediments |
| Schist | Flaky minerals such as mica give glittery, foliated texture | Sediments buried deep in mountain belts, eg siltstones |
| Gneiss | Medium/coarse grain; quartz, feldspar and mica with darker layers or lines | High pressure and temperature, from sediment or granite; abundant deep under continents |
| Migmatite | Mixture of dark schist and light granitic rock; highly folded | Extensive deep metamorphism of sediments |
| Eclogite | Coarse grain; mostly green pyroxene and red garnet | Very high temperature and pressure close to mantle |
| Amphibolite | Coarse grain; often foliated; mostly hornblende | Highly metamorphosed igneous dolorite |
| Marble | Crystalline, soft and sugary; made of calcium carbonate | Limestone heated by igneous intrusion |
| Hornfels | Fine grain; dark coloured with quartz, mica and pyroxene | Sediments closest to hot igneous intrusion |
| Quartzite | Medium grain; of even texture with fused quartz crystals; very hard | Sandy sediment heated by intrusion or regional metamorphism |
| Serpentinite | Coarse grain; green serpentine minerals | Intense metamorphism of olivine-rich rock |

## Igneous rocks

Igneous rocks result from volcanic activity in the Earth's crust and upper mantle. Principal igneous rocks are described below.

| Rock | Texture | Type | Composition | Origin |
|------|---------|------|-------------|--------|
| Granite | Coarse | Acid | >20% quartz, K-feldspars, mica | Intrusive batholiths |

| Rock | Texture | Type | Composition | Origin |
|------|---------|------|-------------|--------|
| Pegmatite | Coarse | Acid | >20% quartz, mica | Deep batholiths and dykes |
| Diorite | Coarse | Intermediate | Plagioclase feldspar and hornblende | Dykes associated with granite |
| Syenite | Coarse | Intermediate | Little or no quartz, otherwise like granite | Dykes and sills |
| Gabbro | Coarse | Basic | Plagioclase, pyroxene and olivine | Large layered intrusions |
| Larvikite | Coarse | Intermediate | Feldspar crystals with pyroxene, mica and amphibolite banks | Small sills |
| Anorthosite | Coarse | Basic | >90% plagioclase feldspar | Layered intrusions, on Moon |
| Dolerite | Medium | Basic | <10% quartz with plagiocase and pyroxene | Dykes and sills near basalt |
| Dunite | Medium | Ultra-basic | Almost entirely olivine | Deep sourced intrusions |
| Kimberlite | Coarse | Ultra-basic | Dense ferro-magnesian minerals | Pipes of deep ancient volcanoes |
| Peridotite | Coarse | Ultra-basic | No quartz or feldspar, mostly olivine and garnet | Caught up in intrusions |
| Rhyolite | Fine | Acid | As granite | Explosive volcanic eruptions |
| Obsidian | Glassy | Acid | Silica-rich glass | Rapid cooling of acid lava |
| Lamprophyre | Medium | Acid to basic | Amphibole pyroxene and biotite | Dykes and sills around granite |
| Andesite | Fine | Intermediate | Mainly plagioclase | Volcanoes above subduction zones |
| Trachyte | Fine | Intermediate | <10% quartz, rich in alkali feldspar | Lava flows, dykes and sills |
| Basalt | Fine | Basic | Plagioclase and pyroxene | Volcanic eruptions |

| Rock | Texture | Type | Composition | Origin |
|------|---------|------|-------------|--------|
| Tuff | Fine | Acid to basic | Consolidated volcanic fragments | Thrown out by volcanic vents |
| Pumice | Fine | Acid to basic | Glass and minute silicate crystals | Rapidly quenched frothy lava |

# CLIMATE AND ENVIRONMENT

## BIOSPHERE

The whole of the environment in which life can flourish is known as the biosphere. It consists of three main parts: the atmosphere, the hydrosphere and the lithosphere.

| Name | Description |
| --- | --- |
| Atmosphere | The air surrounding the Earth |
| Hydrosphere | All the water on the surface of the Earth |
| Lithosphere | The crust of the Earth, including the surface and deeper down |

## BIOMES, ECOREGIONS AND HABITATS

Biomes and ecoregions are terms used to describe regions of the biosphere that are characterized by their physical features and the species that live there. The use of these classifications varies, but some broad categories are listed. Each species has a particular habitat, a place that meets its environmental requirements, which is found within a biome or an ecoregion.

### Desert

Deserts are extremely dry, harsh environments and only well-adapted plants and animals are able to flourish there. They are covered with sand, stones or rocks. Hot dry deserts, such as the Sahara (North Africa) and the Kalahari (south-western Africa), have infrequent rainfall. Cold deserts, such as the Gobi (Mongolia and China) and the Atacama (Chile), experience their precipitation as snow rather than rainfall.

### Tundra

Tundra describes vast, relatively flat zones, with permanently frozen subsoil. Its vegetation consists of dwarf trees and shrubs, grasses, sedges, mosses and lichens. Areas of tundra are found mainly in the Arctic regions of Alaska, northern Canada, and Siberia, but also on the fringes of the Antarctic region.

### Taiga

Taiga describes areas of pine forest that spread across much of subarctic North America and Eurasia, with tundra to the north and steppe to the south. It is also known as Boreal forest or coniferous forest.

### Broad-leaf and mixed forest

Broad-leaf and mixed forests occur in temperate areas of the world, such as Europe, North America and parts of Russia, China and Japan. Many of the trees are deciduous, dropping their leaves as they become dormant for the winter. The forest floor is mainly covered in undergrowth.

### Temperate rainforest

Some areas of the world have temperate rain forests, which occur in mountainous land near the coast. These have a higher rainfall than other temperate forests. Temperate rain forests are found in South America, the Pacific coast of North America, eastern Europe, Australia, New Zealand and Japan.

### Tropical rainforest

Tropical rainforests contain very tall trees that form a dense canopy. This blocks most light from reaching the forest floor, so tropical rainforests have very little undergrowth. They support an incredible diversity of plant and animal species. Tropical rainforests are mainly found in tropical Asia, Africa and South America.

> ## Nature's Pharmacy
>
> Many drugs have been developed from tropical rainforest plants. These include the anti-malarial drug quinone from the bark of the yellow cinchona, the breast cancer treatment taxol from the bark of the Pacific yew, and the anti-leukaemia drug vincristine from the rosy periwinkle. But the pharmacy may be closing early – the rosy periwinkle is already extinct in the wild due to deforestation for timber.

### Scrublands

Scrublands are covered with low-growing shrubs and stunted trees. The land can be flat or mountainous. Scrublands are known by different names in different parts of the world.

| Name | Location |
| --- | --- |
| Chaparral | North America |
| Fynbos | South Africa |
| Mallee | Australia |
| Maquis | Europe |
| Matorral | Chile |

### Grasslands

Grasslands can be found in many parts of the world, and have different names. They are found in both temperate and tropical climates.

| Name | Location |
| --- | --- |
| Pampas | South America |
| Prairie | North America |
| Savanna | Africa |
| Steppe | Asia and central Europe |
| Veld or veldt | South Africa |

## Wetlands

Wetlands are waterlogged spongy areas of land. Some wetlands are permanent, while others are seasonal. They include bogs, marshes, moors, fenland and swamps.

## Aquatic ecoregions

Aquatic ecoregions include both marine (salt water) and freshwater areas. There is variation in how aquatic ecoregions are described: some people consider that there is an aquatic biome, while others divide this into a marine biome and a freshwater biome. Yet another group of people have the view that biomes are land-based zones and that aquatic zones should not be described in terms of biomes.

### Marine ecoregions

Marine ecoregions include coral reefs, where the water is warm and shallow, river estuaries, and oceans. The open ocean can be divided into three main zones: pelagic, benthic and abyssal. The parts where there is enough light for photosynthesis are described as photic or euphotic, while the deeper, darker parts are described as aphotic.

| Ecoregion | Description | Examples of organisms |
|---|---|---|
| Coral reef | Warm shallow sea surrounding the reef | Coral, fish, molluscs, sea stars |
| Estuary | Brackish water at the mouth of a river | Wading birds, small fish, plants, molluscs and crustaceans |
| Ocean – Pelagic | Open ocean, near the surface; the upper part includes the photic zone | Fish, marine mammals, seaweed, plankton |
| Ocean – Benthic | Deep sea and ocean floor | Sponges, sea stars, anenomes, microorganisms |
| Ocean – Abyssal | Ocean trenches | Invertebrates, ancient fish, sulphur-metabolizing bacteria |

### Freshwater ecoregions

Freshwater ecoregions include lakes and rivers. Xeric (dry) basins do not have much permanent surface freshwater but tend to have freshwater springs. Many types of organism live in freshwater ecoregions, including plants, mammals, birds, amphibians and fish.

## Endolithic ecoregion

The endolithic ecoregion has only recently been discovered. It consists of cracks in the rock deep down in the Earth's crust, where specialized microorganisms can live. These include bacteria and algae.

## CLIMATIC ZONES

> The earth may be divided into zones, approximating to zones of latitude, such that each zone possesses a distinct type of climate.

### Tropics

The tropics are a single zone of wet climate near the equator. The climate may be constantly wet, or it may be monsoonal (with wet and dry seasons). The tropical savanna has dry winters. The average temperature is not below 18°C (65°F).

| | |
|---|---|
| Amazon forest | Congo Basin |
| Malaysia | Indonesia |
| South Vietnam | South-East Asia |
| India | Australia |
| Africa | |

### Subtropical zones

The subtropical zones are two zones of steppe and desert climate (transition through semi-arid to arid).

| | |
|---|---|
| Sahara | Australia |
| Central Asia | Kalahari |
| Mexico | |

### Mediterranean zones

The Mediterranean zones have a rainy climate with mild winters; the coolest month has temperatures above 0°C (32°F) but below 18°C (65°F).

| | |
|---|---|
| California | Parts of Chile |
| South Africa | South-West Australia |
| Southern Europe | |

### Temperate zones

Temperate zones have a rainy climate, including areas of temperate woodland, mountain forests, and plains with no dry season. They are influenced by seas, and experience rainfall all year and only small changes in temperature. The average temperature is between 3°C (37°F) and 18°C (65°F).

| Most of Europe | New Zealand |
| --- | --- |
| Asia | Parts of Chile |
| North-West and North-East USA | |

### Boreal zones

Boreal zones are found in the northern hemisphere, and have a climate with a great range of temperature. In some areas the most humid month is in summer and there is ten times more precipitation than the driest part of winter. In other areas the most humid month is in winter and there is ten times more precipitation than in the driest part of summer. In the coldest period, temperatures do not exceed 3°C (37°F); in the hottest period, temperatures do not drop below 10°C (50°F).

| Prairies of USA | Parts of Russia |
| --- | --- |
| Parts of South Africa | Parts of Australia |

### Polar caps

The polar caps consist of tundra and ice-cap, and have a snowy climate with little or no precipitation. There is permafrost in the tundra; vegetation includes lichen and moss all year and grass in the summer. The highest annual temperature in the polar regions is below 0°C (32°F), while in the tundra the average temperature is 10°C (50°F).

| Arctic regions of Russia and North America |
| --- |
| Antarctica |

## CYCLES OF LIFE

A number of cycles operate in the biosphere to circulate substances needed for life. For this reason, some people view the biosphere as being like a living organism itself (see **Key concepts: Gaia hypothesis**).

### Nitrogen cycle

The nitrogen cycle is the continuous circulation of nitrogen and its compounds between the Earth and its atmosphere, resulting from the activity of living organisms.

Nitrogen taken up by plants is incorporated into proteins, and when such plants are subsequently eaten by animals, it is incorporated into animal protein. The waste products of animals, together with the decomposing remains of dead plants and animals, are broken down by nitrifying bacteria to form ammonia. Ammonia is oxidized by other bacteria firstly to nitrites and then to nitrates in a process known as nitrification. The ammonia and nitrates may be used as plant nutrients. Nitrates are also converted to molecular nitrogen (which is released back to the atmosphere) by bacteria that live in waterlogged soils, in a process known as denitrification.

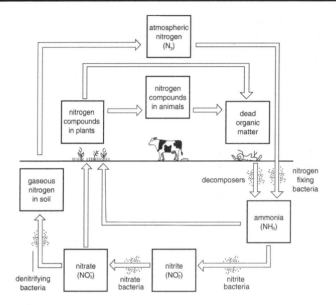

## Carbon cycle

The carbon cycle is the biological circulation of carbon from the atmosphere into living organisms and, after their death, back again. Plants acquire carbon from the atmosphere by photosynthesis (see **Cells: Photosynthesis**), while plants and animals release carbon back to the atmosphere by respiration (see **Cells: Respiration**). The consumption of plants by animals and the decomposition of dead organisms are also part of the cycle.

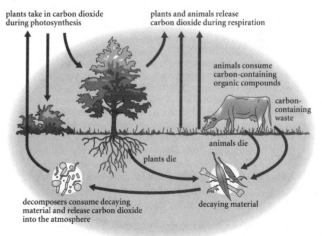

plants take in carbon dioxide during photosynthesis

plants and animals release carbon dioxide during respiration

animals consume carbon-containing organic compounds

carbon-containing waste

animals die

plants die

decomposers consume decaying material and release carbon dioxide into the atmosphere

decaying material

## Hydrological cycle

The hydrological cycle is the circulation of water between the Earth's surface and the atmosphere. Water moves from mountain streams to the sea, travelling along rivers. Evaporation from seas and lakes moves water into the atmosphere, where it condenses to form clouds. Plants also lose water to the atmosphere; this is known as transpiration.

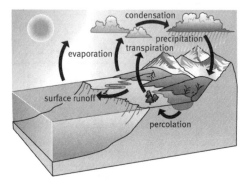

## OZONE LAYER

The ozone layer is a region of the atmosphere where ozone makes up a greater proportion of the air than at any other height. It is located in the stratosphere, between about 20 and 40km (12 and 25mi) above the Earth's surface.

### Importance of the ozone layer

Although the proportion of ozone in the ozone layer is still only a few parts per million, it is extremely important for the environment. It absorbs much of the ultraviolet radiation in sunlight, preventing it from reaching the Earth's surface, where it would otherwise damage living organisms.

### Formation and removal of ozone

Ozone is a triangular molecule consisting of three oxygen atoms. It is formed from oxygen molecules by complex reactions driven by ultraviolet light; this occurs mainly in the tropical stratosphere but atmospheric turbulence distributes the molecules throughout the ozone layer. Ozone is removed from the atmosphere mainly by chain reactions that are sped up by active chlorine- and bromine-based 'free radicals'.

## CHEMICAL IMBALANCES

Human activities can cause an imbalance in the amounts of naturally occurring substances.

### Ozone

Release of man-made pollutants has increased the supply of free radicals in the atmosphere. These molecules can initiate thousands of ozone-destroying cycles before they are themselves removed. The imbalance between formation and destruction of ozone that this has caused has contributed to the development of a hole in the ozone layer over Antarctica. Pollutants of this type include the refrigerants and aerosol propellants known as CFCs (chlorofluorocarbons).

## Carbon dioxide

Carbon dioxide occurs naturally – it is a product of respiration. The level of carbon dioxide should be kept in balance, as plants and trees take it up through photosynthesis. However, the burning of fossil fuels, which are formed from fossilized plants and animals, alters this balance because carbon that has been stored for a long time is released as carbon dioxide in a short time, increasing the amount present in the atmosphere.

## Greenhouse effect

A layer of carbon dioxide, water vapour and other gases in the atmosphere acts somewhat like a greenhouse, trapping heat from the Sun near the Earth's surface. An increase in this greenhouse effect, due mainly to increased carbon dioxide release, is thought to be an important factor in global warming – the gradual rise in temperature of the atmosphere and oceans. CFCs also act as 'greenhouse gases'.

## Acid rain

Nitrogen oxides and sulphur dioxide occur naturally in small quantities due to lightning and volcanic activity. However, levels have increased substantially due to emissions from the burning of fossil fuels. These oxides dissolve in water, leading to increased acidity in rainwater. Acid rain is implicated in damage to forests and the stonework of buildings, and increases the acid content of soils and lakes, harming crops and fish.

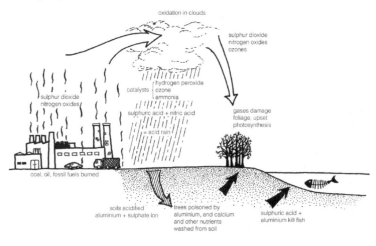

## CLOUDS

Clouds are formed by the condensation or freezing of water vapour on minute particles in the atmosphere. They play an important role in regulating climate, by absorbing and reflecting certain parts of the Sun's radiation. Cloud formation occurs when air masses move upward as a result of convection currents, unstable conditions, etc, and in so doing cool rapidly.

### Types of clouds

Clouds are usually classified into ten main types according to their height and shape.

Meteorologists use feet to measure cloud height; to convert to metres, multiply by 0.3048.

### Low clouds

The base of low clouds is usually surface–7000ft.

**Stratus (St)**

Cloud base: usually surface–1500ft.

Colour: usually grey.

**Cumulonimbus (Cb)**

Cloud base: usually 1000–5000ft.

Colour: white above with dark underside.

**Cumulus (Cu)**

Cloud base: usually 1200–6000ft.

Colour: white in sunlight but dark underside.

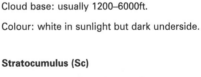

**Stratocumulus (Sc)**

Cloud base: usually 1200–7000ft.

Colour: grey or white, with shading.

### Medium clouds

The base of medium clouds is usually 7000–17 000ft, although Nimbostratus may be much lower.

**Nimbostratus (Ns)**

Cloud base: usually 1500–10 000ft.

Colour: dark grey.

### Altocumulus (Ac)

Cloud base: usually 7000–17 000ft.

Colour: grey or white, with shading.

### Altostratus (As)

Cloud base: usually 8000–17 000ft.

Colour: greyish or bluish.

## High clouds

The base of high clouds is usually 17 000–35 000ft. High clouds are composed of ice crystals.

### Cirrus (Ci)

Cloud base: usually 17 000–35 000ft.

Colour: white.

### Cirrocumulus (Cc)

Cloud base: usually 17 000–35 000ft.

Colour: white.

### Cirrostratus (Cs)

Cloud base: usually 17 000–35 000ft.

Colour: white.

## Clouds and temperature

Low cumulus and cumulonimbus clouds reflect the Sun's heat and light radiation – that is why they are bright on top but dark underneath. Their reflection of heat reduces the temperature at the Earth's surface. High cirrus clouds trap radiation that is reflected from the Earth's surface, so they keep the surface warm.

## Global dimming

Global dimming describes a reduction in the amount of light that reaches the Earth's surface. It is thought to occur due to pollutant particles such as soot, which can reduce the size of water droplets in clouds. Clouds that contain a larger number of smaller droplets can reflect a greater proportion of sunlight, reducing the amount that reaches the Earth.

# SPACE

## THE SUN

The Sun is a typical, average-sized star. The layer we see is the photosphere, the lowest layer of the solar atmosphere. Above the photosphere lies the chromosphere, which is about 10 000km thick and is visible as a pinkish glow during a total solar eclipse. The outermost layer is the corona.

### Composition of the Sun

The Sun consists of nearly 75% hydrogen, 25% helium and about 1% heavier elements. It is effectively a nuclear reactor – the high temperatures at its core allow nuclear fusion of hydrogen to make helium. This produces the Sun's energy (see **Energy, light and radioactivity: Nuclear reactions**).

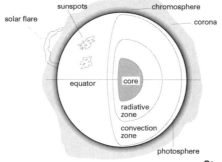

**Structure of the Sun**

### Activity of the Sun

The activity of the sun varies, and this causes various detectable events.

#### Sunspots

Sunspots are cool dark regions (4500K, 4200°C, 7600°F) in the photosphere that can last a few hours or several months. They are caused by fluctuations in the Sun's magnetic field. The number of sunspots rises and falls in a cycle of approximately 11 years, affecting the Earth's atmosphere and therefore telecommunications.

#### Solar flares

Solar flares are bright hydrogen arcs which emit ultraviolet radiation and X-rays (see **Energy, light and radioactivity: Electromagnetic radiation**). They are usually associated with sunspots, and may be accompanied by magnetic storms on the Earth and by the aurora (see **The Earth: The atmosphere**).

#### Solar wind

The solar wind is a steady flow of matter from the corona and is responsible for keeping the tails of comets always pointing away from the Sun.

**Greater Gravity**

Gravity at the surface of the sun is 274 m/sq sec (900 ft/sq sec) – 28 times higher than gravity on earth.

## Time facts

| | |
|---|---|
| Age | 4.6 billion–4.7 billion years |
| Predicted total lifespan | 10 billion years |
| Time taken for Sun to rotate on its axis | 26.8 days (of solar equator, as seen from Earth) |
| Time taken for Sun to travel round galaxy | 220 million years |

## Distance facts

| | |
|---|---|
| Distance from Earth (mean) | 150 million km (93 million mi) |
| Distance from centre of galaxy | 25 000 light years |

## Size facts

| | |
|---|---|
| Diameter | 1 392 500km (864 950mi) |
| Surface area | 6087 billion sq km (2350 billion sq mi) |
| Volume | $1.4122 \times 10^{18}$ cu km ($3.388 \times 10^{17}$ cu mi) |
| Mass | $1.989 \times 10^{30}$ kg ($4.385 \times 10^{30}$ lb) |

## Density facts

| | |
|---|---|
| Mean density | $1.409 \, \text{g cm}^{-3}$ (87.96 lb/cu ft) |
| Density at centre | $150 \, \text{g cm}^{-3}$ |
| Density of photosphere (surface) | $10^{-3} \, \text{g cm}^{-3}$ |
| Density of chromosphere | $10^{-6} \, \text{g cm}^{-3}$ |

## Heat and light facts

| | |
|---|---|
| Luminosity | $3.83 \times 10^{27}$ kW |
| Core temperature | 15 million K (15 million°C, 27 million°F) |

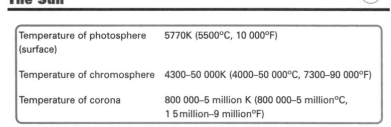

| Temperature of photosphere (surface) | 5770K (5500°C, 10 000°F) |
| --- | --- |
| Temperature of chromosphere | 4300–50 000K (4000–50 000°C, 7300–90 000°F) |
| Temperature of corona | 800 000–5 million K (800 000–5 million°C, 1 5 million–9 million°F) |

## Solar eclipses

The eclipse begins in the first country named. In an annular eclipse, the apparent size of the Moon is too small for a total eclipse and a bright ring of the Sun remains visible. Eclipse data is given for the years 2001–20.

| Date | Type of eclipse | Visibility path |
| --- | --- | --- |
| 21 Jun 2001 | Total | Southern Atlantic Ocean, southern Africa, Madagascar |
| 14 Dec 2001 | Annular | Pacific Ocean, Central America |
| 10 Jun 2002 | Annular | Indonesia, Pacific Ocean, Mexico |
| 4 Dec 2002 | Total | Southern Africa, Indian Ocean, Australia |
| 31 May 2003 | Annular | Iceland, Greenland (Denmark), Scotland (UK) |
| 23 Nov 2003 | Total | Antarctica |
| 8 Apr 2005 | Annular/Total | Pacific Ocean, Panama, Venezuela |
| 3 Oct 2005 | Annular | Atlantic Ocean, Spain, Libya, Indian Ocean |
| 29 Mar 2006 | Total | Atlantic Ocean, Libya, Turkey, Russia |
| 22 Sep 2006 | Annular | Guyana, Atlantic Ocean, Indian Ocean |
| 7 Feb 2008 | Annular | Antarctica |
| 1 Aug 2008 | Total | Arctic, Siberia (Russia), China |
| 26 Jan 2009 | Annular | Southern Atlantic Ocean, Indian Ocean, Borneo (Indonesia) |
| 22 Jul 2009 | Total | India, China, Pacific Ocean |
| 15 Jan 2010 | Annular | Africa, Indian Ocean, China |
| 11 Jul 2010 | Total | Pacific Ocean, southern Chile |
| 20–21 May 2012 | Annular | China, North Pacific, North America |
| 13 Nov 2012 | Total | North Australia, Pacific |
| 9–10 May 2013 | Annular | Australia, Pacific |
| 3 Nov 2013 | Total | Atlantic, Central Africa, Ethiopia |
| 20 Mar 2015 | Total | North Atlantic, Arctic |
| 9 Mar 2016 | Total | Indonesia, Pacific |
| 1 Sep 2016 | Annular | Atlantic, Africa, Madagascar, Indian |

| | | Ocean |
|---|---|---|
| 26 Feb 2017 | Annular | Pacific, South America, Atlantic, Africa |
| 21 Aug 2017 | Total | Pacific, North America, Atlantic |
| 2 Jul 2019 | Total | Pacific, South America |
| 26 Dec 2019 | Annular | Middle East, Sri Lanka, Indonesia, Pacific |
| 21 Jun 2020 | Annular | Africa, Middle East, China, Pacific |
| 12 Dec 2020 | Total | Pacific, South America, Atlantic |

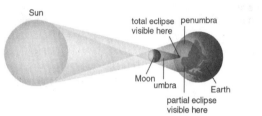

**Solar Eclipse**

## THE SOLAR SYSTEM

For satellites, the first figure gives the total number. The names of the major satellites are listed with those closest to the planet first; the years of discovery are given in parentheses. (See also **The Earth: Earth facts**.)

S = Sun
1 = Mercury
2 = Venus
3 = Earth
4 = Mars
5 = Jupiter
6 = Saturn
7 = Uranus
8 = Neptune
9 = Pluto

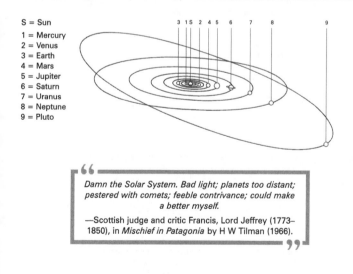

> *Damn the Solar System. Bad light; planets too distant; pestered with comets; feeble contrivance; could make a better myself.*
>
> —Scottish judge and critic Francis, Lord Jeffrey (1773–1850), in *Mischief in Patagonia* by H W Tilman (1966).

## Mercury

Mercury was known in prehistoric times. It was named after the Roman god of merchants, the messenger of the gods, possibly because of its fast movement.

| | |
|---|---|
| Diameter at equator | 4878 km (3031 mi) |
| Maximum distance from the Sun | 69.4 million km (43 million mi) |
| Minimum distance from the Sun | 46.8 million km (29 million mi) |
| Length of year | 88 days |
| Length of day | 58 days 16 hours |
| Atmosphere | Almost none; traces of oxygen, sodium, and helium |
| Surface gravity | $3.7\,m\,s^{-2}$ (12.2 ft/sq sec) |
| Rings | None |
| Satellites | None |

### Hot and Cold

In 1991, radar observations led scientists at the California Institute of Technology to propose that Mercury may have water ice at its north pole. The Sun is low in the sky at the poles, and there are craters whose sides are shaded from it where the ice could form. These areas can have temperatures as low as –150°C (–235°F), in contrast to the 425°C (800°F) temperatures in the hottest parts of the planet. The ice may have come from comets or from gas inside the planet.

## Venus

Venus was known in prehistoric times. It was named after the Roman goddess of love, because of its brightness. Most of its surface features are named after female figures.

### Sultry Venus

Venus has an extreme greenhouse effect due to the high concentrations of carbon dioxide in its atmosphere. The surface temperature reaches 450°C (840°F) – this is hotter than Mercury's surface, even though Venus is further from the Sun.

| Diameter at equator | 12 104 km (7521 mi) |
| --- | --- |
| Maximum distance from the Sun | 109 million km (67.6 million mi) |
| Minimum distance from the Sun | 107.6 million km (66.7 million mi) |
| Length of year | 224.7 days |
| Length of day | 243 days |
| Atmosphere | Mainly carbon dioxide and nitrogen; clouds of sulphuric acid |
| Surface gravity | 8.87 m s$^{-2}$ (29 ft/sq sec) |
| Rings | None |
| Satellites | None |

### Earth

See **The Earth: Earth facts**.

### Mars

Mars was known in prehistoric times. It was named after the Roman god of war, because of its red colour.

| Diameter at equator | 6794 km (4222 mi) |
| --- | --- |
| Maximum distance from the Sun | 249.2 million km (154.5 million mi) |
| Minimum distance from the Sun | 207.3 million km (128.5 million mi) |
| Length of year | 687 days |
| Length of day | 24 hours 37 minutes 23 seconds |
| Atmosphere | Carbon dioxide, nitrogen, argon |
| Surface gravity | 3.71 m s$^{-2}$ (12.2 ft/sq sec) |
| Rings | None |
| Satellites | 2: Phobos (1877), Deimos (1877) |

## Jupiter

Jupiter was known in prehistoric times. It was named after the Roman god of the sky and its attributes.

| | |
|---|---|
| Diameter at equator | 142 800 km (88 700 mi) |
| Maximum distance from the Sun | 817.4 million km (506.8 million mi) |
| Minimum distance from the Sun | 741.6 million km (459.8 million mi) |
| Length of year | 11.86 years |
| Length of day | 9 hours 50 minutes 30 seconds |
| Atmosphere | Mainly hydrogen and helium |
| Surface gravity | $20.87\,\mathrm{m\,s^{-2}}$ (68.5 ft/sq sec) |
| Rings | Yes |
| Satellites | Almost 60: Io (1610), Europa (1610), Ganymede (1610) and Callisto (1610) |

### Almost a Star

Jupiter is a proto-star. If it had been 50–100 times more massive, hydrogen fusion in its interior would have caused it to shine like our Sun. Its many satellites and rings are almost like a solar system.

## Saturn

Saturn was known in prehistoric times. It was named after the Roman god of fertility and agriculture.

### Exploring Saturn

The Cassini-Huygens mission was launched in 2004 by NASA and the European Space Agency. Over the course of several years, the mission will send back information about Saturn. Some of its images and data will be of Saturn's rings, which are already known to consist largely of water ice from the *Voyager* missions of the 1980s. The mission will also provide data about Titan, Saturn's largest moon, whose atmosphere is probably like the Earth's was before life began.

| Diameter at equator | 120 536km (74 900mi) |
| --- | --- |
| Maximum distance from the Sun | 1.5 billion km (937.6 million mi) |
| Minimum distance from the Sun | 1.3 billion km (834.6 million mi) |
| Length of year | 29.46 years |
| Length of day | 10 hours 14 minutes |
| Atmosphere | Mainly hydrogen and helium |
| Surface gravity | $7.2\,ms^{-2}$ (23.6ft/sq sec) |
| Rings | Yes |
| Satellites | At least 30: Mimas (1789), Enceladus (1789), Tethys (1684), Dione (1684), Rhea (1672), Titan (1655), Hyperion (1848), Iapetus (1671) |

## Uranus

Uranus was discovered in 1781. Its discoverer, the English astronomer William Herschel, wanted to name it Georgium Sidus ('the Georgian planet') after the reigning British monarch. However, the name Uranus came into more common use in around 1850. In Greek mythology Uranus was the god of the heavens.

| Diameter at equator | 51 118km (31 765mi) |
| --- | --- |
| Maximum distance from the Sun | 3 billion km (1.8 billion mi) |
| Minimum distance from the Sun | 2.7 billion km (1.7 billion mi) |
| Length of year | 84.01 years |
| Length of day | 16–28 hours[1] |
| Atmosphere | Hydrogen, helium, methane |
| Surface gravity | $8.43\,ms^{-2}$ (27.7ft/sq sec) |
| Rings | Yes |
| Satellites | At least 20: Ariel (1851), Umbriel (1851), Miranda (1948), Titania (1787), Oberon (1787) |

[1] Different latitudes rotate at different speeds.

## Neptune

Neptune was discovered in 1846. It was the first planet to be discovered by mathematical calculations, rather than observation. In Roman mythology, Neptune was the god of the sea.

| | |
|---|---|
| Diameter at equator | 49 492km (30 754mi) |
| Maximum distance from the Sun | 4.5 million km (2.8 billion mi) |
| Minimum distance from the Sun | 4.4 billion km (2.7 billion mi) |
| Length of year | 164.79 years |
| Length of day | 18–20 hours[1] |
| Atmosphere | Methane, hydrogen, helium |
| Surface gravity | $10.7\,m\,s^{-2}$ (35.14ft/sq sec) |
| Rings | Yes |
| Satellites | 11: Proteus (1989), Triton (1846), Nereid (1949) |

[1] Different latitudes rotate at different speeds.

### Far Out

Neptune is usually the eighth planet from the Sun. But for 20 of every 248 Earth years (most recently 1979–99) it becomes the ninth, the furthest planet, as Pluto moves closer to the Sun than Neptune.

### An Influential Family

Because of its distance from the sun, Pluto is a dark and cold planet. The name 'Pluto' was suggested by an eleven-year-old girl from Oxford named Venetia Burney, who felt that the god of the underworld seemed like a suitable namesake for such a place. By coincidence, Venetia's great-uncle Henry Madan had suggested the names of the two moons of Mars – Phobos and Deimos – over fifty years earlier, in 1878.

### Pluto

Pluto was discovered in 1930 by the US astronomer Clyde Tombaugh. It is named after the Roman god of the underworld.

| | |
|---|---|
| Diameter at equator | 2300 km (1429 mi) |
| Maximum distance from the Sun | 7.3 billion km (4.5 billion mi) |
| Minimum distance from the Sun | 4.4 billion km (2.7 billion mi) |
| Length of year | 247.7 years |
| Length of day | 6 days 9 hours |
| Atmosphere | Almost none; probably seasonal traces of methane, nitrogen and carbon monoxide |
| Surface gravity | 0.81 m s$^{-2}$ (2.7 ft/sq sec) |
| Rings | None |
| Satellites | 1: Charon (1978) |

#### Pluto Puzzle

Pluto may not actually be a planet at all. Some scientists believe instead that it is just one of the biggest of a large number of icy bodies known as the Kuiper belt. This orbiting belt is thought to be the origin of some of the solar system's comets.

#### The Tenth Planet?

In 2003, a possible tenth planet was discovered to be orbiting the Sun, three times further away than Pluto. However, Sedna, named for the Inuit god of the ocean, should probably be classified as a planetoid rather than a planet. A new candidate for tenth planet, larger and more distant than Sedna, was discovered in 2005.

#### Temporary Moon

Earth has a second satellite, discovered in 1986. Cruithne, named for the first Celtic people to inhabit the British Isles, is probably not a true moon because it isn't in a permanent orbit around the Earth. However, it is predicted to remain in orbit for around 5000 years.

## THE MOON

No one knows for certain where the Moon comes from. The most probable theory suggests that a body approximately the size of Mars once hit the Earth, and that the Moon is part of the debris from that collision. Others suggest that it may originally have been part of the Earth that broke away, or that it was separate and just happened to be caught by the Earth's gravity, or even that it formed gradually over time.

| | |
|---|---|
| Diameter | 3476 km (2160 mi) |
| Average distance from Earth | 384 467 km (238 908 mi) |
| Orbital period | 27.32 days |
| Age | Approx 4.6 billion years |
| Atmosphere | Trace elements only; water ice has, however, been detected at the poles |
| Mean surface temperature (day) | 107°C (225°F) |
| Mean surface temperature (night) | −153°C (−245°F) |
| Surface gravity | 1.62 m s$^{-2}$ (5.3 ft/sq sec) |
| Mass | 7.3483 × 10$^{22}$ kg (16.2 × 10$^{22}$ lb) |
| Density | 3.341 g cm$^{-3}$ (208.572 lb/cu ft) |

### Lunar seas

The Romans thought that the dark areas visible on the surface of the Moon were lunar 'maria' or seas. Modern astronomy has shown instead that they are dry plains filled with volcanic rocks. However, how they formed is still unclear.

| Latin name | English name | Latin name | English name |
|---|---|---|---|
| Lacus Mortis | Lake of Death | Mare Humorum | Sea of Moisture |
| Lacus Somniorum | Lake of Dreams | Mare Imbrium | Sea of Showers |
| Mare Australe | Southern Sea | Mare Ingenii[1] | Sea of Geniuses |
| Mare Crisium | Sea of Crises | Mare Marginis | Marginal Sea |
| Mare Fecunditatis | Sea of Fertility | Mare Moscoviense[1] | Moscow Sea |
| Mare Frigoris | Sea of Cold | Mare Nectaris | Sea of Nectar |
| Mare Humboldtianum | Humboldt's Sea | Mare Nubium | Sea of Clouds |

| Latin name | English name | Latin name | English name |
|---|---|---|---|
| Mare Orientale[1] | Eastern Sea | Palus Epidemiarum | Marsh of Epidemics |
| Mare Serenitatis | Sea of Serenity | Palus Nebularum | Marsh of Mists |
| Mare Smythii | Smyth's Sea | Palus Putredinis | Marsh of Decay |
| Mare Spumans | Foaming Sea | Palus Somnii | Marsh of Sleep |
| Mare Tranquillitatis | Sea of Tranquillity | Sinus Aestuum | Bay of Heats |
| Mare Undarum | Sea of Waves | Sinus Iridum | Bay of Rainbows |
| Mare Vaporum | Sea of Vapours | Sinus Medii | Central Bay |
| Oceanus Procellarum | Ocean of Storms | Sinus Roris | Bay of Dew |

[1]On the far side of the Moon.

## Phases of the Moon

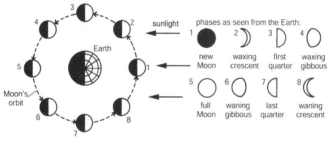

## Tides

Gravitational forces between the Earth and the Moon have a significant effect on the Moon, making it orbit around the Earth. However, they also affect the Earth by pulling the seas towards the Moon. This creates tides as the Moon moves round the earth.

### Spring and neap tides

Gravitational forces between the Sun and the Earth also contribute towards tides, although they have less of an effect. When the Moon and the Sun are lined up, the tides are at their strongest and are called spring tides. This happens during a new Moon or a full Moon. During the first and last quarter, the Sun and the Moon pull the sea at right angles to each other, so the effect is much smaller. These tides are called neap tides.

### Tidal Power

The land, as well as the sea, is affected by tides. The Earth's crust is deformed slightly but it isn't very noticeable. However, the gravitational effect of the Earth on the Moon has a bigger effect, because the Earth is so much larger than the Moon. The Moon's surface is, on average, deformed by about 20 metres (65ft).

## Lunar eclipses

The eclipse begins in the first country named. Eclipse data is given for the years 2000–20.

| Date | Type of eclipse | Time of mid-eclipse (UT[1]) | Where visible |
| --- | --- | --- | --- |
| 21 Jan 2000 | Total | 04.45 | North America, part of South America, south-western Europe, western Africa |
| 16 Jul 2000 | Total | 13.57 | Pacific, Australia, South-east Asia |
| 9 Jan 2001 | Total | 20.22 | Europe, Asia, Africa |
| 5 Jul 2001 | Partial | 14.57 | Asia, Australia, Pacific |
| 16 May 2003 | Total | 03.41 | Americas, Europe, Africa |
| 9 Nov 2003 | Total | 01.20 | Americas, Europe, Africa, western Asia |
| 4 May 2004 | Total | 20.32 | Europe, Africa, Asia |
| 28 Oct 2004 | Total | 03.05 | Americas, Europe, Africa |
| 17 Oct 2005 | Partial | 12.05 | Eastern Asia, Pacific, North America |
| 7 Sep 2006 | Partial | 18.53 | Australia, Asia, eastern Africa |
| 3 Mar 2007 | Total | 23.22 | Europe, Asia, Africa |
| 28 Aug 2007 | Total | 10.39 | Australia, Pacific, part of North America |
| 21 Feb 2008 | Total | 03.27 | Americas, Europe, Africa |
| 16 Aug 2008 | Partial | 21.12 | Europe, Africa, western Asia |
| 31 Dec 2009 | Partial | 19.23 | Asia, Africa, Europe |
| 26 Jun 2010 | Partial | 11.39 | Pacific Rim |
| 21 Dec 2010 | Total | 08.17 | North and South America |
| 15 Jun 2011 | Total | 20.12 | Asia, Africa, Europe |
| 10 Dec 2011 | Total | 14.32 | Pacific, Australia, East Asia |
| 4 Jun 2012 | Partial | 11.03 | Pacific, Australasia |
| 25 Apr 2013 | Partial | 20.09 | Asia, Africa, Europe |
| 14 Apr 2014 | Total | 07.47 | North and South America |
| 8 Oct 2014 | Total | 10.54 | Pacific, Australia, western Americas |
| 4 Apr 2015 | Partial | 12.01 | Pacific, Australasia |

| Date | Type of eclipse | Time of mid-eclipse (UT[1]) | Where visible |
|---|---|---|---|
| 28 Sep 2015 | Total | 02.47 | Africa, Europe, Americas |
| 7 Aug 2017 | Partial | 18.21 | Asia, Africa, Australia |
| 31 Jan 2018 | Total | 13.30 | Pacific, Australia, Asia |
| 27 Jul 2018 | Total | 20.22 | Asia, Africa, part of Europe |
| 21 Jan 2019 | Total | 05.12 | Americas, part of Europe |
| 16 Jul 2019 | Partial | 21.31 | Asia, Africa, Europe |

[1] Universal Time, equivalent to Greenwich Mean Time (GMT).

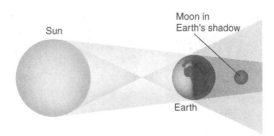

**Lunar Eclipse**

## STARS

### Constellations

A constellation is composed of stars which appear to form a distinctive group as seen from the Earth. The grouping of stars into constellations makes it easier to locate particular stars in the sky. There are 88 constellations in total. Latin names, and their English equivalents, are given.

| Latin name | English name | Latin name | English name |
|---|---|---|---|
| Andromeda | Andromeda | Boötes | Herdsman |
| Antlia | Air Pump | Caelum | Chisel |
| Apus | Bird of Paradise | Camelopardalis | Giraffe |
| Aquarius | Water Bearer | Cancer | Crab |
| Aquila | Eagle | Canes Venatici | Hunting Dogs |
| Ara | Altar | Canis Major | Great Dog |
| Aries | Ram | Canis Minor | Little Dog |
| Auriga | Charioteer | Capricornus | Sea Goat |

| Latin name | English name | Latin name | English name |
|---|---|---|---|
| Carina | Keel | Lupus | Wolf |
| Cassiopeia | Cassiopeia | Lynx | Lynx |
| Centaurus | Centaur | Lyra | Harp |
| Cepheus | Cepheus | Mensa | Table |
| Cetus | Whale | Microscopium | Microscope |
| Chamaeleon | Chameleon | Monoceros | Unicorn |
| Circinus | Compasses | Musca | Fly |
| Columba | Dove | Norma | Level |
| Coma Berenices | Berenice's Hair | Octans | Octant |
| Corona Australis | Southern Crown | Ophiuchus | Serpent Bearer |
| Corona Borealis | Northern Crown | Orion | Orion |
| Corvus | Crow | Pavo | Peacock |
| Crater | Cup | Pegasus | Winged Horse |
| Crux | Southern Cross | Perseus | Perseus |
| Cygnus | Swan | Phoenix | Phoenix |
| Delphinus | Dolphin | Pictor | Easel |
| Dorado | Swordfish | Pisces | Fishes |
| Draco | Dragon | Piscis Austrinus | Southern Fish |
| Equuleus | Little Horse | Puppis | Ship's Stern |
| Eridanus | River Eridanus | Pyxis | Mariner's Compass |
| Fornax | Furnace | Reticulum | Net |
| Gemini | Twins | Sagitta | Arrow |
| Grus | Crane | Sagittarius | Archer |
| Hercules | Hercules | Scorpius | Scorpion |
| Horologium | Clock | Sculptor | Sculptor |
| Hydra | Sea Serpent | Scutum | Shield |
| Hydrus | Water Snake | Serpens | Serpent |
| Indus | Indian | Sextans | Sextant |
| Lacerta | Lizard | Taurus | Bull |
| Leo | Lion | Telescopium | Telescope |
| Leo Minor | Little Lion | Triangulum | Triangle |
| Lepus | Hare | Triangulum Australe | Southern Triangle |
| Libra | Scales | Tucana | Toucan |

| Latin name | English name | Latin name | English name |
| --- | --- | --- | --- |
| Ursa Major | Great Bear | Virgo | Virgin |
| Ursa Minor | Little Bear | Volans | Flying Fish |
| Vela | Sails | Vulpecula | Fox |

## Twinkle Twinkle Little Star

Because stars are so far away, starlight has to travel a great distance to reach the Earth, and stars appear only as tiny points of light in the sky. They twinkle because of rapid changes in their brightness caused by atmospheric turbulence. This effect is called scintillation. Planets are nearer to the Earth, meaning that they appear larger in the sky. Their light is stronger and less susceptible to atmospheric turbulence, so they don't twinkle.

## Constellation maps

The following star maps of the northern and southern skies are an average of how the stars appear, which varies with the time of year and exact location.

**The Northern Sky**

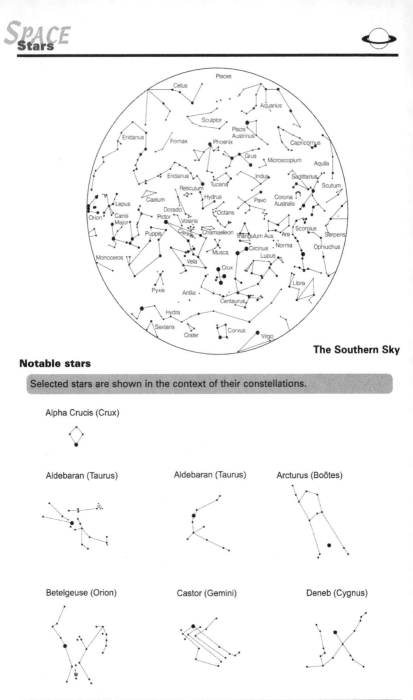

**The Southern Sky**

## Notable stars

Selected stars are shown in the context of their constellations.

Alpha Crucis (Crux)

Aldebaran (Taurus)

Aldebaran (Taurus)

Arcturus (Boötes)

Betelgeuse (Orion)

Castor (Gemini)

Deneb (Cygnus)

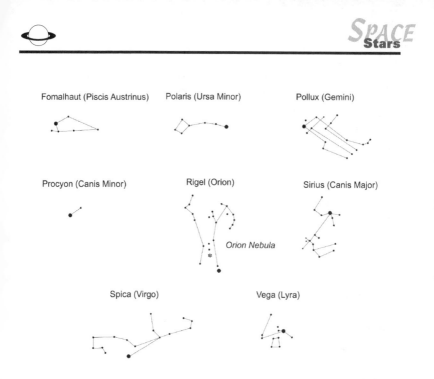

Fomalhaut (Piscis Austrinus)   Polaris (Ursa Minor)      Pollux (Gemini)

Procyon (Canis Minor)          Rigel (Orion)             Sirius (Canis Major)

                               Orion Nebula

            Spica (Virgo)              Vega (Lyra)

## Brightest stars in the sky

The apparent brightness of a star is represented by a number called its magnitude. The larger the number, the fainter the star; the faintest stars visible to the naked eye are slightly fainter than magnitude six. Very bright stars have a value lower than zero. Only approximately 6000 of the billions of stars in the sky are visible to the naked eye. The apparent magnitude takes distance from the Earth into account, and describes how stars actually appear, whereas the absolute magnitude describes how bright a star would appear if it were at a set distance away. The table below gives the Sun and the twenty next brightest stars visible from the Earth (see also **Measurement: Scales**)

| Star name | Distance (light years) | Apparent magnitude | Absolute magnitude |
|-----------|------------------------|--------------------|--------------------|
| Sun | 0.0000158 | −26.8 | +4.8 |
| Sirius A | 8.6 | −1.46 | +1.4 |
| Canopus | 98 | −0.72 | −8.5 |
| Arcturus | 36 | −0.06 | −0.3 |
| Alpha Centauri A | 4.3 | −0.01 | +4.4 |
| Vega | 26.5 | +0.04 | +0.5 |
| Capella | 45 | +0.05 | −0.7 |

| Star name | Distance (light years) | Apparent magnitude | Absolute magnitude |
|---|---|---|---|
| Rigel | 900 | +0.14 | −6.8 |
| Procyon A | 11.2 | +0.37 | +2.6 |
| Betelgeuse | 520 | +0.41 | −5.5 |
| Achernar | 118 | +0.51 | −1.0 |
| Beta Centauri | 490 | +0.63 | −5.1 |
| Altair | 16.5 | +0.77 | +2.2 |
| Alpha Crucis | 120 | +0.83 | −4.0 |
| Aldebaran | 68 | +0.86 | −0.2 |
| Spica | 220 | +0.91 | −3.6 |
| Antares | 520 | +0.92 | −4.5 |
| Pollux | 35 | +1.16 | +0.8 |
| Fomalhaut | 22.6 | +1.19 | +2.0 |
| Deneb | 1500 | +1.26 | −6.9 |
| Beta Crucis | 490 | +1.28 | −4.6 |

## Nearest stars

The table gives the Sun and the twenty next nearest stars to the Earth.

| Star name | Distance (light years) | Apparent magnitude | Absolute magnitude |
|---|---|---|---|
| Sun | 0.0000158 | −26.8 | +4.8 |
| Proxima Centauri | 4.3 | +11.05 | +15.5 |
| Alpha Centauri A | 4.3 | −0.01 | +4.4 |
| Alpha Centauri B | 4.3 | +1.33 | +5.7 |
| Barnard's Star | 5.9 | +9.54 | +13.3 |
| Wolf 359 | 7.6 | +13.53 | +16.7 |
| Lalande 21185 | 8.1 | +7.50 | +10.5 |
| Sirius A | 8.6 | −1.46 | +1.4 |
| Sirius B | 8.6 | +8.68 | +11.6 |
| Luyten 726 8A | 8.9 | +12.45 | +15.3 |
| UV 726 8B | 8.9 | +12.95 | +15.3 |
| Ross 154 | 9.4 | +10.60 | +13.3 |
| Ross 248 | 10.3 | +12.29 | +14.8 |

| Star name | Distance (light years) | Apparent magnitude | Absolute magnitude |
|---|---|---|---|
| Epsilon Eridani | 10.8 | +3.73 | +6.1 |
| Ross 128 | 10.8 | +11.10 | +13.5 |
| Luyten 789-6 | 10.8 | +12.18 | +14.6 |
| 61 Cygni A | 11.1 | +5.22 | +7.6 |
| 61 Cygni B | 11.1 | +6.03 | +8.4 |
| Epsilon Indi | 11.2 | +4.68 | +7.0 |
| Procyon A | 11.2 | +0.37 | +2.7 |
| Procyon B | 11.2 | +10.70 | +13.0 |

## Lengthy Light Year

A light year sounds as though it should be a measurement of time. In fact, it's the distance light travels in a year. The speed of light is very high – around 300 000 kilometres (186 000 miles) per second – so a light year is a very long distance. It's equivalent to about nine trillion kilometres.

### Astronomical telescopes

Light telescopes are used for looking at distant objects such as stars and planets. Because the object of interest is far away, the light rays coming from it are very nearly parallel. In some types of telescope, a lens called the objective lens bends the parallel rays to form an image of the object. The image is magnified by another lens in the eyepiece of the telescope. These telescopes are called refracting telescopes, and have very high resolution. In other telescopes, the objective lens is replaced by a curved mirror called a parabolic reflector. These telescopes are known as Newtonian telescopes; their resolution is lower than refracting telescopes but they collect more light so they are better for studying very distant objects.

Radio telescopes are used to gather radio waves from the Sun, hot gas clouds and active galaxies. They use a large parabolic 'dish' antenna, or an array of these antennae, to gather distant radio waves to a focal point.

### Life cycle of stars

A star is a sphere of matter held together entirely by its own gravitational field, generating energy by means of nuclear fusion reactions deep in its interior (see **Energy, light and radioactivity: Nuclear reactions**). Stars shine as a result of the heat and light energy generated by these reactions. A star will go through several different stages during its lifetime, which can be billions of years.

### nebula

A cloud of gas and dust. As this matter contracts under gravity, the beginnings of the star are created.

### main-sequence star

Eventually the star stops contracting and nuclear fusion reactions begin. The main reaction converts hydrogen into helium. Energy is emitted as heat and light, and the star begins to shine. Stars spend most of their life at this stage, during which their temperature and brightness will barely change. Our Sun is a main-sequence star.

### red giant

Eventually reactions in the star's core stop as all the hydrogen is exhausted. This happens more quickly with bigger, brighter stars. The star expands, swells up greatly and shines more brightly but with a reddish colour. The surface becomes cooler while the core becomes much hotter. Eventually, new nuclear fusion reactions start up, converting helium to carbon and oxygen. In larger red giants this happens gradually, while in smaller ones it happens suddenly in an event called the helium flash.

### supernova

The star explodes, radiating enormous amounts of energy into space. But the core of the star can collapse under its own gravitational field.

*smaller, less massive stars*

*larger stars*

### white dwarf

The star implodes, collapsing into a small, very dense body. It is nearing the end of its life. The remains may eventually cool into a *black dwarf*, which no longer emits visible light.

### neutron star

If a star has insufficient gravity to collapse entirely, it will become a tiny body, a mass of neutrons only a few miles across, but of very high density.

### black hole

The core collapses in on itself to the point where its gravity is so strong that nothing, not even light, can escape. (See also **Black Holes**).

## Pulsars

A pulsar ('pulsating star') is a type of neutron star that rotates rapidly and has a strong magnetic field. Pulsars act as radio sources characterized by extremely regular bursts of radio waves, which they emit in a small cone, like the light beam from a lighthouse. A pulse is observed when the cone sweeps across a radio telescope.

The pulse rate varies between pulsars, and gradually slows down as the rotation of the pulsar gets slower. The rate of decline of pulsars suggests that they remain detectable for a few million years. Pulsars are formed as an endpoint in the evolution of a relatively young massive star.

### The Crab Nebula

One of the fastest current pulsars is in the Crab Nebula, which pulses 30 times per second. Before it was discovered, astronomers thought that all dying stars turned into white dwarfs. However, they knew that white dwarfs couldn't vibrate that quickly. Studying the Crab Nebula turned out to be very important in discovering the existence of neutron stars.

## BLACK HOLES

It is impossible to see a black hole directly, because no light can escape from it. This means that it is very difficult to prove that they exist, but there is very good evidence that they do.

### Singularities

The proposed structure of a black hole includes a region in the centre called a singularity, at which the density of the black hole becomes infinitely high. This could be a single point if the black hole is still, or a doughnut shape if it is spinning.

### Event horizons

A boundary called the event horizon surrounds the black hole. This is the boundary beyond which the speed needed to pull away from the black hole's gravity, known as the escape velocity, is greater than the speed of light. This means that everything, including light, that crosses the event horizon gets sucked into the black hole and is unable to get back out.

### Accretion disc

Matter swirls round the black hole, like water swirling down a plug-hole, forming an accretion disc. The material from the inside edge of the accretion disc gets sucked over the event horizon and into the centre of the black hole. As this happens, energy is released in the form of X-rays; these can be detected around the outside.

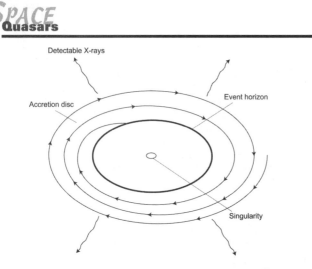

Detectable X-rays

Accretion disc

Event horizon

Singularity

**Structure of a Black Hole**

## QUASARS

A quasar ('quasi-stellar radio source') is an extremely distant object, usually more than a billion light years from Earth.

Though they are far away, quasars appear very bright in the sky, showing that they must be giving out a large amount of energy. Astronomers think that this could be caused by matter falling towards a supermassive black hole in the middle of the quasar.

## GALAXIES

A galaxy is a large family of stars, interstellar gas and dust, held together by their mutual gravitational force. Each galaxy is usually isolated by almost empty space from its neighbouring galaxies. Galaxies are the basic large-scale components from which our universe is constructed.

Galaxies come in a bewildering variety of forms and sizes, but can be classified into three types: spiral, elliptical and irregular. They are found in clusters; our galaxy is part of a cluster called the Local Group, which also includes the Andromeda galaxy.

### The Milky Way

The Milky Way, a hazy band of stars visible in the night sky, is the edge of our own galaxy. There are around 200 billion stars in the whole of the Milky Way.

### Spiral galaxies

Spiral galaxies are flat discs of stars with two spiral arms emerging from the nuclear region, and account for around a quarter of all galaxies including the Milky Way.

The arms are rich in interstellar matter, and they play a key role in star formation.

### Elliptical galaxies

Most galaxies are elliptical. They range from almost spherical up to a ratio of about 3:1 for length relative to diameter. They contain hardly any dust or gas, so there is very little star formation.

### Irregular galaxies

Irregular galaxies have no clear morphology; many very active galaxies, which emit unusually large amounts of radiation from a compact central source, fall into this category.

---

*Radio Galaxies*

About one galaxy per million is a giant radio galaxy. These are an intense source of cosmic radio waves, caused by spiralling electrons that move at speeds close to the speed of light. Their total luminosity is around a million times brighter than a normal galaxy.

---

## COMETS

The solid nucleus of a comet is usually several kilometres in diameter. It consists of ice, dust and solid particles, like a large, dirty snowball.

### Comet structure

When the comet passes close to the sun, a cloud of gas and dust is ejected from the nucleus, forming a huge head or coma many thousands of kilometres in diameter.

Radiations from the sun elongate the gas and dust to form one or more tails, often extending millions of kilometres in space. These tails point away from the sun but, as the comet recedes, the tail gets shorter until the comet returns to its original state.

---

*Deep Impact*

In 2005, NASA ran its Deep Impact mission, which launched a 370kg (820lb) impactor into the path of the comet Tempel 1. The mission will provide information of the composition of the comet. Not everyone is happy about this, however – a Russian astrologer sued NASA for 'deforming her horoscopes'.

---

### Sources of comets

#### Kuiper belt

Short-period comets (those which take less than 200 years to orbit the Sun) come from the Kuiper belt, a large ring of icy bodies orbiting the Sun just beyond Neptune.

## Oort cloud

Long-period comets take much longer to orbit the Sun (up to 30 million years) and originate in the Oort cloud, a cloud of frozen comet nuclei approximately 15 trillion kilometres (9 trillion miles) away from the Sun. It is estimated that the Oort cloud contains approximately 10 trillion comets.

## Selected comets

There have been over 850 comets recorded to date; approximately ten new comets are discovered each year. Some notable comets are listed below.

| Comet | First seen | Period of orbit (years) |
| --- | --- | --- |
| Halley | 240 BC | 76.1 |
| Tycho | 1577 | Unknown |
| Kirch (Newton) | 1680 | 8814 |
| De Chéseaux | 1744 | Unknown |
| Lexell | 1770 | 5.6 |
| Encke | 1786 | 3.3 |
| Flauergues | 1811 | 3094 |
| Pons-Winnecke | 1819 | 6.34 |
| Great Comet | 1843 | 512.6 |
| Donati | 1858 | 1950 |
| Tebbutt | 1861 | 409.1 |
| Swift-Tuttle | 1862 | 125 |
| Cruls | 1882 | 758.4 |
| Wolf | 1884 | 8.4 |
| Morehouse | 1908 | Unknown |
| Daylight Comet | 1910 | Unknown |
| Schwassmann-Wachmann 1 | 1925 | 15 |
| Arend-Roland | 1957 | Unknown |
| Mrkos | 1957 | Unknown |
| Humason | 1961 | 3000 |
| Seki-Lines | 1962 | Unknown |
| Ikeya-Seki | 1965 | 880 |
| Tago-Sato-Kosaka | 1969 | 420 000 |
| Bennett | 1970 | 1680 |
| Kohoutek | 1973 | 75 000 |

| Comet | First seen | Period of orbit (years) |
|---|---|---|
| West | 1975 | 500 000 |
| IRAS-Araki-Alcock | 1983 | Unknown |
| Hale-Bopp | 1995 | 2400 |
| Hyakutake | 1996 | 18 000 |

### Halley's Comet

One of the best-known and brightest comets is Halley's Comet. First recorded in 240BC, when it was seen over China, the comet is visible from Earth approximately every 76 years. Most famously it appeared at the Battle of Hastings in 1066, an event depicted in the Bayeux Tapestry. The comet was named after the English astronomer Edmond Halley (1656–1742), who successfully predicted the years in which it would return. Halley's Comet was last seen in 1986, and won't be visible from Earth again until 2061.

## ASTEROIDS

Asteroids, also known as 'minor planets', orbit the Sun. They are large chunks of rock and metal, ranging in size from less than a kilometre to hundreds of kilometres in diameter.

Most asteroids are found in the Asteroid Belt, orbiting the Sun between Mars and Jupiter. This region may contain millions of asteroids. Some asteroids are captured by Jupiter's gravitational pull, and are called Trojan asteroids. Other asteroids have a very elliptical orbit and come close to the centre of the solar system; these are the ones that can collide with the inner planets, including the Earth. Approximately 20 000 asteroids have already been catalogued. The largest of these is Ceres, which was discovered in 1801 and is 940km (584mi) in diameter.

## METEOROIDS

Meteoroids are small lumps of rock and metal, and can originate from the Asteroid Belt or from comets.

Meteoroids vary in size from a few micrometres to many metres or even kilometres in diameter. Meteoroids can enter the Earth's atmosphere at speeds of up to 70km/s (45mi/sec). They normally burn up at a height of approximately 100km (60mi). Smaller meteoroids that burn up in the Earth's atmosphere are known as meteors or 'shooting stars'. Meteoroids or fragments of meteoroids that reach the Earth's surface are called meteorites.

## Annual meteor showers

Meteors appear to radiate from the named star region.

| Shower | Dates | Maximum activity |
| --- | --- | --- |
| Quadrantids | 1–6 Jan | 3–4 Jan |
| Lyrids | 19–25 Apr | 22 Apr |
| Alpha-Scorpiids | 20 Apr–19 May | 28 Apr–10 May |
| Eta Aquariids | 1–8 May | 5 May |
| Delta Aquariids | 15 Jul–10 Aug | 28 Jul–5 Aug |
| Perseids | 27 Jul–17 Aug | 11–14 Aug |
| Orionids | 15–25 Oct | 21 Oct |
| Taurids | 25 Oct–25 Nov | 4–14 Nov |
| Leonids | 14–20 Nov | 17–18 Nov |
| Geminids | 8–14 Dec | 13–14 Dec |
| Ursids | 19–24 Dec | 22–23 Dec |

## COSMIC RAYS

Cosmic rays are extremely energetic particles moving through the universe near to the speed of light. They comprise atomic nuclei that are accelerated to very high energies. The proportions of different types of nuclei in the cosmic rays are very similar to the relative proportions of each atomic element found in the universe as a whole; this is known as the cosmic abundance. These observations are very important because cosmic rays are the only particles we can detect that have crossed the galaxy.

### Sources of cosmic rays

#### High-energy rays

The rays of the very highest energy may well be coming from quasars and active galactic nuclei. They were created by unknown processes, probably explosive in nature, that pose a real challenge to modern astrophysics.

#### Lower-energy rays

Lower-energy cosmic rays are generated by sources within our own galaxy. They probably originate in supernova explosions, remnants like the Crab Nebula, and pulsars. These cosmic rays are trapped by the magnetic field of the galaxy, probably for tens of millions of years. The direction of an incoming cosmic ray, therefore, tells us nothing directly about its origin. Solar flares are a source of the lowest-energy cosmic rays.

# ENERGY, LIGHT AND RADIOACTIVITY

## ENERGY

Energy is defined as the capacity to do work, and is measured in units called joules. It can be emitted from a source as radiation. Energy can be converted from one form to another, but can never be destroyed (see **Key concepts: Thermodynamics**).

### Mechanical energy

Mechanical energy is energy possessed by objects due to their movement, position or other properties. It includes kinetic energy and potential (stored) energy.

#### Kinetic energy

The energy of moving objects is called kinetic energy. It can be calculated by the formula $E = \frac{1}{2}mv^2$, where E is energy (in joules), m is the mass of the object (in kilograms) and v is the velocity (speed, in metres per second). This means that, as an object moves faster, it rapidly gains kinetic energy. It also means that if two objects of different masses are moving at the same speed, the heavier one has more kinetic energy.

#### Elastic potential energy of objects

If energy is stored by deforming a material, it is known as elastic potential energy. Examples include a coiled spring and a stretched elastic band. The more the material is stretched or compressed, the greater its elastic potential energy.

#### Gravitational potential energy

If an object is held high up, it has gravitational potential energy because it can fall down when released. Gravitational potential energy can be calculated by the formula $E = mgh$, where E is the energy (in joules), m is the mass of the object (in kilograms), g is the gravitational force (in metres per square second; this has a value of around 9.8 on Earth) and h is the height (in metres). This means that objects higher up have more gravitational potential energy.

### Thermal energy

Thermal energy is really a form of kinetic energy, as it involves movements and vibrations of molecules and atoms. The higher the temperature of an object or material, the more thermal energy it has. If an object is warmer than its surroundings, it transfers thermal energy to them in the form of electromagnetic radiation (see **Electromagnetic radiation**); this is known as heat.

> *At what time does the dissipation of energy begin?*
> —Scottish physicist William, Lord Kelvin (1824–1907), when his wife proposed an afternoon walk (quoted in *Memories of a Scientific Life* by A Fleming, 1934).

## Chemical energy

Chemical energy is really a form of potential energy, as it is energy that is stored in the chemical bonds of a substance (see **Atoms, elements and molecules: Chemical bonds**). Breaking chemical bonds can result in the conversion of the stored energy into other forms. This occurs with the burning of fuel and breakdown of food. Batteries convert chemical energy into electrical energy.

## Electrical energy

Electrical energy is another form of potential or stored energy (see **Electricity and magnets: Electricity**). It is stored through the attractions and repulsions of charged subatomic particles such as protons and electrons (see **Atoms, elements and molecules: Subatomic particles**).

## Nuclear energy

Nuclear energy is stored in the nucleus of each atom, due to the interactions between the subatomic particles in the nucleus (see **Atoms, elements and molecules: Subatomic particles**). Nuclear energy can be released from atoms and converted into other forms during nuclear fission or fusion reactions, when subatomic particles within the atoms are rearranged (see **Nuclear reactions**).

## WAVES

Waves are the way in which energy moves from one place to another. Most waves need to travel through a liquid or gas of some kind, known as a medium. The energy carried by the wave displaces particles in the medium, making them vibrate or oscillate around their original position without any permanent change taking place. Some wave terms and types are described below.

| Term | Description | Units |
|------|-------------|-------|
| Period | Time taken for each complete oscillation | Seconds |
| Frequency | Number of complete oscillations per second | Hertz |
| Wavelength | Distance between two successive similar points | Metres |
| Velocity | Speed at which the wave travels in a given direction | Metres per second |

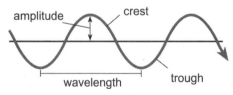

**Wave Structure**

high                                          low

**Wave Frequency**

## Frequency and wavelength

The frequency and wavelength of waves are closely connected, with higher frequency waves having a shorter wavelength. The frequency of a wave (in hertz) can be calculated by dividing its speed (in metres per second) by its wavelength (in metres). Similarly, the wavelength can be calculated by dividing the speed by the frequency.

## Longitudinal waves

Longitudinal waves travel by making particles vibrate backwards and forwards in line with the direction of the wave.

When a longitudinal wave travels, the medium is alternately bunched up (compression) and stretched out (rarefaction). Sound waves are longitudinal waves; in air, they travel at a speed of around 330 metres per second (1000 ft per second).

## Transverse waves

Transverse waves travel by causing vibrations at right-angles to the direction of the wave.

Waves that travel along a string are transverse. Electromagnetic radiation also consists of transverse waves, but these waves are unusual because they can travel through empty space (see **Electromagnetic radiation**).

*Longitudinal* (medium is compressed and rarefied)

*Transverse* (medium is disturbed at right angles to direction of wave)

**Types of Waves**

## Interference

> Interference is an interaction between two or more waves of the same frequency, emitted from different sources.

Constructive interference occurs at points where the waves are in phase, with their peaks and troughs coinciding. Where the peaks and troughs are out of phase and do not coincide, the interference is destructive. Light and dark bands, corresponding to areas of constructive and destructive interference, can be seen as a result of interference between two equivalent single-colour beams of light.

*wave 1* — —
*+ wave 2* - - -
*= wave 3* ———

*Constructive* (waves 1 and 2 in phase)

*Destructive* (waves 1 and 2 out of phase)

## Reflection

> If a wave reaches a boundary between two different substances, it may be bounced straight back, a phenomenon known as reflection.

Reflection can occur when light travels through the air and meets a mirror. If sound is reflected from a wall, we hear it as reverberations or echoes.

## Refraction

> When a wave reaches an interface between two different media, part of it may be bent rather than reflected. This is called refraction.

Waves with short wavelengths are refracted more than those with long wavelengths; for example, blue light is refracted more than red light.

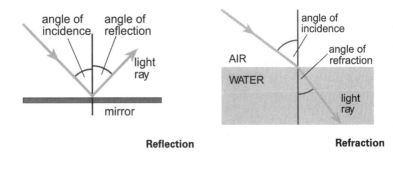

**Reflection**

**Refraction**

---

## Refraction Rainbows

White light is made up of all the colours of the rainbow. If it is shone through a glass triangular prism, the colours are diffracted by different amounts, a process called dispersion. This causes a rainbow-like multi-coloured spectrum to emerge from the prism. Real rainbows are caused by sunlight being refracted by raindrops.

### Diffraction

Waves can spread out when they are obstructed by obstacles or have to pass through a hole, a process called diffraction.

Diffraction is most noticeable when the size of the obstruction is similar to the wavelength of the waves.

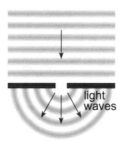

light waves

## Waves or Particles?

The English physicist Thomas Young did experiments to show that light can undergo diffraction and form interference patterns; these supported his theory that light is made up of waves rather than particles. More recently, physicists have realised that light has properties of both waves and particles (see **Key concepts: Quantum mechanics**).

## ELECTROMAGNETIC RADIATION

Electromagnetic radiation can be thought of as transverse waves. As the name suggests, the waves that comprise electromagnetic radiation have both electrical and magnetic components.

Because electromagnetic waves travel by changing electrical and magnetic fields, they do not need a physical medium. This means that electromagnetic radiation can travel through a vacuum. It can also be described as 'particles' or 'packets' of energy, known as photons.

## Electromagnetic spectrum

> Electromagnetic waves exist as a spectrum, ranging from very short to very long wavelengths.

The shorter wavelengths have high frequency and high energy, while the longer wavelengths have lower frequency and lower energy. A number called Planck's constant, after the German physicist Max Planck, relates the frequencies and energies of the waves. The electromagnetic spectrum can be divided into several categories, although it is a continuous spectrum so there are no clear boundaries.

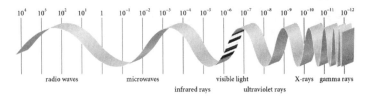

### The Speed of Light

The existence of electromagnetic waves was predicted by the Scottish physicist James Clerk Maxwell, and demonstrated by the German physicist Heinrich Hertz. Maxwell predicted that electromagnetic waves, including light, would travel at a constant speed, which turns out to be just under 300 000 000 metres per second (186 000 miles per second) in a vacuum.

## Radio waves

> Electromagnetic waves that have wavelengths of longer than about 10cm are known as radio waves.

As their name suggests, radio waves are used to transmit radio broadcasts. A carrier wave is modulated (altered) by mixing in a wave carrying the sound to be transmitted. The amplitude of the carrier is modulated in AM radio, while the frequency is modulated in FM radio.

### Radio bands

A number of radio bands have been designated by the International Telecommunications Union.

| Abbreviation | Name | Frequency | Wavelength |
| --- | --- | --- | --- |
| ELF | Extremely low frequency | 3–30 Hz | 100 000 km to 10 000 km |

| Abbreviation | Name | Frequency | Wavelength |
|---|---|---|---|
| SLF | Superlow frequency | 30–300 Hz | 10 000 km to 1000 km |
| ULF | Ultralow frequency | 300 Hz–3 kHz | 1000 km to 100 km |
| VLF | Very low frequency | 3–30 kHz | 100 km to 10 km |
| LF | Low frequency | 30–300 kHz | 10 km to 1 km |
| MF | Medium frequency | 300 kHz–3 MHz | 1 km to 100 m |
| HF | High frequency | 3–30 MHz | 100 m to 10 m |
| VHF | Very high frequency | 30–300 MHz | 10 m to 1 m |
| UHF | Ultrahigh frequency | 300 MHz–3 GHz | 1 m to 10 cm |
| SHF | Superhigh frequency | 3–30 GHz | 10 cm to 1 cm |
| EHF | Extremely high frequency | 30–300 GHz | 1 cm to 1 mm |

### FM and AM radio frequencies

FM radio broadcasts use frequencies in the VHF band; in most of the world the frequencies are between 87.5 and 108 MHz. AM radio is divided into three frequency ranges.

| Abbreviation | Name | Frequency | Radio band |
|---|---|---|---|
| LW | long wave | 153–279 kHz | LF |
| MW | medium wave | 531–1620 kHz | MF |
| SW | short wave | 2.31–25.82 MHz | MF/HF |

### Television broadcasting

In the UK, terrestrial television is broadcast in the UHF radio band. Some countries also use parts of the VHF band for their television broadcasts.

### Microwave ovens

Microwave ovens use electromagnetic radiation to cause vibrations in the water molecules contained in food. This happens because different parts of the water molecule differ slightly in their charge, and constantly try to re-align themselves with the shifting electric field produced by the microwaves. The energy given to the water by the microwaves then spreads throughout the food as heat. Microwave ovens are built from metal to contain the microwaves; the door is covered by a metal mesh, the holes in which are smaller than the 12cm wavelength of the microwaves, preventing them from escaping.

Electromagnetic Radiation

## Microwaves

Microwave radiation has wavelengths of between 0.3 and 30cm.

Microwaves can be produced by a device called a magnetron, which passes electrons through electrical and magnetic fields to make them spin, causing cavities in the magnetron to resonate at microwave frequencies. Microwave radiation is important for communications, including radar, satellite communication and wireless internet connections.

## Infrared (IR) radiation

Infrared radiation has frequencies that are below those of visible red light; its wavelength range is from approximately 750nm to 1mm.

Infrared radiation is linked to heat, because everyday objects that are warmer than room temperature, such as people and hot drinks, emit electromagnetic radiation mainly in the infrared range. Infrared radiation can be classified according to how far it is from the red end of the visible spectrum.

| Name | Approximate wavelengths |
|------|-------------------------|
| Near | 0.75–1.5 µm |
| Intermediate | 1.5–20 µm |
| Far | 20–1000 µm |

### Infrared Spectroscopy

A technique called infrared spectroscopy is based on the fact that infrared radiation can make chemical bonds vibrate. Different bonds have different resonant frequencies at which they are most likely to vibrate. The bonds can also move in different ways: stretching, scissoring, wagging, twisting and rocking. Every molecule therefore has a different pattern of vibrations, depending on the type of bonds it contains and the ways in which they tend to move. Infrared spectroscopy can be used to help identify molecules and determine their structures.

## Visible light

Visible light consists of electromagnetic waves of wavelengths that can be detected by the human eye. These range from 380 to 780nm, although in practice the range that can be detected comfortably by most people is around 400 to 700nm.

| Colour | Approximate wavelengths |
|--------|-------------------------|
| Red | 780–620 nm |
| Orange | 620–590 nm |
| Yellow | 590–550 nm |
| Green | 550–500 nm |
| Blue | 500–450 nm |

| Colour | Approximate wavelengths |
|---|---|
| Indigo[1] | 450–440 nm |
| Violet | 455–380 nm |

[1] Indigo is not always recognized as a separate colour

## Ultraviolet (UV) radiation

Ultraviolet radiation has frequencies that are higher than those of visible violet light. It has wavelengths of from approximately 380nm down to about 10nm. UV radiation is classified according to how far it is from the violet end of the visible spectrum.

| Name | Approximate wavelengths |
|---|---|
| Near ultraviolet | 380–300 nm |
| Middle ultraviolet | 300–200 nm |
| Extreme ultraviolet | 200–10 nm |

### Dangerous Rays

Ultraviolet radiation is strongly absorbed by DNA molecules, and causes inappropriate bonds to form between the bases that code for genes (see **Genetics: DNA**). It is therefore mutagenic (cancer-causing), and exposure through strong sunlight leads to an increased risk of skin cancer.

## X-rays

X-rays are electromagnetic waves of short wavelength, ranging from around 10nm down to about 100pm.

X-rays are produced when high-speed electrons strike a solid target. Electrons passing near a nucleus in the target decelerate and 'lose' energy, which is emitted as a continuous spectrum of radiation known as *bremsstrahlung* (German for 'braking radiation'). In addition, the electrons may 'bounce' electrons in the target atoms up to higher energy levels; when they drop back down, they give out X-rays of specific wavelengths. This is the characteristic X-ray spectrum of the target, and is specific to the target element. High energy X-rays are a form of ionizing radiation and also have enough energy to break chemical bonds.

### X-ray crystallography

X-rays can be used to study the crystal structures of substances by means of a machine called a diffractometer. A beam of X-rays is directed at the crystallized substance. The X-rays are diffracted when they hit electrons in the atoms of the substance, and interference of the diffracted rays makes characteristic patterns that can be viewed on photographic film. The arrangement of atoms in space can be worked out from the distribution of intensity in the diffraction pattern. Work carried out by the English X-ray crystallographer Rosalind Franklin played a key part in determining the structure of DNA (see **Genetics: DNA**).

## Gamma rays

Gamma rays are high-energy electromagnetic waves that generally have wavelengths shorter than about 100pm.

There is actually some overlap between the wavelengths of the highest energy X-rays and the lowest energy gamma rays, because X-rays and gamma rays are properly defined by how they are emitted, rather than their wavelengths. Gamma rays are emitted during radioactive decay, usually at the same time as alpha particles or beta particles. They are a form of ionizing radiation and also have enough energy to break chemical bonds.

## NON-IONIZING RADIATION

The lower-energy waves from the electromagnetic spectrum do not cause ionization (changes in charge) of atoms or molecules.

| | |
|---|---|
| Radio waves | Visible light |
| Microwaves | Ultraviolet radiation |
| Infrared radiation | |

## IONIZING RADIATION

Ionizing forms of radiation can cause atoms or molecules to lose or gain electric charges.

Forms of radiation that can cause ionization have both very high energy and the ability to interact with electrons. As well as the more energetic parts of the electromagnetic spectrum, ionizing radiation is also emitted in the form of particles. Ionizing forms of radiation are particularly harmful to living creatures because they can penetrate tissues and they release considerable energy when they collide with biological molecules.

### Alpha particles

An alpha particle consists of two protons and two neutrons.

Alpha particles can be emitted when unstable forms of an element undergo a process called radioactive decay. These unstable forms are called radionuclides. Alpha radiation can easily be blocked by a sheet of paper but, if it enters the body through swallowing or breathing, it can do a lot of damage because it is extremely ionizing and is strongly absorbed.

### Beta particles

A beta particle is a single electron that is emitted during radioactive decay.

Beta radiation is less ionizing than alpha particles but can penetrate further, requiring a sheet of aluminium to block it.

## Gamma rays

Gamma rays are extremely high frequency electromagnetic energy without mass or charge, emitted during radioactive decay.

Gamma radiation is less ionizing than alpha or beta radiation but can travel a long way and penetrate deeply. Thick layers of dense materials such as lead or concrete are needed to block it.

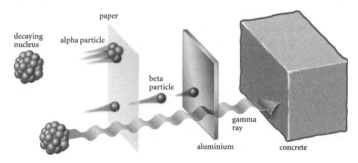

paper

decaying nucleus

alpha particle

beta particle

gamma ray

aluminium

concrete

**Types of Ionizing Radiation**

### X-rays

X-rays are electromagnetic energy, generally of a lower wavelength than gamma rays.

X-rays are not emitted during natural radioactive decay but can be produced artificially. They have very similar properties to gamma rays.

### Cosmic rays

Cosmic rays are a mixture of highly energized radiations from outer space (see **Space: Cosmic rays**).

### Sources of ionizing radiation

Of the ionizing radiation received by everyone continuously, on average about 87% occurs naturally from radon gas in the ground (59%), radioactive elements in rocks (16%), cosmic rays (11%), and radioactive potassium in food and drink (14%). Only 13% comes from artificial sources: medical investigation procedures (12%), nuclear fallout (0.4%), work-related exposure (0.2%), nuclear discharges (0.1%) and other sources (0.4%).

## RADIOACTIVE DECAY

Radioactive decay is a term used to describe the spontaneous breakdown of the nuclei in an unstable material.

It is down to chance as to whether a particular atomic nucleus will undergo radioactive decay. However, it is possible to measure the overall rate of decay and to know what the general probability is that a particular nucleus will decay. This probability is constant, meaning that the level of radioactivity drops as time goes on, because there are fewer unstable nuclei left that could decay. The time taken for the level of radioactivity to halve remains constant, and is called the half-life.

## Cloud chamber

A cloud chamber is a device for visualizing ionizing radiation. One type of cloud chamber contains alcohol vapour in a clear container with a source of ionizing radiation inside. The container has a flexible base that can be moved to lower the pressure inside. This makes the vapour 'super-saturated' so that the gas is on the point of condensing to form a liquid. Ionizing radiation passing through the gas triggers the condensation, creating a vapour trail through the gas, similar to those produced by aeroplanes.

## MEASURING RADIOACTIVITY

Radioactivity is measured in various units, which vary in how much they relate to the effects on living organisms.

| Property measured | Units | Description |
| --- | --- | --- |
| Activity | Becquerels or Curies | Rate of disintegration of atomic nuclei |
| Exposure | Coulombs per kg dry air or Röntgens | Ability to ionize air |
| Absorbed dose | Grays or Rads | Energy absorbed from radioactivity |
| Dose equivalent | Sieverts | Absorbed dose, adjusted for tissue sensitivity and radiation type |

## Geiger counter

A Geiger counter is a device for measuring the level of ionizing radiation. The main part of it is called a Geiger-Müller tube. This consists of a metal container filled with unreactive gas at low pressure. A metal electrode runs along the middle of the container, and there is a high voltage between the container and the electrode. In the absence of ionizing radiation, the gas consists of atoms and acts as an insulator between the electrode and the container. However, when ionizing radiation passes through, the gas is ionized and a current can flow. The current increases as more radiation ionizes the gas. A Geiger counter has a meter to read the current, and often has a loudspeaker so that each disintegration of a radioactive nucleus can be heard as a click.

## NUCLEAR REACTIONS

Nuclear reactions occur when two nuclei, or subatomic particles from nuclei, collide and produce different products.

The combined mass of the products is usually slightly less than the combined mass of the starting materials. The 'missing' mass corresponds to the subatomic particles that previously held the nuclei together (see **Atoms, elements and molecules: Subatomic particles**), and is released as energy (see **Key concepts: Special theory of relativity**), in the form of high speed particles or gamma rays.

> 66
>
> *The energy produced by the breaking down of the atom is a very poor kind of thing. Anyone who expects a source of power from the transformation of these atoms is talking moonshine.*
>
> —New Zealand physicist Ernest, Lord Rutherford (1871–1937) made this rather inaccurate prediction in about 1933.
>
> 99

### Nuclear fission

Nuclear fission reactions occur when a subatomic particle, usually a neutron, collides with a heavy, unstable atom that contains too many neutrons in its nucleus. The atom splits into two or more fission products, including lighter atoms, neutrons and ionizing radiation.

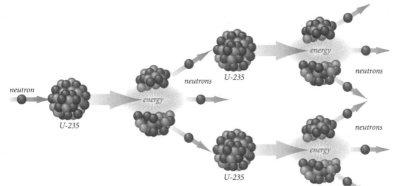

### Fission chain reactions

If several neutrons are released as a result of one neutron colliding with an atom, a chain reaction can occur. Nuclear power stations harness the energy released by nuclear fission chain reactions involving uranium or plutonium. Fission chain reactions were also used in the first atomic bombs.

## Nuclear fusion

Nuclear fusion reactions occur when the nuclei of two atoms join together to make one bigger nucleus. An example is the fusion of two nuclei from certain forms of hydrogen called deuterium and tritium, producing a helium nucleus. Fusion reactions always require that energy is put in to start them off. Fusion of the lighter types of nucleus tends to release more energy than is put in, while fusion of heavier nuclei tends to absorb more energy than is released.

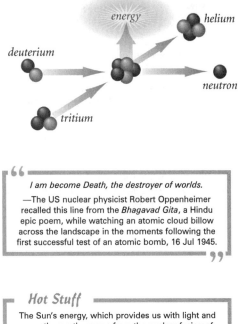

*energy*

*helium*

*deuterium*

*neutron*

*tritium*

> **❝**
>
> *I am become Death, the destroyer of worlds.*
>
> —The US nuclear physicist Robert Oppenheimer recalled this line from the *Bhagavad Gita*, a Hindu epic poem, while watching an atomic cloud billow across the landscape in the moments following the first successful test of an atomic bomb, 16 Jul 1945.
>
> **❞**

### Hot Stuff

The Sun's energy, which provides us with light and warmth, mostly comes from the nuclear fusion of two radioactive forms of hydrogen (deuterium and tritium) to make helium. The world's first power station based on the same fusion reaction, the International Thermonuclear Experimental Reactor (ITER), was given the go-ahead in 2005. The fuel is easier to produce than the enriched uranium needed for fission. If the project is successful, it could therefore lead to much cheaper nuclear energy.

# ELECTRICITY AND MAGNETS

Electricity is a form of energy associated with the separation or movement of charged particles.

> **"**
>
> *Why sir, there is every possibility that you will soon be able to tax it!*
>
> —English physicist Michael Faraday (1891–1867) to W E Gladstone, the Prime Minister, when asked whether electricity would be useful.
>
> **"**

### Electric charge

Symbol: **Q**          Unit: **coulomb**          Abbreviation: **C**

There are two types of electric charge, carried by subatomic particles. Protons have a charge known as 'positive', while electrons have an equal but opposite 'negative' charge. Differing charges attract one another, while like charges repel. Electric charge can not be created or destroyed. It can, however, be moved between atoms or molecules.

### Types of electricity

Electricity is the name given to an imbalance of electric charge. Electric charges can be stationary, in which case the electricity is known as static electricity. Moving charges are called dynamic electricity or, more commonly, electric current.

### Static electricity

Static electricity can be generated by rubbing, or even just touching, two different materials together. It occurs when one material pulls electrons away from the atoms at the surface of the other material, leading to an imbalance of charge. Static electricity tends to build up when the materials are insulators that cannot allow the charges to move through them and disperse.

### Van de Graaff generator

A large amount of static electricity can be generated by using a Van de Graaff generator. A rubber belt is driven at high speed around a roller and picks up extra electrons due to slight slippage. These are passed to a metal dome, which accumulates the negative charges. Van de Graaff generators can be used as a source of electricity for X-ray machines and have also been used in particle accelerators to study subatomic particle collisions.

### Electric potential

Symbol: **V**          Unit: **volt**          Abbreviation: **V**

The electric potential is a measure of how much an electric field can push electric charges. If a charge is at a particular point in an electric field, the electric potential is the amount of energy held by the charge as a result of being there.

Electric potential is defined as the work done to bring a very small positive charge to the place from an infinitely long distance away. The electric potential in volts is equivalent to the energy per unit charge in joules per coulomb.

### Attractive Amber

The precious fossil resin known as amber is not only attractive in a visual sense. When it is rubbed with a cloth, a negative electric charge is built up, and it can attract dust or other particles. The Greek word for amber is *elektron*, which is how the negatively-charged electron got its name.

## Voltage

| Symbol: *V* | Unit: **volt** | Abbreviation: **V** |

Voltage is a measure of the difference in electric potential between two points in an electric field. It is therefore also called potential difference.

When there is a potential difference between two points, charges tend to move between the points in order to release the energy they have and to try to equalize the potentials. This causes electric current to flow.

## Electric current

| Symbol: *I* | Unit: **ampère (amp)** | Abbreviation: **A** |

Electric current is a flow of moving electrical charges. The charge carriers are electrons, which carry negative charge towards the positive side of the circuit. However, current is considered to flow in the opposite direction, from positive to negative; this is called 'conventional current' and is used for historical reasons. The current in amps is equivalent to the flow of charge in coulombs per second.

### Current Affairs

When a current of 1 amp is flowing through a wire, around $6 \times 10^{18}$, or six quintillion, electrons pass through the wire each second. This is more than the total estimated number of insects on Earth.

## Electric fields

An electric field is a region in which forces are exerted on any electric charge present. The strength of an electric field can be measured as force per unit of charge, in newtons per coulomb, or as the potential difference across a set distance, in volts per metre. These measurements are equivalent. Electric field is represented by the symbol *E*.

## Conductors, insulators and dielectrics

### Conductors

Materials that allow current to flow easily are known as conductors. They have 'gaps' in the arrangements of electrons surrounding each atom, and this allows electrons to move between the gaps, in the same way that the tiles can move in a sliding tile puzzle.

### Insulators

Materials through which current cannot easily flow are called insulators. They have electron arrangements without any 'gaps', so the electrons are unable to move around.

### Dielectrics

Insulating materials are used in electrical components called capacitors, when they are known as dielectrics.

## Resistance

| Symbol: **R** | Unit: **ohm** | Abbreviation: Ω |

Resistance is a measure of how difficult it is for a current to flow through a material. The resistance in ohms is equivalent to the voltage across the material in volts divided by the current flow in amps (see **Key concepts: Ohm's law**). Resistance occurs because electrons cannot usually move through the lattice structure of a material with complete efficiency; instead they scatter and collide, losing energy in the form of heat.

### Temperature and resistance

Higher temperatures increase resistance because the lattice vibrates more, making electron flow even less efficient.

### Impurities and resistance

Impurities in the material can also increase resistance, due to flaws in the lattice.

## Power

| Symbol: **P** | Unit: **watt** | Abbreviation: **W** |

Power is the rate at which energy is transferred. It can apply to electrical energy and other energy forms. For electrical energy, the power in watts is equivalent to the current in amps multiplied by the voltage in volts.

## Capacitance

| Symbol: **C** | Unit: **farad** | Abbreviation: **F** |

Capacitance is a measure of how much charge an object can hold when a particular voltage is applied to it. Capacitance occurs when two conductors are insulated from each other, so that current is unable to flow between them. Instead, charge builds up on the two conductors. The capacitance in farads is equivalent to the charge at a given potential, in coulombs per volt.

## Electrochemical cells

An electrochemical cell is a single device that converts stored chemical energy into electrical energy.

### Chemical reactions in cells

An electrochemical cell has two compartments, each with an electrode immersed in a solution or gel, known as the electrolyte, that contains positively-charged ions. A chemical reaction takes place between the electrode and the electrolyte in each half of the cell.

| Electrode | Reaction | Description |
| --- | --- | --- |
| Anode | Oxidation | Loss of electrons; atoms become positively-charged ions |
| Cathode | Reduction | Gain of electrons; positively-charged ions become atoms |

### Ion and electron movements

The two halves of the cell are joined by a connection called a salt bridge, to allow ions to move between them without the solutions mixing. However, electrons also need to move between the compartments; this happens when the electrodes are connected together to form an electrical circuit. The chemical reactions therefore make current flow through a wire connecting them.

### Electrochemical series

The voltage that will be produced by a cell, and the type of reaction that will take place at each electrode, depends on the materials used. This can be predicted by looking up the position of the materials in a list called the electrochemical series.

### Batteries

A group of cells that are used together as one unit is known as a battery. The devices that are commonly known as 'batteries' are usually in fact cells, as they are single devices rather than groups.

### Electromotive force

An electrochemical cell has a theoretical voltage between its electrodes, which depends on the two chemical reactions taking place. This is called the electromotive force, or emf. However, if the voltage between the electrodes is measured when a current is flowing, it is never as high as the emf. This is because the cell itself has some resistance to current flow, which 'wastes' some of the electrical energy.

## Circuits

A circuit is a conducting path (often wire) along which electrons can flow. It connects one end of a source of electrical energy to the other end, with various electrical components in between.

The electrical energy source in a circuit creates a potential difference between its two ends, and this causes current to flow along the wires of the circuit. A circuit can be compared with water being pumped around a pipeline.

| Electrical circuit | Water circuit equivalent |
|---|---|
| Battery | Pump |
| Wire | Pipes |
| Electric potential | Water pressure |
| Current | Flow rate of water |
| Charge | Volume of water in the pipes |
| Resistance | Narrower pipes |

## Electrical components

Various electrical components can be connected into a circuit by two or more terminals.

### Switches

Switches allow a circuit to be completed or broken, so that current flow to other devices can be controlled.

### Resistors

Resistors are components that have high resistance to current flow. When current flows through a resistor, electrical energy is converted to heat.

### Variable resistors and potentiometers

Variable resistors are resistors that have one of their terminals connected to a slider, allowing the proportion of the resistor in the circuit to be altered. They are also called rheostats. If both ends of the resistor are connected into a circuit and the slider is connected to a third wire, a variable voltage can be extracted from the circuit. This is called a potential divider or potentiometer.

### Filaments

A filament is a fine wire with very high resistance. It gets hot enough to glow when a current passes through it because it gives out electromagnetic radiation, some of which is in the visible light frequency range (see **Energy, light and radioactivity: Electromagnetic radiation**). This is called incandescence. Some of the radiation is also at lower wavelengths, including infrared. Filaments are used in electric light bulbs.

### Capacitors

Capacitors use the property of capacitance to store electrical energy. They are often made from a dielectric (insulating) material sandwiched between two conducting plates. Opposite charges build up on the conducting plates but current cannot flow due to the insulation between them.

### Diodes

Diodes are devices that are made from two different semiconductor materials, one of which (the n-doped layer) has extra electrons and the other (the p-doped layer) extra positive 'holes'. The junction between these two layers only allows current to flow in one direction. (See also **Materials: Electronics materials**.)

### LEDs

A light emitting diode, or LED, is a special type of diode that emits light when current is passed through it. The light emission is caused by changes in the amount of energy posessed by electrons in the diode; when an electron in an LED loses energy, it gives it out in the form of visible light. Different types of LED can give out different colours of light, depending on the amount of energy lost by the electrons.

### Photodiodes

Photodiodes work in the opposite way to LEDs – light falling on a photodiode gives electrons enough energy to move electrons through the semiconductor material, causing a current to flow. Photodiodes are used to generate electricity from sunlight in solar panels. They can also be used as light sensors, as the amount of current they generate increases with the amount of light.

### Transistors

Transistors are formed from a 'sandwich' of semiconductor material (see **Materials: Electronics materials**). They are made in two varieties: n-p-n transistors have a layer of p-doped material between two layers of n-doped material, while p-n-p transistors have a layer of n-doped material between two layers of p-doped material. They can therefore be thought of as two diodes placed back-to-back.

The middle part of the transistor is called the base. In a p-n-p transistor, a small current flowing from the base to one of the ends, known as the emitter, can control a larger current flowing from the emitter to the other end, known as the collector. (The emitter and collector are reversed in an n-p-n transistor.) Transistors are therefore used as amplifiers. They can also be used as switches, and connected together to make logic gates.

### Logic gates

Logic gates are devices that give an output that depends on one or more inputs. They can therefore be used to make a circuit alter its behaviour under different circumstances. The output can be on or off, usually represented by the binary numbers 1 and 0 respectively. In electrical circuits, logic gates are often made from transistors, and the on and off states correspond to the presence or absence of a voltage.

| Gate | Number of inputs | Conditions for output to be on |
|------|------------------|-------------------------------|
| NOT | 1 | Input is off |
| OR | 2 or more | At least one input is on |
| NOR ('not or') | 2 or more | No inputs are on |
| EOR ('exclusive or') | 2 | One input is on, but not both |
| EX-NOR ('exclusive nor') | 2 | Both inputs must be the same (on or off) |
| AND | 2 or more | All inputs are on |
| NAND ('not and') | 2 or more | Not all of the inputs are on |

## *Nifty NAND Gates*

Any logic gate can be built by combining two-input NAND gates, and whole series of these gates can be used to carry out complex mathematical calculations. Even the most complicated electrical computer processors could be built this way, as they operate using logical procedures.

## Direct and alternating current

### Direct current

Direct current (DC) always flows in the same direction. It has a constant voltage, and would be drawn as a straight horizontal line on a graph of voltage against time.

### Alternating current

Alternating current (AC) regularly changes direction and would therefore be drawn as a wave on a graph of voltage against time, with the amplitude (height) of the wave equal to the voltage. The voltage moves between equally large positive and negative values, which represent the two directions of current flow, and passes through zero. Because the voltage varies, the voltage stated on AC power supplies has to be an average value. A special type of average, known as the root mean square, is used – an ordinary average would give a value of zero, which wouldn't be very informative.

## MAGNETS

Magnets can attract certain metals, and attract and repel each other. Their ability to line up with the Earth's own magnetic field allows them to be used in a compass to find direction.

## Magnetic poles

There are two types of magnetic pole, which are named north and south to correspond with the Earth's poles. If a magnet is allowed to spin freely on a thread, the end that ends up pointing north is the north pole, while the end that points south is the south pole.

## Magnetic field

Magnets are surrounded by a magnetic field, which then influences other materials. Any change in a magnetic field produces a force.

The field can be thought of as a set of arrows running from the north pole to the south pole, and can be visualized by placing a magnet under a piece of paper and sprinkling iron filings on the paper. The field lines for a bar magnet and a horseshoe magnet are shown, as well as those between pairs of bar magnets.

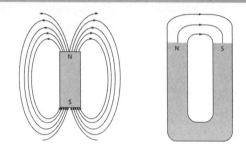

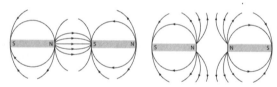

### Magnetic imaging

The nuclei of some elements, including hydrogen, tend to line up in certain directions when they are placed in a magnetic field. Radio waves at a particular frequency can make the nuclei resonate, flipping backwards and forwards between these directions. This technique is called nuclear magnetic resonance, or NMR, and is used to work out the structure of molecules. The resonance of hydrogen nuclei in water molecules can be used to produce images of the human body in a safe and non-invasive way; this is known as magnetic resonance imaging, or MRI.

### Magnetic flux density

| Symbol: **B** | Unit: **tesla** | Abbreviation: **T** |
|---|---|---|

Magnetic flux density is a measurement of the strength of a magnetic field.

### Magnetic flux

| Symbol: **ø** | Unit: **weber** | Abbreviation: **Wb** |
|---|---|---|

Magnetic flux is a measure of the strength and extent of a magnetic field. It takes into account the magnetic flux density and the area of material through which the magnetic flux is measured.

## Attraction and repulsion

Like poles repel each other, but opposite poles are attracted to each other. If the north pole of one magnet is brought close to the south pole of a second magnet, the magnets are drawn towards one another. If the magnets are brought together so that the north poles are facing one another, they will try to push each other away.

## Theory of magnetism

### Electron spin

Magnetism is caused by the arrangement of electrons in a material. The electrons have a property called spin, which produces a tiny magnetic field. The direction of this field depends on the spin direction of the electron, which can be either 'up' or 'down', and there is always one electron of each type in an electron pair.

### Spin alignment

In most materials the effects of the 'up' and 'down' electrons cancel out, but if these become aligned, the magnetic fields combine to make the material magnetic. Alignment occurs at the level of the electrons within an atom, the atoms within a section of the material known as a domain, and the arrangement of the domains.

## Types of magnetism

There are four types of magnetism: diamagnetism, paramagnetism, ferromagnetism and ferrimagnetism.

| Type | Relative effect | Direction relative to field | Timescale |
| --- | --- | --- | --- |
| Diamagnetism | Very weak | Opposite | Temporary |
| Paramagnetism | Weak | Same | Temporary |
| Ferromagnetism/ ferrimagnetism | Strong | Same | Permanent |

### Diamagnetism

All materials can become diamagnetic when placed in a magnetic field, where all of the electrons line up to oppose the magnetic field.

### Paramagnetism

Some materials can experience paramagnetism because some of the electrons in the atoms are unpaired, and the numbers of electrons with each type of spin are not balanced. The 'leftover' electrons line up in the same direction under the influence of a magnetic field.

### Ferromagnetism

Iron, nickel and cobalt are ferromagnetic. They have unpaired electrons, as with paramagnetism, but the spins of these electrons tend to stay lined up in the same direction even when they are not in an externally applied magnetic field.

### Ferrimagnetism

Ferrimagnetic materials include the mineral magnetite and also have unpaired electrons. The spins of the electrons tend to line up in opposite directions but the spin is greater in one direction than the other, and the overall effect still produces magnetism. The material must contain more than one chemical element in order for the spins to be different, so ferrimagnetism does not occur in pure metals.

## ELECTROMAGNETISM

Electricity and magnetism are closely interrelated. The combination of electric and magnetic fields is known as electromagnetism.

Changes in a magnetic field can produce an electric current, and the movement of electrical charges can produce a magnetic field. The electromagnetic force is one of the four fundamental forces (see **Key concepts: Theory of Everything**).

### Solenoids

A solenoid is a coil of wire through which an electric current can be passed. When the current flows, the electric field produces a magnetic field around the coil. The field lines look similar to those of a bar magnet.

Permanent magnets can be made by placing a piece of steel inside a solenoid, so that the magnetic field surrounding the solenoid magnetizes the steel. A solenoid whose current can be switched on and off is known as an electromagnet. Switching the current on or off turns the magnet on and off. This is used in crane arms in scrapyards, where an electromagnet is turned on to pick up scrap iron, and turned off again to drop it.

### Electromagnetic induction

The physicist Michael Faraday worked out that electric current, magnetic field and force (producing movement) are all related. He showed that if any one of the three changes, at least one of the others also changes as as result, a principle known as Faraday's law. The current, magnetic field and force are all at right-angles to each other.

#### Using movement to change current

If a wire is moved through a magnetic field, the magnetic field lines are disturbed and a current is induced in the wire. This is the principle behind an electric generator.

#### Using current to change movement

If a current is sent through a wire in a magnetic field, this also disturbs the field and the wire moves as a result. This is the basis of electric motors.

### Using current to change the magnetic field

If a current is sent through a fixed wire in a magnetic field, the field is changed. This method of changing the field is used to magnetize cassette or video tapes in recording equipment.

### Using the magnetic field to change current

If a wire is in a magnetic field that is changing, for example when magnetic tape is run past the wire, a current will be induced in the wire. This is the principle behind playing video and cassette tapes.

### Why perpetual motion machines can't work

It might seem as though the motor and generator effects could produce a 'perpetual motion' machine, where a moving wire in a magnetic field could induce a current, which could then make the wire move more, and so on. However, when a moving wire induces a current, the force produced tries to move the wire back the other way, so energy is always needed to keep motors and generators running.

---

**Mass spectrometry**

Mass spectrometry is a technique for determining atomic mass, and is often used to analyse a mixture of molecules. The sample is bombarded with electrons to give all the molecules present a negative charge. The charged particles are accelerated along a tube using positive charges to attract them, and electromagnetic fields are used to bend the stream of particles. The amount by which different particles are sent off course allows their masses to be calculated, because lighter particles are deflected more than heavier ones.

---

## Transformers

The relationship between electrical and magnetic fields can be used to change the current and voltage of an AC current. A device that can do this is called a transformer, and consists of two coils of wire. A current is passed through the first coil, inducing a magnetic field that induces a current in the second coil.

Voltage and current can be altered by using coils with different numbers of turns. The coil with more turns has a higher voltage but lower current, while the one with fewer turns has a lower voltage but higher current. The current multiplied by the voltage gives the same result for both coils.

## Electromagnetic radiation

Electric and magnetic fields exist together in the form of electromagnetic radiation (see **Energy, light and radioactivity: Electromagnetic radiation**). The electric and magnetic fields 'feed' off one another, rising and falling due to Faraday's law. As the magnetic field strength increases, it increases the strength of the electrical field, which then tries to produce a magnetic field in the opposite direction. This decreases the magnetic field, which in turn decreases the electric field, so the magnetic field can increase again. This means that each field increases and decreases, but they do so out of phase rather than at the same time. The two fields are always at right-angles to one another. This phenomenon is called polarization.

# NUMBERS AND SHAPES

The numbers used in science and mathematics are based on the number system known as Arabic numerals. In fact, they are derived from India.

## Natural numbers

The natural numbers are the 'counting' numbers.

1, 2, 3, 4, 5 ...

## Whole numbers

The whole numbers are zero and the 'counting' numbers.

0, 1, 2, 3, 4, 5 ...

## Integers

The integers are negative whole numbers, zero and positive whole numbers.

... –5, –4, –3, –2, –1, 0, 1, 2, 3, 4, 5 ...

## Rational numbers

Rational numbers are numbers that can be expressed as a fraction of two integers. The rational numbers include all of the integers as well as the fractional numbers between them.

0.75 is a rational number because it is equal to ¾.

2.6666... is a rational number because it can be written ⁸⁄₃.

## Irrational numbers

Irrational numbers are numbers that cannot be expressed as a fraction of two integers. However, they can still be expressed as solutions to a type of equation called a polynomial that is made up of rational numbers.

The square root of 2, written $\sqrt{2}$, is an irrational number.

## Transcendental numbers

Two well-known irrational numbers have special symbols. They are known as transcendental numbers, and cannot be expressed as solutions to a polynomial equation made up of rational numbers.

**e** is the base of the natural system of logarithms, a system important in studying decay curves. Its value is 2.718 to three decimal places.

**π** (pi) is the ratio of the circumference of a circle to its diameter. Its value is 3.142 to three decimal places.

> *Do not worry about your difficulties in mathematics,*
> *I assure you that mine are greater.*
>
> —Albert Einstein (1879–1955).

### A Bigger Piece of Pi

Although π is often represented as 3.142, it actually has an infinite number of decimal places, and there is a tradition of attempts to recite from memory as many of these as possible. In 2005, Akira Haraguchi of Japan was reported to have smashed the world record – if verified, his public recitation of π to 83 431 decimal places will nearly double the previous record, which was set in 1995. In terms of pure showmanship, however, Haraguchi's achievement is somewhat overshadowed by that of Mats Bergsten of Sweden, who, several months earlier, managed to recite π to 9778 decimal places whilst juggling three balls.

## Real numbers

The real numbers comprise all of the rational and irrational numbers.

## Imaginary numbers

The square roots of negative numbers cannot be calculated in the set of real numbers. In the imaginary numbers, the square root of –1 is defined as a quantity called $i$, allowing this problem to be overcome.

## Complex numbers

A complex number is made up of a real part and an imaginary part. This type of number is used extensively by physicists and electrical engineers.

$3 + i$ is an example of a complex number. Engineers often use the letter $j$ rather than $i$ to avoid confusion with their symbol for electrical current.

> *Whenever you can, count.*
>
> —English scientist Sir Francis Galton (1822–1911), in
> *The World of Mathematics*, edited by J R Newman
> (1956).

## LARGE NUMBERS

The names of large numbers formerly differed between the UK and the USA. In the UK, a billion was one million millions, rather than one thousand millions as given below. International economics has led to the US system becoming increasingly used worldwide and by scientists. The US system is given below; to find the former British equivalents from billion to decillion, increase the power by 6 each time (hence one billion becomes $10^{12}$ and one trillion becomes $10^{18}$). One British centillion is $10^{600}$.

| thousand | $10^3$ | 1 000 |
| million | $10^6$ | 1 000 000 |
| billion | $10^9$ | 1 000 000 000 |
| trillion | $10^{12}$ | 1 000 000 000 000 |
| quadrillion | $10^{15}$ | 1 000 000 000 000 000 |
| quintillion | $10^{18}$ | 1 000 000 000 000 000 000 |
| sextillion | $10^{21}$ | 1 000 000 000 000 000 000 000 |
| septillion | $10^{24}$ | 1 000 000 000 000 000 000 000 000 |
| octillion | $10^{27}$ | 1 000 000 000 000 000 000 000 000 000 |
| nonillion | $10^{30}$ | 1 000 000 000 000 000 000 000 000 000 000 |
| decillion | $10^{33}$ | 1 000 000 000 000 000 000 000 000 000 000 000 |
| googol | $10^{100}$ | 1 followed by 100 zeros |
| centillion | $10^{303}$ | 1 followed by 303 zeros |
| googolplex | 10 to the power of a googol | 1 followed by a googol of zeros |

## PRIME NUMBERS

A prime number is a natural number that can be divided by exactly two numbers – 1 or the number itself. For example, 11 is a prime number, as it is only divisible by 1 or 11. The number 1 is not prime, as it can only be divided by one number. The prime numbers between 1 and 50 are listed.

2, 3, 5, 7, 11, 13, 17, 19, 23, 29, 31, 37, 41, 43, 47...

## SIGNS AND SYMBOLS

Some signs and symbols used in mathematics are listed.

| + | plus; positive; underestimate | $\infty$ | infinity |
| – | minus; negative; overestimate | $\rightarrow$ | approaches the limit |
| ± | plus or minus; positive or negative; degree of accuracy | $\sqrt{}$ | square root |
| ∓ | minus or plus; negative or positive | $\sqrt[3]{}, \sqrt[4]{}$ | cube root, fourth root, etc. |
| | | ! | factorial ($4! = 4 \times 3 \times 2 \times 1$) |
| x | multiplies (colloq. 'times') (6x 4) | % | percent |

| | | | |
|---|---|---|---|
| · | multiplies (colloq. 'times') (6.4); scalar product of two vectors (A·B) | ' | prime; minute(s) of arc; foot/feet |
| ÷ | divided by (6÷4) | " | double prime; second(s) of arc; inch(es) |
| / | divided by; ratio of (6/4) | ⌒ | arc of circle |
| — | divided by; ratio of ($\frac{6}{4}$) | ° | degree of arc |
| = | equals | ∠, ∠s | angle(s) |
| ≠, ≠ | not equal to | ⋛ | equiangular |
| ≡ | identical with | ⊥ | perpendicular |
| ≢, ≢ | not identical with | ‖ | parallel |
| : | ratio of (6 : 4); scalar product of two tensors (X : Y) | ◯, ⑤ | circle(s) |
| :: | proportionately equals (1 : 2 :: 2 : 4) | △, ⚠ | triangle(s) |
| ≈ | approximately equal to; equivalent to; similar to | □ | square(s) |
| | | ▭ | rectangle |
| > | greater than | ▱ | parallelogram |
| ≫ | much greater than | ≅ | congruent to |
| ≯ | not greater than | ∴ | therefore |
| < | less than | ∵ | because |
| ≪ | much less than | $\stackrel{m}{=}$ | measured by |
| ≮ | not less than | △ | increment |
| ≥, ≧, ⋛ | equal to or greater than | Σ | summation |
| ≤, ≦, ⋜ | equal to or less than | Π | product |
| ∝ | directly proportional to | ∫ | integral sign |
| ( ) | parentheses | ▽ | del: differential operator |
| [ ] | brackets | ∩ | union |
| { } | braces | ∪ | interaction |
| — | vinculum: division ($\overline{a-b}$); chord of circle or length of line ($\overline{AB}$); arithmetic mean ($\overline{X}$) | | |

**Mathematical Signs and Symbols**

## GREEK ALPHABET

Lower-case letters from the Greek alphabet are often used to represent unknown quantities in formulae and equations. Greek letters are also used to represent certain scientific concepts (see **Measurement: SI units**).

| Letter name | Lower-case | Upper-case | Letter name | Lower-case | Upper-case |
|---|---|---|---|---|---|
| alpha | α | A | epsilon | ε | E |
| beta | β | B | zeta | ζ | Z |
| gamma | γ | Γ | eta | η | H |
| delta | δ | Δ | theta | θ | Θ |

| Letter name | Lower-case | Upper-case | Letter name | Lower-case | Upper-case |
|---|---|---|---|---|---|
| iota | $\iota$ | I | rho | $\rho$ | P |
| kappa | $\kappa$ | K | sigma | $\sigma$ | $\Sigma$ |
| lambda | $\lambda$ | $\Lambda$ | tau | $\tau$ | T |
| mu | $\mu$ | M | upsilon | $\upsilon$ | Y |
| nu | $\nu$ | N | phi | $\varphi$ | $\Phi$ |
| xi | $\xi$ | $\Xi$ | chi | $\chi$ | X |
| omicron | o | O | psi | $\psi$ | $\Psi$ |
| pi | $\pi$ | $\Pi$ | omega | $\omega$ | $\Omega$ |

## POLYGONS

### Names of polygons

A polygon is a many-sided plane (flat) figure. Polygons are therefore two-dimensional. If all the sides are the same length, a polygon can be described as regular.

| Number of sides | Polygon |
|---|---|
| $n$ | $n$-gon |
| 3 | Triangle, trigon |
| 4 | Tetragon, quadrilateral |
| 5 | Pentagon |
| 6 | Hexagon |
| 7 | Heptagon |
| 8 | Octagon |
| 9 | Nonagon, enneagon |
| 10 | Decagon |
| 11 | Undecagon, hendecagon |
| 12 | Dodecagon |
| 13 | Tridecagon, triskaidecagon |
| 14 | Tetradecagon, tetrakaidecagon |
| 15 | Pentadecagon, pentakaidecagon |
| 16 | Hexadecagon, hexakaidecagon |
| 17 | Heptadecagon, heptakaidecagon |
| 18 | Octadecagon, octakaidecagon |
| 19 | Enneadecagon, enneakaidecagon |
| 1000 | Chiliagon |

Other names have been proposed for larger polygons using a system of prefixes but the form *n*-gon, eg 76-gon for a figure with 76 sides, is more common. The name myriagon has been proposed for a polygon with 10 000 sides.

> *Let no one ignorant of geometry enter my door.*
> —Tradition has it that this was inscribed over the door of Plato's Academy.

## Triangles

The three internal angles of a triangle always add up to 180°. If one of the angles is 90°, the triangle is said to be a 'right-angled triangle' (see **Key concepts: Pythagoras's theorem**). Triangles can be classified according to the number of sides of equal length. They have many interesting properties, including the relationships between their angles and the length of their sides. The study of triangles and their properties is called trigonometry.

| Triangle | Number of equal sides |
| --- | --- |
| Equilateral | 3 equal sides |
| Isosceles | 2 equal sides, 1 different |
| Scalene | No equal sides |

## Quadrilaterals

A four-sided polygon is normally called a quadrilateral or tetragon. However, some of these shapes have special names, depending on their internal angles and the lengths of their sides. The internal angles of a quadrilateral always add up to 360°.

| Shape | Internal angles | Length of sides |
| --- | --- | --- |
| Kite | Not 90° | Each pair of adjacent sides is equal |
| Square | All 90° | All equal |
| Rectangle | All 90° | Each pair of parallel sides is equal |
| Rhombus | Not 90° | All equal |
| Parallelogram | Not 90° | Each pair of parallel sides is equal |
| Trapezium | Not 90° | One pair of parallel sides is equal |

## Circles

Circles are flat shapes that have a single curved edge. All parts of this edge are the same distance from a point at the centre of the circle.

The length of the edge, ie the distance around the circle, is called the circumference. The diameter of a circle is the distance across it, through the centre point. The radius is the distance from the centre point to the edge, so it is always equal to half the diameter. The ratio between the circumference and the diameter of a circle is fixed, and is equal to the number π or 'pi' (see **Types of numbers**).

## POLYHEDRA

### Names of polyhedra

A polyhedron is a three-dimensional shape with flat faces and straight edges. The edges meet at points; each of these is called a vertex and they are collectively called vertices. The numbers of faces, vertices and edges are related by the formula:

**Faces + Vertices – Edges = 2**

| Number of faces | Polyhedron |
| --- | --- |
| 4 | Ttetrahedron |
| 5 | Pentahedron |
| 6 | Hexahedron |
| 7 | Heptahedron |
| 8 | Octahedron, octohedron |
| 9 | Enneahedron |
| 10 | Decahedron |
| 11 | Undecahedron |
| 12 | Dodecahedron |
| 20 | Icosahedron |
| 1000 | Chiliahedron |

### Platonic solids

If the faces of a polyhedron are all the same shape, it is described as regular. There are five regular polyhedra, known as the Platonic solids because they were described by the Greek philosopher Plato.

| Regular polyhedron | Faces | Shape of face |
| --- | --- | --- |
| Tetrahedron | 4 | Equilateral triangle |
| Cube | 6 | Square |
| Octahedron | 8 | Equilateral triangle |
| Dodecahedron | 12 | Pentagon |
| Icosahedron | 20 | Equilateral triangle |

## Other solids

Some irregular polyhedra and other solids have special names.

| Name | Faces | Description |
|------|-------|-------------|
| Pyramid | 5 | Square base plus four triangular faces |
| Cylinder | 3 | Two flat circular faces plus one curved face |
| Cone | 2 | One flat circular face plus one curved face |
| Sphere | 1 | One curved face |

> "
> *Treat nature in terms of the cylinder, the sphere, the cone, all in perspective.*
>
> —French painter Paul Cézanne (1839–1906), in *Paul Cézanne* by Emile Bernard (1925).
> "

## CONIC SECTIONS

A conic section is the curved figure produced when a plane (flat surface) intersects a cone. Depending on the angle at which it cuts through the cone, it may be a circle, ellipse, hyperbola or parabola. Two special cases of intersection give rise to a single point or straight lines rather than a curved figure. *V* is the vertex of the right cone.

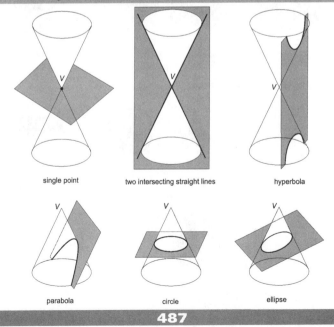

single point

two intersecting straight lines

hyperbola

parabola

circle

ellipse

---

*Picking up by Paraboloid*

Satellite dishes are in the form of paraboloids –
three-dimensional shapes that are related to the two-
dimensional parabola. This shape enables satellite
dishes to receive incoming parallel radio waves and
focus them to a point.

## AREAS AND VOLUMES OF SHAPES

The value of $\pi$, the ratio of the circumference of a circle to its diameter, is used in some of the formulae below.

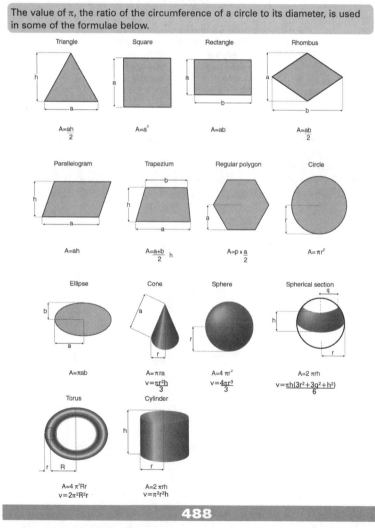

Triangle
$$A = \frac{ah}{2}$$

Square
$$A = a^2$$

Rectangle
$$A = ab$$

Rhombus
$$A = \frac{ab}{2}$$

Parallelogram
$$A = ah$$

Trapezium
$$A = \frac{a+b}{2}\,h$$

Regular polygon
$$A = p \times \frac{a}{2}$$

Circle
$$A = \pi r^2$$

Ellipse
$$A = \pi ab$$

Cone
$$A = \pi ra$$
$$v = \frac{\pi r^2 h}{3}$$

Sphere
$$A = 4\pi r^2$$
$$v = \frac{4\pi r^3}{3}$$

Spherical section
$$A = 2\pi rh$$
$$v = \frac{\pi h(3r^2 + 3q^2 + h^2)}{6}$$

Torus
$$A = 4\pi^2 Rr$$
$$v = 2\pi^2 R^2 r$$

Cylinder
$$A = 2\pi rh$$
$$v = \pi^2 r^2 h$$

## TOPOLOGY

> Topology is the study of shapes and their properties.

### Surfaces and holes

An important aspect of topology for solid objects is the number of surfaces and holes they have. For example, a sphere has one curved face and no holes. A torus (ring doughnut) also has one curved face but it has a hole in it.

### Topological equivalence

Shapes are topologically equivalent if it is possible to turn one into the other without 'tearing' or 'sticking' any parts of the shape. A rectangle and a square are topologically equivalent because a square can be stretched to make a rectangle. A torus and a coffee-cup are topologically equivalent because a coffee-cup, like a torus, has a single hole in it (through the handle). The main part of the cup could be made by stretching and squashing the torus without having to tear or stick it. A sphere is not topologically equivalent to a torus because they have different numbers of holes.

**Topological Equivalence of a Torus and a Coffee-Cup**

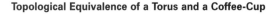

### Tie-ing the Knot

Topologists also study knots, and this recently led to something of a sartorial revolution when two theoretical physicists from the University of Cambridge used knot theory to work out 85 ways of tying a tie. Their research was published in the journal *Nature* and in a book (imaginatively titled *The 85 Ways to Tie a Tie*). Previously, people had only tied their ties in four ways: the Windsor, Half-Windsor, Four-in-Hand, and Pratt Knot. These four ways were all predicted by the research, and featured in the 13 results that were declared aesthetically pleasing.

*'Tie knots, we realised, are equivalent to persistent random walks on a triangular lattice.'*

—Thomas Fink and Yong Mao in *The 85 Ways to Tie a Tie* (1999).

## SYMMETRY

> The symmetry of a shape relates to whether, and how, different parts of the shape correspond to one another.

3-fold
rotational
symmetry

2-fold
reflectional
symmetry

translational
symmetry

### Reflectional symmetry

A shape has reflectional symmetry if each point on one side of a central line – the line of symmetry – has a corresponding point on the other side of the line. Shapes with reflectional symmetry can be folded in half along the line of symmetry and the two halves will lie exactly on top of one another. If a mirror is placed on the line of symmetry, the whole shape will still be seen.

### Rotational symmetry

An image has rotational symmetry if it can be rotated around a central point and still match its original shape. The number of positions in which it can match itself is called the order of symmetry. For example, if a square is rotated, it matches itself four times in a complete rotation, so its order of symmetry is equal to four.

### Translational symmetry

A shape has translational symmetry if it is made up of repeating units, and if each unit can be slid along to match the next unit without being flipped or turned.

## FIBONACCI NUMBERS

> The Fibonacci series of numbers starts with the numbers 0 and 1; each successive number is then the sum of the previous two. The series therefore starts:
>
> **0, 1, 1, 2, 3, 5, 8, 13, 21, 34, 55, 89, 144 ...**
>
> The series is named after the Italian mathematician Leonardo Pisano, who was known as Fibonacci.

### Fibonacci's rabbits

Fibonacci is said to have derived the series by considering a population of rabbits, in which each pair becomes mature at one month old and gives birth to a single pair during each month after that. The following table shows how many pairs of adult (A) and baby (B) rabbits exist at the end of each month. At each step, every A becomes AB (the adults plus their new baby pair) and each B becomes A (the babies maturing).

Fibonacci noticed that the total number of pairs at the end of each month was a member of the Fibonacci series. In fact, the number of adult pairs also follows the series, but lags one place behind.

| Month | Rabbit pairs | Total pairs | Adult pairs |
|---|---|---|---|
| 1 | A | 1 | 1 |
| 2 | AB | 2 | 1 |
| 3 | ABA | 3 | 2 |
| 4 | ABAAB | 5 | 3 |
| 5 | ABAABABA | 8 | 5 |
| 6 | ABAABABAABAAB | 13 | 8 |

### The golden ratio

The golden ratio is usually represented by the symbol φ (phi), and is also called the golden mean or golden number. The ratio of the golden number to 1 is equal to the ratio of 1 to 'the golden number minus 1'. This can be written as an equation:

$$\frac{\varphi}{1} = \frac{1}{1-\varphi}$$

The golden number is an irrational number, with an infinite number of decimal places, so it can never be written down accurately. It is approximately equal to 1.618.

$$\frac{1.618034...}{1} = \frac{1}{0.618034...}$$

The ratio of two consecutive numbers from the Fibonacci series gets closer and closer to the golden ratio as the numbers are taken from further and further along the series. For example, $3 \div 2$ is 1.5 (too low), $5 \div 3$ is 1.666... (too high), $8 \div 5$ is 1.6 (too low), $13 \div 8$ is 1.625 (too high), $21 \div 13$ is 1.615... (too low) and so on. The numbers 'bounce' either side of the actual golden number but, by the time $89 \div 55$ is reached, the value is already at 1.618181818... – and those are only the twelfth and eleventh numbers in the series.

### The golden rectangle

A rectangle with lengths of sides that are in the golden ratio is called a golden rectangle. Sectioning off the biggest possible square from a golden rectangle leaves another golden rectangle. If this is done repeatedly, a spiral can be drawn through the corners that looks extremely similar to the Fibonacci spiral (see **Fibonacci spiral**).

## Fibonacci series in nature

Fibonacci's rabbit model isn't very realistic, as it doesn't take into account the fact that some of the rabbits might die! However, the number series occurs in nature for real. Flowers such as sunflowers have their seeds arranged so that they form two sets of spirals, one curving in each direction. The numbers of spirals in each set are always two consecutive numbers from the Fibonacci series. The same pattern can be seen in the arrangement of the hard 'leaves' of a pine cone. The arrangements of leaves round a plant stem are often related to the Fibonacci series as well.

## Fibonacci spiral

A Fibonacci spiral is drawn by constructing adjoining boxes of areas that correspond to the numbers in the Fibonacci series. The spiral itself runs through the corners of each box.

The Fibonacci spiral is seen in nature, for example in nautilus shells.

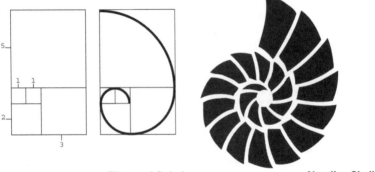

**Fibonacci Spiral**                    **Nautilus Shell**

## FRACTALS

Fractals are geometric shapes that contain ever smaller repeats of the same shapes. They are graphic representations of iterative (endlessly repeating) mathematical functions that involve complex numbers. Two famous types of fractals are the Julia set, devised by the French mathematician Gaston Julia, and the Mandelbrot set, devised by the Polish-born mathematician Benoit Mandelbrot.

## Koch's snowflake

A simple example of a fractal is Koch's snowflake, which is constructed by drawing a triangle and, for each side, removing the middle section and replacing it with two lines of equal length. The replacement of the middle section of each line is then repeated endlessly.

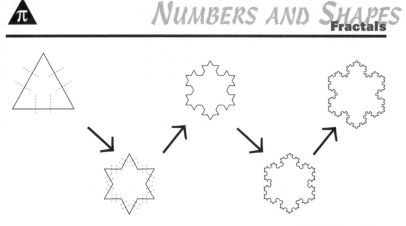

**Koch's Snowflake**

### Infinite perimeter and finite area

Koch's snowflake has an infinitely long perimeter. However, if a circle is drawn around the original triangle, the snowflake will always fit inside that same circle. The area of the shape gets closer and closer to a fixed value as more and more iterations are carried out. Koch's snowflake is therefore said to have a finite area – this is a common property of fractals.

---

*Mathematical Vegetables*

Romanesco, a lime-green relative of cauliflower and broccoli, has florets arranged in two sets of spirals, like a sunflower's seeds; just like the sunflower, the numbers of spirals are consecutive numbers in the Fibonacci series. Also, like fern fronds, Romanesco has fractal properties – each floret is a miniature version of the whole head of Romanesco, and is in turn made up of tiny versions of the same shape. It doesn't taste too bad, either.

---

❝

*Mathematics possesses not only truth, but supreme beauty – a beauty cold and austere, like that of sculpture.*

—English mathematician and philosopher Bertrand Russell (1872–1970), in *The Principles of Mathematics* (1903).

❞

---

### Fractal dimensions

Whereas a line is one-dimensional, and a polygon two-dimensional, a fractal on a flat surface has a 'fractal dimension' that lies between 1 and 2. The fractal dimension of Koch's snowflake is approximately 1.261.

> *Clouds are not spheres, mountains are not cones,*
> *coastlines are not circles, and bark is not smooth,*
> *nor does lightning travel in a straight line.*
>
> —Polish-born mathematician Benoit Mandelbrot
> (b. 1924), in *Fractal Geometry in Nature* (1982).

## Fractals in nature

### Ferns

The branched structures of some fern fronds show fractal properties. Each frond of these ferns has branched structures that look like a miniature version of the whole leaf. These structures themselves can also be branched.

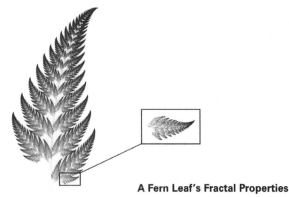

**A Fern Leaf's Fractal Properties**

### British coastline

The coastline of Britain is often used as an example of a fractal. If you wanted to measure its length, you could try to lay an extremely long piece of string around the coast. The problem is that the length measured would depend on whether the string goes around every headland, every rocky outcrop in each headland, every rock in each outcrop, every bump in each rock, or every atom in each bump. As with Koch's snowflake, the coastline could therefore be said to have a fractal dimension of between 1 and 2.

> *The advance and perfecting of mathematics are*
> *closely joined to the prosperity of the nation.*
>
> —Napoleon Bonaparte

> *Mathematics is the door and key to the sciences.*
>
> —English scientist and philosopher Roger Bacon
> (c.1214–1292), in *Opus Majus*, 1267 (translated by
> Robert Belle Burke, 1928).

# MEASUREMENT

## SCALES

### Decibel scale

A decibel is a term used to express a level of sound. It is the tenth part of a bel, a measure for comparing the intensity of noises, which was named after Alexander Graham Bell (1847–1922) who invented the telephone.

| Source | Decibel level (dB) |
|---|---|
| Breathing | 10 |
| Whispering | 20 |
| Conversation | 50–60 |
| Vacuum cleaner | 80 |
| Traffic | 60–90 |
| Pneumatic drill | 110 |
| Jet aircraft | 120 |
| Space vehicle launch | 140–170 |

### Wentworth scale

The Wentworth scale is one of the main scales used in geology to describe the general dimensions of grains in a rock, especially sediment. It was devised by Chester K Wentworth (1891–1969), a US geologist.

| Name | Dimension[1] |
|---|---|
| Boulder | greater than 256 mm |
| Cobble | 64–256 mm |
| Pebble | 4–64 mm |
| Gravel | 2–4 mm |
| Sand | $1/16$–2 mm |
| Silt | $1/256$–$1/16$ mm |
| Clay | less than $1/256$ mm |

[1] To convert millimetres to inches, multiply by 0.0394.

### Mohs' hardness scale

The relative hardness of solids can be expressed using a scale of numbers from 1 to 10, each relating to a mineral (1 representing talc, 10 representing diamond). The method was devised by Friedrich Mohs (1773–1839), a German mineralogist. Sets of hardness pencils are used to test specimens to see what will scratch them; other useful instruments for testing include: fingernail (will scratch a specimen with a hardness of 2.5 or lower), copper coin (3.5 or lower), steel knife (5.5 or lower), and glass (6.0 or lower).

| Talc | 1 | Fluorite | 4 | Quartz | 7 | Diamond | 10 |
|------|---|----------|---|--------|---|---------|----|
| Gypsum | 2 | Apatite | 5 | Topaz | 8 | | |
| Calcite | 3 | Orthoclase | 6 | Corundum | 9 | | |

## Beaufort scale

The Beaufort scale was developed by the English admiral and hydrographer Sir Francis Beaufort, to classify wind speeds.

| Beaufort number | Wind name | Windspeed in kph (mph) | Average wave height in m (ft) |
|-----------------|-----------|------------------------|-------------------------------|
| 0 | Calm | <1 | 0 |
| 1 | Light air | 1–5 (1–3) | 0 |
| 2 | Light breeze | 6–11 (4–7) | 0–0.3 (0–1) |
| 3 | Gentle breeze | 12–19 (8–12) | 0.3–0.6 (1–2) |
| 4 | Moderate breeze | 20–28 (13–18) | 0.6–1.2 (2–4) |
| 5 | Fresh breeze | 29–38 (19–24) | 1.2–2.4 (4–8) |
| 6 | Strong breeze | 39–49 (25–31) | 2.4–4 (8–13) |
| 7 | Near gale | 50–61 (32–38) | 4–6 (13–20) |
| 8 | Gale | 62–74 (39–46) | 4–6 (13–20) |
| 9 | Strong gale | 75–8 (47–54) | 4–6 (13–20) |
| 10 | Storm | 89–102 (55–63) | 6–9 (20–30) |
| 11 | Violent storm | 103–117 (64–72) | 9–14 (30–45) |
| 12–17 | Hurricane | >118 (>73) | >14 (>45) |

## pH scale

pH or pH value is a number used to express degrees of acidity or alkalinity in solutions (see **Atoms, elements and molecules: Acids, alkalis and bases**). The title comes from the German word *Potenz*, meaning power, and H, the symbol for hydrogen.

The scale ranges from 0 to 14; a pH below 7 indicates acidity, and one above 7 alkalinity. A solution with a pH of 7 is neutral. The scale actually represents the concentration of positively charged hydrogen ions in the solution. For example, a solution with a pH value of 3 has a concentration of $10^{-3}$, or 0.001, moles per litre, while a pH value of 5 indicates $10^{-5}$, or 0.00001, moles per litre. The higher the pH number, the lower the concentration of the hydrogen ions.

## Apparent magnitude scale

The ancient Greek astronomer Hipparchus first classified the stars according to their apparent 'magnitude' (luminosity). His scale ranged from one, for the brightest stars, to six, for the faintest stars visible to the naked eye. Today the scale extends further in both directions, with the brightest objects taking negative numbers (see **Space: Stars**).

| Magnitude number | Example |
|---|---|
| −26.7 | The Sun |
| −12.7 | The Moon |
| −4.7 | Venus at its brightest |
| 0 | Vega |
| +6 | Stars just visible with the naked eye |
| +10 | Stars just visible with binoculars |
| +22 | Stars just visible with a large telescope |

### Red Hot Chilli Peppers

The hotness of chillis is measured using Scoville units, named after the German pharmacologist Wilbur Scoville, who devised the scale in 1912. Originally a taste test, the Scoville rating is now determined by measuring the concentration of capsaicin in each type of chilli, using high-performance liquid chromatography.

## CONSTANTS

Values given are the 2002 recommended values.

### Universal constants

| Quantity | Symbol | Value |
|---|---|---|
| Speed of light in a vacuum | $c$ | $299\ 792\ 458\,\text{m}\,\text{s}^{-1}$ |
| Newtonian constant of gravitation | $G$ | $6.6742 \times 10^{-11}\,\text{N}\,\text{m}^2\,\text{kg}^{-2}$ |
| Planck constant: relates the energy of electromagnetic radiation (eg light) to its frequency | $h$ | $6.6260693 \times 10^{-34}\,\text{J}\,\text{s}$ |
| Rydberg constant: relates the frequencies of atomic spectrum lines in a given series | $R_\infty$ | $10\ 973\ 731.568\,\text{m}^{-1}$ |

## Standard values

| Quantity | Symbol | Value |
|---|---|---|
| Acceleration due to gravity | $g_n$ | $9.80665 \, m\,s^{-2}$ |
| Molar mass of $^{12}C$ | $M\,(^{12}C)$ | $12 \times 10^{-3} \, kg\,mol^{-1}$ |
| Standard atmospheric pressure | $p$ | $101\,325 \, Pa$ |

## Subatomic particle constants

| Quantity | Symbol | Value |
|---|---|---|
| Proton rest mass | $m_p$ | $1.67262171 \times 10^{-27} \, kg$ |
| Neutron rest mass | $m_n$ | $1.67492728 \times 10^{-27} \, kg$ |
| Electron rest mass | $m_e$ | $9.1093826 \times 10^{-31} \, kg$ |
| Classical electron radius | $r_e$ | $2.817940325 \times 10^{-15} \, m$ |
| Elementary charge: the charge on an electron or proton | $e$ | $1.60217653 \times 10^{-19} \, C$ |

### Compton wavelengths

A Compton wavelength is the wavelength associated with the mass of a particle

| | | |
|---|---|---|
| Proton Compton wavelength, $h/m_p c$ | $\lambda_{c,p}$ | $1.3214098555 \times 10^{-15} \, m$ |
| Neutron Compton wavelength, $h/m_n c$ | $\lambda_{c,n}$ | $1.3195909067 \times 10^{-15} \, m$ |
| Electron Compton wavelength, $h/m_e c$ | $\lambda_{c,e}$ | $2.426310238 \times 10^{-15} \, m$ |

## Physico-chemical constants

| Quantity | Symbol | Value |
|---|---|---|
| Avogadro constant: the number of molecules in a mole | $N_A$ | $6.0221415 \times 10^{23} \, mol^{-1}$ |
| Atomic mass unit, $m_u = M\,(^{12}C)/12$ | $m_u$ | $1.66053886 \times 10^{-27} \, kg$ |
| Gas constant: relates the pressure of an ideal gas to its temperature and volume | $R$ | $8.314472 \, J\,mol^{-1}\,K^{-1}$ |
| Molar volume: the volume occupied by one mole of an ideal gas, $RT/p$ ($T=273.15K$, $p=101\,325Pa$) | $V_m$ | $0.022413996 \, m^3\,mol^{-1}$ |
| Boltzmann constant, $R/N_A$ | $k$ | $1.3806505 \times 10^{-23} \, J\,K^{-1}$ |

## SI UNITS

SI units (Système International d'Unités) are an internationally accepted metric system for measuring physical properties. There are seven basic units, from which many other units can be derived. The units can be modified to represent smaller or larger quantities by adding standard prefixes.

### SI basic units

| Concept | Symbol | Name of Unit | Abbreviation |
|---|---|---|---|
| Mass | $m$ | kilogram | kg |
| Length | $l$ | metre | m |
| Time | $t$ | second | s |
| Amount of substance | | mole | mol |
| Thermodynamic temperature | $T$ | kelvin | K |
| Electric current | $I$ | ampere | A |
| Luminous intensity | $I$ | candela | cd |

### SI-derived units

| Concept | Symbol | Special name | Abbreviation | Equivalent units |
|---|---|---|---|---|
| Plane angle | $\alpha, \beta, \theta$, etc | radian | rad | $(= 180°/\pi)$ |
| Solid angle | $\Omega, \omega$ | steradian | sr | |
| Area | $A, a$ | | | $m^2$ |
| Volume | $V, v$ | | | $m^3$ |
| Velocity | $v, u$ | | | $m\,s^{-1}$ |
| Acceleration | $a$ | | | $m\,s^{-2}$ |
| Density | $\rho$ | | | $kg\,m^{-3}$ |
| Moment of inertia | $I$ | | | $kg\,m^2$ |
| Momentum | $p$ | | | $kg\,m\,s^{-1}$ |
| Angular momentum | $L$ | | | $kg\,m^2\,s^{-1}$ |
| Force | $F$ | newton | N | $kg\,m\,s^{-2}$ |
| Torque (moment of force) | $T\,(M)$ | | | $N\,m$ |
| Work (energy, heat) | $W\,(E)$ | joule | J | $N\,m$ |

| Concept | Symbol | Special name | Abbreviation | Equivalent units |
|---|---|---|---|---|
| Potential energy | $V$ | joule | J | N m |
| Kinetic energy | $T\ (W)$ | joule | J | N m |
| Heat (enthalpy) | $Q\ (H)$ | joule | J | N m |
| Power | $P$ | watt | W | $J s^{-1}$ |
| Pressure (stress) | $p\ (\sigma, f)$ | | | $N m^{-2}$ |
| Surface tension | $\gamma$ | | | $N m^{-1}$ |
| Viscosity, dynamic | $\eta, \mu$ | | | $N s m^{-1}$ |
| Viscosity, kinematic | $v$ | | | $m^2 s^{-1}$ |
| Electric charge | $Q$ | coulomb | C | A s |
| Electric potential (potential difference) | $V$ | volt | V | $W A^{-1}$ |
| Electric field strength (electric force) | $E$ | | | $V m^{-1}$ |
| Electric resistance | $R$ | ohm | $\Omega$ | $V A^{-1}$ |
| Reactance | $X$ | ohm | $\Omega$ | $V^{-1}$ |
| Impedance | $Z$ | ohm | $\Omega$ | $V A^{-1}$ |
| Conductance | $G$ | siemens | S | $\Omega^{-1}$ |
| Susceptance | $B$ | siemens | S | $\Omega^{-1}$ |
| Admittance | $Y$ | siemens | S | $\Omega^{-1}$ |
| Frequency | $f$ | hertz | Hz | $s^{-1}$ |
| Magnetic flux | $\Phi$ | weber | Wb | V s |
| Magnetic flux density | $B$ | tesla | T | $V s m^{-2}$ |
| Mutual inductance | $M$ | henry | H | $V s A^{-1}$ |
| Self inductance | $L$ | henry | H | $V s A^{-1}$ |
| Capacitance | $C$ | farad | F | $C V^{-1}$ |
| Luminous flux | $\Phi$ | lumen | lm | cd sr |
| Illumination | $E$ | lux | lx | $lm m^{-2}$ |
| Activity of a radioactive substance | $A$ | becquerel | Bq | $s^{-1}$ |
| Absorbed dose of radioactivity | $D$ | gray | Gy | $m^2 s^{-2}$ |
| Radioactivity dose equivalent | $H$ | sievert | Sv | $m^2 s^{-2}$ |
| Catalytic activity | | katal | kat | $mol s^{-1}$ |

## SI prefixes

| Factor | Prefix | Symbol |
|--------|--------|--------|
| $10^{24}$ | yotta | Y |
| $10^{21}$ | zetta | Z |
| $10^{18}$ | exa | E |
| $10^{15}$ | peta | P |
| $10^{12}$ | tera | T |
| $10^{9}$ | giga | G |
| $10^{6}$ | mega | M |
| $10^{3}$ | kilo | k |
| $10^{2}$ | hecto | h |
| $10^{1}$ | deca | da |
| $10^{-1}$ | deci | d |
| $10^{-2}$ | centi | c |
| $10^{-3}$ | milli | m |
| $10^{-6}$ | micro | m |
| $10^{-9}$ | nano | n |
| $10^{-12}$ | pico | p |
| $10^{-15}$ | femto | f |
| $10^{-18}$ | atto | a |
| $10^{-21}$ | zepto | z |
| $10^{-24}$ | yocto | y |

## CONVERSION FACTORS

Some notable non-SI units are listed, along with the conversion to equivalent SI units.

| Unit name | Symbol | Quantity | SI equivalent |
|-----------|--------|----------|---------------|
| acre | | area | $0.405\,hm^2$ |
| Ångström | Å | length | $0.1\,nm$ |
| astronomical unit | AU | length | $0.150\,Tm$ |
| atomic mass unit | amu | mass | $1.661 \times 10^{-27}\,kg$ |
| bar | bar | pressure | $0.1\,MPa$ |
| barn | b | area | $100\,fm^2$ |
| barrel (US) = 42 US gal | bbl | volume | $0.159\,m^3$ |
| British thermal unit | Btu | energy | $1.055\,kJ$ |

| Unit name | Symbol | Quantity | SI equivalent |
|---|---|---|---|
| calorie | cal | energy | 4.186 J |
| cubic foot | ft$^3$ | volume | 0.028 m$^3$ |
| cubic inch | in$^3$ | volume | 16.387 cm$^3$ |
| cubic yard | yd$^3$ | volume | 0.765 m$^3$ |
| curie | Ci | activity of radionuclide | 37 GBq |
| degree = 1/90 right angle | ° | plane angle | $\pi$ /180 rad |
| degree Celsius | °C | temperature | 1K |
| degree Centigrade | °C | temperature | 1K |
| degree Fahrenheit | °F | temperature | 5/9 K |
| degree Rankine | °R | temperature | 5/9 K |
| dyne | dyn | force | 10 $\mu$N |
| electronvolt | eV | energy | 0.160 aJ |
| erg | erg | energy | 0.1 $\mu$J |
| fathom (=6ft) | | length | 1.829 m |
| fermi | | length | 1 fm |
| foot | ft | length | 30.48 cm |
| foot per second | ft s$^{-1}$ | velocity | 0.305 m s$^{-1}$ |
| gallon (UK) | gal | volume | 4.546 dm$^3$ |
| gallon (US) (= 231in$^3$) | gal | volume | 3.785 dm$^3$ |
| gallon (UK) per mile | | consumption | 2.825 dm$^3$ km$^{-1}$ |
| gauss | Gs, G | magnetic flux density | 100 $\mu$T |
| grade = 0.01 rt angle | | plane angle | $\pi$/200 rad |
| grain | gr | mass | 0.065 g |
| hectare | ha | area | 1 hm$^2$ |
| horsepower | hp | energy | 0.746 kW |
| inch | in | length | 2.54 cm |
| kilogram-force | kgf | force | 9.807 N |
| knot | | velocity | 1.852 km h$^{-1}$ |
| light year | l.y. | length | 9.461 × 10$^{15}$ m |
| litre | l | volume | 1 dm$^3$ |

| Unit name | Symbol | Quantity | SI equivalent |
|---|---|---|---|
| maxwell | Mx | magnetic flux | 10 nWb |
| metric carat | | mass | 0.2 g |
| micron | μ | length | 1 μm |
| mile (nautical) | | length | 1.852 km |
| mile (statute) | | length | 1.609 km |
| mile per hour (mph) | mile h$^{-1}$ | velocity | 1.609 km h$^{-1}$ |
| minute = (1/60)° | ' | plane angle | $\pi$/10800 rad |
| oersted | Oe | magnetic field strength | 1/4$\pi$ kA m$^{-1}$ |
| ounce (avoirdupois) | oz | mass | 28.349 g |
| ounce (troy) = 480gr | | mass | 31.103 g |
| parsec | pc | length | 30 857 Tm |
| phot | ph | illuminance | 10 klx |
| pint (UK) | pt | volume | 0.568 dm$^3$ |
| poise | p | viscosity | 0.1 Pa s |
| pound | lb | mass | 0.454 kg |
| pound-force | lbf | force | 4.448 N |
| pound-force/in$^2$ | | pressure | 6.895 KPa |
| poundal | pdl | force | 0.138 N |
| pounds per square inch | psi | pressure | 6.895 × 10$^3$ kPa |
| rad | rad | absorbed dose | 0.01 Gy |
| rem | rem | dose equivalent | 0.01 Sv |
| right angle = $\pi$/2 rad | | plane angle | 1.571 rad |
| röntgen | R | exposure | 0.258 mC kg$^{-1}$ |
| second = (1/60)' | " | plane angle | $\pi$/648 mrad |
| slug | | mass | 14.594 kg |
| solar mass | M | mass | 1.989 × 10$^{30}$ kg |
| square foot | ft$^2$ | area | 9.290 dm$^2$ |
| square inch | in$^2$ | area | 6.452 cm$^2$ |
| square mile (statute) | | area | 2.590 km$^2$ |
| square yard | yd$^2$ | area | 0.836 m$^2$ |
| standard atmosphere | atm | pressure | 0.101 MPa |

| Unit name | Symbol | Quantity | SI equivalent |
|---|---|---|---|
| stere | st | volume | $1\,m^3$ |
| stilb | sb | luminance | $10\,kcd\,m^{-2}$ |
| stokes | St | viscosity | $1\,cm^2\,s^{-1}$ |
| therm (= $10^5$Btu) | | energy | $0.105\,GJ$ |
| ton (= 2 240lb) | | mass | $1.016\,Mg$ |
| ton-force | tonf | force | $9.964\,kN$ |
| ton-force/in$^2$ | | pressure | $15.444\,MPa$ |
| tonne | t | mass | $1\,Mg$ |
| torr (mm mercury) | torr | pressure | $0.133\,kPa$ |
| X unit | | length | $0.100\,pm$ |
| yard | yd | length | $0.915\,m$ |

## MEASURING DEVICES

Some notable measuring devices, and the properties they measure, are listed.

| Device | Used for measuring | Device | Used for measuring |
|---|---|---|---|
| Accelerometer | Acceleration | Galvanometer | Electric currents |
| Altimeter | Height | Geiger counter | Radioactivity |
| Ammeter | Electric current | Geothermometer | Subterranean temperatures |
| Anemometer | Wind | Gravimeter | Variations in the earth's surface gravity |
| Barometer | Atmospheric pressure | | |
| Calorimeter | Heat capacities | Hyetometer, ombrometer, pluviometer | Rainfall |
| Chronometer | Time | | |
| Cryometer | Low temperatures | | |
| Decelerometer | Deceleration | Hygrometer | Humidity of the air or of other gases |
| Dosimeter | Radiation | | |
| Dynamometer | Force | Inclinometer | Slopes |
| Evaporimeter, evaporometer | Rate of evaporation | Interferometer | Wavelengths, wave speeds, angles, etc |
| Flowmeter | Rate of flow of a fluid in a pipe | | |
| | | Luxmeter | Illumination |
| Focimeter | Focal length of a lens | Magnetometer | Strength/direction of a magnetic field |

| Device | Used for measuring | Device | Used for measuring |
|--------|--------------------|--------|--------------------|
| Mileometer, milometer | Miles that a vehicle has travelled | Speedometer | Speed at which a vehicle is travelling |
| Odometer | Distance travelled by a wheeled vehicle | Sphygmomanometer, sphygmometer | Arterial blood pressure |
| | | Tachometer | Velocity |
| Ohmmeter | Electrical resistance | Theodolite | Horizontal and vertical angles |
| Optometer | Vision | Thermometer | Temperature |
| Pedometer | Paces (approximate distance walked) | Vaporimeter | Vapour pressure or vapour |
| | | Velocimeter | Velocity |
| Photometer | Luminous intensity | Vibrograph, vibrometer | Vibrations |
| Pulsimeter | Strength or quickness of the pulse | Viscometer, viscosimeter | Viscosity |
| Pyrometer | High temperatures | | |
| Respirometer | Breathing | Voltmeter | Electromotive force |
| Seismometer | Intensity and duration of earthquakes | Volumeter | Volumes of gases and liquids |
| Spectrometer | Refractive indices | Wattmeter | Circuit power |
| | | Wavemeter | Wavelengths |

## *In the Eye of the Beholder?*

An unofficial unit of measurement is the millihelen, generally defined as the amount of beauty required to launch one ship. The idea for this unit derives from a line in Christopher Marlowe's play *Doctor Faustus* (1604) which refers to the legendary beauty Helen of Troy as 'the face that launched a thousand ships'.

## TEMPERATURE CONVERSION

The methods for converting between the common temperature scales are given. Carry out these operations in sequence.

| To convert | To | Equation |
|---|---|---|
| °Fahrenheit | °Celsius | − 32, × 5, ÷ 9 |
| °Celsius | °Fahrenheit | × 9, ÷ 5, + 32 |
| °Celsius | Kelvin | + 273.15 |
| Kelvin | °Celsius | − 273.15 |

## RELATIVE SIZES

### Getting bigger

Each row of the table is 1000 times larger than the previous row.

| Relative size | Magnitude | Units used for measurement | Example |
|---|---|---|---|
| 1 | $10^0$ | metre | height of an adult man (approx 1.8m) |
| Thousand times bigger | $10^3$ | kilometres | height of Ben Nevis, the UK's highest mountain (1.3km) |
| Million times bigger | $10^6$ | thousands of kilometres | diameter of the Moon (approx 3475km) |
| Billion times bigger | $10^9$ | millions of kilometres | diameter of the Sun (1.4 million km) |
| Trillion times bigger | $10^{12}$ | billions of kilometres | distance from Saturn to the Sun (1.3–1.5 billion km) |
| Quadrillion times bigger | $10^{15}$ | light years (1 ly = $9.4 \times 10^{15}$ metres) | distance from the Sun to nearest star (Proxima Centauri – 4.3 ly) |
| Quintillion times bigger | $10^{18}$ | thousands of light years | distance from the Sun to the centre of our galaxy (approx 25 thousand ly) |
| Sextillion times bigger | $10^{21}$ | millions of light years | distance to the next galaxy (Andromeda – 2.25 million ly) |

> *I ask you to look both ways. For the road to a knowledge of the stars leads through the atom; and important knowledge of the atom has been reached through the stars.*
>
> —English astonomer Sir Arthur Stanley Eddington (1882–1944), in *Stars and Atoms*, lecture 1 (1928).

## Getting smaller

Each row of the table is 1000 times smaller than the previous row.

| Relative size | Magnitude | Units used for measurement | Example |
|---|---|---|---|
| 1 | $10^0$ | metre | height of an adult man (approx 1.8 m) |
| Thousand times smaller | $10^{-3}$ | millimetre | length of a red ant (5 mm) |
| Million times smaller | $10^{-6}$ | micrometre | diameter of a red blood cell (7 μm) |
| Billion times smaller | $10^{-9}$ | nanometre | diameter of DNA helix (2 nm) |
| Trillion times smaller | $10^{-12}$ | picometre | radius of a hydrogen atom (25 pm) |
| Quadrillion times smaller | $10^{-15}$ | femtometre | size of a proton (approx 1 fm) |

> *He uses statistics as a drunken man uses lamp-posts – for support rather than illumination.*
>
> —Scottish writer Andrew Lang (1844–1912).

# INDEX

**B**

## D

## E

## G

imaginary numbers 481
immune system 35, 289, 305
immunity 35
immunoassays 291
immunology 35
immunosuppressant drugs 314
imprinting 35
incandescence 473
incus 288
index 28
indigenous 35
indium 366
induction 35, 85, 95, 478
inert gases *see* noble gases
inertia 35, 246
infectious diseases 35, 296–299
infinity 36
inflationary universe model 242
influenza 297, 358
information entropy 117
infrared radiation 36, 90, 106, 462
infrared spectroscopy 462
infrasound 36
Ingenhousz, Jan 88
innate immune responses 289–290
inner ear 288
inorganic compounds 36
insects 351
insulators 36, 471
insulin 114, 279, 299
integers 36, 480
integration 36
intelligent design 122
inter- 36
interference 458
intermediate vector bosons 256
internet 462
intestine 313
intra- 36
introvert 350
invertebrates 36
in vitro fertilization 36, 121
involuntary muscle 274
iodine 97, 308, 366, 372
ionic bonds 373
ionic compounds 107, 375
ionization 36
ionizing radiation 464, 466
ionopause 408
ionosphere 408
ions 36, 373; *see also* anions; cations
iridium 366
iris 287
iron 281, 308, 365, 478
irrational numbers 37, 480
ibn Ishaq, Hunayn 69
island chains 410
iso- 37
isoleucine 320, 378
isomers 37
isosceles 485
isotopes 37, 113, 363
isotropic 384
-itis 37

IVF *see* in vitro fertilization

## J

Jacob, François 166
Jacobi, Carl Gustav Jacob 166
Jansky, Karl 115, 166
Janssen, Pierre 104
Java Man 109
Jeans, Sir James Hopwood 167, 229
Jeffrey, Lord Francis 431
Jeffreys, Sir Alec 121, 167
jejunum 281
jellyfish 349
Jenner, Edward 90, 167
Jerne, Niels Kai 167
jet stream 37
Johanson, Donald 120, 167
Johnson, Phillip 122
joints 271, 299
Joliot-Curie, Frédéric 168
Joliot-Curie, Irène 168
Joule, James 97, 98, 168, 231
Joule effect 97
joules 98, 455
Joyce, James 362
Julia, Gaston 492
Julian calendar 66, 75
Julia set 492
junctions 329
Jung, Carl Gustav 168
Jupiter 76, 77, 434
Jurassic period 402, 404
Just, Ernest 114

## K

kala-azar 297
kangaroos 356
Kant, Immanuel 168
Kármán, Theodore von 106
Katz, Sir Bernard 169
Keir, James 87
Kekulé von Stradonitz, August 103
Kelvin, Thomson William, 1st Baron 99, 169, 231, 455
Kelvin scale 37
Kendrew, Sir John 169
Kepler, Johannes 4, 76, 77, 169, 245
Kepler's laws of planetary motion 76, 77, 245–247
keratin 394
Khorana, Har Gobind 119, 169
al-Khwarizmi, Muhammad ibn Musa 69, 170
kidneys 270, 279, 282–283
Kilby, Jack S 119
kinematics 37
kinetics *see* dynamics
kinetic theory of gases 84, 228–229
kingdoms 37, 343, 344; *see also* eubacteria; archaea; protista; fungi; plants; animals
Kinsey, Alfred Charles 170

Lowry, Martin 178
'Lucy' (*Australopithecus afarensis*) 120
Ludwig, Karl Friedrich Wilhelm 101
lumen 328
luminescence 39
lunar eclipses 73, 440–441
lunar seas 438–439
lungs 270, 285
luteinizing hormone 278
lutetium 366
Lwoff, André Michel 178
Lyapunov, Aleksandr 264
Lyell, Sir Charles 95, 178, 237
lymph 286
lymphatic system 286
lymph nodes 286
lymphocytes 286, 290, 294
Lynden-Bell, Donald 178
Lyon, Mary Frances 178
Lysenko, Trofim Denisovich 179
lysine 320, 379
lysis 39
lysosomes 330
lysozyme 289

# M

McCarty, Maclyn 318
McClintock, Barbara 179
Mach, Ernst 179
Mach number 39
Macintosh, Charles 94
Mackay, Alan Lindsay 8
Maclaurin, Colin 83
MacLeod, Colin 318
Macleod, John 114, 179
McMillan, Edwin Mattison 179
macrophages 294
magma 39
magnesium 308, 366
magnetic field 39, 476; Earth's 385, 405, 407
magnetic flux 476–477
magnetic flux density 476
magnetic imaging 476
magnetic poles 475
magnetic resonance imaging 476
magnetism 39, 477
magnetron 462
magnets 72, 75, 85, 475–478
magnitude (brightness) 39, 445, 497
magnitude (size) 39
Maiman, Theodore 119
malacology 39
malaria 83, 98, 297
malleability 384
malleus 288
Malpighi, Marcello 81, 180
Malthus, Thomas 90
mammals 355–356
Mandelbrot, Benoît 265, 492, 494
Mandelbrot set 492
manganese 366
Manhattan Project 116

manic depression *see* bipolar disorder
Manson, Patrick 98
Mantell, Gideon 180
mantle 39, 406, 409
Mao, Yong 489
Marconi, Guglielmo, Marchese 111, 180
Marfan, Antoine 304
Marfan syndrome 304
Margulis, Lynn 180, 238
Mariotte, Edmé 229
Mariotte's law *see* Boyle's law
Markov, Andrei 180
Mars 77, 105, 433; landings on 120, 124; possible life on 123
Marsh, James 89
Marsh, O C 181
marsupials 356
mass 39
mass-energy relation 248
mass number 363
mass spectrometry 479
mastodons 39
materials 384–396; properties of 384–385
mathematical signs and symbols 482–483
mathematics 39
matrix 39
Maupertuis, Pierre-Louis Moreau de 258
Maury, Matthew 101
mauveine 101
Maxwell, James Clerk 103, 105, 181, 229, 248, 460
Maxwell's equations 103
May, Sir Robert 265
Maynard Smith, John 181
Mead, Margaret 181
measles 297, 358
measurement 495–507; measuring devices 504–505
mechanics 40
Medawar, Sir Peter 2, 181
medicines 308–316
medulla oblongata 276
meiosis 40, 335–336, 340
Meissner, Walter 396
Meissner effect 396
Meitner, Lise 182
meitnerium 366
melanoma 302
melatonin 278
melting point 385
membrane 40, 328
Mendeleev, Dmitri 104, 182
mendelevium 366
Mendel, Gregor 103, 182, 223, 323
Mendel's laws 103, 221
meninges 276
menstrual cycle *see* female sexual cycle
menstruation 279, 293
mental health disorders 305–306
mercury (element) 366
Mercury (planet) 432
Mesmer, Franz 87
meso- 40
mesolithic 399

mesons 363
mesopause 408
mesophyll 331
mesosphere 408
mesothelioma 302
Mesozoic era 402
metabolism 40, 278, 282
metallography 40
metals 374, 386
metamorphic rocks 40, 415
metaphase 323, 335
metastasis 40, 300
Metchnikoff, Elie 107, 111
meteorites 9, 40, 453
meteoroids 40, 104–105, 453
meteorology 40
meteors 40, 103, 453; meteor showers 454
methane 409
methionine 320, 379
Metre-Kilogram-Second system *see* MKS system
metrology 40
mice 356
Michell, John 85
Michelson, Albert 182
microchip 119
microfilaments 329, 335
microorganisms 40, 296
microscopes 75, 80, 81, 327, 329
microtubules 329, 335
microwave background 41
microwave ovens 461
microwave radiation 40, 462
midbrain 276
middle ear 288
Miescher, Friedrich 104
Milankovitch, Milutin 240
Milankovitch theory 240–241
Milky Way 41, 76, 450
Miller, Stanley 118, 338
Miller, William Hallowes 97
Millikan, Robert 112, 182
million 482
millipedes 351
Milne, John 109
Milstein, Cesar 120, 183
mineralocorticoids 279
mineralogy 41
minerals (dietary) 307–308
minerals (geological) 412–413
minks 356
Miocene series 399
Mitchell, Maria 183
mitochondria 328, 332, 345
mitosis 41, 107, 334–335, 336
Mittasch, Alwin 381
MKS system 41
Möbius, August Ferdinand 101, 183
Möbius strip 101
modulation 41
Moh, Hugo von 100
moho 406
Mohs, Friedrich 87, 495
Mohs' hardness scale 87, 495–496
Moivre, Abraham de 84

molar volume 498
molecules 41, 373–374
moles (chemistry) 41, 228, 232
molluscs 41, 351, 352; habitats of 420; in Mesozoic era 402
molybdenum 366
momentum 246
monkeys 356
mono- 41
monoclonal antibodies 120, 291
monocotyledons 348
monocytes 294
Monod, Jacques 183
monomers 390
monotremes 356
Montagnier, Luc 121, 183
Montagu, Lady Mary Wortley 83
mood-stabilizing drugs 315
the Moon 76, 78, 438–441; first person on 120; first photograph 97; phases of 439
Morgagni, Giovanni 86
Morley, Edward 183
Moro, Antonio Lazzaro 84
morphine 315, 316
morphology 41
Morse, Samuel 98
Morton, William T G 99
Morveau, Louis Bernard Guyton de 89
moths 351
motors 95, 478
Mottelson, Ben Roy 184
mountain ranges 409–410
MRI *see* magnetic resonance imaging
MRSA 297
mucus 289
Müller, Paul 116
Müller, Walther 114
Mullis, Kary Banks 184
multi- 42
multiple sclerosis 299
mumps 298
muscles 270, 271, 272–274; *see also* skeletal muscle; involuntary muscle; cardiac muscle
muscular 272
mussels 352
mutants 323
mutations 42, 300, 321, 340
mycology 42
myelin 299
myo- 272
myofibrils 272
myology 42
myosin 272
myriapods 351

## N

NAD 332
NADH 332, 333
nadir 42
NADP 332
NADPH 332
Napier, John 76, 77, 184

## O

## Q

## R